HANDBOOK OF ECONOMICS AND ETHICS

To Amartya Sen

Handbook of Economics and Ethics

Edited by

Jan Peil

Radboud University, Nijmegen, The Netherlands

Irene van Staveren

Radboud University, Nijmegen, and Institute of Social Studies, The Hague, The Netherlands

Edward Elgar
Cheltenham, UK • Northampton, MA, USA

Published by
Edward Elgar Publishing Limited
The Lypiatts
15 Lansdown Road
Cheltenham
Glos GL50 2JA
UK

Edward Elgar Publishing, Inc.
William Pratt House
9 Dewey Court
Northampton
Massachusetts 01060
USA

A catalogue record for this book is available from the British Library

Library of Congress Control Number: 2009921520

PEFC
PEFC/16-33-111
CATG-PEFC-052
www.pefc.org

ISBN 978 1 84542 936 2 (cased)

Printed and bound by MPG Books Group, UK

Contents

Figures

Tables

Contributors

Sabina Alkire, Director of the Oxford Poverty and Human Development Initiative, University of Oxford, UK.

Jack Amariglio, Professor of Economics, Merrimack College, USA.

Drucilla K. Barker, Professor and Director of Women's Studies at the University of South Carolina, USA.

Albino Barrera, Professor of Economics and Humanities, Providence College, Rhode Island, USA.

Robin L. Bartlett, Bank One Professor of Economics, Denison University, USA.

Günseli Berik, Associate Professor of Economics and Gender Studies, University of Utah, Salt Lake City, USA.

Ken Binmore, Professor of Economics, University College, London, UK.

Hilde Bojer, Associate Professor, Department of Economics, University of Oslo, Norway.

Luigino Bruni, Associate Professor of Economics at the University of Milano-Bicocca, Italy.

Samuel Cameron, Professor of Economics, Department of Development and Economic Studies, University of Bradford, UK.

Rutger Claassen, Assistant Professor in Political Philosophy, Department of Political Science, Leiden University, The Netherlands.

Jeffrey H. Cohen, Associate Professor of Anthropology, Ohio State University, USA and former President of the Society for Economic Anthropology.

Ricardo Crespo, Professor of Economics, Austral University, and Researcher at the National Council of Scientific Investigation, Argentina.

John B. Davis, Professor of History and Philosophy of Economics at University of Amsterdam, The Netherlands, and Professor of Economics at Marquette University, USA.

George DeMartino, Associate Professor of Political Economy at the Josef Korbel School of International Studies, University of Denver, USA.

Paul Downward, Institute of Sport and Leisure Policy, Loughborough University, UK.

Gary A. Dymski, Director, University of California Center Sacramento, and Professor of Economics, University of California, Riverside, USA.

Juliana Essen, Acting Director, University Writing Program and Visiting Professor of Composition and Rhetoric at Soka University of America, USA.

Ben D'Exelle, Researcher at the Institute of Development Policy and Management (IOB), University of Antwerp, Belgium.

John Field, Director of the Centre for Research in Lifelong Learning, University of Stirling, UK.

Deborah M. Figart, Dean of the School of Graduate and Continuing Studies and Professor of Economics, The Richard Stockton College of New Jersey, USA.

Edward Fullbrook, University of the West of England, UK.

Des Gasper, Institute of Social Studies, The Hague, The Netherlands.

Johan J. Graafland, Professor of Economics, Business and Ethics, Tilburg University, Tilburg, The Netherlands.

Nicolas Gravel, Professor of Economics, University of the Mediterranean (Aix-Marseille II), Groupe de Recherche en Economie Quantitative d'Aix-Marseille (GREQAM) and Institut d'Economie Publique (IdEP), France.

Marco E.L. Guidi, Professor of History of Economics at the University of Pisa, Italy.

Lawrence Hamilton, Professor, Department of Politics, University of Johannesburg, South Africa, and Affiliated Lecturer, Department of Politics and International Studies (POLIS), Cambridge University, UK and a Life Member of Clare Hall, Cambridge.

Shaun P. Hargreaves Heap, Professor of Economics at the University of East Anglia, Norwich, UK, and has held visiting positions at Concordia University in Montreal and Sydney University.

Tom De Herdt, Professor and Vice-Chair of the Institute of Development Policy and Management (IOB), University of Antwerp, Belgium.

Johannes Hirata, Professor of Economics, University of Applied Sciences, Osnabrück, Germany.

Bernard Hodgson, Professor of Philosophy, Trent University, Peterborough, Ontario, Canada, and Editor for Philosophical Foundations, Journal of Business Ethics.

Rolph van der Hoeven, Professor of Employment and Development Economics, Institute of Social Studies, The Hague, The Netherlands.

Ronald Inglehart, Professor of Political Science at the University of Michigan, USA, and directs the World Values Survey.

Rhys Jenkins, Professor of Development Economics at the School of Development Studies, University of East Anglia, UK, and a founder member of the International Research Network on Business, Development and Society.

Prue Kerr, Honorary Research Fellow of the Discipline of English, Communication and

Cultural Studies, School of Social and Cultural Studies, University of Western Australia, Australia.

Celia Lessa Kerstenetzky, Professor of Economics and Director of the Inequality and Development Centre, Federal Fluminense University, Brazil.

Arjo Klamer, Professor of Economics of Art and Culture, Erasmus University Rotterdam and Dean Academia Vitae, University College in Deventer, both in The Netherlands.

Serge-Christophe Kolm, Ecole des Hautes Etudes en Sciences Sociales, Paris, France.

Eric van de Laar, Ethicist in the Catharina Hospital Eindhoven, The Netherlands.

Odd Langholm, Professor Emeritus, Norwegian School of Economics, Bergen, Norway.

Mark A. Lutz, Professor Emeritus of Economics, University of Maine, Orono, USA.

Yahya M. Madra, Assistant Professor of Economics, Gettysburg College, USA.

Anne Mayhew, Professor Emerita at the University of Tennessee, Knoxville, Tennessee, USA.

Andrew Mearman, Senior Lecturer in Economics, Bristol Business School, University of the West of England, UK.

Ellen Mutari, Associate Professor of Economics and Coordinator of Women's Studies, The Richard Stockton College of New Jersey, USA.

Robert H. Nelson, Professor, School of Public Policy, University of Maryland, College Park, Maryland, USA.

Bart Nooteboom, Professor of Innovation Policy, Tilburg University, Tilburg, The Netherlands.

Pippa Norris, McGuire Lecturer in Comparative Politics, John F. Kennedy School of Government, Harvard University, USA.

John O'Neill, Professor of Political Economy, Philosophy, School of Social Sciences, The University of Manchester, UK.

J.B. (Hans) Opschoor, Professor of Economics of Sustainable Development at the Institute of Social Studies, and Professor of Environmental Economics at the Free University, The Netherlands.

Narendar Pani, Professor, School of Social Sciences, National Institute of Advanced Studies, India.

Stephen D. Parsons, School of English, Performance and Historical Studies, De Montfort University, UK.

Jan Peil, Assistant Professor of Economics, Radboud University Nijmegen, The Netherlands.

Ingrid Robeyns, Professor of Practical Philosophy, Erasmus University Rotterdam, The Netherlands.

Carlos Rodriguez-Sickert, PhD Economics at University of Cambridge and Assistant Professor, Pontificia Universidad Catolica de Chile, Instituto de Sociologia, Chile.

David F. Ruccio, Professor of Economics and Policy Studies, University of Notre Dame, USA, and editor of *Rethinking Marxism: A Journal of Economics, Culture & Society*.

Darla Schumm, Associate Professor of Religious Studies, Hollins University, USA.

William Schweiker, Edward L. Ryerson Distinguished Service Professor of Theological Ethics, University of Chicago, Illinois, USA.

Jonathan Seglow, Senior Lecturer in Political Theory, Department of Politics and International Relations, Royal Holloway, University of London, UK.

Esther-Mirjam Sent, Professor of Economic Theory and Policy, Radboud University Nijmegen, The Netherlands.

Irene van Staveren, Professor of Economics and Christian Ethics, Radboud University Nijmegen, and Associate Professor of Feminist Development Economics, Institute of Social Studies, both in The Netherlands.

Peter N. Stearns, Provost and Professor of History, George Mason University, USA.

Andy Sumner, Research Fellow at the Institute of Development Studies, Sussex. Also a Council Member of the Development Studies Association, UK.

Kari Wærness, Professor in the Department of Sociology, University of Bergen, Norway.

William Waller, Professor of Economics, Hobart and William Smith Colleges, USA.

Vivian Walsh, Distinguished Visiting Scholar in Economics and Philosophy at Muhlenberg College, USA.

Patrick J. Welch, Professor of Economics, Saint Louis University, USA.

Samuel Weston, Assistant Professor, Department of Economics, University of Dallas, Irving, Texas, USA.

Mark D. White, Associate Professor, Department of Political Science, Economics, and Philosophy, College of Staten Island, and The Graduate Center, CUNY, USA.

Jonathan B. Wight, Professor of Economics and International Studies, Robins School of Business, University of Richmond, USA.

Rodney Wilson, Professor of Economics, Durham University Institute for Middle Eastern and Islamic Studies, UK.

Stuart D. Yoak, Executive Director, Center for the Study of Ethics and Human Values, Washington University and Adjunct Professor, John M. Olin School of Business, Washington University, St Louis, USA.

Acknowledgements

In the first place, we warmly thank our authors. We are pleased that so many accepted our invitation to contribute to this volume, economists as well as philosophers/theologians and in some cases other social scientists. Furthermore, we are grateful for the enormous help we received from Haroon Akram-Lodhi, Gani Aldashev, Marcel Becker, Daniel Bell, Jos de Beus, Jeroen van Bouwel, Bé Breij, Geoffrey Brennan, Irene Breugel, Andries Broekhuijsen, Vivienne Brown, Maurizio Bussolo, Cara Beed, Clive Beed, Satya Chakravarty, Charles Clark, Gerhard Clever, William Clohesy, David Crocker, Charles Dannreuther, Lei Delsen, Steven DeLue, Severine Deneulin, David Dequech, Wilfred Dolfsma, Peter Dorman, Richard Dougherty, Sheila Dow, Stavros Drakopoulos, John Dupré, Zohreh Emami, Ben Fine, Russell Arben Fox, David George, Michele Gilman, Floris Heukelom, Susan Himmelweit, Geoff Hogdson, Toine Van de Hoogen, Andre van Hoorn, Bernd Irlenbusch, Zamir Iqbal, Richard Jolly, Steve Keen, Theo van de Klundert, Tony Lawson, Michelle Luijben, Patrick Mardellat, Charles McCann, Julie Nelson, Herman Noordegraaf, Mark Peacock, Renee Prendergast, Jack Reardon, Geert Reuten, Donna Rowen, Kala Saravanamuthu, Gerhard Scherhorn, Jan Aart Scholte, Nathalie Sigot, Peter Söderbaum, Ulrich Thielemann, Henk Tieleman, Kea Tijdens, Gaute Torsvik, Thanh-Dam Truong, Rudi Verburg, David Vogel, Jana Vyrastekova, Anthony Waterman, Patrick Welch, Charles Wilber, Jon Wisman, Stuart O. Yoak Stefano Zamagni and Eyal Zamir.

We are grateful to Cambridge University Press for the permission to include an edited extract of chapter 7 'Religion, the Protestant Ethics, and Moral Values' from *Sacred and Secular*, by Pippa Norris and Ronald Inglehart (Cambridge University Press, 2004).

Finally, we are grateful for the financial support of the Department of Economics of Radboud University Nijmegen which made this *Handbook* possible.

Introduction
Irene van Staveren and Jan Peil

Ethics and economics: the revival of economics as a moral science
From Adam Smith until John Maynard Keynes economics was widely understood as a moral science. Smith was Professor of Moral Philosophy in Glasgow while Keynes explicitly recognized economics as a moral science throughout his work. During the twentieth century, however, the centrality of neoclassical economics came to marginalize the ethical dimensions of economics. The stronghold of positivism over the discipline, particularly since Lionel Robbins's influential claim in 1932 that welfare economics should not compare levels of utility between individuals but leave that to politics, shifted ethical concerns to the equity side of the Paretian welfare criterion, which portrays efficiency and equity as trade-offs. This heritage leaves us today with a strong belief across the discipline that there are positive economics and normative economics and that the two are not only distinct but also each other's opposite.

Recently, however, the dichotomy between positive and normative economics that is portrayed in textbooks, models and empirical analyses has come under increasing attack. First, critical economists and philosophers challenge the fact/value dichotomy underlying modern science, including economics (Walsh 2000, 2003; Putnam 2002, 2003; Putnam and Walsh 2007). Putnam, a philosopher, argues 'that the whole idea of dividing up a thick ethical concept, such as cruelty or bravery, into a "purely descriptive part" (one which can be fully characterized in "value-free language") and a "purely evaluative art" is a philosopher's fantasy' (Putnam 2003, p. 396). He continues more precisely for economists, saying 'the world we inhabit when we describe the world for purposes the economist is interested in – is not describable in "value neutral" terms. Not without throwing away the most significant *facts* along with the "value judgments"' (ibid., emphasis in original). Walsh, an economist, confirms Putnam's view of economists, stating that 'a fact/value dichotomy (of which logical positivism was the early 20th century version) still underlies the beliefs and practices of economists today' (Walsh 2003, p. 321). He adds that the concept of rationality as the maximization of any goal 'is profoundly reductionist – boiling down "rationality" to sheer efficient maximization – fits like a glove the mathematics of constrained maximization. For both its formal convenience *and* its emptiness it is beloved of economists' (ibid., p. 345, emphasis in original). Amartya Sen is among the very few contemporary economists and Nobel Prize winners who has consistently rejected such economic reductionism, whether it is through the concept of rationality, welfare economics or efficiency, while developing an alternative paradigm around capabilities and human development which acknowledges the interwovenness of economic behaviour and morality (Sen, 1987, 1992, 1997).

The orthodox interpretation of Hume's is/ought distinction as an opposition finds less and less support among economists, who challenge dichotomies such as reason/emotion, preference/constraint, market/state, self-interest/altruism and statistical significance/substantive significance (see for example, van Staveren 2001, pp. 89–90). Of course, there is a fundamental difference between *distinguishing* between facts and values (which is necessary for conceptual reasons as well as to do justice to the different meanings of these concepts) and placing them in a *dichotomous* relation. The problem with a dichotomous positioning of fact and value and positive and normative economics is that one excludes the other and is favoured over the other, often without any ground other than that the favoured notion is not the unfavoured notion. Contrary to such dichotomies, values are part of economic analysis, alongside and frequently intertwined with facts, rather than being separated from facts in the form of policy recommendations following a supposedly value-free analysis. This connection between facts and values is revealed in economic terms such as 'freedom of choice', 'equilibrium' and 'efficiency' as being 'optimal'.

Second, experimental game theory has revealed that agents generally do not behave like the stereotype rational economic man, acting out of self-interest even when doing something for others (hedonistic altruism). A recent volume with state-of-the-art contributions from experimental game theory, entitled *Moral Sentiments and Material Interests* (Gintis et al. 2005) clearly shows that the rational economic man has had its time. The volume provides mounting evidence against the standard motivational assumption and instead reveals that strong reciprocity is the more prevalent motivation among human beings in various settings. The editors define strong reciprocity as 'a predisposition to cooperate with others, and to punish (at personal cost, if necessary) those who violate the norms of cooperation, even when it is implausible to expect that these costs will be recovered at a later date' (Gintis et al. 2005, p. 8). Strong reciprocity, hence, transcends the dichotomy between self-interest and altruism which characterizes most economic analysis today. Again, in the words of the editors, 'people are often neither self-regarding nor altruistic. Strong reciprocators are *conditional cooperators* (who behave altruistically as long as others are doing so as well) and *altruistic punishers* (who apply sanctions to those who behave unfairly according to the prevalent norms of cooperation)' (ibid., emphasis in original). Gintis and colleagues conclude with a call for a serious rethinking of economics in light of their model of strong reciprocity.

But such calls for rethinking have often fallen on deaf ears, even beyond the narrow confinements of neoclassical economics, as Kahneman, an economic psychologist, noted in his 2002 Nobel lecture. 'Theories in behavioural economics have generally retained the basic architecture of the rational model, adding assumptions about cognitive limitations designed to account for specific anomalies' (Kahneman 2003, p. 1469). The main reasons we see for the limited impact of innovative mainstream and heterodox empirical research on ethics in the economy is that these insights *cannot* simply be added on to the dominant paradigm. Attempts to do this are ethically weak, unconvincing, or right out perverse, as is the case for the inclusion of moral preferences in the rational choice model. This attempt simply reduces doing good by agent A to agent B to a 'warm glow' feeling for agent A motivated by agent A's preference maximization, not motivated by B's need, or only instrumentally so.

We are not under the illusion that this *Handbook of Economics and Ethics* will be able to trigger the necessary paradigmatic shift. But we do hope that this collection will contribute to the expansion of a critical mass of theoretical and empirical research that challenges the still common beliefs and practices of positivism in much of today's economics. With this as its motivation, the *Handbook* is a collection of 75 entries on the intersections between economics and ethics. It covers a wide range of topics – from key economists such as Smith and Keynes to the major ethical theories of utilitarianism, deontology and virtue ethics, and from basic economic concepts like markets and prices to key economic questions surrounding poverty, inequality and sustainability.

The purpose of the *Handbook* is twofold. First is the practical goal of providing a reference, a companion for academic economists, students and ethicists, as well as for policy-makers who may be confronted with the ethical dimensions of economic policies. For this reason, we have kept the entries short and supplemented them with extensive reference lists for further reading. The *Handbook*'s second aim is to contribute to the challenging task of addressing the calls, referred to above, to reconsider the relationship between ethics and economics. To this end, we have collected a wide diversity of entries, theoretical as well as policy-oriented, analytical as well as empirical, having one common characteristic that makes them suitable for the ambitious task ahead. That characteristic is to go beyond the fact/value dichotomy that characterizes today's welfare economics, behavioural economics, evolutionary economics, new institutional economics and even to some extent normative economics. All of the entries in this *Handbook* focus on the intersections between ethics and economics, how the two are related in diverse ways, rather than assuming that they are necessarily trade-offs, or that ethics should come into the analysis only after presumably morally-neutral economic questions have been addressed.

At the same time, the entries are in many ways diverse; not only because of the wide diversity of authors who were willing to contribute to the *Handbook*, but also because we as editors did not want to force any particular framework upon the contributions. Hence, some entries are richly descriptive, such as, for example, the entry on corporate social responsibility, whereas others offer original analysis, of which the entry on postmodernism is a good example. Another consequence of our relatively open approach is that no unified message can be found of how economics and ethics are precisely related. There is not just one way in which the two connect, and there is not just one way through which these connections speak to economic theory.

It is up to the reader to judge whether we have succeeded in striking a balance between coverage and diversity, on the one hand, and helping the 'rethinking economics project' further beyond the fact/value dichotomy, on the other hand.

References

Gintis, Herbert, Samuel Bowles, Robert Boyd and Ernst Fehr (2005), *Moral Sentiments and Material Interests: The Foundations of Cooperation in Economic Life*, Cambridge, MA: MIT Press.

Kahneman, Daniel (2003), 'Maps of bounded rationality: psychology for behavioral economics', *American Economic Review*, **93** (5), 1449–75.

Putnam, Hilary (2002), *The Collapse of the Fact/Value Dichotomy*, Cambridge, MA: Harvard University Press.

Putnam, Hilary (2003), 'For ethics and economics without the dichotomies', *Review of Political Economy*, **15** (3), 395–412.

Putnam, Hilary and Vivian Walsh (2007), 'Facts, theories, values and destitution in the works of Sir Partha Dasgupta', *Review of Political Economy*, **19** (2), 181–202.

Sen, Amartya (1987), *On Ethics and Economics*, Oxford: Basil Blackwell.

Sen, Amartya (1992), *Inequality Re-examined*, New York: Russell Sage Foundation.

Sen, Amartya (1997), *On Economic Inequality*, expanded edition, Oxford: Oxford University Press.

Staveren, Irene van (2001), *The Values of Economics. An Aristotelian Perspective*, London: Routledge.

Walsh, Vivian (2000), 'Smith after Sen', *Review of Political Economy*, **12** (1), 5–25.

Walsh, Vivian (2003), 'Sen after Putnam', *Review of Political Economy*, **15** (3), 315–94.

1 Altruism
Jonathan Seglow

The term 'altruism' was coined by Auguste Comte in the 1830s, derived from the Latin 'alteri huic' which literally means 'to this other'. It soon became the centrepiece of an ethics stressing our social duties to other people. The term gained particular currency in the nineteenth century with the decline of traditional societies in which people's duties were based on their rank or station. With the rise of more impersonal industrial societies, the question of what obligations people had to others became an issue. However, the idea of behaviour which puts the interests of others before oneself was discussed by Aristotle, Jesus, Aquinas and many other ethicists before Comte (Scott and Seglow 2007, Ch. 1). Altruism has fallen out of favour among contemporary moral philosophers largely because it has come to be associated with supererogatory (praiseworthy but not required) duties, and these have received relatively little attention compared with stricter obligations – of social justice for example.[1] Altruism remains a concern of evolutionary biologists seeking to explain why humans among other selfish animals promote the interests of others, as well as of social psychologists who similarly explore the nature of altruistic motivation (Monroe 1994; Scott and Seglow 2007, Ch. 3, 4).

Economists have long been interested in altruism (Phelps 1975; Collard 1978; Kolm 1983), though one writer claimed, perhaps unfairly, it's been a 'painful nuisance' for them (Lunati 1997, p. 50). Pareto, Edgeworth, Walras and Smith are among those who investigated altruism. Of them, Smith's treatment is best known. 'It is not from the benevolence of the butcher, the brewer or the baker that we expect our dinner', he famously wrote in *The Wealth of Nations*, 'but from their regard to their own interest' (Smith [1776] 1976, pp. 26–7). Others spoke of 'the Adam Smith problem' (Kolm 1983, p. 22; 2000, p. 16) which concerned how the self-interested assumptions of *The Wealth of Nations* can be squared with the expansion of our empathetic sentiments, as Smith urged in *The Theory of Moral Sentiments* (1759). Recent work has recontextualized Smith, however, resisting his recruitment as a public choice theorist before his time. According to Muller, Smith believed that commercial society created institutional incentives for people to attain virtues that conduced to both their private and the public good. These included prudence, self-control, deferred gratification, respect for others and sensitivity to others' needs (Muller 1993). The rising level of material comfort in a market society enables the masses to escape their dependence on elites and expand their sympathy and concern for others. Human beings have a natural desire to feel emotionally related to others and to identify with them (Peil 1999, pp. 83–100). Our desire for approval means we measure our behaviour by others' standards, causing us to strive for wealth and power as things generally valued, but at the same time acting as a check on our egoistic tendencies. Altruism, for Smith, is motivated above all by our desire to act in a manner that elicits others' praise (Muller 1993, p. 106) – a point to which we shall return.

Before investigating altruism further, we need some definitions. Assume that individuals are self-interested, an axiom of rational choice. The self-interested individual may, however, be perfectly altruistic or perfectly selfish, or, as is most likely, somewhere between the two. It depends on the source of one's utility. If I *only* gain utility through seeing you succeed in your goals, then I am perfectly altruistic; if conversely my utility is routed only through success in my own goals and preferences, and I am indifferent to yours, then I am selfish. Yet in both cases I am self-interested in the sense that I attend exclusively to my own utility, whatever the source of it is.[2] Most people enjoy utility gains through success in their own endeavours but also partly by enjoying the successes of others, particularly those close to them. A world of perfect altruists is a logical impossibility, since every last person would be exclusively concerned with others' preferences, leaving no preferences of their own. (Two altruists arguing over who should have the last seat on a bus: 'After you', 'No, after you!')

In its assumption that much overtly altruistic behaviour is powered by more self-interested considerations, economics has an affinity with socio-biological accounts of altruism. On the socio-biological account, altruism is a sacrifice of reproductive success ('fitness') on the part of the individual in order that at least some members of the group enjoy a rise in fitness (Simon 1993, p. 158). This is a rational choice if the fitness lost by the altruist is less than that gained by the group. Indeed, at the genetic level it is a self-interested choice insofar as group members share the altruist's genes. It is possible to determine which choices are altruistic, in this technical rendering, and which are on any account selfish. On this basis, Simon (1993) urged a less a priori and more empirically informed economics.

How genuine is altruistic behaviour? Is there a self-interested or other-regarding motive to an individual's benefiting others? As a behavioural science concerned with observable preferences, economics has difficulty distinguishing when A's promotion of B's welfare is actually motivated by A's altruism from when it is a strategic way of advancing A's own self-interest (Elster 2006). Individuals seek to advance others' goals not just because they care about them, but to boost their own reputation, to achieve social approval (one likes to be thought good and indeed needs to be thought so according to Smith), to trigger return goods from a strong reciprocator or to avoid punishment if the other is powerful. However, if self-interestedly motivated altruistic acts can be put to work in an incentive structure geared to the good of all, then it may not matter if they are not genuinely altruistic. In the United States, for example, there is a strong norm of charitable giving amongst some of the population; non-givers may experience some shame if givers are motivated largely by the desire to avoid shame. Many prohibitions, such as norms against littering and other kinds of anti-social behaviour, work in much the same way (Elster 2006, pp. 194–8). On the other hand, an advocate of the self-interested agent, for the sake of consistency, still needs to take account of every source of well-being, and an individual whose altruism is merely behavioural may lose out on sources of well-being that only a genuine motivational altruism can provide. As Frey (1997) points out, behavioural (not genuine) altruists suffer, first, from impaired self-determination, as they are captive to an incentive structure designed by others and do not set their own altruistic ends; second, they do not enjoy the heightened self-esteem that comes from having one's genuine altruism acknowledged by others; and third they are denied the expressive possibility of communicating their genuinely altruistic motives to other people. It is fair to say that economics has been more interested in the effects of altruistic behaviour rather than agents' motives, whatever they are. Frey's work reminds us there may be costs in doing so.

Along similar lines, Andreoni, who has written extensively on philanthropy, fears that economics may be poorly suited to explaining it – a possibility discussed by others too (Andreoni 2006, p. 1205; Sugden 1982). Notwithstanding this, philanthropy is a central area in which economists interested in altruistic behaviour have been able to apply their theories – sometimes altruism and charity are even equated (Khalil 2004). There are also other reasons to examine altruism. In the United States, philanthropic activity amounts to about 5 per cent of gross national product.[3] Older, better-educated citizens tend to give more, and in the United States at least, their preferred recipients have some religious affiliation, amounting to nearly half of all donations. The super-wealthy in the United States are usually very generous, but donate less to religiously associated causes. Charities operate as competitive market agents, employing ever more sophisticated strategies to increase their 'market share'. Individuals' giving preferences tend to be interdependent; one study found that peer group effects are significant insofar as people adjust their giving to what is deemed the socially correct amount (Andreoni and Scholz 1998).

In some cases it is not easy to distinguish philanthropic from more market-motivated behaviour, for example, where individuals who donate blood or organs are rewarded for their gifts through tax breaks, reimbursement for hospitalization and lost time, payments from their insurance company and so on. Notwithstanding this, organ donation (in contrast to standard gifts of time and money) is commonly seen as one of the most praiseworthy philanthropic gestures an individual can make (Hamish 1992). Richard Titmuss's classic account of blood donation places value on donors' trust that their fellow citizens would give the same gift in return should the need arise (Titmuss [1970] 1997). Blood donation helps to bind citizens together as an ethical community in which civic solidarity flourishes (Page 1996, pp. 94–102). Set against this, Kenneth Arrow complained that the prohibition on selling blood curtails liberty, while the marketization of blood alongside a donor system gives individuals a new freedom to sell their blood, while retaining their old freedom to donate it (Arrow 1972; compare Singer 1973). Indeed, a marketized system existing *alongside* a donor system means unpaid donors can more easily demonstrate their altruism and social virtue by opting for the latter (Machan 1997, pp. 252–3).

The problem philanthropy poses for altruism arises from the so-called 'warm glow' effect. Individual givers gain much well-being from the activity of giving itself: experiencing sympathy, doing what is right and receiving gratitude and recognition in return. As charities grow larger, the marginal benefit of each extra donation is reduced, and the warm glow effect tends to crowd out other kinds of motivations. Experimental results confirm the importance of the warm glow. In one game, individuals preferred donating some fraction of 100 units as a public good over withdrawing from the same number of units already publicly committed that fraction they wanted for themselves (Andreoni 1995). Consistent with this, recent work has theorized the notion of personally making a difference (Duncan 2004). If the latter is taken seriously as an effect, and not just as an intention, then donors may cut their contributions (or switch them elsewhere) as their marginal effect declines. Elster (2006, p. 204) suggests that many charitable endeavours are performed for the inner audience. One wants to be able to esteem oneself for a reason; individuals do give considerable amounts even when no one else knows of their philanthropy (Frey and Meier 2004). Whether self-esteem and the warm glow should count in social welfare is a complex question (Andreoni 2006, pp. 1223–30). The same money given may be coercively transferred through the tax system, the standard view being that this crowds out philanthropic transfers (Andreoni and Payne 2003).

The family is another area in which altruistically-minded economists have produced interesting results. In his well-known *Treatise on the Family* Becker argues that altruism is peculiarly common in families, because they tend to be smaller and contain a denser network of interactions than economic enterprises, both of these making other-regarding behaviour easier to perform (Becker 1981, p. 299). Marriage 'markets' tend to match altruistic folk with self-interested spouses who prefer to benefit from their partner's altruism, creating a stable arrangement where both gain in different ways. (Two altruists married to each other would suffer from the 'after you' problem, and two people eager to benefit from others' altruism would enjoy less utility than if they married altruists.) Becker's well-known rotten kid theorem states that if the head of a family is impartially concerned with the good of all of its members, and 'rotten kids' can augment the family's wealth leaving the head with more to disburse, then they will surely do so. This is a further example of simulated altruism (Becker 1974). Stark has conceived of families' willingness to marry out their daughters to wealthy families as a way of buying insurance for themselves in their old age (Stark 1995, pp. 13, 8). Further, while on the face of it, it is more rational for families in developing countries to send sons rather than daughters abroad to lucrative jobs since sons tend to earn more and hence have more income to send back, many families prefer to send daughters because girls tend to remit a higher proportion of their income and thus in many cases will secure a greater income stream for their parents and siblings back home (ibid., pp. 74–7).

If altruistic behaviour, within families, towards charities and elsewhere, augments social welfare then it may not matter if many of its motives are less than pure. However, as Corts (2006) showed, we cannot always assume that altruism does produce aggregate welfare gains. This is chiefly because altruists encounter coordination problems which more self-interested individuals are able to avoid. For example, a husband and wife might each sacrifice something valuable for themselves – time, money, a valuable possession that one might need to sell – in order to buy a present for the other. But if the gift a wife presents to her husband is less than the utility she sacrificed to procure it, and the same holds for her husband's gift to her, the aggregate social welfare outcome is lower than if each had chosen to be selfish.[4] Corts shows that if several players are only partially altruistic, so that each person's utility is a part-function of their own success and a part-function of at least one other person's success, then total social welfare may not be optimized.

Pure selfishness would make the world simpler, if not more pleasant, but the evidence is that individuals rarely behave purely selfishly. A couple of examples from game theory illustrate our tendency towards altruistic behaviour. In the one-shot ultimatum game, the proposer, in possession of 100 units, makes an offer to share a fraction with the respondee which she can either accept or reject. If she rejects it, both get nothing. A crude rational choice model would see the respondee accept offers of just one unit on the grounds that anything is better than nothing. In fact, offers of below 25–30 units tend to be rejected, illustrating a strong norm of fairness; respondees feel insulted if offers fall below what they consider just. The ultimatum game has been tested in the United States, Germany, Russia, Israel, Japan and among remote tribes in Indonesia and across the Pacific Islands with fairly consistent results (Fehr and Schmidt 1999; Carrerer 2003, Ch. 2). Age, ethnicity, gender and other demographic variables also have weak effects.

The proposer's offer may or may not be motivated by fairness. In the knowledge that, were the proposer in the respondee's shoes, the norm of fairness would be important, the proposer may make a relatively generous offer for purely strategic reasons (Elster 2006, p. 189). In the dictator game, by contrast, recipients are powerless; proposers simply choose which offer to make. The first time this was tested, three-quarters of proposers chose to split $20 equally between themselves and the recipient; and only one-quarter elected to keep $18, handing over just $2 (Kahneman et al. 1986). However, in subsequent experiments when dictators could choose precisely what fraction to share, offers were less generous. In one game where dictators disbursed money to actual welfare recipients, those recipients who were seen to have a stronger preferences for working were offered more (Fong 2007).

Two parties each prepared to give to the other often enter mutually *reciprocal* beneficial relationships. Closely related to altruism, reciprocity differs in that it is bi-directional, A gives to B *and* B gives to A. Reciprocity is also distinguished from exchange, which shares its bi-directionality. With exchange, however, exemplified in the economic market, giving is *conditional* on receiving something in return at the same time; with reciprocity there is merely the expectation that this will be forthcoming (Kolm 2006, p. 25). Why should individuals expect this? Individuals may reciprocate because they like the giver, because they self-interestedly want the giving to continue, out of gratitude towards the giver or a desire to retain the 'moral balance' and not be indebted, as well as considerations of fairness. That last motive is useful in explaining schemes of 'generalized reciprocity' when the individual from whom givers enjoy a return may not be the same as the person to whom they gave. Reciprocity usually serves social integration, but generalized reciprocity means a degree of solidarity can be maintained over far larger numbers of people. When practices of reciprocity benefit all, and individuals are prepared to maintain them, the result can be a stable economic society of mutual benefit. Perhaps because of this, reciprocity is endemic to human society. Marcel Mauss's classic of comparative anthropology *The Gift* (1924), argues that, contrary to what anthropologists such as Malinowski believed, human history shows there are no unreciprocated gifts; giving *always* establishes an expectation of return (Mauss [1924] 2002). Mauss's thesis that (reciprocal) gifts in ritualized settings promote social integration provides insights for today's thinking about gift economies (as opposed to market economies). But the claim that there are no free gifts is a radical and hardly plausible one (how could there then be altruism?), and it is certainly not entailed by the truth that reciprocity is endemic.

Strong reciprocity tends to occur when individuals share and cooperate, and in addition are liable to punish, even at some personal cost, free-riders and others who violate cooperative norms (Bowles and Gintis 2004). Strong reciprocity stabilizes other-regarding norms without recourse to hierarchical authority, but unfortunately it cannot always be guaranteed. Some of the most intractable problems in the economics of altruism occur when it is so essential that individuals get their due that practices of reciprocity are institutionalized and backed by coercive sanctions as in the tax-funded welfare state. One could argue, as noted above, that any kind of genuine altruism is crowded out here (Seglow 2002), though Harris (1987) maintains that, though forced to give, taxpayers still have the choice of whether to give *altruistically*. The evidence shows that individuals will accept sanctions on defaults from altruism if those sanctions are perceived as fair (Fehr and Rockenbach 2003). The difficulty then becomes how to harness this sense of fairness to the forced nature of tax-giving, especially given that many citizens believe that welfare subsidizes those who in reality have little claim on our giving (Gilens 1999).

Notes

1. Monroe's (1996) moral-psychological notion of a common humanity is an important exception to this trend.
2. What economics has difficulty explaining is persons who care about others' welfare exclusively *for the sake of the other*, without reference to their own utility at all.
3. In most European states, private philanthropic activity is far less, but public transfers are correspondingly higher.
4. Of course, we would need to factor into this the utility that comes from giving itself.

References

Andreoni, James (1995), 'Cooperation in public goods experiments: kindness or confusion?' *American Economic Review*, **85** (4), 891–904.
Andreoni, James (2006), 'Philanthropy', in Serge-Christophe Kolm and Jean Mercier Ythier (eds), *Handbook of the Economics of Giving, Altruism and Reciprocity*, Vol. 2, Amsterdam: Elsevier, pp. 1201–69.
Andreoni, James and A. Payne (2003), 'Do government grants to private charities crowd out giving or fund-raising?' *American Economic Review*, **93** (3), 792–812.
Andreoni, James and John K. Scholz (1998), 'An econometric analysis of charitable giving with interdependent preferences', *Economic Inquiry*, **36** (3), 410–28.
Arrow, Kenneth (1972), 'Gifts and exchanges', *Philosophy and Public Affairs*, **1** (4), 343–62.
Becker, Gary (1974), 'A theory of social interactions', *Journal of Political Economy*, **82** (6), 1063–93.
Becker, Gary (1981), *A Treatise on the Family*, Cambridge, MA: Harvard University Press.
Bowles Samuel and Herbert Gintis (2004), 'The evolution of strong reciprocity: cooperation in heterogenous populations', *Theoretical Population Biology*, **65** (1), 17–28.
Carrerer, Colin (2003), *Behavioural Game Theory*, Princeton, NJ: Princeton University Press.
Collard, David (1978), *Altruism and the Economy: A Study in Non-Selfish Economics*, Oxford: Martin Robertson.
Corts, Kenneth (2006), 'When altruism lowers total welfare', *Economics and Philosophy*, **22** (1), 1–18.
Duncan, Brian (2004), 'A theory of impact philanthropy', *Journal of Public Economics*, **88** (9–10), 2159–80.
Elster, Jon (2006), 'Altruistic behaviour and altruistic motivations', in Serge-Christophe Kolm and Jean Mercier Ythier (eds), *Handbook of the Economics of Giving, Altruism and Reciprocity*, Vol. 1, Amsterdam: Elsevier, pp. 183–206.
Fehr, Ernst and Bettina Rockenbach (2003), 'Detrimental effects of sanctions on human altruism', *Nature*, 422, 137–40.
Fehr, Ernst and Klaus M. Schmidt (1999), 'A theory of fairness, competition and cooperation', *Quarterly Journal of Economics*, **114** (3), 817–68.
Fong, Christina (2007), 'Evidence from an experiment on charity to welfare recipients: reciprocity, altruism and the emphatic responsiveness hypothesis', *The Economic Journal*, **117** (522), 1008–1024.
Frey, Bruno S. (1997), *Not For The Money: An Economic Theory of Personal Motivation*, Cheltenham, UK and Lyme, US: Edward Elgar.
Frey, Bruno S. and Stephan Meier (2004), 'Pro-social behavior in a natural setting', *Journal of Economic Behavior and Organization*, **54** (1), 65–88.
Gilens, Martin (1999), *Why Americans Hate Welfare*, Chicago, IL: Chicago University Press.
Hamish, Stewart (1992), 'Rationality and the market for blood', *Journal of Economic Behaviour and Organisation*, **19**, 125–43.
Harris, David (1987), *Justifying State Welfare*, Oxford: Basil Blackwell.
Kahneman, Daniel, Jack L. Knetsch and Richard Thaler (1986), 'Fairness as a constraint on profit-seeking: entitlements in the market', *American Economic Review*, **76** (4), 728–41.
Khalil, Elias L. (2004), 'What is altruism?' *Journal of Economic Psychology*, **25** (1), 97–123.
Kolm, Serge-Christophe (1983), 'Altruism and efficiency', *Ethics*, **94** (1), 18–65.
Kolm, Serge-Christophe (2000), 'The theory of reciprocity', in Louis-André Gérard-Varet, Serge-Christophe Kolm and Jean Mercier Ythier (eds), *The Economics of Reciprocity, Giving and Altruism*, Basingstoke: Macmillan, pp. 115–41.
Kolm, Serge-Christophe (2006), 'Introduction to the economics of giving, altruism and reciprocity', in Serge-Christophe Kolm and Jean Mercier Ythier (eds), *Handbook of the Economics of Giving, Altruism and Reciprocity*, Vol. 1, Amsterdam: Elsevier.

Lunati, M. Teresa (1997), *Ethical Issues in Economics: From Altruism to Co-operation to Equity*, Basingstoke: Macmillan.

Machan, Tibor M. (1997), 'Blocked Exchanges Revisited' *Journal of Applied Philosophy*, **14** (1), 249–62.

Mauss, Marcel ([1924] 2002), *The Gift*, ed. Mary Douglas, London: Routledge.

Monroe, Kristen (1994), 'A fat lady in a corset: altruism and social theory', *American Journal of Political Science*, **38** (4), 861–93.

Muller, Jerry Z. (1993), *Adam Smith: In His Time and Ours*, Princeton, NJ: Princeton University Press.

Page, Robert (1996), *Altruism and the British Welfare State*, Aldershot: Avebury.

Peil, Jan (1999), *Adam Smith and Economic Science: A Methodological Reinterpretation*, Cheltenham, UK and Northampton, MA, USA: Edward Elgar.

Phelps, Edmund (ed.) (1975), *Altruism, Morality and Economic Theory*, New York: Russell Sage Foundation.

Scott, Niall and Jonathan Seglow (2007), *Altruism*, Buckingham: Open University Press.

Seglow, Jonathan (2002), 'Altruism and freedom', in Jonathan Seglow (ed.), *The Ethics of Altruism*, special issue of *Critical Review of International Social and Political Philosophy*, **5** (4), 145–63.

Simon, Herbert A. (1993), 'Altruism and economics', *American Economic Review (Papers and Proceedings)*, **83** (2), 156–61.

Singer, Peter (1973), 'Altruism and commerce: a defense of Titmuss against Arrow', *Philosophy and Public Affairs*, **2** (3), 312–20.

Smith, Adam ([1759] 2002), ed. K. Haakonssen, *The Theory of Moral Sentiments*, Cambridge: Cambridge University Press.

Smith, Adam ([1776] 1976), *An Enquiry into the Nature and Causes of the Wealth of Nations*, ed. R.H. Campbell and Andrew S. Skinner, Oxford: Clarendon Press.

Stark, Oded (1995), *Altruism and Beyond*, Cambridge: Cambridge University Press.

Sugden, Robert (1982), 'On the economics of philanthropy', *Economic Journal*, **92**, 341–50.

Titmuss, Richard ([1970] 1997), *The Gift Relationship*, London: LSE Books.

See also the entries on: Economic antropology; Egoism; Fairness; Self-interest; Utilitarianism.

2 Thomas Aquinas
Odd Langholm

In the history of economic ideas, Thomas Aquinas (1225–74) is the foremost representative of Scholasticism, that is, the system of Christian philosophy taught in the schools of Western Europe in the Middle Ages. This assessment is usually based on Aquinas's contribution of four articles dealing with exchange and value and with loans and usury in his *Summa Theologiae* (II–II, 77, 1–78, 4). However, Aquinas dealt with economic subjects elsewhere in that work and in a number of other works as well. He also belonged to a tradition that included many important contributors to scholastic economics, some before him, on whom he drew, and some after him, who further developed his ideas. What singles him out, in the eyes of both his contemporaries and his scholastic successors and from the historian's perspective, is his powerful intellect combined with his common sense and moderation.

Thomas Aquinas was the youngest son of an Italian count. He was born around 1225 at Roccasecca near Aquino, a small town between Rome and Naples. Having spent his boyhood as an oblate at the Benedictine abbey of Monte Cassino, Aquinas left without taking monastic vows and enrolled in the arts faculty of the University of Naples. While studying there he became attracted to the ideals of the mendicant friars and joined the more recently founded Dominican order. After some initial opposition from his aristocratic family he was permitted to travel to Paris where he came under the influence of Albert the Great. After graduating as a master of theology, he taught at the University of Paris and in Dominican *studia* in Italy, while a steady stream of works issued through the pens of his secretaries. In 1274, at less than fifty years of age, he fell ill while on his way to the Council of Lyons and died at the Cistercian abbey of Fossanova, not far from his birthplace. Thomas Aquinas was canonized in 1323, and in 1576 Pope Pius V declared him a doctor of the church.

St Thomas discussed economic activity against the historical background of a patristic tradition that questioned the possibility of anyone engaged in trade being saved. He cited the example of Christ's eviction of the traders from the temple, and drew upon the contemporary categorical claim by a faction of the Franciscan order that abnegation of wealth was a measure of economic virtue. Aquinas stated firmly that the end of man is not of this world and that material wealth is irrelevant from that perspective. In this earthly life, however, the exercise of virtue is impaired by bodily defects. Since the body depends on material things for its preservation, material wealth is necessary and desirable in an instrumental sense (*Sum. Theol.* I–II, 4, 6–7). On the other hand, excessive wealth may impede the love and fear of God. A distinctive feature of riches is that one easily gets entrapped by avarice, which tends to infinity (*Sententia Libri Politicorum* I, 8). Appetite for inordinate wealth is sinful because it can make a man a slave of wealth rather than its master (*Sum. Theol.* I–II, 108, 3). Wealth in itself is not at fault, but the abuse of wealth. The same is true of poverty (*Summa Contra Gentiles* III, 134). Poverty, like wealth, is an instrument. Perfection of the Christian life does not, however, reside in poverty in the sense that where there is more poverty there is necessarily more perfection (*Sum. Theol.* II–II, 185, 6). As a matter of fact, the poor are easy prey to the lure of lucre (*Sum. Theol.* II–II, 186, 3). Poverty is good insofar as it liberates humans from the vices associated with wealth, but if it impedes the benefits that wealth can bring, namely, the necessary material support of oneself and of others, poverty is an unfortunate state (*Contra Gentiles* III, 133).

Whereas part of Aquinas's message was addressed to those of the mendicant friars who overrated the state of voluntary poverty, his warning against falling victim to avarice was meant as much for laypeople. By the Middle Ages, private property had long since been instituted by law. The scholastic masters were disinclined to argue against secular institutions on this level. From classical and patristic sources, Aquinas and his contemporaries inherited a natural law doctrine according to which all property was originally common, people worked together in harmony and shared the fruits of their labour, an idyll shattered by the Fall of Man. The fundamental principles of natural law remained in force, but an addition to it had to be made in view of humankind's present state, which ordained division of property (*Sum. Theol.* I–II, 94, 5; II–II, 66, 2).

Aristotle had earlier suggested a number of reasons why property ought to be private. Common ownership was unproductive, a cause of trouble and, as Aquinas added (not one inclined to place his premises in humanity's baser nature), a cause of disorder (*Sent. Pol.* II, 4; *Sum. Theol.* II–II, 66, 2). A duty of charity to succour the needy still remained in force. To deny charity to those in real need he saw as a mortal sin (*Quodlibet* VI, 12). If the poor are made to starve amidst the surplus of the wealthy, the original precepts of natural law might be reactivated (*Sum. Theol.* II–II, 66, 7). In cases of 'urgent and manifest need', Thomas Aquinas asserted, taking another's property is not to be reckoned as theft in an ethical sense (*Sum. Theol.* II–II, 32, 5). 'In extremé need all is common' (*Sum. Theol.* II–II, 32, 7).

Unfortunately, because of the Fall, charity cannot rule the marketplace. When Aquinas turned to exchange of property for a recompense, all that the moral theologian can insist on and hope for, is justice; that is, to give each of the exchangers their due. Now 'justice by its name implies equality' (*Sum. Theol.* II–II, 58, 2). 'A sale is just when the price accepted equals the thing sold' (*Quodl.* II, 10). These statements derive from Aristotle and apply to barter, in terms of which Aristotle's analysis in the *Nicomachean Ethics* is couched, as well as to buying and selling. They are valid in positive law and in the moral law, but their interpretation and enforcement is different in each case. If a certain seller, without committing fraud or applying physical duress, by normal bargaining can manage to dispose of a commodity at more than the just price, positive law will not prosecute (which does not mean that it commends such conduct), unless the divergence is manifestly unreasonable. The moral law, on the other hand, leaves nothing unpunished that is contrary to virtue and insists on the just price. It does not follow, however, that it is necessary, or indeed possible, to determine the just price with the utmost precision. The just price consists rather of a kind of estimate (*Sum. Theol.* II–II, 77, 1).

Aquinas envisaged two factors on which to base such estimates, namely, human need (the demand side of the exchange equation) and cost (the supply side). Both are established in his commentary on Aristotle's *Ethics*. In *Ethics* (V, 5), a cast of characters representing different occupations is introduced: a builder, a shoemaker, a farmer and a doctor. This cast mutually exchange their products and services. According to Aristotle, 'The number of shoes exchanged for a house must correspond to the ratio of builder to shoemaker.' What could this cryptic statement mean? What determines the ratio between exchangers? Aristotle asserts that the cause of exchange, the reason why people engage in mutual exchange, is the need each party has for the product or service offered by the other party. Aquinas, adhering closely to his teacher Albert the Great, suggests, as one explanation, that need is not only the cause of exchange, it is also the natural measure of the just value of the things exchanged (*Sententia Libri Ethicorum* V, 9). Now in the version of the Latin translation used by Aquinas, the word rendered here as 'need' is *indigentia*, which also permits the translation 'demand', provided that it is not associated too closely with the modern notion of aggregate market demand. Aristotle's strange formula relates to individual person-to-person exchange, and it offers no further suggestion as to how Aquinas conceived of *indigentia* in an exchange context.

In the same chapter of his *Ethics* commentary, still following Albert the Great, Aquinas mentions the alternative estimate of justice in exchange, that of cost. As many shoes should be exchanged for a house, as the builder exceeds the shoemaker 'in labour and expenses'. As is to be expected, a large and varied literary output like that of Thomas Aquinas contains many remarks about labour, some of them enumerating its blessings and rewards but not all equally relevant to economics. Labour chases away idleness, macerates the body, aids the poor and, obviously and necessarily, provides for one's own bodily sustenance (*Sum. Theol.* II–II, 187, 3; *Contra Gentiles* III, 135; *Quodl.* VII, 17).

One should be wary about almsgiving to able beggars, who rather ought to work (*Contra Impugnantes* 7, 11), whereas those who do work should be paid at least a sub-sistence wage (*Contra Impugnantes* 7, 7). Poor manual labourers should be paid without delay lest they lack food (*Sum. Theol.* I–II, 105, 2). These ideas are brought to bear on the labour of merchants. A man may intend the moderate gain which he seeks to acquire by trading for the upkeep of his household, or for the assistance of the needy; or again, a man may take to trade for some public advantage, for instance, lest his country lack the necessaries of life, and seek gain, not as an end, but as a payment for his labour (*Sum. Theol.* II–II, 77, 4).

The cost (labour and expenses) principle and the need (or demand) principle both appear in an analytical model that may be called Thomas Aquinas's 'double rule' of just pricing. In reply to the question of whether anyone may lawfully sell a thing for more than it is worth, Aquinas suggests this should be considered from two viewpoints. From a general point of view, buying and selling can be seen to have been instituted for the benefit of both parties. The exchange is then based on the principle of equality and selling above or buying below the value of the good is unjust and unlawful.

In special cases, however, buyer and seller may value the good differently. First, con-sider a case where the potential buyer is in great need of (*multum indiget*) a thing and the potential seller will be harmed by parting with it. In such a case the just price will depend not only on the thing sold, but also on the loss that the sale brings on the seller, who may lawfully sell the thing for more than it is worth in itself, though not for more than it is worth to the seller. Second, suppose the buyer is in need, whereas the seller does not suffer the particular loss assumed in the first case. It would then be unlawful to overcharge the buyer (*Sum. Theol.* II–II, 77, 1).

The first part of this double rule establishes a principle of indemnity; the seller's loss is an instance of what is now called 'opportunity cost'. The second part embodies a prohibition of economic coercion. Need is a just measure of goods in exchange but is not to be exploited under unusual circumstances. Aquinas does not tell us what he means by value 'in itself' (*secundum se*). There is no reason to believe that he had some inherent value in mind, divorced from human estimation. On the contrary, he emphasized the essential difference between value according to the scale of natural perfection and value in the economic order (*Sum. Theol.* II–II, 77, 2; *Sent. Eth.* V, 9). Perhaps value in itself can be taken to mean some sort of normal value in exchange. Some later scholastics took it to mean market value. This interpretation lacks a basis in Aquinas, but it may be worth pointing out that the question of lawfulness of selling a thing for more than it is worth does not arise if the parties have access to a market operating under normal competitive conditions.

On a par with economic coercion, a purchase or sale may be rendered unjust on account of fraud. 'Fraudulence' appears in the title of Thomas Aquinas's question about justice in exchange in the *Summa Theologiae* and is more specifically the subject of its second and third articles. They are mostly concerned with defective goods and with the seller's obligation to reveal defects. Aquinas denounces falsification with regard to substance, quantity and quality of merchandise and discusses what kinds of withholding of information amount to fraud in the moral sense. As pointed out elsewhere, the right of buyers and sellers to outwit one another granted them in civil law does not extend to a general license to commit fraud (*Quodl.* II, 10). Buyers and sellers should use measures established by public authority or custom in each place of trade. A seller is obliged to reveal hidden defects in goods if they are likely to cause danger or loss. In the case of manifest defects, where the buyer has the opportunity to inspect the merchandise, the seller is not obliged to offer the former all advantages. The sale is morally valid if he charges a reduced price that seems just considering the defect. If he were to have the defect publicly announced, a price even below that level might be difficult to obtain. Sometimes a merchant should be allowed to withhold information that does not pertain specifically to the merchandise but may yet have an influence on price. A trader who carries victuals to a certain location where they fetch a high price owing to scarcity need not reveal knowledge of the imminent arrival of plentiful supplies (which would cause an anticipated drop in prices) but may trade at the current price. It would be an act of great virtue to lower the price but as a matter of justice there is no obligation to do so (*Sum. Theol.* II–II, 77, 2–3).

If a price is increased because payment is delayed or decreased because of advance payment, usury may be involved in the sale. In such transactions profits are due merely to the passage of time; but time belongs to God. Scholastic literature abounds in case discussion of hidden usury. Aquinas was less occupied with details than with general principles. From a general point of view, economic exchange involving a time element can be interpreted as a combination of an instantaneous sale and a loan. In this regard, Aquinas's main contribution is his analysis of usury in straight monetary loans. Usury in scholastic terminology meant the payment (or the hope of payment) of an amount in excess of the principal in a loan of money (or, in theory, a loan of any natural fungible). Aquinas cautiously acknowledged certain extrinsic (non-usurious) titles to interest, covering loss on the part of the creditor due to the loan, but this was a subject for the future and for the canonists rather than the theologians. He shared the common scholastic opinion that usury was divinely forbidden, citing Luke, 6:35: 'Lend, hoping for nothing again' (*Sum. Theol.* II–II, 78, 1). The scholastics also believed it possible to establish a natural law case against usury, suggesting a number of arguments to this effect. Aquinas mentioned some of these arguments briefly, rejecting others. He based his own case on three arguments, namely, that from the sterility of money, that from the consumptibility of money and an argument from economic coercion.

As regards the sterility argument, which derives from Aristotle's *Politics*, Aquinas did not fall victim to the simplistic interpretation of sterility in a biological sense, money being barren metal unable to breed (which probably cannot be attributed to Aristotle either). It is rather that money is barren in a certain moral sense. The usurer attempts to make money by means of money. This is against the purpose for which money was invented, which is to serve as a means and measure in exchange (*Sent. Pol.* I, 8). Usury is an unnatural and sinful use of money.

The argument from the consumptibility of money depends entirely on Aquinas's metalist conception of money, that is, of money as specie, as coin made of rare precious material (*Sum. Theol.* II–II, 78, 1; *Sent. Pol.* I, 7). There are some things, he argued, whose use is not the consumption of the things themselves, for instance, a house, which can be leased for a period of time without being demolished, and the same is true of a horse or a dress. There are other things, however, whose use is the consumption of the things themselves, such as wine, whose use is the drinking of it, whereby its substance is consumed. Such is the case of money as well. Money borrowed is not consumed the way wine or other natural fungibles are consumed but it is borrowed in order to be exchanged for other things and in that transaction the money (that is, the actual pieces of coin) is consumed and completely gone, the loan subsequently being repaid in kind:

> When therefore someone lends money on the agreement that the money be repaid in full and over and above this will have a price for the use of the money, it is clear that he sells separately the use of the money and the substance of the money itself; but the use of money is nothing other than its substance, therefore he sells that which does not exist or sells the same thing twice, namely the money whose use is its consumption, and that is manifestly contrary to natural justice. (*De Malo* XIII, 4; cf. *Sum. Theol.* II–II, 78, 1; *Quodl.* III, 19)

This is as far as Aquinas goes in his main statements of the argument, but elsewhere he refers briefly to things consumed in use as 'having no usufruct' (*Sum. Theol.* II–II, 78, 3). The idea that money has no *use value* separate from its monetary value is another way of saying that it is barren.

Moreover, if someone is made to pay for the non-existent use value of barren money, that person cannot be considered to do so completely voluntarily but must be assumed to be subject to some duress. Modern critics have maintained that scholastic price doctrine and scholastic usury doctrine are based on different principles. Through his economic coercion argument, Aquinas places them under the same formula. In his commentary on the *Nichomachean Ethics* he paraphrases Aristotle's discussion of physical coercion, citing the example of the captain of a ship in a storm at sea who jettisons cargo to avoid shipwreck, but does so with a 'mixed will' (*Sent. Eth.* III, 1). In one of his late discussions of usury, Aquinas must counter the objection that the borrower pays usury knowingly and willingly. His reply runs as follows:

Granted that the usurer does not apply absolute force he nevertheless applies a certain mixed force on him, in that the necessity of having to accept the loan imposes a serious condition so that he must return more than he is given. And it is similar if one reduced to need were to be sold a certain thing for more than its worth, for that would be an unjust sale just as a usurious loan is unjust. (*De Malo* XIII, 4)

By thus questioning, on a broad scale, the ethics of the use of economic power, Thomas Aquinas identifies what has remained the core issue of economic ideological dispute ever since.

Bibliography

Thomas Aquinas (1884), *Opera omnia*, Rome.
Langholm, Odd (1992), *Economics in the Medieval Schools*, Leiden: Brill.
Weisheipl, James A. (1974), *Friar Thomas d'Aquino: His Life, Thought and Works*, Oxford: Basil Blackwell.

See also the entries on: Aristotle; Catholic Social Thought; Needs and Agency; Prices; Religion.

3 Aristotle
Ricardo Crespo

Introduction

In his *Lives of the Philosophers*, Diogenes Laertius depicts a very well-known portrait of Aristotle's life and work, characterizing him as a morally good person. Diogenes transcribes Aristotle's last will and testament, in which the philosopher expressed in detail the caring for his relatives and freeing of his slaves. This concern for all of them reflects the non-ethereal nature of his *Ethics*, which is firmly rooted and embedded in matter and time. Diogenes writes of Aristotle's teachings, 'virtue was not sufficient of itself to confer happiness; for that it had also need of the goods of the body, and of the external goods'. Hence, we are obliged to look after not only virtue but also these goods. According to Aristotle, as quoted by Diogenes, 'things which are ethical . . . concern politics, and economy, and laws'. In effect, Aristotle conceived economics as one of the practical sciences (*epistème praktikè*), which were the ethical sciences. For him, the highest practical science was politics, to which economics, as the other practical sciences, was subordinated.

However, we must clarify two points. First, the connection between economics and ethics, according to Aristotle, is not direct and intrinsic. Aristotle used the term *oikonomikè*, here translated as 'the economic'. Second, strictly speaking, Aristotle's concept of 'the economic' differs from today's economics. At the beginning of an article on the Aristotelian notion of economy, Christian Rutten (1987, p. 289) notes the following:

> Firstly, 'the economic' of Aristotle does not correspond at all with that that in our time is called the economy. Secondly, this does not mean that we do not find in Aristotle . . . developments about the economic reality in the today sense. Thirdly, this does not mean in advance that there is not any relation, in Aristotle's thought, between 'the economic', on the one hand, and production, distribution and consumption of material goods, on the other hand.

This chapter starts by explaining the meaning of 'the economic' for Aristotle. It then reflects on a re-elaborated conception of Aristotle's notion of the economic. These concepts – the original and the re-elaborated one – are distinguished by writing the original notion of 'the economic' in quotation marks and the re-elaborated notion without them. Third, the ethical character of the economic is argued. Fourth, the connection between the economic and virtues is explored, followed by a look at the economic's embeddedness in politics and at gender considerations.

'The economic'

In the primitive sense used by Aristotle, *oikonomikè* is household management.[1] As such, it deals with three relations: the householder as husband, the householder as father and the householder as master of slaves and of other properties.[2] This last relation with properties is the most relevant for our analysis. In this respect, with the term *oikonomikè*, Aristotle referred to the use of wealth in the house. Aristotle defined *oikonomikè* in close relation with chrematistics (*chrèmatistikè*). This last is the art of acquiring or producing the things used by *oikonomikè* (*Politics* I, 8, 1256a 10–2). For Aristotle, chrematistics is subordinate to *oikonomikè*. Aristotle considers chrematistics to be the instrument of *oikonomikè* (*Politics* I, 10, 1258a 27–34).

These Aristotelian conceptions of 'the economic' and chrematistics must be considered within the context of Aristotle's ideas about human beings and their insertion in society. For Aristotle, the human being is essentially political.[3] For him, however, the *polis* is a concept that entails deeper consequences for human beings and closer relationships between them than the contemporary meaning of society. For Aristotle, *polis* is the realm in which human beings act freely and morally, develop their virtues and achieve fulfilment. It is in the *polis* that human beings may *live well* and may finally achieve self-realization or happiness (*eudaimonia*). Conversely, the house (*oikia*) is the realm of necessity, in which human beings only *live*, merely satisfying their basic needs. Therefore, the house is not the right place for freedom and, consequently, there is no place in the house for moral life. For this reason, strictly speaking, there is no direct relation between the management of the house, that is, 'the economic', and ethics according to Aristotle. Thus, given this distinction between the free and moral realm of politics and the necessary and not moral realm of household management ('the economic'), the term 'political economy' would constitute for Aristotle, as Hannah Arendt (1959, p. 28) notes, a contradiction in terms (see also Barker 1959, p. 357).

From 'the economic' to the economic

There are two potentially complementary ways of walking the path from 'the economic' – unconcerned with ethics – to the economic – an ethically relevant concept. The first is to show that this distinction of realms does not apply directly as described above in the case of 'the economic'. The second is to identify the Aristotelian concepts that correspond to current economics and to analyse them.

Concerning the first way, we may consider two quotations from Aristotle. To start, Aristotle had the following to say about chrematistics:

> [It] is a form of acquisition which the manager of a household must either find ready to hand, or himself provide and arrange, because it ensures a supply of objects, necessary for life and useful to the association of the polis or the household. (*Politics* I, 8, 1256b 26–30; compare also I, 10, 1258a 19–21; I, 11, 1259a 33–6)

Elsewhere, he affirms:

> We may make the assumption that property is part of the household, and that the art of acquiring property is a part of household management (*oikonomías*); and we may do so because it is impossible to live well (*eû zèn*), or indeed to live at all (*zèn*), unless the necessary conditions are present. (*Politics* I, 4, 1253b 23–5)

These quotations mix elements of both realms – the house and the *polis*. It seems that 'the economic' has to do both with the house and the *polis*, with the necessary and the useful, with 'to live at all' and 'to live well'. Thus, when we consider *oikonomikè* and chrematistics together it seems that Aristotle's *oikonomikè* is more than household management, as, indeed, many economic and philosophy historians maintain. If 'the economic' also has to do with the realm of the *polis*, it enters into morality. This is consistent with other

Aristotelian statements, such as the subordination of 'the economic' to politics and the moral disqualification of unlimited chrematistics.

Taking the second approach, the question is, 'Where do we find current political economy in the Aristotelian system?' Chrematistics is not the right place to look because it would correspond to contemporary production, commerce and finance. In Aristotelian thought, the tasks of political economy are subsumed into politics, and they relate not only to those actions concerning the 'necessary' or the 'useful' for the *polis*, but also the activities of 'the economic' related to the *polis* performed by the owner of the house. This is then an enlarged re-elaborated notion of the economic according to Aristotle. This broader notion deals not only with the house, the life and necessity, but also with the *polis*, with what is useful and free and thus moral, and with the good life and happiness.

The economic and ethics

Accepting this enlarged and re-elaborated concept of the economic, let us try to develop through Aristotelian arguments the scope and consequences of this notion.

Oikonomikè is an adjective and as such calls for a noun: 'The economic what?' The answer is multiple. The economic applies to several things and not univocally. Using Aristotle's terminology, we may say that it is a homonymous *pròs hèn* term, that is, an analogical term. It has a main or 'focal' meaning and other 'derivative' meanings. These different meanings correspond to different entities to which the adjective applies. The focal meaning is economic action, which is Aristotle's definition of *oikonomikè*. As explained, he settled this definition by relating it to the definition of *chrèmatistikè*. *Oikonomikè* is the use (*chrèsasthai*) of wealth, while *chrèmatistikè* refers to its provision, production or acquisition. 'To use' is a human action. In sum, the economic is for Aristotle a human action: the action of using wealth. The derivative meanings of *oikonomikè* are economic capacity, economic habit and economic science (economics), all of which are oriented to the suitable use of wealth (Crespo 2006).

The kind of action that the economic is signals its ethical character. Aristotle distinguished two kinds of human actions. The first is *immanent* actions. These are actions for which the end is the action itself, such as seeing, thinking and living. Moreover, the end of an immanent action is or remains within the agent. These actions are performed 'because it is noble to do so' (*Nicomachean Ethics* III, 7, 1115b 23). The second is *transitive* actions, in which the 'result is something apart from the exercise, [thus] the actuality is in the thing that is being made' (*Metaphysics* 1050a 30–1). The results of transitive actions transcend and are different from the agent, for example, any good produced. Except for fully immanent actions, such as thinking or loving, all human actions are both immanent and transitive. Let us exemplify this. When a person works there are two 'results'; that is, the 'objective' result, such as the product or service (transitive), and the 'subjective' modification, such as an increase in ability or self-fulfilment of the agent as well as the morality of the act (immanent). For Aristotle, this last, immanent aspect is the most relevant, it is the one sought for its own sake, and for no further reason. Aristotle said, 'we call that which is in itself worthy of pursuit more complete than that which is worthy of pursuit for the sake of something else' (*Nicomachean Ethics* I, 7, 1097a 30–1). That is, Aristotle attributed more relevance to the immanent aspect of action – that which in itself is worthy of pursuit – because it is the aspect for which the end is the very fulfilment or perfection of the agent. In this way, Aristotle linked the immanent (or practical) aspect of an action to its morality. For him the external aspect of action is instead instrumental.

The economic action is an action of using, in Greek, *chrèsasthai.* What kind of action, immanent or transitive, is *chrèsasthaï*? 'To *use*' is a transitive action insofar as the thing used is consumed or wasted when used. However, the complete action of the economic is to use what is necessary to satisfy the agent's requirements to live well; this is a predominantly immanent consideration of use (the proper perfection).[4] Thus the economic action has a moral aspect.

Aristotle also considered chrematistics as a human action: a technique that ought to be subordinate to the economic (at both the *oikonomikè* and the *politikè* levels). He further distinguished two kinds of chrematistics: one subordinate to *oikonomikè*, limited and natural, and another unnatural, not subordinate to *oikonomikè*, looking unlimitedly for money. Concerning that last he affirms, 'this second form [leads] to the opinion that there is no limit to wealth and property' (*Politics* I, 9, 1257a 1). He calls it 'justly censured' (*Politics* I, 10, 1258b 1). Both forms of chrematistics use money as an instrument. What happens is that some people may, due to their unlimited desire, take what is an instrument as an end. This mistaken type of chrematistics infects other behaviours:

> [It leads to use of] each and every capacity in a way non consonant with its nature. The proper function of courage, for example, is not to produce money but to give confidence. The same is true of military and medical ability: neither has the function of producing money: the one has the function of producing victory, and the other that of producing health. But those of whom we are speaking turn all such capacities into forms of the art of acquisition, as though to make money were the one aim and everything else must contribute to that aim. (*Politics* I, IX, 1258a 6–14)

Thus, while there is a kind of chrematistics that is perverse, it is unthinkable that the economic can be harmful. As every good act, the economic requires of virtues to realize itself. Moreover, for Aristotle, the economic is part of politics. These last two points are developed in the next sections.

The economic and virtues
As every good action when repeated, the economic tends to shape virtues, which in turn facilitate the performance of these very actions. Virtues are good habits and the thus resulting actions. Habits are ways of being, firmly fixed possessions developed by the repetition of the same actions. According to Aristotle, the main means to foster these actions are education and law.

What do we expect from the economic and what are the corresponding virtues? According to Aristotle, we need the economic because 'it is impossible to live well, or indeed to live at all, unless the necessary conditions are present' (*Politics* I, 4, 1253b 25), and 'it is therefore the greatest of blessings for a state that its members should possess a moderate and adequate fortune' (*Politics* IV, 11, 1296a 1). Happiness is an activity conforming to virtue, and 'still, happiness . . . needs external goods as well. For it is impossible or at least not easy to perform noble actions if one lacks the wherewithal' (*Nicomachean Ethics* I, 8, 1099a 31–3). Thus, for Aristotle, chrematistics and economic actions should assure that everybody succeeds in possessing what they need to achieve the *Good Life*. This goal has various aspects in which virtues collaborate.

One of the problems of economics is to face uncertainty. In this sense, virtues can render future affairs more predictable. The probability of habits originating stable behaviours is larger if these are morally good (virtues). According to Aristotle, the incontinent are unpredictable; instead, the virtuous or continent are more predictable because of their perseverance. 'A morally weak person', he says, 'does not abide by the dictates of reason' (*Nicomachean Ethics* VII, 9, 1151b 25–7). 'A morally strong person remains more steadfast and a morally weak person less steadfast than the capacity of most men permits' (*Nicomachean Ethics* VII, 10, 1152a 26–7). Thus, the probability of economic coordination is larger among virtuous people, for they have a stable character and their conduct can be anticipated. Coordination is easier within a group of people who possess an ethical commitment and a common *ethos*.

Further, virtues foster the economic process in other ways. Practical wisdom, which is an intellectual and ethical virtue, helps people to act accurately, assessing the real situation, helping to avoid errors. Justice helps people to act in the way prudence indicates. In fact, for Aristotle market relations are regulated by justice, under which commercial vices fade away. People strongly committed to justice do not free-ride. It must also be noted that Aristotle devoted the largest part of his *Nicomachean Ethics* (Books VIII and IX) to friendship. This virtue, which fosters social cohesion, develops in situations where justice is insufficient. In fact, justice is not necessary between friends. Liberality or generosity (Book IV, 1) also helps overcome problems of disequilibrium, through individual or collective action. In sum, in an imperfect world, virtues help to reduce error and act as a balm. They foster coordination and reduce costs.

Virtues, for Aristotle, are always political. They can be developed and consolidated only within the interaction of a community. Thus economic virtues are embedded in a political environment. Consequently, the economic is tied to the historical, cultural, social and political factors surrounding it. Therefore, the economic is also closely related to politics and the political community. On the other hand, coordination, as a result of individual actions, is possible when agents act prudently, applying a set of socially recognized values to concrete situations and actions. The knowledge of these shared social values is a matter of the most architectonical of Aristotle's practical sciences, politics.

The economic and politics

Human beings are political animals. To be political means to share a common sense of what is expedient and inexpedient, just and unjust, good and evil (*Politics* I, 2). Sharing and trying to behave in a virtuous way is the end of human beings in society and the way to achieve happiness. Thus, for Aristotle 'the end is the same for one man and for a civil community' (*Nicomachean Ethics* I, 2, 1094b 7–8). Aristotle's concept of civil society, that is, *polis*, is a unity of families. What kind of being is a unity of families? It is one which belongs in the category of 'relation' (*prós ti*). The basis of the particular relation of families that constitutes a *polis* is the orientation of all their actions towards an end. What end? Let us hear Aristotle:

> What constitutes a polis is an association of households and clans in a *Good Life* (*eû zèn*), for the sake of attaining a perfect and self-sufficing existence (*autárkous*) ... The end (*télos*) and purpose of a polis is the *Good Life*, and the institutions of social life are means to that end. A polis is constituted by the association of families and villages in a perfect and self-sufficing existence; and such an existence, in our definition, consists in a life of true felicity and goodness. It is therefore for the sake of good actions (*kalôn práxeon*), and not for the sake of social life, that political associations must be considered to exist. (*Politics* III, IX, 1280b 29–35; 1280b; 1281a 4)

That is, the final goal of *polis* subsumes the final end of *oikonoimikè* as action. For Aristotle, politics as the practice and science of the *Good Life* is morality in itself and the economic (and also *oikonomiké*) is an action and science subordinated to it. It receives its ends from politics and politics has need of it; the economic is one of the conditions of society's existence and unity. Extrapolating to nowadays, we may say market relations may foster the unity and existence of society (*Politics* VII, 1, 1324a 1). However, for this re-elaborated Aristotelian conception, the market cannot work well outside of political society and its goals. Otherwise it would fall into what Aristotle called 'censured chrematistics'. The well working of the market does not happen in a vacuum but in political society. The realm of virtues is the *polis*. They foster individual actions that lead the market to attain the community's shared values.

Ontologically the Aristotelian *polis* is an order – a quality – of relations composed by the actions of people. The order is given by the fact that they aim for a common goal which is a shared thought and intention of those people. This is to say, society is an accidental stable reality that finally exists inhering in the people that compose it. We may infer that the market is also an accidental reality, a net or order of relations – of buyers and sellers, people who exchange; the order or unity comes from the coincidence of a number of wills willing to buy or sell in order to satisfy needs, and this coincidence is achieved thanks to prices. This net of relationships belongs to the broader net of the whole of society, and is a prerequisite of it.

For Aristotle, both society and the market are natural in the sense that they are institutions demanded by human nature in order to achieve its fulfilment. However, for Aristotle natural in the realm of human beings does not mean 'spontaneous' or 'automatic'. Right actions in the *polis* and the market are to be performed with effort, they are not given facts. This does not mean that there cannot be some institutions which help in this task and work quite automatically. Precisely, one task of politics and economics is to find out and shape these institutions.

In sum, for Aristotle the economic is one condition of the *polis*, which is the place of human fulfilment or morality, and it must be subordinate to politics.

The gender perspective

In her introduction to *Feminist Interpretations of Aristotle*, Cynthia Freeland (1993, p. 15) asserts 'it is no longer acceptable to read Aristotle's works while ignoring issues of gender'. Aristotle has been objected to for relegating women to a second place, specifically to the area of the household, because of his patriarchal bias. For him, man's virtue is to command and woman's virtue entails obeying (*Politics* I, 13, 1260a 23–4). However, it has been highlighted, in Aristotle's defence, that he considers man and woman to have the same essence, to be specifically equal (Deslauriers 1993, p. 139) and to both be citizens (*Politics* I, 13, 1260b 19; II, 9, 1269b 15) oriented towards the ends of life (*Nicomachean Ethics* VIII, 12, 1162a 21–2).

The differences between men and women remarked on by Aristotle lie in their functions (*erga*) in the house (*Nicomachean Ethics* VIII, 12, 1162a 22) – in other words, a gender division of labour. For some authors, they stem from 'an unreflective belief' (Deslauriers 1993, p. 159) based on sociological observation (Hirshman 1993, p. 229).

Other authors suggest that feminist theories may profit from an updating of Aristotle's ideas. Ruth Groenhout (1993) notes that the ethics of care may be fruitfully complemented by Aristotle's ethics. Irene van Staveren (2001) applies this ethics to economics. Martha Nussbaum's work highlights not only Aristotle's contribution to feminism, but also to a required new conception of economics, for Aristotle 'insists on an exhaustive scrutiny of all existing distributions and preferences in the name of the basic needs all human beings have for functioning' (1993, p. 249).

Conclusion

Modern economics takes ends as given. An Aristotelian re-elaborated notion of 'the economic' makes sense only if it aims to ends: to live and to live well. This perspective confers an intrinsic ethical character to Aristotle's notion of the economic, which is elaborated today in the capability approach. Both in the domestic sphere and in society, economic resources should be oriented to the achievement of those ends. This can be done with the assistance of virtues, which help human beings to overcome their tendencies endlessly to desire the means. It can all be obtained only within the boundaries of the *polis*, which is the community in which human fulfilment can be achieved, according to Aristotle.

Notes

1. There are many articles or parts of books dealing with Aristotle and economics. The most focused and exegetical book on Aristotle's thought on economics is Meikle (1995).
2. For a short discussion of the gender perspective of the language that Aristotle uses, see below.
3. Slaves were not part of the *polis*. Concerning women, see the later section on gender. Concerning children, Aristotle takes into account that they 'grow up to be partners in the government in the polis' (*Politics* I, 13, 1260b 19–20).
4. *To chrèsasthai* is the 'substantivization' of the Greek verb *chráo* in its 'middle voice' infinitive aorist form. The middle voice has a reflexive use that is coherent with the possible predominant sense of *práxis* of *chrèsasthai*. The French and Spanish translations show this characteristic: 'se server' (fr.); 'procurarse de', 'servirse de' (sp.). *Chresoméne*, another form used by Aristotle to signify the action of *oikonomiké*, is another form of *chráo*, a future middle participle that indicates finality.

References

Arendt, Hannah (1959), *The Human Condition*, New York: Doubleday.
Aristotle (1924), *Metaphysics*, translated by W.D. Ross, Oxford: Clarendon Press.
Aristotle (1954), *Nicomachean Ethics*, translated and introduced by Sir David Ross, Oxford: Oxford University Press.
Aristotle (1958), *Politics*, edited and translated by Ernest Barker, Oxford: Oxford University Press.
Barker, Ernest (1959), *The Political Thought of Plato and Aristotle*, New York: Dover Publications.
Crespo, Ricardo (2006), 'The ontology of "the economic": an Aristotelian perspective', *Cambridge Journal of Economics*, **30**, 767–81.
Deslauriers, Marguerite (1993), 'Sex and essence in Aristotle's *Metaphysics* and biology', in Cynthia Freeland (ed.), *Feminist Interpretations of Aristotle*, University Park, PA: Pennsylvania State University Press, pp. 138–67.
Diogenes Laertius (2007), *The Lives and Opinions of Eminent Philosophers*, translated by C.D. Yonge, www.classicpersuasion.org/pw/diogenes/dlaristotle.htm, 1 September, 2007.
Freeland, Cynthia (ed.) (1993), *Feminist Interpretations of Aristotle*, University Park, PA: Pennsylvania State University Press.
Groenhout, Ruth (1993), 'The virtue of care: Aristotelian ethics and contemporary ethics of care', in Cynthia Freeland (ed.), *Feminist Interpretations of Aristotle*, University Park, PA: Pennsylvania State University Press, pp. 171–200.
Hirshman, Linda Redick (1993), 'The Book of "A"' in Cynthia Freeland (ed.), *Feminist Interpretations of Aristotle*, Pennsylvania: The Pennsylvania State University Press, pp. 201–47.
Meikle, Scott (1995), *Aristotle's Economic Thought*, Oxford: Oxford University Press.
Nussbaum, Martha (1993), 'Aristotle, feminism, and needs for functioning', in Cynthia Freeland (ed.), *Feminist Interpretations of Aristotle*, University Park, PA: Pennsylvania State University Press, pp. 248–59.
Rutten, Christian (1987), 'L'économie chez Aristote', *Les Cahiers de l'Analyse des Donées*, **XIII** (3), 289–94.
Staveren, Irene van (2001), *The Values of Economics: An Aristotelian Perspective*, London: Routledge.

See also the entries on: Feminism; Individualism; Realism; Virtue Ethics.

4   Jeremy Bentham
Marco E.L. Guidi

Jeremy Bentham (London, 1748–1832), a legal philosopher and the founder of the utilitarian tradition in ethics, which was further developed by John Stuart Mill and Henry Sidgwick, laid the cornerstones of his moral philosophy in *An Introduction to the Principles of Morals and Legislation* ([1789a] 1970, hereafter *IPML*). His early writings on legislation reveal the typical attitude of an eighteenth-century philosopher who aimed to become the counsellor of the enlightened sovereigns of that age. Bentham also took an interest in political economy, publishing 'Defence of usury' ([1787] 1952–54), a pamphlet in which he criticized legal fixation of the interest rate. He then wrote 'Manual of political economy' ([1793–5] 1952–54), and a series of practical albeit sometimes unrealistic proposals concerning fiscal and monetary policy. Perhaps Bentham's best-known project was the panopticon prison (Bentham [1791] 1962), a circular building in which the convicts were to be constantly under the eye of an inspector. The panopticon was never built: disappointed by the failure of this scheme, which he attributed to the corruption of the British political system, Bentham turned to political radicalism around 1810. He set out the principles of his theory of representative democracy based on universal suffrage in *Constitutional Code* ([1830] 1983). In the same period, he wrote a 'guide' to private ethics entitled 'Deontology' ([1814–31] 1983).

This chapter deals with Bentham's utilitarian ethics (Section 4.1) and its relationships with the development of economics (Section 4.2). It focuses on the normative aspects of Bentham's moral thought, ignoring questions concerning hedonistic psychology and the theory of motivation which are related to economic analysis and social engineering rather than ethics.

4.1   Bentham's utilitarianism
In the famous *incipit* of *IPML* Bentham wrote, 'Nature has placed mankind under the governance of two sovereign masters, *pain* and *pleasure*. It is for them alone to point out what we ought to do, as well as to determine what we shall do' (Bentham [1789a] 1970, p. 11). This definition introduces a clear distinction between positive (or 'expository') and normative (or 'censorial') ethics, while arguing that both must adopt pleasure and pain as a standard of analysis (Harrison 1983, pp. 106–12). The positive side contains a theory of human action inheriting from Anglo-French sensationalist philosophy the basic hedonistic assumption that human beings make their choices in order to increase pleasure and reduce pain. The normative side recommends as a criterion of right and wrong the 'principle of utility', or the 'greatest happiness principle' (GHP). This principle states that an action is morally correct if and only if no alternative produces a greater happiness in those who are involved by it, and an action is morally binding if any alternative produces a lesser amount of happiness in the same aggregate of individuals. Happiness is pleasure or absence of pain. More precisely, happiness or 'well-being' is a balance between pleasure and pain and can be augmented either by increasing the former or by reducing the

latter. In more familiar terms, the GHP directs us to choose that action that maximizes total happiness. Bentham initially adopted Francis Hutcheson's formula 'the greatest happiness of the greatest number' – the literal phrasing of which he almost certainly found in the English translation of Cesare Beccaria's *On Crimes and Punishments* (*Dei delitti e delle pene* 1767) (Shackleton 1972; Burns 2005). But he eventually considered this definition ambiguous, since it might imply the total sacrifice of a minority to the happiness of the majority.

Bentham's utilitarianism belongs to the family of axiological ethical theories. These theories connect the morality of an action to some 'good' or intrinsic value associated with it. They differ from deontological approaches, which relate the morality of an action to the universal rules which inspire it. In particular, the principle of utility defines a 'consequentialist' ethical theory, as it considers only the 'good' associated with the con-sequences of actions (Pettit 1991). Furthermore, the hedonistic variety of utilitarianism that Bentham espoused gives only pleasure and absence of pain an intrinsic value among consequences. Bentham also considered that, although a method of deliberation based on common sense and legal rules is useful in ordinary life, the weighting of hedonistic con-sequences must be repeated for every act (act-utilitarianism). Finally, the universalistic character of utilitarianism is made evident by the consideration that it indistinctly applies to all sentient beings, including animals.

It could be argued that Bentham's formulation of the utility principle makes the 'natu-ralistic fallacy' for which George E. Moore (1903) reproached classical utilitarianism, since it defines 'good' in terms of a natural property ('pleasant'). But it certainly respects Hume's is/ought distinction, for the GHP is never recommended as a consequence of the *fact* that people desire pleasure and avoid pain. In Chapter 2 of *IPML*, Bentham ([1789a] 1970, pp. 17–33) defends the utilitarian rule by way of rational argumentation, highlighting its superiority vis-à-vis rival principles.

It is evident from the above definitions that the GHP requires the 'felicific calculus', that is, a measure of the value of pleasures and pains. This aspect is examined in Chapter 4 of *IMPL*. Here the value of a pleasure or pain is said to depend on seven 'circum-stances'. Four of these refer to individual pleasures and pains considered by themselves: 'intensity', 'duration', 'certainty or uncertainty' (that is, probability) and 'propinquity or remoteness' (basically, time-span) (Bentham [1789a] 1970, p. 38). Two refer to the 'ten-dency' of an act, that is, to its remote or indirect consequences. These are 'its *fecundity*, or the chance it has of being followed by sensations of the *same* kind' (ibid., p. 39, italics in the original), and 'its *purity*, or the chance it has of not being followed by sensations of the *opposite* kind' (ibid.) The final circumstance is the 'extent' of a pleasure or pain, that is, 'the number of persons to whom it *extends*' (ibid.) That last is crucial when the action is 'other-regarding', involving the interest of persons other than the agent. In a short manuscript note of the early 1780s entitled 'Value of pain and pleasure', part of which was published by Elie Halévy ([1901–03] 1995, I, pp. 300–8), and then transcribed by David Baumgardt (1952, pp. 554–66), Bentham shows awareness of other aspects of the arithmetic of pleasures and pains. First, he defines the unit of pleasure as the least perceivable quantity of pleasure with regard to intensity and duration. Second, he acknowledges the principle of decreasing marginal utility, arguing that the increments of pleasure are less than proportional to the increments of its cause.

As Bentham points out in 'Deontology', this method of calculation implies that every positive balance between the sum of pleasures enjoyed and the sum of pains suffered by a single individual or group of individuals is a state of happiness or 'well-being', however small its value (Bentham [1814–31] 1983, pp. 130–31). The same procedure holds both for the valuation of the consequences of a single act, and for that of the whole life of an individual. Bentham criticized Maupertuis, who equated happiness with a state of mind in which pleasure is experienced 'in a high and as it were superlative degree' (ibid., p. 132), since such a view entailed unnecessary pessimistic conclusions. However, Bentham's optimistic attitude should not be confused with conservative laissez-faire: the goal of maximizing total happiness implies that every improvement an individual or the legislator can introduce is not only morally approved, but is also morally binding. Utilitarianism has indeed been accused of the opposed shortcoming of being too demanding on individuals.

Another feature of the GHP is that it implies equal consideration of interests. In Bentham's hedonistic terms, the happiness of every individual counts only for its amount and not for any other characteristic of its bearer. As John Stuart Mill commented in 'Utilitarianism' ([1861] 1969), 'Bentham's dictum, "everybody to count for one, nobody for more than one"[,] might be written under the principle of utility as an explanatory commentary' (ibid., p. 257).

This impartiality requirement implies that self-preference cannot be approved as a universal rule of behaviour. As Mill observed, utilitarianism goes so far as to recommend enlightened self-sacrifice (ibid., p. 217). This implication has been overshadowed by an interpretation of Bentham's philosophy which goes back to Jean-Baptiste Say ([1833] 2003) and was sanctioned by Halévy ([1901–03] 1995). According to this interpretation, the GHP is interchangeable with the enlightened interest principle (EIP). The latter assumes that human beings are inevitably self-interested, yet can be educated to pursue their 'considered' interests, taking into account the way in which their own psycho-physical constitution, other people and the external environment react to their choices. Individuals 'ought to' choose what they 'would' choose, were they perfectly informed about the remote consequences of their acts. It is clear that the EIP, strictly considered, suggests prudence rather than disinterestedness in other-regarding actions. Individuals are not required to take into account the consequences of their choices on the happiness of others, unless in an indirect way, as far as the others' happiness affects their own. This is the crucial difference between the EIP and the GHP, which recommends maximizing the happiness of all the individuals involved. The GHP requires human beings to set aside their self and take into equal consideration the interests of others.

It could be objected that in many circumstances the practical suggestions of both principles converge. However, there are cases in which the conduct suggested by the GHP is not that which maximizes the enlightened interest of the agent. It is true that Bentham himself, in *Constitutional Code*, argued that in public life 'self-regard' constantly prevails over 'other-regard' and that individuals tend to promote their own private interest at the expense of the public interest (Bentham [1830] 1983, pp. 118–20). But this was no more than a prudent political maxim, as shown by the fact that at the same time Bentham was working on 'Deontology', in which he argued that individuals are able to act sympathetically and that the growth of benevolence is the key to a happier society.

It is easy to see that the GHP implies interpersonal and intra-personal comparisons of utility. At this point, a distinction must be introduced between three principles: (i) equal consideration of interests, (ii) interpersonal equivalence between units of pleasure and (iii) equal capacity for happiness.

The principle of equal consideration of interests has already been expounded. It remains only to remark that it contains two distinct characteristics: anonymity or impersonality (that is, in evaluating the happiness of different individuals it is not morally significant *whose* happiness it is) and equal weight or equiproportionality (that is, to equal needs is due equal consideration, and to unequal needs equiproportional consideration).

The second principle, that of interpersonal equivalence, means that the units of pleasure of each individual are considered equal. It does not imply that these units are objectively equal, only that they are assumed to be so by the observer. Like Marshall after him, Bentham clearly states our inability to derive a direct measure of the intrinsic value of the pleasures enjoyed by different individuals, and thus we must resort to an indirect scale or 'thermometer'. This scale is provided by the money individuals are willing to spend for goods. When two persons spend the same amount of money for the same quantity of a good, we should assume that their pleasure is equal (Baumgardt 1952, p. 560).

The third principle stipulates that, paraphrasing Edgeworth (1881, p. 57),[1] individuals have *an equal* capacity for happiness vis-à-vis one another, when for the same amount of means they obtain *the same* amount of pleasure, and for the same increment whatsoever of means *the same* increment of pleasure. Although in some passages of his works Bentham formulates something close to this principle (see Bentham [1788] 2002, pp. 68–9), it is unclear whether he is presenting an empirical or an axiological argument. If the argument is empirical, it should be contrasted with the chapters of *IPML* in which Bentham argues that the sensibility to pleasures of different qualities differs from individual to individual according to circumstances (Bentham [1789a] 1970, p. 51). The equal capacity argument would then imply that an individual's higher sensibility to a certain kind of pleasure is compensated by a lower sensibility to another, and vice versa in a different individual, so that, on average, both have the same capacity for pleasure. The principle could then be reformulated in the following way: taking a basket composed of all the goods preferred by all individuals (in which different individuals give different weights to the single items), an individual has an equal capacity for happiness vis-à-vis another, when for the same amount whatsoever of *this basket* they obtain the same amount of pleasure, and for the same increment whatsoever of *this basket* the same increment of pleasure. If, in contrast, Bentham intended to formulate an axiological argument, this means that one individual's capacity for pleasure has the same intrinsic value as that of another. As a consequence, whatever the psychological differences between individuals, from the point of view of the GHP, each must be 'counted for one'. In this case, the argument tends to conflate with the principle of equal consideration of interests. Bentham seems, however, to place himself on the more prudent level of *epoché*, when he states, 'Lacking the power to determine the relative degree of happiness that different individuals are susceptible of, it is necessary to start with the assumption that the degree is the same for all' (Bentham [1788] 2002, p. 68; Mack 1962, p. 449).

Another significant feature of Bentham's utilitarianism is the so-called doctrine of the 'subordinate ends of legislation', whose main conclusions can be extended to the general domain of ethics. (A further characteristic of Bentham's utilitarianism is that it makes no distinction between private and public ethics.) This doctrine was expounded in 'Principles of the civil code' (Bentham [1801] 1962), a text in which the French-Swiss editor of Bentham's works, Etienne Dumont, first published in 1801 some manuscripts of the 1780s. Here, Bentham stated that although the GHP is the 'end in view' of every act of the legislator, there are some 'subordinate' ends which may contribute to the attainment of the chief goal. These are security, subsistence, abundance and equality. Subsistence and abundance are the main objects of political economy. As Adam Smith had demonstrated, these goals are generally fulfilled through the private initiative of economic agents, and government interference is often 'nugatory', if not deleterious. Bentham endorses this view, although he argues that there are cases in which public intervention improves the functioning of the market. Conversely, security and equality are the products of civil and penal legislation, although their consequences spread in many ways over the economic sphere through taxation and regulation.

Between the goals of security and equality there is a peculiar dialectic. On the one hand, the GHP, qualified by the above-illustrated principles (decreasing marginal utility, equal consideration of interests, interpersonal equivalence of the units of pleasure, equal capacity for pleasure), furnishes a strong argument in favour of equality: *ceteris paribus*, assuming an unequal distribution of fortunes, every transfer of resources from those who possess more to those who have less increases total utility, since the marginal utility of goods decreases as quantities increase. 'The more nearly the actual proportion approaches to equality, the greater will be the total mass of happiness' (Bentham [1801] 1962, p. 305).

On the other hand, 'axioms of mental pathology' explain the capital importance attributed to the security of persons and property. These axioms depend in turn on a type of pleasure that plays a peculiar role in producing happiness: the 'pleasure of expectation'. Human beings make plans about their personal relationships and the use of goods. Not only will these activities produce actual pleasures in the future, but expectation is itself a pleasure, and one of a *durable* kind. Any limitation of liberty and personal integrity, and any loss of property produces an intense 'pain of disappointed expectation'. Moreover, this pain has a special 'fecundity' of its own, as it produces 'evils of second' and 'third order' (Bentham [1843] 1962, p. 230), respectively, the 'fear of loss' (or 'alarm') and the 'destruction of industry' (Bentham [1801] 1962, p. 310). Based on this is the 'axiom' that 'by the nature and constitution of the human frame, sum for sum, enjoyment from gain is never equal to suffering from loss' (Bentham [1800–04] 1952–54, p. 348). In case of compulsory redistribution of resources, the advantages of equality are counterbalanced by the evils associated with threat to security. Notice that it is the goal of security that guarantees individual liberty under the protection of the law. In Bentham's utilitarian ethics, there is no room for an independent value of liberty or autonomy: the unconditional respect of liberty cannot be recommended if there are cases in which its consequences are ethically reprehensible. Nevertheless, liberty has a fundamental instrumental value, and it must be invariably respected in self-regarding choices, where every individual is the best judge of what is conducive to his/her own happiness. This is the ground on which, in 'Defence of usury', Bentham argues in favour of the liberty of credit.

If equality must succumb to security, this does not mean that there is no circumstance in which redistribution can be promoted. For example, 'escheat' or death duties – especially in case of collateral successions – generate no pain of disappointment (Bentham

[1801] 1962, pp. 312–13; see also Bentham [1789b] 2002). More generally, every reform must be gradual and provide full compensation for vested interests. If perfect equality cannot be attained, a good society is one 'in which, while the fortune of the richest . . . is greatest, the degrees between the fortune of the least rich and that of the most rich are most numerous, – in other words, the gradation is most regular and insensible' (Bentham [1843] 1962, p. 230).

4.2   The place of Bentham's ethics in the history of economics

Although Ricardo declared in a letter to Maria Edgeworth that 'my motto, after Mr. Bentham, is "the greatest happiness to the greatest number"', his commitment to utilitarianism was rather weak (Cremaschi 2004). The case is obviously different with John Stuart Mill, who developed utilitarian ethics in his works 'On liberty' ([1859] 1977) and 'Utilitarianism' ([1861] 1969). In the latter, after mentioning Bentham's 'dictum' on the equal consideration of interests, Mill insisted that this principle necessarily implies 'an equal claim to all the means of happiness, except in so far as the inevitable conditions of human life, and the general interest, in which that of every individual is included, set limits to the maxim; and those limits ought to be strictly construed' (p. 258). His *Principles of Political Economy* ([1848] 1969) – especially Book 2 'Distribution' and Chapter 6 of Book 4, 'Of the Stationary State' – turn around the argument that a system based on the principle of private property is superior to communistic and socialistic organizations only inasmuch as it does not 'aggravate the inequality of chances arising from the natural working of the principle' (p. 986). Mill's proposals on the limitation of the right of bequest and of collateral inheritance (ibid., Book 2, Ch. 2) derive directly from the utilitarian justification of equality. In *Principles*, Mill also discusses the question of unequal capacities for pleasure. In his view, neither the acquired nor the natural 'diversity of tastes and talents' justifies unequal consideration and unequal treatment. On the contrary, different capacities must be compensated by positive action in order to produce an equality of chances (ibid., p. 979).

On the other side of the channel, Say was responsible for the success of utilitarianism among the economists of the French laissez-faire school. His doctrine of enlightened interests was joined with a firm belief in the self-regulation of the sphere of production and exchange. Political economy was considered the fundamental body of knowledge that would educate individuals to understand their long-term interests and legislators to acknowledge the natural limits to state intervention.

Through Mill, and especially through Sidgwick, Bentham's utilitarianism had a decisive impact on British marginalism. William Stanley Jevons drew heavily on *IPML* to formulate the theory of the 'final degree of utility' on which he based his economic analysis. He found in Bentham's 'felicific calculus' the elements he required to reframe political economy as a natural science. In Chapter 1 of *The Theory of Political Economy* ([1871] 1971), however, Jevons declared that his study was confined to individual motives and to the '*mechanics of utility and self-interest*' (p. 21, italics in the original) and that it never attempted 'to compare the amount of feeling in one mind with that in another' (ibid., p. 14). Although he had 'no hesitation in accepting the Utilitarian theory of morals' (ibid., p. 23), an analysis of general utility had no place in this work. The last work he published, *The State in Relation to Labour* ([1882] 1910), adopted utilitarian ethics to examine the role of government in economic affairs.

A more intriguing case is that of Francis Ysidro Edgeworth. He wrote *New and Old Methods of Ethics* ([1874] 1962) and *Mathematical Psychics* (1881) under the joint influence of Sidgwick's *Methods of Ethics* (1874) and Alfred Barratt's (1877) defence of egoism based on evolutionist arguments (Peart and Levy 2004). In a way, he tried to reconcile these opposed sources of inspiration. Edgeworth drew from Sidgwick and Herbert Spencer the distinction between 'egoistic hedonism' and 'universalistic hedonism' and applied it to economic analysis. The perspective of 'egoistic hedonism', already adopted by Jevons, assumed perfectly self-interested individuals who aimed to maximize their individual utility in exchange. It was in this part of his analysis that Edgeworth produced his best known contributions to economic theory, the use of indifference and contract curves to examine the 'final settlements' generated by exchange. These tools allowed him to express what is now known as the limit theorem, arguing that perfect competition is 'an asymptotic property of a sequence of exchange economies' and that under perfect competition Walrasian equilibrium and core equilibrium coincide (Hildebrand 1993, pp. 477–8). In all other cases, that is, when the number of competitors is limited, the result of exchange is indeterminate and there arises a need for 'a principle of arbitration'. At this stage individuals would resort to the ethical intuition acquired in the course of evolution that '[a]ny individual experiencing a unit of pleasure-intensity during a unit of time is to "count for one"' (Edgeworth 1881, p. 8). Having in mind this reformulation of Bentham's equal consideration principle, the same individuals would be reluctant to leave to hazard or power the choice of an appropriate allocation, as recommended by Barratt and other advocates of Darwinism. 'Universalistic hedonism' (the GHP) would then emerge as an answer to the ethical requirements of those individuals.

However, Edgeworth was persuaded that evolutionist biology and empirical psychology had demonstrated that individuals differ in their capacity for pleasure, and that this difference is due to genetic inheritance rather than education. In these circumstances, the dictate of the GHP would be '*the distribution of means as between the equally capable of pleasure is equality; and generally is such that the more capable of pleasure shall have more means and more pleasure*' (Edgeworth 1881, p. 64, italics in the original). Similar inegalitarian conclusions apply to the distribution of labour. Francis Galton's influence is evident in Edgeworth's contention that the GHP implies '[t]he *quality of population should be the highest possible evolution*' (ibid., p. 68, italics in the original). But the means of education are scarce, and 'it is probable that the highest in the order of evolution are most capable of education and improvement' (ibid.) Again, priority should be given to the most capable. Finally, 'universalistic hedonism' enjoins the rule of maximizing happiness across generations. But combined with unequal capacity and with Malthus's principle of population, this goal implies 'that to substitute in one generation for any number of parents an equal number each superior in capacity (evolution) is beneficial for the next generation' (ibid., p. 70). And it could be demonstrated that this advantage is equal 'for all time' (ibid., p. 71). Thus, hedonistic utilitarianism combined with the assumption of unequal capacities for pleasure entails unequal distribution and eugenics.

Three decades later, Arthur C. Pigou published *Wealth and Welfare* (1912), the book that gave birth to welfare economics. One of the fundamental propositions he advanced was that 'economic welfare is likely to be augmented by anything that, leaving other things unaltered, renders the distribution of the national dividend less unequal' (Pigou 1912, p. 24). Pigou pointed out that this proposition relies on the assumption of 'equal temperament' (ibid.) amongst individuals. He implicitly objected to Edgeworth's suggestion that unequal capacities for pleasure are a result of nature and heredity. Most such differences, he said, derive from education, and capacities are susceptible to improvement (ibid., p. 26). Although Pigou was not totally adverse to compulsory eugenics in some 'extreme' cases, he argued that redistributive policies that improve the condition of the poor can favour the emergence of human potentialities that are repressed by the social environment (ibid., pp. 58–9).

Conclusions

The trajectory of hedonistic act-utilitarianism came to an end with Pareto's critique of cardinal utility in economics and Moore's attack on naturalism in moral philosophy. Strictly speaking, the implications of utilitarian ethics for economic distribution and individual liberty discussed in this chapter make sense only within the hedonistic variety of utilitarianism. Nevertheless, the principle of equal consideration of interests continues to play a central role in contemporary neo-utilitarian approaches, as demonstrated in the works of John Harsanyi (1977) and Peter Singer (1993). This principle is at the basis of the favourable view by which most utilitarians look to substantive equality. The discussions originated by Bentham reveal that careful examination of empirical and axiological assumptions is necessary to avoid extremely inegalitarian conclusions that run counter to our moral intuitions.

Notes

The author wishes to thank Philip Schofield for his useful comments on a former version of this article. Usual disclaimers apply.
1. Edgeworth's original (inegalitarian) version of this passage sounds as follows: 'An individual has greater *capacity for happiness* than another, when for the same amount whatsoever of means he obtains a greater amount of pleasure, *and also* for the same increment (to the same amount) whatsoever of means a greater increment of pleasure.'

References and further reading

Barratt, Alfred (1877), 'The "suppression" of egoism', *Mind*, **2** (6), 167–86.
Baumgardt, David (1952), *Bentham and the Ethics of Today*, Princeton, NJ: Princeton University Press.
Bentham, Jeremy ([1787] 1952–54), 'Defence of usury', in William Stark (ed.), *Jeremy Bentham's Economic Writings*, Vol. I, London: Allen and Unwin, pp. 121–207.
Bentham, Jeremy ([1788] 2002), 'Considérations d'un Anglois sur la composition des Etats-Généraux y compris réponses aux questions proposées aux Notables & c. 1788', in Philip Schofield, Catherine Pease-Watkin and Cyprian Blamires (eds), *Rights, Representation and Reform: Nonsense Upon Stilts and Other Writings on the French Revolution*, Oxford: Clarendon Press, pp. 63–146. The English translations quoted in this chapter are taken from the appendix to Mary P. Mack (1962), *Jeremy Bentham: An Odyssey of Ideas 1748–1792*, London, Melbourne and Toronto: Heinemann.
Bentham, Jeremy ([1789a] 1970), *An Introduction to the Principles of Morals and Legislation*, critical edition ed. J.H. Burns and H.L.A. Hart, London: Athlone Press.
Bentham, Jeremy ([1789b] 2002), 'Supply: new species proposed', in Philip Schofield, Catherine Pease-Watkin and Cyprian Blamires (eds), *Rights, Representation and Reform: Nonsense Upon Stilts and Other Writings on the French Revolution*, Oxford: Clarendon Press, pp. 205–26.
Bentham, Jeremy ([1791] 1962), 'Panopticon; or, the inspection house', in John Bowring (ed.), *The Works of Jeremy Bentham*, Vol. IV, New York: Russell & Russell, pp. 37–172.
Bentham, Jeremy ([1793–5] 1952–54), 'Manual of political economy', in William Stark (ed.), *Jeremy Bentham's Economic Writings*, Vol. I, London: Allen and Unwin, pp. 219–73.
Bentham, Jeremy ([1801] 1962), 'Principes du code civil' in *Traités de législation civile et pénale*; English

translation, 'Principles of the civil code', in John Bowring (ed.), *The Works of Jeremy Bentham*, Vol. 1, New York: Russell & Russell, pp. 297–580.

Bentham, Jeremy ([1800–04] 1952–54), 'Institute of political economy', in William Stark (ed.), *Jeremy Bentham's Economic Writings*, Vol. 3, London: Allen and Unwin, pp. 303–80.

Bentham, Jeremy ([1814–31] 1983), 'Deontology', in Amnon Goldworth (ed.), *Deontology Together with a Table of the Springs of Action and the Article on Utilitarianism*, Oxford: Clarendon Press.

Bentham, Jeremy ([1830] 1983), *Constitutional Code*, Vol. I, ed. F. Rosen and J.L. Hume, Oxford: Clarendon Press.

Bentham, Jeremy ([1843] 1962), 'Pannomial fragments', in John Bowring (ed.), *The Works of Jeremy Bentham*, Vol. 3, New York: Russell & Russell, pp. 211–30.

Burns, James H. (2005), 'Happiness and utility: Jeremy Bentham's equation', *Utilitas*, **17** (1), 46–61.

Creedy, John (1986), *Edgeworth and the Development of Neoclassical Economics*, London: Blackwell.

Cremaschi, Sergio (2004), 'Ricardo and the utilitarians', *European Journal of the History of Economic Thought*, **11** (3), 377–403.

Crisp, Roger (1997), *Mill on Utilitarianism*, Abingdon: Routledge.

Dinwiddy, John (1989), *Bentham*, Oxford: Oxford University Press.

Edgeworth, Francis Y. (1877), *New and Old Methods of Ethics*, Oxford and London: Parker & Co.

Edgeworth, Francis Y. (1881), *Mathematical Psychics*, London: Kegan Paul.

Guidi, Marco E.L. (1990), '"Shall the blind lead those who can see?" Bentham's theory of political economy', in D. Moggridge (ed.), *Perspectives on the History of Economic Thought*, Vol. II, *Classical, Marxians and Neo-Classicals*, Aldershot, UK and Brookfield, US: Edward Elgar.

Guidi, Marco E.L. (2002), 'Bentham's economics of legislation', *Journal of Public Finance and Public Choice*, **20** (2–3), 165–89.

Guidi, Marco E.L. (2004), '"My own Utopia": the economics of Bentham's *Panopticon*', *European Journal of the History of Economic Thought*, **11** (3), 405–31.

Halévy, Elie ([1901–03] 1995), *La formation du radicalisme philosophique*, Paris: Alcan, Paris; critical edition edited by Monique Canto-Sperber, Paris: Puf; Translated into English (not including the appendices) and published in 1928 as *The Growth of Philosophical Radicalism*, London: Faber & Faber.

Harsanyi, John C. (1977), *Rational Behavior and Bargaining Equilibrium in Games and Social Situations*, Cambridge: Cambridge University Press.

Harrison, Ross (1983), *Bentham*, London: Routledge and Kegan Paul.

Hildebrand, Werner (1993), 'Francis Ysidro Edgeworth: perfect competition and the core', *European Economic Review*, **37**, 477–90.

Jevons, William S. ([1871] 1971), *The Theory of Political Economy*, 4th edition, London: Macmillan.

Jevons, William S. ([1882] 1910), *The State in Relation to Labour*, 4th edition, London: Macmillan.

Maas, Harro (2005), *William Stanley Jevons and the Making of Modern Economics*, Cambridge: Cambridge University Press.

Mack, Mary P. (1962), *Jeremy Bentham: An Odyssey of Ideas 1748–1792*, London, Melbourne and Toronto: Heinemann.

Mill, John S. ([1848] 1969), *Principles of Political Economy*, in John M. Robson (ed.), *The Collected Works of John Stuart Mill*, Vols II–III, Toronto and London: University of Toronto Press and Routledge & Kegan Paul.

Mill, John S. ([1859] 1977), 'On liberty', in John M. Robson (ed.), *The Collected Works of John Stuart Mill*, Vol. XVIII, *Essays on Politics and Society*, Toronto and London: University of Toronto Press and Routledge & Kegan Paul, pp. 213–310.

Mill, John S. ([1861] 1969), 'Utilitarianism', in John M. Robson (ed.), *The Collected Works of John Stuart Mill*, Vol. X, *Essays on Ethics, Religion and Society*, Toronto and London: University of Toronto Press and Routledge & Kegan Paul, pp. 203–59.

Moore, George E. (1903), *Principia Ethica*, Cambridge: Cambridge University Press.

Peart, Sandra J. (1996), *The Economics of W.S. Jevons*, London: Routledge.

Peart, Sandra J. and David M. Levy (2004), 'Sympathy and its discontents: "Greatest happiness" versus the "general good"', *European Journal of the History of Economic Thought*, **11** (3), 453–78.

Pettit, Philip (1991), 'Consequentialism', in Peter Singer (ed.), *A Companion to Ethics*, Oxford: Blackwell, pp. 230–240.

Pigou, Arthur C. (1912), *Wealth and Welfare*, London: Macmillan.

Rosen, Frederick (2003), *Classical Utilitarianism from Hume to Mill*, London: Routledge.

Say, Jean-Baptiste ([1833] 2003), 'Essai sur le principe d'utilité', in Charles Comte (ed.), *Mélanges et Correspondances d'Economie Politique: Ouvrage Posthume de J.-B. Say*, Paris: Chamerot; critical edition in Gilles Jacoud and Philippe Steiner (eds), *J.-B. Say: Leçons d'Economie Politique, Oeuvres Complètes*, Vol. 4, Paris: Economica, pp. 130–54.

Schofield, Philip (2006), *Utility and Democracy. The Political Thought of Jeremy Bentham*, Oxford: Oxford University Press.

Shackleton, Robert ([1972] 1988), 'The greatest happiness of the greatest number: the history of Bentham's phrase', *Studies in Voltaire and the Eighteenth Century*, reprinted in Robert Shackleton, *Essays on Montesquieu and on the Enlightenment*, Oxford: Voltaire Foundation, pp. 375–89.
Sidgwick, Henry ([1874] 1962), *The Methods of Ethics*, 7th edition, London: Macmillan.
Singer, Peter (1993), *Practical Ethics*, Cambridge: Cambridge University Press.
Skorupski, John (1989), *John Stuart Mill*, London: Routledge.

See also the entries on: Deontology; Positive-normative distinction in British history of economic thought; Utilitarianism.

5 Buddhist economics
Juliana Essen

Introduction

'Buddhist economics' – isn't that an oxymoron? This surprisingly common query is likely prompted by Buddhism's stereotype of saffron-robed monks who, after renouncing all worldly possessions and sensations, meditate their way to *nibbana*[1] in peaceful solitude. This image may be at odds with that of a Wall Street stockbroker, the quintessential capitalist, yet few Buddhists are actually monks. Most are ordinary laypeople trying to make a good life (and better rebirth) for themselves and their families. While Buddhist teachings (*dhamma*) are geared toward the monastic community, the Buddha also provided ethical guidelines to address the householder's particular needs, aspirations and societal roles. The guidelines relating to an individual's economic activity – including work and subsequent wealth accumulation, consumption and investment – are the focus here. More precisely, since Buddhism's ontology and objective differ from those of Western capitalism, the economic means and ends resulting from each ideology logically differ, as does the currency valued: money versus *kamma* or merit.

Though Buddhism is ultimately concerned with individual enlightenment, Buddhist principles have been applied to communities, firms and nations and bear some relevance for the global economy as well. It must be noted that there is a dearth of literature on Buddhist economics. This contribution then, is an early attempt in this nascent field to expound a theory of Buddhist economics based on scant scholarly work, early Theravada Buddhist scripture[2] and an example from the author's field study of an operational model of Buddhist economics. Due to space limitations and other considerations, this short chapter stops short of evaluating current economic practice and the strengths and weaknesses of Buddhist ethics as a fix.

Buddhist basics

This section briefly reviews Buddhist ontology and the practical teachings that serve as the foundation for Buddhist economic ethics. Buddhism's central doctrine, the Four Noble Truths, teaches that there is suffering (*dukkha*); the cause of suffering is craving or desire (*tanha*); there is an end to suffering; and the way to end suffering is the Eightfold Path. The Buddhist theory of conditionality, also known as dependent origination (*paticca samuppada*), offers insight into the origin of individual suffering through a 12-link chain of dependently arising conditions (ignorance, volitional impulses, consciousness, body and mind, six sense bases, sense contact, feeling, craving, clinging, becoming, birth, and ageing and death, which have despair as their by-product). There is no first cause, as each depends on the existence of another to come into being, and at the same time, each conditions the arising and existence of yet another. On a few occasions, the Buddha also declared that all things in the world arise continuously in this same way: conditioned by another and subject to the natural law of cause and effect. The gloss that Buddhists believe in the 'interconnectedness of all life' stems from these more complex

31

ideas. Thus no entity exists independently or permanently, not even the self. Contrary
to the Western assumption of an atomistic self, Buddhism teaches non-self (*anatta*) and
the release of attachment to ideas of 'me' and 'mine' (Swearer 1989). When the Buddha
spoke of enlightenment, *nibbana*, he was referring to the absolute understanding of these
truths that ends suffering.

Returning to the fourth Noble Truth, the Buddha outlined a practical way to end
suffering though the Eightfold Path. To escape the cycle of rebirth (*samsara*) and attain
nibbana, individuals must practice the Eightfold Path according to their own capabilities.
The eight aspects of the path are right view, right effort, right thought, right speech, right
action, right livelihood, right mindfulness and right concentration. These eight components are practised simultaneously and aim to promote and perfect the three divisions of
Buddhist training: morality (*sila*), mental development (*samadhi*) and wisdom (*panna*).
The texts elaborate on how to follow the path and cultivate *sila*, *samadhi* and *panna*, but
the various Buddhist schools and sects disagree as to which practices are most conducive
to enlightenment.

While monks and nuns devote their lives to such endeavours, laypeople typically find
them too challenging or incompatible with everyday life. Fortunately, there is another
doctrinally derived option available for lay salvation: *kamma*, the consequences of intentional thought and action that may positively or negatively affect this life and the next
(Keyes 1983). *Kamma* is not an exclusively Buddhist concept. Nevertheless, Buddhism
holds that the laws of causal dependence governing nature encompass human behaviour,
such that 'good deeds bring good results; bad deeds bring bad results' (Payutto 1995).
Nothing can change past *kamma*, but an individual may balance its negative effects by
improving future *kamma* through meritorious actions.

Buddhist economic ethics for the individual
Regarding the monk and the stockbroker, Buddhist economics and mainstream Western
economics are not necessarily radically opposed. Like its Western sibling, the Buddhist
model is based on individual rational choices concerning material well-being. The accumulation of wealth is allowed and in many cases encouraged, contrary to popular belief.
Significant differences emerge, however, upon closer examination of rational choice, the
objectives of economic activity, the nature of desire, appropriate means of satisfying
desires, conceptions of work and attitudes toward wealth, particularly how to consume
and disperse it.

First take 'economic man': the Enlightenment era rational actor model situates the
individual as an isolated unit whose behaviour is predictable by adherence to rationality.
Neoclassical economic theory of methodological individualism presents this individual
as using instrumental or means-to-ends rationality, calculating choices of comparable
value to arrive at the optimal outcome: maximization of self-interests, whether for profit
or some other form of satisfaction.

A Buddhist version of this model based on the theory of conditionality and the law of
causality (call it the rational Buddhist householder) looks a bit different. The Buddhist
sense of self is connected to other entities rather than being isolated, and an individual's
actions have consequences arising in a non-linear fashion, possibly resulting in a *kammic*
boomerang. This clearly expands an individual's notion of 'self-interest'. As such,
where the neoclassical economic man's rational process stops at satisfying a demand,

the rational Buddhist householder would first factor into his or her choices the possible effects on all spheres of human existence: individual, society and nature (Payutto 1995).

Readers responding that worrying about *kamma* is irrational are urged to reconsider their basis of rationality. Sociologist Max Weber (1958) distinguished two kinds of rationality: formal or instrumental rationality (on which economic man is based) and value rationality, which constitutes acting in accordance with one's values or that which is intrinsically valuable, perhaps of an ethical, aesthetic or religious nature. Anthropologists such as Gudeman and Rivera (1990) further argue that rationality is contextually dependent. Take for example a woman on her way to the market who refuses to sell her heavy load to a foreigner offering more than the market value; she may be perceived as behaving irrationally until one considers that she places greater value on long-term social relationships with market trading partners than a one-time monetary gain (Plattner 1989).

Regarding the objective of economic activity, Buddhist and mainstream Western economic models profoundly diverge. Buddhist economics does not promote material well-being for its own sake but as a necessary condition for spiritual development toward the ultimate goal, *nibbana*. To illustrate the relationship between spiritual and material development, the Venerable Prayudh Payutto (1992) relates a story from the Buddhist scriptures: one day, the whole town of Alavi gathered to hear the Buddha speak, but he insisted on waiting for a single poor peasant he sensed was ready for enlightenment. The peasant arrived exhausted and hungry. When the Buddha saw his condition, he asked the crowd for food and let him eat his fill before he began teaching. Listening to the discourse, the peasant entered the first stage of enlightenment. The Buddha later explained to the monks why he had waited: hunger is a great source of suffering, and 'when people are overwhelmed and in pain through suffering, they are incapable of understanding religious teaching' (Payutto 1992, p. 88). Hence the provisioning of basic material needs – food, shelter, clothing and medicine – serves as the foundation for human spiritual advancement.

With the minimum material comfort to support spiritual growth as its objective, it may seem that there is little motivation to be productive in the Buddhist economic model. The capitalist economy, after all, is driven by desires, and Buddhists are supposed to rid themselves of this source of suffering. On the contrary, Buddhism distinguishes between two kinds of desires. *Tanha*, the subject of the second Noble Truth, is craving for pleasurable feelings associated with both the tangible and intangible such as status or fame. This desire stems from ignorance and is viewed negatively. *Chanda* is positive desire for well-being and benefit. It is based on *panna* or intelligent reflection and leads to right effort and action. A Buddhist would argue that economic activity can and should be prompted by the latter form of desire – and possibly by the more specific desire to turn money into merit.

To satisfy such desires, an individual must perform some productive or livelihood activity. E.F. Schumacher, the first Western scholar to explore this subject, observed that since the Eightfold Path included right livelihood, 'there must be such a thing as Buddhist economics' (1973, p. 56; also see Daniels 2005). Right livelihood is guided by *chanda* and allows the individual to keep the five basic householder precepts (abstain from killing or harming life, lying, stealing, engaging in sexual misconduct, and consuming sense-altering substances). The Buddha specified the following unwholesome livelihoods a householder should *not* pursue: trading in weapons, flesh (human and animal), intoxicants and poison (*Anguttara Nikaya* III, p. 207). Right livelihood also requires diligence, an important Buddhist virtue captured in the Buddha's last words, 'work out your own salvation with diligence', and in the Buddha's directives for house-holders to achieve happiness in the present lifetime: diligent acquisition, followed by careful conservation, having virtuous friends and living within one's means (*Anguttara Nikaya* IV, p. 281).

Yet work may be more than just the means to satisfy material needs. Some Buddhist schools and sects, most notably Zen, view work as an opportunity to practice *samadhi* or 'open eye' meditation. Concentration prevents distractions, thereby allowing people to work more efficiently and carefully with fewer mistakes and accidents. Ideally they can also work together more harmoniously by controlling thoughts, feelings, speech and action according to the Eightfold Path. In theory, as individuals' mental states improve, so too does the quality of their work and social interactions. (For more on this topic, see Essen 2005 as well as the ideas of premier Thai Buddhist philosopher Buddhadasa Bhikkhu, for example, Swearer 1989.)

When most Buddhist householders work, however, they simply receive a pay cheque and may even accumulate wealth, just like their capitalist counterparts. The Buddha did not forbid wealth as long as it was gained according to *dhammic* norms (for example, through right livelihood). In fact, Buddhists may perceive wealth to be favourable for two reasons. First, wealth is a sign of virtue because it is partly a result of good *kamma*. That is, wealth accumulated through right livelihood is good; therefore, it is a suitable reward for meritorious actions (Sizemore and Swearer 1990). Second, surplus wealth is necessary to make more merit or good *kamma*, as described below.

Wealth accumulation is not so much the issue for Buddhists as what happens after-wards. Along with the benefits of wealth come increased potential for attachment to money, material goods and the resulting status as well as the craving for more. With this in mind, the Buddha advised householders to divide their wealth into four parts: one part for daily needs and obligations, two parts for investment and one part for future savings (*Digha Nikaya* III, p. 188). He also specified five uses of wealth: to provide for oneself and one's family, to share with friends, to save for emergencies, to make the fivefold offerings (to relatives, guests, the departed, the government and the deities) and to support spiritual teachers and monks (*Anguttara Nikaya* III, p. 45). Of these, two uses warrant further consideration: personal consumption and giving.

While a monk's personal consumption is certainly minimal, the Buddha did not advo-cate deprivation. As established, material well-being is necessary for spiritual advance-ment. Moderation is a better approach to Buddhist consumption as evidenced by the following story of Buddhism's beginnings: on a walk outside his palace one day, Sidartha Gotama encountered an old man, a sick man, a dead man and a holy man. He took these four meetings as signs that life is impermanent – that he himself would die someday, and that being the case, all his riches were meaningless. Acting on this realization, Sidartha renounced his worldly life and set out to find the truth about suffering and happiness. He quickly determined the severe self-deprivation of the forest holy men to be another form of suffering; subsequently, the Buddha charted his own path to end suffering, the Eightfold Path, and called it the Middle Way of neither extreme luxury nor extreme asceticism. The question of what is sufficient – not merely to sustain life but to give a sense of well-being – is to be continually re-evaluated by each individual at different levels of spiritual attainment. The aim, though, is to consume less.

Assuming a steady rate of diligent wealth accumulation (and no debt), reduced consumption permits greater opportunity for giving. This is desirable not simply because generosity is a householder virtue, but because, as a Thai nun once declared, 'Giving is the Heart of Buddhism.' Giving away surplus allows Buddhists to practice non-attachment to material objects as well as to possessive feelings; it is training in selflessness, non-self or *anatta*. A Thai college student made the point simply as she stood next to a cremation platform: 'You can't take it with you.' According to Phra Rajavaramuni (1990), an esteemed Thai scholar monk, lay and monastic training in Theravada countries tend to differentiate charity (*dana*), morality (*sila*) and mental development (*bhavana*) as the three bases of meritorious action. These are emphasized over higher training in *sila*, *samadhi* and *panna*. *Dana* is religious giving, not some ethic for social justice, and it is hierarchical, the highest form of which is directed at the Buddha and the monastic community (*sangha*). Phra Rajavaramuni suggests the stress on giving has to do with lay concern for good social relationships; other scholars (for example, Gutschow 2004) point to the reciprocal relationship between monasteries and households, material support flowing one way (that is, donations to temples) and spiritual support flowing the other. This cooperation between monks and laity creates the optimal context for the pursuit of salvation.

From the lay perspective, giving results in merit, the currency of spiritual wealth, which can be viewed as an investment for a better future in this lifetime and an even better rebirth. The rational Buddhist householder wanting to maximize spiritual wealth must choose between 'fields of merit', optimal recipients for giving. According to the concept of *dana*, the more noble and accomplished the recipient, the higher the field of merit. Keeping in mind that giving is but one of three categories of merit-making activities, a typical ranking of such activities in Thailand might include completely financing the construction of a temple, becoming a monk, having a son become a monk, contributing money to repair a temple, giving food daily to monks, observing every Buddhist Sabbath and strictly observing the five precepts (Tambiah 1968, p. 69). Most laypeople tend to rank morality and mental development low because they perceive these practices as beyond their capabilities; giving, then, is the preferred method. A final note here: the doctrinal definition of *dana* as religious giving is rather narrow; however, in practice many 'socially engaged' Buddhists (for example, Queen and King 1996) aim to benefit the wider community of monastics, ordinary people and the environment they live in. This approach to giving may be inspired by the ideal individual characteristics, known as the Four Sublime States: goodwill (*metta*), compassion (*karuna*), sympathetic joy (*mudita*) and equanimity (*upekkha*).

Buddhist economic ethics for communities, firms, nations and the global economy

Though Buddhism is fundamentally concerned with individual salvation, the economic ethics presented above may be applied to associations of individuals. This section presents a survey of work on Buddhist economic ethics for communities, firms, nations and the global economy.

The intentional, cooperative communities established by the Santi Asoke Buddhist Reform Movement of Thailand illustrate how individual Buddhist ethics might contribute to community development (Essen 2005). Through personal cultivation of non-attachment and Buddhist work attitudes, members of the Srisa Asoke Buddhist Centre turned a barren cemetery into a bustling village with a common hall for both religious and secular activities, tree-lined lanes of wooden houses on stilts, facilities for cultivating mushrooms, weaving cloth and recycling trash, organic vegetable and herb gardens in every available space, reforested areas with walking paths, a museum, a convenience store, a library, a rice mill, a boarding school for 200 students and more. Moreover, the fact that all seven such Asoke communities thrived throughout the nation's economic troubles is a testament to the value of 'meritism', the Asoke version of Buddhist economics.

The Asoke case is surely an unusual one, but Buddhist principles are also at work in many ordinary communities. Wanna Prayukvong (2005), a Thai scholar of management science, showed how community development in one southern Thai village is facilitated by the two prerequisites of the Eightfold Path. The first prerequisite is to associate with good people; this is an external factor and may be likened to social capital. The second, systematic attention/reflection, is an internal factor, which may be viewed as human capital. This study aimed to demonstrate how communities with leaders possessing these qualities succeeded in their development efforts and pointed to the need for development agencies to invest first in fostering these two factors.

Another handful of scholars is beginning to apply theories of Buddhist economics to firm structure and behaviour. Julie Nelson (2004), a feminist economist, starts from the idea that Buddhist ontology is relational. She then argues that among the different options for relationships, mutuality (mutual respect, consideration and support) is the most beneficial. Nelson recognizes that mutuality may be symmetric or asymmetric (characterized by unequal power) yet maintains that power may be used constructively. This conceptualization may be advocated to improve a firm's internal and external relationships. David Bubna-Litic (1995) similarly explores the relevance of Buddhist 'interbeing' for ethical business practices, particularly long-term strategic planning including the content of decisions as well as the decision-making process.

Because Buddhism adapts easily to new contexts, it may be tailored to a modern Buddhist nation's economic plan. Traditionally, a reciprocal relationship has existed between *sangha* and state, whereby the ruler offers protection and the *sangha* offers legitimation in return. Moreover, as a former prince, the Buddha had much to say about good governance. King Asoka's illustrious reign of India during the third century BC is seen as a realization of the Buddhist political ideal and a charter for all succeeding Theravada kingdoms (Tambiah 1978). However, considering economic conditions in Burma (Schumacher's inspiration), simply being a Buddhist nation does not ensure that the ethics will be applied. That requires right view, right thought, right effort, and right action on the part of the leaders. A prime contemporary example is the King of Thailand who promoted his 'new theory' for a 'sufficiency economy' shortly after the economic crisis of 1997 to provide better subsistence and protection from market fluctuation. This approach was well received in the north-east, the poorest region; unfortunately, it did not proliferate perhaps due to the business-tycoon prime minister's conflicting agendas. Hence the greatest difficulty for a nation wanting to implement Buddhist economic ethics may be dealing with the influence of capitalism, both within its borders and from its trading partners.

That leaves the global economy. Though concerned scholars, practitioners and global citizens may find Buddhist economic ethics quite appealing, anthropologists and feminist economists (for example, Gibson-Graham 1996) caution against facilely replacing the dominant neoliberal economic model with a Buddhist one. Instead, economic pluralism is advocated, consisting of the myriad of approaches to material and social well-being that are culturally and environmentally appropriate. This is essential for a vital global economy because, quite simply, different problems require different solutions. Nevertheless, it is possible and even desirable that actors in the global economy learn from these different approaches for a more environmentally sustainable and socially just way of being in the world. Indeed, the Buddha counselled the householder to accumulate wealth as a bee collects nectar from a flower, that is, without destroying the flower (Thero 1997). Let the flower represent the world in which we live, and that seems sage advice.

Notes

1. This work uses Pali, the language of early Theravada texts.
2. In light of the vociferous debate on whether modern environmental ethics may be derived from Buddhist scriptures (for example, Schmithausen 1997), the present author judiciously cites only original Theravada texts and examples from Theravada countries rather than later Mahayanan interpretations.

References

Buddhist texts: *Anguttara Nikaya*, vols. III and IV, and *Digha Nikaya* vol. III, *Sutta Pitaka*, Lancaster, UK: Pali Text Society.

Bubna-Litic, David (1995), 'Buddhist ethics and business strategy making', *Journal of Buddhist Ethics*, online conference on Buddhism and human rights, jbe.gold.ac.uk/1995conf/bubna.txt, 1 June 2006.

Daniels, Peter (2005), 'Economic systems and the Buddhist world view: the 21st century nexus', *Journal of Socio-Economics*, **34**, 245–68.

Essen, Juliana (2005), *'Right Development': The Santi Asoke Movement of Thailand*, Lanham, MD: Lexington Books.

Gibson-Graham, J.K. (1996), *The End of Capitalism (As We Knew It)*, Oxford: Blackwell.

Gudeman, Stephen and Alberto Rivera (1990), *Conversations in Colombia: The Domestic Economy in Life and Text*, Cambridge: Cambridge University Press.

Gutschow, Kim (2004), *Being a Buddhist Nun: The Struggle for Enlightenment in the Himalayas*, Cambridge, MA: Harvard University Press.

Keyes, Charles (1983), 'Introduction: the study of popular ideas of karma', in Charles Keyes and Daniel E. Valentine (eds), *Karma: An Anthropological Inquiry*, Berkeley, CA: University of California Press.

Nelson, Julie (2004), 'Beyond small-is-beautiful: a Buddhist and feminist analysis of ethics and business', Tufts University Global Development and Environment Institute Working Paper No. 04–01, http://www.ase.tufts.edu/gdae/publications/working_papers/04-01BeyondSmall.pdf, 1 June 2006.

Payutto, Ven. Prayudh (1992), *Buddhist Economics: A Middle Way for the Market Place*, Bangkok: Buddhadhamma Foundation.

Payutto, Ven. Prayudh (1995), *Good, Evil, and Beyond: Kamma in the Buddha's Teaching*, Bangkok: Buddhadhamma Foundation.

Plattner, Stuart (1989), *Economic Anthropology*, Palo Alto, CA: Stanford University Press.

Prayukvong, Wanna (2005), 'A Buddhist economic approach to the development of community enterprises: a case study from Southern Thailand', *Cambridge Journal of Economics*, **29**, 1171–85.

Queen, Christopher and Sallie King (eds) (1996), *Engaged Buddhism: Buddhist Liberation Movements in Asia*, Albany, NY: State University of New York Press.

Rajavaramuni, Phra (1990), 'Introduction', in Russell F. Sizemore and Donald K. Swearer (eds), *Ethics, Wealth, and Salvation: A Study in Buddhist Social Ethics*, Columbia, SC: University of South Carolina Press.

Schmithausen, Lambert (1997), 'The early Buddhist tradition and ecological ethics', *Journal of Buddhist Ethics*, **4**, 1–74.

Schumacher, Ernst F. (1973), *Small is Beautiful: Economics as if People Mattered*, London: Blond and Briggs.

Sizemore, Russell F. and Donald K. Swearer (eds) (1990), *Ethics, Wealth, and Salvation: A Study in Buddhist Social Ethics*, Columbia, SC: University of South Carolina Press.

Swearer, Donald K. (1989), *Me and Mine: Selected Essays of Bhikkhu Buddhadasa*, Albany, NY: State University of New York Press.
Tambiah, Stanley J. (1968), 'The ideology of merit and the social correlates of Buddhism in a Thai village', in Edmund Leach (ed.), *Dialectic in Practical Religion*, Cambridge: Cambridge University Press.
Tambiah, Stanley J. (1978), 'Sangha and polity in modern Thailand: an overview', in Bardwell L. Smith (ed.), *Religion and Legitimation of Power in Thailand, Laos, and Burma*, Chambersburg, PA: ANIMA Books.
Thero, Ven. Melpitiye Wimalakitti (1997), 'Buddhist perspectives on the natural and social environment', in Peter Gallay-Pap and Ruth Bottomley (eds), *Toward an Environmental Ethic in Southeast Asia*, Phnom Penh, Cambodia: The Buddhist Institute.
Weber, Max (1958), *The Protestant Ethic and the Spirit of Capitalism*, New York: Charles Scribner's Sons.

See also the entries on: Consumerism; Individualism; Rationality; Religion.

6 Capability approach
Ingrid Robeyns

What is the capability approach?

The capability approach is a broad normative framework for the evaluation and assessment of individual well-being and social arrangements and the design of policies and proposals about social change in society. Its roots can be traced back to, among others, Aristotle, Adam Smith and Karl Marx. Nonetheless, it has become especially well known in the past three decades through the work of economist and philosopher Amartya Sen (for example, 1980, 1985, 1990, 1992, 1993, 1999) and classicist and philosopher Martha Nussbaum (1988, 1995, 2000, 2003, 2006). The capability approach is employed in a wide range of academic disciplines, most prominently development studies, welfare economics, social policy and political philosophy. It can be applied to evaluate inequality, poverty, the well-being of an individual or the well-being of the different members of a group (whether the average, or other aspects of the distribution). It can also be employed as an alternative evaluative tool for social cost-benefit analysis, or as a framework for the design and evaluation of policies. These latter range from welfare state design in affluent societies to development policies by governments and non-governmental organizations in developing countries.

The literature includes a wide variety of studies, from the very abstract to applied empirical works. The capability approach also provides the theoretical foundations for the human development paradigm, which is often described as an alternative to neoliberalism and the so-called 'Washington Consensus' in development thinking (Fukuda-Parr 2003). It is not a theory that in itself explains poverty, inequality or well-being. Instead, it provides a range of concepts and a normative framework within which to conceptualize and evaluate these phenomena. Applying the capability approach to issues of policy and social change therefore often requires the addition of explanatory theories.

In this chapter, the capability approach is explained and discussed with a special focus on how it relates to economics and ethics. As will be argued, the capability approach differs from standard economic analysis in at least four ways. First, it starts from a different set of foundational concepts. Second, the comprehensive and multidimensional nature of these core concepts leads to the strong interdisciplinary character of the approach and its closely related reliance on a broad range of methodologies. Third, the capability approach explicitly acknowledges that all evaluative or prescriptive analyses, including those from welfare and development economics, have normative and ethical moments that should be explicitly addressed rather than hidden behind approaches and methodologies that give the false impression of being entirely objective and non-normative. Finally, capability analyses often lead to conclusions that differ from those reached using standard economic methods and theories.

Core concepts and claims

The core concept of the capability approach is the notion of a person's capabilities, that is, the set of things that a person is effectively able to do and to be. This contrasts with approaches that concentrate on people's happiness or desire-fulfilment, or on income, expenditures and consumption. Capability theorists argue that our evaluations and policies should emphasize what people are effectively able to do and to be, the quality of their life and removing obstacles in their lives so that they have more freedom to live the kind of life which, upon reflection, they have reason to value. A key analytical distinction in the capability approach is that between the means and the ends of well-being and development. Only the ends have intrinsic importance, although means are instrumental to reaching the goals of increased well-being, justice and development. However, in concrete situations these distinctions often blur, since some ends are simultaneously also means to other ends (for example, the capability of being in good health is an end in itself, but also a means for being able to work).

According to the capability approach, the ends of well-being, justice and development should be conceptualized in terms of people's capabilities to function, that is, their effective opportunities to undertake the actions and activities that they want to engage in, and to be the kind of person they want to be. These beings and doings, called 'functionings', together constitute what makes a life valuable. Functionings include working, resting, being literate, being healthy, being part of a community, practising a religion and so forth. The distinction between achieved functionings and capabilities is between that which is realized and that which is effectively possible, in other words, between achievements on the one hand, and freedoms or valuable options from which one can choose on the other. What is ultimately important is that people have the freedoms or valuable opportunities (capabilities) to lead the kind of life they want to lead, to do what they want to do and to be the person they want to be. Once they effectively have these substantive opportunities, they can choose those options which they most value. For example, every person should have the opportunity to be part of a community and to practise a religion, but if someone prefers to be a hermit or an atheist, they should also have this option.

The capability approach evaluates policies according to their impact on people's capabilities. It asks whether people are being healthy and whether the means or resources necessary for this capability are present, such as clean water, access to medical facilities, protection from infections and diseases and basic knowledge of health issues. It also asks which social and economic institutions are most suitable to expanding people's valuable capabilities. It asks whether people have genuine opportunities to be well-nourished, and whether the conditions for this capability, such as having sufficient food supplies and food entitlements, are being met. It asks whether people have access to a high-quality educational system, to real political participation, and to community activities which provide support in coping with the struggles of daily life and which foster real friendships. For some of these capabilities, the main input will be financial resources and economic production, but for others it can also be political practices and institutions, such as the effective guaranteeing and protection of freedom of thought, political participation, social or cultural practices, social structures, social institutions, public goods, social norms, traditions and habits.

In sum, the capability approach covers all dimensions of human well-being. Development, well-being and justice are regarded in a comprehensive and integrated manner, and much attention is paid to the links between material, mental and social well-being, or in other words, to the economic, social, political and cultural dimensions of life.

Means, ends and conversion factors

A crucial distinction in the capability approach, which has special relevance if one wants to know how it differs from standard economic practices, is the distinction between the means and the ends of well-being. The ends of well-being are a person's functionings and capabilities. The means of well-being are resources, though in a broad sense, as these include goods, services and other aspects that play an instrumental role in the production of well-being, including social capital and people's time allocations. Resources should therefore not necessarily be thought of as exchangeable for income or money – as this would restrict the capability approach to analyses and measurements related to the market only, which is not intended. Since resources are generally understood much more narrowly in economics (in contrast to the broad definition of political philosophy), it may be advisable to use an alternative terminology, such as 'capability inputs'.

The relation between capability inputs and capabilities is influenced by *conversion factors*, which may be classified in three categories. First, *personal conversion factors* (for example, metabolism, physical condition, sex, reading skills and intelligence) influence how a person can convert the characteristics of the capability input into a functioning. If a person is disabled, or in poor physical condition, or has never learned to cycle, then the bicycle will be of limited help in enabling the functioning of mobility. Second, *social conversion factors* (for example, public policies, social norms, discriminatory practices, gender roles, societal hierarchies and power relations) and, third, *environmental conversion factors* (for example, climate, geographical location) play a role in the conversion of characteristics of the input to the individual functioning. If there are no paved roads, or if a government or the dominant societal culture imposes a social or legal norm that women are not allowed to cycle without being accompanied by a male family member, then it becomes much more difficult or even impossible for a woman to use the resource to enable the functioning. Hence, knowing the resources a person owns or can use is not sufficient to know which functionings they can achieve. We also need to know much more about the person and the circumstances in which they are living.

The central role of the conversion factors also highlights the importance of human diversity in the capability approach. The approach takes account of human diversity in two ways: by its focus on the plurality of functionings and capabilities as the evaluative space and by the explicit focus on personal, social and environmental conversion factors of inputs into functionings. A focus on functionings and capabilities does not imply that resources, including income, are no longer relevant or important from a capability perspective. While functionings and capabilities are of ultimate normative concern, other aspects of well-being, and the inputs generating well-being, can be important as well. Indeed, in their evaluation of development in India, Jean Drèze and Amartya Sen (2002) stressed that working within the capability approach in no way excludes the integration of an analysis of resources or other means. Income analyses and capability analyses can provide complementary insights, and there are many cases where both are relevant, such as when one is interested in poverty measurement (Ruggeri Laderchi et al. 2003).

An alternative to utilitarianism and income metrics
The capability approach proposes an alternative to other evaluative approaches, such as the welfarist or utilitarian approaches and income- or resource-based theories. Sen rejects welfarist theories because, whatever their further specifications, they rely *exclusively* on utility and thus exclude non-utility information from moral judgements (for example, Sen 1979). Sen is concerned not only with the information that is included in a normative evaluation, but also with the information that is excluded. The non-utility information that is excluded by utilitarianism could be a person's additional physical needs as a result of physical impairment, but could also be moral principles, such as the deontological principle that men and women should be paid the same wage for the same work. For a utilitarian, this principle has no intrinsic value, and men and women should not be paid the same wage as long as women are satisfied with lower wages. But it is counter-intuitive, Sen argues, that such principles not be taken into account in our moral judgements. Thus, the first normative theories that Sen attacks are those that rely exclusively on mental states. This does not mean that Sen thinks mental states, such as happiness, are unimportant and have no role to play; rather, it is the exclusive reliance on mental states that the capability approach rejects.

The capability approach also entails a critique of how economists have applied the utilitarian framework for empirical analysis in welfare economics. Economists use utility as the focal variable in theoretical work, but translate this into a focus on income in their applied work. But in order for income to be a good indicator of individual welfare, let alone well-being, several strong assumptions must be made (Kuklys and Robeyns 2005, pp. 14–20). First, the income metric would need to account for all non-market contributions (whether negative or positive) to individual well-being, such as care work, public goods or externalities. Second, income metrics are unable to account for heterogeneity of needs, as captured in the notion of the conversion factors. Here it should be granted that some recent research has applied techniques such as equivalence scales to account for disabilities – but not for all other differences in personal and social conversion factors. Third, income metrics are generally based on rough assumptions about sharing within the household, which means they are unable to account for intra-household inequalities of well-being or opportunities. Thus, while income generally is an important means to well-being and freedom, it can only serve as a rough proxy for what matters intrinsically, namely people's capabilities.

Selecting capabilities
The multidimensional nature of the capability approach raises several concerns among economists, including the question of how to know which dimensions are to be included. How should we select or identify the capabilities that matter? Perhaps this is not possible in the first place. Many mainstream economists are weary of making explicit value judgements; and selecting relevant capabilities requires precisely such normative judgements (Sugden 1993). But it is illusionary and deceiving to think that, in contrast to the capability approach, traditional income approaches in economics are not normative. Rather, the differences are that income metrics have become the standard in economics (and hence we do not question them as much as new approaches), that income has the advantage of providing a common currency in which to sum the multiple dimensions of well-being, and that most countries have much better income statistics than data on functionings and capabilities.

For some economists, the capability approach cannot become operational as long as we do not know how to select (or, as they sometimes put it, 'identify') the relevant capabilities. Sen (2004) responded to these criticisms by pointing out that the problem is not with the listing of the important capabilities, but with the endorsement of one predetermined list of capabilities. He further argues that this is not the task of the theorist. For Sen the selection of capabilities is the task of the democratic process. We cannot make one definitive list of capabilities, as these lists are used for different purposes, and each purpose might require its own list. For example, the founders of the *Human Development Report* (UNDP 1990–2007) decided to include in their index those dimensions that they considered appropriate for the purpose at hand, namely inter-country comparisons of universal basic capabilities. Moreover, lists of capabilities are used in different social, cultural and geographical settings, which will also influence the selection. Finally, Sen stresses that public discussion and reasoning can lead to a better understanding of the value and role of specific capabilities. Nussbaum (2000, 2003) in contrast, proposes a universal list of human capabilities that each government should guarantee to each citizen up to a minimum threshold. However, she has always stressed that her list is of highly general capabilities, which should be made more specific by the local populations.

Yet if we follow the procedural route, it remains unclear how these processes of public reasoning and democracy will take place, and how we can ensure minimal conditions of fair representation. Moreover, not all applications of Sen's capability approach allow for fully democratic discussions among all those affected. Hence more work is needed on the principles or procedures that should be used to select capabilities in those circumstances. Some of this work has recently been taken up by scholars such as Alkire (2002) and Robeyns (2003). While a recent survey of how the capability approach has been put into practice illustrates that the approach can be applied and does lead to insights that are different from mainstream economic analysis (Robeyns 2006), it is also clear that not enough work has yet been done on the kind of democratic institutions that the 'capability approach in practice' would require, nor on methodologies to guide social scientists who want empirically to assess capability or functioning levels.

Methodologies and interdisciplinarity of the capability approach
The differences between the capability approach and standard approaches in welfare and development economics are not just in the different sets of concepts and normative breadth of the information taken into account when analysing development or well-being issues. Nor does it lie purely in the explicit recognition of the normative nature of those analyses. An equally important, but much less discussed, characteristic of the capability approach is its interdisciplinary nature and reliance on a broad set of methodologies.

The capability approach is a truly interdisciplinary field, whereby scholars unite around research questions (for example, how to develop a new set of social indicators) or topics (for example, gender or education), rather than starting from a disciplinary framework. In addition, the methodologies used are diverse, including standard tools from analytical philosophy (Cohen 1993; Nussbaum 2006; Sen 1990), critical analysis based on qualitative empirical work (Unterhalter 2003), standard quantitative economic methods (Alkire 2002), and quantitative methods not widely used in economics such as factor analysis (Schokkaert and van Ootegem 1990), fuzzy sets theory (Chiappero Martinetti 2000; Qizilbash and Clark 2005) and advanced statistical methods (Kuklys

2005). Yet some economists have argued that the capability approach is still too narrow in the concerns that it addresses, and needs to be further broadened if it wants to address issues such as structural power differences or the importance of care (Gasper and van Staveren 2003; Hill 2003).

So far, the capability approach has attracted most attention from heterodox economists, philosophers and other social scientists. This can probably be explained by the fact that the approach is much more 'verbal' than 'mathematical', and its underlying philosophical and methodological principles do not naturally lend themselves to highly abstract modelling, especially if simplified or stylized assumptions are used. Applications of the capability approach are also much richer with respect to the information that they use, but this is done at the cost of being unable to construct simple models, to conduct full measuring or to construct full rankings. The more an economist (or an economic community such as a particular faculty) values minimalist models, or parsimony, the more difficult it will be to work within the capability paradigm in a non-reductionist way, and to account for factors such as culture, the unpaid economy, caring, identities, the symbolic order and so forth with a sufficiently rich understanding.

The methodological upshot seems to be that the capability approach would benefit from a broad and methodologically pluralistic understanding of economics. By the same token, a broadening of economics would benefit from paying more attention to the core concepts of the capability approach and the lessons that can be learned from its applications.

The capability approach, ethics and economics
Given the above description of the capability approach in relation to economics, what can we conclude regarding its relation to ethics and economics? We can look at this relationship in various ways. We could ask whether the capability approach is particularly related to one traditional ethical theory, such as consequentialism (briefly, the view that our individual and collective actions should be guided by the goodness or badness of their consequences), deontology (the view that actions should be guided by moral rules and duties, rather than by an evaluation of the consequences) or virtue ethics (the view that emphasizes virtues and moral character). The form of utilitarianism that dominates economics is a particular kind of consequentialism, which evaluates the consequences of actions in terms of their preference satisfaction. This type of consequentialism the capability approach clearly rejects, but the capability approach is consistent with types of consequentialism that evaluate actions and social states in terms of people's functionings and capabilities. However, given the underspecified nature of the capability approach, one can also construct capability theories that are more in line with deontological thinking or virtue ethics. These are all possible within the broad family of the capability approach as can be discerned from the literature. Amartya Sen has some sympathies for deontological thinking, as seen from his endorsement of the importance of freedoms, basic liberties and the crucial role of agency (for example, Sen 2003), whereas Martha Nussbaum, especially in her earlier work, has more affinity with Aristotelian virtue ethics (for example, Nussbaum 1988).

We can also ask which substantive ethical differences the capability approach makes. There are at least two. First, the capability approach redefines the moral value of freedom from a negative notion of freedom to a notion of positive freedom or substantive opportunity freedom. This has implications for the economic analysis of the market and public policies: the answer to the question of which is more desirable will depend on people's functionings and capability levels. It follows that, rather than advocating that either markets or the government lead to a more desirable outcome, their relative usefulness will depend on the specific context. Second, the capability approach redefines well-being from a narrow materialistic notion of economic welfare to a much broader quality of life notion. This too can have radical consequences for economic analysis. For example, it explains behaviour that mainstream economics would regard as irrational, such as choosing a lower material standard of living in order to have more time for family, the community or unpaid projects that one chooses on moral, ideological or religious grounds, rather than on grounds of utility maximization.

References

Alkire, Sabina (2002), *Valuing Freedoms: Sen's Capability Approach and Poverty Reduction*, New York: Oxford University Press.

Chiappero Martinetti, Enrica (2000), 'A multi-dimensional assessment of well-being based on Sen's functionings approach', *Revista Internazionale di Scienza Soziali*, **58**, 207–39.

Cohen, Gerald A. (1993), 'Equality of what? On welfare, goods and capabilities', in Martha Nussbaum and Amartya Sen (eds), *The Quality of Life*, Oxford: Clarendon Press, pp. 9–29.

Drèze, Jean and Amartya Sen (2002), *India: Development and Participation*, Oxford: Oxford University Press.

Fukuda-Parr, Sakiko (2003), 'The human development paradigm: operationalizing Sen's ideas on capabilities', *Feminist Economics*, **9** (2/3), 301–17.

Gasper, Des and Irene van Staveren (2003), 'Development as freedom – and as what else?' *Feminist Economics*, **9** (2/3), 137–61.

Hill, Marianne (2003), 'Development as empowerment', *Feminist Economics*, **9** (2/3), 117–35.

Kuklys, Wiebke (2005), *Amartya Sen's Capability Approach: Theoretical Insights and Empirical Applications*, Berlin: Springer.

Kuklys, Wiebke and Ingrid Robeyns (2005), 'Sen's capability approach to welfare economics', in Wiebke Kuklys, *Amartya Sen's Capability Approach: Theoretical Insights and Empirical Applications*, Berlin: Springer, pp. 9–30.

Nussbaum, Martha (1988), 'Nature, functioning and capability: Aristotle on political distribution', *Oxford Studies in Ancient Philosophy*, supplementary volume, 145–84.

Nussbaum, Martha (1995), 'Human capabilities, female human beings', in Martha Nussbaum and Jonathan Glover (eds), *Women, Culture and Development*, Oxford: Clarendon Press, pp. 61–104.

Nussbaum, Martha (2000), *Women and Human Development: The Capabilities Approach*, Cambridge: Cambridge University Press.

Nussbaum, Martha (2003), 'Capabilities as fundamental entitlements: Sen and social justice', *Feminist Economics*, **9** (2/3), 33–59.

Nussbaum, Martha (2006), *Frontiers of Justice. Disability, Nationality, Species Membership*, Cambridge, MA: Harvard University Press.

Qizilbash, Mozaffar and David Clark (2005), 'The capability approach and fuzzy poverty measures: an application to the South-African context', *Social Indicators Research*, **74**, 103–39.

Robeyns, Ingrid (2003), 'Sen's capability approach and gender inequality: selecting relevant capabilities', *Feminist Economics*, **9** (2/3), 61–92.

Robeyns, Ingrid (2006), 'The capability approach in practice', *Journal of Political Philosophy*, **14** (3), 351–76.

Ruggeri Laderchi, Caterina, Ruhi Saith and Frances Stewart (2003), 'Does it matter that we do not agree on the definition of poverty? A comparison of four approaches', *Oxford Development Studies*, **31**, 243–74.

Schokkaert, Erik and Luc van Ootegem (1990), 'Sen's concept of the standard of living applied to the Belgian unemployed', *Recherches Economiques de Louvain*, **56**, 429–50.

Sen, Amartya (1979), 'Personal utilities and public judgements: or what's wrong with welfare economics?' *Economic Journal*, **89**, 537–58.

Sen, Amartya (1980), 'Equality of what?' in Sterling McMurrin (ed.), *The Tanner Lectures on Human Values*, Salt Lake City, UT: University of Utah Press, pp. 195–220.

Sen, Amartya (1985), *Commodities and Capabilities*, Amsterdam: North Holland.

Sen, Amartya (1990), 'Justice: means versus freedoms', *Philosophy and Public Affairs*, **19**, 111–21.

Sen, Amartya (1992), *Inequality Re-examined*, Oxford: Clarendon Press.

Sen, Amartya (1993), 'Capability and well-being', in Martha Nussbaum and Amartya Sen (eds), *The Quality of Life*, Oxford: Clarendon Press, pp. 30–53.

Sen, Amartya (1999), *Development as Freedom*, New York: Knopf.

Sen, Amartya (2003), *Rationality and Freedom*, Cambridge, MA: Harvard University Press.

Sen, Amartya (2004), 'Capabilities, lists, and public reason: continuing the conversation', *Feminist Economics*, **10** (3), 77–80.

Sugden, Robert (1993), 'Welfare, resources, and capabilities: a review of *Inequality Re-examined* by Amartya Sen', *Journal of Economic Literature*, **31**, 1947–62.

UNDP (1990–2007), *Human Development Report*, Oxford and New York: Oxford University Press.

Unterhalter, Elaine (2003), 'The capabilities approach and gendered education: an examination of South African complexities', *Theory and Research in Education*, **1** (1), 7–22.

See also the entries on: Human development; Needs and well-being; Amartya Sen; Utilitarianism.

7 Catholic social thought
Albino Barrera

Moral philosophy is a constitutive part of economics as a social science. The economy is, after all, a human institution whose primary end is the integral development of the person in body, mind and spirit. This interdisciplinary approach is a fundamental contribution of Catholic social thought to contemporary economic science. Its principal legacy is evident in the branch of social economics, which weaves together the study of economics, human dignity, ethics, theology and philosophy. The *Review of Social Economy*, especially in its first few decades when it was the academic journal of the Catholic Economic Association, illustrates such scholarship. Significantly, this association was founded in 1941, at a time when the discipline was increasingly subscribing to Lionel Robbins's view of economics as a value-free science, as conveyed in his famous *Essay on the Nature and Significance of Economic Science* (1932).

The association has since dropped its original name and greatly diversified its interests beyond Catholic social thought. Nevertheless, the Association for Social Economics, as it is now known, is still distinctive within heterodox economics for its commitment to addressing socio-economic questions that impinge on values and human flourishing. Msgr John A. Ryan of Roosevelt-era New Deal fame and Bernard Dempsey are two notable offshoots of this school of thought in the last century. Of late, this strand has given rise to economic personalism and the *Journal of Markets and Morality*. Economic personalism seeks to provide a better anthropology for economic analysis through interdisciplinary scholarship.

Moving forward, 'theological economics' emerged as a sub-field of economic thought which studies the contributions of Jewish, Christian, Islamic and other religious traditions to normative economics. Catholic social thought is a significant part of this field given its long-standing, fairly well-developed and ongoing thinking on economic life.

Scope and method
Catholic social thought does not purport to do positive economic analysis. Its interest is in examining the economy not as a subject in itself but in how economic agency intersects the moral life. In terms of ethical methodology, it combines a deontological approach (for example, scriptural precepts), a teleological articulation of its understanding of the needs that flow from human nature and a call for virtue in social living. It draws from Revelation, philosophy and the social sciences. Through faith, it accepts Revelation as God's self-revelation through the Sacred Scripture, Tradition and the Magisterium of the Church. Consequently, Catholic social thought spans from the Hebrew Scriptures, to the New Testament, to the Patristic Fathers, to the scholastic doctors and the modern papal and episcopal social documents.

Philosophy and the empirical sciences are also vital sources for Catholic social thought, because of its view that morality is intelligible. Such an approach is fortuitous because theological reflection is often discounted in pluralistic and secular societies. However, since Catholic social thought is also steeped in natural-law reasoning, it is adept at shifting between philosophy and theology in making its case, depending on the receptivity (or lack thereof) to religious ethics in the public square of ideas and debate.

The contributions of Catholic social thought to normative economics are not systematic treatises but rather theological and philosophical reflections on the particular socio-economic problems of the day, with the more recent teachings taking advantage of insights offered by the human (social) sciences. Thus, it is a living tradition marked by both continuity and change as it grapples with new problems in a constantly evolving economy. Despite being spread over a long period of time and despite having to deal with different kinds of problems in radically dissimilar economies (for example, ancient, feudal and industrial), there is nonetheless a discernible pattern of regularities, underlying axioms and overarching themes running throughout the entire tradition. After all, these various teachings share a similar starting point (Revelation) and rely on the use of both faith and reason.

Anthropology

To appreciate the distinctive contribution of Catholic social thought to economic ethics requires an understanding of its anthropology. Creation is not a random event. There is a purpose for which everything has been created, including economic activity. Every creature has received and, in turn, communicates a particular dimension of God's goodness and perfections according to its mode of being and operation. In the case of human beings, this entails the proper use of their two signal faculties of reason and will, the ability to know and to love. There is a reflexive nature to the human act, in that our actions return to define and form who we are. Thus, human beings truly live up to the fullness of their creation in the image and likeness of God to the degree that they achieve moral excellence through the reasoned use of their freedom. In the case of the goods of the earth, besides reflecting the perfections and the grandeur of God, they are also meant to supply the needs of human beings.

The seemingly perennial clash of interests between the individual and the community is more apparent than real. After all, the goal of the community is to provide the most propitious conditions and all the assistance required for its individual members to flourish in life. For its part, the person reaches the heights of moral excellence only through an act of self-giving, which is possible only in community. Thus, far from being inherently in conflict with each other, the person and the community are in fact necessary conditions for one another. Human life can be viewed as a threefold gift: a gift of the self, a gift of each other and a gift of the Earth.

Given these foundational premises, Catholic social thought does not subscribe to some of the axioms of the heuristic model of neoclassical economics, such as methodological individualism, self-interestedness and non-satiety in consumption. Individual economic agency is admittedly the animating core of economic life, as methodological individualism points out. However, it cannot be separated from the larger community in which it is nurtured and within which it operates. Individuals are the key factor, but they are effective only as persons within a community. Moreover, the characteristic self-interested quality of *homo oeconomicus*, while an important assumption in formal modelling, is not truly descriptive of the human person. Selflessness in human experience is, in fact, more commonly observed and desired than is generally acknowledged. Furthermore, the assumption of 'more is better' (for example, in consumption or accumulation) is also problematic, because wealth acquisition is not an end, but is merely a means to the much higher end of moral excellence. Economic life is not an end in itself; it is merely a means, albeit an important one, to human flourishing.

Herein lies a key difference between Catholic social thought's normative economics and mainstream, positive economics. While Catholic social thought starts off with an objective end for which the economy exists (human well-being), neoclassical economics embraces a liberal openness of decentralized, subjective ends in which individuals are free to set their respective preferences. After all, neoclassical economics views its task merely as a value-free exercise of putting scarce resources to their most valued uses and not to specify ends that must be pursued.

Conceptual framework
In addition to its anthropological premises, a second distinctive contribution of Catholic social thought to the field of economic ethics is its conceptual framework for assessing the socio-economic problems of our day. This is an array of useful principles slowly accumulated, handed down and refined over time as this tradition grappled with the attendant ethical dilemmas of a constantly evolving economy through the ages, from the ancient, classical period, to the medieval era, and then to our own modern industrial age.

The bedrock of Catholic social thought is the protection and promotion of human dignity within an overarching common good. Compared to all other creatures, human beings are the only ones to have been created for their own sake and imbued with moral agency, for the purpose of sharing in divine life and happiness. They have an open-standing personal invitation for eventual union with God for all eternity. They have been saved by Jesus Christ and are sustained by God in continued existence. These are the core elements that endow human beings with an inalienable human dignity. Economic life is about facilitating the completion of the human quest to requite this proffered divine friendship, both by supplying the material needs for continued existence and by providing the occasion for growth in moral perfection through virtuous economic activity. Indeed, far from being mundane, economic life is important for both the material and spiritual dimensions of human flourishing. The many other principles of this tradition flow from this foundational axiom of human dignity.

The principle of integral human development contends that genuine human advancement is primarily a moral phenomenon, and not solely or principally economic in nature as is commonly believed. Development is truly integral only if the individual thrives as a whole person, in body, mind and spirit. It is human only to the degree that the person internalizes the values of truth, love, friendship and justice. Every person is responsible for his or her own development. The community has a collective duty to ensure that every person has all of the necessary means and assistance to attain such integral human development, which is the full actualization of the person's human dignity.

The principle of the universal destination of the goods of the earth stipulates that the fruits of the earth are meant for the benefit of all, regardless of how titles of ownership are divided. Thus, there is an implicit 'social mortgage' on private properties. This claim is based on the understanding that the earth was created and given by God as a bequest to all of humanity, excluding no one (Genesis 1–2). In laissez-faire capitalism, legal ownership confers on proprietors the right to use and dispose of their properties in whatever way they please as long as they do not hurt anybody and are not in violation of the law; just use automatically flows from just ownership. Not so for Catholic social thought, for which just ownership and just use are not identical. Each must live up to a different set of criteria. The right to property ownership has an attendant just use obligation that is satisfied only when the property in question is utilized for the benefit not only of the owner but also for others, especially those who are propertyless. In fact, in dire emergencies, properties held in private become common in use. A further extension of this principle is the superfluous income criterion, which calls on people to use their excess earnings or wealth for the benefit of the needy. Superfluity is measured in terms of the relative unmet needs of others.

The universal destination of the goods of the earth principle has been extensively employed in all periods of tradition. Its perennial use to address social questions is not surprising considering that economics, by its nature, is about the allocation of scarce goods. The principle in fact claims that every person ought to be able to satisfy his or her needs. The name of the principle is modern, but its spirit is not. We see the intent of this principle at work, for example, in the various economic precepts of the Old Testament, such as the gleaning law, lending grain or money without interest and the return of ancestral land to its original owners. The same spirit is evident in the radical, voluntary divestment of the early Christian community which held all properties in common for the use of all according to need.

The principle of subsidiarity calls on higher bodies not to arrogate for themselves functions that lower bodies or individuals are able to perform. Human beings are not endowed with a perfected reason and will at the time of their birth. These signal faculties have to be formed and nurtured if they are to be exercised properly. In fact, people will most likely spend their entire lives learning how to use their freedom in a reasoned and virtuous manner. To engender this facility in the use of free will, it is necessary to furnish people with the opportunity to use these faculties and to learn from both their triumphs and their inevitable occasional mistakes. Thus, we have the principle of subsidiarity that calls for giving people a wide berth and space to do what they are able to do and should be doing for themselves. Obviously, this principle is an important building block of the market economy, because of its reliance on private initiative, which is the critical ingredient in Schumpeter's (1942, 81–86) gales of creative destruction.

The principle of socialization is the mirror image of the principle of subsidiarity. It calls for higher bodies to intervene and assist lower bodies or individuals if the latter are no longer able to perform functions on behalf of the common good. The term 'socialization' comes from the papal encyclical *Mater et Magistra* (1961) and describes modern society's increasing complexity and interdependence to the point where individuals are no longer able to accomplish what they used to do for themselves. Ever wider circles of cooperation are needed among people. This is a significant principle for economic ethics because it recognizes a legitimate and active role for government in socio-economic life. In fact, one could make this statement even stronger by noting that it is not merely a legitimate option for government to be involved, it is, in fact, an obligation to do so when the common good is at risk or poorly served. Furthermore, we can extend the obligation of this principle to include any moral agent (for example, individuals, firms, nongovernmental bodies and so on) with the necessary capacity and resources to step in whenever such assistance is needed on behalf of the common good. Acting as the Good Samaritan, in this case, is not a supererogatory act; it is an obligation. In the policy arena, this principle is especially important in refocusing the constant debate over the choice of small versus large government. The nub of the issue is not the size of the government per se, but the unattended requirements of the common good.

The principle of solidarity calls for an active and genuine solicitude for the welfare of others, because we see in them ourselves and a fellow child of God. Consequently, we are able to empathize with each other's hopes, dreams, sorrows and struggles. Justice is about giving people their due. This requires precise measurements, which are not always possible in practice. Solidarity's ethos of mutual respect, trust and care picks up where justice leaves off. While justice is measured in what it apportions, love is unmeasured in its self-giving. Consequently, this principle is the response of last resort for many unresolved, grey areas in economic ethics.

The preferential option for the poor goes all the way back to the prophetic writings of the Old Testament. Attending to the plight of the destitute and the helpless is not a gratuitous act of mercy; it is a requirement of justice. We are responsible for each other's well-being, as per the principle of solidarity. This duty takes on even greater weight and significance when it is the welfare of those living on the fringes of the community that is at risk. Moreover, assistance is provided in direct proportion to the severity of a neighbour's unmet needs. The more extreme the marginalization and poverty, the greater is the obligatory aid.

The primacy of labour principle is founded on the central importance of work in integral human development. Work is a necessary avenue for self-realization and perfection because through labour, humans secure their basic needs, exercise the duties of stewardship over their personal gifts and the earth, serve as 'co-creators' in the creative activity of God, share in the sufferings of Christ through the toil and hardships of work, contribute to the common good, participate in the social order and express themselves and their creativity. Given these manifold functions of human work, the community must ensure that people are provided with meaningful opportunities for employment that pays a living wage. Moreover, human labour cannot be treated as if it were just a factor of production, no different from inputs, such as raw materials and machinery. The dignity of human labour has priority over capital, profits or whatever other factors may be deemed to be important in business operations. After all, the economy is meant to be at the service of the human person, and not vice versa.

Finally, the principle of stewardship notes that we should not approach the goods of the earth or our natural talents with a proprietary attitude. Rather, we are invited to view these as a trust committed to us for our use as we seek integral human development for one another.

These major principles, and other minor ones that we lack the space here to cover, are all subsumed under the umbrella of the 'common good'. The common good in general terms is defined as the sum of those conditions that provide a propitious, nurturing environment for humanity to live truly as a family and for the attainment of integral human development for every person. It is impossible to list all these conditions exhaustively given the richness of human life. However, it is possible to ascertain some of the minimum conditions that must be satisfied if there is to be a truly common good. Two of these minimum conditions include due order in all of the vital relationships that make a community what it is (person to God, people to one another, community to the marginalized, community to its members and stewardship of the earth) and due proportion in the sharing of the finite goods of the earth. The preceding principles provide further specification and content to what due order and due proportion require, given the particular context of the social questions to be addressed.

Political economy

By its own account, Catholic social thought does not claim to be a 'third way', midway between laissez-faire capitalism and Marxism. It is content to limit itself merely to outlining the requirements of a human economy and the manner by which economic life can be used as a stepping stone, rather than an obstacle, to moral perfection and virtue. Catholic social thought is critical of laissez-faire capitalism for its indifference to deleterious market outcomes and processes that demean rather than ennoble the human person. It also vigorously disagrees with Marxism's call for the abolition of private property ownership, with its materialist anthropology, and with its pessimistic view of an intrinsic class conflict. Catholic social thought argues that the right to private ownership of property per se comes with human nature and is, consequently, not even within the power of the state to confer or to take away. Moreover, as we have seen in its bedrock principle of human dignity, Catholic social thought stresses the rich spiritual dimension and possibilities of the human person, even as it celebrates the goodness of all creation, including the material. Furthermore, class conflict is not the unavoidable lot of human beings because of their capacity for the reasoned and virtuous use of their freedom.

Catholic social thought is also distinctive in its characteristic balance in approaching political economy. Take the case of the clash between labour and management. Marxism resolves this tension by simply dismissing the claims of capitalists through its refusal to acknowledge the right to private ownership of property. On the other hand, laissez-faire capitalism simply calls for the protection of private property and private initiative, as workers themselves would eventually benefit from the trickle-down effects of a vibrant capitalist entrepreneurship, the proverbial 'tide that raises all boats'. Catholic social thought subscribes to neither of these but affirms the right to private ownership (and therefore the claims of capitalists), even while affirming the obligations attendant on such property ownership, as in the provision of gainful and humane conditions of employment for workers. Note the delicate balance struck in resolving the competing claims.

Another example of balance in Catholic social thought's approach to political economy is its understanding of human rights. Long before modern human rights language came into vogue, this tradition already championed the spirit of economic rights, as seen in the precepts of the Sacred Scripture. However, unlike modern liberalism, Catholic social thought does not treat human rights in isolation of the larger milieu of the common good's obligations that give rise to such rights to begin with. Humans enjoy inalienable rights not as ends in themselves but as means with which to discharge their duties. For example, Catholic social thought defends the right to private property ownership based on its instrumental value in satisfying basic human needs. Rights are inseparable from their concomitant obligations.

The cautious balance of Catholic social thought is also evident in its approach to many other facets of the economy: the promotion of the good of both the individual and the community; the advancement of both the person's material and spiritual development; the legitimate role of both the private sector and government as agents of development;

the pursuit of both efficiency and equity as macroeconomic goals; the call for both healthy competition and familial cooperation; the use of both market and non-market mechanisms for allocation; the affirmation of both a personal and a social dimension to economic activity and gifts.

This balance is also reflected in the conceptual tools examined in the preceding section. Catholic social thought's principles cannot be used piecemeal. They must be employed together as a single framework of analysis in order to prevent their abuse or extension beyond their intended purposes. These principles not only mutually reinforce one another; they also counterpoise one another's claims and prevent extremes. For example, the principle of subsidiarity cannot be used as justification for the complete abolition of welfare assistance under the pretext that it breeds dependency and prevents people from doing what they should be doing for themselves. This is a misuse of the principle, because of the principle of socialization (which calls for intervention when the common good is at risk), the principle of the universal destination of the goods of the earth (satisfaction of the basic needs of all), the principle of solidarity (mutual solicitude) and the preferential option for the poor. Many examples of abuses can be cited. However, it suffices here to note that these principles can be used only in conjunction with one another in addressing social problems.

Catholic social thought's characteristic balance allows for a much more comprehensive approach to resolving problems, but it also makes their resolution much more difficult and requires more effort and prudent judgement. This is unavoidable in light of its high expectations of the power of economic life to produce good. Using theological language, we can describe economic security as a twofold divine gift: (i) because of the satisfaction of our material needs, but more importantly (ii) because God provides for us through one another. We are invited to participate in the divine providence and governance of creation. This is economic life's most promising possibility. Using philosophy and the empirical sciences alone, we can describe economic security as flowing from personal effort and striving, mutual support and collaboration, and an appreciation for the earth as providing sufficient material provisions for all.

References and further reading

Barrera, Albino (2001), *Modern Catholic Social Documents and Political Economy*, Washington DC: Georgetown University Press.

National Conference of Catholic Bishops (1986), *Economic Justice for All*, Pastoral Letter on Catholic Social Teaching and the US Economy, Washington DC: National Conference of Catholic Bishops.

O'Brien, David and Thomas Shannon (1992), *Catholic Social Thought: The Documentary Heritage*, Maryknoll, NY: Orbis.

Phan, Peter (1984), *Social Thought*, Message of the Fathers of the Church series, Vol. 20, Wilimington, DE: Michael Glazier.

Pontifical Council for Justice and Peace (2004), *Compendium of the Social Doctrine of the Church*, Rome: Vatican.

Review of Social Economy (early decades), This is the academic journal of the Catholic Economic Association, which subsequently became the Association for Social Economics.

Robbins, Lionel (1932), *An Essay on the Nature and Significance of Economic Science*, London: Macmillan.

Ryan, John (1996), *Economic Justice: Selections from Distributive Justice and a Living Wage*, ed. Harlan Beckley, Louisville, KY: Westminster John Knox Press.

Schumpeter, Joseph (1942), *Capitalism, Socialism and Democracy*, New York: Harper.

Vatican Council II (1965), *Gaudium et spes*, Pastoral Constitution on the Church in the Modern World, Rome: Vatican.

See also the entries on: Dignity; Economic anthropology; Social economics; Religion.

8 Code of ethics for economists
Robin L. Bartlett

Introduction

The American Economic Association (AEA) and the International Economic Association, unlike most professional associations, do not have codes of ethics to guide their members in conducting their daily professional activities. Yet there is general agreement among most professionals that without codes of ethics, significant harm can be done both directly and indirectly. Moreover, in business settings, employees who lose the direct recognition and economic rewards they deserve may be less trusting of the system, less motivated to do their best, and less willing to work collaboratively, all of which are counterproductive. In academic settings, instructors may lose confidence in their abilities, students may quit doing their best and the acquisition or creation of economic knowledge may proceed at a much slower pace than otherwise would be the case.

While some professionals may abuse the power of their relative position, others may abuse their power as experts. Economists are presumed to have more knowledge and understanding of how individuals decide to allocate scarce resources and how the economy operates than the average individual on the street. Members of the press, colleagues in other disciplines, students and co-workers defer to economists' knowledge on relevant topics. A layperson may have difficulty evaluating the quality of statements made by economists. They assume (i) that economists possess the education, skills and information to make such statements; (ii) that economists are truthful about what they know; and (iii) that economists are honest about the limitations and purposes to which their knowledge can be applied. These assumptions may be seen as part of an unwritten ethical contract that serves as a basis for the individual to accept the validity of what an economist says. The public allows economists to go about their professional activities and asks for advice and guidance that they then use in their own work. Economists may say, 'Let the buyer beware.' However, given the accelerating growth of and access to knowledge and the rise of specialization within and across fields, this unwritten contract between economists and the general public is now more important than ever.

Economists recently began arguing for a code of ethics. Enders and Hoover (2004) recommend a code of ethics for economists because a sizeable majority of the editors they questioned attributed plagiarism and other unethical behaviour to poor training and mentoring. Margolis (2003) suggests that economists might find an ethical code helpful to sustain 'motivation and adherence to noble practices even in the most difficult or tedious moments of collecting data, cleaning data sets, running regressions, writing up results, or responding to reviewers' (p. 12). DeMartino (2005) concludes that a code of ethics for economists would at the very least make these professionals more aware of issues and encourage them to reflect critically on the possible ethical repercussions of their work.

A code of ethics would guide economists to make the right decisions at ethical junctures in the process of creating and debating economic knowledge and anticipating the direct and indirect effects of sharing it with the world. Once economic ideas become widely accepted and find their way into the public domain, a code of ethics would dictate that economists are responsible for the possible use, intended and unintended, of these ideas. Given the rapidly changing nature of the economics profession, the increased globalization of trade, and the seemingly growing political unrest in the world, the potential impact of reactions to economists' actions is multiplying exponentially. Doing the right thing at ethical junctures increases economic knowledge, safeguards the general public's trust and also keeps government legislators at bay.

The need for a code of ethics for economists
A number of factors contribute to the growing need for a code of ethics for economists:

- The composition of membership of the profession has changed dramatically since the establishment of the AEA in 1885.
- Interdisciplinary work has become more commonplace.
- The potential impact of policy recommendations is unknown.
- Funding agencies increasingly require applicants to provide assurances that they will do no harm.

Diversity of membership
The current membership of the AEA no longer resembles the elite group of predominantly Anglo-Saxon males who founded the association. Most of them were employed by top academic institutions in the United States, the United Kingdom and Western Europe, and they shared a common cultural heritage. The economics profession is now more diverse. Women have made significant progress, entering economics and moving up its academic ranks. People of colour – Africans, Asians and Latin Americans – are also making their way into the profession, though at a much slower pace. The proportion of international students enrolled in the top PhD-granting programmes of the United States has grown from 50 per cent in 1985 to 70 per cent in many programmes. The AEA has a rising international membership as well. Thus, the moral instincts, cultural values and prejudices of today's budding and boomer economists are likely very different and more varied than those of the association's founders.

A significant proportion of economists who belong to the AEA no longer work in academia. Many are practitioners in businesses, non-profit organizations and governments or work as private consultants. As reported incidents of professional misconduct and self-interested behaviour increased over the past decade, many of these businesses rushed to write codes of ethics to ward off potential government interventions. Most business and government organizations thus now have codes of ethics and procedures for enforcing them. These codes define acceptable behaviours, encourage high standards of practice, provide benchmarks for self-evaluation, outline professional responsibilities and establish a sense of professional identity.

In some sense, academic economists are in a different line of work than non-academic economists. Rather than competing in markets, academic economists observe and think about markets. However, the days of monastic scholars are long past, and the worlds of academic and non-academic economists have merged to accommodate the growing demand for advanced degrees and marketable skills. Institutions of higher education are no longer safe havens for open discussions, contemplation and debate. They are now big businesses satisfying consumer demands. As a result, academic economists face many of the same ethical dilemmas that non-academic economists confront in their day-to-day professional activities: how to interact with co-workers (colleagues), clients (students), employers (administrators), products (discipline) and society (society).

Interdisciplinary work
Given the multidimensional nature of many economic issues, academic and non-academic economists are increasingly collaborating with professionals whose backgrounds are in other disciplines and who use different methodologies. Recently, neuroscientists and economists collaborated to learn where economic decisions are made in the human brain. Experimental, behavioural, feminist, institutional and political economists are all crossing disciplinary boundaries and learning new theoretical and methodological approaches to help them better understand economic issues. Similarly, government economists collaborate with lawyers and accountants to write effective legislation. Forensic economists find themselves working with actuaries and medical professionals to determine the economic worth of individuals.

Public trust in economics and economists is nonetheless diminishing, and to some extent economists' trust in one another is declining as well. Working across disciplines adds complexity, and cooperation with colleagues from other disciplines reveals the importance of the subtle signals professionals send to one another, and how they might be misinterpreted in the absence of consensus on how to proceed. For example, protocols vary for listing authors contributing to a work. Authorship credit is less meaningful in some disciplinary cultures where cooperation is encouraged. What constitutes plagiarism may also vary by disciplinary culture (Redden 2007). Few economists may think about the ethical consequences of the listing of authors or what constitutes plagiarism, but a code of ethics may encourage them to do so.

Impact of policy recommendations
Despite the significant time, talent and effort that goes into economic analysis, economists cannot prove their theories or know for certain the possible impacts of policy actions based upon them (DeMartino 2005). As a result, economists have an obligation to consider how their work may affect targeted markets or populations. For example, a recent survey of 80 economists by Whaples (2006) found that all agreed that eliminating tariffs and other barriers on trade was the right thing to do. The average response rating (on a five-point scale) was 4.18, indicating very strong agreement amongst these economists about trade policy.

Average individuals on the street, however, would probably strongly disagree with the economists. Their casual empiricism and theorizing based on their own observations might suggest that eliminating trade barriers between countries benefits some workers and harms others; and of those harmed, marginalized workers are harmed the most. Average individuals might thus have a sense of fairness that calls into question recommendations strongly supported by economists.

Funding issues
Webster (2006) notes that until recently, codes of ethics 'reflected a professional concern for the client, especially concerns over the unintended consequences of scientific research,

managing risks and reducing or removing harm to individuals' (p. 39). Now, funding agencies, private and public, are increasingly requiring codes of ethics. Foundations and government agencies, particularly in Europe, want to be assured that their monies will do no harm, because ultimately they as funders will be held responsible. Members of boards of directors do not want to see their names in headlines or be prosecuted for their funds being used either for unethical purposes or in unethical ways.

Potential challenges
Codes of ethics are not without their critics (Matthews 1991) and critiques (Jamal and Bowie 1995). Critics contend that codes of ethics inhibit competition and the creation of new ideas that competition generates. Yet whether competition produces more and superior results is still unclear. The rush to tenure or promotion presents numerous ethical dilemmas that may damage the quality of economic work. For example, young colleagues may find it difficult to choose between finishing a paper with unverified data and taking the additional time for data confirmation. The ethical decision would be to take the time and be sure. The economic decision would be to weigh the potential costs and benefits of not taking the time, including the accompanying risks, against the costs and benefits of taking the time. Hoover (2006) uses game theory to suggest that plagiarism could be a successful strategy. In a recent study of journal editors, Enders and Hoover (2004) found that cutting corners and plagiarism are not unusual in economics. Moreover, they found the chance of exposure is small.

Critics also contend that codes of ethics generate cumbersome additional paperwork and procedures with their associated review boards, needlessly increasing the cost of professional work. Rules and regulatory boards are an anathema to economists. Some worry that adopting a code of ethics may lead to increased monitoring of the profession by outside groups. Identifying who is a member of the profession is another concern. Siegfried (2006) points out that the AEA does not even have a definition of an economist. The only requirement to be a member of the AEA is to pay dues.

Another potential problem is that codes of ethics can be racist and gendered. Those who are called upon to write codes of ethics bring with them their own cultural values and prejudices. What seemed the right thing to do 200 years ago might not seem the right thing to do today. For example, many thought slavery in the United States was the right thing based on the Bible. The 'latest' 'scientific' findings reinforced these beliefs and fortified slaves' position in society. The same can be said about women, homosexuals and other marginalized populations around the world.

Developing and implementing a code of ethics for economists
Economists can draw upon the work of other professions and professional organizations for guidance in developing a code of ethics. The Economic Developers Association of Canada (2008), the German Association of Political Consultants (2007) and the American Political Science Association (2004) all have and continue to revise their codes of professional ethics. In addition, comprehensive codes of ethics are provided specifically for scientists and social scientists by the Economic and Social Research Council (2006) and Israel and Hay (2006) in the United Kingdom, by CODEX (2007) operated by the Swedish Research Council in cooperation with the Centre for Bioethics at Uppsala University and Karolinska Institutet in Sweden, and by the Committee on Science,

Engineering, and Public Policy (1995) in the United States. The American Association of University Professors (AAUP 1987) maintains a code of professional ethics for academics to guide them in their processes of research, to set a standard of respect and integrity in their interactions with students, colleagues and administrators, and to establish an expectation of civic responsibility. All of economics' sister social sciences have endorsed the AAUP code.

These codes are built upon a mission statement and a set of general principles. Three general principles can be extracted from these codes: be truthful, be respectful of oneself and others, and leave the world at least the same or preferably an even better place. In short, do no harm and try to do some good.

It is important that the general principles of an ethics code and the code of ethics itself be consistent with an organization's mission statement. The current AEA mission statement, adopted in 1885, sets before the general public the goals the organization wants to accomplish:

● 'The encouragement of economic research, especially the historical and statistical study of the actual conditions of industrial life.
● The issue of publications on economic subjects.
● The encouragement of perfect freedom of economic discussion'. (AEA 2006)

The language is archaic, the scope is narrow and the tone unwelcoming. Not only does the wording need to be updated and clarified, but the topics considered also require expansion. The tone of the mission statement should invite the diversity of alternative explanations and methodologies used by today's economists.

The mission statement for a code of ethics for economists should reflect the fact that economists are studying a global market and non-market economy. Though the industrial component of aggregate economic activity has survived in various stages of economic development around the world, it is not the most important nor is it the only component of aggregate economic activity under investigation. The growing numbers of heterodox economists have pointed out glaring omissions in the topics considered by mainstream economists. Moreover heterodox economists are critical of the assumptions and performance of neoclassical economics. As yet, however, much of their work has been dismissed as politically motivated, as sociology or some other social science, and as insufficiently rigorous.

All explanations of economic activity must receive a fair hearing and be debated side by side. One way to accomplish this would be to have AEA journals publish work by mainstream economists alongside work of heterodox economists on the same topic. Otherwise, mainstream and heterodox economists will continue to read their own work in their own journals and there will be no real debate. If economists do not give different explanations and approaches equal consideration, economic knowledge cannot advance, and the splintered knowledge that currently exists may cause more harm than contested knowledge. Topics, and not alternative models and techniques, should dictate the dividing lines between journals. In addition to giving the range of work done by economists a legitimate hearing, the works of other scientists and social scientists, as well as interdisciplinary teams, should be welcomed.

Finally, academic freedom is the cornerstone of academic work and this should probably hold true for non-academic work as well. Economists must be able to say what they think, no matter how agreeable or disagreeable their statement may be to other economists or to their superiors. At the same time, avoiding conflicts of interest and maintaining the interest of the institutions as priorities would help professionals to respectfully agree to disagree.

A sample code of ethics for economists

The AAUP *Statement of Professional Ethics* (1987) provides a good starting point for developing a code of ethics for economists. Substituting the word 'economists' for the word 'professors' in the AAUP code creates an example of how such a code for econo-mists might look. The adapted AAUP code of ethics for academic economists is presented in Box 8.1. In reading the adapted code, academic economists will see that economists are indeed a subset of all professors. The code as presented could be expanded and modified as other professions have done to include non-academic economists.

BOX 8.1   A SAMPLE CODE OF ETHICS FOR ECONOMISTS

1. Economists, guided by a deep conviction of the worth and dignity of the advancement of knowledge, recognize the special responsibilities placed upon them. Their primary responsibility to their subject is to seek and to state the truth as they see it. To this end economists devote their energies to developing and improving their scholarly competence. They accept the obligation to exercise critical self-discipline and judgement in using, extending and transmitting knowledge. They practise intellectual honesty. Although economists may follow subsidiary interests, these interests must never seriously hamper or compromise their freedom of inquiry.

2. As teachers, economists encourage the free pursuit of learning in their students. They hold before them the best scholarly and ethical stand-ards of their discipline. Economists demonstrate respect for students as individuals and adhere to their proper roles as intellectual guides and counsellors. Economists make every reasonable effort to foster honest academic conduct and to ensure that their evaluations of students reflect each student's true merit. They respect the confidential nature of the relationship between professor and student. They avoid any exploitation, harassment or discriminatory treatment of students. They acknowledge significant academic or scholarly assistance from them. They protect their academic freedom.

3. As colleagues, economists have obligations that derive from common membership in the community of scholars. Economists do not discrimi-nate against or harass colleagues. They respect and defend the free inquiry of associates. In the exchange of criticism and ideas, economists show due respect for the opinions of others. Economists acknowledge academic debt and strive to be objective in their professional judgement of colleagues. Economists accept their share of faculty responsibilities for the governance of their institution.

4. As members of an academic institution, economists seek above all to be effective teachers and scholars. Although economists observe the stated regulations of the institution, provided the regulations do not contravene academic freedom, they maintain their right to criticize and seek revision. Economists give due regard to their paramount responsibilities within their institution in determining the amount and character of work done outside it. When considering the interruption or termination of their service, economists recognize the effect of their decision upon the programme of the institution and give due notice of their intentions.

5. As members of their community, economists have the rights and obligations of other citizens. Economists measure the urgency of these obligations in light of their responsibilities to their subject, to their students, to their profession and to their institution. When they speak or act as private persons, they avoid creating the impression of speaking or acting for their college or university. As citizens engaged in a profession that depends upon freedom for its health and integrity, economists have a particular obligation to promote conditions of free inquiry and to further public understanding of academic freedom.

Note: Adapted from the American Association of University Professors' Code of Conduct of Professional Conduct.

All of the other social sciences have accepted their responsibilities towards their discipline, colleagues, students, institutions and society. The AEA could, at the very least, endorse this code before moving forward with articulating a code for itself. Davis (2007) suggests that a small committee be constituted to read the numerous codes of ethics and to develop underlying principles that may, or may not, be unique to the economics profession. The committee that starts the process should be diverse, including economists from academic and non-academic organizations, younger and older economists, economists from teaching and research universities and those from different racial, cultural and religious backgrounds.

Some organizations implement their ethics code by constituting a review board to hear cases of impropriety. Education is another key aspect of implementation. The AEA and other such organizations could sponsor sessions on the code of ethics for economists at their annual meetings. Newer economists who attend these sessions would learn about the potential benefits of such a code. Senior economists attending the sessions would become familiar not only with the relevance of the code to their work, but also with their responsibility to mentor their junior colleagues.

Awards, such as the ten best ethical departmental training programmes, could signify the professional and disciplinary priority of adhering to a common code of ethics. Such awards and the recognition they bring encourage compliance by example. An example is the list of the 100 best corporate citizens (Raths 2006), which is anxiously awaited each year to see who is recognized for doing the right things. A good reputation is good for business. Doing the right thing builds trust among the public and lowers transaction costs.

Conclusion

The adoption of a code of ethics for economists by the profession could open up the profession to new ideas and methodologies. If a code of ethics increases discussion and debate, the discipline will certainly benefit, through an increased and broader understanding of the many facets of economic issues and the variety of ways to analyse them. Economists are not defined only by the techniques they use but also by the issues they address. An accepted code of ethics would take economics to new frontiers of economic understanding and public policy and additionally minimize collateral harm.

References

American Association of University Professors (1987), *Statement of Professional Ethics*, www.aaup.org, 13 November, 2006.

American Economic Association (1923), *Mission Statement*, www.vanderbilt.edu/AEA/gen_info.htm, 6 November, 2006.

American Political Science Association (2004), *A Guide to Professional Ethics in Political Science*, Washington DC: The American Political Science Association.

CODEX (2004), *Codes of Professional Ethics*, www.codex.vr.se/codex_eng/codex/oversikter/etik/yrkesetik. html, 16 November, 2007.

Committee on Science, Engineering, and Public Policy (1995), *On Being a Scientist: Responsible Conduct in Research*, Washington DC: National Academy Press, www.nap.edu/readingroom/books/obas/contents/ introduction.html, 22 May 2006.

Davis, Michael (2007), 'Eighteen rules for writing a code of professional ethics', *Science and Engineering Ethics*, **13** (2), 171–89.

DeMartino, George (2005), 'A professional ethics code for economists', *Challenge*, **48** (4), 88–104.

Economic and Social Research Council (2006), *Research Ethics Framework*, Swindon, UK: Economic and Social Research Council.

Economic Developers Association of Canada (2008), http://www.epac-apec.ca/cont-ang/ethical-stds.htm, 14 September 2008.

Enders, Walter and Gary A. Hoover (2004), 'Whose line is it? Plagiarism in economics', *Journal of Economic Literature*, **42** (2), 487–93.

German Association of Political Consultants (2007), *Code of Conduct*, www.degepol.de/eng/become_a_ member/basic_documents/code_of_conduct/, 16 November, 2007.

Hoover, Gary A. (2006), 'A game-theoretic model of plagiarism', *Atlantic Economic Journal*, **34** (4), 449–54.

Israel, Mark and Iain Hay (2006), *Research Ethics for Social Scientists*, London: Sage Publications.

Jamal, Karim and Norman E. Bowie (1995), 'Theoretical consideration for a meaningful code of professional ethics', *Journal of Business Ethics*, **14**, 703–14.

Margolis, Joshua D. (2003), 'Preparing for ethical challenges', *The Committee on the Status of Women in the Economics Profession Newsletter*, (Winter), 12–14.

Matthews, Robin C.O. (1991), 'The economics of professional ethics: should the professions be more like business?' *Economic Journal*, **101** (407), 737–50.

Raths, David (2006), '100 Best Corporate Citizens for 2006', *Business Ethics: The Magazine of Corporate Responsibility*, Spring, **20** (1), www.business-ethicz.com/whats_new/100best.html#Social_Data, 22 May, 2006.

Redden, Elizabeth (2007), 'Cheating across cultures', *Inside Higher Ed*, 24 May, file://Volumes/Media/Users/ bartlett/Desktop/Cheating%20and%20Culture.webarchive, 30 October, 2007.

Siegfried, John J. (2006), *American Economic Association*, Unpublished manuscript, Vanderbilt University, USA.

Webster, Andrew (2006), 'Social science ethics: the changing context for research', *Clinical Ethics*, **1**, 39–40.

Whaples, Robert (2006), 'Do economists agree on anything? Yes!' *The Economists' Voice*, **3** (9), Article 1, www. bepress.com/ev/vol3/iss9/art1, 15 January 2007.

See also the entry on: Teaching economics.

9 Consumerism
Peter N. Stearns

'Consumerism' refers to an attachment to purchasing goods not necessary for personal or familial survival, and a value system that makes this attachment an important part of personal and social evaluation. Elements of consumerism go back deeply into history. For example, some interest in personal adornment began early in the experience of our species. Nonetheless, the phenomenon is predominantly modern and dependent on modern economic and cultural systems. Ethical concerns about consumerism have also multiplied in modern times, operating in some tension with this widespread interest.

Aristocracies and their monied imitators in many premodern societies displayed consumerist impulses – like the Roman senators and their wives who eagerly dressed in silks from China. Often, greater consumerism was part of an aristocratic transition from a warrior past to a more sophisticated, often more urban style of life. Western crusaders in the Holy Land picked up a number of consumer interests from the more polished upper class of the urban Middle East, for example.

Consumerism, however, was limited in most premodern societies in several ways. First, and most obviously, the bulk of the population did not have a sufficient margin above subsistence to afford any elaborate display of consumerism. Many other customs limited consumerism as well. Religious commitments often commanded significant economic resources, such that churches and mosques displayed a society's extra wealth, pre-empting much personal consumerism. Other customs also constrained such tendencies. Urban artisans, for example, emphasized standard uniforms for public display, rather than more individualized consumerist attire. The notion of standardization and group conformity was intended to limit exhibitions of personal wealth. Some of the same constraints applied to peasant village life, where exceptional display drew critical comment. Many societies periodically enforced limits on consumerism by attacks on excess and through sumptuary laws – an early distinctive statement of ethical concern. Thus Renaissance consumerism was attacked in the pious crusades of reformers like Savanorola. The Chinese emperor periodically punished upper-class consumers, including women, who seemed unduly indulgent, even involving executions, as recently as the eighteenth century. Obviously, these traditions of restraint and religious alternatives could help feed ethical approaches to modern consumerism once it did develop.

Modern consumerism took shape first in Western Europe in the seventeenth and eighteenth centuries. The exploration of this pre-industrial consumerism is one of the real discoveries of social historians during the past twenty years, for previously it was assumed that consumerism flowed from industrialization rather than the other way around. Toward the middle of the seventeenth century, the Dutch began to display a passion for purchasing tulips, and when the flowers were unavailable, they bought pictures of tulips – one of the world's first clear consumer fads. More consistently, Europeans began to enjoy international goods like sugar, tea and coffee (regarding that last, explicitly copying a consumer enthusiasm that first developed in the Middle East).

By the early eighteenth century, European consumer interests had spread to home furnishings and tableware, including tea and coffee services to accommodate the new products more stylishly. Enthusiasm for fashionable clothing spread as well, as attested by a flourishing market for second-hand clothes and by rapidly rising rates of clothing thefts. Wills began to bequeath cherished consumer goods to particular heirs, suggesting that these goods were invested with emotional as well as financial value.

Along with these new behaviours and motives came a growing consumer apparatus, again, throughout much of urban Western Europe. Shops became more common, and they began to improve their displays. Advertising increased, taking advantage of weekly and then daily newspapers; aristocrats were induced to lend their names to products like razors and shaving strops. Shopkeepers introduced other innovations, such as 'loss leaders' – products offered at cut prices in hopes that consumers would enter a store and buy other items as well – and consumer credit. Much of what we would recognize today as the world of consumerism was available by 1800.

Historians have worked hard to identify causes for these major changes, and of course there are debates and disputes; but the attempt to explain the origins of modern consumerism is a vital part of figuring out the more basic meanings of the phenomenon.

Three factors, operating in combination, seem particularly important. Obviously, the new extent of consumerism depended on growing wealth for a substantial segment of the West European population, though decidedly not for all. But prosperity by itself did not guarantee consumerism. After all, wealth could have been used for more ornate churches or public buildings, or lower levels of work. Why the consumerist use?

Factor one involves the new range of goods available, initially from rising levels of international trade. Sugar, spices, tea, coffee and, soon, imported or import-imitated goods like china table settings clearly spurred new tastes. Tulips, brought in from the Ottoman Empire, had the same effect. Soon, Europeans themselves became adept at making desirable consumer goods for their own populations. Cotton cloth was an example, for its cheapness but also for its bright colours which created a widely accessible sense of style.

Factor two – and these factors operated in combination – involved new cultural impulses associated with growing secularism and especially the rise of early Romantic thinking. New interest in emotional expression and sensuality, shared by Romantic novelists and actual courting couples by the eighteenth century, had clear consumerist implications. The desire to adorn the body, particularly for women, and even to embellish the family through commercial indulgence, tapped these new cultural roots and in turn reinforced them.

Social issues define factor three. A more commercial economy and, by the eighteenth century, rising populations created tremendous difficulty for many individuals to achieve recognized status markets. Guilds weakened in many cases, as artisan masters became more exclusionary; many journeymen were blocked from advance and from some of the social satisfactions of guild solidarity. More obviously still, many peasants could no longer count on inheriting land from their parents, because of commercial pressures and population growth. They could survive and sometimes moderately prosper as domestic manufacturing workers earning money wages, but they could not achieve conventional village status. In this context, more individualistic badges of identity and achievement were essential, and consumerism increasingly did the trick. Domestic manufacturing workers were leading rural consumerists, often headed by young people who could also establish an identity separate from parental control by purchasing urban-style clothing and the like.

A version of this pattern applied to women. Women were increasingly barred from some key crafts from the seventeenth century onward, and in Protestant areas they also lost religious outlets. Opportunities to buy new goods and organize family consumerism (particularly around furnishings and meals) provided an alternative outlet. This might help to explain why, though women did not necessarily buy more than men, they displayed signs of greater emotional attachment to goods.

These causes illuminate the seriousness of consumerism. The phenomenon can seem, and be, quite frivolous, but it had deeper explanations and meanings. It could help people translate cultural innovation and compensate for social uncertainties. It could enable individuals to quietly defy older power structures and find some self-expression. These factors continue to sustain consumerism in more recent times, and beyond the West alone.

Not surprisingly, the nature and novelty of early modern consumerism provoked a great deal of criticism, some of it ethical in a broad sense. There was widespread comment on the social inappropriateness of consumer choices. From the mid-eighteenth century to the mid-nineteenth century, many commentators expressed shock that the lower classes were dressing just like their betters. This was distressing itself in hierarchical terms, but it also suggested that poor people were wasting scarce resources on frivolous goods, thus exposing their families and themselves to greater poverty. A similar criticism was directed toward women, with some men delighting in claiming that profligate consumerist women were wasting their husbands' hard-earned wages. Obviously this line of comment remains alive today, as in criticisms of African Americans who buy showy cars or athletic shoes, defying their betters and leading their families toward ruin or welfare. Such social commentary is unethical in its foundation, but it could also generate, or constrain, ethical commentary.

A second set of attacks focused on religious factors and the clash between materialist consumerism and proper spiritual goals. Many ministers fulminated against the false gods of the age. Health criteria were also invoked, sometimes linked to a sense of moral punishment for excess, with attacks on the impact of indulgence on the body, particularly of course in food and drink. Foreign-ness was another early theme. Several British intellectuals around 1750 attacked the growing use of 'French' umbrellas and the associated new notions of comfort, arguing that they undermined British hardiness. The French Revolution brought radical praise for simplicity of style – the *sans-culottes* – against aristocratic pretence and (often female) frivolity. All of these channels were amplified as consumerism expanded.

Consumerism wavered in the early decades of the actual Industrial Revolution. Many workers were too poor to indulge, or eager to use any margin to buy time away from work, in days off, rather than to pursue consumerist goals. Still, attacks on workers' spending habits continued, with arguments that these, rather than low wages, explained poverty. Religious objections multiplied as consumerism spread to the United States, buoyed by imports of European clothing styles and restaurants and new interest in amenities like watches. Religious revivals in the 1830s and 1840s frequently attacked modern materialism. Several popular lecturers combined criticisms of consumerism with charges of sexual immorality, urging a return to simple habits and pure foods as an antidote to this combined degeneracy. Large audiences attended the purity lectures, and new foods like Graham crackers (named after Sylvester Graham, one of the movement's leaders) and Kellogg cereals sought to further the simplicity goals.

Advancing industrialization from the 1850s onward extended consumerism in several ways. More people, throughout the Western world, began to depend extensively on consumer success. The rise of department stores both reflected and encouraged greater consumerism, with eye-catching displays and a deliberate profusion and variety of goods. Shopping itself became a rising pastime. Advertisements became more emotional and visual. A new disease, 'kleptomania', reflected the extreme of the phenomenon. Revealingly, most mainstream religions began to make their peace with consumerism, arguing that stylish dressing, for example, was a sign of God's favour and an enjoyment of His blessings. This connection even visited Utah Mormons by the later nineteenth century, as they started to indulge in catalogue purchases from urban centres further east.

Modern consumerism also spread geographically. Department stores opened in Russia by the 1850s, catering of course to the upper classes. By 1900 similar stores were launched in places like Tokyo and Shanghai, initially in foreign sections of town but gradually attracting local interest too.

Predictably, attacks on consumerism also mounted, with arguments shifting somewhat but with political consequences ensuing in certain cases as well. Several major lines of commentary developed, virtually wherever consumerism took hold or intensified. Older themes persisted, particularly in heightened criticism of the frivolity and vulnerability of women – the subject of a major novel by Emile Zola (2002). The fact that most kleptomaniacs were women provided further grist for the mill, though American commentators were a bit less misogynist than their European counterparts. Thus when Thorsten Veblen (1979), in his *Theory of the Leisure Class*, offered a powerful critique of the false goals of consumers, he focused on artificiality with ample concern for men and women alike.

Growing attacks centred on department store owners and, increasingly, advertisers, for so blatantly pandering to unnecessary impulses and making people believe that such impulses were true needs. The idea that consumers were being lured by the greedy forces of commercial capitalism gained new strength, and when taken to the extreme fanned fires of anti-Semitism on the grounds that Jews were disproportionately involved in commerce.

The political left joined the chorus as well. Socialists participated in attacks on voracious department store magnates. They were also often disappointed that their party members and trade unionists so frequently preferred consumer fare over opportunities to engage in political discussions or to read serious books at the local party centre.

Anti-consumerist politics crescendoed after World War I, again on both the right and the left. A basic plank of fascism and Nazism involved attacks on consumerism as distracting from traditional national loyalties, including customary dress, displaced by skimpy fashions, and as vaunting individualism over devotion to state and leader. Fascist organizations pushed rhetoric further in principle than in practice, but there were efforts to organize mass leisure in terms of group bonding and simple pleasures rather than consumerist outlets.

Communists, victorious in Russia, faced an obvious dilemma: should they strive to beat consumerism at its own game, offering the working class greater pleasures than capitalism could muster, or should they seek an alternative set of goals? As they organized state-run department stores, communist leaders spoke of a purer socialist consumerism, but in fact, partly because of other production priorities, the regime managed only a fairly shoddy array of consumer choices, with much more attention going to group leisure and party ceremonies. Communist parties in Western Europe ultimately made greater accommodations for consumerism, organizing fashion shows and the like as part of party activities.

Growing ability to manipulate consumer interests led to more explicitly ethical evaluation as well. In the United States, the Progressive movement of the late nineteenth and early twentieth centuries included considerable attention to false advertising, to exploitative credit practices and to fraudulent or dangerous product quality. Consumer quality advocates did not argue that consumerism was bad, but that its exploitation by capitalists often led to deficient standards and price gouging. In some areas, cooperative movements sought to offer more reliable and reasonably priced goods. Consumer watchdog groups also emerged, publicizing their tests of product claims. In areas such as food quality, actual legislation and protection served to regulate product quality, where the marketplace alone could not be trusted.

Discussions about consumerism and children surged in the early twentieth century and continue today. Many experts questioned the desirability of introducing children to consumerism too early. Consumer products, including media fare, like commercial radio shows and comic books in the United States, seemed undesirable. Yet efforts to regulate enjoyed only fitful success. Typically, alternative consumer products, designed to improve educational capacity or physical health, provided the most popular response.

As consumerism spread beyond the West, other concerns arose, though in some cases they echoed Western criticism. Where consumer products emanated from imperialist countries, they might be doubly tainted. Successful product boycotts were organized as part of nationalist campaigns in India and elsewhere. Japanese leaders, uneasy about the individualistic components of consumerism and also eager to promote savings and investment, undertook a deliberate anti-consumerist campaign in the 1920s and 1930s. 'Moral suasion groups' provided instructions on savings, particularly to the lower classes, while claiming to protect communities against the 'winds of extravagance and habits of luxury'. Under Mao, Chinese communism vigorously opposed consumerism, urging uniform dress styles such as the Mao jacket. Intellectuals in many countries bemoaned the impact of consumer tastes on traditional values and styles. For example, the Nigerian novelist Chinua Achebe's *No Longer at Ease* (1961) explored how consumer tastes prevented a young urbanite from following convention on the occasion of his mother's death, while commentators from La Paz in Mexico, to Yukio Mishima in Japan, worried about loss of cultural identity amid a sea of standardized consumer goods.

Consumerism advanced further, and spread more widely across the globe, in the decades after World War II. The global economy itself depended increasingly on the production and distribution of consumer goods, with durable goods like automobiles but also a growing array of media products leading the list. The spread of malls as well as department stores symbolized the extension of the phenomenon. While advertising and international marketing played a key role, motives remained complex. Young people in Shanghai, interviewed at a McDonald's restaurant, indicated that they did not particularly like the food but enjoyed the sense of being connected to the wider world and being seen in such a contemporary place; the chance to individuate themselves from their parents' tastes and control played a role as well.

Polls suggested that while people in consumer societies were no happier than others over time, the advent of consumerism created a measurable increase in perceived satisfaction. In many cases also, no clear alternatives to consumerism seemed available. Many Chinese and Russians, after the effective collapse of communist ideology, saw in material acquisitions the only goals available. In the United States the triumph of consumerism, and its centrality in politics and economy, were symbolized by official reactions to the 11 September terrorist attacks, which combined promptings to fear with pleas to continue shopping.

Commentary on consumerism changed in the contemporary era, partly because in many places its advance seemed hard to challenge, and partly because some previous critiques had merged with fascist or communist reactions that had been thoroughly discredited. Attacks from the left had also been muted by working-class gains in consumerism in many societies. The rise of religious fundamentalism, though aimed at targets broader than mere consumerism, represented the most systematic reactions to consumer styles and commitments in the contemporary world; implicit anti-consumerism played a significant role, for example, in the Iranian revolution of 1979, though signs of continued consumer interests persist in Iranian society.

Movements to assure more consistent quality in consumer goods and to guard against misleading advertising and sales techniques constituted an ongoing ethical and political check on the most rampant exploitation of consumer interests. Commentary on impacts on children continued, directed for example against the violence of many media products aimed at the young. By the early twenty-first century, another round of health concerns – focused on the global epidemic of childhood obesity – intermixed some ethical injunctions as well.

Spiralling consumerism generated new watchdog movements, designed to attack not only excessive manipulation through misleading advertisement, but also products that were unsafe. Leaders like Ralph Nader, concerned about consumer excess in general, focused attention on automobiles and other expensive, potentially dangerous items whose manufacturers cut corners in the interest of expanding profit margins. Expansion of essentially consumer practices into other areas, such as 'selling' political candidates, also raised ethical concern.

Nowadays, the most sweeping ethical criticism of contemporary consumerism, outside of the religious domain, has two principal foci. The first is the environmental movement, which though not new, manifested growing strength from the 1960s onward. This movement built on themes emerging first in student protest and directed toward heedless consumerism and on growing evidence of environmental damage from consumer-related industries and products. Pressure on individuals to restrain certain types of consumerism and on consumer outlets in the interest of limiting further environmental deterioration had mixed success, but the emergence of 'green' parties and related organizations offered regular commentary on consumerism from the standpoint of environmental ethics.

The second new prong involved growing awareness of labour exploitation, particularly in many so-called 'Third World' economies, in the manufacture of consumer products.

Several international non-governmental organizations emerged to publicize abuses, and a number of successful protests targeted multinational corporations such as Nike sporting goods. As with environmentalism, results remained varied and inconsistent.

Both environmental and labour concerns, and some interest in protecting traditional cultures, fed an anti-consumerist element in protests against globalization, beginning with the demonstrations in Seattle in 1999.

Thus, over its roughly three centuries of existence, and still today, modern consumerism has provoked varied ethical and moral commentary. Arguments have shifted somewhat over time, particularly as certain strands seemed outdated (the social hierarchy component, for example, or unduly blatant misogyny) or led to clearly unacceptable political consequences (fascism and to a certain degree communism). But new concerns, most recently environmentalism, maintain or even enhance ethical anxieties regarding consumerism. Though many individuals have been visibly constrained, the phenomenon has hardly yielded ground, neither in intensity nor in its growing geographical scope. In some instances, as in the commercial exploitation of 1960s youth culture, purveyors of consumerism have been able to convert erstwhile counter-cultures into new opportunities for sales. The tension between this dominant cultural expression and recurrent ethical critiques and constraints forms a pervasive aspect of contemporary life throughout the urban world. Ethical commentary, in fact, seems built into consumerism itself, through efforts to moderate excess and fraud, and, recurrently, to question the moral validity of the phenomenon.

References and further reading

Achebe, Chinua (1961), *No Longer at Ease*, London: Fawcett Premier.
Annals of the American Academy of Political and Social Science (2007), special issue, 611 (May).
Bevir, Mark and Frank Trentmann (eds) (2007), *Governance, Consumers and Citizens: Agency and Resistance in Contemporary Politics*, Basingstoke: Palgrave Macmillan.
Breckenridge, Carol (ed.) (1993), *Consuming Modernity: Public Culture in a South Asian World*, Minneapolis, MN: University of Minnesota Press.
Brewer, John and Roy Porter (eds) (1993), *Consumption and the World of Goods*, London: Routledge.
Cross, Gary (2000), *An All-Consuming Century: Why Commercialism Won in Modern America*, New York: Columbia University Press.
Douglas, Mary and Baron Isherwood (1996), *The World of Goods: Toward an Anthropology of Consumption*, London: Routledge.
Horowitz, David (1993), *The Morality of Spending: Attitudes Toward the Consumer Society in America*, Chicago, IL: I.R. Dee.
Stearns, Peter N. (2006), *Consumerism in World History: The Global Transformation of Desire*, London: Routledge.
Veblen, Thorsten (1979), *The Theory of the Leisure Class*, New York: Penguin.
Watson, James (ed.) (1998), *Golden Arches East: McDonald's in East Asia*, Palo Alto, CA: Stanford University Press.
Williams, Rosalind (1982), *Dream Worlds: Mass Consumption in Late Nineteenth Century France*, Berkeley, CA: University of California Press.
Zola, Emilé (2002), *Au Bonheur des Dames*, London: Penguin.

See also the entries on: Aristotle; Identity; Needs and agency; Scarcity.

10   Corporate social responsibility
Rhys Jenkins

What is corporate social responsibility?
Corporate social responsibility (CSR) is defined in a variety of ways. Meanings differ across authors and organizations and have evolved over time. One of the leading corporate organizations advocating CSR, the World Business Council for Sustainable Development (WBCSD 2002), has defined it as 'the commitment of business to contribute to sustainable economic development, working with employees, their families, the local community and society at large to improve their quality of life' (quoted in Blowfield and Frynas 2005, p. 501).

As this definition illustrates, CSR is often linked to the concept of sustainable development, which includes the social and environmental as well as the economic impacts of business. It also emphasizes the role of a broader range of stakeholders rather than seeing firms as accountable solely to their shareholders. Many definitions explicitly mention the voluntary nature of CSR and emphasize that it involves going beyond compliance with legal obligations.

The philanthropic activities of companies are also often viewed as part of CSR, although this is more debatable. What is novel about CSR in recent years is that it affects (or claims to affect) companies' core activities. In other words it is 'pre-profit' in the sense that it has the potential to affect the profits that companies make (positively or negatively) as opposed to 'post-profit', that is, affecting the distribution of profit after it has been earned. Charitable donations by companies fall into the latter category and should be distinguished from changes in the ways that firms do business as a result of taking up CSR.

The rise of CSR
At its most general level, CSR is about the relationship between business and society. Its antecedents go back to the early days of the Industrial Revolution in Britain and Robert Owen's textile mills in New Lanark, and its evolution can be traced through the 'New Model' employers of the 1850s and 1860s in England and the 'Industrial Betterment' movement in the United States during the last quarter of the nineteenth century.

The 1960s and 1970s
The recent history of CSR has been marked by the growing significance of transnational corporations in the second half of the twentieth century. This period saw two major waves of CSR activity. The first came in the late 1960s and 1970s, partly in response to corporate scandals involving corruption and political interference by transnational corporations in the affairs of foreign countries. The emblematic case was the US transnational International Telephone and Telegraph Company's attempts to destabilize the democratically-elected government of socialist President Salvador Allende in Chile in the early 1970s.[1]

Another issue that attracted attention in the 1970s was investment by transnational corporations in Apartheid South Africa. The international campaign to boycott South Africa eventually pressured these companies to withdraw. In this context, many companies adopted the Sullivan principles, which were drawn up to assure investors and the public that businesses were acting responsibly in South Africa and were not complicit in the oppression of the black majority. For many companies this was their first explicit adoption of ethical principles for their business activities.

The late 1960s also saw health professionals in developing countries raising concerns about the impacts of the increasing use of breast-milk substitutes on infant health and nutrition. This gave rise to a strong nongovernmental organization-led campaign in the 1970s against the marketing practices of Nestlé and other manufacturers. In response to public criticism, the International Council of Infant Food Industries (ICIFI) adopted the Code of Ethics and Professional Standards for Advertising, Product Information and Advisory Services for Breast-Milk Substitutes in 1975 (Richter 2001, Ch. 3).

1990s to the present

The second wave of CSR activity dates from the 1990s, when corporations started to come under criticism for their global environmental and labour practices. The emergence of global 'value chains' in which buyers in the North control a web of suppliers in the South led to calls for corporations to take responsibility not only for aspects such as quality and delivery dates, but also for working conditions and environmental impacts throughout the chain. At the same time, the increased significance of brands and corporate reputation rendered leading companies particularly vulnerable to bad publicity. The same global communications developments which enabled corporations to control production activities on an ever-widening scale also facilitated the international transmission of information about working conditions at overseas suppliers, contributing to increased public awareness and facilitating campaigning activities.

Once again, companies responded to bad publicity surrounding their activities by espousing CSR. Many firms sourcing consumer goods from developing countries adopted supplier codes of conduct following scandals about the labour practices of their subcontractors.

Environmental issues also became a matter of increasing public concern, as attention focused on the Earth Summit held in Rio in 1992. In the run-up to the summit, the corporate sector resisted suggestions that any form of environmental regulation should be applied to transnational corporations, instead promoting self-regulation through voluntary codes and charters. During the 1990s, major transnational corporations in the oil and other extractive industries, such as Shell, BP and Rio Tinto, came to be seen as leaders in terms of the environmental dimensions of CSR. They also incorporated the protection of human rights into their business principles, following the negative publicity about Shell's activities in the Niger Delta and BP's operations in Colombia in the mid-1990s.

Trends

The scope of CSR has broadened over time. In the nineteenth century the main emphasis was on 'good works' and the treatment of the firm's own workers in terms of issues such as working conditions and housing. In the 1960s and 1970s the emphasis extended to include relations with consumers and governments. In the former case the emphasis was on product safety and consumer information and education leading to the development of some specific codes of conduct on marketing practices. In terms of relations with governments, the main emphasis was on corruption, in the wake of the bribery scandals revealed by the US Securities and Exchange Commission in the mid-1970s.

In the 1990s, sustainable development, with its emphasis on environmental and social issues, came to the fore as a central plank of CSR. Labour rights emerged as a key issue too, with the scope of application extended to suppliers as well as those who were directly employed by the corporation. In the late 1990s, protection of human rights was added to the CSR agenda. Thus, not only has the CSR agenda broadened in terms of the issues addressed, it has also expanded in terms of the range of stakeholders covered.

The growth of CSR manifests in several ways. Many companies have adopted CSR statements which set out their business principles. An increasing number of companies report on their social and environmental performance as well as their economic performance. It has even become fashionable to describe this as the 'triple bottom line'. More than 2000 companies now produce CSR reports (Vogel 2005, p. 6). There has also been a rise in codes of conduct covering such areas as environmental performance and labour rights (Jenkins 2001). These include corporate codes adopted by individual companies, those developed by business associations and multi-stakeholder codes drawn up in association with nongovernmental organizations or trade unions. In 2000, the United Nations launched its Global Compact with nine principles of corporate responsibility (subsequently expanded to ten). By 2006, the compact had been signed by more than 2500 corporations in 90 countries.

Perspectives on CSR

CSR is a controversial subject with passionate advocates and trenchant critics at both ends of the political spectrum. The different perspectives can be categorized according to their view of the impact of CSR on the profitability of the individual businesses that adopt it and on society in general. Table 10.1 classifies the perspectives, which are elaborated below.

The 'business case' for CSR

CSR advocates explicitly conceive the relationship between corporate profitability and social responsibility in 'win-win' terms. Here, the conventional CSR wisdom is that companies that do good, do well, as exemplified in numerous business texts, surveys of corporate executives and company statements (Vogel 2005, pp. 19–24).

Table 10.1   Contrasting perspectives on CSR

		Impact on business	
		Raises profit	Reduces profit
Impact on society	Good	Business case	Robin Hood
	Bad	Engineering consent	Libertarian

Source: Own elaboration based on *The Economist, The Good Company* supplement, 22 January 2005, p. 8.

A number of arguments have been put forward to support the view that social responsibility contributes to profitability and shareholder value. First, it is said to enable companies to attract, motivate and retain staff, which helps to increase productivity. Second, it is said to have positive effects on the marketing side, in terms of developing markets, building brand reputation and encouraging consumer loyalty. Third, it purportedly helps reduce risk to future profits and share price from environmental disasters and clean-up costs or from negative publicity arising from mistreatment of workers or violation of human rights. It may also help attract investment from the emerging 'ethical' and 'green' funds which screen companies in terms of their environmental and social policies and performance. Finally, it is often argued, particularly in relation to environmental issues, that greater corporate responsibility promotes innovation and competitiveness (Porter and van der Linde 1996).

The 'Robin Hood' view

The second view sees CSR in terms of a shift of resources from shareholders to other stakeholders. According to Arthur Laffer, the 'father' of supply-side economics, 'what CSR means, really, is redistribution of wealth' (Gupte 2005). In contrast to the claims made in support of the 'business case', the Robin Hood view does not share the belief that the benefits of CSR outweigh the costs at the corporate level.

In fact, a multitude of costs must be taken into account. Adopting CSR requires firms to devote additional resources, which could be used more profitably elsewhere, to stakeholder consultation, monitoring and auditing. There are further costs when CSR is implemented if it requires, for example, pollution abatement equipment to be installed in order to reduce environmental damage or employees to be paid higher wages. In contrast to the 'business case' approach, this view sees no guarantee that additional environmental outlays will be compensated by 'innovation offsets' or that increased wages will bring about higher productivity.

In addition to these direct costs, CSR also distracts managers from their primary role, which is to maximize shareholder value. The multidimensional nature of CSR makes it difficult for managers to set clear objectives, and it is impossible to maximize along all of the dimensions of the triple bottom line.

In the case of most modern corporations, where there is separation of ownership and control between shareholders and managers, the idea of CSR is also viewed as posing an ethical challenge. Since profits are owned by the shareholders, not the managers, corporate philanthropy, and by extension CSR measures that reduce profits in order to achieve some social benefit, could be construed as managers in effect robbing owners by indulging their charitable instincts at the expense of shareholders (*The Economist* 2005).

'Libertarian' views

Many critics on the right go even further, arguing that CSR is bad both for profits and for society as a whole. They cite the sometimes perverse effects of well-intentioned actions taken in the name of CSR. A much-heard example is the case of Bangladesh, where thousands of children lost their jobs in garment export factories in 1993 and 1994 as a result of the concerns about child labour; these children ended up working in even more exploitative conditions as a result (Vogel 2005, p. 98).

Advocates of the libertarian position take a broader view than the effects of individual corporate actions, focusing on the more generally negative impacts of CSR. The starting point of this analysis is the view attributed to Adam Smith: 'By pursuing his own interest he [the individual] frequently promotes that of the society more effectively than when he really intends to promote it.' In this vein, it is said to be the 'invisible hand' that ensures the welfare of society. CSR, by interfering with market forces, leads to misallocation (as well as misappropriation) of resources and as a result reduces the overall level of social welfare.

There are many ways in which CSR is said to lead to resource misallocation (Henderson 2001, Ch. 6). It threatens competition (which is central for efficient resource allocation) by raising barriers to entry and disadvantaging small and medium-sized firms. Large, incumbent firms within an industry are better able to adopt CSR, but then if threatened by 'less responsible' firms are quick to call for a 'level playing field'. This is particularly evident at the international level, where attempts to impose higher labour or environmental standards in developing countries are seen in those countries as disguised protectionism on the part of the North. CSR is also perceived as the thin end of the wedge leading to increased state regulation and the erosion of economic freedom.

'Engineering consent'[2]

At the opposite end of the critical spectrum are those who regard CSR as primarily a public relations exercise by companies to defuse criticism, with no significant social benefits and which may indeed have negative effects. This view sees large transnational corporations, which are often leaders in adopting CSR, as a cause of many of the social and environmental ills which CSR is meant to address. According to Christian Aid (2004, p. 2), 'CSR is a completely inadequate response to the sometimes devastating impact that multinational companies can have in an ever-more globalised world – and it is actually used to mask that impact.' Environmental critics have termed CSR 'greenwash'.

As well as scepticism about the motives that lie behind its adoption, this points to a weakness of CSR, that is, its being perceived as '95 per cent rhetoric and 5 per cent action' (see Vogel 2005, p. 12). The measures adopted in the name of CSR, such as voluntary codes of conduct, rarely have teeth in terms of monitoring performance or sanctioning violations (Jenkins 2002).

The negative effects of CSR highlighted by these critics arise from the way in which they mislead the public and suggest that corporations can regulate themselves, obviating the need for state regulation. Such fears are reinforced by statements from business organizations and consultants promoting CSR on precisely these grounds. Similarly, trade unions worry that CSR and codes of conduct covering labour rights are becoming a substitute for workers' self-organization and labour legislation (Justice 2002).

Beyond the four views

Although it is useful to classify the different views of CSR in this way, it can also be misleading if the categories are interpreted as applying universally. An alternative approach rejects such universality and argues instead for a more contingent position. Thus, Vogel (2005, p. 3) discussing the 'business case' approach to CSR claims 'it makes sense for some firms in some areas under some circumstances'. Whether one looks at CSR in terms of its impact on business or on society as a whole, outcomes are seen as being highly context-dependent. This challenges both the uncritical advocacy of CSR in the 'business case' and the rejection of CSR as either creeping socialism or a capitalist con trick.

Evidence of the impacts of CSR

Impact on corporate performance
A key question concerning CSR is whether it improves or detracts from a company's financial performance. This has become particularly central because of the recent emphasis in much of the CSR literature on the 'business case', in other words, on establishing that it pays to be 'green' or 'ethical'. This has given rise to a vast literature examining the empirical relationship between financial performance and various measures of environmental or social responsibility. The results have been mixed, however, with some studies showing a positive relationship and others a negative one, while some fail to find any statistically significant relationship. Whilst one group of reviewers have concluded that the bulk of the evidence confirms the existence of a positive relationship (Orlitzky et al. 2003), others remain sceptical (Margolis and Walsh 2003; Vogel 2005, Ch. 2). The lack of consensus has generated a continuing stream of papers attempting to refine earlier analyses and present new data.

Sceptics point to a number of difficulties in establishing the causal relationship between CSR and financial performance, which is at the heart of the 'business case'. They question the direction of causality, pointing out that more profitable firms may increase their environmental expenditures or social action because they have the profits to do so. Correlations may also reflect the omission of variables that affect both financial performance and social responsibility, since many studies fail to include control variables. The studies also use a variety of different measures both of financial performance and CSR, precluding cross-study comparisons. Finally, the failure to find a systematic relationship may simply reflect the fact that CSR is not sufficiently costly to affect profitability.

Even if these problems were resolved and a clear relationship were established between financial performance and CSR, there is still the question of how this should be interpreted. Advocates of the business case claim that it indicates that CSR makes business sense for all companies. However, it could also mean that there is a market niche to be filled by firms which behave responsibly, but not that all firms would be more profitable if they behaved more responsibly.

The social and environmental impacts of CSR
In contrast to the vast literature on the impact of CSR on business performance, very little systematic attention has been devoted to its impact on society (or the environment). What there is consists mainly of case studies which provide a very partial evaluation of the overall impact of CSR. The lack of systematic research on the social and environmental impacts of CSR reflects the inherent difficulties of analysing such impacts. The difficulties in measuring CSR and selecting appropriate indicators for financial performance which are faced in studies of the impact of CSR on business are relatively minor compared to the problems of evaluating its impact on the wider society. The multidimensional nature of the social impacts means that they cannot be reduced to a single measure even if the focus is confined to one area, such as the impact on labour or the environment.

Furthermore, it is necessary to evaluate indirect as well as direct effects of CSR when considering the impacts on society as a whole. Take for example the case of child labour. A firm may ban its suppliers from employing children, the direct effect being a reduction in child labour. But without complementary measures, the step could simply lead to increased employment of children elsewhere in the economy. Thus, what appears to be a positive result in terms of direct effects has minimal (and possibly even negative) effects for society as a whole.

A detailed review of the case study literature would be out of place here. Suffice to say the results of these studies are varied, and though this partly reflects the prejudices of the authors, it also reflects the diversity of outcomes of CSR initiatives in different contexts. Nevertheless, several tentative generalizations can be suggested.

First, the extent to which CSR has led to positive outcomes tends to vary according to the issue being addressed. For example, in the case of labour, impact seems to have been greater in terms of preventing child labour and upholding health and safety standards than on wages, overtime restrictions and the right to form trade unions (Vogel 2005, p. 107). This reflects the scope of public concern in the North about these issues and the existence of well-organized nongovernmental organizations putting pressure on companies. It also demonstrates the extent to which specific issues pose a threat to a firm's basic operations and its profitability. Children can be replaced in factories at relatively low cost. Yet restrictions on overtime might challenge the whole model of flexible response to changes in consumer demand on which export production in some sectors is based.[3]

The extent and impact of CSR also differ across industries and firms. Industries and companies that export to the North are most subject to public pressure. Thus, CSR has been taken up in industries which produce consumer goods such as clothing and footwear. The visibility of a company and the degree to which it relies on branding and reputation also affect the extent to which profits may be threatened by revelations of irresponsible behaviour and negative social or environmental impacts (Klein 2000). Greater intensity of competition in an industry may have negative effects because firms struggling for survival do not usually have the resources to devote to CSR. That means it is often firms in oligopolistic sectors which are best placed to pursue such policies. Where firms do have a margin of discretion, the personal commitment of top management can also play a role in influencing social and environmental outcomes.

The impact of CSR can also differ between countries. It is more likely to have a positive impact on welfare in countries with a strong civil society, high levels of transparency and a well established rule of law. In the absence of these, CSR is likely to remain window-dressing. For example, voluntary standards such as those of the Forest Stewardship Council (FSC) have been more effective in improving forestry practices in North America and Europe than in curbing tropical forest destruction in South-East Asia, Latin America and sub-Saharan Africa (Vogel 2005, pp. 117–21).

Finally it is important to bear in mind that CSR may have losers as well as winners; and thus it may benefit only *some* people. The shift to concentrate production in factories in the football-stitching industry in Sialkot, Pakistan, so as to better monitor child labour, led many women homeworkers to lose out (Brill 2002). Similarly, in the Kenyan horticulture industry, smallholders have tended to be displaced by large commercial growers and the exporters' own farms as suppliers for the major export corporations (Dolan and Humphrey 2000).

Notes

1. See Sigmund (1980, p. 147–9) for a brief account and references to the various US Senate hearings on this case.
2. This term is taken from Richter (2001).
3. See Oxfam (2004, Ch. 2) for evidence of the way in which the tight turn-around times required in global value chains lead to pressure to work overtime to meet shipping deadlines.

References

Blowfield, Michael and Jedrzej G. Frynas (2005), 'Setting new agendas: critical perspectives on corporate social responsibility in the developing world', *International Affairs*, **81** (3), 499–513.

Brill, Lucy (2002), 'Can codes of conduct help home-based workers?' in Rhys Jenkins, Ruth Pearson and Gill Seyfang (eds), *Corporate Responsibility and Labour Rights: Codes of Conduct in a Global Economy*, London: Earthscan, pp. 113–123.

Christian Aid (2004), *Behind the Mask: The Real Face of Corporate Social Responsibility*, London: Christian Aid.

Dolan, Catherine and John Humphrey (2000), 'Governance and trade in fresh vegetables: the impact of UK supermarkets on the African horticulture industry', *Journal of Development Studies*, **37** (2), 147–76.

The Economist (2005), 'The good company: a survey of corporate social responsibility', 22 January.

Gupte, Pranay (2005), 'Arthur Laffer: corporate social responsibility detrimental to stockholders', *New York Sun*, 19 January.

Henderson, David (2001), *Misguided Virtue: False Notions of Corporate Social Responsibility*, London: Institute of Economic Affairs.

Jenkins, Rhys (2001), 'Corporate codes of conduct: self-regulation in a global economy', Technology, Business and Society Paper No. 2, Geneva: United Nations Research Institute for Social Development.

Jenkins, Rhys (2002), 'The political economy of codes of conduct', in Rhys Jenkins, Ruth Pearson and Gill Seyfang (eds), *Corporate Responsibility and Labour Rights: Codes of Conduct in a Global Economy*, London: Earthscan, pp. 13–30.

Justice, Dwight W. (2002), 'The international trade union movement and the new codes of conduct', in Rhys Jenkins, Ruth Pearson and Gill Seyfang (eds), *Corporate Responsibility and Labour Rights: Codes of Conduct in a Global Economy*, London: Earthscan, pp. 90–100.

Klein, Naomi (2000), *No Logo*, London: Flamingo.

Margolis, Joshua D. and James P. Walsh (2003), 'Misery loves companies: rethinking social initiatives by business', *Administrative Science Quarterly*, **48**, 268–305.

Orlitzky, Marc, Frank L. Schmidt and Sara L. Rynes (2003), 'Corporate social and financial performance: a meta-analysis', *Organization Studies*, **24** (3), 403–41.

Oxfam (2004), *Trading Away Our Rights: Women in Global Supply Chains*, Oxford: Oxfam International.

Porter, Michael and Claas van der Linde (1996), 'Green and competitive: ending the stalemate', in Richard Welford and Richard Starkey (eds), *The Earthscan Reader in Business and Environment*, London: Earthscan, pp. 61–77.

Richter, Judith (2001), *Holding Corporations Accountable: Corporate Conduct, International Codes and Citizen Action*, London: Zed Press.

Sigmund, Paul E. (1980), *Multinationals in Latin America: The Politics of Nationalization*, Madison: The University of Wisconsin Press.

Vogel, David (2005), *The Market for Virtue: The Potential and Limits of Corporate Social Responsibility*, Washington DC: Brookings Institution Press.

See also the entries on: Labour standards; Sustainability.

11 Deontology
Mark D. White

In philosophical ethics, a significant dichotomy between two popular moral theories informs many ethical debates, whether general or specific, academic or practical. One group of theories is often described as *teleological*, in which moral priority is given to the 'good', however it may be defined, and the goal or end (*telos*) is to promote or maximize the quantity of good. A common theory of this type is *consequentialism*, which defines 'good' in terms of the outcomes or consequences of actions. *Utilitarianism* is a specific form of consequentialism in which the goodness of outcomes is defined as the sum total of individuals' utilities generated in the respective states of the world. As we will see below, mainstream economics is intrinsically consequentialist or, more specifically, utilitarian in both its modelling of individual behaviour, as well as in its evaluation of institutions, law and policies.

The other group of theories is known as *deontological*, and is much more difficult to define. It is usually understood in the negative, as being non-teleological or non-consequentialist, but positive definitions have been suggested as well, focusing on concepts such as respect, dignity, rights and duties. In a two-part article, Gerald Gaus (2001a, 2001b) dissected the term and found no less than *ten* different uses of it in the philosophy literature (2001b, pp. 189–90). He organized these into two groups: the first generally finds deontological systems of ethics to be those that give consideration of the 'right' priority over the 'good'. In this regard, Gaus (2001a, p. 28) cites Frankena's 'almost classic definition':

> Deontological theories . . . deny that the right, the obligatory, and the morally good are wholly, whether directly or indirectly, a function of what is nonmorally good or what promotes the greatest balance of good over evil for self, one's society, or the world as a whole. (Frankena 1973, p. 15)

The implication is that deontological ethics will sometimes demand acts that result in less good consequences, or prohibit acts that would further good outcomes, because of some moral defect in the act itself which serves as a constraint on good-maximizing action.[1]

Of course, there is enormous room for argument here. What counts as good? For instance, can the rightness of an act be counted amongst its consequences?[2] Such inclusion, endorsed by ideal utilitarians such as Rashdall (1907), would make consequentialism much broader and more general, but at the same time stretches its very fabric (rendering it unrecognizable to classical utilitarians). It also conflicts with another understanding of deontology which denies maximization, optimization or trade-offs between certain intrinsic, incalculable values such as justice and dignity. In such a view, including rightness among the good consequences to be maximized implies that some of these values may be traded off for others, which these varieties of deontology forbid.

One practical application of this understanding of deontology is the treatment of rights, which Ronald Dworkin (1977) famously referred to as 'trumps' against consequentialist policies. The acknowledgment of rights implies that the specific interest protected by the right takes precedence over the general interest, and cannot be sacrificed for the greater good. 'Rights do not determine a social ordering but instead set the constraints within which a social choice is to be made, by excluding certain alternatives, fixing others, and so on' (Nozick 1974, p. 166). Of course, rights also limit individual action, not just social decision-making, but as the latter often has more serious ramifications, those limits are often emphasized more. Philosophers who take an extreme view of these prohibitions, and hold that no consequentialist considerations can override a deontological constraint, are known as *absolutist deontologists*. However, most modern deontologists are *moderate deontologists*, who believe that rights violations can be justified if the consequences of adhering to them are sufficiently dire. (For instance, both Dworkin and Nozick, to the extent they are deontologists, are moderate; see Ellis 1992 for more on moderate deontology.)

The second group of theories sees the essence of deontology in the reasons it provides agents to act (Gaus 2001b), focusing on individual actions rather than social decisions and policies. In this sense, the classic distinction is between agent-relative and agent-neutral obligations (or constraints) (Scheffler 1982).[3] Agent-neutral obligations are universal in the sense that they apply to any individual facing a particular set of circumstances falling under that obligation. Rules deriving from utilitarian considerations are agent-neutral, because the identity of the agent is irrelevant; in a gross oversimplification of utilitarianism, every person is required to take those actions that will maximize utility. On the other hand, agent-relative obligations are specific to a certain person, and obligate or constrain that person in ways that may not promote or maximize the general good. (Of course, this is simply a specific instance of giving the right priority over the good, consistent with the discussion above.) Common examples include refusing to kill one person to save several others – a person is bound not to kill, even if that killing would save more lives and increase total utility. Such agent-relative obligations are often traced to an inviolable value, such as respect for persons, most clearly present in the ethics of Immanuel Kant. This respect, which cannot be traded off for other values, including the goodness of outcomes, places limits on what agents can do to promote or maximize the good (similar to Nozick's side-constraints).

As stated above, mainstream economics is fundamentally utilitarian in two important ways.[4] First, the standard economic model of individual decision-making represents agents as choosing actions to maximize their preference satisfaction (or 'utility', understood formally as an index of said preferences, not a mental state such as pleasure). Second, welfare economics is based on maximizing the sum total of individuals' levels of preference satisfaction or utility, with the assumption that each person's preferences are linked to their well-being. Because of these broadly consequentialist foundations, mainstream economics encounters several problems when confronted with deontological ethics. First, I will discuss the problems caused by deontological concepts such as commitment and duty, or desire-independent reasons in general, for the standard preference-satisfaction model of choice. Second, I will discuss the relevance of deontology for welfare economics and policymaking, in reference to the broader right/good distinction.

Individual decision-making, preferences and desire-independent reasons

The standard model of economic choice – constrained preference satisfaction against a background of perfect or imperfect information – is consistent with David Hume's desire/belief model of choice, which is the standard model of the philosophy of action (Davidson

1980). In both, agents' reasons for acting are contained entirely in their preferences and information, which in turn completely determine and explain their choices. In other words, no reason for action exists that cannot be represented by a preference informed by the available information (and knowledge of the limitations of such). From this point on, I will abstract away from informational issues and focus simply on preferences as determinants of choice in the standard model.

In his famous 1977 paper, Amartya Sen criticized the 'rational fools' implied by this approach. He suggested instead the possibility of commitment as a motivating force and explanatory factor in choice. This represents a distinct break from the preference-satisfaction or desire/belief framework of choice, and parallels the debate regarding desire-independent reasons in philosophy (Searle 2001). The aspect in which we are most interested here is that commitment provides an opening for deontological values and principles to be incorporated into economics. Using the commitment framework, agents can act on principles, duties or values without representing them as preferences which can be substituted for others. In other words, this allows for absolute considerations in economic models of choice, influences which are not subject to considerations such as prohibitively high opportunity cost or diminishing marginal benefit.

Other scholars have attempted to work deontological concepts explicitly into the economic choice model. One example is Amitai Etzioni (1987, 1988, 1990), who bases his proposal for a socio-economics in part on deontology, which he describes as holding that 'actions are morally right when they conform to a relevant principle or duty' (1988, p. 12). Etzioni further holds deontological ethics to judge the intrinsic quality of an act, not its consequences. Later, he elaborates on the deontological aspects of personal ethics using four criteria: 'moral acts reflect an imperative, a generalization, and a symmetry when applied to others, and are motivated intrinsically' (ibid., pp. 41–2). These descriptors are consistent with the discussion above; where Etzioni strays from deontology as commonly understood when he models moral decision-making as resulting from maximization behaviour, parallel to the maximization of utility as self-interest. To his credit, he does not posit a self-interested motivation for ethical behaviour, but instead holds that what is maximized in ethical cases is 'a kind of satisfaction, a kind of moral worth . . . One has a sense of *affirmation*, or having done what is required, reestablished one's values, adhered to one's higher self, resisted impulses and urges, and been of virtue' (ibid., p. 45, emphasis in the original). This 'moral utility', beside 'pleasure utility', provide the motivation for ethical and self-interested behaviour, respectively. But maximization itself denies the absoluteness of deontological values and the impossibility of trade-offs between them – and in fact, the imperative nature of moral rules that Etzioni emphasized as a hallmark of deontological ethics.

Others have recognized this problem as well. In his article 'Deontology and economics', John Broome (1992) cites Etzioni's bi-utility model as being essentially teleological, since it aims toward maximizing a quantity of a good, in this case moral utility or affirmation (alongside pleasure utility). Furthermore, Broome explains that any teleological system of ethics can be incorporated into the preference-satisfaction or utility-maximization model of economics, provided that 'preferences' and 'utility' are understood in their formal sense (which Etzioni rejects as empty; see 1988, pp. 30–1). In support of this general view of preferences, he quotes Lionel Robbins (1935, p. 95): '[O]ur economic subjects can be pure egoists, pure altruists, pure ascetics, pure sensualists or – what is much more likely – bundles of all these impulses.' Insofar as an agent's ethics are teleological, or have 'the structure of good . . . a maximizing structure' (Broome 1992, p. 276), they can be represented in standard economic models of choice, including Etzioni's 'deontological' bi-utility system.

However, as we have seen, deontological ethics are often characterized (negatively) as non-teleological (as Broome does), so persons who adhere to deontological ethical systems, rules, or principles may pose a problem for economic models of maximization. As described above, Sen popularized one way of incorporating deontological factors in choice through the concept of commitment, and a substantial literature has emerged discussing this development.[5] Many heterodox economists, as well as scholars outside economics (such as Etzioni), have also incorporated deontological thinking into their work. For instance, social economists, who emphasize the role of ethics in economics, often emphasize deontological factors. Lanse Minkler (1999) builds on Sen by formalizing commitment and applying his model to the deontological ethics of W.D. Ross and Immanuel Kant, and Mark D. White (2004) explicitly models Kantian duties using a modified version of the standard constrained preference-satisfaction framework. Irene van Staveren (2007) recognizes the superiority of deontology over utilitarianism as a basis for incorporating ethics into economic choice, but prefers a third option, virtue ethics (van Staveren 2001). Given the wide array of understandings of deontological ethics, it may be premature to declare them incompatible with mainstream economic modelling, while many heterodox economists have embraced them.[6]

Welfare economics, policy and the right/good distinction

'If deontological moralities affect people's behaviour in important ways, then economics is in for a shock' (Broome 1992, p. 282). Not only does the inclusion of deontological factors impact choice models in 'shocking' ways, but it obviously calls into question the foundations and tools of normative welfare economics and the policy recommendations resulting from it. In mainstream economics, the consequences of changes in institutions, laws or policies are evaluated according to their efficiency, usually understood as either Pareto optimality or Kaldor-Hicks efficiency. Both concepts are essentially consequentialist, though Pareto has more respect for some deontological values, depending on its interpretation (especially regarding consent). But as we will see, neither can accommodate deontological values such as intrinsic rights, the dignity of persons and a protected domain of personal liberty.[7]

For instance, Kaldor-Hicks efficiency endorses a proposed change if the resulting total gains to some parties exceeds the total losses to others, with the gains and losses measured in terms of persons' willingness to pay. Although the 'winners' from the change receive enough benefit to compensate the 'losers' and still enjoy net gain, such compensation is not necessary; it is merely 'hypothetical'. Since those who lose from the policy are not compensated, it is very likely they would not consent, in which case imposing such a change is an affront to their dignity as persons worthy of respect. Furthermore, any rights that may be violated by the change – such as property rights in eminent domain cases favouring other private interests – are ignored by the Kaldor-Hicks criterion, and count only insofar as the right-holders are willing to pay to preserve them; they have no intrinsic value in the decision process. As Richard Posner writes in reference to the role of rights in the study of law and economics, 'absolute rights play an important role in the economic theory of the law'. However, 'when transaction costs are prohibitive, the *recognition of absolute rights is inefficient*' (1983, p. 70, emphasis added).

The well-known Pareto criterion, which endorses a change if it makes at least one person better off and no one worse off, seems less offensive to deontological concerns than Kaldor-Hicks. But this is true only insofar as it respects the consent requirement, which in its strictest form would demand that any party affected by the change agree to it in advance. This would ensure that no one is harmed by change according to their own standards, although the transaction costs of acquiring actual consent from any sizeable group of people would be very high, which is why supporters of a strict consent requirement have been called 'fanatics' (Posner 1983, p. 97). Practical issues aside, when consent is merely inferred from estimates of affected persons' self-interest, no matter how accurate the assessment, the absence of actual consent is problematic in several ways. First, as with Kaldor-Hicks efficiency, the inability to consent to changes that affect one's life, even positively, is an affront to the inherent dignity of persons. Second, and perhaps more importantly, agents may have reasons to refuse consent that are not based on self-interest, or even preferences in general, but on principles such as justice or fairness, as discussed above with reference to Sen's introduction of commitment into economic models of rationality. For example, a tax cut that saves every taxpayer 10 per cent of his or her tax liability may be seen as unfair by those who pay less taxes because it benefits high payers by a larger absolute amount. Those taxpayers may oppose such a plan, based on a principle of fairness, even though it increases their disposable income; therefore their consent cannot be inferred from their self-interest alone.[8]

This leads to the broader issue of the disconnect between preferences and well-being, casting further doubt on consequentialist policymaking based on the welfare of individuals. It is well known among philosophers and economists that preferences do not necessarily track welfare. Most utilitarian philosophers who endorse preference-satisfaction recommend that preferences be 'cleaned up' prior to the evaluation of their satisfaction. But deontology introduces another complication: not only do desire-independent reasons for choice (such as Sen's commitment) destroy the identity of preference and choice, but they also split choice from welfare, because choices can be made on bases other than personal well-being. As Sen writes, commitment 'drives a wedge between personal choice and personal welfare, and much of traditional economic theory relies on the identity of the two' (1977, p. 94). Note that this critique is not normative or ethical, but methodological, in the sense that the presence of deontological choice factors among agents (regardless of the researcher's own opinion of them) severs the link between preferences, choice and welfare that Sen correctly identifies as essential to models of both rational choice and welfare economics. Even if we adopt utilitarian standards of policy evaluation, recognition of agents' deontological motivation produces the 'shock' referred to in the quote by Broome at the start of this section.

Conclusion

Deontology does pose challenges to mainstream economics, but they are being increasingly met, by both orthodox and heterodox economists. Scholars are following Sen's lead in modelling various forms of commitment and duty within the constrained preference-satisfaction framework of individual choice. Can government policymaking similarly incorporate deontological values into its consequentialist decision-making procedures? Of course, all real-world governments already do this – in the United States, for example, the Bill of Rights enumerates certain actions, such as those that prohibit freedom of speech, that the government may not take regardless of how beneficial their consequences may be. It is in this sense that Dworkin and Nozick held that rights (and other deontological concepts) serve as constraints on policymaking, ensuring that these values are respected at the same time that social welfare is promoted within these constraints. There may be disagreements about which values are to be given lexical priority and which can be traded off to advance others, but all governments grant some considerations deontological status.

This discussion also points to more fundamental issues with the social decision-making process itself that cannot be remedied simply by acknowledging limits on policy tools. Acknowledging that persons act on reasons based on commitment and duty as well as preferences casts into doubt the measurement of well-being based on preference-satisfaction, as well as inferences regarding consent. If taken seriously, these arguments suggest turning to alternative consequentialist measures such as objective well-being based on income, capabilities or primary goods, which do not require any estimation of personal well-being or satisfaction, or the anti-consequentialist 'minimal state' of classical liberalism, in which the government does not take an active interest in the welfare of its citizens, but instead restricts itself to enforcing rights against interference. Both of these proposals, as well as further alternatives to welfarism, have been discussed at length in the literature on political philosophy as well as heterodox economics, but need to be debated more frequently in mainstream economics as well – not simply as instrumentalist strategies to increase well-being or utility, but as tools to guarantee that deontological values such as rights and dignity are acknowledged and intrinsically respected.

Notes

1. This conflates several of Gaus's distinct definitions; see Gaus (2001a) for more detail.
2. For example, Sen (1982) advocates including the disvalue of rights violations in consequentialist evaluation.
3. Sen discusses a similar topic using the term 'evaluator relativity' or 'position relativity' (1982, 1983); he claims that such considerations can be included in consequentialist evaluation.
4. Many of the papers in Sen and Williams (1982) discuss the utilitarian nature of mainstream economics.
5. A recent symposium in the journal *Economics & Philosophy* (Peter and Schmid 2005) discusses various aspects of Sen's concept of commitment, which can also be viewed through the lens of virtue ethics (van Staveren 2001, pp. 12–15).
6. Game theorists have 'simulated' deontological principles using *rule-utilitarian* arguments, which require only that agents follow rules or institutions that maximize utility in general, even though they may not maximize utility in any particular instance of applying them. For instance, Robert Frank (1988) provides an evolutionary explanation for the development and sustenance of the trait of honesty. To Frank, an agent who can convey honesty will often (but not always) secure better terms of trade, and thereby gain enhanced potential for survival and reproduction. Furthermore, sincere (not feigned) honesty is rewarded because such persons will more reliably be able to convey honesty by avoiding the 'tells' that often give away liars. However, honesty thus derived is not deontological in the nonconsequentialist sense, because at its root it is motivated by ends, not duty per se.
7. The last is well known from Sen's argument regarding 'the impossibility of a Paretian liberal' (1970); see also Sen (1979, pp. 549–54).
8. See Coleman (1980, pp. 127–9) and Dworkin (1980, pp. 275–80) for critical analysis of the consent justification of Pareto and Kaldor-Hicks efficiency.

References

Broome, John (1992), 'Deontology and economics', *Economics and Philosophy*, **8**, 269–82.
Coleman, Jules L. (1980), 'Efficiency, utility and wealth maximization', reprinted (1988) in *Markets, Morals and the Law*, Cambridge: Cambridge University Press, pp. 95–132.

Davidson, Donald (1980), *Essays on Actions and Events*, Oxford: Oxford University Press.

Dworkin, Ronald (1977), *Taking Rights Seriously*, Cambridge, MA: Harvard University Press.

Dworkin, Ronald (1980), 'Why efficiency?' reprinted (1985) in *A Matter of Principle*, Cambridge, MA: Harvard University Press, pp. 267–89.

Ellis, Anthony (1992), 'Deontology, incommensurability, and the arbitrary', *Philosophy and Phenomenological Research*, **52**, 855–75.

Etzioni, Amitai (1987), 'Toward a Kantian socio-economics', *Review of Social Economy*, **45**, 37–47.

Etzioni, Amitai (1988), *The Moral Dimension: Toward a New Economics*, New York: The Free Press.

Etzioni, Amitai (1990), 'Toward a deontological socioeconomics', in Mark A. Lutz (ed.), *Social Economics: Retrospect and Prospect*, Boston, MA: Kluwer Academic Publishers, pp. 221–33.

Frank, Robert H. (1988), *Passions within Reasons: The Strategic Role of the Emotions*, New York: W.W. Norton.

Frankena, William K. (1973), *Ethics*, 2nd edition, Englewood Cliffs, NJ: Prentice-Hall.

Gaus, Gerald F. (2001a), 'What is deontology? Part one: orthodox views', *Journal of Value Inquiry*, **35**, 27–42.

Gaus, Gerald F. (2001b), 'What is deontology? Part two: reasons to act', *Journal of Value Inquiry*, **35**, 179–93.

Minkler, Lanse (1999), 'The problem with utility: toward a non-consequentialist/utility theory synthesis', *Review of Social Economy*, **57**, 4–24.

Nozick, Robert (1974), *Anarchy, State, and Utopia*, New York: Basic Books.

Peter, Fabienne and Hans Bernhard Schmid (2005), 'Symposium on rationality and commitment: introduction', *Economics & Philosophy*, **21**, 1–3.

Posner, Richard A. (1983), *The Economics of Justice*, 2nd edition, Cambridge, MA: Harvard University Press.

Rashdall, Hastings (1907), *The Theory of Good and Evil*, Oxford: Oxford University Press.

Robbins, Lionel (1935), *An Essay on the Nature and Significance of Economic Science*, 2nd edition, London: Macmillan.

Searle, John (2001), *Rationality in Action*, Cambridge, MA: MIT Press.

Scheffler, Samuel (1982), *The Rejection of Consequentialism*, Oxford: Oxford University Press.

Sen, Amartya (1970) 'The impossibility of a Paretian liberal', reprinted (1982) in *Choice, Welfare and Measurement*, Cambridge, MA: Harvard University Press, pp. 285–90.

Sen, Amartya (1977), 'Rational fools: a critique of the behavioural foundations of economic theory', reprinted (1982) in *Choice, Welfare and Measurement*, Cambridge, MA: Harvard University Press, pp. 84–106.

Sen, Amartya (1979), 'Personal utilities and public judgments: or what's wrong with welfare economics', *Economic Journal*, **89**, 537–58.

Sen, Amartya (1982), 'Rights and agency', *Philosophy and Public Affairs*, **11**, 3–39.

Sen, Amartya (1983), 'Evaluator relativity and consequential evaluation', *Philosophy and Public Affairs*, **12**, 113–32.

Sen, Amartya and Bernard Williams (eds) (1982), *Utilitarianism and Beyond*, Cambridge: Cambridge University Press.

Staveren, Irene van (2001), *The Values of Economics: An Aristotelian Perspective*, London and New York: Routledge.

Staveren, Irene van (2007), 'Beyond utilitarianism and deontology: ethics in economics', *Review of Political Economy*, **19**, 21–35.

White, Mark D. (2004), 'Can *homo economicus* follow Kant's categorical imperative?' *Journal of Socio-Economics*, **33**, 89–106.

See also the entries on: Efficiency; Immanuel Kant; Amartya Sen.

12 Dignity
Mark D. White

The word 'dignity' has many meanings, most of them interconnected in some way, but with widely varying emphases. In some cases, it names a self-referential quality, similar to self-respect; this is how most ancient philosophers used the term. For the purpose of ethics and economics (and this chapter), dignity may be best understood as an intrinsic quality of persons which accords them some degree of respect. This version is well known through the writings of Immanuel Kant, but has been discussed and elaborated upon – with significant differences – by other philosophers as well. It also features prominently in constitutions and other foundational documents of many nations and international organizations, such as in the United Nations Charter, as well as the United Nations Declaration of Human Rights (Schachter 1983). In this sense, dignity is often an individualistic counterweight to consequentialist systems of ethics, such as utilitarianism, which is often accused of obscuring the distinction between individual persons due to a disregard for their inherent dignity (for example, see Rawls 1971, pp. 27–30). Following from its roots in classical utilitarianism, mainstream economics must share in this charge; however, heterodox economists – especially social economists – have made significant strides in incorporating various meanings of dignity into their work.

This chapter begins with a review of several important philosophical analyses of dignity. While dignity has been discussed by a wide array of philosophers and from many viewpoints, due to space limitations I have chosen to focus on the work of Immanuel Kant, Alan Gewirth and scholars in the Catholic tradition, because theirs are the conceptions of dignity economists most often use. Accordingly, after the philosophical survey, the chapter turns to the use of the concept of dignity in the economics literature, by both mainstream and heterodox economists.

Philosophers on dignity
Immanuel Kant's moral philosophy is perhaps best known for its emphasis on duties, which are derived from the categorical imperative, which is Kant's formulation of the moral law and which must be followed out of respect for the moral law in order to generate truly moral action. But these formalistic details of Kant's system are ultimately based on his claim that all rational beings have an intrinsic, objective and unconditional dignity based on their capacity for autonomous choice, independent of any external or internal influences aside from the moral law itself (Kant 1785, pp. 436, 440).

Kant famously contrasted things and persons, the former having a price and the latter possessing a dignity above price: 'whatever has a price can be replaced by something else as its equivalent . . . whatever is above all price, and therefore admits of no equivalent, has a dignity' (1785, p. 434). In this sense, persons, who are to be regarded as 'ends in themselves', possess a dignity which is incalculable and incomparable, resisting summation or substitutability (1785, p. 428; 1797, pp. 434–5).[1] As such, dignity is the basis for the version of the categorical imperative that Sullivan (1989, Ch. 14) names the 'Formula for the respect of the dignity of persons': 'Act in such a way that you treat humanity, whether in your own person or in the person of another, always at the same time as an end and never simply as a means' (Kant 1785, p. 429). This is often seen as the most humanistic form of Kant's moral law, as it emphasizes respect for persons (including oneself) based on their inherent worth.

Alan Gewirth is a notable modern philosopher who has written extensively on human worth and dignity. Gewirth defines dignity as signifying 'a kind of intrinsic worth that belongs equally to all human beings as such, constituted by certain intrinsically valuable aspects of being human' (1992, p. 12).[2] His conception of dignity is grounded similarly to Kant's, in that Gewirth maintains that persons have dignity and worth based on their agency, or capacity for purposeful action. He argues that since persons act intentionally towards ends, those ends must have value to them, and that value extends to persons as well, granting them dignity. Furthermore, since persons are essentially alike in this aspect, each person must recognize the dignity of every other, resulting in the intrinsic dignity of all persons.[3] Finally, like Kant, he believes that rights derive from dignity, as opposed to others who say that dignity is either a result of, or equivalent to, having rights (see Gewirth 1992, pp. 11–13).

However, Gewirth derives much different conclusions from his concept of dignity than does Kant. In the standard interpretation, Kantian ethics makes strong demands regarding negative duties (such as 'do not kill' and 'do not lie'), but less stringent ones concerning positive duties (such as beneficence and aid). As a result, persons have a right to be free of interference, but not a right to well-being or welfare. As such, Kantian dignity is usually understood to imply a strong version of classic liberalism, similar to that of Robert Nozick (1974), in which the state performs a largely negative function, protecting individuals from each other, without providing positive assistance or guaranteeing welfare.[4] On the other hand, Gewirth's conception of dignity grants persons a right not only to freedom but also to well-being, which it is the responsibility of every individual, as well as the state, to recognize and support. Therefore, Gewirth's philosophy, while foundationally similar to Kant's, leads to a more proactive, somewhat egalitarian vision of government, which has a duty to ensure the well-being of its citizens.[5]

An emphasis on human dignity is also seen in many documents from the Catholic philosophical tradition, which holds that 'the dignity of the human person is rooted in his creation in the image and likeness of God' who 'created man a rational being, conferring on him the dignity of a person who can initiate and control his own actions' (*Catechism*, paras 1700, 1730). As with Kant and Gewirth, the Catholic conception of dignity stems from persons' autonomy and freedom of will: 'By virtue of his soul and his spiritual powers of intellect and will, man is endowed with freedom, an outstanding manifestation of the divine image' (*Catechism*, para. 1705).[6] In the Catholic tradition, the dignity of persons implies a responsibility to promote the common good of all: 'It is necessary that all participate, each according to his position and role, in promoting the common good. This obligation is inherent in the dignity of the human person' (*Catechism*, para. 1913). In terms of the state, 'public authorities are bound to respect the fundamental and inalienable rights of the human person' (*Catechism*, para. 1907), for 'these rights are prior to society and must be recognized by it. They are the basis of the moral legitimacy of every authority' (*Catechism*, para. 1930).

Nonetheless, there is an important egalitarian thread in Catholic thought deriving from the dignity of persons: 'Their equal dignity as persons demands that we strive for fairer and more humane conditions. Excessive economic and social disparity between individuals and peoples of the one human race is a source of scandal and militates against social justice, equity, human dignity, as well as social and international peace' (*Catechism*, para. 1938). However, there is a strong emphasis on charitable works, in the spirit of solidarity, to balance state intervention and welfare programmes, placing Catholic teaching based on dignity between the extremes of Kant and Gewirth.

Economics and dignity

Mainstream economics

Dignity is seldom mentioned by mainstream economists, whose dominant paradigm is rooted in classical utilitarianism, both in terms of its modelling of individual behaviour and its policymaking based on welfare economics. To the mainstream, individual choice is deterministic, leaving no room for true choice and free will, from which true human dignity derives (in all three concepts surveyed above). Welfare economics is based on maximizing total social welfare or utility, and therefore sanctions trade-offs between the well-being of individuals, neglecting any rights they may have by virtue of their essential dignity.

But heterodox economists – especially social economists – have critiqued the refusal of mainstream economists to recognize and respect the dignity of the economic agents they model. They have also made advances in incorporating concepts of dignity into economic discourse.

Mainstream models of economic decision-making are based on maximizing expected utility (an index of preference satisfaction defined over lotteries) within constraints based on the agent's economic resources and environment. Decisions in this model are determined completely by preference, beliefs and constraints, leaving no room for true choice or agency. As we saw above, dignity is based on the free will, agency or autonomy of rational agents; it is because of the capacity for true choice that human beings have intrinsic worth. But the standard economic model leaves no room for choice, and therefore denies 'agents' any true agency, and by extension, dignity.[7]

One way in which mainstream economics may seem to respect the dignity of persons is their adherence to the doctrine of consumer sovereignty, which holds that persons' own preferences (as revealed by their choices) are to be used in social policy decisions (as well as market interactions), regardless of policymakers' opinions regarding those preferences.[8] But rather than reflecting respect for dignity, most economists support this doctrine for pragmatic and epistemic reasons: since they believe that one's preferences define one's well-being, and further that no one knows better than oneself what those preferences (and therefore well-being) are, preferences – reflected in one's market choices – should be the only basis of information used in social policy. In other words, consumer sovereignty and respect for individual choice is rarely based on the inherent dignity of persons, but instead on questionable value judgements concerning the nature of preferences and well-being (Redmond 2000).

In matters of policymaking, mainstream welfare economics displays its neglect of dignity by utilizing summed measures of utility or well-being that obscure the distinction between individuals (as Rawls wrote) and ignore the essential rights of persons. Evaluative standards, such as the Kaldor-Hicks efficiency test, endorse changes that benefit some persons at the expense of others, regardless of rights, justice or fairness, all closely related to, or derived directly from, dignity (Lutz 1995, p. 187; White 2006). Rights are valued only insofar as they increase welfare, rendering them purely instrumental, rather than intrinsic, as implied by their derivation from essential human dignity. Even the Pareto principle, which requires that any policy proposal make at least one person better off and no one worse off, fails to respect human dignity because it does not require consent from affected parties (although, ironically, the presumption of consent is often used to justify Pareto improvements). Policies are judged to be Pareto improvements based on third-party estimates of financial or material well-being, but deny that persons may refuse to consent to a policy on grounds of rights, justice, fairness or other nonpecuniary principles. While actual consent would safeguard the dignity of persons by respecting their true preferences and principles, a Pareto standard which merely infers consent based on 'average' preferences does not (White 2008).

Heterodox economics

Not surprisingly, given their historical ties with Catholic economics, social economists are the leaders in recognizing the importance of dignity to economics, as shown by the number of their seminal writings that focus on it.[9] Mark Lutz (in frequent collaboration with psychologist Kenneth Lux) is perhaps the most prominent social economist to have emphasized dignity as a missing element in mainstream economics. In his 1995 presidential address to the Association of Social Economics (Lutz 1995), he discussed the importance of human dignity to a social economic outlook. In addition to the critiques of 'rational economic man' and welfare economics discussed above, Lutz also criticizes scientific positivism (which considers only observable, measurable phenomena), cultural and moral relativism (which denies any objective ethical values), commercial advertising (which he claims manipulates consumers, using them as mere means to increase profit) and neglect of ecological sustainability (which would value the dignity of future generations).[10] Most notably, he embraces Gewirth's conception of dignity, along with Gewirth's call for a proactive government and welfare state.

Another application of dignity cited in Lutz (1995, 1999) is that firms should be owned and operated by labour as opposed to capital. Based on Kant's version of dignity and his much-cited person/thing distinction, David Ellerman (1988, 1990) has argued that respect for the dignity of workers implies that the current wage-labour system in which capital hires labour is immoral, because the latter is used simply a means to the end of the former. Ellerman likens this arrangement to voluntary slavery, which would be forbidden by Kant as sacrificing one's autonomy. But White (2003) argues against this interpretation of Kantian dignity, distinguishing between voluntary slavery, which may be irreversible, and an employment agreement, which the worker is free to abandon at will. He also points to Kant's requirement not to treat persons *merely* as means, but at the same time as ends, and argues that if the worker agrees to a work assignment and a wage, and is able to leave this employ (within the limits of the employment contract), the employer is respecting the workers as ends in themselves; otherwise, commerce itself would grind to a halt.

John B. Davis (2006), as part of his ongoing work exploring the nature of the individual in economics, has recently focused on dignity as an important normative part of a person's identity. Drawing on Feinberg's (1970) connection between dignity and the ability to claim rights, Davis links the two senses of dignity cited at the beginning of this chapter, writing that self-respect (self-referential dignity) depends critically on 'a socially accepted capacity to claim rights' (2006, p. 79). He concludes that 'for the socially embedded individual conception, freedom, dignity, and human rights produce a structure of values that provide an account of the moral autonomy and independence of the individual' (2006, p. 79). Shifting to policy recommendations, Davis focuses on the elimination of humiliation, identified by Avishai Margalit (1996) as the 'violation of human dignity', and writes that 'making human dignity a central value of social-economic policy, then, means changing social institutions to eliminate humiliating institutions' (Davis 2006, p. 81). Examples are those institutions that sustain racial or gender-based discrimination. In this way, Davis maintains, societal institutions can respect the essential dignity and autonomy of the members of that society, bringing it closer to what Margalit terms a 'decent society'.

While social economists have dominated the move to integrate concepts of dignity into the economics literature, other non-mainstream economists have also emphasized the issue. Timothy P. Roth (2002) has argued, along the lines of the standard reading of Kant (along with Rawls), that respect for the dignity of persons requires a minimalist government, and he analyses mainstream welfare economics and public choice theory on these grounds. Austrian economists, especially intellectual descendants of Ludwig von Mises (1949), hold similar views regarding dignity and the role of the state.[11] Though their language varies, feminist economists focus on the dignity and autonomy of women, in addition to their health and material well-being when arguing for improvements to economic theory and policymaking. Most notably, Amartya Sen's (1993) capabilities approach to human well-being and development is grounded in part on considerations of human dignity, based on Sen's earlier work on agency and well-being (1985, 1987), with increasing emphasis on women's agency (1999, Ch. 8).[12]

Conclusion
Even considering the attention given to it by social economists, dignity is a largely ignored concept in the economics literature. Given the impersonal nature of classical utilitarianism, this omission is certainly understandable, but nonetheless inexcusable. Economists of all schools and approaches should reflect on how they represent persons in their work, both theoretical and empirical, and ask themselves (i) if those persons have the free choice and agency that is necessary for true human dignity and (ii) if their intrinsic dignity is taken into account in policy analysis and welfare economics.[13] These considerations are essential to respecting the inherent dignity of those whose decisions we as economists study in our work.

Notes
1. See Hill (1980) for detailed discussion of these properties of Kantian dignity.
2. Gewirth distinguishes between this 'intrinsic' dignity and 'empirical' dignity; the latter corresponding more to the phrasing 'acting with dignity' or 'being dignified'.
3. This argument is laid out in detail in terms of rights in Gewirth (1978, Chs 1–3), and he reformulates it in terms of dignity in Gewirth (1992).

4. There are scholars who disagree with this reading of Kant. They claim that Kant did support an active welfare state (for example, see Kaufman 1999).
5. See Gewirth (1996) for an extended treatment of the political implications of his concept of dignity.
6. The links between Catholic and Kantian understandings of dignity and autonomy are clear in Pope Paul VI's writing, 'Hence man's dignity demands that he act according to a knowing and free choice that is personally motivated and prompted from within, not under blind internal impulse nor by mere external pressure. Man achieves such dignity when, emancipating himself from all captivity to passion, he pursues his goal in a spontaneous choice of what is good, and procures for himself through effective and skilful action, apt helps to that end' (*Gaudium et Spes* 17).
7. See Lutz (1995, pp. 181–2) and White (2007) for more on the absence of true choice in economic models of decision-making.
8. See Persky (1993) for a historical overview of the various understandings of the term 'consumer sovereignty', of which the one cited here is relatively modern.
9. See, for instance, O'Boyle (2001) and Wilber (2004), in addition to works cited below.
10. Many of these themes are further explored in Lutz and Lux (1988) and Lutz (1999), as well as other work cited in Lutz (1995).
11. The fact that economists on both the left and the right can embrace dignity is explained by the ambiguity of the claims that dignity allows individuals to make: from negative claims against interference (from standard readings of Kant) to positive claims to assistance (as in Gewirth, as well as alternative readings of Kant).
12. Despite his Nobel Prize, I classify Sen's contribution here as heterodox because the capability approach has been embraced mainly by heterodox economists and other social scientists rather than mainstream economists. Indeed, due to his emphasis on women's issues, feminist economists claim him as one of their own (Agarwal et al. 2003).
13. One issue that has been insufficiently dealt with in both the economics and philosophical literatures is the dignity of mentally impaired and developmentally disabled persons, who may not have the capacity of free will and agency from which dignity is commonly derived. While such persons certainly deserve to be treated with dignity, it is an open question whether they possess dignity in the sense described above. Obviously, a negative answer to that question casts doubt on the derivation of dignity from free will and agency.

References

Agarwal, Bina, Jane Humphries and Ingrid Robeyns (2003), 'Exploring the challenges of Amartya Sen's work and ideas: an introduction', *Feminist Economics*, **9** (2–3), 3–12.
Catechism of the Catholic Church (1994), www.vatican.va/archive/ccc/index.htm, accessed 3 March, 2009.
Davis, John B. (2006), 'The normative significance of the individual in economics', in Jane Clary, Wilfred Dolfsma and Deborah M. Figart (eds), *Ethics and the Market: Insights from Social Economics*, London: Routledge, pp. 69–83.
Ellerman, David P. (1988), 'The Kantian person/thing principle in political economy', reprinted in 1995 in *Intellectual Trespassing as a Way of Life: Essays in Philosophy, Economics, and Mathematics*, Lanham, MD: Rowman & Littlefield, pp. 87–101.
Ellerman, David P. (1990), *The Democratic Worker-Owned Firm*, Boston, MA: Unwin Hyman.
Feinberg, Joel (1970), 'The nature and value of rights', reprinted in 1980 in *Rights, Justice, and the Bounds of Liberty: Essays in Social Philosophy*, Princeton, NJ: Princeton University Press, pp. 143–58.
Gewirth, Alan (1978), *Reason and Morality*, Chicago, IL: The University of Chicago Press.
Gewirth, Alan (1992), 'Human dignity as the basis of rights', in Michael J. Meyer and W.A. Parent (eds), *The Constitution of Rights: Human Dignity and American Values*, Ithaca, NY and London: Cornell University Press, pp. 10–28.
Gewirth, Alan (1996), *The Community of Rights*, Chicago, IL: The University of Chicago Press.
Hill, Thomas E., Jr (1980), 'Humanity as an end in itself', *Ethics*, **91**, 84–90.
Kant, Immanuel (1785), *Grounding for the Metaphysics of Morals*, reprinted in 1993, trans. James W. Ellington, Indianapolis, IL: Hackett Publishing Company.
Kant, Immanuel (1797), *The Metaphysics of Morals*, reprinted in 1996, trans. and ed. Mary Gregor, Cambridge: Cambridge University Press.
Kaufman, Alexander (1999), *Welfare in the Kantian State*, Oxford: Oxford University Press.
Lutz, Mark A. (1995), 'Centering social economics on human dignity', *Review of Social Economy*, **53**, 171–94.
Lutz, Mark A. (1999), *Economics for the Common Good: Two Centuries of Social Economic Thought in the Humanistic Tradition*, London: Routledge.
Lutz, Mark A. and Kenneth Lux (1988), *Humanistic Economics: The New Challenge*, New York: The Bootstrap Press.
Margalit, Avishai (1996), *The Decent Society*, Cambridge, MA: Harvard University Press.

Mises, Ludwig von (1949), *Human Action*, Auburn, AL: Ludwig von Mises Institute.
Nozick, Robert (1974), *Anarchy, State, and Utopia*, New York: Basic Books.
O'Boyle, Edward J. (2001), 'Personalist economics: unorthodox and counter-cultural', *Review of Social Economy*, **59**, 367–93.
Paul VI (1965), *Gaudium et Spes*, www.newadvent.org/library/docs_ec21gs.htm, 3 March, 2009.
Persky, Joseph (1993), 'Retrospectives: consumer sovereignty', *Journal of Economic Perspectives*, **7**, 183–91.
Rawls, John (1971), *A Theory of Justice*, Cambridge, MA: Harvard University Press.
Redmond, William H. (2000), 'Consumer rationality and consumer sovereignty', *Review of Social Economy*, **58**, 177–96.
Roth, Timothy P. (2002), *The Ethics and Economics of Minimalist Government*, Cheltenham, UK, and Northampton, MA, USA: Edward Elgar.
Schachter, Oscar (1983), 'Human dignity as a normative concept', *American Journal of International Law*, **77**, 848–54.
Sen, Amartya (1985), 'Well-being, agency and freedom: the Dewey Lectures 1984', *Journal of Philosophy*, **82**, 169–221.
Sen, Amartya (1987), *On Ethics & Economics*, Oxford: Blackwell.
Sen, Amartya (1993), 'Capability and well-being', in Martha C. Nussbaum and Amartya K. Sen (eds), *The Quality of Life*, Oxford: Oxford University Press, pp. 30–53.
Sen, Amartya (1999), *Development as Freedom*, New York: Knopf.
Sullivan, Roger J. (1989), *Immanuel Kant's Moral Theory*, Cambridge: Cambridge University Press.
White, Mark D. (2003), 'Kantian dignity and social economics', *Forum for Social Economics*, **32** (2), 1–11.
White, Mark D. (2006), 'A Kantian critique of neoclassical law and economics', *Review of Political Economy*, **18**, 235–52.
White, Mark D. (2007), 'Does *homo economicus* have a will?', in Barbara Montero and Mark D. White (eds), *Economics and the Mind*, London: Routledge, pp. 143–58.
White, Mark D. (2008), 'Social law and economics and the quest for dignity and rights', in John B. Davis and Wilfred Dolfsma (eds), *The Elgar Companion to Social Economics*, Cheltenham, UK and Northampton, MA, USA: Edward Elgar, pp. 575–94.
Wilber, Charles K. (2004), 'Ethics, human behavior, and the methodology of social economics', *Forum for Social Economics*, **33** (2), 19–50.

See also the entries on: Catholic social thought; Immanuel Kant; Rights.

13 Discrimination
Deborah M. Figart

Discrimination is usually defined as the act of treating 'equals' unequally. It therefore violates one formulation of Immanuel Kant's categorical imperative that 'equals should be treated equally'. Economic discrimination is unequal treatment based on group identity in labour markets, housing markets, education markets and other markets. As explored in detail below, such discrimination violates norms of commutative justice (fair exchange) and distributive justice (fair distribution of resources).

Although discrimination can occur in a variety of markets, labour-market discrimination has received the bulk of economists' attention. Labour-market discrimination occurs in hiring, promotion, conditions of work and wage-setting. Moreover, discrimination in one of these areas tends to have implications for others. For example, occupational segregation of men and women into different job categories is one of the causes of wage differentials. Wages, the most easily measured outcomes of labour-market discrimination, have been the primary focus of empirical research. Because wages are the primary means of provisioning in market economies, access to jobs paying relatively higher wages provides a degree of power and autonomy in the public sphere and within the household. Wage inequality therefore has implications for an individual's ability to achieve a quality of life.

Neoclassical theories of discrimination
Economic definitions of discrimination generally derive from the basic framework of unequal treatment of equals. However, as Amartya Sen (1992, p. ix) cogently argued, the significant question in any discussion of inequality is 'equality of *what*?' For mainstream economic theories of discrimination, especially those grounded in neoclassical economics, the answer is productivity. Rational employers hire workers when the value of their contribution to the firm's productivity is at least equal to their wages. With the added assumptions of declining marginal returns from labour inputs in the short run and competitive labour and product markets, this behavioural proposition leads to the conclusion that equilibrium wages gravitate toward the point where they are equivalent to the market value of workers' productive contributions. Wage discrimination, then, consists of remunerating employees differently when they have equivalent productivity. From an ethical standpoint, the equivalence of contribution and reward represents a fair exchange according to the commutative justice principle.

Discrimination interferes with fair wage-setting (commutative justice) by violating the equivalency of productivity and remuneration. An economy built on free markets requires for its efficiency that certain normative rules be followed, and these rules constrain individuals' behaviour, in this case, discriminatory behaviour.

The troubling question for economists is how economically irrational behaviour, such as discrimination, can persist over time. Unless the members of different groups (for example, men and women) differ in their productivity, rational employers would be expected to hire cheaper categories of labour until wages equalize. Mainstream economists are therefore divided into those who are sceptical of persistent discrimination and those who seek to reconcile the existence of discrimination with prevailing theory (see Blau and Kahn 2000; Maume 2004).

The first group, grounded in human capital theory, argues that apparent wage inequality must be explainable by legitimate factors affecting the relative productivity of different workers (see, for example, O'Neill 2003). Focusing on labour supply issues, they suggest that unequal productivity is at the root of unequal pay. For example, women's rational decisions to invest less in their human capital, based on their anticipation of intermittent labour market participation and household responsibilities, would explain both occupational segregation and wage differentials.

Similarly, underfunded schools in inner cities might inadequately prepare some racial-ethnic minorities for high-skilled jobs. The resulting inequality is thus generated by factors outside of the labour market. Under such formulations, no discrimination, and therefore no ethically troubling behaviour, is occurring. Human capital theory, especially as applied to gender inequality, can be interpreted as emphasizing a utilitarian approach to ethics, in which individuals' subjective assessments of their own well-being are not challenged. Women are presumed to make choices that improve their own welfare.

In contrast with supply-side human capital theory, two neoclassical approaches acknowledge the existence of discrimination. Both can be seen as constructing arguments of why the wages of individual members of certain groups are not set at the appropriate price.

First, Gary Becker revived discrimination as a topic for serious study by neoclassical economists with his landmark book *The Economics of Discrimination*, published in 1957(1971). In this work, Becker defines discrimination in monetary terms. That is, a person (an employer, co-worker or consumer) is said to have a 'taste for discrimination', similar to a (dis)taste for strawberries, in that they would pay to maintain social or psychological distance from members of a particular group. Reflecting on the concept in 2002, Becker succinctly argued, 'Discrimination comes from prejudice, and I translate that into a monetary amount – how much you are willing to pay' (Clement 2002). One discriminates when one forfeits income in order to indulge this preference. By this definition, discrimination is never profitable for the employer. Imperfectly competitive markets, however, permit discrimination to persist. Deregulation and free trade, by enhancing market competition, should reduce discrimination (Black 1999).

The second neoclassical approach, the theory of statistical discrimination, suggests that discrimination may persist because it is rational under conditions of imperfect information. Employers, according to this theory, cannot fully predict the potential productivity of future employees. To compensate, they use screening devices to select between applicants, including generalizations about racial or gender groups. According to Kennelly (2003), statistical discrimination consists of 'using characteristics associated with groups as substitutes for information about individuals' (p. 184). Such generalizations are often based on ignorance or outdated information; and, even if statistically true about the group 'average', the generalization may not apply to an individual group member. Nevertheless, as in Becker's definition, statistical discrimination is unethical because it violates the commutative justice principle.

Heterodox theories of discrimination

There are several problems with these three neoclassical frameworks and their narrow focus on the commutative principle as applied to productivity and remuneration. Within most neoclassical frameworks, pre-labour-market discrimination and socialization are treated as exogenous, not part of the study of economics and markets. Yet as several scholars note, there are feedback effects (or cumulative causation) between the labour market and other social institutions, including the family (England 1992, pp. 108–12; Bruegel and Perrons 1995, pp. 111–12; Blau and Kahn 2000, p. 82). Women and racial-ethnic minorities who perceived discrimination in the past may be discouraged from training for nontraditional jobs or making other investments in their human capital. This results in a productivity gap attributable to prior discrimination (D'Amico 1987). Alternatively, those who overcome barriers to entry may be relatively *more* qualified and *more* productive than their co-workers without receiving additional compensation.

Wage discrimination may also encourage couples to adopt a traditional division of labour between market and domestic labour. David Neumark and Michele McLennan (1995), for example, found empirical evidence that self-reported experiences of discrimination increased the probability of women changing employers, marrying and having children. Although they did not find that women who reported discrimination accumulated less human capital, they did note that the expectation of discrimination could be shared by the 'control' group, that is, women without direct experience of bias. While the debate between supply-side human capitalists and neoclassical discrimination theorists is divided between two options–either individuals choose certain jobs (supply-side) or employers discriminate (demand-side)–in reality, these dynamics of choice and constraint cannot be isolated from each other.

Barbara Bergmann's landmark formulation of the crowding hypothesis formalizes the feedback problem (see Bergmann 1974). Past and current discrimination restricts women and racial-ethnic minorities to a small subset of occupations, a phenomenon termed 'occupational segregation'. Occupational segregation can also result from organizational policies and practices (Kmec 2005). An abundant supply of workers (crowding) in these limited occupations drives down wages. Employers can afford to hire white men at a premium only if their competitors do the same, passing on higher prices to consumers. Discrimination is therefore profitable and sustainable only if it is a generalized practice (see also Myrdal 1944). The existence of separate labour markets for different groups maintains industry and individually-based wage differentials, as well as differences according to occupation. The crowding hypothesis, however, is unable to account for within-occupation gender wage differentials (Solberg 2005). There is also substantial regional variation in occupational segregation by gender and race, indicating less rigidity than Bergmann's initial formulation suggests (McCall 2000; Cohen and Huffman 2003).

Bergmann's crowding theory is one example of an institutional theory of discrimination. The scope of institutional discrimination is broader than merely the short-sightedness or ignorance of employers adhering to stereotypes and assumptions; rather, it relates to *structural* features of labour markets and employment practices (see, for example, Shulman 1996). These structural features can be relatively rigid because of cumulative causation. Segmented labour market theory, for example, posits that racial-ethnic minorities and women who are employed in the 'secondary sector' of the labour market are not paid commensurate with their productivity due to employment barriers (Boston 1990). Segmentation takes new forms with structural economic shifts and changes in managerial practices. For example, contemporary flexibility policies create separate labour markets, with organizational 'insiders' enjoying traditional employment relations and 'outsiders' having non-standard work arrangements (Kalleberg 2003).

Structural theories of discrimination, both within institutional economics and within radical political economy, also focus on the interaction between market forces and the factors that determine bargaining power (Mason 1995). Darity et al. (2005) have posited racial identity as itself a type of productive property, generating wealth for members of dominant groups who therefore resist any weakening of their property rights. These heterodox approaches, therefore, move beyond commutative justice to explore the implications of discrimination for distributive justice, meaning fair distribution of society's resources.

While neoclassical theory treats wages as simply the price of labour, heterodox political economy distinguishes labour (or labour power) from other commodities traded in markets (see Figart et al. 2002; Figart and Mutari 2004). Because wages are also necessary to reproduce the labour force in a market economy, employers are ethically bound to pay a 'living wage', one that guarantees minimal subsistence, regardless of workers' productive contributions to the product. Living wage arguments note that many of the factors affecting the market value of an individual's productive contribution, including the price of the good or service contribution, technologies employed in production and how much bargaining power workers have, are beyond the individual's control (Robinson 2004).

Feminist theories of discrimination
Both mainstream and heterodox accounts of discrimination, however, tend to treat discriminatory wage differentials as simply distortions of appropriate wage levels. For heterodox political economists, structural barriers and customs preventing the flow of labour between segmented labour markets are obstacles to the equalization of wage rates for workers with equal potential productivity. Further, both mainstream and structural theories tend to presume that the basic occupational structure of the economy and the relative quality of jobs are determined a priori of the gender or racial-ethnic assignment of workers. In other words, both approaches assume that gender and race-ethnicity do not factor into the construction of the 'places' in an occupational structure; they merely determine the places to which a particular worker has access.

Empirical research by gender scholars into the processes by which discrimination occurs, however, indicates that socially constructed notions of gender (and race-ethnicity, class, age and so on) actually shape the available places (Nelson and Bridges 1999; Skuratowicz and Hunter 2004; Reskin and Bielby 2005). When an employer creates a position with opportunities for training and upward mobility but requiring periods of extensive overtime, for example, the job is implicitly 'white' and 'male'. A part-time job with expectations of high turnover and therefore little career development carries the embedded image of a 'mommy track' job.

Similarly, the net wage penalties for being in 'care work' occupations and for being a mother are still substantial (Budig and England 2001; England et al. 2002). Part of the reason, therefore, that 'good' and 'bad' job characteristics tend to cluster within specific jobs and occupations is the implicit gender and racial-ethnic labelling of work. This occurs because wages are more than a price (as depicted in neoclassical theory) and a living (as asserted by heterodox theory), they are also a social practice (see Figart et al. 2002). As a social practice, wages can reinforce or redefine how people can live.

Attention to such discriminatory processes requires us to expand our definition of discrimination. The capabilities approach, pioneered by Amartya Sen and Martha Nussbaum (Sen 1992; Nussbaum and Sen 1993; Nussbaum 1999), provides an alternative framework for ethical social theory that can illuminate our understanding of discrimination by breaking the assumed link between productivity and remuneration as the primary lens for wage-setting. Capabilities theorists emphasize equal worth regardless of productive contributions to a market economy; such equality is rooted in human dignity (Nussbaum 1999). This emphasis on dignity is shared by heterodox economists working from a deontological perspective (van Staveren 2007). However, capabilities theorists incorporate processes and subjective assessments of well-being rather than simply equal outcomes. Such an approach requires attention to the diverse attributes that individuals may possess and the diverse definitions of well-being that individuals may consider important. Sen and his followers posit a definition of equality that can be reconciled with the pervasive human diversity: '[equal] capability to achieve functions that he or she has reason to value' (Sen 1992, p. 4).

Capabilities theory shares this vision with social practice theory as articulated by gender theorists. Both concepts emphasize the importance of access to material resources as part of the true freedom to shape one's life (Robeyns 2003). Yet access to resources, including equal wages, is insufficient if one is not positioned to utilize these resources, either because of physical differences or due to cultural barriers (Nussbaum 1999). For example, in the 1980s and 1990s, middle-class women in the United States were better positioned to reap the benefits of equal opportunity policies than were their working-class counterparts (Blau and Kahn 2000). Inequality of capabilities, rather than inequality per se, is thus defined as problematic. Equality of capabilities, however, is not reducible to equal outcomes.

A more comprehensive approach to labour-market discrimination views it as 'a multidimensional interaction of economic, social, political, and cultural forces in both the workplace and the family, resulting in differential outcomes involving pay, employment, and status' (Figart 1997, p. 4). Perceptions of fairness may be as significant to workers' flourishing as concrete indicators of occupational success, according to capabilities theorists (see Gagnon and Cornelius 2000). Yet disadvantaged groups may develop 'adaptive preferences', internalizing cultural norms and social constraints (Nussbaum 2001). In this regard, capabilities theory attempts to negotiate a middle ground between objective and subjective ethical standards. Such a broad approach, however, poses measurement difficulties, as articulated by numerous scholars. The next section considers these difficulties and the ways in which capabilities theorists are overcoming them.

Methodology and measurement
How discrimination is defined has implications for how it is measured. Placing human diversity at the centre of discussions of discrimination has led scholars to reconsider how to measure discrimination and its opposite, sometimes referred to as 'equal opportunities' (Beckley 2002; Cornelius and Gagnon 2004). As noted by Beckley, 'equal capability does not produce equality of results' (2002, p. 109). Traditional methods for quantifying the

extent of discrimination and progress toward equal opportunities presume a direct connection between opportunities and outcomes. They are also premised on the assumption that all workers should be similarly positioned to take advantage of equal opportunities once they have been provided.

Conventional economic methods for documenting the existence and extent of wage discrimination derive from the assumption that market forces should produce wage relativities that can be explained by individual variations in productivity. Regression analysis, with wages (specifically, the natural log of wages) as the dependent variable, allows researchers to incorporate independent variables for as many wage determinants as possible, including measures of human capital and structural variables thought to affect productivity (such as industry, occupation and union status). These methods seek to 'explain' as much of the differential as possible with these explanatory variables.

To assess discrimination, the race and gender characteristics of interest to the researcher can be incorporated as a series of dichotomous (or dummy) variables in a regression of pooled data (that is, data on different demographic groups are combined). A second methodology, developed by Ronald Oaxaca (1973), involves separate wage regressions for groups of interest, such as men versus women. This latter method indirectly estimates the degree of discrimination as the 'unexplained' portion of the wage differential between two groups. Based on the assumption that human capital and other productivity-related variables are legitimate bases for wage differentials, Oaxaca's approach has come to be called the 'residual method' because it defines discrimination as the portion of wage differentials that is 'left over' after the best possible specification of wage determinants (see Darity and Mason 1998).

Human capital theorists have never been able to statistically explain the full wage gap using human capital variables (Darity and Mason 1998; Blau and Kahn 2000; Maume 2004). Some mainstream economists continue to escalate both the number of variables and the complexity of regression techniques to minimize the unexplained residual in order to buttress theories that discount the existence of discrimination.

Problems with these methodologies parallel problems with neoclassical definitions of discrimination. The mean values of other variables specified in the models may be affected by the feedback effects of discriminatory processes. A related problem is that the use of dummy variables implicitly conceives of race and gender as independent of other specified wage determinants. Even the dummy variables themselves are not truly independent. Discrimination experienced by women of colour is not simply additive of race and gender discrimination as separate processes. Although such multicollinearity is not technically fatal to wage regressions, the correlation among variables becomes more important if we are interested in the relative size of coefficients rather than simply their statistical significance. The extent of discrimination, rather than merely its existence, is the more economically significant measure.

Recently, efforts have been made to sketch alternative methods for evaluating the degree of inequality based on a capabilities perspective. Nussbaum (1999) pioneered these efforts when she began to develop a list of 'central human functional capabilities' that could be used to assess the status of women and disadvantaged groups. Ingrid Robeyns (2003) has sought an approach that balances context with the need to assess social justice, arguing that there needs to be agreement on the appropriate, democratic processes for determining the capabilities relevant to a particular context. For gender equality assessment, she developed a list of fourteen capabilities. Among these are 'paid work and other projects' (being able to work in the labour market or to undertake projects, including artistic ones) and 'time-autonomy' (being able to exercise autonomy in allocating time). Also relevant to the discussion at hand is the capability for 'domestic work and nonmarket care', which Robeyns defines as 'being able to raise children and to take care of others' (2003, pp. 71–2).

Cornelius and Gagnon (2004) focus more explicitly on applying capabilities theory to equal opportunities/diversity management in the workplace. They provide 'key design principles or elements' that managers should use to develop workplace inequality measures (see also Gagnon and Cornelius 2000). These innovative approaches are laying the groundwork for the development of new measures, but as yet there is no clear consensus about how to evaluate progress within the capabilities perspective. What is clear is that multiple measures, including ones that provide voice and agency for affected groups, are essential.

References

Becker, Gary S. ([1957] 1971), *The Economics of Discrimination*, Chicago, IL: University of Chicago Press.

Beckley, Harlan (2002), 'Capability as opportunity: how Amartya Sen revises equal opportunity', *Journal of Religious Ethics*, **30** (1), 107–35.

Bergmann, Barbara R. (1974), 'Occupational segregation, wages and profits when employers discriminate by race or sex', *Eastern Economic Journal*, **1** (2/3), 103–10.

Black, Sandra E. (1999), 'Investigating the link between competition and discrimination', *Monthly Labor Review*, **122** (12), 39–43.

Blau, Francine D. and Lawrence M. Kahn (2000), 'Gender differences in pay', *Journal of Economic Perspectives*, **14** (4), 75–99.

Boston, Thomas D. (1990), 'Segmented labor markets: new evidence from a study of four race-gender groups', *Industrial and Labor Relations Review*, **44** (1), 99–115.

Bruegel, Irene and Diane Perrons (1995), 'Where do the costs of unequal treatment for women fall?' *Gender, Work and Organization*, **2** (3), 110–21.

Budig, Michelle J. and Paula England (2001), 'The wage penalty for motherhood', *American Sociological Review*, **66** (2), 204–25.

Clement, Douglas (2002), 'An interview with Gary Becker', *The Region*, **16** (2), 16–25.

Cohen, Philip N. and Matt L. Huffman (2003), 'Individuals, jobs, and labor markets: the devaluation of women's work', *American Sociological Review*, **68** (3), 443–63.

Cornelius, Nelarine and Suzanne Gagnon (2004), 'Still bearing the mark of Cain? Ethics and inequality measurement', *Business Ethics: A European Review*, **13** (1), 26–40.

D'Amico, Thomas F. (1987), 'The conceit of labor market discrimination', *American Economic Review*, **77** (2), 310–15.

Darity, William A., Jr and Patrick L. Mason (1998), 'Evidence on discrimination in employment: codes of color, codes of gender', *Journal of Economic Perspectives*, **12** (2), 63–90.

Darity, William A., Jr, Patrick L. Mason and James B. Stewart (2005), 'The economics of identity: the origin and persistence of racial identity norms', *Journal of Economic Behavior & Organization*, **60** (3), 283–305.

England, Paula (1992), *Comparable Worth: Theories and Evidence*, New York: Aldine de Gruyter.

England, Paula, Michele J. Budig and Nancy Folbre (2002), 'Wages of virtue: the relative pay of care work', *Social Problems*, **49** (4), 455–73.

Figart, Deborah M. (1997), 'Gender as more than a dummy variable: feminist approaches to discrimination', *Review of Social Economy*, **55** (1), 1–32.

Figart, Deborah M. and Ellen Mutari (2004), 'Wage discrimination in context: enlarging the field of view', in Dell P. Champlin and Janet T. Knoedler (eds), *The Institutionalist Tradition in Labor Economics*, Armonk, NY: M.E. Sharpe, pp. 179–89.

Figart, Deborah M., Ellen Mutari and Marilyn Power (2002), *Living Wages, Equal Wages: Gender and Labor Market Policies in the United States*, London: Routledge.

Gagnon, Suzanne and Nelarine Cornelius (2000), 'Re-examining workplace equality: the capabilities approach', *Human Resource Management*, **10** (4), 68–88.

Kalleberg, Arne L. (2003), 'Flexible firms and labor market segmentation', *Work and Occupations*, **30** (2), 154–75.

Kennelly, Ivy (2003), '"That single-mother element": how white employers typify black women', in Ellen Mutari and Deborah M. Figart (eds), *Women and the Economy: A Reader*, Armonk, NY: M.E. Sharpe, pp. 183–98.

Kmec, Julie A. (2005), 'Setting occupational sex segregation in motion', *Work and Occupations*, **32** (3), 322–54.

Malinowski, Bronislaw (1922), 'Argonauts of the Western Pacific: An Account of Native Enterprise and Adventure in the Archipelagoes of Melanesian New Guinea', George Routledge & Sons Ltd.

Mason, Patrick L. (1995), 'Race, competition and differential wages', *Cambridge Journal of Economics*, **19** (4), 545–67.

Maume, David J., Jr (2004), 'Wage discrimination over the life course: a comparison of explanations', *Social Problems*, **51** (4), 505–27.

McCall, Leslie (2000), 'Gender and the new inequality: explaining the college/non-college wage gap', *American Sociological Review*, **65** (2), 234–55.

Myrdal, Gunnar (1944), *An American Dilemma: The Negro Problem and Modern Democracy*, New York: Harper.

Nelson, Robert L. and William Bridges (1999), *Legalizing Gender Inequality: Courts, Markets, and Unequal Pay for Women in America*, Cambridge: Cambridge University Press.

Neumark, David and Michele McLennan (1995), 'Sex discrimination and women's labor market outcomes', *Journal of Human Resources*, **30** (4), 713–40.

Nussbaum, Martha (1999), 'Women and equality: the capabilities approach', *International Labour Review*, **138** (3), 227–45.

Nussbaum, Martha C. (2001), 'Adaptive preferences and women's options', *Economics and Philosophy*, **17** (1), 67–88.

Nussbaum, Martha C. and Amartya Sen (eds) (1993), *The Quality of Life*, Oxford: Clarendon Press.

O'Neill, June (2003), 'The gender gap in wages, circa 2000', *American Economic Review*, **93** (2), 309–14.

Oaxaca, Ronald (1973), 'Male-female wage differentials in urban labor markets', *International Economic Review*, **14** (3), 693–709.

Reskin, Barbara F. and Denise D. Bielby (2005), 'A sociological perspective on gender and career outcomes', *Journal of Economics Perspectives*, **19** (1), 71–86.

Robeyns, Ingrid (2003), 'Sen's capability approach and gender inequality: selecting relevant capabilities', *Feminist Economics*, **9** (2–3), 61–92.

Robinson, Tony (2004), 'Hunger discipline and social parasites: the political economy of the living wage', *Urban Affairs Review*, **40** (2), 246–68.

Sen, Amartya (1992), *Inequality Reexamined*, New York: Russell Sage Foundation and Harvard University Press.

Shulman, Steven (1996), 'The political economy of labor market discrimination: a classroom-friendly presentation of theory', *Review of Black Political Economy*, **24** (4), 47–64.

Skuratowicz, Eva and Larry W. Hunter (2004), 'Where do women's jobs come from? Job resegregation in an American bank', *Work and Occupations*, **31** (1), 73–110.

Solberg, Eric J. (2005), 'The gender pay gap by occupation: a test of the crowding hypothesis', *Contemporary Economic Policy*, **23** (1), 129–48.

Van Staveren, Irene (2007), 'Beyond utilitarianism and deontology: ethics in economics', *Review of Political Economy*, **19** (1), 21–35.

See also the entries on: Equity; Feminism; Inequality.

14   Economic anthropology
Jeffrey H. Cohen

Economic anthropology might seem at some level an odd title for a field. Perhaps it is neither completely economic nor entirely anthropological. Certainly, economic anthropologists have been described as posers by their critics; not fully understanding the implications of economic theory nor embracing the ethnographic realities of anthropological research. Yet a second and more satisfying way to think about economic anthropology is as a field that borrows from economic theory while applying anthropological practices to understand the human dimensions of economic behaviour, this most social of processes (see Herkovits's original statement [1940] 1965).

The roots of economic anthropology, in fact, lie in bridging economic and anthropological concerns. As can be imagined, such bridge building has come with a great deal of conflict and debate concerning what constitutes 'the economy' for a given group. Debates among economic anthropologists have raged concerning how we define the economy, how we approach economic motivations and how we can best explain the social and cultural basis of economic practices.

Early work in anthropology sought to understand the economics of people who were assumed to live well outside the market systems, capitalist frameworks and rational actions that define Western economic practices. This research was informed not by concerns for economic processes, but rather by the assumption that anthropologists would encounter some form of production, systems of exchange and consumption regardless of the society or culture studied. Paul Bohannon (quoted in Dalton 1961, p. 12) described the situation as follows: 'the anthropologist is not asking the same set of questions as the economist. The business of anthropology is not economics; it is rather something we might call "ethno-economics".' In other words, anthropologists were conducting research in non-Western settings, and in those settings it was assumed anthropologists would not encounter 'economies' per se, but instead activities like production that were economic in nature – or at least in a comparative sense. That these categories fit Western concepts meant little as the anthropologists, at least at this stage, were concerned with how production, trade and consumption fit into 'the provisioning of material goods which satisfy biological and social needs' (Dalton 1961, p. 6).

This perspective is obvious in work by Bronislaw Malinowski. Working in the Trobriand Islands of Papua New Guinea in the early decades of the twentieth century, Malinowski argued that this horticultural society could not be explained using contemporary economic models (1921, 1922). An exploration of production among the Trobriand Islanders revealed that farming was not about simply producing food. Instead, farming, and most importantly yam cultivation, was linked to elaborate systems of magic and ritual and these ritual practices tied families together through kinship and marriage. The yam cultivator worked not for himself but rather grew yams to feed his sister's husband, earning his status not through an effort made for himself, but for his brother-in-law. Furthermore, he grew far more yams than could easily be consumed, and often many yams were left to rot. How could we explain such a complex and complicated system by assuming the cultivator was a 'rational actor' maximizing his utility? As Malinowski described the system and the Trobriand Islanders who were a part of it, 'we find a state of affairs where production, exchange and consumption are socially organized and regulated by custom, and where a special system of traditional economic values governs their activities and spurs them on to efforts' (Malinowski 1921, p. 15).

Similarly, and in the guise of archaeology and history, the economic anthropologist sought to understand provisioning, craft production and trade in the past and through time. Most important in this vein was the work by Karl Polanyi who defined a three-staged typology of exchange relationships that described economic development ([1944] 1957). The three stages, reciprocity, redistribution and market exchange marked not only different economic realities, in Polanyi's argument; they characterized extremely different moral universes and were associated with very different political or control structures.

The stages that Polanyi defined were associated with evolutionary changes in human social relationships. Polanyi assumed that human social relations were founded in reciprocal, symmetrical (or socially balanced) face-to-face systems. One can think here of early hominid and human bands moving about the landscape in search of food, shelter and the like. As complexity increased – and Polanyi had no doubt that human social life evolved – reciprocal relationships were replaced by redistributive ones. In parallel, the symmetrical, face-to-face systems where leadership was achieved rather than earned were replaced by asymmetrical hierarchies. Chiefdoms took the place of tribal systems and were themselves later replaced by kingdoms and empires. Finally, market systems developed and economic complexity reached its apex. Face-to-face systems disappeared to be replaced by faceless, price-driven and self-interested market behaviour, which Polanyi describes as the 'great transformation' ([1944] 1957).

Reciprocity (often framed as gift-giving, and see Mauss 1990), describes exchanges between individuals who are coequal and that take place in face-to-face settings – or what Marshall Sahlins describes as putative altruism (1972, p. 193). Perhaps more importantly, these face-to-face exchanges are conducted in the context of long-term relationships between individuals who know and trust one another. Critical too, is a sense of obligation that goes hand-in-hand with the reciprocal exchanges. Polanyi describes reciprocity as 'acts of barter . . . usually embedded in long-range relations implying trust and confidence, a situation that tends to obliterate the bilateral character [or the contractive nature] of the transaction' ([1944] 1957, p. 61). In other words, where we might expect the exchange to play into the hands of one of its participants, say as a way to maximize a less-than-advantageous hand at a metaphorical card game (see Weiner 1992), in fact, people work together and do not abuse the bonds of friendship, kinship and trust that characterize their reciprocal exchanges. They do this because they live in a face-to-face setting ruled by thick layers of social code, rules and regulation that limit the self-interested goals of 'economic man' and place an extremely high cost on the abuse of the social system. Characterized as a small-scale society with limited leadership, reciprocity was embedded in other social relationships. Polanyi describes the situation succinctly, 'the outstanding discovery of recent historical and anthropological research is that man's economy, as a rule, is submerged in his social relations' ([1944] 1957, p. 46). Thus, 'economic' relationships like reciprocity were part of a larger symmetrical system allowing human societies to interact with the natural world and each other in an honest, trusting fashion (Polanyi [1944] 1957).

Redistributive systems, like reciprocal ones, are embedded in broad social and cultural processes. In other words, like reciprocity, redistribution takes place within the context of cultural beliefs and social practices that define economic outcomes. However, where the reciprocal system is defined by symmetrical groups (sharing leadership, ownership and so forth) in the redistributive system we find centrifugal forces at work. Hierarchies exist and enable surplus to be accumulated in a central place and by a central figure (a chief or ruler, tax collectors and the like). Nevertheless, these hierarchies are not built upon the individual and his or her economic might. Rather, in the redistributive model, a central authority enacts culturally defined acts of distribution that build upon socially obligated giving by the common folk. Thus, even though the situation is hierarchical and authority is held by a limited number of centralized figures, there is no abuse as social rules and cultural norms are maintained.

The final stage in Polanyi's model of economic evolution is the rise and development of the market system. Here exchange is no longer embedded in culture, production is not defined by social rules and consumption is a personal choice rather than a group decision. In place of culturally defined and socially circumscribed action, the market is, according to Polanyi, 'directed by market prices and nothing but market prices' (ibid., p. 43). Furthermore, because the market system is tied only to price and the logic of money as a universally transferable medium, the social foundation and cultural norms that mediated economic or economic-like relationships become generally useless. In fact, Polanyi goes so far as to suggest that society is less than marginal to the market – in a market setting, social life and cultural beliefs are isolated from the market which is, itself, a self-regulating system. As Polanyi maintains, 'instead of economy being embedded in social relations, social relations are embedded in the economic system' (ibid., p. 57).

One consequence of Polanyi's model is an assumption that morality (and the pressure to act morally) declines as complexity increases from reciprocity, through redistribution and finally to the market. In fact, Polanyi is quite clear in his evaluation of the development of economics from its reciprocal roots to the current market-driven world. He states, 'Whether hailing the fact [the market] as the apex of civilization or deploring it [again the market] as a cancerous growth' the market is not natural yet the result is a 'self-regulating system of tremendous power' (ibid.).

Of course, the problem that faces us and as we now see it in economic anthropology, but also in economics in general, is that there is no evolutionary hierarchy of economic types. In other words, economic and social evolution do not follow set paths moving from a starting point in reciprocity through redistribution and finally to the market. Furthermore, the embedded quality of reciprocal relationships is not necessarily lost in the market. The social contracts and cultural beliefs that characterize reciprocity are often clearly at work in market systems. The opposite is also quite apparent, reciprocal ties are often abused and misused and that misuse can be quite calculated. Furthermore, these processes can happen in the past as well as the present. Timothy Earle's discussions of Pacific, northern European and South American economic development (2002) make this point quite clearly. There is no a priori evolutionary path that economic systems follow, and even as economic systems become more complex, it is not necessary for political systems to develop in tandem or even before the market. In other words, we should not be surprised when market ties develop directly from the social linkages that are characterized by reciprocal and redistributive relationships, and when seemingly 'primitive' organizational systems give rise to complex exchange systems (see, for example, Plattner 1989). That a relationship between a buyer and a seller is instrumental does not mean it is, by definition, void of social meaning and cultural relevance. Furthermore, long-term market relationships are often loaded with social significance and cultural meaning (Mintz 1961). Katharine N. Rankin brings this rethinking of markets to contemporary issues as she critiques neoliberal reforms in Nepal and shows that the disregard of local beliefs can and does undermine planned development (2004). Finally, we cannot forget the real and symbolic violence that can be framed in reciprocal relationships. Weiner, in her reanalysis of Malinowski's work on gifts and kula among the Trobriand Islanders clearly shows how women manipulate linkages for their benefit and short circuit recipro-cal ties for profit, even as they remain deeply committed to the importance of reciprocity in the organization of social life (1992).

Richard Wilk, in his overview of economic anthropology suggests that the debate over the moral underpinnings of economic (and therefore human behaviour) 'looks mainly at what people think and believe about the world in order to explain their actions. This perspective underlies what can be called *cultural economics*' (Wilk 1996, p. 38, italics in the original). In effect, Polanyi's argument reflects a belief that market economics (and all of its associated baggage) represents a certain kind of culture (or lack of culture) even as reciprocal and redistributive systems represent alternative systems – systems rooted in cultural beliefs and shared morality that the market lacks (see Dalton 1971).

We've moved well beyond such restricted models of the economy. It is not so simple as the statement that contemporary economic anthropology realizes the importance of cultural beliefs and social practices to economic life in general, but that such a belief in the importance of culture and social practices is balanced against the realization that for most people and through most times, we are also involved in maximizing and making (within cultural, social, political and economic boundaries) rational choices (Schneider 1974). Additionally, we also recognize the important role social relationships play in organizing economic institutions.

Perhaps as importantly, most economic anthropologists also see individuals as 'eco-nomic actors' or social actors who are involved in making choices (economic and oth-erwise) about the world around them. Or, put another way, social actors make rational decisions and maximize utility, even as that utility is defined locally. A key example comes from the work of Stephen Gudeman, who shows how cultural beliefs frame economic interpretations. He argues, 'The economy consists of two realms, which I call commu-nity and market. Both facets make up economy, for humans are motivated by social fulfilment, curiosity, and the pleasure of mastery, as well as instrumental purpose, com-petition, and the accumulations of gains' (2001, p. 1). In other words, we make the best choices we can. Profit is not always the motive, but as social actors who exist in various realms, home and the market or the private and the public, our behaviours and decisions balance needs, wants and cultural beliefs as well as social practices (see also Cancian 1992; Portes and Sensenbrenner 1993; White 1994).

Economic anthropologists are interested not only in productive relationships and how individuals engage one another but also in markets through ethnographic space and archaeological time. Economic anthropologists tend to explore three realms: production, exchange and consumption. In the past, consumption was seen as little more than an exercise in defining the subsistence strategies of a population – what Wilk (2002, p. 243) describes as a 'utilitarian theory of consumption'. A group is defined as a foraging society. Foragers are organized through reciprocity and there is little additional consumption to worry about once we understand how foraging functions. The situation was similar when anthropologists studied horticulturalists, subsistence agriculturalists and the like. To study consumption meant to study the ways in which a group organized and maintained itself over time. There was little or no concern with the social, cultural and symbolic meaning of goods (with the exception of ritual meaning) and there was even less concern with the connection of the individual to the goods consumed.

Mary Douglas's (1975) work on consumption, symbolism and society began a process that continues today and focuses on the complex nature of consumption, and the link between consumption and culture, symbolism and the individual (see Acheson 2002, p. 45). From this beginning, economic anthropologists have moved on to explore the social meaning of consumption. We focus not only on the relationships that exist between and among individuals involved in exchanges and transactions, something that Mauss recognized in his pioneering work on gift-giving (1990), but also on the cultural and social meaning of the things exchanged (Appadurai 1986, 2006). Consumption is not simply a utilitarian drive in a non-Western social group; rather it is a complex social process that is rich with cultural meaning. Furthermore, that meaning extends to the very goods that are consumed – each is rich, no matter how trite they may seem – and we can study goods from the smallest items bought and sold between friends on street corners to the largest exchanges that take place between nation-states (see, for example, Werner and Bell 2004). Karen T. Hansen's (2000) discussion of *salaula* or second-hand clothing businesses in Zambia is a fine example of such work. The consumption of second-hand clothing reflects the colonial history of Zambia and beliefs about the importance of 'fine Western clothing' and contemporary global economic relationships. As importantly, the rise of *salaula* and the arrival of economic and political reforms combined to destroy Zambia's local clothing industry. Finally, the very meaning of the clothing – goods imported from the United States – and the way those clothes are worn also has a bearing on prices, and outcomes which include symbolical organization of Zambian ideas of modernity, gender and belonging.

Economic anthropologists also continue to acknowledge and focus upon new issues as they arise. The gendered nature of economic behaviour and outcomes is one such critical area (Clark 2003). Economic anthropologists were (and remain) critical players as we focus on economic relationships that are not male, public and 'rational'. Over and over, economic anthropologists break the boundary that is often defined as separating male and female economic behaviour. The anthropologist is able to show where competition marks relationships among women, even though original analyses often assumed that all women were nominally powerless and of equal status within groups.

Economic anthropologists are also engaged in discussion of globalization, transnationalism, development and new economic institutions including anthropological analyses of stock markets, multinational corporations and the changing economic landscape of former communist countries. These avenues of research emphasize the cultural qualities of economic behaviour and the local character of social behaviour. Thus, we explore not how Western capitalist models overwhelm local systems – perhaps what economist and development specialists thought might occur following upon Rostow's conceptualization of economic growth (1960) – but instead the ways in which local systems adapt, adopt and innovate, and of course sometimes fail to cope with change. Eric Wolf, in his monumental study of this process, *Europe and the People without History*, reminds us that the process of change is not a one-way street, rather there has always been give and take as systems respond to external forces, and conquerors as well as the conquered adapt (1997).

Ecology, landscape and environment also continue to influence and guide our studies. However, where once the economic anthropologist saw the environment as a benign setting upon which humans secured a living (as foragers, horticulturalists and the like, Forde 1934), we now understand that the environment is an actor on the social and economic stages that frame human behaviour (Netting 1993). Thus, we look at how humans use the landscape but also how the landscape influences and motivates outcomes, in other words, the landscape or environment gain agency and are active in the creation of social as well as economic realities. Finally, a new area for economic anthropology is developing around experimental economics and efforts to understand how social actors negotiate reciprocal as well as self-interested motivations and to follow these processes in the real world rather than the laboratory (Ensminger 2002; Henrich et al. 2004).

There was a time, and not so long ago, when economic anthropologists were interested in production, exchange and consumption as if each were a discrete process and part of long, unchanging traditions found among non-Western and tribal people. Furthermore, these processes were unblemished by concepts like maximization and utility. Non-Western people and prehistoric groups were not interested in securing profit; rather, as Marshall Sahlins argued in *Stone Age Economics* they were motivated by having enough (1972). More did not matter, and the individual was submerged in the broader needs and necessities of the group – the band, tribe or community. Finally, there was little doubt that the people we focused on were morally complex – we might even go so far as to say, morally righteous. Of course, this morality came from putting the community before the individual and worrying about feeding the band rather than making a singular profit. Thus, in a sense, being economically isolated meant that morality was not an issue.

Today, we know the world is far more complex and that it is much harder to classify behaviours and their outcomes and it is incredibly difficult to determine the moral nature of the group let alone the individual. We know that social actors are very good at framing their behaviours (whatever they may be, and whatever their overall positive or negative impact) as not only rational, but also as socially sanctioned and culturally meaningful and typically moral. Furthermore, we are just as capable of showing that while we are moral in our behaviours, our neighbours are not. In 1992, villagers I worked with disparaged communities that were nearby, telling me that they were full of thieves and hooligans; and that I risked great violence if I left the safety of 'my' site (Cohen 1999). Of course, an anthropologist working in any of these other communities would have heard a similar story from the villages they were living in. We are quite able to moralize about the qualities of our own behaviours even as we trash our neighbours. Where does this leave us? Certainly, if economic anthropology is to be effective, maybe it is best simply to ignore the question of morality, but that seems a cop-out rather than a solution. Many economic anthropologists argue that we cannot look for morality, rather if we do our work well, morality will find us, we will hear it in the stories that are told, whether the teller is a rural peasant in Mexico, the chairperson of the board of a major corporation or something in between. In other words, our interests and our methods have shifted from categorizing economic behaviour to looking at outcomes, possibilities, contests and processes that define economic space for individual social actions as well as community, cultures and societies at large. We've also started to apply the tools of economic anthropology, tools defined in the analysis of rural, tribal peoples (those anthropological populations) in non-anthropological settings: boardrooms, stock markets and the like. Finally, we now realize that to understand the economy does not just mean we should study it, but also that we 'anthropologize' it – in other words, we look at the social and cultural basis of economic behaviour, of moral action and immoral practices.

References

Acheson, James (2002), 'Transaction cost economics: accomplishments, problems, and possibilities', in Jean Ensminger (ed.), *Theory in Economic Anthropology*, Vol. 18, Society for Economic Anthropology Monograph Series, Walnut Creek, CA: AltaMira, pp. 27–58.

Appadurai, Arjun (1986), 'Introduction: commodities and the politics of value', in Arjun Appadurai (ed.), *The Social Life of Things*, Cambridge: Cambridge University Press, pp. 3–63.

Appadurai, Arjun (2006), 'The thing itself', *Public Culture*, **18**(1), 15–21.

Cancian, Frank (1992), *The Decline of Community in Zinacantan: Economy, Public Life and Social Stratification, 1960–1987*, Stanford: Stanford University Press.

Clark, Gracia (ed.) (2003), *Gender at Work in Economic Life*, Walnut Creek, CA: AltaMira Press.

Cohen, Jeffrey H. (1999), *Cooperation and Community: Economy and Society in Oaxaca*, Austin: University of Texas Press.

Dalton, George (1961), 'Economic theory and primitive society', *American Anthropologist*, **63**(1), 1–25.

Dalton, George (1971), *Economic Anthropology and Development:Essays on Tribal and Peasant Economies*, New York: Basic Books.

Douglas, Mary (1975), *Implicit Meaning: Essays in Anthropology*, London: Routledge and Kegan Paul.

Earle, Timothy (2002), *Bronze Age Economics*, Boulder: Westview Press.

Ensminger, Jean (ed.) (2002), *Theory in Economic Anthropology*, Walnut Creek, CA: AltaMira.

Forde, C. Daryll (1934), *Habitat, Economy, and Society*, New York: E.P. Dutton.

Gudeman, Stephen (2001), *The Anthropology of Economy*, Malden, MA: Blackwell Publishers.

Hansen, Karen Tranberg (2000), *Salaula: The World of Secondhand Clothing and Zambia*, Chicago: University of Chicago Press.

Henrich, Joseph et al. (eds) (2004), *Foundations of Human Sociality: Economic Experiments and Ethnographic Evidence from Fifteen Small-Scale Societies*, Oxford: Oxford University Press.

Herskovits, Melville J. ([1940] 1965), *Economic Anthropology: The Economic Life of Primitive Peoples*, New York: W.W. Norton & Company, Inc.

Malinowski, Bronislaw (1921), 'The primitive economics of the Trobriand Islanders', *Economic Journal*, **31**(121), 1–16.

Mauss, Marcel (1990), *The Gift: The Form and Reason for Exchange in Archaic Societies*, trans. W.D. Halls, New York: WW Norton.

Netting, Robert McC. (ed.) (1993), *Smallholders, Householders: Farm Families and the Ecology of Intensive, Sustainable Agriculture*, Stanford: Stanford University Press.

Plattner, Stuart (1989), 'Introduction', Stuart Plattner (ed.), in *Economic Anthropology*, Palo Alto: Stanford University Press, pp. 1–20.

Polanyi, Karl ([1944] 1957), *The Great Transformation*, Boston, MA: Beacon Press.

Portes, Alejandro and Julia Sensenbrenner (1993), 'Embeddedness and immigration: notes on the social determinants of economic action', *American Journal of Sociology*, **98**(6), 1320–50.

Rankin, Katharine Neilson (2004), *The Cultural Politics of Markets: Economic Liberalization and Social Change in Nepal*, Toronto: University of Toronto Press.

Rostow, Walt W. (1960), *The Stages of Economic Growth*, Cambridge: Cambridge University Press.

Sahlins, Marshall David (1972), *Stone Age Economics*, Chicago: Aldine-Atherton.

Schneider, Harold K. (1974), *Economic Man: The Anthropology of Economics*, New York: Free Press.

Weiner, Annette (1992), *Inalienable Possessions: The Paradox of Keeping-While-Giving*, Berkeley: University of California Press.

Werner, Cynthia and Duran Bell (eds) (2004), *Values and Valuables: From the Sacred to the Symbolic*, Vol. 21, Society for Economic Anthropology Monograph Series, Walnut Creek, CA: AltaMira Press.

White, Jenny B. (1994), *Money Makes Us Relatives: Women's Labor in Urban Turkey*, Austin: University of Texas Press.

Wilk, Richard R. (1996), *Economies and Cultures: Foundations of Economic Anthropology*, Boulder, CO: Westview Press.

Wilk, Richard R. (2002), 'When good theories go bad: theory in economic anthropology and consumer research', in Jean Ensminger (ed.), *Theory in Economic Anthropology*, Vol. 18, Society for Economic Anthropology Monograph Series, Walnut Creek, CA: AltaMira, pp. 239–50.
Wolf, Eric R. (1997), *Europe and the People without History*, Berkeley: University of California Press.

See also the entry on: Market.

15 Efficiency
Irene van Staveren

Introduction

The dominant economic theory, neoclassical economics, employs a single economic evaluative criterion: efficiency. Moreover, it assigns this criterion a very specific meaning. Other – heterodox – schools of thought in economics tend to use more open concepts of efficiency, related to common sense understandings of cost-saving and preventing waste. Also, to assess the state of an economy, heterodox schools of thought tend to draw upon additional evaluative criteria, such as stability, equity and sustainability. Economics' widespread concern with efficiency is, of course, implied in the well-known definition of the subject as 'the study of the allocation of scarce resources to alternative ends'. Here, the aspect regarded as mattering most is simply which allocation of resources helps to achieve the most ends.

However, efficiency has not always dominated economic evaluation. For Adam Smith, a good economy was characterized not only by efficiency in exchange, but also by moral sentiments underlying the functioning of markets. A market economy, Smith argued in his *Wealth of Nations*, should combine efficiency and equity: 'It is but equity, besides, that they who feed, cloath and lodge the whole body of the people, should have such a share of the produce of their own labour as to be themselves tolerably well fed, cloathed and lodged' (Smith [1776] 1981, p. 96). John Stuart Mill considered a good economy one that provides freedom for all agents, including the socially and politically marginalized, such as women. This requires not only the negative freedom of markets, but also positive freedom, guaranteed by entitlements, such as embodied in the Poor Laws in England which Mill ([1848] 1917, pp. 754–7) defended in *Principles of Political Economy*. For Karl Marx ([1867] 1969), to mention a third classical economist, an economy that would allow exploitation of labour through unequal ownership of resources was a bad economy, because it limited the freedom of a whole class to own the product of its labour. Classical economists, hence, regarded freedom, justice and equality as equally important criteria for economic evaluation.

It was only in the twentieth century that efficiency came to dominate economic evaluation through the development of welfare economics by economists such as Arthur Pigou and Vilfredo Pareto. Welfare economics, of course, could not exist without a measure of welfare, and these thinkers opted for a utilitarian approach. The consequentialist ethics of utilitarianism is concerned with what Jeremy Bentham phrased 'the greatest happiness for the greatest number'. Today, 'Pareto efficiency' is widely used in economics. It refers to the situation in which no one can be made better off without making anyone else worse off – irrespective of who would be affected or to what extent. So, only total utility counts, not its distribution. This prohibition of interpersonal utility comparisons rules out redistribution and invokes a strong form of the liberal 'no-harm principle'; that is, any redistribution that harms at least one person is regarded as morally bad, irrespective of the good it would bring to others. Hence, Pareto efficiency is not a morally neutral criterion but expresses a strong liberal – even libertarian – ethics through the application of a strict no-harm principle towards redistribution.

Critiques of Pareto efficiency

Utilitarianism and the prohibition of interpersonal utility comparisons
As explained above, Pareto efficiency has been defined in utilitarian terms, through the development of welfare economics. Utility is a fully commensurable individual measure of well-being that assumes individuals maximize their utility by satisfying their preferences. In other words, they follow their self-interest, even when satisfying other-directed preferences: altruism exists only when it increases the utility of the altruist to a larger extent than self-directed actions would have done, with given prices and constraints. As a consequence of the entirely individualistic subjective utility space of evaluation, Pareto efficiency ignores a more social and political, or democratic, assessment of valued ends, capacities and efforts of economic agents.

So, in the widely applied criterion of Pareto efficiency, redistribution of resources is only allowed as long as it makes at least one person better off without making *anyone* else worse off. No redistribution is allowed if even one person would become worse off, regardless of whether that one person would be only a bit worse off, whereas many others would benefit. In other words, equity is portrayed as a trade-off with efficiency. The logic behind this trade-off is that if the state were to tax the income (or land or any other resource) of the rich and pass the proceeds on as a subsidy to the poor, this would create disincentives, decreasing efficiency. The rich would no longer be willing to invest to innovate and expand if the marginal benefits of that effort were taxed away. The poor, on the other hand, would no longer do their best to find employment, be entrepreneurial and work hard, because they would receive welfare support anyway. This logic clearly rests on a reductionistic view of humans as entirely self-interested with a dislike of work – indeed, the assumption of economic rationality in neoclassical economics.

Surprisingly, the subjective and individualistic straitjacket of Pareto efficiency may not actually promote the most efficient outcome for an economy. This can be explained with the help of the principle of diminishing marginal returns, which states that a last added unit generates less value than a previously added unit (of a production factor, income or consumer good). Now, applying this to total utility, it may well be that when some resources are shifted from those with low marginal utilities (generally the rich) to those with high marginal utilities (generally the poor), total utility would increase because of a more efficient resource use. The poor would benefit more from such redistribution than the rich would lose. Hence, with given resources, more total utility could be achieved. But the definition of Pareto efficiency does not allow such redistribution, even though in resource terms it would be more efficient – resulting as it does in more total utility with the same amount of resources. This leads to the conclusion that Pareto efficiency is not really about maximum efficiency, but rather about relative maximum utility, that is, total utility constrained by a strong no-harm principle. In other words, Pareto efficiency allows for the waste of resources – land, food or health care – by the affluent.

Perfect competition

The first fundamental welfare theorem holds that Pareto efficiency occurs in a situation of perfect competition. Now, perfect competition occurs in an ideal market without externalities, barriers to entry or exit or economies of scale. Obviously, real-world markets are almost never perfectly competitive. Markets often create externalities, exhibit collusion or value-chain control by firms or generate increasing returns to scale leading to monopolistic tendencies. Hence, Pareto efficiency is largely a theoretical construct with very little relation to real markets. Moreover, as Amartya Sen (1987) explained so well, in the real world, economic agents do not behave like the typical neoclassical 'rational economic man' – they do not act exclusively competitively, pursuing their own interests. Real-world economic agents also care for others and follow norms of justice, and therefore also help to further the well-being of others, sometimes even at the cost of their own well-being. Hence, as Walter Schultz (2001) recognized, economic behaviour has a morally laden interpersonal dimension which is not captured by the first fundamental welfare theorem. Agents need to have particular moral characteristics – rights and responsibilities – in order to bring about and support perfectly competitive markets. In particular, agents need to refrain from free-riding, resist blocking others from participation and not be tempted to dump external costs on third parties. Self-interest is clearly not enough for markets to flourish and efficiency to emerge.

In addition to the abovementioned assumptions about perfect competition, the one-to-one relationship between Pareto efficiency and perfect competition in the first fundamental welfare theorem builds on a hidden assumption as well. This is the limitation of efficiency to the realm of exchange, while assuming that exchange by definition is beneficial for both parties. The applicability of Pareto efficiency to other realms of the economy – such as the supply of public goods by the state or unpaid transactions within and between households – is very limited (except in the case of so-called 'market failures'). This excludes much of women's work from welfare analysis, as such work largely takes place unpaid in households, creating a gender bias in the concept of Pareto efficiency (Barker 1995). At the same time, the market-only focus of Pareto efficiency regards public goods as, at most, second-best compared to market supply. Pareto efficiency takes for granted that agents will be able to survive when exchange in perfectly competitive markets is not mutually beneficial. In other words, Pareto efficiency assumes that autarky – self-reliance – is always a feasible option, living off of one's wealth, savings, own-account production or access to commons, in cases where possible exchanges do not satisfy both parties. This is what Sen (1981) called 'trade-independent security'. Distress sales may be regarded by libertarians as voluntary in a static sense, but they undermine an agent's resource base and hence crowd out productive capacity in the long run. This is generally not efficient in a dynamic sense, making people dependent on others or the state. In the real world, without perfect markets, but with the important influence of power and uncertainty, most people who experience a disadvantaged exchange position have very few resources to live from, except their labour power. Hence, many people have no trade-independent security. Even their labour may not be in demand. Due to a lack of nutrition and health (Dasgupta 1993), one's labour may not earn sufficient market value for survival (Kurien 1996). Or a combination of factors may lead to low demand for labour, including lack of aggregate demand (Walsh 1996).

Hence, the strong no-harm principle of libertarianism benefits the status quo of the distribution of endowments, which, however, does not necessarily imply the most efficient allocation of resources from a dynamic perspective.

Compensation
The second fundamental welfare theorem, that of the Kaldor-Hicks compensation, is an addition to Pareto efficiency that allows for some form of redistribution. This is limited to a lump-sum redistribution of resources from winners (those who gain from free markets) to losers (those who, temporarily or due to exogenous shocks to the economy, do not gain from exchange), to the extent that winners keep a net advantage in order to buy the losers' cooperation, that is, their voluntary exchange. The objective of such redistribution is not so much *fairness* between winners and losers in the optimum but the *feasibility* of reaching the optimum from a political economy perspective.

Again, this theorem is an entirely theoretical construct. In the real world it is unlikely that winners will sufficiently compensate losers, because of the difference in bargaining power between the two groups. So it is unlikely that prices will change in order to seduce losers into the exchange (for example, with higher wages) or that the winners will accept a tax rise for the benefit of the losers. The existence of winners and losers in free markets itself creates a difference in bargaining power, so that the losers, without having adequate trade-independent security, are unlikely to be compensated for their cooperation with the winners.

In conclusion, these three critiques indicate that Pareto efficiency is not at all a value-neutral evaluative criterion, but one strongly intertwined with values. Pareto efficiency favours the status quo of competitive market outcomes based on given distributions, relying on a strong no-harm principle which disallows any effective form of redistribution, while measuring efficiency in total utility outcome, rather than minimum resource use, thus condoning various forms of waste.

Cost-benefit analysis
Since utility is unmeasurable, empirical welfare analysis relies on the monetary measurement of welfare levels using incomes and prices. This allows for interpersonal comparisons and, hence, for redistributions that might improve equity as well as efficiency. In practice, money-metric efficiency analysis is applied through cost-benefit analysis, which helps to evaluate the efficiency of a particular economic outcome, or to compare the efficiency of policy alternatives. A problem with shifting from subjective utility space to welfare measured in monetary terms is that estimations need to be made for costs and benefits that are not priced. This difficulty has been solved by including findings of willingness to pay surveys. Such surveys result in lists of virtual prices for non-priced resources (such as nature) and outcomes (such as a loss of social cohesion), which are then used in analyses (Zerbe 2001).

However, as a method of assessing efficiency, cost-benefit analysis has received much critique from heterodox schools of thought (see for an accessible discussion Ackerman and Heinzerling 2004). It has been viewed as having at least four shortcomings. First, income is said to be a poor indicator of well-being across different income classes. This makes it likely that the willingness to pay for particular non-priced goods will differ between classes: the poor are less able to pay but in fact may benefit more from certain policies. At the same time, the value of income to people has decreasing marginal returns, so that beyond a certain level of income, subjective well-being no longer improves with GDP growth (Easterlin 2001). Money, then, becomes a less reliable measure to assess well-being at higher levels of income. Recently, this difficulty has been addressed with happiness studies, which use surveys ranking self-reported life satisfaction (Frey and Stutzer 2002). But whereas happiness studies may fill some gaps in cost-benefit analysis, they are designed to assess people's experienced satisfactions, not their expected satisfactions, and these are still individualistic.

Second, some valued subjective goods simply cannot be measured in monetary terms and made commensurable with other valued ends, not even with willingness to pay studies. For example, some may enjoy listening to birds in a park but are unable or unwilling to attach a monetary value to this, while others' satisfaction from consumer goods increases with the knowledge that others are worse-off and declines when neighbours' consumer patterns appear more luxurious than their own. Moreover, not all possible effects of a policy can be foreseen, due to uncertainties. Even when a project is carried out as planned there are likely to remain externalities, feedback effects and lock-in situations that limit future choices. This, in the words of Richard Wolff (2004, p. 171), makes 'efficiency analysis . . . an illusion'. Others are less pessimistic, but agree that 'technical optimization is not feasible' (Alkire 2002, p. 232) because of incommensurabilities between priced and non-priced items in cost-benefit analysis.

Third, compensation is not always possible. This is obviously the case with tragic human or environmental losses or the prevention of these. For example, it is simply not possible to reduce the number of traffic deaths to zero by spending more money on traffic regulation and control. A dramatic reduction in road accidents requires not only money but also changes in behaviours and attitudes, such as no alcohol use when driving; and some traffic deaths are caused by bad luck and factors beyond our control. Moreover, some goods are priceless in a moral sense – how would one, for example, answer a question such as 'For how much would you be willing to change your religion?' The question of how much one is willing to pay for a particular outcome may not only be fictitious insofar as the payment is concerned, but also rather unrealistic in terms of the desired outcome. This puts the whole exercise on shaky ground.

Fourth, even if cost-benefit analysis is applied at the aggregate level, including a wide variety of social costs and benefits for a large group of people, its outcome may have very unequal distributional effects, as Peter Söderbaum (2004) argues. A net benefit accruing to one group may jeopardize human rights, destroy ecological values such as biodiversity, or have other irreparable consequences for another group, as is the case in the displacement of people for the building of dams. In fact, many cost-benefit analyses, in their effort to calculate net outcomes, tend to underestimate negative human impacts (Alkire 2002, p. 219).

This critique of cost-benefit analysis points to the need for other concepts of efficiency that do not regard markets and prices as neutral. Instead, an understanding of efficiency is required that does not put efficiency and equity in opposition and recognizes that efficiency cannot escape morality.

Alternative measures of efficiency

In heterodox economics, we find two approaches to alternative measures of efficiency. Neither is as well developed as Pareto efficiency, and probably never will be, as both are less formalized, more open and concerned with social as well as individual values.

One alternative is that developed in the capability approach of Amartya Sen. It shifts the evaluative space from utility to opportunity freedom, while keeping in place the consequentialist orientation and the strong no-harm principle of Paretian welfare economics. The evaluative criterion is the 'weak efficiency of opportunity-freedom' defined as follows: '[A] state of affairs is weakly efficient in terms of opportunity-freedom if there is no alternative feasible state in which everyone's opportunity-freedom is surely unworsened and at least one person's opportunity-freedom is surely expanded' (Sen 2002, p. 518). This efficiency criterion favours economic outcomes that increase the range and significance of the options available to individuals over outcomes that reduce options or increase these only for a small group. Sabina Alkire (2002) applied this efficiency notion to a micro-credit case study. She showed that loans for the poor in developing countries may improve people's options in a variety of ways, ranging from provision of more stable incomes to improved self-esteem, stronger supportive social relations and more meaningful participation in religious ceremonies. Compared to a cost-benefit analysis evaluation, which is unable to put a monetary value on some of these opportunity expansions, Alkire argues that the efficiency criterion derived from the capability approach appears better able to assess incommensurable outcomes and to value these in the project participants' own terms. The efficiency gain is not so much monetary, although the project needs to fulfil some basic financial criteria of viability, but in terms of human development. It results in the expansion of real and valued opportunities in the short run, but also in the long run, because it makes people more participatory in the economy.

The second alternative approach starts from the view that efficiency has intrinsic value. More than half a century ago, home economist Margaret Reid (1934) made this intrinsic value of efficiency explicit by redefining efficiency as the minimization of waste: first, the waste of means of production (for example, unused land owned by big landowners in the presence of landless farmers); second, inefficient production methods (for example, household production of food, whereas communal kitchens would generate economies of scale); third, production of goods that harm objective well-being (for example, growing tobacco rather than food); and fourth, when the rich consume at luxurious levels whereas the poor lack a basic standard of living (which keeps the poor below a minimally acceptable living standard and at a low level of labour productivity).

The strength of Reid's formulation of efficiency as the minimization of waste is that it goes beyond the common opposition of efficiency and equity: it points out the relationship between the two. This relationship has recently received revived attention, in particular in the literature on increasing returns (Arthur 1994). At the macro level, for example, studies show that GDP growth can benefit substantially from universal access to education for the poor, especially for girls, whose enrolment rates are much lower than those of boys in some parts of the world (Klasen 2002). At the micro level, studies show that in African farm-households redistribution of land, labour and fertilizer from men's cash crops to women's food crops increases total household output by 10 to 40 per cent (Udry et al. 1995). Finally, ecological economics also draws on the relationship between equity and efficiency. For example, it has been pointed out how much grain goes to waste in the production of meat, which results in less food available for a growing world population (Rifkin 1992). Applications of such more open and less subjective measures of efficiency make use of complex techniques, most of them multi-criteria methods, taking externalities and other feedback effects into account as well as uncertainties by applying a multiple stakeholder perspective and using the precautionary principle. Alternative approaches to efficiency thereby move away from utilitarianism and cost-benefit analysis and instead emphasize substantial well-being outcomes for the population as a whole, in a positional analysis, addressing ideological orientations, alternatives and consequences, including irreversibilities (Söderbaum 2006).

Conclusion

Efficiency is not a value-neutral evaluative criterion. In neoclassical economics, the notion of efficiency is founded upon a utilitarian ethics with a strong version of the liberal no-harm principle. Moreover, it is measured in utility space rather than resource space, so it does not guarantee minimization of waste. In heterodox economic traditions, efficiency has always been regarded as non-neutral and related to equity. Heterodox approaches recognize that equity may help to crowd in production and productivity by those who otherwise remain without resources and must depend on charity, crime or the state.

References

Ackerman, Frank and Lisa Heinzerling (2004), *Priceless: On Knowing the Price of Everything and the Value of Nothing*, New York: New Press.
Arthur, Brian (1994), *Increasing Returns and Path Dependence in the Economy*, Ann Arbor, MI: University of Michigan Press.
Alkire, Sabina (2002), *Valuing Freedoms: Sen's Capability Approach and Poverty Reduction*, Oxford: Oxford University Press.
Barker, Drucilla (1995), 'Economists, social reformers, and prophets: a feminist critique of economic efficiency', *Feminist Economics*, **3** (1), 1–51.
Dasgupta, Partha (1993), *An Inquiry into Wellbeing and Destitution*, Oxford: Clarendon Press.
Easterlin, Richard (2001), 'Income and happiness: towards a unified theory', *Economic Journal*, **111** (473), 465–84.
Frey, Bruno and Alois Stutzer (eds) (2002), *Happiness and Economics. How the Economy and Institutions Affect Well-Being*, Princeton, NJ: Princeton University Press.
Klasen, Stephan (2002), 'Low schooling for girls, slower growth for all? Cross-country evidence on the effect of gender inequality in education on economic development', *World Bank Economic Review*, **16** (3), 345–73.
Kurien, C.T. (1996), *Rethinking Economics: Reflections Based on a Study of the Indian Economy*, New Delhi: Sage.
Marx, Karl ([1867] 1969), *Capital: A Critique of Political Economy*, ed. Friedrich Engels, Hamburg: Meissner.
Mill, John Stuart ([1848] 1917), *Principles of Political Economy*, ed. W.J. Ashley, London: Longmans Green.
Mintz, Sidney (1961), 'The Question of Caribbean Peasantries: A Comment', *Caribbean Studies*, **1**, 31–34.
Reid, Margaret (1934), *Economics of Household Production*, New York/London: Wiley/Chapman & Hall.
Rifkin, Jeremy (1992), *Beyond Beef: The Rise and Fall of the Cattle Culture*, New York: Dutton.
Schultz, Walter (2001), *The Moral Conditions of Economic Efficiency*, Cambridge: Cambridge University Press.
Sen, Amartya (1981), *Poverty and Famines: An Essay on Entitlement and Deprivation*, Oxford: Clarendon Press.
Sen, Amartya (1987), *On Ethics and Economics*, Oxford: Basil Blackwell.
Sen, Amartya (2002), *Rationality and Freedom*, Cambridge, MA: The Belknap Press of Harvard University Press.
Smith, Adam ([1776] 1981), *An Inquiry into the Nature and Causes of the Wealth of Nations*, Indianapolis, IN: Liberty Fund.

Söderbaum, Peter (2004), 'Decision processes and decision-making in relation to sustainable development and democracy – where do we stand?' *Journal of Interdisciplinary Economics*, **15** (1), 41–60.

Söderbaum, Peter (2006), 'Democracy and sustainable development – what is the alternative to cost-benefit analysis?' *Integrated Environmental Assessment and Management*, **2** (92), 182–90.

Udry, Christopher, John Hoddinott, Harold Alderman and Lawrence Haddad (1995), 'Gender differentials in farm productivity: implications for household efficiency and agricultural policy', *Food Policy*, **20** (5), 407–23.

Walsh, Vivian (1996), *Rationality, Allocation, and Reproduction*, Oxford: Clarendon Press.

Wolff, Richard (2004), 'The "efficiency" illusion', in Edward Fullbrook (ed.), *A Guide to What's Wrong with Economics*, London: Anthem, pp. 169–75.

Zerbe, Richard (2001), *Economic Efficiency in Law and Economics*, Cheltenham, UK and Northampton, MA, USA: Edward Elgar.

See also the entries on: Equity; Amartya Sen; Utilitarianism.

16   Egoism
John O'Neill

The term 'egoism' is used both to refer to a theoretical claim about human dispositions and to refer to a particular human disposition itself. Egoism as a theoretical claim can take two forms – descriptive and normative. Descriptively it refers to the claim that individuals are only concerned with their own interests. Normatively it refers to the claim that they ought to be only concerned with their own interests. This normative claim can be understood as an ethical claim – that it is morally right that individuals only pursue their own interests – or as a claim about rationality – that rational individuals ought only to pursue their own interests. Egoism is also used to refer to a disposition of character rather than a doctrine. One says that a person is egoistic or that they exhibit the virtue or vice of egoism. While the theoretical doctrines will be discussed below, this chapter uses the term primarily to refer to a disposition of character. Used as such it often appears in both empirical and normative discussions of market economies. The assumption that agents in market economies are egoists, concerned only with the pursuit of their own self-interest, appears in both explanatory and normative claims about market economies. It appears in normative arguments that are critical of the scope of market economies and also in arguments in their defence.

The perfectionist argument against markets from egoism
One common argument against markets from egoism is a perfectionist argument that runs in outline as follows:

1.   Egoism is a vice of character.
2.   Markets foster egoism.
3.   Ideal economic institutions should not foster the development of the vices.
4.   Hence, markets are not ideal economic institutions.

   The practical upshot of this argument can take more or less radical forms. The less radical form is that spheres of non-market altruistic behaviour should be protected from incursions of market norms. Something like this argument is defended, for example, by Richard Titmuss in his rejection of markets in blood. In markets, individuals do not act out of concern for others, but out of self-interest. Sustaining spheres of public gift, such as that of blood donation, is a condition of sustaining social solidarity (Titmuss 1970). The more radical form is that the market should be replaced by non-market forms of economic organization that foster social ties. This position is defended by Marx in *On the Jewish Question*, where he characterizes the market as a 'sphere of egoism' (Marx 1974, p. 220) that leaves individuals alienated from their 'species-being', specifically from their nature as social beings. In political emancipation achieved through the liberal state, the individual lives a social life as a citizen in the political state, but in an illusory form. Human emancipation requires individuals to realize their social nature in their economic life (ibid., p. 236). In this view, the development of the virtues constitutive of the best life for agents requires non-market socialist institutions.

A defender of the market might respond to this argument by denying one or more of the premises. Thus, one possible response is to deny the first premise, that egoism is a vice. This response in part turns on what is meant by egoism. The term 'egoism' along with many other concepts to describe self-seeking dispositions in economic and political debates emerged relatively recently, in the mid-eighteenth century. The concepts of private and public 'interests' are older, but the use of these terms to describe economic advantage is similarly recent, emerging in the seventeenth and eighteenth centuries (Hirschman 1977, pp. 31–42).

The term 'egoism' employed in the critical sense is a successor of a number of more specific vice concepts used to describe unlimited acquisitiveness, such as *pleonexia*, greed and avarice. Eighteenth-century economic writers such as Mandeville still use specific vice terms, such as avarice (Mandeville 1988, Vol. I, pp. 25 and 100ff.) Hume often uses the term 'self-interest' interchangeably with 'avarice', 'love of gain' or avidity, 'the interested affection', most notably in *A Treatise of Human Nature*. The successful development of commercial society requires the redirection of the 'interested affection' through institutional principles for the 'stabilization' and 'transference' of property and the possibility of mutual promising through which the passion of self-interest is redirected to control itself (Hume 1978, part II, sections III–V).

However, there is another older term that is sometimes used in the same conceptual space as egoism but which is more ambivalent, that is 'self-love'. Classical philosophical and biblical texts use the concept of self-love in both a narrow negative sense and a wide non-negative sense. Aristotle, for example, claims that while the term can be used describe the narrow pursuit of 'the biggest share of money, honours and bodily pleasures', and is commonly thus understood, proper self-love involves an appropriate conception of the goods of life and as such incorporates wider attachments to others: the virtuous are proper self-lovers (Aristotle 1985, IX). In biblical texts, the concept is sometimes used in a narrow negative sense to describe vices of character – such as covetousness and pride (Timothy 2:3) – and sometimes in a neutral or positive sense, most notably in the commandment 'love thy neighbour as thyself' (Leviticus 19:18; Matthew 19:19, 22:39). The distinction between different senses of self-love is stated with clarity by Aquinas: 'Love of self is common to all in one way; in another way it is proper to the good; in a third way it is proper to the wicked' (Aquinas 1952, II.II.25.7). The first refers to the desire for self-preservation, the second to self-love founded upon a proper conception of what it is to flourish as a human being, the third to self-love founded upon a misconception of human flourishing involving the pursuit of a narrow set of goods. On this account the proper response to the egoist understood as a self-lover in the third sense is that he has misidentified the goods of life.

Some eighteenth-century writers draw a related contrast between 'immoderate' or 'excessive' self-love and 'reasonable' self-love (Butler 1983, II.9). This distinction is central to Butler's apparently paradoxical point that it is not in a person's interests to be motivated by the excessive pursuit of self-interest. 'Immoderate self love does very ill consult its own interests; and how much soever a paradox it should appear, it is certainly true that even from self-love we should endeavour to get over all inordinate regard to and consideration of ourselves' (Butler 1983, IV.8). The paradox allows Butler to conclude that benevolence, acting for the good of others, is not contrary to self-love: 'there is no peculiar contrariety between self-love and benevolence, no greater competition between these than between any other particular affections and self-love' (ibid., IV.12). Implicit in the last remark is a more general point that self-love is a second-order affection that presupposes more specific passions and interests to give it content:

> The very idea of an interested pursuit necessarily presupposes particular passions or appetites; since the very idea of interest or happiness consists in this, that an appetite or affection enjoys its object. It is not because we love ourselves that we find delight in such and such objects, but because we have particular affections towards them. Take away these affections, and you leave self-love absolutely nothing at all to employ itself about. (ibid., Preface.37)

A similar distinction between the different senses of 'self-love' is also to be found in Hume's *Enquiries*. Thus he notes that it is improperly used in a narrow sense: 'Avarice, ambition, vanity and all passions vulgarly, though improperly, comprised under the denomination of *self-love*' (Hume 1975, p. 221). In contrast to that account, Hume echoes Butler's claim that self-love in its proper sense is a second-order affection that is parasitic on first-order passions (Hume 1975, pp. 253–4).

To the extent that egoism is a counterpart of self-love, the question of whether egoism is a vice in part turns on which sense the term is being employed. Consider, for example, Smith's much-quoted passage:

> It is not from the benevolence of the butcher, the brewer, or the baker that we expect our dinner, but from their regard to their own interest. We address ourselves, not to their humanity but to their self-love, and never talk to them of our own necessities but of their advantages. (Smith 1981, I.II.2)

The term self-love in the passage is open to both narrow and broad interpretations. In the narrow sense, it is a claim that agents are moved by concern for the accumulation of some narrow range of goods, say 'the biggest share of money'. Particular vice terms such as 'avarice' or 'the love of lucre' could replace the term 'self-love'. In the broader sense, it is to say that we address others as independent individuals with their own projects. The claim interpreted in the narrow sense does portray commercial society as a sphere that fosters a particular set of vices. In the broader sense, which is closer to Smith's use of the term, it need not have that implication. The first premise of the argument from egoism against markets employs the concept of egoism to refer to self-love in the narrower sense. This is the sense in which critics of commercial society such as Marx and Titmuss use the term. A central question will then be the empirical one of whether markets do foster egoism in this sense.

Thus, a second possible response to the argument against markets from egoism is to reject the second premise, that egoistic behaviour is fostered by markets. There are at least two ways this argument could run. One found in much economic theory is to appeal to egoism as a theoretical claim. Egoism is a universal disposition of human beings that is to be found in all societies. The explanatory story should run not in terms of market institutions fostering egoism, but rather in the opposite direction. The development of institutions such as markets is to be explained in terms of the behaviour of rational agents who have a prior disposition to maximize their expected utility. Given that humans are self-interested, the normative argument should also run in the opposite direction: market institutions best realize the satisfaction of human well-being, because they run with the grain of basic human motivations. This argument is examined in more detail below. A second form that an argument against the claim that markets foster egoism might take is to accept that institutions do play some part in explaining human motivations, but to claim that the standard story of markets promoting egoism in the sense in which it is a vice is false. It might be argued that markets suitably constrained and designed can have the opposite effect of civilizing human agents, developing independence and conditions of mutual trust and respect between agents. The argument between the critics and defenders of market institutions again turns on an empirical question of the kinds of character that are in fact fostered by market economies.

A third response is to reject the third, perfectionist, premise. It is not part of the purpose of market institutions to foster virtues and eliminate vices of character. To assume that markets should have that purpose relies upon a particular conception of the good, and liberal economic institutions should be neutral between different conceptions of the good. The arguments between perfectionists and defenders of liberal neutrality are discussed elsewhere in this volume (see the chapter on the market). However, one response might be to shift the argument into non-perfectionist territory by reformulating it in terms of the conditions for justice rather than the human good. The argument might run as follows:

1. Egoistic behaviour is incompatible with respect for justice.
2. Markets promote egoistic behaviour.
3. Hence, markets promote unjust behaviour.

The practical conclusion again could be more radical – arguing for a different economic system founded on justice – or less radical, for example, defending constraints on free market activity to render it consistent with a just distribution of goods.

Another response is to accept the perfectionism of the third premise, but to claim that the standards of an ideal institution are set too high. Thus, one might accept that markets can corrupt the character in fostering a form of egoism, but allow that the moral loss is defensible in terms of other goods that follow, be this the development of other virtues, such as independence and autonomy, or other goods, such as the general improvements of welfare. For example, classical economists like Smith held that while the motivations that moved commercial society might corrupt the character, they had indirect beneficial consequences. Smith's invisible hand appears in *The Theory of Moral Sentiments* to refer to the indirect link between the 'selfishness and rapacity' of the rich in their pursuit of 'vain and insatiable desires' and the advancement in the 'interest of society' (Smith 1982, IV.1.10). Desires founded in self-deception promote activity 'to cultivate the ground, to build houses, to found cities and commonwealth, and to invent and improve all the sciences and arts which ennoble and embellish human life' (ibid.) Such invisible hand arguments have been central to arguments for market economies from egoism. How far they are true is an empirical question. What they do entail is the existence of a systemic tension within commercial society, between forces that move accumulation and any beneficial consequences that might flow from it (O'Neill 1998, Ch. 4).

The argument for markets from self-interest
Arguments from egoism have been central not only to critics of market economies, but also to their defenders. The market economy, it is claimed, runs with the grain of human nature. It is able to motivate individuals who are egoistic. Since markets run with the

grain of human nature, they produce outcomes that could be defended from the stand-point of the impartial altruist. As Arrow and Hahn put it:

> There is by now a large and fairly imposing line of economists from Adam Smith to the present who have sought to show that a decentralised economy motivated by self interest and guided by price signals would be compatible with a coherent disposition of economic resources that could be regarded, in a well defined sense, as superior to a large class of possible alternative dispositions. (1971, pp. vi–vii)

In contrast, alternative arrangements of the kind that socialists have traditionally defended are said to make unrealistic demands on the altruism of agents, requiring unre-alistically self-sacrificial behaviour on the part of individuals. The consequence is that they fail to meet the needs and aspirations of individuals.

These arguments start from assumptions of egoism understood as a theoretical claim. There are at least two versions of those assumptions. The first is an empirical claim about the nature of human motivation:

1a. Humans are by nature self-interested.

The second is a normative claim about what is required by rational agents:

1b. All rational agents are self-interested.

Given either premise the argument would then run in outline as follows:

2.   Markets are able to motivate and coordinate the actions of self-interested agents in ways that produce better outcomes than any alternative economic arrangement.
3.   Hence, markets are better economic arrangements than any alternative.

The second premise of this argument takes us into large questions in economic theory that are beyond the scope of this chapter. Here, we focus instead on the two versions of the first premise.

Why might someone believe either version of the first premise? One common argument for (1a) appeals to Darwinian theory and the limits of biological altruism, where biological altruism refers to behaviour that benefits the reproductive success of others at the cost of an organism's own reproductive success. However any such argument faces at least two difficulties. First, Darwinian theory is consistent with some forms of biological altruism, such as kin altruism. Second, the appeal to evolutionary theory in support of (1a) depends on an unsupported inference from the limits of biological altruism to the limits of psychological altruism, where psychological altruism refers to behaviour that aims at improving the welfare of others. There is no reason to assume that psychological altruism undermines reproductive success, or that psychological egoism improves repro-ductive success. The concepts of biological and psychological altruism thus need to be kept distinct (Sober 1994).

The assumption (1b) that egoism is a requirement of rationality is sometimes taken to be a starting point of economic theory. Rational agents will aim to maximize their expected utility. However, whatever the defensibility of this claim, it does not commit one to the assumption that the agent is an egoist who acts out of self-interest. The assumption merely amounts to the claim that the agent is concerned with maximizing the satisfaction of a set of consistent preferences under the constraint of a finite budget. Merely acting consistently from one's own preferences does not entail that one is acting only to satisfy one's own interest. It all depends what preferences an agent has: 'The postulate that an agent is characterized by preferences rules out neither the saint nor Genghis Kahn' (Hahn and Hollis 1979, p. 4). To claim a person is an egoist one needs to make a set of assumptions about the narrowly constrained nature of the agent's utility function.

There is an old, still widespread argument for the claim that egoism is necessarily built into the structure of behaviour of agents who pursue what they value. Here is a hedonistic version of the argument. Suppose someone values something for impersonal reasons and hence apparently acts towards it in a disinterested, selfless fashion:

1. If something is of value for someone, that person will find satisfaction in treating it in the appropriate way.
2. Satisfaction is a form of pleasure.
3. Hence, if something has value for someone, that person will gain pleasure from treating it in the appropriate way.
4. Hence, when the person treats the object in the appropriate way, the person's aim was pleasure.
5. Hence, the valued object is really only a means to a selfish end – to gain personal pleasure.

The argument is often taken to be illustrated by Hobbes's reported response to a challenge as to why he was so generous to 'a poor and infirm old man [who] craved his alms'. Hobbes is reputed to have answered, 'Because . . . I was in pain to consider the miserable condition of the old man; and now my alms, giving him some relief, doth also ease me' (Aubrey 1949).

The argument is fallacious: (4) does not follow from (3). That you gain pleasure from something does not entail that it is only a means to pleasure. When you act generously to someone you care for, what you value is the other person. The fact that you gain pleasure from so acting only shows how much you care for that person. The point is made pithily by Hume:

> [T]hey found, that every act of virtue or friendship was attended by a secret pleasure; whence they concluded, that friendship and virtue could not be disinterested. But the fallacy is obvious. The virtuous sentiment or passion produces the pleasure, and does not arise from it. I feel a pleasure in doing good to my friend, because I love him; but do not love him for the sake of that pleasure. (Hume 1985a, pp. 85–6)

Criticism of attempts to reduce all other-regarding preferences to a concern for one's own well-being has been developed more recently by Sen who draws a distinction between sympathy and commitment. One acts from sympathy when concern for another directly affects one's own well-being, and one acts out of that concern as a means of improving one's own well-being. Like Hobbes before the beggar, one contributes to the well-being of others to ease one's own distress: 'behavior based on sympathy is in an important sense egoistic, for one is oneself pleased at others' pleasure and pained at others' pain, and the pursuit of one's own utility may thus be helped by sympathetic action' (Sen 1979, p. 95). One acts from commitment when one acts out of concern for others for reasons of principle or duty, such that, even if so acting improves one's own well-being, this is not the reason for the choice: 'one acts on the basis of concern for duty which, if violated could cause remorse, but the action is really chosen out of the sense of duty rather than just to avoid the illfare resulting from the remorse that would occur if one were to act otherwise' (Sen 1979, p. 96). Sen's distinction opens space for rational non-egoistic behaviour. However, it is not clear that this formulation of the distinction opens it quite enough. It appears to fail to leave space for non-egoistic concern for others that is not based on duty or principle, space of the kind that Hume's criticism of egoism inhabits. If I do good for friends, I do not act from duty but from direct concern for another. Their interests become my own.

Institutions and the scope of egoism

In the explanation of market behaviour, economic theory often assumes a more narrowly constrained utility function according to which individuals pursue preferences for an ever-increasing bundle of commodities. Two questions might be raised about this assumption. The first is how far it does capture the behaviour of actors in markets. The second is whether the assumption is confined to the behaviour of actors in markets. The first as we noted above is an empirical question. A negative answer to the second question forms the starting point of standard public choice theory. If it is true that individuals act as rational self-interested agents in the marketplace, 'the inference should be that they will also act similarly in other and nonmarket behavioral settings' (Buchanan 1972, p. 22). In principle, the assumption applies in any social setting, be it politics, the family, science, universities or any other association, although it is in the sphere of politics that it is most normally applied: we should reject 'the conventional wisdom which holds that the market is made up of private citizens trying to benefit themselves, but that government is concerned with something called the public interest' (Tullock 1970, p. v).

However, there are good reasons to be sceptical of the claim that an agent's utility function is constant across different institutional settings. Different institutions define agents' interests in different ways. As classical economists recognized, the very development of market motivations can be undermined by the dominance of non-market institutional forms. Hume, for example, notes that commerce is 'apt to decay in absolute governments . . . because it is less *honourable*' (Hume 1985b, p. 93). In societies where honours, 'birth, titles and place', are defined as the object of one's interest, 'traders will be tempted to throw up their commerce, in order to purchase some of those employments, to which privileges and honours are annexed' (Hume 1985b, p. 93).

Conversely, one argument for market boundaries is that the conception of self-interest fostered by markets undermines the systems of rewards that define what it is to do well in non-market spheres. Individuals can have distinct interests under different descriptions in different institutional settings – for example, as a scientist or a parent. If markets foster egoism, it is in virtue of defining an individual's interests in a particularly narrow fashion in terms of the acquisition of an increasing bundle of commodities. Where market mechanisms enter non-market spheres the pursuit of goods outside this narrow range is institutionally defined as an act of altruism (O'Neill 1998, Chs 11–12). The assumption that egoism, in the sense of the love of gain, is universal in all institutional settings is false.

References

Aquinas, Thomas (1952), *Summa Theologica*, Chicago, IL: William Benton.
Aristotle (1985), *Nicomachean Ethics*, trans. Terence Irwin, Indianapolis, IN: Hackett Publishing Company.
Arrow, Kenneth J. and Frank Hahn (1971), *General Competitive Analysis*, San Francisco, CA: Holden-Day.
Aubrey, John (1949), 'A brief life of Thomas Hobbes, 1588–1679', in *Brief Lives*, London: Secker and Warburg.
Buchanan, James M. (1972), 'Towards analysis of closed behavioural systems', in James M. Buchanan and Robert D. Tollison (eds), *Theory of Public Choice*, Ann Arbor, MI: University of Michigan Press.
Butler, Joseph (1983), *Five Sermons Preached at the Rolls Chapel*, ed. Stephen Darwell, Indianapolis, IN: Hackett Publishing Company.
Hahn, Frank and Martin Hollis (eds) (1979), *Philosophy and Economic Theory*, Oxford: Oxford University Press.
Hirschman, A.O. (1977), *The Passions and the Interests*, Princeton, NJ: Princeton University Press.
Hume, David (1975), *Enquiries Concerning Human Understanding and Concerning the Principles of Morals*, Oxford: Clarendon Press.
Hume, David (1978), *A Treatise of Human Nature*, Oxford: Clarendon Press.
Hume, David (1985a), 'Of the dignity or meanness of human nature', in *Essays Moral, Political, and Literary*, Indianapolis, IL: Liberty Press.
Hume, David (1985b), 'Of civil liberty', in *Essays, Moral, Political, and Literary*, Indianapolis, IL: Liberty Press.
Mandeville, Bernard (1988), *The Fable of the Bees or Private Vice, Publick Benefits*, Indianapolis, IL: Liberty Press.
Marx, Karl (1974), *On the Jewish Question*, in *Early Writing*, ed. Lucio Colletti, Harmondsworth: Penguin.
O'Neill, John (1998), *The Market: Ethics, Information and Politics*, London: Routledge.
Sen, Amartya (1979), 'Rational fools', in Frank Hahn and Martin Hollis (eds), *Philosophy and Economic Theory*, Oxford: Oxford University Press, pp. 87–109.
Smith, Adam (1981), *An Inquiry into the Nature and Causes of the Wealth of Nations*, Indianapolis, IL: Liberty Press.
Smith, Adam (1982), *The Theory of Moral Sentiments*, Indianapolis, IL: Liberty Press.
Sober, Elliot (1994), 'Did evolution make us psychological egoists?' in *From a Biological Point of View*, Cambridge: Cambridge University Press.
Titmuss, Richard M. (1970), *The Gift Relationship*, London: Allen and Unwin.
Tullock, Gordon (1970), *Private Wants, Public Means*, New York: Basic Books.

See also the entries on: Altruism; Homo economicus; Market; Scarcity; Self-interest.

17   Epistemology
Edward Fullbrook

Empiricism and ethics

In the social sciences, economics especially, epistemology and ethics are inextricably linked. Within any science, different perspectives on a particular field may suggest different possibilities for human intervention in that field; or they might suggest the same interventions but evaluate them differently. In the social sciences these possibilities relate directly to the human realm and so inevitably pertain to ethical and political judgements. Historically, economists have glossed over this interdependence between their epistemological choices and ramifications for ethical issues.

One can regard economics as a science in a post-Enlightenment sense only to the extent that it is grounded on an empirical epistemology. Empiricism, in the broadest sense, is the idea that experience is fundamental to our knowledge of the world. Unlike rationalism, empiricism exhibits caution regarding claims to knowledge. It refuses notions of privileged access to the world. Instead, it recognizes the eccentricity and incompleteness of all perspectives, and therefore discrepancies between conceptions of things and the things themselves. In lieu of appeals to authority, empiricism democratizes science by making the replication of observations carried out from the same cognitive perspective but by different individuals the criterion of authentic science.

One consequence, often overlooked, of this epistemology is that it relativizes knowledge to the kinds of experiences we have. Experience-based knowledge depends not only on the object of inquiry but also on the *cognitive perspective* (questions asked, criteria for selecting facts, conceptual categories, framework of analysis and so on) that the inquirer brings to the task. Knowledge arrived at empirically emerges as an entanglement of two sources of inputs, one from the world, be it natural or social, and another from the inquirer.

Human subjectivity does not dissolve when one moves from being a consumer to thinking about and observing the world, not even when thinking about and observing economies. The subjectivity of the human mind is an irreducible feature of reality. Nowhere is this more in evidence than in the practice of empiricism. The problem or question selected for investigation is always someone's problem, whose 'facts' are always a selection from experience, that are then organized into various selected conceptual categories, and which are then subjected to a selected framework of analysis. Inevitably, each of these four selection stages involves value choices influenced by the social context of the selection processes, such as the known predilections of a PhD examining committee, and by the desires and the social, personal and intellectual characteristics of those making the choices.

The significant elements of cognitive perspectives are diverse and open to various combinations, each offering a particular viewpoint on the field of inquiry. By the very nature of scientific practice, scientists utilizing the same cognitive perspective in a field come to see themselves as a group with group interests. If relatively strong in number, such a group may become inclined to promote itself by discouraging or even stopping empirical inquiry in its field from cognitive perspectives, especially promising ones, other than its own. Such a state of affairs constitutes a *degenerate empiricism*, as it wishes to limit inquiry to a single vantage point, thereby holding back the advancement of knowledge.

Degenerate empiricisms are more likely to emerge and persist in the social sciences than in the natural sciences. This tendency exists because, as noted, the possibilities brought to light by the social sciences pertain directly to the human realm and so inevitably suggest or call for the making of ethical and political judgements. Making them would be difficult even if everyone brought the same system of values to bear on the possibilities. But they do not, and so some people will wish to highlight some possibilities and to obscure others. This creates a strong additional source of motivation for restricting empirical inquiry. Individuals both in and out of a science may become ethical or political partisans of the implications suggested by one cognitive perspective and so promote it by blocking the use of others. Let us explore these ideas in more detail.

In considering cognitive perspectives it helps to highlight the difference between those which are incompatible and those which are merely non-equivalent. Harvard philosopher Hilary Putnam (2004, pp. 48–9) explains the difference:

> But the fact that the contents of a room may be partly described in the terminology of fields and particles and the fact that it may be partly described by saying that there is a chair in front of a desk are not in any way 'incompatible,' not even 'at face value': the statements 'the room may be partly described by saying there is a chair in front of a desk' and 'the room may be partly described as consisting of fields and particles' don't even *sound* 'incompatible.' And they are not cognitively equivalent (even if we do not bar the fantastic possibility of defining terms like 'desk' and 'table' in the language of fundamental physics, the field-particle description contains a great deal of information that is not translatable into the language of desks and chairs). That we can use both these schemes without being required to reduce one or both of them to some single fundamental and universal ontology is the doctrine of pluralism.

Epistemology in the natural sciences

The key adjective in the above is 'partly'. Because any cognitive perspective can only partly describe an object, a non-degenerate empiricism prefers two perspectives to one when they are compatible but not equivalent. Sometimes scientists may prefer to keep two even when they are incompatible. Twentieth-century and contemporary physics is a paragon example. To describe the fundamentals of the physical universe it deploys two cognitive perspectives which are fundamentally incompatible (Bohm 1983, p. 176):

- General relativity conceives of space and time as continuous; quantum theory conceives of them as discontinuous.
- General relativity conceives of matter as particulate; quantum theory conceives of it as a wave-particle duality.
- General relativity conceives of physical objects as having actual properties; quantum theory describes them as having only potential properties within the given physical situation.
- General relativity conceives all physical reality as determinate and all events as in principle having a causal explanation; quantum theory admits indeterminacy and events incapable of causal explanation.

Some physicists, Einstein most famously, have held out the hope of someday reconciling the two perspectives. However, no physicist of note, least of all Einstein, who was a founder of both approaches, has suggested that the use of either (including the technologies that it has made possible) should be curtailed pending such reconciliation. On the contrary, in the main the empiricism of physics is resolutely non-degenerate, meaning that it accepts descriptions from more than one cognitive perspective as long as their observations meet the replication criterion. Physicist David Bohm provides a further elaboration of the doctrine of pluralism defined by Putnam above:

> What is called for is not an *integration* of thought, or a kind of imposed unity, for any such imposed point of view would itself be merely another fragment. Rather, all our different ways of thinking are to be considered as different ways of looking at the one reality, each with some domain in which it is clear and adequate. One may indeed compare a theory to a particular view of some object. Each view gives an appearance of the object in some aspect. The whole object is not perceived in any one view but, rather, it is grasped only *implicitly* as that single reality which is shown in all these views. When we deeply understand that our theories also work in this way, then we will not fall into the habit of seeing reality and acting toward it as if it were constituted of separately existent fragments corresponding to how it appears in our thought and in our imagination when we take our theories to be 'direct descriptions of reality as it is'. (Bohm 1983, pp. 7–8)

The story in economics could not be more different. Historically economists investigating the economics realm from different cognitive perspectives have regarded one another at the very least as rivals and usually as enemies. This is reflected in the custom among economists of referring to pursuits for economic knowledge from different perspectives not as 'fields' which complement each other, but as 'schools' which do battle against one another. This comes about partly because economists generally are in denial about the partiality of their vision of economic reality, and partly and more importantly because, as noted above, in economics different epistemological choices suggest different ethical/political choices, and the latter are allowed to determine the former.

Epistemology and ethics in economics

There are two ways in which the interdependence between epistemology and ethics in economics may come about. The individual economist may in the first instance already adhere to a particular set of ethical or political beliefs and choose the cognitive perspective (that is, the school) that lends support to it. Or indoctrination in a particular school may lead the economist to adopt the ethical perspective that it suggests with the result being that he or she comes to disdain attempts to advance economic knowledge from other cognitive perspectives.

Economics' predilection for choosing emotive and normative words, such as 'rationality', 'choice', 'freedom', 'equity' and 'efficiency', to designate its concepts actively encourages the conflation of epistemological and ethical choices. But more fundamental is that the intrinsic interchange between epistemology and ethics in the human sciences makes it extremely difficult at the analytical level to maintain the distinction between fact and value.

For example, neoclassical economics, especially in its more formalistic forms, is founded on the strictly normative idea that an optimum or preferred state is always a maximum or a minimum. Seldom is it presented in the classroom as such. But this omission may be due to ignorance more often than to ethical failure. Genuine confusion here emerges easily because of the collective unawareness of the fact that in the social sciences epistemological choices suggest ethical ones. A look at the maximum/minimum analytical framework illustrates the point.

With the advent of Samuelson's tautological concept of revealed preferences, neoclassical economics tried to unhook itself from utilitarianism so as to champion itself as value-free. Even if our age is less credulous of such claims, it remains easy to miss the primary source of the implicit value structure. Although many neoclassicalists dispensed with the cardinal utility concept, their analysis remained wedded to the same notion of optimum (and equilibrium and methodological individualism) because that was the only one their maxima/minima calculus, borrowed from classical mechanics, permitted. In the context of physical bodies, that calculus is ethically neutral, but when applied to human affairs and when the value-laden word 'optimum' is attached to those maxima and minima, the calculus becomes ethically charged.

Even so, this need not create a problem. One can dream of the day when economists, like physicists, refuse to indulge degenerate empiricism. If other (non-neoclassical) cognitive frameworks were presented and some of the possibilities that they outlined were acknowledged as alternatives to the neoclassical 'optimums', so that facts (for example, maximums) were distinguished from preferred states (for example, neoclassical optimums), then the conflation between fact and value, now endemic, would be much less likely to result. This example illustrates the general case: without pluralism it is impossible for economics to maintain the distinction between fact and value.

Of course the conflation of fact and value that takes place under degenerate empiricism in the social sciences is not always inadvertent. Sometimes, when the ethos permits, it results from a more deliberate use of language and so raises ethical questions on a more personal but nonetheless epistemological level. But whether accidental or deliberate, merging the ethical and epistemological dimensions of a body of knowledge generated by a degenerate empiricism is the standard recipe for making an ideology. In economics any cognitive perspective could be used to this end and many have, some notoriously, like Marxist economics in the past and neoclassical economics today (Fullbrook 2005). Because of the latter's current stranglehold on the economics profession, it makes sense to turn to it for examples of degenerate practice. I will consider four.

Rational choice
The Newtonian metaphysics of neoclassical economics if known would embarrass many partisans of liberal democracy. Like Newton's, the neoclassical model presumes determinacy. This requires that the properties of its determinants be fixed. In both theories the determinants are individuals, in Newton's case bodies and in neoclassical economics persons. Obviously this condition is inconsistent with freedom of choice. This does not necessarily obviate the usefulness of this cognitive approach in economics if practised non-degenerately. But when the approach mutates into an ideology, this attribute becomes a serious liability and so requires concealment.

For this concealment, neoclassical economics has invented an elaborate rhetorical device. Conjoining two emotive words, it coined the term 'rational choice' to refer to a situation in which its model precludes the possibility of choice. 'Rationality' means that an agent's 'choices' are in conformity with an ordering or scale of preferences. The 'rational' agent is required to 'choose' among the alternatives available that option which is highest-ranking. 'Rational behaviour' here means behaviour in accordance with some prior ordering of alternatives in terms of relative desirability.

For this approach to have any predictive power, it must be assumed that the preferences do not change during the period of time being considered. So the basic condition of neoclassical rationality is that individuals must *forgo* choice in favour of some past reckoning, thereafter acting as automata.

This conceptual elimination of freedom of choice, in both its everyday and philosophical meanings, gives neoclassical theory the hypothetical determinacy that its Newtonian inspired metaphysics require. No indeterminacy; no choice. No determinacy; no neoclassical model. The neoclassical contrivance of 'rational choice' is an example, an extreme one admittedly, of what can happen when in the social sciences a cognitive perspective becomes degenerate.

Efficiency
Like rationality, nearly everyone considers 'efficiency' a good idea. It is hard to imagine a more value-laden word. This makes the word attractive to many economists, especially when addressing the public. Yet the meaning of 'efficiency' always depends on what one chooses to count. Members of the public are inclined to believe that economists use the word to mean approximately what they themselves construe. This is seldom the case. For example, suppose five firms all manage to lower by the same amounts the production cost and selling price of a standard product that they all produce. One does it by cutting its workers' pay, another by working employees longer hours, another by getting materials at lower prices from a poorer country, another by replacing some of its workers with robots and another by inventing machinery improvements that allow it to cut work hours with no loss of output, profit, jobs or pay. Are all of these changes equally efficient (or inefficient)? A neoclassical economist would answer yes, because the five firms all end up producing the same product at the same cost and selling it at the same price. For them that is all that matters.

Market
In neoclassical economics the term 'market' is habitually used, sometimes in the same sentence, often in the same paragraph, to signify both a brute fact (as in 'the Chinese market for mobile phones') and a normative and hence ethical idea as when a government is said to interfere with 'the market's free operation' or 'the market is distorted and its prices artificial'. This rhetorical bridging of the is/ought divide is a powerful device, be it intentional or not, for ideological indoctrination. Do economists, especially those who teach, have an ethical obligation to avoid encouraging such conflations between facts and their ethical values?

Economic growth
Like the term 'market', the neoclassical mainstream uses the term 'economic growth' in both a factual and a normative sense, so the one meaning has come to infer the other. It presumes that 'economic growth' always represents a good thing. The mainstream defines the term precisely, it being any increase in a country's gross or net national product. Yet the implications of this definition are seldom apparent, as a few examples illustrate.

If a family decides to forgo home-cooked meals in favour of more expensive fast-food ones, their additional expenditure counts as economic growth. If parents decide to pay for a nursery to care for their children instead of continuing to do so themselves, the amount they pay for the care counts as economic growth. Even more worrying, social breakdown, epidemics and pollution are treated as engines of 'economic growth'. Social breakdown leads to increased expenditures for prisons, police and alarm systems. Epidemics result in increased expenditure for medicines and stays in hospitals. Pollution and congestion lead to huge expenditures to escape them, for example, commuting from the suburbs, double glazing and air-conditioning. All of these phenomena, which most ethical systems would deplore, contribute significantly to economic growth as defined by the neoclassical mainstream, which holds it to be a good thing.

Expenditure incurred in repairing environmental damage caused by human activity is what ecologists call 'defensive expenditure'. Jean Gadrey explains how the ecological economist, beginning from a different epistemological position, casts these expenditures in another ethical light, from an ecological perspective:

> [E]xpenditure (and the corresponding output) incurred in repairing the damage caused by human actions should not be counted as a positive contribution to 'real' wealth. If such damage (pollution, crime, road accidents, etc.) reduces well-being and makes it necessary to produce goods and services (whose value is X) in order to repair or defend, there can be no question of X being counted as a positive item in any measurement of 'real' wealth. And since the conventional measure of GDP counts the defensive output X as a positive item, which is acceptable from a purely economic perspective, X must be deducted from GDP in order better to identify 'real' wealth (that which contributes to well-being). (Gadrey 2004, pp. 265–6)

Conclusion

Of course the suggestion here is not that neoclassical economists favour social breakdown, epidemics and pollution. Rather, these are illustrations of how in the social sciences cognitive perspectives, quite innocent in and of themselves, can lead, intended or otherwise, to ethical positions. Each of the four examples has an epistemological dimension and an ethical one. But when the knowledge base from which the ethical discussions take place is tightly controlled, the outcomes of those discussions are in effect prearranged. This is a standard tactic of ideologies in general and of neoclassical economics in particular. By refusing to recognize the legitimacy of economic knowledge coming from cognitive perspectives other than its own, neoclassical economics forces ethical questions into a framework of controlled ignorance and thereby predetermines their 'answers'.

In economics, no less than in other fields, empiricism offers the possibility of making different epistemological choices when approaching an object of inquiry. Because each approach views the economic realm from a different perspective (areas of interest, procedures of observation, categories of facts and analytical frameworks) they create different representations of the economy, all of them partial, some or all of them useful and each egregiously inaccurate if it categorically denies the legitimacy of other representations. This by itself would be bad enough. But in economics, as in other social sciences, degenerate empiricism subverts and in many cases pre-empts ethical debate by concealing possible configurations of and actions in the human realm and also by generally obfuscating the distinction between fact and value. In these ways, what should be a pursuit of knowledge is subverted into the construction and dissemination of ideology.

References

Bohm, David (1983), *Wholeness and the Implicate Order*, London: Routledge.
Fullbrook, Edward (2005), 'Concealed ideologies: a PAE view of ideology in economics', *Revue de Philosophie Economique*, summer, 131–47.
Gadrey, Jean (2004), 'What's wrong with GDP and growth? The need for alternative indicators', in Edward Fullbrook (ed.), *A Guide to What's Wrong with Economics*, London: Anthem Press, pp. 265–6.
Putnam, Hilary (2004), *Ethics without Ontology*, Cambridge, MA: Harvard University Press.

See also the entries on: Positive versus normative economics; Rationality.

18 Equity
Bernard Hodgson

By 'equity' for the purposes of this chapter we shall understand the principles of moral justice as they apply to economic activities. More particularly, we shall concentrate on the issue of distributive justice or the criteria for the fair allocation of the material benefits and burdens among the participants in a particular economy. However, such an inquiry also has significant implications for questions concerning commutative and social justice. We shall pursue these implications from a contemporary vantage point at the intersection of philosophy and economics. The perspective taken within the latter discipline is that of the 'orthodox' tradition of classical and neoclassical theory. As we shall learn, an analysis of moral equity within economic ethics faces a deep conundrum.

The initial standpoint and its criticism

A good deal is at stake philosophically in addressing questions of justice. Of all moral ideals, the criteria of justice seem based in the provenance of pure reason itself. Most critically, the imperatives of justice do not permit individuals to make exceptions in their own favour. This practical consistency or impartiality rule is most compelling when understood as an extension of our basic intuitive repugnance to avowing a formal contradiction (x is M and x is not M) to practical contexts bearing on the avower. For example, I should be allocated good B in circumstances C but not another person P in the same circumstances. Barring exceptive conditions, from the point of view of justice, persons as persons are moral equals.

Aristotle, characteristically, was among the first to get to the precise heart of the matter with his general view that, according to the meaning of justice, equals should be treated equally and unequals unequally but only in proportion to their relevant difference. The relevant difference, for Aristotle, had to be one of merit or desert. Moreover, and critically, Aristotle understood that, in its root meaning, justice is a *virtue*, a categorically desirable dispositional trait of human character by which each individual is inclined to render unto each other individual what is his/her due. As Aristotle comments, 'we see that all men mean by justice that kind of state of character which makes people disposed to do what is just and makes them act justly and wish for what is just' (Aristotle, p. 106).

It is noteworthy that the perspective in neoclassical economics on questions of distributive justice begins along essentially Aristotelian lines (Friedman 1962, Ch. 10). In particular, it is claimed that if the natural mechanisms of an unconstrained market are left to run their course, then all workers (indeed all factor services) are considered to be treated in a fair or impartial manner. Unequal returns in income for the service of different kinds of workers will be in exact proportion to the unequal desert of such workers as calculated by the value of their marginal product – that is, the increase in revenue of the total output from the addition of one worker of that type. So understood, laissez-faire libertarians have argued that the distributive share of purchasing power that one deserves in a perfectly competitive economy is according to a well-grounded criterion of that for which one is responsible. A particular worker freely chooses a certain kind of employment and is due a return equal to what such productive effort contributes to the aggregate product. If we were to define commutative justice as the fair return an individual or group should receive from other individuals in exchange for a certain transaction with them, we might say that, from the viewpoint we are examining, the criterion of commutative justice is equivalent to that of distributive justice, for individuals would receive a distributive allocation of material reward equal to the productive value of their labouring transactions with other economic actors.

Reference to the free choices of workers bespeaks the classical moral ideal affirmed by advocates of the capitalist market system – that is, that this system gives expression to 'natural liberty' in our communal economic life more adequately than any alternative form of economic organization. The fundamental sense of such liberty, in both classical and neoclassical economic thought, is the 'negative' one wherein economic agents are free from external constraint in acting as they choose – unconstrained, in particular, by state command of any market decisions they might make. This conception of human freedom has reinforced the conception of moral justice explained above by argument of a 'natural right' sort, which has recently been discussed within the scope of the principle of 'self-ownership'. In the words of the Oxford philosopher, G.A. Cohen, the principle states that 'every person is morally entitled to full private property in his own person and powers. This means that each person has an extensive set of natural rights (which the law of the land may or may not recognize) over the use and fruits of his body and capacities' (Cohen 1995, p. 127). Accordingly, as ethically interpreted, the 'marginal product' allocation of a competitive market economy fully and precisely satisfies an individual's right to self-ownership. For all individuals are receiving a distributive share of income which they morally deserve in consistency with this right – namely, a compensation commensurate with the difference the activation of each individual's own self and capabilities makes to the social product.

Understandably, such a standpoint has spawned a potent reply from more unreservedly egalitarian theorists. We are reminded that any individual's contribution to the social product is a function of his or her original endowment in external and internal resources: the degree of physical capital and productive talent one possesses. However, it is frequently unjustified to assign moral responsibility for such assets to certain individuals, as they are often due to social contingencies or genetic inheritance beyond these individuals' capabilities to control. In upshot, the conclusion is drawn that awarding unequal shares according to unequal marginal product is not to comply with an adequate principle of moral desert, but simply is morally arbitrary.

In terms of redistributive justice for those not responsible for their disadvantages in productive assets, egalitarians basically suggest two levels of rectification. At the first level, Ronald Dworkin, for one, proposes that compensation be directed to the equalization across individuals of the economic value of both internal and external resources, but not for their uncoerced preference orderings of commodity bundles, or preference for leisure over labour (Dworkin 1981, pp. 283–345). In a more radical vein, G.A. Cohen opts for a standard of 'equal access to advantage', arguing, against Dworkin, that sometimes an individual's preferences themselves will be causally determined by genetic endowment or social conditioning that are really conditions of 'brute luck' beyond the person's capacity for choice (Cohen 1989, pp. 906–44). Consider, for example, an individual born with a highly sensitive receptivity to refined music, generating an expensive preference for attendance at performances of elite orchestras as compared with other forms of entertainment, but such attendance is precluded by this individual's sparse income. According to Cohen, such a preference should be underwritten by public funding.

Despite their differences in identifying the factual content of responsible choice, egalitarian theorists such as Dworkin and Cohen are at one in claiming that libertarian advocates of the freedom of free markets have been insufficiently sensitive to the empirical access to free choice that real-life economic agents actually possess. Most critically, insofar as individual agents within a capitalist market economy have insubstantial endowments of external capital or internal talent, they will *ipso facto* have little access to the 'positive' liberty of moral autonomy, of the freedom to be self-determining for their material well-being or to be in control of the quality of their economic existence.

The master argument

Libertarian advocates of unconstrained markets are not expected to be silenced by the preceding criticism of egalitarian philosophers. For libertarian marketeers regularly invoke a 'fall-back' argument in reply to egalitarian theses. (We may refer to this as the 'master argument' for the distributive justice of laissez-faire capitalism.) The reply begins with a basic observation of contemporary political economy that neoclassical economic theory continues the ethico-scientific tradition of the 'invisible hand', while seeking to provide a more rigorous clarification of its moral import. Put in summary terms, neoclassical general equilibrium theory implies that if individual producers and consumers are left free to act in a solely self-regarding fashion to maximize their own profits and utilities in a perfectly competitive market, then, as an unintended consequence, the common good or social utility will be 'Pareto maximized' (Arrow 1983, pp. 120–2). More precisely, 'common good' is here defined in classical utilitarian fashion as the satisfaction of the totality or aggregate of given individual consumer desires but as consistent with a Paretian distributive constraint – namely, any movement from such a 'Pareto-optimal' state will make at least one consumer worse off in terms of the satisfaction of his/her de facto wants. It is in this light that the economist Tjalling Koopmans remarks, 'the idea that perfect competition in some sense achieves efficiency in the maximization of individual satisfaction runs through the whole of classical and neo-classical literature' (Koopmans 1961, p. 41).

Indeed, egalitarian philosophers could themselves concede that the Pareto-efficient production of an array of goods that did reflect the free choices of individuals acting on their strongest preferences would, other things being equal, constitute a socially desirable consequence of substantial moral force. However, serious questions of ethical fairness or distributive justice have traditionally haunted such consequentialist reasoning in moral thought. The situation for a capitalist economy as conceived by orthodox economics is no exception to this rule. It is arguable, furthermore, that neoclassical theory only reinforces the 'knots' of the problem. For general equilibrium theory only demonstrates that there will be a *set* of Pareto-optimal equilibria, each member of which is generated by different distributions of 'original endowments' – that is, allocations of ownership of factors of production across individual members of a particular society. Moreover, due to a relatively meagre share of initial endowments, and hence income, an economic actor may receive a similarly meagre share of final product, and thus subjective utility, at a competitive market equilibrium, but this market share may be clearly reprehensible from the point of view of distributive justice. Hence, a final moral appraisal of the various possible Pareto-optimal social outcomes cannot be made unless and until an ethically defensible criterion of fairness is provided to determine an ethically acceptable initial distribution of factor endowments, and, thus, the comparative moral worth of the distinct Pareto-optimal consequences to which such distributions lead. But what would be such a well-founded principle of distributive justice?

From the perspective of the theoretical analysis of competitive capitalism, it must be said that neoclassical economics speaks with a certain forked tongue on this matter.

In the first instance, on the problem of whether the private market system provides distributive justice to its participants, neoclassical theorists are disposed to take refuge behind the rather shop-worn veil of their standard claim to value-neutrality *qua* scientists. That is, they insist that a final moral appraisal of the various possible Pareto-optimal social outcomes of a capitalist market economy is beyond the economist's provenance as a scientist. Indeed, they contend that such an appraisal demands not only an extra-scientific, but also an *extra-market* judgement of distributive justice by the relevant political community whose criterion will either legitimate the status quo, or prescribe either (i) a more equitable distribution of the final product or (ii) a fairer distribution of factor ownership, or both.

However, there is a methodological sleight of hand in this official arm's length posture and the claim to value-neutrality underpinning it. For this is not all that is said: neoclassical welfare economists typically continue with a certain substantive commentary on the abstract theoretical constructions of equilibrium analysis, and in so doing, seek to entrap market critics in a systemic dilemma. Put concisely, they further argue that the basic measures available to a private market system to apply communal principles of moral justice to redress de facto distributive injustice would necessitate severe and intractable inefficiencies as defined by a free market economy. Most particularly, expectation of the redistribution of either final product or original factor endowments would undermine the self-interested *incentives* for material gain of individual entrepreneurs and workers. In the straightforward words of economist D.M. Winch, 'If such attempts are made to superimpose equity on the competitive equilibrium, then its efficiency is jeopardized. If income transfers are achieved by progressive taxation, then the marginal conditions of optimality that follow from the motivational assumptions of the competitive model are violated' (Winch 1971, p. 99). And, as we shall see, such incentives are understood within mainstream economic thought to be the primary springs of economic productivity and growth. Accordingly, such neoclassical commentary concludes, there is no coherent way, in principle, of *integrating* redistributive justice with the allocative efficiency provided by competitive capitalism. But if this is so, neoclassical economics is not ethically neutral with respect to questions of social equity, nor is the conclusion of the commentary a purely factual scientific proposition without serious normative implications.

Among the pivotal features of recent social thought is the fact that politically influential philosophers, of both libertarian and liberal persuasion, have found the pattern of reasoning of the master argument a compelling one. Thus, among the former group, David Gauthier bluntly argues that the findings of neoclassical welfare economics demonstrate that a perfectly competitive market society is politically ideal, indeed that such a social order would not even require moral constraints because, claims Gauthier, 'the coincidence of utility-maximization and [Pareto] optimization in free interaction removes both the need and rationale for the constraints that morality provides' (Gauthier 1986, p. 93; see also Nozick 1974, Ch. 7; Narveson 2003). In the liberal group, Thomas Nagel, somewhat reluctantly, but clearly, accedes to the force of the incentive rationale: 'As acquisitive individuals they must force their socially conscientious selves to permit talent-dependent rewards as the unavoidable price of productivity, efficiency, and growth' (Nagel 1991, p. 115).

Recently there has been an attempt to adapt conceptions of Pareto or John Rawls in an effort to put formally rigorous contemporary dress on what is perhaps the oldest of the arguments set forth to justify the productive structures of competitive capitalism. In effect, a *displacement thesis* is endorsed, namely, a repositioning of the traditional ideal of justice from the Aristotelian conception of the moral virtue of the individual agents participating in the politico-economic order to that of the agreement of rational self-interested individuals to the rules defining the institutional structure of the order. In technical terms, the order is ethically legitimated by means of a consensual 'social contract' among such individuals directed to their expectation of mutual advantage from complying with the rules of the contract.

For our purposes, the most critical rules, of course, are those investing radically unequal private ownership in initial resources in a capitalist market economy. In response to egalitarian views, it is argued that the self-regarding motivation of economic actors to apply their own talents and energy to the physical capital at their command supplies the basic motor force for the productive activities characteristic of competitive markets. Of course, without the freedom to exercise one's own capabilities in productive enterprise, such a motor force would remain inactivated. It is further contended that the creative capabilities released by such freedom resolves the challenge from egalitarians that such a free enterprise system would distribute the final product unfairly, because very unequally. For the opportunity to use private resources in innovative reshapings of capitalist production is such that, as a rule, this politico-economic order would deliver such a bountiful volume of aggregate output of goods and services that, either

- in Pareto superior terms, everyone's material well-being would be higher than in alternative forms of economic organization, or
- at least, in an application of Rawls's 'difference principle', if you were to be one of the worst off, you could expect to be better off than your counterparts within different economic systems (Rawls 1971, Sections 13 and 46).

Most importantly, given these prospects, it is concluded that rational men would assent to the institutional arrangements of competitive capitalism as essentially just. (It should be clarified here that Rawls himself emphasizes that differences or inequalities in the distribution of income and wealth are to be judged from the position of an initial baseline of equality; that is to say, an equal distribution of such goods is to be preferred unless an unequal distribution is to the greatest benefit of the least advantaged; Rawls 1971, pp. 76 and 303). It should also be mentioned that sometimes in the literature the focus on an institutional framework for distributive justice is classified as an inquiry into social justice, whereas at other times the concept of social justice is simply considered equivalent to that of distributive justice. We shall observe that this is not a trivial matter.

Rejoinder to the master argument
The above master argument for market capitalism is of considerable historical and current significance. However, it can be challenged from the perspective of moral philosophy along the following lines (Hodgson 2004).

In its very foundation, the argument sins against Aristotle in not correctly accepting that justice is, at basis, a virtue of human character. If we were to subscribe to the displacement thesis, then we would be willing to accept the prospect that as long as it delivered Pareto-superior or difference principle results, an entirely just social order could be populated by entirely unjust individual persons, since the latter could rationally agree to the order. But the displacement thesis is a replacement thesis: a cynical shift from the first principles of justice to a counterfeit of justice. In real-life terms, highly driven market maximizers, favourably positioned in terms of external capital or productive talent, can be, and typically are, completely indifferent to what is due, as a matter of moral justice, to those who occupy other kinds of competitive positions. There is no disposition by such self-regarding maximizers to respect a baseline of equality in their dealings with less favoured market actors unless an advantageous outcome for the latter can be identified to warrant unequal treatment. There is simply the single-minded pursuit of the greatest obtainable utility or profit by individual consumers and producers; indeed, whatever inequality results in the distribution of consumer goods or capital is expected as the foreseeable consequence of such pursuit. Moreover, even if there were hard empirical evidence that such single-mindedness would bring about a Pareto-superior outcome, or at least an improvement in the prosperity of the least advantaged, it does not follow that even universal assent to such expected consequences could be construed as pre-eminently rational. For such assent would be established by deliberately overriding the aforementioned primitive axiom of consistency demanded in the practical domain of treating each person as a moral equal, barring a relevant exceptive condition. Universal assent to an inconsistent judgement cannot redeem the judgement.

Moreover, we need to recognize that the underlying pattern of motivation in the market capitalist order entrenches the inequity just outlined. For the primary source of unfairness in a political economy, the disposition in the character of some human beings to treat equal persons unequally to themselves in access to material goods, is not self-interested motivation per se. In fact, if we were to define the economic problem as that of the allocation of resources to productive processes to meet consumer desires, and the level of such desire was sufficiently *moderate*, the economic problem could be resolved without injustice. Rather, as Aristotle explained, the unjust individual is characteristically motivated by a certain pathological *form* of self-interest – that of *pleonexia*: sheer acquisitiveness, the desire for more as such for oneself (Aristotle, Bk. V, Chs 1–2, esp. 1129a, Bk. IX, 1168b). It was this primary affect which gave rise to the secondary character trait of injustice, that of a proclivity to grasp more than one's fair share of what is due to oneself, and to be indifferent to the original entitlement to equal shares of other persons as moral equals – in Kantian terms, as equal-ends-in-themselves.

But just such *pleonexia* is the fundamental motivation of the agents turning the wheels of the competitive market machine articulated by neoclassical economics. In terms of neoclassical consumer theory, allegedly rational agents consistently satisfy a non-satiation axiom, that is to say, they always prefer more of available commodities. Or, as Gauthier accurately puts the structural logic of this situation, 'Appropriation has no natural upper bound. Economic man seeks more' (Gauthier 1986, p. 318). Considered as such, economic man would be the wrong natural kind to play fair as the acquisitive aggrandizement or 'possessive individualism' driving his choices in the market would render him increasingly insensitive to the moral claims of others to the just partitioning of material possessions within the social order.

Conclusion

We may briefly close by raising the question of the ultimate prospect of fusing a competitive capitalist economy with a morally just social order. Indeed, this is perhaps the foremost problem for the formation of political policy in our era. Nevertheless, our inquiries above lead us to conclude that there is no clear resolution to this concrete social problem. In fact, we observed that the philosophico-economic address of the issue has yet to extract itself convincingly from a deep conundrum in the form of an entrenched dilemma: if we seek a maximally efficient production of goods and services at an adequate level of growth to meet consumer demand on an increasingly global scale, then we need to acknowledge that the prime mover of such productivity will be the 'economic man' or self-regarding maximizer of orthodox economics. If we are morally serious about introducing distributive justice into economic relations within a particular society, let alone the international community, then we need to acknowledge that a radically different kind of economic agency will have to evolve than the one expressed by classical and neoclassical economics and the competitive market order represented by such theory. The new economic agents will need to break out of atomistic market fetters, recognize their essential connectedness, not separateness, in terms of their ontological identity as persons, and thereby become capable of conceiving other agents as something other than classical market beings – that is, as something other than competitive rivals. Yes, such agents would be more naturally disposed in their character to heed the call of Aristotelian virtue and ensure that the material goods of a community, no doubt even the global one, are distributed among its members according to what is rightly due each member. Unfortunately, however, there is no a priori guarantee that such other-regarding agents will be suitably motivated to enact the economic efficiency and productivity required to provision the material well-being of a continually expanding, globalized domain of consumers. In sum, our discussion must end on a regrettable note of scepticism concerning the prospect of reconciling market efficiency and moral equity in the real world.

References

The literature on the problem of distributive justice within the economic order is voluminous and increasing. The list below consists only of works referenced in the text above. But they themselves make reference to a considerable body of additional relevant literature. A useful recent anthology on the topic is Clayton and Williams (2004).

Aristotle, *Nicomachean Ethics*, reprinted in 1980, trans. David Ross, rev. J.I. Ackrill and J.O. Urmson, Oxford: Oxford University Press.
Arrow, Kenneth J. (1983), 'Economic equilibrium', in *General Equilibrium: Collected Papers*, Vol. 2, Oxford: Blackwell, pp. 107–32.
Clayton, Matthew and Andrew Williams (eds) (2004), *Social Justice*, Oxford: Blackwell.
Cohen, Gerald A. (1989), 'On the currency of egalitarian justice', *Ethics*, **99**, 906–44.
Cohen, Gerald. A. (1995), *Self-Ownership, Freedom, and Equality*, Cambridge: Cambridge University Press.
Dworkin, Ronald (1981), 'What is equality? Part 2: Equality of resources', *Philosophy and Public Affairs*, **10**, 283–345.

Friedman, Milton (1962), *Capitalism and Freedom*, Chicago, IL: University of Chicago Press.
Gauthier, David (1986), *Morals by Agreement*, Oxford: Oxford University Press.
Hodgson, Bernard (2004), 'On economic men bearing gifts and playing fair', in Bernard Hodgson (ed.), *The Invisible Hand and the Common Good*, Berlin and New York: Springer Verlag, pp. 279–98.
Koopmans, Tjalling C. (1961), *Three Essays on the State of Economic Science*, New York: McGraw-Hill.
Nagel, Thomas (1991), *Equality and Partiality*, New York: Oxford University Press.
Narveson, Jan (2003), 'The invisible hand', *Journal of Business Ethics*, **46**, 210–22.
Nozick, Robert (1974), *Anarchy, State and Utopia*, New York: Basic Books.
Rawls, John (1971), *A Theory of Justice*, Cambridge, MA: Harvard University Press.
Winch, David (1971), *Analytical Welfare Economics*, Harmondsworth: Penguin.

See also the entries on: Aristotle; Efficiency; Justice.

19 Ethics of care
Kari Wærness

A new moral discourse on care comes into being

Feminist academic work on the issue of care developed rapidly in many Western countries after it was put on the agenda in the 1970s and experienced a renaissance as an academic topic in the 1980s. We can distinguish between, on the one hand, studies that place emphasis on care as *work* and, on the other hand, those that place emphasis on the *emotional aspects* (Abel and Nelson 1990; see also Finch and Groves 1983). Both were important constituents of the growing scientific discourse on care and within both care was studied as physically and emotionally demanding unpaid work that women carry out in the home. This early work was later criticized because it was too one-sided, for focusing only on the caregivers and not on those who receive care and for discussing unpaid care and not care as paid and professional work (Morris 1991/92).

In contrast, the Nordic discourse, even then, included both paid and unpaid care work. One reason for this could be that crucial state welfare services were already defined as 'care', and a different research tradition based on socio-economic welfare expertise was already established long before there was any feminist research. 'Caregiving work' was defined as only a part of smaller caring activities, delimited to help, support, and services given on a consistent and reliable basis to persons who according to generally accepted social norms are dependent: the children, the ill, the disabled, and the frail elderly. Caring in relations between independent adults who in principle could care for themselves was defined as something else, either as expressions of friendship or as personal services. In all these kinds of caring, feeling concern for, and taking charge of the well-being of others in face-to face-relations is a common defining characteristic (Wærness 1984a). The focus on both unpaid and paid care work led to the cognition that public home care services could be valued as better and preferable to informal family care among frail elderly, because such services made it possible to maintain the same kind of 'intimacy at a distance' and reciprocity in family relations as before (Wærness 1989). (For further theoretical discussions on care and care work along this line, see Himmelweit 1999 and Meagher 2006.)

Feminist research on care in the Nordic countries developed parallel to the earlier established welfare research which during the last two decades has been influenced by more market economic thinking. Feminist researchers criticized this socio-economic planning perspective, as not based on an adequate understanding of the distinctive nature of care and therefore often generating reforms and measures that go against the 'logic' or 'rationality' of caring (Wærness 1984b, 2006).

Both planning research and feminist research in this area are normative in the sense that researchers speak both about the facts of what is and what would be good, desirable and possible. The normative perspective is, however, more clearly expressed in feminist research, where morals, human values, and authors' own views on values are more often discussed.

The heated debate on Gilligan's 'ethics of care'
Since the 1990s, the US-led debate on care has contributed to the development of an international discourse on 'the feminist ethics on care'. The most internationally known and influential study on care of a more moral philosophical nature came from the American educational psychologist Carol Gilligan (1982). Her book *In a Different Voice: Psychological Theory and Women's Development*, which launched the ethic of care as a field of study, became an immediate focus of controversy and one of the most widely discussed books in the humanities and social sciences of our time.

Another American pioneer on the ethics of care, Nel Noddings (1984) also came from the field of education. She emphasized the importance of 'caring for' others through an actual relationship, as opposed to 'caring about' others in the abstract, and argued that care involves an empathetic response to the particular needs of individuals. Sensitivity and responsiveness to the feelings, concerns and particular circumstances of individuals, an attitude which Wærness (1984b) has defined as a vital part of 'the rationality of caring', are critical and invaluable qualities for care-workers in the public care services. This has also been strongly argued in feminist economics (Folbre 1995; Himmelweit 1999; Nelson 1999).

One question in the heated debate on Gilligan's and to a lesser extent on Noddings's contributions to the ethics of care, was whether men and women had a fundamentally different approach to morality. Even if Gilligan never said that her 'different voice' always was a female one and Noddings dedicated her book to her caring husband, many critics have worried about the undesirable implications of resurrecting the 'womanly virtues' that traditionally have been used to keep women in the 'private' sphere.

These questions have not however in any way hindered the wide interdisciplinary impact of Gilligan's work, in part due to her claims about the value of women's experiences. Her ideas became particularly important in moral philosophy, where the abstractions of ethicists have dominated the field, allowing little if any reference to the reality of people's moral lives (Larrabee 1993). Caring has also become an important theoretical issue in the professional education of workers in various parts of the modern welfare state (Gordon et al. 1996).

The ethics of care as an accepted philosophical position
Even though Gilligan's research still is controversial, recognition of an ethics of care developed from her work in psychology and defined in contrast to the established ethics of justice seems to be an accepted philosophical position today, a position also related to historical antecedents in the work of some Western philosophers, going back to Aristotelean virtue ethics (Furrow 2005). The ethics of care takes our responsibilities within relationships as the foundation for moral values. The guiding thought is that people need each other in order to lead a good life and that they can only exist as individuals through caring relationships with others. The central theme in this ethics might be expressed in the following way: we all need both to care and be cared for to be fully human. The ethics of care takes caring relationships such as that of parent, friend, nurse and teacher as the paradigm for how we ought to treat others generally. Relationships in which one person cares for another or in which there is mutual care are the crucible ones in which we develop moral capacities. Unlike in other moral theories, for the ethics of care, emotions are central to our capacity to reason effectively. The model of the social

actor in this theory is not the instrumental rational actor that dominates economics, but what Hochschild (1975) has named 'the sentient actor' (that is, the actor who is both rational and feeling at the same time). A critique of the instrumental rational actor, *homo economicus*, has been the basis for many works in feminist economics on care (for example, England and Folbre 1999; Folbre 1995; Himmelweit 1995; Nelson 1999). In feminist economics today we also find more general critical works on the separative model of the self upon which not only neoclassical economics but also theories of rational choice more generally are based (for example, England and Kilbourne 1990; Nelson 1996 and 2003).

Care as process and practice

Tronto (1993) has suggested that as an alternative to defining morality in terms of thinking we should focus on care as a process and emphasize care as a practice. Analysing the ethics of care from this angle leads to the awareness that the analysis will be incomplete if we do not also make care a key topic of political discourse. The ethics of care must be discussed on the basis of both a moral and a political context. This implies that the established boundaries between morality and politics and between private and public have to be breached, and that the role of feelings in moral assessments must be included in academic discourse. Tronto suggests that we analyse care as a social process consisting of four different stages: (i) *caring about* (recognizing a need for care), (ii) *taking care of* (assuming some responsibility for the need and determining how to respond to it), (iii) *care-giving* (the direct meeting of needs for care) and (iv) *care-receiving* (the recipient's situation after the care has been given). Analysis of all the four stages should be done in relation to the core values of the ethic of care: attentiveness, responsibility, competence and responsiveness. When defining care in this way it becomes clear that there are many opportunities for conflict over both values and the allocation of scarce resources in the form of money and time. This approach helps to analyse more concretely how the division of labour in caring is gendered, raced and classed, how this changes over time and how it differs between countries. It also offers a broad starting point for renewing the normative frameworks of social policy in European welfare states to base it on empirical research on unpaid and paid care (Gardiner 1997; Sevenhuijsen 1998; Picchio 2003; Bettio and Plantenga 2004).

The care ethic and modern welfare policy

In the Western world today a 'relocation of politics', that is a weakening of the nation-state is taking place, simultaneously with a 'relocation of care', somewhat of a move from women to men, somewhat less from home and more from outside services, and a considerable increase in the need of care in the health services as a result of people living longer with chronic illnesses (Sevenhuijsen 2003). These changes imply that daily care more than ever is the subject of political action and negotiation. That these changes also involve both what is defined as 'crises of care' and a 'care drain' of domestic and professional care workers from the countries of the South to the countries of the North (Anderson 2001; Ehrenreich and Hochschild 2003; Wærness 2006) adds to the importance of integrating ethical and political discourse. This relocation of care enables some of the values of the ethics of care to be transferred into the public sphere where their suitability to assess the quality of care can be determined. In order to solve the specific problems in the real world of care, we require a way of thinking, which is contextual and descriptive, rather than formal and abstract. The ethics of care and the rationality of caring suggest that personal knowledge and a certain ability and opportunity to understand what is specific in each caring situation are important prerequisites in order to be able to provide good care. Human and moral qualities in public care can only be elicited in situations where there is not a lot of bustle, but where there is enough *quiet*, so that those requiring help are confident and sure that their helpers recognize their specific needs. In other words; that in his or her state of helplessness, a person feels to be in good hands. This means that each helper must not be too busy. So far mainstream economic studies on 'efficiency' in the public services do not seem have taken into consideration this important aspect of care-giving work. The usual economic measures of efficiency do not have relevance for care provision due to its relational character, and suggestions of alternative measures have become a topic in feminist economics (Donath 2000; Himmelweit 2007). The need for such alternative measures in modern health and welfare policy seems urgent. Further, with the growth of research on care in feminist economics and on the ethics of care there seems to be a growing recognition that the ethics of care may also be of some relevance in wider domains including activities unrelated to caring for dependents. Today we even find the ethics of care discussed in business ethics (see for instance Furman 1990; French and Weis 2000).

The ethics of care is inherently characterized by a relational ontology both in its descriptive and normative respects. The argument is that care, justice and freedom are three different value domains that have to be balanced in all economic activities (van Staveren 2001), and that the concrete framing of this balance has to differ according to what is the main concern of any particular economic activity. The ethics of care should dominate and at the same time be the most demanding in terms of practical norms, in those activities involved in taking care of the most dependent and vulnerable members of society. In these activities the asymmetry in power between the carers and the cared-for often makes caring a difficult balancing act between responsibility for the other – a responsibility that can turn into unacceptable forms of paternalism (or maternalism) both in unpaid and paid care – and a respect for the integrity of the other, which can border on indifference and neglect (Eliasson-Lappalainen and Milsson 1997). Low pay and a devaluation of caring skills in modern society add to this problem. Studies trying to find out why care is undervalued and low paid (Nelson 1999; Folbre and Nelson1999; Folbre and Weisskopf 1998; England et al. 2002) could be of great importance as a tool for a new policy to change this situation.

References

Abel, Emily and Margaret Nelson (eds) (1990), *Circles of Care: Work and Identity in Women's Lives*, New York: State University Press.

Anderson, Bridget (2001), *Doing the Dirty Work? The Global Politics of Domestic Labour*, London: Zed Books.

Bettio, Francesca and Janneke Plantenga (2004), 'Comparing care regimes in Europe', *Feminist Economics*, **10** (1), 85–113.

Donath, Susan (2000), 'The other economy: a suggestion for a distinctively feminist economics', *Feminist Economics*, **6** (1), 115–123.

Ehrenreich, Barbara and Arlie R. Hochschild (eds) (2003), *Global Woman: Nannies, Maids and Sex Workers in the New Economy*, London: Granta.

Eliasson-Lappalainen, Rosemari and Ingrid Motevasel Milsson (1997), 'Ethics of care and social policy', *Scandinavian Journal of Social Welfare*, **6**, 189–96.

England, Paula and Nancy Folbre (1999), 'The cost of caring', in Ronnie Steinberg and Deborah M. Figart (eds), *The Annals of the American Academy of Political and Social Science*, 561, Special Issue on Emotional Labor, 39–51

England, Paula and Barbara Kilbourne (1990), 'Feminist critiques of the separative model of the self: implications for rational choice theory', *Rationality and Society*, 2 (2), 156–72.

England, Paula, Michelle Budig and Nancy Folbre (2002), 'Wages or virtues: the relative pay of carework', *Social Problems*, 49, 455–73.

Finch, Janet and Dulcie Groves (eds) (1983), *A Labour of Love: Women, Work and Caring*, London: Routledge & Kegan Paul.

Folbre, Nancy (1995), '"Holding hands at midnight": the paradox of caring labor', *Feminist Economics*, 1 (1), 73–92.

Folbre, Nancy and Julie Nelson (1999), 'For love or money?', *Journal of Economic Perspectives*, 14 (4), 123–140

Folbre, Nancy and Thomas Weisskopf (1998), 'Did Father know best? Family, markets and the supply of caring labor', in Avner Ben-Ner and Louis Putterman (eds), *Economics, Values and Organization*, Cambridge: Cambridge University Press.

French, Warren and Alex Weis (2000), 'An ethics of care or an ethics of justice', *Journal of Business Ethics*, 27 (1–2), 125–36.

Furman, Frida K. (1990), 'Teaching business ethics: questioning the assumptions, seeking new directions', *Journal of Business Ethics*, 9 (1), 31–8.

Furrow, Dwight (2005), *Ethics: Key Concepts in Philosophy*, New York/London: Continuum.

Gardiner, Jean (1997), *Gender, Care and Economics*, London: Macmillan Press.

Gilligan, Carol (1982), *In a Different Voice: Psychological Theory and Women's Development*, Cambridge, MA: Harvard University Press.

Gordon,Suzanne, Patricia Brenner and Nel Noddings (eds) (1996), *Caregiving, Reading in Knowledge, Practice, Ethics and Politics*, Philadelphia, PA: University of Pennsylvania Press.

Himmelweit, Susan (1995), 'The discovery of "unpaid work": the social consequences of the expansion of work', *Feminist Economics*, 1 (2), 1–9.

Himmelweit, Susan (1999), 'Caring labor', *Annals of American Academy of Political and Social Science*, 561, 27–38.

Himmelweit, Susan (2007), 'The prospects for caring: economic theory and policy analysis', *Cambridge Journal for Economics*, 31, 581–99.

Hochschild, Arlie R. (1975), 'The sociology of feeling and emotion: selected possibilities', in Marcia Millman and Rosabeth M. Kanter (eds), *Another Voice*, New York: Anchor Books, pp. 280–307.

Larrabee, Mary J. (1993), *An Ethic of Care: Feminist and Interdisciplinary Perspectives*, London: Routledge.

Meagher, Gabrielle (2006), 'What can we expect from paid carers?', *Politics and Society*, 34 (1), 33–53.

Morris, Jenny (1991/92), '"Us" and "Them"? Feminist research, community care and disability', *Critical Social Policy*, 11 (3), 22–39.

Nelson, Julie A. (1996), *Feminism, Objectivity and Economics*, London: Routledge.

Nelson, Julie A. (1999), 'Of markets and martyrs: is it OK to pay well for care?', *Feminist Economics*, 5 (3), 43–59.

Nelson, Julie A. (2003), 'Once more, with feeling: feminist economics and the ontological question', *Feminist Economics*, 9 (1), 109–18.

Noddings, Nel (1984), *Caring: A Feminine Approach to Ethics and Moral Education*, Berkeley: University of California Press.

Picchio, Antonella (2003), *Unpaid Work and the Economy: A Gender Analysis of the Standards of Living*, London and New York: Routledge

Sevenhuijsen, Selma L. (1998), *Citizenship and the Ethics of Care, Feminist Considerations on Justice, Morality and Politics*, London and New York: Routledge.

Sevenhuijsen, Selma L. (2003), 'The place of care: the relevance of the feminist ethic of care for social policy', *Feminist Theory*, 4, 179–97.

Staveren, Irene van (2001), *The Values of Economics: An Aristotelian Perspective*, London: Routledge.

Tronto, Joan C. (1993), *Moral Boundaries: A Political Argument for an Ethic of Care*, New York: Routledge.

Wærness, Kari (1984a), 'Caring as women's work in the welfare state', in Harriet Holter (ed.), *Patriarchy in a Welfare Society*, Oslo: Universitetsforlaget, pp. 67–87.

Wærness, Kari (1984b), 'The rationality of caring', *Economic and Industrial Democracy*, 5 (2), 185–212; reprinted in A.S. Saasson (ed.) (1987), *Women and the State*, London: Hutchinson and S. Gordon (ed.) (1996), *Caregiving*, Philadelphia: PENN.

Wærness, Kari (1989), 'A more symmetrical family – a greater demand for public care?', in K. Boh, G.B. Sgritta and M.B. Sussman (eds), *Marriage and Family Review: Cross-Cultural Perspectives on Families, Work and Change*, New York: The Haworth Press, pp. 41–67.

Wærness, Kari (2006), 'Research on care: what impact on policy and planning?', in Caroline Glendinning and Peter A. Kemp (eds), *Cash and Care Policy Challenges in the Welfare State*, Bristol: The Policy Press, pp. 21–32.

See also the entries on: Feminism; Homo economicus; Virtue ethics.

20   Fact/value dichotomy
Vivian Walsh

The philosophical roots of the fact/value dichotomy that still haunts neoclassical economics go back at least to David Hume. For Hume, a 'matter of fact' was something that one could see, hear, touch, taste or smell. Arguably, this was a reasonable view for a philosopher to adopt in the eighteenth century. In the early twentieth century, however, the new science confronted philosophers with 'facts' that could not be perceived nor expressed except in mathematics. This directly destroyed another dichotomy – that between fact and theory – while indirectly undermining the fact/value dichotomy as well.

Meanwhile, there was a detailed attack on the fact/value dichotomy by one group of philosophers, and a striking defence of it by another. The attack came from the classical American pragmatists, who argued that facts, theories and values are all necessarily entangled. Since these pragmatists peaked in the late nineteenth and very early twentieth century, however, their work was done before the impact of the new mathematics, logic and science, and was not framed in such a way as to catch the attention of the new science and philosophy. One pragmatist, however, Morton White, *was* young enough to make important contributions, and these will be discussed later.

Logical positivism
The logical positivists in Vienna of the 1920s were deeply impressed by the new axiomatic mathematics and logic, and by the new physical science. Their goal was to serve the new science by clarifying the language available for its formalization, eliminating metaphysical vestiges and constructing an ideal parlance in which an ultimately unified science could be rationally reconstructed. This ambition launched them upon a programme of massive proportions, which ultimately collapsed. Their relevant positivist concepts, however, can be expressed quite simply. They believed that all valid utterances were one of two distinct types. There were factual utterances, like 'the cat is on the mat', which could be tested. And there were *analytic* utterances, which were simply valid manipulations of a language – in effect tautologies, like 'all bachelors are unmarried', or '2 + 2 = 4'. An English speaker will know that the first of these is correct without questioning bachelors, and anyone familiar with the standard notation of arithmetic will recognize the second as correct, given the conventions of this formal language. All utterances which fell into neither of these categories, they claimed, were cognitively meaningless.

It is important to note that the original positivists regarded all natural languages (like English or German) as deeply logically corrupted. It did not surprise them that all sorts of ethical claims (for example) could be made while using (say) English quite correctly. Thus Sir Alfred Ayer[1] pointed out:

> we are not, of course, denying that it is possible to invent a language in which all ethical symbols are definable in non-ethical terms, or even that it is desirable to invent such a language and adopt it in place of our own; what we are denying is that the suggested reduction of ethical to

non-ethical statements is consistent with the conventions of our actual language. (Ayer [1936] 1952, p. 105)

A natural language might contain irreducibly ethical claims, but supposedly this just showed that natural languages contain inextricable metaphysical impurities.

The collapse of the fact/value dichotomy

Leading positivists left Vienna in the 1930s and came to the United States. Thus it happened that the philosopher Hilary Putnam (1994) came to be close to two of the most important positivists, Rudolph Carnap and Hans Reichenbach. Putnam's work therefore is a rich example of how positivism evolved and what happened to it.

The positivists needed two dichotomies, and of these it was not the fact/value dichotomy but their fact/theory dichotomy which did the philosophical heavy lifting (see Putnam 2002, pp. 1–64). The discussions of economists tended to concentrate on the fact/value dichotomy – as if it could have done what the positivists needed on its own. This tendency reveals clearly how little many economists – whether believing in the fact/value dichotomy or not – really know about logical positivism.

The positivists, it should not be forgotten, were passionately interested in the physical sciences and mathematics, and in the project of 'logical translation' – of science into an ideal language. Having dismissed ethics as meaningless, they had no further interest in it.

Given how modernist the Vienna positivists were, it is deeply paradoxical that they still depended on Hume's notion of a fact as something directly perceptible. As Putnam remarks, '[t]he logical positivists themselves were deeply impressed by the successes of relativity theory, which speaks of "curved space-time", and quantum mechanics. The idea that a "fact" is just a sensible "impression" would hardly seem to be tenable any longer' (Putnam 2002, p. 22). What was being offered by science was an inextricable mixture of theory and fact. The logical positivist dichotomy between fact and theory was in ruins.

As W.V.O. Quine wrote:

> The lore of our fathers is a fabric of sentences. In our hands it develops and changes, through more or less arbitrary and deliberate revisions and additions of our own . . . It is a pale gray lore, black with fact and white with convention. But I have found no substantial reasons for concluding that there are any quite black threads in it, or any white ones. (Quine 1963, p. 405)

This was overkill! The recognition that much of science involves an entanglement of fact and theory would have sufficed to kill the logical positivist dichotomy between factual statements and analytic (theoretical) statements. Especially since Quine had powerfully argued earlier that a theory could not be decomposed into a set of individual scientific statements, and each of these tested on its own. Rather, a theory must meet the test of experience 'as a corporate body' (Quine [1951] 1953, p. 41).

But if it was admitted that a theory was a web of entangled black and white threads (of fact and theory, which Quine called 'convention') how could Quine know that there were not also red threads of value interwoven in the texture? This challenge to Quine, to face the consequences of his own position, was first presented to him by his close friend and colleague at Harvard, Morton White. Quine, committing an amazing blunder, never recognized the validity of White's argument, and it remained for Putnam, in a series of works, to drive home the fatal implications of the collapse of the fact/theory dichotomy for the survival of the fact/value dichotomy. A few words about the construction of models and about theory choice, which may appeal to economists, must suffice here.

Even elementary microeconomics textbooks always point out, correctly, that in constructing a model one must *simplify*. Models, they sometimes add, are like maps. What, then, is put on a map? Those features which are important for the buyer. True, but this is an evaluation – if anything is! The texts do not stress that what is featured in a model is what is *valued* by those who pay for it. To lay bare the values implicit in a model, one should look for what is left out. The values at issue may be very well-known ones. There is, however, a more sophisticated sort of value which can be involved in the choice of a new theory. Putnam calls these 'epistemic' values – one could call them 'scientific values'. Testing a new theory in physical science can be very expensive. Thus, many inferior candidates may be eliminated because of their lacking simplicity, coherence, mathematical elegance, the ability to conserve existing theory or the prospect of many fruitful empirical applications, and so on. These are scientific values. Theorists like Amartya Sen, by contrast, have tended to reject accounts of development wholly dependent on gross domestic product and to adopt treatments which focus on what happens to vital human capabilities.

The 'new' welfare economics, and its relation to a weakening positivism

A number of years ago, John Chipman claimed that Paul Samuelson had 'set up welfare economics as a separate discipline: the study of the relationships between economic policies and value judgments' (Chipman 1982, p. 152). He noted that Samuelson's contribution 'grew out of Bergson's seminal work' (ibid.). With this he was referring to Abram Bergson (1938). When Bergson wrote his youthful paper, logical positivism was in its vigorous original form. By the time Samuelson wrote his development and endorsement of Bergson, positivism, settled into its new home in America and Britain, was about to enter its decline. It was about to soften, at the hands of English-speaking philosophers, in ways which importantly affected its influence on economics.

Samuelson, in his famous work ([1947] 1983) would still take positivism very seriously, in a way which the original Vienna positivist founders had certainly deserved while their arguments stood. But the 'new welfare economics' which Samuelson promoted was destined to receive a kind of support from the emerging English-language 'soft' positivism which it would never have had from the Viennese.

Bergson's importance for Samuelson was that he had shown how one could give an account of the results of an economic policy (in output of commodities and so on) without having to endorse the values of the policymakers – just as an anthropologist might study the way a society achieved its goals without adopting those goals: '[T]he scientist does not consider it any part of his task to deduce or verify (except on the anthropological level) the value judgments whose implications he grinds out' (ibid., p. 210). This was no trivial matter, because Samuelson was accepting the position of the original Vienna positivists: 'ethical values have no place in scientific analysis' (ibid., p. 219). The economic scientist could put on, as it were, protective clothing, before handling material infected with values.

It has become customary to attribute the adoption of a fact/value dichotomy in economics to the influence of Lord Robbins. Samuelson, in the work just quoted, lends support to this view: 'It is fashionable for the modern economist to insist that ethical value judgments have no place in scientific analysis. Professor Robbins in particular has insisted upon this point' (ibid.). This belief in Robbins's influence may well be true. His position was complicated, however, in the end leading him to the 'soft' positivism which Morton White identified. The principle target Robbins wished to attack was the interpersonal comparison of utilities. If these comparisons were allowed, then economists could be asked whether it would not be a good idea, in the depths of the Great Depression, to redistribute some of the superfluous income of the rich to the destitute. Some economists at the London School – notably Lord Dalton – strongly favoured this. Robbins first attacked interpersonal comparisons in his book *An Essay on the Nature and Significance of Economic Science* ([1932] 1935). But his argument then rested not on logical positivism, but on metaphysical claims as to the inscrutability of other minds. Ayer would have rejected the other minds argument as metaphysical, and argued that the question of who was starving and who was well off was a testable factual issue!

In later work, Robbins (1938) gave up the other minds issue, and moved towards arguing that interpersonal comparisons were ethical judgements. Logical positivism was well known in Britain by then, and most of those who followed Robbins probably used some knowledge of this. Robbins himself had again a position of his own. Instead of resting his fact/value dichotomy on logical positivism, he turned to Hume for 'the distinction between "ought" and "is"' (Robbins 1971, p. 148). He turned to 'the old fashioned term Political Economy' (ibid., p. 150) as a designation for some of his own works 'to make clear their dependence on judgments of value and to distinguish them from pure science' (ibid.) Here he is responding to 'readers who will jump to the conclusion that I deny the importance of judgments of value' (ibid., p. 149).

Well, the Vienna Circle certainly denied the importance – even the meaningfulness – of judgements of value! But Britain was beginning to develop, by the 1950s, a species of 'soft' positivism. A notable feature of this was its Humean tendencies. The Vienna Circle borrowed their notion of a fact from Hume, but they were much more severe in their insistence on the utter meaninglessness of value utterances. As Putnam has noted, Hume certainly denied that ethics was about matters of fact. But '[i]n Hume's case, the thesis was not meant to rule out the possibility of a philosopher's writing a textbook on morals, whereas in Carnap's case it certainly was so meant' (Putnam 2002, p. 19). 'Carnap's purpose was to *expel* ethics from the domain of knowledge' (ibid., p. 20). It should perhaps not surprise us that when positivism began to be adopted by British philosophers, it started to be affected by a tradition which was still marked by the influence of David Hume.

The original Viennese positivism had cracked under the pressure of the deep problems the results of physical science posed, and under the impossible demands of their project of logical translation. Perhaps some of the new 'soft' positivists did not understand – or were even unaware of – all this. The English-speaking positivists were not primarily concerned with physical science, or even with symbolic logic and pure mathematics. They were chiefly concerned with the roles of facts and values in natural languages. But, as we already know, even the Vienna positivists recognized that in a natural language values were impossible to eliminate. Being a consistent positivist in this situation was a tall order. There were reasons, however, why this might not have been evident for some time.

Under the influence of Wittgenstein, younger philosophers, especially at Oxford, were coming to realize the powers and subtleties of natural languages. So the question as to what could and could not legitimately be done with value words was not one which they were willing to regard as decided without deep and lengthy investigation. Soft positivism would get a run for its money. This is the period about which Morton White's works are an invaluable source.

The contribution of Morton White

White came on stage at just the right time to see how the original hard positivism morphed into its later, Anglican form. Having thoroughly understood the dogmas of the Vienna Circle, seen Quine's demolition of the fact/theory dichotomy, and having pressed Quine unsuccessfully to abandon the fact/value dichotomy, White was totally free from any unwarranted belief in even the original positivism. Indeed, his deep pragmatist roots had made any conversion to the Vienna faith highly unlikely from the beginning. By 1950, when his first book of relevance to these issues came out, he had clearly absorbed the ideas of the later Wittgenstein and of Oxford philosophers such as John Austin, Gilbert Ryle and Sir Peter Strawson, who were freed from the Cambridge dominance of mathematics and symbolic logic, and returning to the serious analysis of natural language instead of the positivist quest for the Holy Grail of a perfect, ideal language. Beside White, by the mid-1950s, it was the Vienna positivists who looked dated.

By the time White wrote *Toward Reunion in Philosophy* (1956), the original 'hard' positivist position was being given up as positivism went into retreat. Some of his most interesting arguments, therefore, consist of explorations of the confusions which result when philosophers still influenced by positivism faced the delicately probing scalpel of an Austin or a Strawson. Efforts were made to put together a mellower, or softer positivism – this was especially true of ethics and of that starved unacknowledged child of ethics known as the 'new' welfare economics.[2]

Morton White was, of course, well aware that, for the original founders of logical positivism, the argument that there were irreducibly ethical words, phrases and sentences in natural languages would not have been seen as posing any problem. They would have simply pointed out that this feature of natural languages was one of the reasons why serious scientific discourse needed to be conducted in a logically chaste, constructed language, from which these (and other) impurities had been eliminated. Sir Alfred Ayer was thus (as we have seen) consistent with the original logical positivist position when he argued that 'it is possible to invent a language in which all ethical symbols are definable in non-ethical terms' (Ayer [1936] 1952, p. 105). He was similarly so in concluding that 'what we are denying is that the suggested reduction of ethical to non-ethical statements is consistent with the conventions of our own language' (ibid.)

Once the original hard positivism had morphed into what White calls 'ethical positivism', however, a fundamental change had taken place on this issue. As White notes, 'it is important to stress the fact that most ethical positivists formulate their theses so that they apply to sentences in ordinary languages' (White 1956, p. 202). Contrasting Ayer's hard positivism with these mellowed soft 'positivists', White notes, '[t]here are indeed those among the emotivists who pride themselves on their feeling for ordinary language and on the fact that their conclusions are the result of their sensitive understanding of what they sometimes call the living context in which language is written and spoken' (ibid.)

White is quite clear that these 'positivists' have cut themselves off from the foundations of the original Viennese positions which had made possible 'the rational reconstruction-ist's elimination of metaphysical sentences' (ibid.), and from the deep implications which the original position supposedly had for science (by then refuted by Quine). There was no reason, of course, why this small segment of the original great positivist ship to which these survivors clung should have been thought capable of floating on its own.

The rise, in this period, of the 'emotivist' theory of ethical utterances can thus be seen as the natural child of a decayed positivism and a misunderstanding of ordinary language. As White puts it, the original positivists were now followed by 'moderates', who con-ceded that ethical sentences might have cognitive meaning but that this was not the key to ethical discourse. The moderates focused their attention on emotive meaning, 'a kind of Christmas cheer generously sprinkled on sentences like "I approve of this" in order to produce a shiny ethical judgment' (ibid., p. 227). It will cause no surprise that White regretfully observes, 'We shall be forced to reject this point of view' (ibid., p. 228).

As Putnam insists, the original 'hard' positivists were great philosophers and followed a route which, at the time, it was of profound importance to investigate. The 'soft' positiv-ists carefully dissected by White were arguably given, by him, more than they deserved. White's work on this literature, however, has considerable importance because of the effect of soft positivism on a highly influential group of social scientists during the later twentieth century. I refer of course to the wave of neoclassical economists that dominated world debate from just after World War II up to such recent events as the scandal caused by the disastrous results of the Washington Consensus interpretation of globalization.[3] The work of economists like Stiglitz, and the widespread disillusion even within neoclas-sical circles with its formal models of general equilibrium, suggest the beginnings of rising dissent within the ranks.

'Thick' ethical concepts

Another feature of White's work concerns his position on what Putnam calls 'thick' ethical concepts. Putnam, following Iris Murdoch (1970), long maintained that a single word, like 'cruel', 'simply ignores the supposed fact/value dichotomy and cheerfully allows itself to be used sometimes for a normative purpose and sometimes as a descrip-tive term' (Putnam 2002, p. 35). It is therefore surprising that – as far as I can find – this is *not* adopted by White. As recently as 1986 he remarked, 'it will be evident that I do not advocate the abandonment of the distinction between normative and descriptive sentences' (White 1986, p. 661). White's pragmatist holism makes him a true blue advo-cate of what might be called macro entanglement, but not of the *micro* entanglement (of which Murdoch was perhaps the original champion) of a single word, or even of a single sentence (see White 1981, 1986).

Now in a social science, and perhaps especially in mathematical economics, where an entire model is often the focus of interest, it may be asked whether the micro entanglement of a single word is likely to figure in an important way. Are not models – and even theories – to be judged as corporate bodies in Quine's fashion? It happens, however, that there is remarkable support from some mathematical economists for the importance of micro entanglement. For most of his life, Amartya Sen has been deeply influenced by Maurice

Dobb. Sen recently reinforced this by comparing Dobb's concept of 'rich description' with Putnam's treatment of entanglement. Some ordinary uses of a word like 'exploitation' are examples of Dobb's concept of 'rich description'. Other important contributors to the analysis of development have echoed this theme without any reference to Dobb. In 1993 Sir Partha Dasgupta, for example, wrote,

> [C]oncepts like *undernourishment* and *disease* and *destitution* on the face of it have only a descriptive content. In fact, there is an evaluative content as well, in that there is no way of saying what our ethical evaluation of the state of undernourishment, or disease, or destitution should be, or can be, without our having to use words *like* undernourishment, or disease, or destitution. (Dasgupta 1993, pp. 6–7, emphasis in the original)

Dasgupta cites Putnam and tells the reader that the concept of entanglement 'will influence the way I will throughout argue in this book' (ibid., p. 6). He leaves no room for doubt that, for him, entanglement is a property that can be concentrated in a single word: writing as he does especially of the truly poor, he finds the concept of well-being 'an elusive one, and it is hard to identify it accurately. So my strategy will be to explore a starker notion, that of *destitution*' (ibid., p. 8, emphasis in the original).

What destitution is for Dasgupta, arguably the concept of exploitation was for Dobb. Sen quotes Dobb's argument on 'exploitation':

> [Exploitation is] neither something 'metaphysical' nor simply an ethical judgment (still less 'just a noise') as has sometimes been depicted: it is a factual description of a socio-economic relationship, as much as is Marc Bloch's apt characterization of Feudalism as a system where feudal Lords 'lived on the labour of other men'. (Dobb 1973, p. 145, cited in Sen 1987, p. 911)

Sen explored Dobb's concept of rich description on several occasions, noting recently that 'the need for richer description is quite pervasive in the subject of economics, despite the minimalist inclinations of contemporary economics. Indeed, 'rich description' is a general directional priority that, I argue, is both important and badly neglected in contemporary economics' (Sen 2005, p. 110).

As author of a theory of development which characterizes this process as involving the fulfilment of a number of vital human capabilities, Sen is thoroughly entitled to inherit Dobb's concept of rich description – which as he is well aware is extremely close to that of entanglement. Moreover, with Sen's work on the capability approach, the demolition of the fact/value dichotomy in economics is now well on its way.

Notes

Comments from Stephanie Blankenberg and Geoff Harcourt are gratefully acknowledged.
1. Ayer was a member of the Vienna Circle, and his early book (cited above) offers a clear introduction to the original positivist position for English-speaking, non-philosopher readers.
2. Readers interested in the relationship between welfare economics and ethics might wish to see Philippe Mongin (2006), Sir Partha Dasgupta (2005) and Putnam and Walsh (2007).
3. See for example Joseph E. Stiglitz (2003), and for a discussion from the point of view of the present paper, Hilary Putnam and Vivian Walsh (2007).

References

Ayer, Alfred J. ([1936] 1952), *Language, Truth and Logic*, New York: Dover Publications.
Bergson, Abram (1938) 'A reformulation of certain aspects of welfare economics', *Quarterly Journal of Economics*, **52**, 310–34.

Chipman, John S. (1982), 'Samuelson and consumption theory', in George R. Feiwel (ed.), *Samuelson and Neoclassical Economics*, Hingham, MA: Kluwer, pp. 31–71.

Dasgupta, Partha (1993), *An Inquiry into Well-Being and Destitution*, Oxford: Clarendon Press.

Dasgupta, Partha (2005), 'What do economists analyze and why: values or facts?' *Economics and Philosophy*, **21**, 221–78.

Dobb, Maurice H. (1973), *Theories of Value and Distribution since Adam Smith: Ideology and Economic Theory*, Cambridge: Cambridge University Press.

Mongin, Philippe (2006), 'A concept of progress for normative economics', *Economics and Philosophy*, **22**, 19–54.

Murdoch, Iris (1970), *The Sovereignty of 'Good'*, London: Routledge and Kegan Paul.

Putnam, Hilary (1994), *Words and Life*, ed. James Conant, Cambridge, MA: Harvard University Press.

Putnam, Hilary (2002), *The Collapse of the Fact/Value Dichotomy and Other Essays*, Cambridge, MA: Harvard University Press.

Putnam, Hilary and Vivian C. Walsh (2007), 'Facts, theories values and destitution: a response to Sir Partha Dasgupta', *Review of Political Economy*, **19** (2), pp. 181–202.

Quine, W.V.O. ([1951] 1953), 'Two dogmas of empiricism', in *From a Logical Point of View*, Cambridge, MA: Harvard University Press, pp. 20–46.

Quine, W.V.O. (1963), 'Carnap and logical truth', in Paul A. Schilpp (ed.), *The Philosophy of Rudolph Carnap*, La Salle, IL: Open Court.

Robbins, Lionel R. ([1932] 1935), *An Essay on the Nature and Significance of Economic Science*, London: Macmillan.

Robbins, Lionel R. (1938), 'Interpersonal comparisons of utility: a comment', *Economic Journal*, **48**, 635–41.

Robbins, Lionel R. (1971), *Autobiography of an Economist*, London: Macmillan.

Samuelson, Paul A. ([1947] 1983), *Foundations of Economic Analysis*, Cambridge, MA: Harvard University Press.

Sen, Amartya (1970), *Collective Choice and Social Welfare*, Amsterdam: North Holland.

Sen, Amartya (1987), 'Dobb, Maurice Herbert', in John Eatwell, Murray Milgate and Peter Newman (eds), *The New Palgrave Dictionary of Economics*, Vol. 1, London: Macmillan, pp. 910–12.

Sen, Amartya (1999), *Development as Freedom*, New York: Knopf.

Sen, Amartya (2002), *Rationality and Freedom*, Cambridge, MA: The Belknap Press of Harvard University Press.

Sen, Amartya (2005), 'Walsh on Sen after Putnam', *Review of Political Economy*, **17** (1), 107–13.

Stiglitz, Joseph E. (2003), *Globalization and its Discontents*, New York: W.W. Norton.

Walsh, Vivian C. (2008), 'Freedom values and Sen: towards a morally enriched classical economic theory', *Review of Political Economy*, **20** (2), pp. 199–232.

White, Morton (1956), *Toward Reunion in Philosophy*, Cambridge, MA: Harvard University Press.

White, Morton (1981), *What is and What Ought to be Done, an Essay on Ethics and Epistemology*, New York: Oxford University Press.

White, Morton (1986), 'Normative ethics, normative epistemology, and Quine's holism', in Lewis E. Hahn and Paul A. Schlipp (eds), *The Philosophy of W.V. Quine*, La Salle, IL: Open Court.

See also the entries on: Positive versus normative economics; Amartya Sen.

21 Fairness
Tom De Herdt and Ben D'Exelle

'Fair' is something we ask others to be. It is an injunction to act in a particular way. Before we proceed to describe the particularity of this, it is important to acknowledge that the use of fairness arguments in our conversation with others already presupposes a more complicated reading of human behaviour than the *homo economicus* model would suggest. People do not merely maximize utility given fixed preferences and a set of constraints; others can make them do otherwise. If not, there would be no point in trying to convince a person to do something.

To be sure, there is a large literature on fairness that tries to capture the idea's essence within the standard rational choice paradigm. Though this literature misses a crucial point, it is nevertheless instructive, as it allows us to reach a finer understanding of what people mean by 'fair behaviour'. Fairness injunctions generate three kinds of questions: what moves people to act fairly? What moves people to injunct others to act fairly? And, what do people mean by fairness?

The injunction to act fairly is more ambitious than the injunction to act reasonably and less ambitious than the injunction to act unselfishly. When we expect our dinner from the butcher, the baker and the brewer, we 'address ourselves not to their humanity but to their self-love, and never talk to them of our own necessities but of their advantages', says Adam Smith ([1791] 1979, p. 27). When we invoke fairness arguments, however, we address ourselves to more than people's self-love but to less than their humanity. Max Weber argues,

> When a man who is happy compares his position with that of one who is unhappy, he is not content with the fact of his happiness, but desires something more, namely the right to his happiness, the consciousness that he has earned his good fortune, in contrast to the unfortunate one who must equally have earned his misfortune. (Cited in Scott 1990, p. 68)

Concomitantly, acting fairly 'earns' you the right to your happiness. People are also prepared to forgo private happiness to earn public recognition for doing so. The fair trade movement is fundamentally built on the idea that at least in some circumstances – and particularly in contexts like North-South transactions, in which the parties enjoy vastly different bargaining positions (Maseland and De Vaal 2002), the gains from the trade are not 'earned' in a Weberian sense.

Game experiments may be helpful in refining how people understand fairness and how it impacts on behaviour. That people withdraw from unfair deals even at significant personal cost (or forgone profit) to themselves is borne out by numerous so-called 'ultimatum game' experiments. In an ultimatum game (Güth et al. 1982) one player (the proposer, say, Mr P) receives a fixed amount of money that he must distribute between himself and another player (the respondent, say, Ms R). R can accept or reject, and if she rejects neither player receives anything.

Experimental results typically show that average offers are around 30–40 per cent of the available amount, and most Ps offer half of the available amount of money. At the same time, most offers of less than 20 per cent are rejected (Camerer and Thaler 1995). These results are also valid when the amount of money to be distributed is increased, from $10 to $100 (Hoffman et al. 1996a).

Why would P make a more or less fair proposition? P's behaviour may be interpreted in either of two ways. Either P strategically anticipates R's rejection of inequitable allocations, or he is concerned with an equitable allocation himself. The latter possibility demonstrates what Adam Smith called 'humanity', the former merely signals P's ability to empathize with R. To single out humanity, the ultimatum game was converted into a 'dictator game' by eliminating R's option to reject and thus eliminating any strategic considerations of P. Results show that in most dictator games a considerable amount of non-zero offers are made, although the offers are significantly lower than in ultimatum games (Hoffman et al. 1994). Further research, however, has demonstrated that these results are biased by experimenter effects: dictators make non-zero offers because they care about their image in the eyes of the experimenter. Once such third-party effects are excluded, virtually all positive offers disappear (Hoffman et al. 1996b). Thus, in ultimatum experiments, non-zero offers have to do with reputation and empathy, rather than with humanity and sympathy.

More interesting for our purpose is why R, the responder, rejects. Mere unfairness seems an insufficient explanation. The majority of Rs accept moderately inequitable proposals (that is, offers between 30 per cent and 49 per cent). This suggests that there is no straightforward link between ideas about fairness and inclinations to act on them. In trying to understand people's withdrawal from grossly inequitable situations, researchers have played the ultimatum game with numerous variations and slight alterations. It is impossible to review all of these here. However, we would like to draw attention to some specific elements.

First, the experimental results do not indicate that *dependency* as such is experienced as problematic. Note that the very structure of the ultimatum game reflects an asymmetric relationship between the two players: R's payoff always depends on P's decision. But this is not a reason to systematically reject any proposal made by P. Neither is an *unequal* proposal, as such, a problem. Many respondents accept slightly unequal proposals. Only grossly unequal propositions trigger rejection by the respondents. It can be argued, in this respect, that people find themselves in a 'parallelogram of forces' (Elster 1989, p. 110) constituted by fair treatment on the one side and what they stand to lose by insisting on their social status on the other. The complication is that these forces do not exert a uniform influence on behaviour over the whole range of possible offers. One might think here in terms of an explanatory model of behaviour that distinguishes between direct and virtual determinants of behaviour (Pettit 1995). As long as a particular allocation falls within some bounds, people allow themselves to play for advantage. Beyond those bounds, however, a bell rings and people start to undertake an entirely different kind of action. Only grossly inequitable proposals are demeaning enough to cause moral indignation (Ulmann-Margalit and Sunstein 2001), and so are rejected.[1] As long as the deviation from the fair solution is not too great, it is possible for R to postpone a reading of the outcome as signalling unfairness.

Second, there is no consensus amongst individuals about the threshold at which the bell rings. To be sure, experimental evidence demonstrates that the average rejection rate varies according to age groups (Murnighan and Saxon 1998; Harbaugh et al. 2002), gender categories (Eckel and Grossman 2001) and cultural setting (Henrich et al. 2004). But beyond the averages there exists considerable inter-individual variation in the 'threshold' at which people start to reject an inequitable offer. Even in experimental situations, while trying to isolate as many contaminating factors as possible and to remove every source of ambiguity from the context, variation between individuals remains. Some reject at relatively modest levels of unfairness; others are much more tolerant and accept even very unequal propositions. Based on this insight, Ulmann-Margalit and Sunstein (2001) argue that one of the important roles of what they call 'indignation entrepreneurs' is precisely that they coordinate the responders' labelling of particular allocations as 'humiliating'. They thus clarify a 'fairness norm' from which deviation can be rightfully sanctioned.

Compare this account of fairness norms with rational choice accounts, which explain social norms as evolutionary products. As theoretically elaborated and documented with evidence from hunter-gatherer societies, fairness norms can only emerge when people are able to mutually monitor one another (Binmore 2005) or when 'strong reciprocators' are prepared even to punish unfair behaviour towards others (Gintis 2000; Fehr et al. 2002). For Ulmann-Margalit and Sunstein, the collective action problem of the generation and maintenance of social norms has less to do with the availability of monitoring and punishment mechanisms than with the ability to coordinate perceptions of 'right' and 'wrong'.

Third, the point at which one decides to act on the basis of one's fairness beliefs is not primarily defined in terms of a particular distribution of outcomes. Indeed, fairness is not merely about the final outcome (outcome-based fairness), it is also about procedural fairness, about how one feels treated by the other (see, for example, Anand 2001 and de Cremer and van Knippenberg 2005 for a distinction between the two). In this reading, unequal payoffs are but a symptom symbolizing a relation of dominance of P over R. What counts is P's agency over R. As a proof of the contrary, experiments have demonstrated that Rs readily accept highly unequal allocations when they know that P could not do otherwise (Falk et al. 2003) or when they play against a computer (for example, Blount 1995). We are less reluctant to be dominated by 'chance and circumstances', than to be dominated by others. Likewise, 'the nature of things does not madden us, only ill will does', said Rousseau (cited in Berlin 1958). Conversely, to the extent that people can be convinced that their situation is due to bad luck, they will more readily accept gross inequality. In this sense, a discourse on vulnerability vis-à-vis nature which ignores vulnerability vis-à-vis others may sustain a social order and contribute to the reproduction of poverty (De Herdt and D'Exelle, 2007). Besides bad luck, *circumstances* offer another convincing argument to accept unfair allocations. In an experiment by Roth et al. (1991), for example, multiple buyers each submit an offer to a single seller and only the one with the highest bid is accepted by the seller whereas the other buyers receive nothing. The buyers in the experiment reported by Roth and colleagues are similar to the responders in the ultimatum game, except that there is now more than one R. As each buyer tries to overbid the other buyers, all accept very high prices, far from the equal split. The unequal allocation between buyer and seller is legitimized by the circumstances of competition between buyers.

Fourth, the threshold between acceptable and unacceptable allocations relates in part to the extent to which the end result can be legitimated by each actor's relative contribution. Hoffman et al. (1994) demonstrated that P offered significantly less, and R rejected P's proposal significantly less, when P 'earned' his position – for example, by being the winner in a trivia quiz rather than having been assigned his position by lot.[2] By analogy, Bowles and Gintis (1999) report evidence that US citizens do not so much oppose the US welfare system because it would cost them too much or even because they disagree that 'it is the responsibility of the government to take care of people who cannot take care of themselves'. In fact, in a 1995 *New York Times*/CBS poll, it appeared that twice as many respondents agreed as disagreed on this statement. The issue is rather that US citizens see people actually living on welfare as undeserving of such aid, because their predicament can be attributed, in one way or another, to their own fault. Similarly, race-based opposition to welfare can be traced back to the specific perception that, as a group, 'African Americans are not committed to the work ethic' (Gilens 1999).

The connection between effective allocation of resources and each actor's perceived responsibility deserves further comment. It must be noted that the Hoffman et al. (1994) result does not completely reflect Aristotle's equity formula, which predicts relative outcomes (*O*) on the basis of relative contributions (*C*) (Konow 2000):

$$\frac{C_A}{C_B} = \frac{O_A}{O_B}$$

Indeed, there is not really a tight mathematical relationship between winning a trivia quiz and being entitled to a larger share in an ultimatum game setting. Yet, the performance of both players in the quiz is sufficient both for P to claim a larger share and for R to accept a more unequal distribution. The mere association between the quiz results and the ultimatum game positions is enough to legitimize an unequal distribution. It is in fact rather unsettling how easy it is to modify experimental outcomes just by changing the narrative introducing an experiment (Hoffman and Spitzer 1985; Larrick and Blount 1997). The high sensitivity of ultimatum game outcomes to the precise way in which the game is framed by a particular discourse should not be interpreted as a reliability problem invalidating the experimental outcomes. Yet it does provide information about 'how the mind works in real players' (Hoffman et al. 2000, p. 6) and how real players' behaviour can be modified by alternative discourses, so as either to redress the inequality or confirm the status quo.

Though laboratory experiments allow specifying the conditions under which ill will can madden us, they also by definition create an artificial environment that filters out some aspects of life outside of the laboratory. More particularly, most structured experiments limit themselves to a set of discrete choices with clear payoffs within a pre-specified game. In our view, real life differs from such a situation in a number of respects, which are in themselves quite important as determinants of acceptance or rejection of particular allocations.

First, though laboratory experiments do, for obvious reasons, work with abstract units of measurement to count 'contributions' and 'payoffs', these may be so qualitatively different in real-life situations that any attempt to compare them might be a source of considerable divergence. Look at the battle of the sexes at the household level. There is undoubtedly much less disagreement about the principle that spouses' contributions to household chores must be distributed evenly than about how exactly this principle can be operationalized. For instance, how do household chores compare to a formal job? Even the difference between 'contributions' and 'payoffs' may be open for discussion: is 'child caring' not also a payoff? What about the job satisfaction associated with most high-level jobs? In real life, the assumption of 'common knowledge' on the basis of which experiments are organized is far from self-evident.

Beyond measurement problems, there may be agreement that allocations should be proportionate to each person's contributions, but there may be huge disagreement about the way in which particular events are attributable to one's own or other people's agency, or to nature. Inequalities that can be 'naturalized' as inevitable or as accidental are more readily accepted. Conversely, Sen's entitlement approach to famines (1983) was effectively intended to de-naturalize famine victims and consider them rather as the result of institutional failure than as the victims of the whims of nature. If local discourses have a crucial role to play in the acceptability of unequal claims and obligations, the development of alternative discourses has a crucial role to play in poverty alleviation.[3]

Finally, by necessity experimental games must focus on particular interactions to be able to isolate their effects as neatly as possible. Pursuing the game metaphor, real life is, in contrast, an 'ecology of games' (Long 1958). In real-life game ecologies, people always have the opportunity to at least symbolically redress an outcome they experienced as inequitable in another game. In terms of the ultimatum game, all rejections can indeed be interpreted as ways to oppose the proposal – Hirschman (1970) would call this the 'exit option' – but not all accept that strategies should be interpreted as subscriptions to the underlying fairness norm, or 'loyalty', in Hirschman's terms. Though this is impossible in a laboratory where experiments must be uniformly structured, in open-ended ecologies people may first, officially, accept a proposal but then, later, try to go back in order to redress the situation. The ethnographic account of this possibility was developed by James Scott (1990) under the heading 'hidden transcripts'. People are often not given the opportunity to express their fairness judgements and to influence local distributive processes. In some cases even if they were given the opportunity to express their discontent with the current situation, they would refuse to do so because of a lack of self-confidence or fear of openly entering into a conflict which could make them worse off. This does not mean they accept their plight without any further opposition, however. Their involvement in other interactions may allow them to cultivate alternative discourses and henceforth the disposition to act upon them.

Notes

1. Others talk of 'wounded pride' (Pillutla and Murnighan 1996).
2. This result is confirmed by Gächter and Riedl (2006), who allow players to freely negotiate for a limited amount of time.
3. Note that we do not consider 'information' as such a problem, nor the biased way in which individuals process information (Babcock and Loewenstein 1997). The crucial question is how people come to share their perception of the situation, and this is why we focus on discourses as filters processing information.

References

Anand, Paul (2001), 'Procedural fairness in economic and social choice: evidence from a survey of voters', *Journal of Economic Psychology*, **22**, 247–70.
Babcock, Linda and George Loewenstein (1997), 'Explaining bargaining impasse: the role of self-serving biases', *Journal of Economic Perspectives*, **11** (1), 109–26.

Berlin, Isaiah (1958), *Two Concepts of Liberty*, Oxford: Clarendon Press.

Binmore, Ken (2005), *Natural Justice*, Oxford: Oxford University Press.

Blount, Sally (1995), 'When social outcomes aren't fair: the effect of causal attributions on preferences', *Organizational Behavior and Human Decision Processes*, 63, 131–44.

Bowles, Samuel and Herbert Gintis (1999), 'Is inequality passé? Homo reciprocans and the future of egalitarian politics', *Boston Review*, 23 (6), 23–58.

Camerer, Colin and Richard H. Thaler (1995), 'Anomalies: ultimatums, dictators and manners', *Journal of Economic Perspectives*, 9 (2), 209–19.

De Cremer, David and Daan van Knippenberg (2005), 'Cooperation with leaders in social dilemmas: on the effects of procedural fairness and outcome favorability in structural cooperation', *Organization Behavior and Human Decision Processes*, 91, 1–11.

De Herdt, Tom and Ben D'Exelle (2007), 'La vulnérabilité vis-à-vis d'autres personnes: leçons pour les interventions contre la pauvreté', *Mondes en Développement*, 35 (4), 101–14.

Eckel, Catherine C. and Philip J. Grossman (2001), 'Chivalry and solidarity in ultimatum games', *Economic Inquiry*, 39 (2), 171–88.

Elster, Jon (1989), *The Cement of Society*, Cambridge: Cambridge University Press.

Falk, Armin, Ernst Fehr and Urs Fischbacher (2003), 'On the nature of fair behavior', *Economic Inquiry*, 41 (1), 20–26.

Fehr, Ernst, Urs Fischbacher and Simon Gächter (2002), 'Strong reciprocity, human cooperation and the enforcement of social norms', *Human Nature*, 13, 1–25.

Gächter, Simon and Arno Riedl (2006), 'Dividing justly in bargaining problems with claims: normative judgments and actual negotiations', *Social Choice and Welfare*, 27 (3), 571–94.

Gilens, Martin (1999), *Why Americans Hate Welfare: Race, Media, and the Politics of Antipoverty Policy*, Chicago, IL: University of Chicago Press.

Gintis, Herbert (2000), 'Strong reciprocity and human sociality', *Journal of Theoretical Biology*, 206, 169–79.

Güth, Werner, Rolf Schmittberger and Bernd Schwarze (1982), 'An experimental analysis of ultimatum bargaining', *Journal of Economic Behavior and Organization*, 3, 367–88.

Harbaugh, William T., Kate S. Krause and Steven G. Liday (2002), 'Bargaining by children', University of Oregon Economics Department Working Papers, University of Oregon, Eugene, OR.

Henrich, Joe, Robert Boyd, Samuel Bowles, Colin Camerer, Ernst Fehr and Herbert Gintis (eds) (2004), *Foundations of Human Sociality: Economic Experiments and Ethnographic Evidence from Fifteen Small-Scale Societies*, Oxford: Oxford University Press.

Hirschman, Albert O. (1970), *Exit, Voice, and Loyalty: Responses to Decline in Firms, Organizations, and States*, Cambridge, MA: Harvard University Press.

Hoffman, Elizabeth and M.L. Spitzer (1985), 'Entitlements, rights and fairness: an experimental examination of subjects' concepts of distributive justice', *Journal of Legal Studies*, 14 (2), 259–97.

Hoffman Elizabeth, Kevin McCabe, K. Shachat and Vernon Smith (1994), 'Preferences, property rights, and anonymity in bargaining games', *Games and Economic Behavior*, 7 (3), 346–80.

Hoffman, Elizabeth, Kevin McCabe and Vernon Smith (1996a), 'On expectations and monetary stakes in ultimatum games', *International Journal of Game Theory*, 25 (3), 289–301.

Hoffman, Elizabeth, Kevin McCabe and Vernon Smith (1996b), 'Social distance and other-regarding behavior in dictator games', *American Economic Review*, 86 (3), 653–60.

Hoffman, Elizabeth, Kevin McCabe and Vernon Smith (2000), 'The impact of exchange context on the activation of equity in ultimatum games', *Experimental Economics*, 3, 5–9.

Konow, James (2000), 'Fair shares: accountability and cognitive dissonance in allocation decisions', *American Economic Review*, 90 (4), 1072–91.

Larrick, Richard P. and Sally Blount (1997), 'The claiming effect: why players are more generous in social dilemmas than ultimatum games', *Journal of Personality and Social Psychology*, 72, 810–25.

Long, Norton E. (1958), 'The local community as an ecology of games', *American Journal of Sociology*, 64, 251–61.

Maseland, Robbert and Albert de Vaal (2002), 'How fair is fair trade?', *De Economist*, 150 (3), 251–72.

Murnighan, J. Keith and Michael S. Saxon (1998), 'Ultimatum bargaining by children and adults', *Journal of Economic Psychology*, 19, 415–45.

Pettit, P. (1995), 'The virtual reality of homo economicus', *Monist*, 78 (3), 308–29.

Pillutla M.M. and J.K. Murnighan (1996), 'Unfairness, anger, and spite: emotional rejections of ultimatum offers', *Organizational Behavior and Human Decision Processes*, 68 (3), 208–24.

Roth, Alvin E., Vesna Prasnikar, Masahiro Okuno-Fujiwara and Shmuel Zamir (1991), 'Bargaining and market behavior in Jerusalem, Ljubljana, Pittsburgh and Tokyo: an experimental study', *American Economic Review*, 81, 1068–95.

Scott, James C. (1990), *Domination and the Arts of Resistance: Hidden Transcripts*, New Haven, CT: Yale University Press.

Sen, Amartya (1983), 'Development: which way now?', *Economic Journal*, **93** (372), 742–62.
Smith, Adam ([1791]1979), *An Inquiry into the Nature and Causes of the Wealth of Nations*, ed. R.H. Campbell and A.S. Skinner, Oxford: Clarendon Press.
Ullmann-Margalit, Edna and Cass R. Sunstein (2001), 'Inequality and indignation', *Philosophy and Public Affairs*, **30**, 60–82.

See also the entries on: Equity; Game theory; Inequality.

22 Feminism
Drucilla K. Barker and Darla Schumm

This chapter considers feminism, ethics and economics. In particular, it looks at the parallels between feminist economics and feminist ethics. Recent contributions to these fields question the notion of a universal moral agent and the 'rational economic man', underlining the need to include the voices of women and other marginalized groups and to consider needs and values contextually. The ethics of care has emerged as a central concern for both disciplines.

Economic agents and moral agents

The rational moral agent and the rational economic agent are both instances of the disembodied liberal subject in Enlightenment thought. Within economics, rationality is defined as the ability of individuals to order their preferences (their likes and dislikes) in a manner that is logically consistent and then, given the constraints of income and time, to make choices that maximize their self-interest. The idea that all actions are guided by self-interest has led feminist economists to call attention to the gendered nature of this abstract, disembodied subject, *homo economicus*.

Within ethics rationality is defined as acting according to the tenets of a particular ethical system – deontological, utilitarian, Aristotelian or situational ethics. Like feminist economics, feminist ethics call into question previously held assumptions which claim a universal gender-neutral moral agent who is capable of articulating and asserting universal moral principles. While historically most ethicists have maintained that the universal moral agent is defined as any rational person free from the constraints of gender, race or social location, feminist ethicists have more recently highlighted the gendered nature of the rational moral agent, who is said to directly represent the experiences of men in positions of power and elevated social status.

Alison Jaggar (1992) identifies a fourfold approach to feminist ethics that embodies the shift from claiming that ethics is a gender-neutral enterprise to recognizing the role that gender has played in constructing our understanding of morality and ethics. Jaggar argues that feminist ethics: (i) articulates moral critiques of actions and practices that perpetuate women's subordination, (ii) prescribes morally justifiable ways of resisting such actions and practices, (iii) envisions morally desirable alternatives for such actions and practices, and (iv) takes women's moral experience seriously, though not uncritically. Thus a central focus of feminist ethics is to prioritize the voices and experiences of all persons – women and men – as active moral agents capable of participating in the construction of systems of morals and ethics.

Feminist economists are engaged in a similar enterprise. They have shown that the scientific knowledge claims made by neoclassical economics are inevitably saturated with a variety of contextual values and ethical commitments that reflect the gender, race, class and social status of their practitioners. Indeed, economics is a remarkably homogeneous profession dominated by elite white men. Despite the slow increase in women and racial minorities over the past two decades, the profession as a whole has been famously slow in seeking out socially marginalized viewpoints from which to critically examine the general cultural assumptions that underlie economic knowledge.

The purported gender and race neutrality of the rational economic agent and the distinction between positive and normative economics are commonly accepted assumptions in the profession. However, as the feminist philosopher of science Sandra Harding (1995) has argued, when culturally specific values and interests shape research projects, the assumption of value neutrality legitimates institutions and practices through which distortions and their exploitative consequences are generated, because it allows the objections of marginalized groups to be dismissed as 'special' interests.

A feminist approach to economics, on the other hand, takes an explicitly ethical position. It is centrally concerned with reconstructing economics in a way that will be more responsive to the well-being of women and their families (Strassmann 1999).

Rationality, choice and values
The assumption of rationality is common to both ethics and economics. As stated above, within economics rationality refers to the ability of individuals to order their likes and dislikes in a manner that is logically consistent and, given the constraints of income and time, to make choices that maximize their self-interest. Within ethics, rationality refers to the ability of moral subjects to engage in moral reasoning and to make informed moral choices.

Julie Nelson (1993) has argued persuasively that the emphasis on choice in economics is related to the Cartesian dichotomy between embodiment and rationality. In this view, the abstract, detached, masculine view represents scientific thinking and is radically removed from the concrete, connected, feminine reality of material life. Nelson argues that making the detached *cogito* the object of study in economics means that nature, the body, children and the need for human connectedness remain cut off from masculine concern. Moreover, the emphasis on scarcity suggests that nature is hostile and stingy. This implies a conception of man dominating a passive, but nevertheless threatening, nature. Nelson suggests that instead of conceptualizing economics as a theory of choice, it could be conceived of as a theory of provisioning. This would enable feminist economists to direct their attention away from the theoretical modelling of utility-maximizing behaviour and toward examinations of ways to improve people's economic well-being.

Reconceiving economics in this way entails an explicit consideration of values and ethics, a consideration informed by feminist ethical commitment to eliminate the subordination of women and other marginalized groups. Nelson's suggestion echoes the four principles articulated by Jaggar and reminds us of the importance of including the voices and needs of all persons in economic and ethical conversations.

Feminist ethics and science
Helen Lognino is another feminist philosopher of science who argues that conceiving of science as value free, politically neutral and gender blind results in scientific knowledge that is distinctly androcentric and biased (Longino 1997). Longino's analysis starts from the Quinian under-determination thesis; that is, theories are always under-determined by the data used to support them (Quine 1953). There are multiple ways we can put together our theories of the world that would be consistent with the evidence, and since knowledge

claims about the world face the tribunal of evidence not in isolation but as part of a larger belief system, the same evidence can support a variety of theories. The familiar social science refrain, that correlation does not prove causation, is a good example of under-determination. According to Longino, one of the strategies developed to minimize the threat that the under-determination thesis poses to the scientific status of knowledge claims, is to invoke additional criteria from a pool of cognitive or theoretical values. These values – empirical adequacy, simplicity, accuracy, generality and so forth – are used to adjudicate competing scientific claims.

Longino posits a contrasting set of theoretical values that support feminist goals: empirical adequacy, novelty, ontological heterogeneity, mutuality of interaction, applicability to human needs and diffusion of power. Her purpose in contrasting this with a more traditional set of desiderata is not to show that we have two competing sets of values, but rather to show that in addition to empirical adequacy all theoretical values reflect additional cultural, sociological and political ideals. Since science cannot be value-neutral, the task of feminist scholarship is to carefully articulate what values are being expressed and whose interests are being served.

The feminist values articulated by Longino mesh well with the fourfold approach to feminist ethics articulated by Jaggar. Feminist economic work that does not perpetuate women's subordinate economic position may be examined in terms of Longino's feminist theoretical values. For example, novelty, as a theoretical value, entails privileging theories that postulate different entities, adopt different principles of explanation or investigate what traditional scientific inquiry has not. This is important for feminist economics because conventional economic explanations based on contractual exchanges between rational agents justify male privilege and treat women's subaltern economic position as a result of women's rational choices. Feminist economists admit other types of explanations that take into account gendered social norms such as reciprocity, responsibility and obligation, and so they come to quite different conclusions. The work on globalization and engendering macroeconomic modelling is a good example here.

This novel approach to macroeconomics accounts for the relationship between the economy of monetized production and the non-monetized economy of reproductive labour. The wealth of scholarship in this area has demonstrated that taking the social construction of gender seriously and making unpaid household labour visible fundamentally reshapes our understanding of the paid, market economy. Gendered social expectations not only shape women's experience of work, they also permeate all economic processes including economic globalization. Globalization will exacerbate inequalities between women and men unless gender issues are taken seriously (Benería et al. 2000). This claim echoes Jaggar's ethical injunction to take women's moral experience seriously.

We have chosen in this example to highlight novelty, but one could do this analytic exercise in terms of any or all of the other theoretical values. They are not mutually exclusive; in fact, they build on one another. Likewise, there are a myriad of other examples of the ways in which feminist economists are using feminist values to rewrite economics in ways that explicitly reflect feminist ethics. Alternative explanations of the gender wage gap, of occupational segregation and of intra-household decision-making and resource allocation are just three examples.

We would argue though that ontological heterogeneity has emerged as one of the most significant ethical considerations in feminist economics. Heterogeneity requires that economic theories question the centrality of the rational economic agent and take seriously relations of dependency between people. Likewise, economic agency is considered in ways other than constrained maximization, and social relationships are based on obligation, care and responsibility, as well as self-interest. The vast literature that has emerged on caring labour is a good example of how this approach can construe relationships of dependency and consider the needs of children, the aged and people with disabilities.

Ethics and caring labour
Over the past two decades the relationships between women's roles in social reproduction, women's subordinate position in paid labour markets and the marginalization of caring labour in capitalist economies have emerged as central concerns in feminist economics. Relatively affluent women entering the labour force use some of their income to purchase the domestic services no longer produced in the home, and these services are provided mainly by poor women from minority, working-class or global South immigrant backgrounds. This presents at least two ethical dilemmas. The first is that these caregivers have few options other than to participate in the poorly paid, insecure and devalorized segments of the transnational market for domestic labour. They do so often by forgoing the care of their own children and families. The second, and related ethical dilemma concerns the commodification of care.

Developing an ethics of care has emerged as one priority among feminist ethicists. Carol Gilligan (1982) was one of the earliest thinkers to introduce the idea of care as an ethical framework. In her pivotal work, *In a Different Voice*, Gilligan argues that the process of moral deliberation differs for men and women and that previous mainstream psychological and ethical theories largely represent male approaches to moral deliberation. Gilligan asserts that when facing moral dilemmas women focus on questions pertaining to issues of care and relationality, an ethics of care, while men focus on questions of rights and rules, an ethics of justice.

Gilligan's work was widely criticized among feminist and non-feminist thinkers alike. For feminist scholars, Gilligan's over-simplification of the essential nature of both men and women, her underlying and uncritical assumption of a singular description of women's experience and her implication that women are almost always culturally associated with care and men are almost always culturally associated with justice, represented serious flaws in her argument (Greeno and Maccoby 1986; Luria 1986). Nevertheless, Gilligan made two significant contributions to the debate within feminist ethics regarding care. First, Gilligan's work introduced a tension which has remained a central focus for feminist ethics: how to reconcile an ethics of care with an ethics of justice. Second, in spite of the concerns raised regarding the danger of associating women with an ethics of care in the context of a patriarchal society, Gilligan's work highlighted the need for a rigorous and realistic articulation of a feminist ethics of care.

Joan Tronto (1993) argues that the association of care with women and the private sphere has its roots in the late eighteenth century. During this time, European views of social relations were being transformed from a hierarchical world view to a more democratic one. Simultaneously, moral, social and political concerns were becoming less parochial and more universal. Direct and indirect contact with distant others raised the question, 'To whom does one have a moral obligation?' Answering this question entailed a shift from contextual moral theories to universal ones in both their deonto-logical Kantian form and their teleological utilitarian form. These forms of universal moral reasoning posed dilemmas that moved morality and care from the public sphere of politics and markets into the private sphere of the family and communities. Activities in the public sphere were conceived of in terms of rational calculations while those in the private sphere were conceived of in terms of altruism and care. The morality of the private sphere was a corrective to the amorality of market logic. Although he eschews explicit ethical considerations, the idea that selfishness guides market relations while altruism guides those in the home is evident in the economist Gary Becker's (1981) work on marriage and the family.

Similar to Tronto, Irene van Staveren (2001) argues that care is neither an individual value nor a public and universal value. Rather, care expresses contextual values between persons that arise from contingent needs and human vulnerability. Thus, an ethic of care must be theorized contextually rather than universally. Both Tronto and van Staveren show that the capacity for care is not necessarily an essentially feminine trait, but rather that specific economic, political and cultural changes occurred to create this connection.

Feminist scholars, such as Nel Noddings (1984) and Fiona Robinson (1999), likewise take up challenges presented by Gilligan's early work. Noddings develops an ethics of care based on the centrality of relationality. She argues that an ethics of care begins with the relationship between the person providing care and the person being cared for. Noddings maintains that an ethics of care is not a disinterested project, but that an understanding of real care arises when there is a connection, or relationship, between two people. This point is likewise articulated in feminist economics.

Susan Himmelweit (1995), in an article exploring the emergence of the concept, 'women's work', argues that activities like childcare do not fit into the category 'work' because the work being done is not separable from the person doing it. She argues that although it may seem appropriate to commodify many things formerly produced in the household, endeavours such as childcare, elder-care and caring for the emotional needs of family, friends and colleagues are not amenable to complete commodification. Caring labour should be considered analytically distinct from other sorts of social reproduction. The distinction is that whether paid or unpaid, the quality of care received depends, in part, on the quality of the relationships connecting the givers and the receivers of care. Himmelweit's concern over treating caring labour as work is that it devalues the rela-tional and self-fulfilling aspects of those activities. Moreover, people who perform caring activities are not considered real workers and the work remains devalued and largely invisible.

Anxieties over the commodification of caring labour are likewise found in the work of Nancy Folbre and Julie Nelson. Folbre's (1995) classic article argues that caring labour presents a paradox for feminist economists because the affective nature of care implies that it should be its own reward; however, if it does not command an economic return, its global supply will be diminished. Later, an article by Folbre and Nelson (2000) begins with the concern that many of the activities and tasks that were formerly performed by family or friends – rearing children, caring for the elderly, attending to the emotional needs of friends and workers – are now being performed within relationships based purely on monetary exchange. They draw a distinction between caring for and caring about, and argue that one of the distinctive features of care work is that it is undertaken for both love and money. Their concern is over the effects of commodification on the quality and quantity of care. The problem is that theorizing the affective component as 'caring about' leaves in place its gendered dualisms and does not invite a consideration of the ways in which the social value of caring labour is constituted by the social locations of the givers and receivers of care.

Cultural attitudes toward mothering practices in the United States provide a good example. When an impoverished African-American woman quits her job to care for her young children, social policy represents her as a lazy parasite on the social body. Her labour, rearing her children, has little or no social value. When an affluent white woman does the same thing she is extolled as a 'good mother'. When poor black, Latina or Filipina women are paid to care for the children of the affluent, this labour is suddenly valorized, but remains poorly paid relative to what might be earned by a young woman of European descent. The difference lies not in the nature of the work but rather in the political and cultural representations of the labouring bodies (Barker 2005).

Partly in response to some of the issues around essentialism and care, feminists have expanded their notion of care beyond the private realm. Noddings, for example, expands her ethics of care to the arena of social justice and public policy by arguing that the lessons learned in the domestic sphere regarding care must be applied when addressing social policy issues like homelessness and education. For Noddings, the basis for an ethics of care is first learned at home, but can, indeed must be, the basis for a relevant ethics of care which attends to issues of social justice.

Robinson insists even more emphatically than Noddings on the imperative to incorporate an ethics of care into tackling the social problems of our day. When confronting an issue like poverty, Robinson argues that a rigorous ethics of care must make privileged people aware of their part in perpetuating national and international structures which re-inscribe poverty. It is not enough to donate money to a charity to 'help' poor people; rather an ethics of care must educate the privileged about how their social location contributes to the system of poverty and motivate them to work for social, political and economic reform that instigates real change. Thus, a feminist ethics of care takes seriously the experiences and needs of women (although not at the expense of or to the exclusion of the experiences and needs of men) and is grounded in the caring that occurs in real relationships. It does not, however, limit itself to the private or domestic sphere as some critiques have alleged, but applies a robust understanding of care which insists on social, political and economic reform. Robinson's insight that the everyday practices inscribed by conventional social science accounts obscure the ways in which such practices lead to human suffering opens a space for considering the ethical questions raised by transnational markets for domestic services.

As we have seen, a feminist approach to the role of ethics in economics questions the notion of the universal moral agent as well as the rational economic agent. It does so without substituting a universal woman in their place. It highlights the importance of gender in thinking about morality and ethics, particularly in terms of the distinction between private and public and insists on a contextual rather than a universal conception of ethics. Finally, it insists on considering the voices and concerns of all economically and socially marginalized peoples.

References

Barker, Drucilla K. (2005), 'Beyond women and economics: rereading women's work', *Signs: Journal of Women in Culture and Society*, **30** (4), 2189–209.

Becker, Gary S. (1981), *A Treatise on the Family*, Cambridge, MA: Harvard University Press.

Benería, Lourdes, Maria Floro, Caren Grown and Martha MacDonald (2000), 'Introduction: globalization and gender', *Feminist Economics*, **6** (3), 7–18.

Folbre, Nancy (1995), 'Holding hands at midnight: the paradox of caring labor', *Feminist Economics*, **1** (1), 73–92.

Folbre, Nancy and Julie A. Nelson (2000), 'For love or money or both', *Journal of Economic Perspectives*, **14** (4), 123–40.

Gilligan, Carol (1982), *In a Different Voice: Psychological Theory and Women's Development*, Cambridge, MA: Harvard University Press.

Greeno, Catherine G. and Eleanor E. Maccoby (1986), 'How different is the "different voice"?' *Signs: Journal of Women in Culture and Society*, **11** (2), 310–16.

Harding, Sandra (1995), 'Can feminist thought make economics more objective?', *Feminist Economics*, **1** (1), 7–32.

Himmelweit, Susan (1995), 'The discovery of "unpaid work"', *Feminist Economics*, **1** (2), 1–20.

Jaggar, Alison M. (1992), 'Feminist ethics', in L. Becker and C. Becker (eds), *Encyclopedia of Ethics*, New York: Garland Press, pp. 363–4.

Longino, Helen (1997), 'Cognitive and noncognitive values: rethinking the dichotomy', in Lynn Hankinson Nelson and Jack Nelson (eds), *Feminisms, Science, and the Philosophy of Science*, Dordrecht: Kluwer Academic Publishers, pp. 39–58.

Luria, Zella (1986), 'A methodological critique', *Signs: Journal of Women in Culture and Society*, **11** (2), 316–21.

Nelson, Julie A. (1993), 'The study of choice or the study of provisioning? Gender and the definition of economics', in M.A. Ferber and J.A. Nelson (eds), *Beyond Economic Man: Feminist Theory and Economics*, Chicago, IL: University of Chicago Press, pp. 23–6.

Noddings, Nell (1984), *Caring: A Feminine Approach to Ethics and Moral Education*, Berkeley, CA: University of California Press.

Quine, Willard V.O. (1953), 'Two dogmas of empiricism', in *From a Logical Point of View*, 2nd edition, Cambridge, MA: Harvard University Press.

Robinson, Fiona (1999), *Globalizing Care: Feminist Theory, Ethics and International Relations*, Boulder, CO: Westview Press.

Staveren, Irene van (2001), *The Values of Economics: An Aristotelian Perspective*, London: Routledge.

Strassmann, Diana (1999), 'Feminist economics', in Janice Peterson and Margaret Lewis (eds), *The Elgar Companion to Feminist Economics*, Cheltenham, UK and Northampton, MA: Edward Elgar, pp. 360–71.

Tronto, Joan C. (1993), *Moral Boundaries: A Political Argument for an Ethic of Care*, New York: Routledge.

See also the entries on: Ethics of care; *Homo economicus*; Needs and agency; Rationality.

23 Freedom
Nicolas Gravel

Freedom in economics

In economics, individual freedom is examined through the formalism of *opportunity sets*. Any such opportunity set is interpreted as containing all options that are available for choice to the individual whose liberty is being evaluated. The budget set of standard consumer theory, which consists of all consumption bundles that a consumer can afford given her wealth and prevailing prices, is the most salient example of an opportunity set. The problem of defining freedom in that context amounts to defining what it means for one opportunity set to offer more freedom than another.

Negative or actual freedom?

The formalism of opportunity sets does not *a priori* restrict the nature of the constraints that limit the availability of options. These constraints can be physical (for example, 'I do not have the ability to play piano like Horowitz'), economic (for example, 'I cannot afford to own a second home') or legal (for example, 'I'm not allowed to sunbathe topless at the beach'). Yet some economists believe that the origin of the constraints matters for defining freedom. F.A. Hayek (1960, p. 12) is clearly one of them when he writes:

> [F]reedom refers only to a relation of men to other men, and the only infringement on it is coercion by men. This means, in particular, that the range of physical possibilities from which a person can choose at a given moment has no direct relevance to freedom. The rock climber on a difficult pitch who sees only one way out to save his life is unquestionably free, though we would hardly say he has any choice.

It has become common, after Isaiah Berlin (1969), to refer to the notion of freedom that focuses on constraints resulting only from the behaviour of other individuals – as opposed to those arising from physical or biological impediments – as *negative freedom*. While the view that only negative freedom matters has eloquent defenders, many writers (like Sen 1970; van Parijs 1995; and, before them, Knight 1947) believe that the relevant practical question is that of *actual* power or opportunity to do things rather than negative freedom. The formalism of opportunity sets, which leaves completely open the nature of the constraints that define the set, is compatible with both views. It is even possible, as illustrated by van Hees (1997), to consider a multilevel structure of constraints in which one defines first the set of options that are physically (say) available and then, in the feasible set, the subset of those options that are legally (say) available.

Extent of choice or causation by the will?

Defining freedom through a ranking of opportunity sets may seem an overly specific way of proceeding. For one thing, the approach seems to capture only the 'extent of choice' aspect of the notion. Yet, there are other accounts of freedom that do not seem reducible to the 'extent of choice'. The most important of these is probably that conveyed by the expression 'being one's own master'. Immanuel Kant (1998, p. 52) formulated this as follows:

> Will is that kind of causality attributed to living agents, in so far as they are possessed of reason; and freedom is such a property of that causality that enables them to originate events, independently of foreign determining causes.

This definition of freedom, as absence of determination by causes other than the 'will', irrigated a rich tradition of philosophical thinking, ranging from Kant to Jean-Paul Sartre and Berlin. Despite appearances, such an account of freedom is consistent with the approach based on a ranking of opportunity sets. An opportunity set is interpreted, indeed, as the set of options available for choice to the individual. This availability can be the result of various causes that are interpreted as *external* to the individual 'will'. It is the choice made by the individual, at some later stage, in the set that is the result of the 'will'. To that extent, an individual choosing from a 'large' opportunity set may be seen as exerting more will-power than another person choosing from a smaller opportunity set. For example, an individual choosing not to drink alcohol in a country where alcohol consumption is authorized may be seen as making a freer act than someone forced to abstinence by some prohibitive law.

While the opportunity set approach to freedom is consistent with the notion of liberty as 'causation by the will', it does not ride on it. Perhaps the individual is not making a choice according to will. Perhaps the individual chooses randomly by flipping a coin. One might choose by instinct, or by mechanically maximizing some objective function. In fact, the notion of freedom described here is applicable to animals. A tiger in a cage has fewer opportunities to do things than a tiger in the jungle, though few would be tempted to express the lack of liberty of the tiger in a cage in terms of the tiger's 'will'.

The important feature of the economic approach to freedom is the tight partitioning between things that the individual *can* do, and things that the individual *will* do, irrespective of the forces assumed to govern choices. While many conceptions of freedom would be tempted to distinguish between these forces – choosing out of impulse is not a free act while choosing out of thoughtful deliberation of the will is – the economic approach is incapable in its present state of development to make this distinction. Again, the only distinction made in the approach is that between the things that are available for choice (possibly after instinctive behaviour has eliminated possibilities) and the (usually unique) thing that will be chosen.

Defining freedom without referring to motivations
Some of the literature has defined freedom without explicitly referring to the future choice behaviour of the individual. On what principles should such a definition be based?

Monotonicity with set inclusion
An obvious principle that comes to mind is monotonicity with set inclusion. Two versions of this principle are considered in the literature. A first (weak) version says that adding an option to an opportunity set does not reduce freedom. A second (strong) version says that adding an option strictly increases freedom. The weak version of the principle is hardly disputable. What conception of freedom would consider that making *more*

options available for choice *reduces* freedom? More disputable is the strong principle that adding options to an opportunity set strictly increases freedom. Indeed, several writers have challenged the libertarian character of this principle by arguing that the addition of 'very bad' options, like, for instance, 'the possibility of being beheaded at dawn' (Sen 1988) does not necessarily increase freedom.

It seems however that this kind of argument, which refers to the value of the option from the viewpoint of the motivations underlying an individual's choice, is more a criticism of the attempt to define freedom without explicit reference to these motivations than a criticism of the adequacy of the principle to capture intuition about freedom given this attempt. It seems, after all, hardly disputable that adding options to an opportunity set, provided that the individual keeps the possibility of choosing or not the options, does strictly enlarge the individual's freedom to choose. If I am given the freedom to be beheaded at dawn upon request, hasn't my freedom to end my life in the way I choose increased?

A more immediate criticism of monotonicity with respect to set inclusion is its incompleteness. Suppose that the creation of a network of bicycle paths in a metropolis leads to a reduction in the space available for automobile traffic. Set inclusion does not provide any clue for appraising the impact of such a creation on the freedom to move around in the city. The bicycle paths certainly give more options to cyclists to move around safely, but they remove some of the options offered to car drivers to commute from one point to another. While the incompleteness of set inclusion as a definition of freedom can be serious in appraising the freedom to move in a city, it is not damaging when set inclusion is used to evaluate the economic freedom of an individual exposed to a given price system. For, in such an environment, an individual's wealth provides a (clearly complete) ranking of the budget sets that coincide with set inclusion.

Counting the number of options
An easy way to obtain a complete ranking of opportunity sets that is consistent with set inclusion is to compare sets on the basis of their *number* of available options. This ranking was informally suggested by F.A. Hayek (1960) about fifty years ago. It was given elegant, and widely discussed, axiomatic characterizations by Jones and Sugden (1982) and Pattanaik and Xu (1990). Should we be satisfied with this definition of freedom as the number of available options? Hayek, as well as more recent writers like van Hees (1997) would probably be inclined to answer affirmatively to this question.

Yet, if we leave aside the aforementioned 'beheaded at dawn' criticism, which applies with equal force here, there are at least two reasons for differing from these writers.

First, defining freedom by the number of available options entails the acceptance of the principle that sets containing only one option should all be considered equivalent. This conclusion may not at first seem bothersome. After all, an opportunity set offering only one option provides *no* freedom of choice. It seems therefore all the more normal that these sets be considered as offering the same level of freedom, that is, none. Yet a second thought may make one doubtful about this. Is it that clear that I am equally unfree when I am forced to get dental surgery without anaesthesia as when I am forced to get the dental surgery with anaesthesia? To some extent, this question refers to the value of the options from the viewpoint of the use that the individual will make of them. But to some other extent, there is no compelling reason why all situations in which one is forced to do something should be considered equivalent, especially when the 'thing' that one is forced to do is different.

It is possible to address this kind of concern by considering an *additive generalization* of the ranking of sets according to their number of elements. For instance, one could think of attaching a (non-negative) 'freedom weight' to every conceivable option and to rank sets on the basis of the sum of the weights of their options. Comparing sets on the basis of their number of options is just one particular member of this class of additive rules, in which each option is assigned the same 'freedom-weight'. But there is no reason to limit oneself to this particular member. For instance, it may be believed that the possibility of undergoing dental surgery without anaesthesia has less impact on one's freedom than the possibility of undergoing the same surgery with anaesthesia. The additive generalization of the counting rule was discussed by Klemisch-Ahlert (1993) and axiomatically characterized in Gravel et al. (1998). While it significantly enlarges the class of freedom-based rankings of sets that one may wish to consider, this generalization leaves completely undetermined the question of the choice of the weights attached to the options. Without a specific reason for attaching more weight to dental surgery with anaesthesia than to surgery without anaesthesia – like, for instance, the fact that any reasonable person would prefer going through dental surgery with a anaesthesia than without – why weight them differently? There is, indeed, no reason for weighting them in one way or another. But there is no reason for weighting them equally either. The family of additive rankings of sets has the merit of covering all of the logically conceivable kinds of options weighting that one may wish to consider.

Freedom and diversity

A second problem with the ranking of sets based on their number of elements, also shared by the additive generalization, is the assumption that the contribution of an option to freedom is *independent* of the set to which the option belongs. To take a transportation example once again, suppose that we agree to say that someone who is forced to make a trip using a blue car has the same (null) freedom of choice as someone who is forced to make the same trip using a green bicycle. Suppose now that the possibility of making the trip using a blue bicycle is made available to both individuals. Does this imply that the individual who now has the choice between a blue car and a blue bicycle has the same freedom of choice as the individual who has the choice between a green bicycle and a blue bicycle? Few of us, it seems, would be inclined to answer affirmatively to this question. After all, as Thomas Aquinas put it some 800 years ago, 'An angel is more valuable than a stone. It does not follow, however, that two angels are more valuable than one angel and one stone' (from *Summa contra Gentiles III*, cited in Nehring and Puppe 2002).

Any plausible account of freedom, it seems, should be sensitive to the dissimilarities of the options available for choice, and should attach some importance to the diversity of choice. By failing to express such a sensitivity, additive rankings fail to qualify as completely plausible definitions of freedom. Yet, diversity is a delicate notion. In the last fifteen years, significant efforts have been made toward understanding what it means for one set of objects to be 'more diverse' than another. Approaches have examined the question by taking as given the existence of an underlying notion of pairwise dissimilarities between the objects and by defining diversity as aggregate dissimilarity.

These approaches differ in the information they assume to be available on the pairwise dissimilarities between objects. Some, like Weitzman (1998) and Bossert et al. (2003), have supposed that this pairwise dissimilarity can be measured precisely by a *distance function* that enables one to say things like 'the dissimilarity between a blue car and a blue bicycle is ten times as large as the dissimilarity between a green and a blue bicycle'. Others, like Pattanaik and Xu (2000) or Bervoets and Gravel (2008) make the more prudent assumption that the underlying information on dissimilarity is only qualitative in nature. One also finds approaches, as in Nehring and Puppe (2002), that define diversity with respect to an underlying set of attributes possessed by the options as well as a function that weights these attributes. It is obviously beyond the scope of this chapter to discuss in detail this growing literature on diversity, which I have surveyed elsewhere (Gravel 2007).

Defining freedom with respect to motivations

Choices and preferences

Another branch of the literature defines freedom by making explicit reference to the future choice behaviour of the individual and to the motivations underlying this choice.

From an abstract point of view, choice behaviour can be described by a function that selects, in every opportunity set, a particular option. *A priori*, the choice behaviour can be anything. Yet, if it is completely arbitrary and unpredictable, the choice behaviour can hardly be used to define freedom. Economics commonly assumes that choices are not arbitrary but, instead, are 'instrumentally rational' in the sense that they result from the maximization of some objective. There has been considerable discussion as to what this objective is. Economists of welfarist inclination would be tempted to say that it is somewhat connected to the individual's personal 'well-being'. But a great many other objectives have been considered as well, ranging from several forms of concern for others (altruism or, to the contrary, jealousy and malevolence) to behaviours resulting from 'a sense of duty'. The only feature of the objective that commands a large support is its assumed minimal structure: it produces a complete and transitive ranking of all options. Economists refer to the objectives that govern the individual's choice as the individual's *preferences*. How can these preferences be used to define freedom?

A given preference

If an individual has preferences amongst options and chooses, in every opportunity set, the option that they most prefer, there seems to be an easy answer to this question. One opportunity set offers more freedom than another if, and only if, the choice made in the first set is preferred to that made in the other. Following Bossert et al. (1994), the literature now commonly refers to this ranking as 'the indirect utility ranking'. This ranking is clearly weakly monotonic with respect to set inclusion, since someone who chooses optimally from a set from the viewpoint of some objective cannot lose from the addition of options to the set. If the added options are valuable, the individual will choose them and will consider the enlargement a strict improvement. If none of the added options is valuable, then the individual will not choose them and will, therefore, not lose from their availability. Of course, in the latter case, the individual does not gain either from the availability of the added option. Hence, the indirect utility ranking is not strongly monotonic with respect to set inclusion.

If individual preferences are related to well-being, then the indirect utility ranking of opportunity sets is precisely the ranking of opportunity sets that would be agreed upon by standard welfarist analysis. If this is the case, the indirect utility ranking of opportunity sets attaches no intrinsic importance to freedom and views freedom as an instrumental means of achieving greater well-being. If, on the other hand, the preference does not reflect the individual's well-being but, instead, a more complex 'objective' considered by the individual, say after a 'free deliberation of the will', to be worth pursuing, then the indirect utility ranking may represent a plausible conception of freedom.

A family of preferences

It may be held that freedom is, to some extent, the result of the 'indetermination' of the individual with respect to his or her preferences. A natural way to think of this indetermination is to posit the existence of a 'family of preferences' that could be used by the individual for making choices. The literature gives *two* different interpretations to the family of preferences.

First, the family is interpreted as the set of preferences that the individual *could* possibly have. In such a context of *ignorance* of the future preferences, freedom is considered as synonymous with *flexibility*. Once a family of possible preferences for the individual is defined, the ranking of sets can be viewed as an aggregation of the various indirect utility rankings of the sets, one such ranking for every possible preference. That is, freedom can be defined as the ranking of sets induced by some aggregation of the multiple 'selves' of the individual. There are several ways by which the aggregation can be performed. In Foster (1993), the ranking of sets is simply taken to be the unanimity of all indirect utility rankings of sets. Hence set A offers more freedom than set B if, for every possible preference, the most preferred option in A is preferable to the most preferred option in B. A problem with this ranking is its incompleteness. The ranking is, indeed, unable to compare sets A and B on which there are conflicting views among the individual's multiple selves as to which offers the best option. Kreps (1979) and Arrow (1995) suggest instead a complete ranking of sets based on comparison of the *expected value* of their best option, with expectations taken over all possible selves of the individuals. Puppe (1998), similarly, discusses the possibility of ranking opportunity sets according to the recommendation of a 'majority' of the individual selves. There are obviously many ways of thinking about how an undetermined individual who admits the possibility of having different 'selves' can aggregate them when taking a decision.

In the second interpretation, the family of preferences to which individual freedom refers need not be the possible preferences that the individual may have in the future. It is, rather, interpreted as the set of preferences that *any* 'reasonable' person could have. Pattanaik and Xu (1998) give the example of appraising the impact of a decision authorizing women to join the army on the freedom of some particular woman, 'Delima' say. They argue that such a decision could plausibly be seen as enlarging Delima's freedom, even if Delima is a committed pacifist and is absolutely sure that she would in no circumstance choose to join the army. The reason why, according to these authors, allowing women to enrol in the army can be seen as improving Delima's freedom is that it is conceivable that a 'reasonable person' *could* choose to enrol in the army. The approach obviously leaves aside the politically important question of how to determine when a person, or a preference, is 'reasonable'. Yet, provided that we can answer that question, defining freedom in terms of a family of preferences that a reasonable person could have leads naturally to a focus on those options that could be chosen by some reasonable preference. It is only the availability of those 'essential' options – that is, those options that are optimal from the viewpoint of some reasonable preference – that matters for freedom.

Various rankings of opportunity sets based on their subsets of 'essential' options have been proposed. The most discussed of these is the ranking of sets based on their *number of essential options.* Clearly, for such a criterion to be significantly different from the comparison of sets based on their total number of options, one must have a concept of 'reasonableness' of preference that is sufficiently tight. If any logically conceivable preference is a priori reasonable, then there is no difference between the opportunity set and its subset of essential options – as any option would then be essential. On the other hand, if the set of reasonable preferences is defined too narrowly, there is a risk that the notion of freedom will fail to account for essential opportunities.

Freedom in a social context

The approaches discussed so far focus on the definition of individual freedom in an abstract context where interactions between individuals are ignored. This leaves aside two important issues that are worth a brief mention. The first one concerns the question of how to allocate more justly the freedoms of the different individuals, after these have been properly defined. There is by now a large literature (see, for example, Roemer 1998; or, for a survey, Fleurbaey and Maniquet 2008) that attempts to make more precise the popular slogan of 'equalizing opportunities' as a normatively worthwhile objective.

Much of this literature addresses the issue of equalizing opportunities, not in terms of opportunity sets, but rather, by combining a (freedom-based) respect for individuals' responsibility for some of their decisions with an (egalitarian) concern for equalizing the aspects of the individuals' situation for which the persons cannot be held responsible. It is of course possible to connect this notion of 'responsibility' with that of freedom, as envisaged here, by considering that individuals are not responsible for the opportunity set they face but are responsible for the choice they will be making in that set. There have been attempts in the literature (see, for example, Bossert et al. 1999; Kranich 1996; and Ok 1997) to explore some of the issues raised by the comparisons of distributions of individual opportunity sets. In certain cases (for example, Bossert et al. 1999; Ooghe et al. 2007), the connection between the approach in terms of opportunity sets and of 'responsibility' is made explicit.

The second issue is less explored. It concerns the necessity, for defining freedom, of accounting for the interactions that exist between individuals. Accounting for these interactions is essential to make sense of popular expressions such as 'one's own freedom starts where another person's freedom ends'. From a formal point of view, introducing interactions in the analysis amounts to recognizing the fact that the final consequences of one's own choice also depend upon the choices made by others. This requires one to view an opportunity set as a set of *actions*, and to view each action as a set of all the possible *consequences* that it could have. The final consequence resulting from the choice of a particular action will, in this perspective, depend upon the choice of action made by others. The proper formalism for handling this structure is that of game forms, which describe precisely the actions available to each individual and the consequence that results from any combination of these actions. This formalism has been used by some (see, for example, Deb et al. 1997) as an alternative to the standard formal approach to rights derived from seminal work on the subject by Sen (1970) and Gibbard (1974). Yet much remains to be done in connecting the notion of individual rights to that of freedom. Bervoets (2007) made a recent attempt in this direction.

References

Arrow, Kenneth J. (1995), 'A note on freedom and flexibility', in Kaushik Basu, Prasanta Pattanaik and Kotaro Suzumura (eds), *Choice, Welfare and Development: A Festschrift in Honour of Amartya K. Sen*, Oxford: Oxford University Press, pp. 7–15.

Berlin, Isaiah (1969), *Four Essays on Liberty*, Oxford: Oxford University Press.

Bervoets, Sebastian (2007), 'Freedom of choice in a social context: comparing game forms', *Social Choice and Welfare*, **29**, 295–316.

Bervoets, Sebastian and Nicolas Gravel (2007), 'Appraising diversity with an ordinal notion of similarity: an axiomatic approach', *Mathematical Social Sciences*, **53**, 259–73.

Bossert, Walter, Prasanta Pattanaik and Yongsheng Xu (1994), 'Ranking opportunity sets: an axiomatic approach', *Journal of Economic Theory*, **63**, 326–45.

Bossert, Walter, Marc Fleurbaey and Dirk van de Gaer (1999), 'Responsibility, talent and compensation: a second best analysis', *Review of Economic Design*, **4**, 295–312.

Bossert, Walter, Prasanta Pattanaik and Yongsheng Xu (2003), 'Similarity of options and the measurement of diversity', *Journal of Theoretical Politics*, **15**, 405–21.

Deb, Rajat, Prasanta Pattanaik and Laura Razzolini (1997), 'Game forms, rights and the efficiency of social outcomes', *Journal of Economic Theory*, **72**, 74–95.

Fleurbaey, Marc and Francois Maniquet (2008), 'Compensation and responsibility', in Kenneth J. Arrow, Amartya Sen and Kotaro Suzumura (eds), *Handbook of Social Choice and Welfare*, Vol. 2, Elsevier, forthcoming.

Foster, James (1993), *Notes on effective freedom*, mimeo, Vanderbilt University, Nashville, TN.

Gibbard, Allan (1974), 'A pareto-consistent liberal claim', *Journal of Economic Theory*, **7**, 388–410.

Gravel, Nicolas (2008), 'What is diversity?' in T. Boylan and R. Gekker (eds), *Economics, Rational Choice and Normative Philosophy*, London: Routledge, pp. 15–55.

Gravel, Nicolas, Jean-Francois Laslier and Alain Trannoy (1998), 'Individual freedom of choice in a social setting', in Jean-Francois Laslier, Marc Fleurbaey, Nicolas Gravel and Alain Trannoy (eds), *Freedom in Economics: New Perspectives in Normative Analysis*, London: Routledge, pp. 76–92.

Hees, Martin van (1997), 'On the analysis of negative freedom', *Theory and Decision*, **45**, 175–97.

Hayek, Friedrich A. (1960), *The Constitution of Liberty*, London: Routledge.

Jones, Peter and Robert Sugden (1982), 'Evaluating choices', *International Journal of Law and Economics*, **2**, 47–65.

Kant, Immanuel (1998), *Groundwork of the metaphysics of ethics*, trans. M.J. Gregor, Cambridge, UK: Cambridge University Press.

Klemisch-Ahlert, Marlies (1993), 'Freedom of choice: a comparison of different rankings of opportunity sets', *Social Choice and Welfare*, **10**, 189–207.

Knight, Frank H. (1947), *Freedom and Reform: Essays in Economics and Social Philosophy*, New York: Harper.

Kranich, Laurence (1996), 'Equitable opportunities: an axiomatic approach', *Journal of Economic Theory*, **71**, 131–47.

Kreps, David M. (1979), 'A representation theorem for "preference for flexibility"', *Econometrica*, **47**, 565–77.

Nehring, Klaus and Clemens Puppe (2002), 'A theory of diversity', *Econometrica*, **70**, 1155–90.

Ok, Efe A. (1997), 'On opportunity inequality measurement', *Journal of Economic Theory*, **77**, 300–29.

Ooghe, Erwin, Eric Schokkaert and Dirk van de Gaer (2007), 'Equality of opportunity vs equality of opportunity sets', *Social Choice and Welfare*, **28**, 209–30.

Parijs, Philippe van (1995), *Real Freedom for All: What (If Anything) Can Justify Capitalism?* Oxford: Clarendon Press.

Pattanaik, Prasanta K. and Yongheng Xu (1990), 'On ranking opportunity sets in terms of freedom of choice', *Recherches Economiques de Louvain*, **56**, 383–90.

Pattanaik, Prasanta K. and Yongsheng Xu (1998), 'On freedom and preferences', *Theory and Decision*, **44**, 173–98.
Pattanaik, Prasanta K. and Yongsheng Xu (2000), 'On diversity and freedom of choice', *Mathematical Social Sciences*, **40**, 123–30.
Puppe, Clemens (1998), 'Individual freedom and social choice', in Jean-Francois Laslier, Marc Fleurbaey, Nicolas Gravel and Alain Trannoy (eds), *Freedom in Economics: New Perspectives in Normative Analysis*, London: Routlege, pp. 49–68.
Roemer, John E. (1998), *Equality of Opportunity*, Cambridge, MA: Harvard University Press.
Sen, Amartya (1970), 'The impossibility of a Paretian liberal', *Journal of Political Economy*, **78**, 152–7.
Sen, Amartya (1988), 'Freedom of choice: concept and content', *European Economic Review*, **32**, 269–94.
Weitzman, Martin L. (1998), 'The Noah's Ark problem', *Econometrica*, **66**, 1279–98.

See also the entries on: Capability approach; Individualism.

24 Game theory
Ken Binmore

Introduction
Game theory is sometimes dismissed as an instrument of evil designed to help selfish people exploit their power. However, game theorists believe their subject is ethically neutral. Like logic or mathematics, it can be used on either side of any dispute. When game theorists say what follows from what in a game, they no more offer a value judgement than a mathematician who asserts that $2 + 2 = 4$.

This brief chapter can only touch on how game theory can be used in ethics, much as mathematics is used in physics. My books *Natural Justice* (2005b) and *Game Theory and the Social Contract* (1994, 1998) offer a more comprehensive overview.

Toy games
Game theorists follow John von Neumann in making a virtue out of using the language of parlour games like chess or poker. People are usually able to think dispassionately about the strategic issues that arise in such games without throwing their hands up in horror if the logic leads to an unwelcome destination. But logic is the same whatever the context in which it is applied. The same principle applies to the toy games that game theorists use as examples. It is sometimes said that the world is too complicated to be captured by such simple models, but who learned to solve complicated problems without solving simple problems first?

The Stag Hunt
To illustrate his social contract theory, Jean-Jacques Rousseau ([1762] 1913) tells a story of two hunters, whom I call Adam and Eve. They agree to cooperate in hunting a stag, but when they separate to put their plan into action, each may be tempted to abandon the joint enterprise by the prospect of bagging a hare for themselves. As in Brian Skyrms's (2003) book *The Stag Hunt*, game theorists have interpreted Rousseau's story in terms of the toy game in Figure 24.1, known as the Stag Hunt game.

In the Stag Hunt game, each player has two strategies, dove (*d*) and hawk (*h*). Adam's two strategies are represented by the rows of the payoff table for the Stag Hunt Game in Figure 24.1. Eve's two strategies are represented by its columns. The four cells of the payoff table correspond to the possible outcomes of the game. Each cell contains two numbers, one for Adam and one for Eve. The number in the south-west corner is Adam's payoff for the corresponding outcome of the game. The number in the north-east corner is Eve's payoff.

Each player is assumed to seek to maximize his or her expected payoff. This would be easy if a player knew what strategy the other was going to choose. For example, if Adam knew that Eve was going to choose *dove* in the Stag Hunt game, he would maximize his payoff by choosing *dove* as well. That is to say, *dove* is Adam's best reply to Eve's choice of *dove*, a fact indicated in the payoff table by starring Adam's payoff in the cell that results if both players choose *dove*.

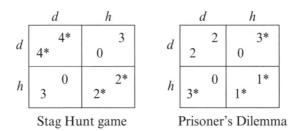

Stag Hunt game   Prisoner's Dilemma

Note: Two toy games: Payoff tables for the Stag Hunt game and the Prisoner's Dilemma. The four cells of the payoff table correspond to the possible outcomes of the game. Each cell contains two numbers, one for Adam and one for Eve. The number in the south-west corner is Adam's payoff for the corresponding outcome of the game. The number in the north-east corner is Eve's payoff. A pair of strategies whose play leads to a cell in which *both* payoffs are starred is a Nash equilibrium.

Figure 24.1   Two toy games

A pair of strategies whose play leads to a cell in which *both* payoffs are starred is called a 'Nash equilibrium'. A Nash equilibrium is therefore a pair of strategies, each of which is a best reply to the other. Nash equilibria are of interest for two reasons. If an authoritative book on game theory records the rational solution to a game, it must be a Nash equilibrium – otherwise it would be rational for at least one player to deviate from the book's recommendation. The second reason is equally important. An evolutionary process that always moves in the direction of better replies can only stop at a Nash equilibrium. Only Nash equilibria can therefore be evolutionarily stable.

The starred payoffs in the payoff table for the Stag Hunt Game show that the game has two Nash equilibria in pure strategies,[1] one in which the players cooperate by both playing like doves, and one in which they defect by both playing like hawks. Adam and Eve therefore have two candidates for a stable social contract[2] in their microcosm of a society. One of these is the Nash equilibrium (d, d). The other is the Nash equilibrium (h, h). The latter equilibrium – in which the players fail to cooperate – is inefficient, in the sense that both players would get a larger payoff at the equilibrium where they both play *dove*.

Several lessons can be learned from the Stag Hunt game. The first is that even very simple games can have more than one Nash equilibrium. Realistic games usually have very large numbers of equilibria. A society operating a stable social contract must therefore somehow have found its way to a solution of the equilibrium selection problem in the game of life that its citizens play. A second lesson is that Nash equilibria do not need to be (Pareto) efficient – all players can sometimes be made better off by moving away from a Nash equilibrium to some other outcome of the game.

A third lesson arises when we ask why the citizens of a society that found itself at a social contract corresponding to the inefficient equilibrium *(h, h)* wouldn't just agree to move to the efficient social contract (d, d). Experts in international relations refer to the Stag Hunt game as the Security Dilemma when using it to explain why matters aren't necessarily so simple.

However hard Adam seeks to persuade Eve that he plans to play *dove* in the future, she will remain unconvinced. Whatever Adam is actually planning to play, it is in his interests to persuade Eve to play *dove*. If he succeeds, he will get *4* rather than *0* if he is planning to play *dove*, and *3* rather than *2* if he is planning to play *hawk*. Rationality alone, therefore, does not allow Eve to deduce anything about his plan of action from what he says, because he is going to say the same thing no matter what his real plan may be.

Attributing rationality to the players therefore is not enough to resolve the equilibrium selection problem, even in a seemingly transparent case like the Stag Hunt game. This is not because game theory says that it is irrational for people to trust each other. Game theorists only say that it is not rational to trust people without a good reason: that trust can't be taken on trust.

Prisoner's Dilemma

When Immanuel Kant described Jean-Jacques Rousseau as the 'Newton of the moral world', it was not because he bought into the discussion of the stag hunt story given above. My own reading of Rousseau is that he was one of the first to claim that it is rational to cooperate in a version of the Prisoner's Dilemma – as stipulated by Kant's categorical imperative (Binmore 1994).

From an ethical perspective, the Prisoner's Dilemma of Figure 24.1, pinpoints the difference in outlook between David Hume and Immanuel Kant. Hume ([1739] 1978) asks, 'What theory of morals can ever serve any useful purpose, unless it can show that all the duties it recommends are also the true interest of each individual?' Kant tells us that we are not behaving morally if we act as we want, even if what we want is to act morally. In game theory terms, Hume's dictum restricts ethics to choosing among the Nash equilibria of our game of life. That is to say, ethics is a system of social norms whose ultimate purpose is to resolve the equilibrium selection problem in games. On the other hand, Kant tells us that individual optimization isn't rational at all, and so Nash equilibria are irrelevant to ethical behaviour.

Kant claimed that a truly rational individual will necessarily observe his categorical imperative: 'Act only on the maxim that you would at the same time will to be a universal law.' If everyone were to choose the same in the Prisoner's Dilemma, everyone would will that they all choose to cooperate by playing *dove*. But it is not a Nash equilibrium to play *dove* in the Prisoner's Dilemma. As the starred payoffs in Figure 24.1 show, the only Nash equilibrium is for both Adam and Eve to play *hawk*. However, the outcome (*h*, *h*) is inefficient because both players would get more by both playing *dove* instead.

A whole generation of scholars swallowed the line that the Prisoner's Dilemma embodies the essence of the problem of human cooperation, and hence that reasons need to be given why game theory's resolution of this supposed 'paradox of rationality' is mistaken. However, game theorists think it just plain wrong that the Prisoner's Dilemma embodies the essence of the problem of human cooperation. On the contrary, they think it represents a situation in which the dice are as loaded against the emergence of cooperation as they could possibly be. If the great game of life played by the human species were the Prisoner's Dilemma, we would not have evolved as social animals (Binmore 1994).

Cooperative game theory

The toy games of the previous section were discussed using the tools of non-cooperative game theory. Why not use the tools of cooperative game theory instead?

The distinction between cooperative and non-cooperative game theory originates in von Neumann and Morgenstern's (1944) *Theory of Games and Economic Behavior*. The first half of this path-breaking work is devoted to two-person zero-sum games, in which a gain for one player is automatically a loss for the other. Von Neumann's famous minimax theorem for such games characterizes their Nash equilibria. The methodology in this part of the book is therefore non-cooperative.

Von Neumann and Morgenstern devote the other half of their book to cooperative game theory, thereby creating an endless source of confusion for critics who mistakenly assume that non-cooperative game theory is exclusively about conflict and cooperative game theory is exclusively about cooperation. However, cooperative game theory differs from non-cooperative game theory only in its abandoning any pretension at explaining *why* cooperation survives in our species. It postulates instead that the players have access to an unmodelled black box whose contents resolve all the problems of commitment and trust that make ethics such a difficult subject. In particular, cooperative game theory takes for granted that the players can negotiate a binding preplay contract before they begin the game, thereby implicitly assuming the existence of an external agency that somehow enforces such contracts.

Nash programme

It is only when foundational questions are at issue that the criticisms of cooperative game theory outlined above are necessarily relevant. For example, in economic applications, one can sometimes argue that the cooperative black box contains all the apparatus of a legal system. The players then honour their contracts for fear of being sued if they do not. In social applications, the black box may contain the reasons why the players care about the effect that behaving dishonestly in the present may have on their reputation for trustworthy behaviour in the future. One can even argue that the black box contains the results of our childhood conditioning, or an inborn aversion to immoral behaviour.

However, in ethical discussions, we presumably want to avoid the Utopian fallacy of imagining that the black box of cooperative game theory contains nothing more than the fond hope that conflict will disappear if only people would behave rationally. John Nash (1951) suggested that the way to respond to the Utopian fallacy is to open the cooperative black box and take a long hard look at what lies inside. Why does it make sense for players to trust each other in some situations and not in others? Why don't they pursue their own interests rather than those of the group to which they belong?

When seeking to answer such questions, we have no choice but to use the methods of non-cooperative game theory. Non-cooperative game theory is therefore the study of games in which any cooperation that may emerge is fully explained by the choice of strategies that the players make. But this can be very hard. Cooperative game theory bypasses all of the difficult *why* questions in the hope of finding simple characterizations of *what* agreement rational players will eventually reach.

Nash therefore regarded cooperative and non-cooperative game theory as complementary ways of approaching the same problem. Cooperative game theory offers easily applied predictions of rational agreements. Non-cooperative game theory provides a way of testing these predictions.

Repeated games

The folk theorem of repeated game theory is a major contribution to political philosophy. It is explained here for the case when the game that gets repeated is the Prisoner's Dilemma (Figure 24.1).

Cooperative payoff regions

In a cooperative analysis, we would first ask what payoff pairs the players could implement in the Prisoner's Dilemma by writing a binding preplay contract. Without transferable utility, the set of such payoff pairs is the cooperative payoff region shaded in Figure 24.2 (which also shows the corresponding region for the Stag Hunt game). For example, the payoff pair (P) can be achieved by writing a contract that specifies (*d*, *d*) is to be played if a commonly observed fair coin falls *heads* and (*d*, *h*) is to be played if it falls *tails*.

Since rational players will not sign a contract that assigns them less than they could get by unilaterally playing *hawk*, we can reduce the set of viable contracts to the darkly shaded set in Figure 24.2. Notice that the unique Nash equilibrium of the Prisoner's Dilemma results in the worst payoff pair (1, 1) in this set.

The folk theorem

A rough-and-ready version of the folk theorem states that any contract that rational players might negotiate in a one-shot game in the presence of an external enforcement agency is also available as a Nash equilibrium when the game is played indefinitely often by very patient players with no secrets from each other.[3] Repetition therefore makes it possible for us to dispense with the various metaphysical substitutes for a real external

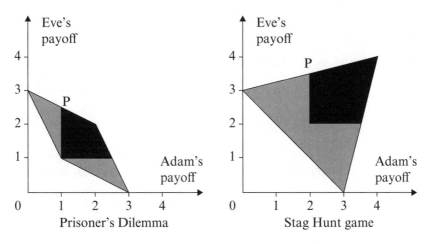

Note: The cooperative payoff regions are shaded. A payoff pair in the darkly shaded regions is a Nash equilibrium of the infinitely repeated game with infinitely patient players. The worst punishment that the opponent can inflict on a player who makes a best reply to the punishment strategy is called the player's minimax value. The darkly shaded region consists of all payoff pairs in the cooperative payoff region that give both players their minimax payoff or more.

Figure 24.2   Prisoner's Dilemma and Stag Hunt game

enforcement agency that are commonly proposed (such as Rawls's (1972) notion of 'natural duty'). Every benefit available with the help of external enforcement is available with only internal policing by the players themselves when the conditions of the folk theorem apply.

In particular, every point in the darkly shaded regions shown in Figure 24.2 can be approximated by Nash equilibrium outcomes in the repeated game if the players are assumed to care nearly as much about their future payoffs as their current payoffs.

Reciprocal altruism
The mechanism that supports efficient Nash equilibria in an indefinitely repeated game is *reciprocity* – as exemplified by the strategy *tit-for-tat* made famous by Axelrod's (1984) *Evolution of Cooperation*.[4] However, tit-for-tat is only one of an infinite number of strategies that can support an efficient equilibrium in the indefinitely repeated Prisoner's Dilemma. For example, the *grim* strategy requires a player to cooperate until the opponent plays *hawk*, which behaviour is then punished relentlessly by always playing *hawk* thereafter. If each player uses *grim*, the result is a Nash equilibrium, since neither player can gain by provoking the punishment that would follow any failure to cooperate. By sticking with *grim*, each player will therefore be making a best reply to the strategy choice of the other. As David Hume ([1739] 1978, p. 521] explains:

> I learn to do service to another, without bearing him any real kindness, because I foresee, that he will return my service in expectation of another of the same kind, and in order to maintain the same correspondence of good offices with me and others. And accordingly, after I have serv'd him and he is in possession of the advantage arising from my action, he is induc'd to perform his part, as foreseeing the consequences of his refusal.

The game theorists of the 1950s who reinvented this idea were unaware of Hume's work. They simply set out to extend Nash's (1951) newly minted equilibrium notion to repeated games, with the result that a number of different researchers came up with versions of the folk theorem simultaneously (Aumann and Maschler 1995). The same idea was reinvented again some fifteen years later by the biologist Robert Trivers (1971), who reached a wider audience by referring to the mechanism behind the folk theorem as *reciprocal altruism*, although no genuine altruism need be involved when the mechanism operates.

Reciprocal altruism explains how a society of selfish Mr Hydes can maintain an efficient social contract no less well than a society of genuinely altruistic Dr Jekylls. We therefore have no need to balk at laboratory experiments and historical studies which suggest that human beings sometimes behave more like Mr Hyde than Dr Jekyll (Ledyard 1995; Sally 1995). Such a conclusion may be unwelcome, but it does not necessarily imply that our current social contract is under threat.

Sustaining and selecting equilibria

This speculative section suggests that deontological philosophers who prioritize the 'right' derive their intuitions from observing how equilibria are *sustained* in our game of life, whereas consequentialist philosophers who prioritize the 'good' derive their intuitions from how new equilibria are *selected* when the underlying game changes.

Rights and duties

Amartya Sen's (1970) definition of a minimal right requires that each citizen be able to dictate what choice society should make over at least one pair of social alternatives. For example, if Adam has a right to decide how he dresses, then his preference will prevail over two social alternatives that differ only in whether he wears his fig leaf or goes naked. This definition leads immediately to Sen's paradox, which says that a transitive social preference cannot allow such a minimal right to each citizen without violating the unanimity requirement that when all citizens prefer one outcome to another, then so must society as a whole.

Gaertner et al. (1992) are typical of critics who take Sen to task for not offering a definition that allows people to exercise their rights *independently* of one another. Sugden (1985, 1986) proposed enriching the available language by saying that we all have a right to choose any strategy available to us in the game of life, but such a definition does not allow us to escape a version of Sen's paradox (Binmore 1998).

In any case, Sugden's definition only captures the idea of Hobbes ([1651] 1986) and Spinoza ([1670] 1951, pp. 200–204) that we have a 'natural right' to take any action within our power (which we surrender when joining with others in a social contract). But what of the rights we enjoy through participating in a civilized social contract? If it makes sense to model a stable social contract as an equilibrium in a society's game of life, then an understanding of our intuitive idea of a right therefore has to be sought by studying how equilibria in our repeated game of life are sustained.

From this point of view, a player's duty simply lies in never deviating from the equilibrium path specified by the social contract. The custom of doing one's duty then survives because those who evade their obligation to honour the social contract suffer sufficient disapproval or punishment to make the deviation unattractive. One can then say that players have a right to take an action if and only if they do not have a duty to refrain from it.

For example, if the game of life is the indefinitely repeated Prisoner's Dilemma, and the social contract being operated calls for both players to use *grim*, then Adam's duties would consist of cooperating with someone who has always cooperated in the past, and relentlessly punishing any other behaviour.

The notion of a right becomes significant only in a game of life with more structure. For example, 'Does Adam have the right to decide whether he goes naked or wears a fig leaf?' To construct a toy game that addresses this issue, we can model Eve as a prude by subtracting a small positive number from her payoffs in the Prisoner's Dilemma in those cases when Adam immodestly turns up to play without his fig leaf. However, we allow Adam's preferences to vary. Before each repetition of the Prisoner's Dilemma, a chance move decides whether he prefers to wear a fig leaf or go naked today by adding or subtracting a small positive number to his payoffs, depending on what he wears. In the repeated version of this new game, it remains an equilibrium for both players use *grim* without any reference to how Adam is dressed. If the social contract requires the play of this equilibrium, then Adam has a right to dress as he pleases. However, if the social contract requires the play of the equilibrium in which both players switch permanently to *hawk* if either fails to cooperate or if Adam appears naked in public, then Adam has no right to dress as he pleases.

Fairness

Social norms can be seen as devices for solving the equilibrium selection problems that arise when we encounter new variants of the game of life. For example, the social norm we implement with traffic signals requires operating one equilibrium of the Crossroads game when the lights are red and another when they are green.

Fairness norms are seldom so simple. Although they did not see their task as solving an equilibrium selection problem, John Rawls (1972) and John Harsanyi (1977) are the best known of several scholars who proposed that fairness norms can be modelled using the device of the *original position*. When rational players make use of this device, they imagine what bargain they would negotiate behind a 'veil of ignorance' that conceals the identity of any party disadvantaged by the deal. The resulting outcome is said to qualify as fair, because no players will wish anyone to be disadvantaged – because they may find themselves to be the one disadvantaged when they emerge from behind the veil of ignorance.

Egalitarianism and utilitarianism

Both Harsanyi (1977) and Rawls (1972) invented a metaphysical enforcement agency that somehow binds the players to whatever hypothetical deal would be reached in the original position. Harsanyi called his enforcement agency 'moral commitment'. Rawls's enforcement agency is called 'natural duty'. Harsanyi's (1977) analysis of bargaining in the original position leads to a utilitarian outcome. Rawls (1972) is led to a form of egalitarianism. Who is right?

Since Harsanyi won a Nobel prize for his contributions to game theory, it will come as no surprise that game theorists argue in his favour. Although Rawls explicitly wrote his *Theory of Justice* (1972) to provide a reasoned alternative to utilitarianism, he escapes being led to the same conclusion as Harsanyi only by the iconoclastic expedient of denying orthodox rational choice theory. However, I am unusual among economists in believing that Rawls's intuition is better than his analysis.

The third and longest part of the *Theory of Justice* is concerned with what Rawls called the 'strains of commitment' and an economist would call 'incentive compatibility'. If one takes his remarks to the logical extreme and denies all commitment possibilities that are not enforced by a real-life enforcement agency, then it is Rawls who triumphs over Harsanyi. The basic reason is almost absurdly simple. When the players emerge from behind the veil of ignorance, a metaphysical coin somehow determines who is to be Adam and who Eve. But how can anyone know whether a metaphysical coin has fallen heads or tails? The usual answer is that this was somehow decided in the past when fate decided who would be the rich man in his castle and who the poor man at the gate; or who would be a man and who a woman in a patriarchal society. But without some commitment device, why should any party disadvantaged by the fall of such a phantom coin feel obliged to honour the hypothetical deal reached in the original position? It might be different if the coin were a real coin tossed right now, but even then there seems no strictly rational reason why someone whose life or freedom is put at risk by the way a coin has fallen should acquiesce in being so disadvantaged.

The way out of this conundrum is simple. The only deals in the original position that are incentive-compatible are those that specify an equilibrium in the game of life that assign Adam and Eve roles between which they are indifferent when in the original position. When this requirement is expressed in game-theoretic terms, the result is that

Adam and Eve will choose a social contract that accords with the 'egalitarian bargaining solution' (Binmore 1994, 1998, 2005b).

Notes

1. The 'pure strategies' in the Stag Hunt game are simply *dove* or *hawk*. Mixed strategies arise when the players randomize over their pure strategies. When mixed strategies are permitted, the Stag Hunt game has a third Nash equilibrium in which each player uses *hawk* with a probability of 1/3.
2. The traditional term 'social contract' is used to describe any consensus within a society to operate according to one convention rather than another. With no source of external enforcement, any stable social contract must be self-policing – and hence a Nash equilibrium of whatever game of life the society plays. When the word 'contract' is used elsewhere, it should be understood in its usual sense as an agreement enforced by some agency external to the players.
3. What happens when we can sometimes keep our bad behaviour secret, as in a large modern society? The jury remains out on the extent to which efficiency can then be sustained in equilibrium.
4. The *tit-for-tat* strategy requires that a player begin by playing *dove,* and continue by choosing whatever action the opponent chose last time. Note that Axelrod's claims for *tit-for-tat* exaggerate its virtues (Binmore 1998). For example, it is false that *tit-for-tat* is evolutionarily stable in the sense of Maynard Smith and Price (1982).

References

Aumann, Robert J. and Michael B. Maschler (1995), *Repeated Games with Incomplete Information*, Cambridge, MA: MIT Press.

Axelrod, Robert (1984), *The Evolution of Cooperation*, New York: Basic Books.

Battalio, Raymond, Larry Samuelson and John van Huyck (2001), 'Optimization incentives and coordination failure in laboratory Stag Hunt games', *Econometrica*, **69**, 749–64.

Binmore, Ken (1994), *Playing Fair: Game Theory and the Social Contract I*, Cambridge, MA: MIT Press.

Binmore, Ken (1998), *Just Playing: Game Theory and the Social Contract II*, Cambridge, MA: MIT Press.

Binmore, Ken (2005a), 'Economic man – or straw man? A commentary on Henrich et al.', *Behavioral and Brain Science*, **28**, 817–18.

Binmore, Ken (2005b), *Natural Justice.* New York: Oxford University Press.

Binmore, Ken, John Gale and Larry Samuelson (1995), 'Learning to be imperfect: the Ultimatum Game', *Games and Economic Behavior*, **8**, 56–90.

Gaertner, Wulf, Prasanta Pattanaik and Kotaro Suzumura (1992), 'Individual rights revisited', *Economica*, **59**, 161–78.

Harsanyi, John (1977), *Rational Behavior and Bargaining Equilibrium in Games and Social Situations*, Cambridge: Cambridge University Press.

Hobbes, Thomas ([1651] 1986), *Leviathan*, ed. C.B. Macpherson, London: Penguin Classics.

Hume, David ([1739] 1978), *A Treatise of Human Nature*, 2nd edition, ed. L.A. Selby-Bigge, revised by P. Nidditch, Oxford: Clarendon Press.

Hume, David ([1758] 1985), 'Of the first principles of government', ed. E. Miller, in *Essays Moral, Political and Literary, Part I*, Indianapolis, IN: Liberty Classics.

Kant, Immanuel ([1793] 1949), 'Theory and practice', ed. C. Friedrich, in *The Philosophy of Kant*, New York: Random House.

Ledyard, John (1995), 'Public goods: a survey of experimental research', in J. Kagel and A. Roth (eds), *Handbook of Experimental Economics*, Princeton, NJ: Princeton University Press.

Maynard Smith, John (1982), *Evolution and the Theory of Games*, Cambridge: Cambridge University Press.

Myerson, Roger B. (1991), *Game Theory: Analysis of Conflict*, Cambridge, MA: Harvard University Press.

Nash, John (1951), 'Non-cooperative games', *Annals of Mathematics*, **54**, 286–95.

Neumann, John von and Oskar Morgenstern (1944), *The Theory of Games and Economic Behavior*, Princeton, NJ: Princeton University Press.

Rawls, John (1972), *A Theory of Justice.* Oxford: Oxford University Press.

Rousseau, Jean-Jacques ([1762] 1913), 'The social contract', in G. Cole (ed.), *Rousseau's Social Contract and Discourses*, London: J.M. Dent, pp. 5–123.

Sally, David (1995), 'Conversation and cooperation in social dilemmas: a meta-analysis of experiments from 1958 to 1992', *Rationality and Society*, **7**, 58–92.

Sen, Amartya (1970), 'The impossibility of a Paretian liberal', *Journal of Political Economy*, **78**, 152–7.

Skyrms, Brian (2003), *The Stag Hunt and the Evolution of the Social Structure*, Cambridge: Cambridge University Press.

Spinoza, Benedict de ([1670] 1951), 'Theologico-political treatise', trans. Robert H.M. Elwes, in *Chief Works of Benedict de Spinoza, Volume I*, New York: Dover.

Sugden, Robert (1985), 'Liberty, preference and choice', *Economics and Philosophy*, **1**, 213–19.

Sugden, Robert (1986), *The Economics of Rights, Cooperation and Welfare*, Oxford: Blackwell.

Trivers, Robert L. (1971), 'The evolution of reciprocal altruism', *Quarterly Review of Biology*, **46**, 35–56.

See also the entry on: Fairness.

25 Globalization
George DeMartino

Introduction

The processes of deepening international economic integration that have accelerated over the past quarter century have brought in their train a range of difficult
theoretical and ethical questions. Does this integration signal a fundamentally new
kind of world economy – commonly referred to as a 'global economy' – in which
(for the first time) the global market directs economic flows and outcomes? Or does
it more prosaically mark a return to the interdependence of earlier historical eras,
when widely dispersed national economies were joined in various configurations? Is
globalization driven by powerful economic forces over which states have little control,
so that political processes and outcomes are now fully determined by economic
interests? Or is global economic integration conditioned, enabled and even directed
by states that continue to enjoy authority over even global economic actors? Finally,
how should we evaluate and perhaps respond to these developments, once we sort
out just what they are?

These and related questions are deeply contested today – not least because scholars and observers who engage them approach the matter from different theoretical
perspectives. It is not at all surprising that political realists differ on these topics from
constructivists, or that economic institutionalists, Marxists and neoclassicalists come to
blows over these developments. There is by now an extensive literature that examines
this terrain. The goal of this chapter is not to review these features of the globalization
debate, but instead to turn attention towards some of the most pressing and challenging *ethical* questions that arise in the context of deepening international economic
integration.

Global integration requires of economists a careful engagement with a range of
ethical matters for which they are, by virtue of their training, largely unprepared.
This is unfortunate and even dangerous. Today, leading economists enjoy enormous
influence over economic policy in the international arena and especially across the
developing world. Not least, this expanding influence is manifest in the increasing
power of the world's leading multilateral agencies (for example, the International
Monetary Fund and the World Bank) to engage in social engineering across the South
and in the transition economies of Central and Eastern Europe. The consequence of
the convergence of the ethical unpreparedness of the economics profession with its
increased influence in the world has been economic policy prescriptions of dubious
ethical content.

Some of the ethical issues discussed below are *sui generis*; others preceded globalization
but are nevertheless exacerbated by it. This chapter explores several of the most pressing
of these. It concludes by turning to the matter of what these issues imply for professional
economic ethics.[1]

Whose values, whose rules?[2]

Global integration brings about a deepening of the economic linkages that bind the diverse communities of the world. These linkages entail inter alia international flows of goods and services, finance, investment and labour. Over the millennia, widely dispersed communities have crafted their own ways of being, replete with distinct judgements over matters both trivial (such as common preferences) and vital (deepest value judgements). With respect to the latter, communities have reached sometimes antagonistic conclusions about matters pertaining to religious practices and freedoms, gender-based rights and obligations, the status of children (both the rights and protections to which they are entitled and the means to which they may be put), the relationship between humanity and the natural environment, appropriate forms of governance (including what are taken to be legitimate forms of association, participation and representation) and much else.

As long as diverse communities were largely self-sufficient and economically insulated from one another, these differences in values, judgements and practices presented no particular challenge for economists. But today we find increasing economic interdependence among communities that differ fundamentally over matters such as those listed above. The economic links now binding China with Europe and the United States come to mind in this regard. This implies that practices in one country might have cross-border spillover effects (Aaron et al. 1994). Moreover, deepening international economic flows require new international rules, norms and institutions to govern the behaviour of those who transact across national borders. The question that arises in this context, then, is whose values and whose rules should govern international economic intercourse. To what degree (and how) should global institutions (such as the World Trade Organization) make space for diverse and perhaps even opposing values and norms? Alternatively, should these institutions adjudicate between the contending values, norms and practices (imposing one set on all agents) when these differences bear on economic interdependence? For instance, whose rules should govern the behaviour of a multinational corporation that invests abroad in a country where the norms and rules of home do not seem to apply, and where the rules of the host country appear not just different, but objectionable or even abhorrent to those at home?

In recent years prominent neoclassical trade theorists have taken the view that ethical preferences abroad are neither better nor worse – they are simply different (Bhagwati and Srinivasan 1996). This conclusion follows from neoclassical theory's deep-seated antipathy to certain sorts of value judgements. In the first instance, this antipathy is expressed as an unwillingness to judge consumer preferences or even to distinguish meaningfully between preferences and values. In the context of globalization, this agnosticism toward preferences yields a steadfast refusal to judge communities' beliefs, norms and practices. Free trade economists have therefore come to embrace a rather severe form of cultural relativism which preaches tolerance (and even celebration) of international differences. In this context, 'free trade' is now taken to imply that the institutions governing trade must not seek to harmonize practices where nations differ (with respect, for instance, to labour rights, environmental protection and other standards). Free-traders argue that differences in these practices represent a natural and entirely legitimate and beneficial source of comparative advantage. This follows from the notion that countries simply choose those standards that accord with the preferences of their inhabitants, and with the opportunity costs that they face (DeMartino 2000).

Heterodox economists have challenged this position on multiple grounds. Some criticize its naivety, arguing that weak labour and other standards are imposed from above on vulnerable populations; they are by no means simply chosen. Hence, using the terminology of choice in this context only serves to mask rather obvious oppressions (Dorman 1988). Others challenge the sustainability of cultural relativism as an ethical position in economics. Not least, the neoclassical refusal to judge preferences (and related norms, standards and practices) does not free the economist from making value judgements, since 'not judging' leads to an acceptance of all preferences that arise – and this *is* a value judgement. This ethical error is obscured by the apparent objectivity of neoclassical economic science, which believes itself to be free of value judgements.

That said, it is by no means obvious how economic theory ought to deal with the matter of cross-national differences in norms, values and practices. What is an appropriate position to take, for instance, when one country loses investment, employment and income as firms migrate to other countries where worker protection or environmental protection is weaker than that at home? What ethical standards ought to guide the formation of international rules to govern international economic flows? Whose values and whose rules ought to prevail? To date, the economics profession has barely begun to think through questions of this sort. Yet doing so is of the utmost importance, given the depth and extent of international economic integration.

Poverty and global inequality
Globalization has made more immediate the continuance (and even deepening) of global poverty and inequality.[3] A number of distinct ethical issues arise in this context. The first set concerns the nature of the 'problem'. How should poverty and inequality be defined and (consequently) measured? Ought we be concerned only with 'absolute' poverty – that is to say, with a community's access to income, nutrition, housing and health-care and its consequent mortality rates? Or should we attend to levels of 'relative' poverty as well and hence, to levels of inequality between the rich and poor? Even this first step, the identification of the problem, is ethically laden since without ethical judgement it becomes entirely arbitrary whether we 'see' any particular distribution of burdens, resources and opportunities as particularly notable or objectionable (see Sen 1992).

The second set of ethical issues concerns 'causes'. How does globalization either deepen or ameliorate problems of poverty and inequality? Answering this question engages social theory and the causal mechanisms embedded therein. But different social theories yield different answers. Recent Marxian accounts of globalization posit mechanisms that deepen inequality and poverty. Yet most neoclassical accounts emphasize what they see as the equalizing effects of globalization and the manner in which it promotes prosperity. Hence, a choice is to be made between contending social theories as we assess the consequences of globalization. But as many have by now argued, selection between alternative social theories is in large measure normatively (as opposed to empirically) driven (Elgin 1989; Goodman 1989). Distinct social theories seek and accomplish different things. They view the world differently (and may even see different worlds) and they reach distinct conclusions about matters such as globalization. The choice of social theory therefore biases the conclusions that observers reach. Without an objective science of theory choice, this initial (and vitally important) decision is a matter of normative rather than scientific judgement.

Third, the continuance of poverty and inequality in the context of globalization raises the particularly thorny ethical question of the geographical borders (or other limits) of our ethical obligations. It may be disturbing to learn that people far away endure terrible poverty, and it is entirely reasonable to take steps to ameliorate this suffering. But is it one's ethical *obligation* to do so? Is a community ethically indictable for circumscribing the terrain of its ethical obligations in ways that exclude some others – be they simply across town or all the way across the globe?

Ethical claims gain force to the degree that they are universal. It is difficult, as Sen (1992) argued, to imagine a compelling defence of any ethical principle that does not treat *all* people equally in some way that is taken to be vitally important. At face value, this might be taken to imply a radical cosmopolitanism, in which each and every one of us must count equally in all ethical judgements, and in which there are no limits to who is 'us'.

Neoclassical theory tends toward this position. The welfarist framework (derived from classical utilitarianism) that underlies its judgements makes no distinctions between people. All count equally in assessing, for instance, whether a policy intervention is Pareto improving. Moreover, in the context of globalization, no normative distinction is permitted between the welfare of those at home and those abroad. This impartiality is among its most valuable normative commitments. And it is one that is shared to varying degrees by most egalitarians, who likewise demand equal treatment for all, where 'all' is taken literally to imply each and every one of the world's inhabitants.

Against this cosmopolitan view it has been argued that we might face varying levels of ethical obligation – represented perhaps by concentric circles – with the greatest obligation to those nearest us, and decreasing obligation to those at increasing distances.[4] It is fairly unobjectionable that we bear the greatest obligation to our own children, siblings, parents and others with whom we share our lives, and that these obligations trump those we may face towards others. Indeed, we might expect to be ethically indicted were we to overlook these 'special obligations', treating our own family members as no more worthy of our attention, assistance and care than others. But if that is the case, might we not similarly have special (though less pressing) obligations to those in our community, which would of necessity entail that we have diminished obligations to others – and especially to those most distant from us? And if this is the case, finally, what obligations do we have when confronting a world of global inequality and distant poverty?

The goal here is not to provide these answers. It is only to emphasize that globalization adds urgency to the question of whether there are boundaries to ethical obligations, how these boundaries are drawn and what they imply. This matter becomes all the more pressing for those economists who embrace normative perspectives that demand the most of us. To get at this, consider the cosmopolitanism of neoclassical theory in comparison with Marxian theory. Both emphasize a kind of freedom and equality as universals. Neoclassical theory prizes 'formal freedom', or the freedom to choose from among the opportunities one faces without undue interference by others (and particularly, the state). This freedom is to be enjoyed equally by all. Marxian theory values 'substantive freedom' which reaches beyond formal freedom to take account of what a person can actually do, achieve or become. This freedom, too, is to be enjoyed equally. There is a formal similarity in that both accounts apply these demands to all who populate the globe. But in the case of the neoclassical theorist, the demand is far easier to meet, since the enjoyment of formal freedom by any one agent is unlikely to bear on the formal freedom enjoyed by others. When the privileged buy up scarce resources, or enjoy spiralling incomes, they may alter the opportunity sets of others, but they do not impinge on the right of others to make their best choices within their own opportunity sets (no matter how paltry these may be). In the Marxian view, this is not the case. In this account, actions by the privileged that diminish the opportunity sets of others are indictable because they diminish others' substantive freedoms. Hence, the exercise of freedom by any one agent may in fact deny substantive freedom to others – and this may require restrictions on the enjoyment of freedoms (see DeMartino 2003).

Globalization therefore presents the most difficult challenge not to neoclassical theorists, but to heterodox economists who value equality of substantive freedoms across the globe. For these economists, increasing international economic interdependence may bear on this equality in important ways. On the one hand, globalization may alter the distribution of substantive freedoms, for better or worse. Heterodox economists must therefore attend to the particular nature of the new economic flows and the rules under which they occur to ensure that they are managed in such a way that, at a minimum, they do not harm those who are worst off. On the other hand, globalization may affect the ability of the privileged to enhance the substantive freedom of the deprived. Globalization, properly managed, might enable new policies that improve the quality of life for those abroad who suffer absolute and relative poverty. But insofar as this is true, there is a greater ethical burden on the privileged to attend to the needs of the deprived. *Ought*, after all, implies *can*, and this means that once a community acquires the capacity to make improvements in the lives of others, it may at the same time acquire the obligation to do so.

The ethical imperatives of democracy
During the 1980s and into the early 1990s many observers argued that globalization had occurred to such an extent and with such force as to render meaningless local (and even national) governance. Global market pressures were seen to enjoy veto power over governments – states that acted in ways that were contrary to the needs of global market actors (be they multinational corporations, global hedge fund investors, or others) would be punished severely with capital flight, currency devaluation and loss of jobs, income and opportunities. Many expressed worry, in particular, about the viability of European social democratic regimes that imposed relatively high tax burdens and restrictions on firms in order to sustain relatively generous welfare systems and protections. Critics of globalization argued that the economic freedoms and pressures would undermine national policy autonomy and, in the extreme, yield policy convergence across the globe.[5]

Against this backdrop there emerged in the mid-1990s a critique of this 'globalization' thesis. Critics argued that globalization either was not occurring to the degree that others claimed or that, in any event, national governments continued to enjoy a much greater degree of policy autonomy than advocates of the globalization thesis suggested (Dicken 2003; Hirst and Thompson 1999; Rhodes 1997). The debate took on important ethical dimensions, since it raised the question of the survival of democratic governance in an era of globalization. The debate is cross-cut by two vectors, each of which entails an ethical dimension. Along one vector are those who advocate the thesis that globalization does in fact involve the transfer of power to global economic actors. Advocates of this thesis nevertheless are divided into two camps. The first views globalization as an ominous and unethical interruption of democratic governance. This group has become the most vocal of globalization's critics. The other camp, including neoclassical economists, views this veto power as at worst benign and at best beneficial, since it leads to rational control over otherwise irrational or even corrupt government (see Friedman 2000). Along the second vector are those who have come to reject the idea that globalization has the powers attributed to it by the globalization thesis advocates. These observers emphasize that national policymaking remains a viable and vital arena of democratic governance. For them, then, objecting to the globalization thesis represents a critical step, ethically driven, to protect democratic governance against the chorus of those who cite its death at the hands of global forces (see Hirst and Thompson 1999).

Ethical obligations of the economist

All of these matters bear on the ethical obligations facing the practising economist, especially those who find themselves in positions to influence the contours of both global and domestic economic policy. The confluence of globalization processes and the deepening dependence of many developing and transition countries on the developed world and its proxy institutions give extraordinary power to economists. Notably, they are often vested with the authority to take actions that bear meaningfully on others. They are in a position to alter livelihoods and other life circumstances of those who populate the communities for which they legislate (or which they advise, especially when that advice is backed by the institutional resources and power of the world's major economic agencies). They are in a position to help, to be sure, but they are also in a position to do substantial harm.

This privileged position of influence obviously involves ethical substance, and raises important ethical dilemmas. But what are these dilemmas precisely? And what *particular* professional ethical imperatives do they entail?

To date, there has been a profound tendency among practising economists at the highest levels of economic governance to view themselves as experts with arcane and specialized knowledge that is unavailable to the non-professional. They are authorized (and perhaps even obligated) to wield this knowledge in the interest of those they serve. Confronting national governments with balance of payment and other crises, economists have scripted economic reforms designed to generate growth and stability. The preferred agenda to achieve these results has been 'neoliberalism', or the transformation away from state-directed economic activity and outcomes to market-mediated activity and outcomes. Economists have undertaken this form of social engineering in the belief that neoliberalism promises more rapid growth than any possible alternative regime.

Across professions, bodies of professional ethics have emerged to guide specialists in their work. This is particularly true of professions that enjoy a relative monopoly of knowledge and expertise not shared by those they serve and where the potential for harm to those served is more or less ineradicable. Law and medicine are exemplary in this regard. In both cases, the typical client cannot begin to amass the expertise required to make appropriate judgements without the help of the professional; and in both cases, interventions that are designed to benefit the client may in fact cause substantial harm – to the client or to others.

The social engineering undertaken by professional economists in the era of globalization exhibits both qualities. Economists enjoy a kind of knowledge that is not shared by those for whom they have legislated or advised policy reform. Moreover, the transition from state-mediated to market-mediated economic activity, regardless of its purported benefits, entails substantial risk of serious harm to those whom this transformation is intended to help. Yet, unlike the doctor or lawyer, practising economists have no body of professional ethics to which to turn, or from which to learn, when performing their work. In the era of globalization, then, economists have re-engineered entire economies, with impacts of truly global scale, without the barest of training in the professional ethical matters that they face.[6]

Perhaps as a consequence, there has been growing interest of late in the ethical stature of the economics profession and the ethical behaviour of leading economists. The scandal at the Harvard Institute of International Development shocked many economists, and forced Harvard to close the institute altogether.[7] Moreover, no less an economist than former World Bank Chief Economist Joseph Stiglitz has begun to ruminate about the ethical deficiencies of economics practice at the highest levels of the International Monetary Fund and World Bank (Stiglitz 2000). At the same time, economists such as Dani Rodrik (1997) have launched internal critiques of the free-trade position, arguing for greater attention to the ethical foundations and implications of this approach. Rodrik argues that there is much greater force to the ethical challenges to globalization that have emerged across the globe, and warns his economist colleagues not to dismiss any and all concerns that raise questions about economists' most cherished principles.

These developments suggest a growing unease and even dissatisfaction within economics about the profession's role on the global stage. There is increasing recognition that leading economists of the past several decades were simply unprepared by their profession for the extraordinary, and consequentially historical, role of social engineer that they came to play. Speaking politely, we might say that the consequences have been mixed. But for many of the world's most desperate and vulnerable, the effects have been catastrophic. Recognizing that much might help to instigate renewed reflection in the profession on the ethical foundations of the field and focus careful attention to what these ethical foundations imply about globalization.

Notes

1. Space constraints preclude a review of the full panoply of ethical issues associated with international economic integration. For example, I will not directly examine the ethical issues surrounding migration or the provision of public goods (such as environmental protection).
2. The material in this section is explored in depth in DeMartino (2000).
3. For data on recent trends in global poverty and inequality, see UNDP (2006).
4. Sen (1992, p. 19) broaches this matter only in passing but provides useful citations of the literature. For Sen, my treatment here might suffer a confusion of 'social' with 'personal' ethics, since social ethics requires impartiality while personal ethics authorizes and perhaps requires particular attachments to particular individuals. For my part, I believe that his distinction is insufficient: even in the field of social ethics we can and must confront the question of the limits to our ethical obligations.
5. DeMartino (2008) explores the ideas in this section in greater detail.
6. DeMartino (2005, forthcoming) explores these matters further.
7. A Harvard economist and a lawyer at the institute were found to have profited personally from their associations with high-ranking government officials during the 1990s when they were helping to direct the privatization of the assets of the Russian government. Specifically, the defendants were charged with 'buying several hundred thousand dollars' worth of Russian stocks, bonds and, perhaps most important, jumping to the head of the queue in order to receive, from the Russian Securities and Exchange Commission they

advised, the first license to offer mutual funds in Russia – a potential goldmine' (Warsh 2004). See Wedel (2001) for a detailed discussion of this matter.

References

Aaron, Henry J., Ralph R. Bryant, Susan M. Collins and Robert Z. Lawrence (1994), 'Preface to the studies on integrating national economies', in Ronald G. Ehrenberg, *Labor Markets and Integrating National Economies*, Washington DC: Brookings Institution.
Bhagwati, Jagdish N. and T.N. Srinivasan (1996), 'Trade and the environment: does environmental diversity detract from the case for free trade?' in Jagdish N. Bhagwati and Robert E. Hudec (eds), *Fair Trade and Harmonization*, Cambridge, MA: MIT Press.
DeMartino, George (2000), *Global Economy, Global Justice: Theoretical Objections and Policy Alternatives to Neoliberalism*, London: Routledge.
DeMartino, George (2003), 'Realizing class justice', *Rethinking Marxism*, **15** (1), 1–31.
DeMartino, George (2005), 'A professional ethics code for economists', *Challenge*, July/August, 88–104.
DeMartino, George (2008), 'The ethical dimensions of the "globalization thesis" debate', in J.B. Davis and W. Dolfsma (eds), *The Elgar Handbook of Socio-Economics*, Cheltenham, UK and Northampton, MA, USA: Edward Elgar.
DeMartino, George (forthcoming), '*I Do Solemnly Swear* ': on the Need for and Content of Professional Economic Ethics.
Dicken, Peter (2003), *Global Shift*, 4th edition. New York: Guilford Press.
Dorman, Peter (1988), 'Worker rights and international trade: a case for intervention', *Review of Radical Political Economics*, **20** (2&3), 241–6.
Elgin, Catherine Z. (1989), 'The relativity of fact and the objectivity of value', in Michael Krausz, *Relativism: Interpretation and Confrontation*, Notre Dame, IN: University of Notre Dame Press, pp. 86–98.
Friedman, Thomas L. (2000), *The Lexus and the Olive Tree: Understanding Globalization*, New York: Farrar, Straus and Giroux.
Goodman, Nelson (1989), 'Just the facts, ma'am', in Michael Krausz, *Relativism: Interpretation and Confrontation*, Notre Dame, IN: University of Notre Dame Press, pp. 80–85.
Hirst, Paul and Graham Thompson (1999), *Globalization in Question*, 2nd edition, Cambridge: Polity Press.
Rhodes, Martin (1997), 'Globalization, labour markets and welfare states: a future for "competitive corporatism"?' in Martin Rhodes and Yves Meny (eds), *The Future of European Welfare*, London: Macmillan.
Rodrik, Dani (1997), *Has Globalization Gone Too Far?* Washington DC: Institute for International Economics.
Sen, Amartya (1992), *Inequality Reexamined*, Cambridge, MA: Harvard University Press.
Sen, Amartya (1999), *Development as Freedom*. New York: Alfred A. Knopf.
Stiglitz, Joseph E. (2000), 'Ethics, economic advice, and economic policy', paper presented at the Inter-American Development Bank, December. Document included in the digital library of the Inter-American Initiative on Social Capital, Ethics and Development, www.iadb.org/etica/documentos/dc_sti_ethic-i.htm, 16 September 2008.
United Nations Development Programme (2006), *Human Development Report 2006*, New York: Palgrave Macmillan.
Warsh, David (ed.) (2004), *The 'Assigned To' Trial*, economicprincipals.com, available at http://www.economicprincipals.com/issues/04.12.05.html, accessed on 6 November, 2008.
Wedel, Janine R. (2001), *Collision and Collusion: The Strange Case of Western Aid to Eastern Europe*, New York: Palgrave.

See also the entries on: Code of ethics for economists; Labour standards; Poverty.

26 Global financial markets
Gary A. Dymski and Celia Lessa Kerstenetzky

Introduction

Insufficient ethical discussion has accompanied the emergence of financial globalization. This essay explores the ethical dimensions of contemporary financial globalization. It first describes financial globalization, focusing on the dramatic impacts of this process, intended and unintended, on social and individual welfare. It then presents some ideas about an ethical benchmark for evaluating the financial globalization process.

Financial globalization in the contemporary age

Global finance involves lending, investment and financial transactions in which creditors or owners are in one country and debtors and assets in another. Equilibrium models suggest there should be substantial gains from opening an economy that has per capita capital levels below the world average to offshore financial flows and institutions.[1] Asset owners would gain an improved risk-to-return opportunity set, while production and employment would increase as a result of increasing overseas loans and investments.

Since the 1970s, financial globalization has accelerated due to deregulation in banking systems across the world. Financial crises have also become increasingly frequent. Two kinds of crises can occur. In a *currency crisis*, a national currency suddenly plummets as those holding it dump it, and demand for the currency disappears. In a *banking crisis*, the structure of financial commitments made between owners, banks and borrowers collapses.

The growing frequency of crises and financial globalization is linked. The reduction in regulatory scrutiny has led to more credit flows to riskier borrowers, and to new practices that have permitted risky financial claims to be distributed more widely than before – even across borders. Furthermore, speculators have more leverage to put pressure on the currencies of nations whose prevailing exchange rates they regard as unsustainable and likely to be devalued. So more banking crises have occurred; and these have sometimes led to currency crises. When financial claims are held across borders, currency markets may react speedily to banking crises. 'Overshooting' and self-fulfilling prophecies are therefore common.

Financial crises, whether enabled by financial globalization or not, cause pain and loss. The extent and distribution of this pain and loss have differed systematically for crises in upper- and lower-income countries. In lower-income countries, financial crises have often caused widespread downturns, with many companies forced into bankruptcy, many jobs lost, and many personal traumas. These strong impacts have been amplified by financial globalization in two ways. First, banking and currency crises have tended to coincide in lower-income nations. These nations have often been perceived by speculators as weak and unable to sustain their policy paths; so any hint of difficulties in meeting the obligations associated with cross-border borrowing crisis triggers speculative currency attacks. These nations' borrowers often count on generating revenue from selling abroad, but when the currencies in which they buy become more expensive and the currency in which they sell loses value, profit margins and the capacity to repay both shrink.

Second, lower-income nations' financial crises often are followed by restrictive macroeconomic policies. Developing-world states are regarded as explicitly or implicitly underwriting lender-borrower arrangements involving economic units within their borders. When these go bad, the state there 'assumes' the bad debt. If it cannot meet these obligations, the International Monetary Fund (IMF) provides emergency financing, and dictates a range of adjustments designed to rid the borrower country of 'bad' fiscal habits and position it to repay its debts. These interventions typically mandate that fiscal expenditures be cut, publicly held assets be privatized and markets opened to overseas firms and owners. This is where social costs of financial crises arise. Cuts in fiscal expenditure mean reduced spending on health, education, retirement programmes and the like. Indeed, the state must often subsidize bankrupt entities to make them attractive to prospective buyers. So the poor get poorer; middle-income families, workers and business-owners lose income and security; and clinics and schools are squeezed. The locus of human costs is usually far removed from those who made the decisions about what should be borrowed and on what terms.

Financial crises affecting upper-income nations have had much milder effects on households and businesses. Even in severe episodes, such as the 1980s United States savings-and-loan crisis or the 1990 Japanese financial crisis, these nations' relatively strong national governments have orchestrated bail-outs without triggering either currency crises or punitive IMF interventions. This pattern has held in the 2007 subprime crisis: the upper-income nations whose banking systems were devastated by large portfolios of non-performing loans have been able to practice expansionary fiscal policy and recapitalize their banks after this crisis deepened in 2008: policies never contemplated in lower-income countries' financial crises. Due to financial globalization, then, the effects of financial crises that started in an upper-income countries reverberates throughout the banking systems, credit structures, and currency values of lower-income countries.

Financial crises also result in the opening of financial markets to new participants and practices. This too has asymmetric effects. In largely open upper-income countries, banking crises only accelerate the openness to competition with which these markets are already familiar. In lower-income countries, however, these crises create huge changes. Prior to crises, domestic banking systems captured virtually all national savings at low interest rates and guided them into targeted investment sectors. After crisis, overseas banks gain the right of entry. They are primarily interested in upscale customers. These upper income customers enjoy enhanced investment opportunities, including the ability to invest in overseas assets. This increase of individual freedom for participants in the upscale financial game comes at the cost of reduced general banking services for the broader mass of people. This is because domestically chartered financial firms, which are now competing with foreign banks, must meet global banking standards which compel them to increase their net revenue relative to their assets. The result is fewer implicit cross-subsidies for very low-balance customers. All customers must now 'carry their own weight'.

Implicit moral perspectives in the theory of developing-country borrowing

How can financial globalization be understood in ethical terms? Neo-liberal economists and officials affiliated with the IMF and World Bank have a broad consensus approach that implicitly extends the moral perspective for assessing a closed economy to the global sphere. This moral perspective invokes the welfare theorems underlying microeconomic theory. A market economy that permits more cross-border financing options entails more individual freedom, and hence more efficiency in resource use, than an economy that does not.

This economistic approach has, in turn, yielded two principal models by which to explain financial crises. One model, applied more to currency crises than to lending crises, attributes these events to 'sunspot' effects, in other words, self-fulfilling prophecies based on nothing more than a spreading fear that a given currency will lose value (see Obstfeld 1986). This 'accidents happen' model leaves open the question of who should be held liable. After all, if *what happened* (the crisis) is independent of *what should have happened in the absence of random noise,* then why should the borrower nation take on obligations of economic agents within its borders? Why should people in the borrower nation suffer reduced incomes and social services?

The second model, applied more to lending than to currency markets, sees lending as a principal-agent game characterized by asymmetric information and moral hazard. Crises of repayment, when they occur, can be traced to borrowers' guile. The borrower's nation, because it has not prevented bad behaviour through appropriate regulations, is ultimately the responsible party. Indeed, asymmetric information models of cross-border lending and crisis treat the entire borrowing nation as one 'agent' in a bargaining game with overseas lenders (see Eaton et al. 1986; also see Dymski 2006a on recent financial crises). This posits a naturalized hierarchy of obligation, in which states can be held accountable by entities across national borders. The fiction that the borrower nation commits national resources as an *agent* in a bargain erases intra-national distributional issues, as well as class and political conflicts. The open question as to whether those uninvolved in cross-border borrowing decisions should pay for others' misjudgements disappears. Consequently, the question of who loses out in crises has drawn virtually no analytical attention from economists. As Polanyi ([1944] 2001) observed more than half a century ago, from this perspective the social damage that often accompanies the liberation of markets, including widening social inequalities, should vanish as a deepening of markets strategy proceeds.

Heterodox economists and analysts affiliated with global civil society movements, focusing on asymmetric global power rather than microeconomic asymmetric information, have developed a scathing critique of these economistic analyses (see Eatwell and Taylor 2000). In this alternative view, financial crises stem from efforts to exploit markets abroad by multinational financial firms, that is, by banks, investment funds and private equity funds, but also pension funds. Such firms often overlend, as a result of competitive pressures, disaster myopia and an excessive focus on short-term returns. This is to say that lenders and not borrowers are primarily to blame. Financial crises often work out to these firms' longer-term advantage, while they push borrower nations' economic units along in the global race to the bottom.

An ethical benchmark for assessing the effects of financial globalization

These differing views of the implications of financial globalization hardly prepare the ground for careful consideration of the possibility of an ethical benchmark for financial globalization. The conceptual polarization reviewed above stands in the way. Those analysts who believe that opening markets will eventually generate more global prosperity see no need for an ethical discussion. These analysts would define as unethical only intentionally unfair behaviour by lenders, thus establishing a narrow standard, which in any case empirical studies are very unlikely to be able to measure.[2] Meanwhile, those convinced that opening markets widens the global rift between rich and poor have already judged the global system as unfair.

Nonetheless, ever more actors – including some transnational institutions[3] – are willing to concede that liberalized financial markets may be deepening global inequality. So an ethical benchmark is needed; this section suggests one.

We begin by subjecting the notions of freedom and efficiency, touched on above, to deeper scrutiny. Freedom is a critical idea. Emancipating human possibilities by eliminating the constraining aspects of frontiers and barriers seems desirable. But how can the idea of freedom accommodate not only efficiency but also social justice?

The approach adopted by neoliberal economists concentrates too much on the property rights and self-ownership aspects of freedom. Market institutions, as freedom-abiding mechanisms for acquiring and transferring legitimate property rights, necessarily deliver end results that are justified, and hence just.

But when freedom is characterized as capabilities, by Sen (1990), as a substantive freedom of choice among lives people have reason to value, or as the comparable concept of real freedom by van Parijs (2003), institutions and their consequences are linked. The freedom that rests in having capabilities then becomes a criterion for evaluating the institutions that generate (or fail to generate) that consequence. The underlying idea is that freedom is meaningful only when it has an opportunities dimension, and when it is envisioned for real people in their heterogeneity – not for a representative, idealized individual.

Real freedom, thus, recognizes not just the formal freedom elements of security and self-ownership, but also the opportunity aspect. It asks what options are open for individuals to choose between meaningful lives, in which they can safely trade property rights and have their self-ownership secured. This enhanced definition of freedom calls attention to the *worth* of freedom for individuals, as Rawls (1971) put it.[4]

This approach accommodates a concern with social justice – that is, with inequalities of real freedom. Here, we follow Rawls's notion that one institutional arrangement is superior to another when it maximizes the advantages (or prospective advantages) of those who are least advantaged in the political community. Rawls proposed this in connection with the so-called 'difference principle', which regulates the distribution of income and wealth while guaranteeing that the priority on the least advantaged is lexicographically subordinate to the implementation of the principles of equal basic liberties and fair opportunities. But if we take 'advantage' to mean real freedom – a contraction of basic liberties and broad opportunities which abides by a 'soft' version of the Rawlsian lexicographic rule (see van Parijs 2003) – and consider market arrangements, then fair efficiency recommends market arrangements that maximize the real freedom of the least advantaged.[5] In this sense, 'real-freedom-for-all' is adopted as a fairness principle.

Universal basic income: implementing real-freedom-for-all
While the circumstances of the least advantaged are not fully captured by their market incomes, one important proposal for operationalizing real-freedom-for-all involves supplementing the market distribution of income by distributing a sizeable, universal and

unconditional basic income (UBI) – mainly in cash, but also in kind (public goods).[6] The UBI is based on a rethinking of property rights. Extant property rights derive from an institutional framework that legitimizes previous distributions of endowments, in turn distributing economic rights of acquisition and transfer based on what people 'own'. But neither natural resources nor accumulations of physical capital and knowledge have natural private owners: property rights over these things have been extended to private owners due to institutional arrangements that privilege the property rights aspects of freedom. If real-freedom-for-all is adopted instead, social fairness dictates that the private owners of common resources should pay a 'rent' to non-owners.

An advantage of UBI as a social redistribution measure is that it is respectful of social and cultural diversity. It is not motivated by a moral concern for assisting the poor. It is substantially about distribution of citizenship rights. That said, many challenges would have to be overcome in implementing the UBI. In particular, since we care about the maximum of real-freedom-for-all, it will be important to maintain a coordinating role for incentives.

An additional advantage comes from the recognition that the somewhat uncertain character of market successes and failures, which constrains us not to treat opportunities exclusively as resources individuals take to the market in order to carve out a living. Those who succeed are sometimes lucky, sometimes more capable or harder working, sometimes better organized to exploit market advantages. Determining the contributions of these various elements even in any one case is impossible; and irregardless, luck is neither a personal merit nor a personal fault.[7] The UBI, by contrast, accommodates such concerns via a straightforward rule that minimizes abstruse and uncertain calculations. It is a rent paid by the lucky private owners of commonly possessed resources to everybody else, stipulated at the highest level consistent with its sustainability.

Ethical questions raised by financial globalization and crisis
Since the 1970s, global financial markets have acquired ever more autonomy, leaving nation-states with ever less control over money and credit. Ironically, then, this globalization process *is* creating a community, irrespective of the intentions of those involved. Offshore decisions by firms, banks, customers and governments affect people's daily lives everywhere, even in remote rural areas of peripheral countries. In a further irony, the very advances in communication and information technologies that have helped release markets from nation-states' control also permit an unprecedented scale of connections between people across countries.

Is any notion of justice applicable to such a wide community? Clearly yes. Capital has never been so free, and yet its hypermobility has been associated with heightened instability and with debt crises which have compromised political communities' capacities to sustain – much less increase – people's real freedom.

Financial globalization has a distributional global impact through both macro and micro channels. At the macro level, financial globalization restricts debtor countries' abilities to design and implement growth and welfare policies, therefore impacting common people. At the micro level, globalization has been in most cases a vehicle for spreading mechanisms of financial exclusion among common people (see Dymski 2007).

Further, financial globalization impacts different people in different ways in crisis and non-crisis periods. In non-crisis periods, cross-border financial flows increase opportunities and returns disproportionately for non-poor people, directly and indirectly. But crises trigger micro and macro adjustments that adversely affect real-freedom-for-all, especially in lower income countries.

This leads directly to the insight that, from a real freedom perspective, the UBI should be applied to the global 'community'; for (i) systemic risks threaten the fiscal capacity of debtor countries to finance a UBI nationally; (ii) exercises of market power by multinational banks within national markets violate market freedoms and extract monies from the vulnerable, deepening inequality and reducing real freedom.[8]

Two institutions that crucially affect these distributive outcomes at the macro level are property rights over an increasingly important asset, 'global liquidity', and the set of financial rules that regulates adjustments in debtor nations after debt crises (see Dymski 2006c). Those possessing global liquidity claim socially wasteful rents that deepen the gulf between the real freedom levels of the rich and non-rich the world over. Biased adjustment rules that throw the burden onto the borrower's shoulders, in turn, are also a source of rents for owners of global liquidity (the lenders), who possess the socially scarce good of monetary security.

A more just world with financial globalization

Creating a more just world – one with more real-freedom-for-all – in the era of financial globalization poses challenges at many levels. As noted, control over global liquidity and over global financial rules is asymmetrically distributed. This permits lender countries to collect rents the legitimacy of which we challenge here. Eliminating these rents to promote more real-freedom-for-all requires both a redistribution of property rights to global liquidity and a revision of transnational financial rules. To reduce the likelihood of systemic crises, which also adversely affect real freedoms, capital flows should be controlled at a transnational level. A Tobin tax on global financial transactions, coordinated by transnational institutions, could both reduce outbreaks of financial crises and fund a global UBI. The Tobin tax, based on a proposal by Yale economist James Tobin, would levy a small percentage-rate tax on some categories of financial asset purchases or sales – specifically, those transactions frequently associated with financial speculation. These fees would especially discourage short-term market transactions attempting to exploit – but often having the effect of worsening – price or rate disparities between assets denominated in different national currencies.

To address micro impacts, states should be able to guarantee low-income people access to finance under fair conditions. This access should be included in the real freedom set. Wealth redistribution would help guarantee this access, since possession of wealth is the key to having access to fair financial conditions. Regulatory reforms or new public institutions, both involving some restructuring of national banking systems, can also ensure this access is provided in a way that is sustainable for those with lower incomes.

A question of global governance

What system of governance can reduce the real-freedom-for-all losses that have accompanied financial globalization? Alternatively, how can a UBI become a core component of the global economic system? Several meta-solutions have been proposed, ranging from a multi-state social contract to a cosmopolitan view of the rights and duties of people and institutions.[9]

The multi-state social contract approach has some limitations. Contemporary states, regardless of how politically accountable they are, cannot adequately look after their citizens in the current situation, because global financial markets react quickly to perceived (or anticipated) policy changes. Despite differences in regulatory capacity, states today face a Catch-22: if they protect themselves via capital controls or other measures, they face the prospect of capital outflows; if they do not, they must consider maintaining austere policies and privatize to reassure global financial markets.[10] Competition between countries for capital inflows is likely to be predatory, and the less income-secure people in these countries are the most likely victims.

Shrinking welfare states and increasingly selective social policies are certainly not ideal from a universal real-freedom perspective. The cosmopolitan idea of global justice asserts that doing better as a world community necessitates that global consumers and producers be reframed as world citizens. Creating a world community necessitates a move from targeting to universalism. Real-freedom-for-all should guide the creation of institutional structures that regulate world economic integration. Then the welfare of a citizen of any country – one whose banks' excessive lending has created social crises elsewhere, one experiencing such crises, one not considered a desirable target for such lending – can be evaluated using a uniform ethical framework.

This framework suggests a global UBI based on a worldwide evaluation of natural resources and social development and focused on advancing the global real freedom of *individuals*. Funds for this grant could come from many different sources.[11] Given that no method of devising a world government has been put forward, operationalizing a global UBI means establishing an effective structure of world governance. To focus on people's real freedom in a world of nation-states will certainly require some means of incorporating intermediary political communities – sub-national, national and regional, as well as transnational – into a multilayered governance structure. It will require application of the principle of subsidiarity, wherein decisions on how to implement policies are taken at the lowest possible level, while higher levels retain oversight. The essential idea is that a multilayered governance structure can deliver the basic real freedoms to global citizens that nation-states no longer can (see Koenig-Archibugi 2002; Thakur and van Langenhove 2006).

In this setting, international financial institutions could play a very different role than at present. For example, they could develop criteria for determining multinational financial firms' fair-share contribution to national, regional or global UBI resource pools. They might develop regulations aimed at both reducing the frequency of crises generated by capital flows and deepening real-freedom-for-all. In short, their mission would shift from mediating or distributing the bads accruing from unbridled competition among countries, to organizing and delivering the benefits of cooperation.[12]

Conclusion

Financial globalization has not yet entered the terrain of serious ethical discussion. As financial crises multiply, however, and have increasingly asymmetric results, the need for this discussion grows more profound. This chapter has suggested, in rough outline, one possible ethical approach to current processes of financial globalization. It argues that because global finance has generated recurrent losses for economically vulnerable countries and individuals, via complex and uncertain cause-effect linkages, an adequate ethical response is called for. This would involve establishing some level of global real-freedom-for-all linked to global finance. Such an approach raises fundamental questions about the uses of markets, the nature of property rights and the nature of human rights.

Notes

1. MacDougall (1960) established the basic theoretical insight; King and Levine (1993) elaborated the implications for allocative efficiency.
2. This has been the trajectory of the economics literature on racial discrimination in US credit markets (Dymski 2006b).
3. Such as the World Bank, as evident in the shift between its 2005 and 2006 editions of the *World Development Report* (World Bank 2005, 2006).
4. There is however an important difference between Sen's and Rawls's proposals regarding the measurement focus, whether on the 'means to freedom' (Rawls) or the 'extents of freedom' (Sen). See Sen (1992).
5. In van Parijs's rendering, 'real-freedom-for-all' is leximin: it prioritizes the least advantaged and then moves up to levels of society that are successively better-off.
6. Van Parijs (2005) provides a critical introduction to the UBI; for a fuller account of this concept see Vanderborght and van Parijs (2005).
7. Kerstenetzky (2002) examines the influence of the factors discussed here.
8. Those adversely affected will have particular demographic, cultural and spatial identities in different countries and regions. Examples are residents of rural areas or *favelas*, women, children and disadvantaged minorities.
9. We take the distinction between a multi-state social contract and a cosmopolitan view from Beitz (1999). The former model is illustrated by Rawls's (1999) proposal for a social contract between 'peoples', whereas the latter stems from treating the global community as a political community (a 'people') and working out the implications in this setting for Rawlsian 'justice as fairness'. Held (1995) represents a seminal contribution on the issue of democracy in the cosmopolitan view.
10. However, the recent cases of China, Malaysia and Chile suggest that new parameters for national policy autonomy may be emerging.
11. Alternatives suggested for financing a global UBI range from progressive income taxes (Frankman 2002) to seigneurage rights over a single global currency (Frankman 2002; Huber 2000), to a uniform global tax on a sustainable level of pollution (van Parijs 2002).
12. Scholte and Schnabel (2002) explore the idea of civil society governance of global finance.

References

Beitz, Charles (1999), 'International liberalism and distributive justice: a survey of recent thought', *World Politics*, **51** (2), 269–96.

Dymski, Gary A. (2006a), 'Banking and financial crises', in Philip Arestis and Malcolm Sawyer (eds), *Handbook of Alternative Monetary Economics*, Cheltenham, UK and Northampton, MA, USA: Edward Elgar, pp. 385–402.

Dymski, Gary A. (2006b), 'Discrimination in the credit and housing markets: findings and challenges', in William Rodgers (ed.), *Handbook on the Economics of Discrimination*, Cheltenham, UK and Northampton, MA, USA: Edward Elgar, pp. 215–59.

Dymski, Gary A. (2006c), 'Money as a positional good and global power asymmetries: reflections on "positional goods and asymmetric development"', *Econômica*, **8** (2) (Niterói, Brazil), pp. 320–27.

Dymski, Gary A. (2007), 'The globalization of financial exploitation', in Amiya Kumar Bagchi and Gary A. Dymski (eds), *Capture and Exclude: Developing Economies and the Poor in Global Finance*, Delhi: Tulika Books, pp. 172–94.

Eaton, Jonathan, Mark Gersovitz and Joseph Stiglitz (1986), 'The pure theory of country risk', *European Economic Review*, **30**, 481–513.

Eatwell, John and Lance Taylor (2000), *Global Finance at Risk*, New York: New Press.

Frankman, Myron J. (2002), 'A planet-wide citizen's income: espousal and estimates', paper presented at the IXth Congress of the Basic Income European Network (BIEN), Geneva, 12–14 September.

Held, David (1995), *Democracy and the Global Order: From the Modern State to Cosmopolitan Governance*, Cambridge: Polity Press.

Huber, Joseph (2000), 'Funding basic income by seigneurage', paper presented at the VIIIth Congress of the BIEN, Berlin, 6–7 October.

Kerstenetzky, Celia Lessa (2002), 'Por que se importar com a desigualdade', *Dados ⊠ Revista de Ciências Sociais*, **45** (4), 649–75.

King, Robert G. and Ross Levine (1993), 'Finance, entrepreneurship, and growth: theory and evidence', *Journal of Monetary Economics*, **32**, 513–42.

Koenig-Archibugi, Mathias (2002), 'Mapping global governance', in David Held and Anthony McGrew (eds), *Governing Globalization: Power, Authority, and Global Governance*, Cambridge: Polity.

MacDougall, Donald (1960), 'The benefits and costs of private investment from abroad: a theoretical approach', *Economic Record*, **36**, 13–35.

Obstfeld, Maurice (1986), 'Rational and self-fulfilling balance-of-payments crises', *American Economic Review*, **76** (1), 72–81.

Parijs, Philippe van (2002), 'Does basic income makes sense as a worldwide project?' Closing plenary address of the Xth Congress of the BIEN, Geneva, 12–14 September.

Parijs, Philippe van (2003), *Real Freedom for All: What (If Anything) Can Justify Capitalism?* Oxford: Clarendon Press.

Parijs, Philippe van (2005), *What's Wrong with a Free Lunch?* Boston, MA: Beacon Press.

Polanyi, Karl ([1944] 2001), *The Great Transformation: The Political and Economic Origins of Our Time*, Boston, MA: Beacon Paperbacks.

Rawls, John (1971), *A Theory of Justice*, Cambridge, MA: The Belknap Press of Harvard University Press.

Rawls, John (1999), *The Law of Peoples*, Cambridge, MA: Harvard University Press.

Scholte, Jan Aart (ed.) with Albrecht Schnabel (2002), *Civil Society and Global Finance*, London: Routledge.

Sen, Amartya (1990), *The Standard of Living: The Tanner Lectures*, ed. Geoffrey Hawthorn, Cambridge, UK: Cambridge University Press.

Sen, Amartya (1992), *Inequality Reexamined*, Cambridge, MA: Harvard University Press.

Thakur, Ramesh and Luk van Langenhove (2006), 'Enhancing global governance through regional integration', *Global Governance*, **12** (3), 233–8.

Vanderborght, Yannick and Philippe van Parijs (2005), *L'Allocation Universelle*, Paris: La Découverte.

World Bank (2005), *World Development Report*, Washington, DC: World Bank.

World Bank (2006), *World Development Report*, Washington, DC: World Bank.

See also the entries on: Globalization; Income distribution.

27 Happiness
Luigino Bruni

Introduction
The 'professors of the dismal science' (Carlyle [1850] 1898, p. 43) have rekindled their interest in happiness. In an editorial note to 'Controversy: economics and happiness' in the *Economic Journal*, Huw D. Dixon (1997, pp. 1812–13) introduced 'three economists from different backgrounds who all believe that happiness must play a more central role in economic science once again'.[1] With the 'once again' Dixon refers back to a period in economic thought when the notion of '*pubblica felicità*' (public happiness) was introduced as the core concept of economic analysis by Italian economists such as Ludovico Antonio Muratori, Antonio Genovesi and others in the mid-1700s. This period ended in the rejection of the utilitarian foundations of choice theory in the first decades of the twentieth century.[2]

The reason for economics' new interest in happiness is well expressed by Andrew J. Oswald, one of the three authors referred to in the 'Controversy' article: 'The importance of the economic performance is that it can be a means for an end. The economic matters interest only as far as they make people happier' (Oswald 1997, p. 1815). The same idea is restated by another of the authors mentioned, Yew-Kwang Ng: 'We want money (or anything else) only as a means to increase our happiness. If to have more money does not substantially increase our happiness, then money is not so important, but happiness is' (Ng 1997, p. 1849). By arguing that happiness should take a more central role in economics once again, economists like Oswald and Ng also call attention to one of the main assumptions of economics since the very beginnings of modern economics in the eighteenth century: the positive and direct nexus between wealth and welfare or 'public happiness'. Economics deals *directly* with wealth and by its concern for growth it *indirectly* aims to contribute to an economic policy of increasing the national well-being.[3]

Recent empirical findings however appear to challenge this assumption and urge economists to rethink economics' subject matter. This chapter discusses these empirical findings – phrased as the 'paradox of happiness' or the 'Easterlin paradox' – and their impact on economists' agendas. Discussing rival explanations, it will show how the paradox is giving way to a revival of Aristotelian or eudaimonian approaches to happiness and economics.

The Easterlin paradox
The rediscovery of happiness in economics is mainly a by-product of a process originating in psychology. In fact, the paper published by Brickman and Campbell in 1971, under the telling title 'Hedonic relativism and planning the good society', can rightly be considered the starting point of the new studies on happiness and its paradoxes related to the economic domain. In their study, the two psychologists extend 'adaptation level' theory to individual and collective happiness, concluding that bettering the objective conditions

of life (income or wealth) bears no lasting effects on personal well-being. Such a thesis should have provoked a serious methodological discussion about the meaning of analysis of the nature and causes of the wealth of nations. Yet it did not; the study remained practically unknown in mainstream economics for years.

By utilizing empirical research on people's happiness, Richard Easterlin managed to open the debate around the 'happiness paradox' – also today called the 'Easterlin paradox'. He made use of two types of empirical data. The first was supplied by the responses to a Gallup poll type of survey in which a direct question was asked – a question which is still at the basis of most empirical analyses on happiness: 'In general, how happy would you say that you are – *very* happy, *fairly* happy, or *not very* happy?' (Easterlin 1974, p. 91). The other data set Easterlin made use of came from more sophisticated research carried out by the humanist psychologist Hadley Cantril (1965), another forerunner of contemporary studies on happiness, concerning people's fears, hopes and satisfaction in 14 countries. The subjects interviewed were asked to express their own 'life satisfaction' on a scale from 1 to 10.

Drawing on both types of data, Easterlin's seminal analyses produced several converging results:

(i)   Within a single country, at a given moment in time, the correlation between income and happiness exists and is robust. 'In every single survey, those in the highest status group were happier, on the average, than those in lowest status group' (Easterlin 1974, p. 100).

(ii)   In cross-sectional data among countries, the positive wealth-happiness association, though present, is neither general nor robust, and poorer countries do not always appear to be less happy than richer countries. In other words, 'if there is a positive association among countries between income and happiness it is not very clear . . . The results are ambiguous' (Easterlin 1974, p. 108).[4]

(iii) National time-series data collected in 30 surveys over 25 years (from 1946 to 1970 in the United States) show that per capita real income rose by more than 60 per cent, but the proportion of people who rate themselves as 'very happy', 'fairly happy' or 'not very happy' remained virtually unchanged.

Today almost all scholars, irregardless of background, agree on the third thesis above, that is, the non-correlation between happiness and income in time series. There is, in fact, evidence that 'over time and across OECD countries rises in aggregate income are not associated with rises in aggregate happiness . . . At the aggregate level, there has been no increase in reported happiness over the last 50 years in the US and Japan, nor in Europe since 1973 when the records began' (Layard 2005, p. 148).

Many economists confirm Easterlin's finding that a causal correlation runs from income to happiness within a single country at a given moment in time and is robust (point (i) above).[5]

Scholars disagree, however, with Easterlin's (1974) point (ii) result, that is, with the cross-country income-happiness correlation. Using data from the World Values Survey, some economists argue that despite Easterlin's thesis a correlation does exist: 'Various studies provide evidence that, on average, persons living in rich countries are happier than those living in poor countries' (Frey and Stutzer 2002, p. 19). Hagerty and Veenhoven

(2003) claim that rising GDP is associated with greater happiness. Replying to this paper and defending his classical thesis, Easterlin (2005b) passes over Veenhoven's criticism of his thesis about international comparisons. Veenhoven (1991) plotted the same data as Cantril, though using the same scale on both axes, and showed that the relationship follows a convex pattern of diminishing returns.[6]

Notwithstanding the critiques, the idea of a very low correlation between happiness and income growth is still widely accepted among economists working on happiness. An example of recent research which confirms this idea is Layard (2005, p. 149):

> [I]f we compare countries, there is no evidence that richer countries are happier than poorer ones – so long as we confine ourselves to countries with incomes over [US] $15,000 per head . . . At income levels below $15,000 per head things are different, since people are nearer to the absolute breadline. At these income levels richer countries are happier than poorer ones. And in countries like India, Mexico and Philippines, where we have time series data, happiness has grown as income levels have risen.[7]

What is happiness?
Before discussing explanations of the happiness paradox it is important to note that economists have no clear conceptual understanding of what happiness is in relation to other similar concepts. Ng (1997) defines happiness as 'welfare'; for Oswald (1997) happiness means 'pleasure' or 'satisfaction'. Easterlin is most explicit, 'I use the terms happiness, subjective well-being, satisfaction, utility, well-being and welfare interchangeably' (2001, p. 465). What is more, the way economists deal with happiness is mostly empirical, and their research is driven by the availability of self-reports on happiness or satisfaction with life. They rely on subjective responses to questionnaires simply asking people, 'How happy are you?'[8] It is fully self-reported without any need to define ex ante what happiness is or should be.

For a more concrete definition of happiness and a better understanding of the indicators used to measure it, we turn to psychology. In psychology, studies on happiness began in the 1950s, and psychologists generally use the expression 'happiness' with more precision than economists. Psychologists distinguish (i) 'life satisfaction', which is a cognitive element; (ii) 'affection', which is the affective component; and (iii) 'subjective well-being' (SWB), defined as a 'state of general well-being, synthetic, of long duration, which includes both the affective and cognitive component' (Ahuvia and Friedman 1998, p. 153).

It is important to note that in these studies of happiness there is a rivalry between two approaches to happiness. The first approach relates to the hedonistic/utilitarian views of Epicurus and Jeremy Bentham on humanity and society (Kahneman et al. 1997). More precisely, 'hedonism' (Kahneman et al. 2004) reflects the view that well-being is equivalent to feeling happy, that is, experiencing pleasure. 'Hedonism, as a view of well-being, has . . . been expressed in many forms and has varied from a relatively narrow focus on bodily pleasures to a broad focus on appetites and self-interests' (Deci and Ryan 2001, p. 144). Sometimes this approach is labelled as 'subjectivist' or 'psychologistic' because of its almost exclusive reference to what people report about their own – subjectively experienced – feelings.

The second approach relates to Aristotle's ethics, in particular to his understanding of happiness as 'eudaimonia'. According to Aristotle, happiness is about the good life and human flourishing, that is, the actualization of human potentials through intrinsically motivated activities in a context of interpersonal relationships. Until recently this approach was almost absent from economists' discussions of wealth and happiness (see Gui and Sugden 2005 for a review). We will return to this view on happiness after a discussion of explanations of the Easterlin paradox, based on hedonistic/utilitarian understandings of happiness.

Individual and social treadmills
The first economist who attempted to explain the paradox was Richard Easterlin himself, in his seminal 1974 paper. His explanation refers to Duesenberry's (1949) relative income theory. According to Duesenberry (1949, p. 32), we are constantly comparing ourselves to some group of people and what others buy influences our choices about what we want to buy. It is the 'keeping up with the Joneses' scenario. The consumption function is constructed upon the hypothesis that our consumption choices relate to our *relative* income – reflecting the difference between our level of income and others' income level – instead of our absolute income. The utility that individuals experience from a certain level of consumption depends on their budget relative to others' budgets.

Without going back to classical authors, who gave prominence to the social dimensions of consumption, at the end of nineteenth century Veblen introduced the notion of 'conspicuous goods', referring to goods people purchase to impress others with their wealth. After all, the most significant acts of consumption are normally carried out in public, under others' gaze. In recent times, Tibor Scitovsky (1976) dealt with the relationship between consumption and status, and Fred Hirsch (1977) coined the term 'positional good'. Contemporary positional theory centres on the concept of *externality*: conspicuous commodities share some characteristics of 'demerit goods' (because they are private goods generating negative externalities), with the typical consequence of Pareto-inefficiency (for over-consumption). In other words, there is a problem of self-deception: people, because of self-deception, consume an excessive amount of conspicuous goods, and, as a consequence, the amount of time devoted to 'inconspicuous consumption' is inefficient (too little) (Easterlin 2005a).

Besides explanations based on the relative consumption hypothesis (Frank 1997, 1999; Ng 1997; Höllander 2001; Richard 2005), there are other explanations as well, based on the 'treadmill' concept introduced from research on happiness in the field of psychology.

Before discussing the new trend of explaining the Easterlin paradox in terms of individual treadmills it is important to note that the relative consumption theory can be rephrased as a 'social treadmill' explanation: more income or consumption delivers hardly any more satisfaction when others' income or consumption keep pace.

The treadmill metaphor, coined by Brickman and Campbell (1971), imagines that one is running constantly and yet remains at the same place because the treadmill one is on is operating at the same pace – or even faster. Key concepts in individual treadmill explanations are 'hedonic adaptation' and 'set point'.

According to the set point theory, there is a level of happiness which remains practically constant during one's lifetime, because personality and temperament variables seem to play a strong role in determining the level of happiness of individuals. Such characteristics are basically innate. In other words, in the long run, we are fixed at hedonic neutrality, and our efforts to make ourselves happier by gaining good life circumstances are only short-term solutions. Therefore, life circumstances, including health and income, often account for a very small percentage of variance in subjective well-being. People initially do react to events (positive as well as negative), but then they return to baseline levels of well-being that are determined by personality factors (Argyle 2001; Lucas et al. 2002). Empirical studies (Lykken and Tellegen 1996), for instance, conclude that more than 80 per cent of the variance in long-term stable levels of subjective well-being can be attributed to inborn temperament. It is on this basis that researchers have claimed that people have inborn subjective well-being 'set points'.[9] The various *shocks* that hit people in their lifetime affect their happiness only temporarily. We inevitably return – that is, there is a 'hedonic adaptation' – to our *set point* after a brief period.

Set-point theory explanations are popular in economics. Their proponents believe happiness to be essentially a congenital matter that mostly depends on subjective elements that are absolute, such as character, genes or the inherited capacity to live with and overcome life's hardships. In other words, there exists a given level of happiness, around which the various experiences of life gravitate. This approach is not far removed from the thesis of Herrnstein and Murray (1994), who in *The Bell Curve* decry the uselessness of social programmes on the basis that people's innate level of intelligence cannot be permanently changed by education.

More recently, Kahneman et al. proposed distinguishing another type of treadmill, the satisfaction one, besides the treadmill based on hedonic adaptation. While 'hedonic treadmill' denotes the treadmill based on adaptation, 'satisfaction treadmill' is based on aspiration, 'which marks the boundaries between satisfactory and unsatisfactory results' (1999, p. 14). Frey and Stutzer (2005) make a similar distinction between the two treadmill effects: 'This process, or mechanism, that reduces the hedonic effects of a constant or repeated stimulus, is called *adaptation* . . . According to aspiration level theory, individual well-being is determined by the gap between aspiration and achievement' (p. 125, emphasis in original).

As their incomes rise, people are induced to seek continuous and ever more intense pleasures in order to maintain the same level of satisfaction. The *satisfaction treadmill* works in such a way that one's subjective happiness (self-evaluation) remains constant even when one's objective happiness improves. In this case, while Mr Brown gets a boost in his objective well-being, because he bought a new car, the fact that he has had a rise in income has also boosted his aspirations about which is the ideal car to own; so his subjective satisfaction level remains the same. This is true even though he may be objectively more comfortable in his new car. Frank (2005) and Layard (2005) suggest policies for offsetting distortions due to such self-deception, for example, that inconspicuous consumption be taxed less than conspicuous consumption.

Explanations from a eudaimonian perspective on happiness

Relative consumption and treadmill explanations are based on a hedonic/utilitarian understanding of happiness: happiness is conceived as the effect of earning income aimed at purchasing commodities. From an Aristotelian eudaimonian perspective this conception is too restrictive and – because of this restriction – even biased. Earning money and purchasing commodities in the context of a market economy is at best only an aspect of what eudaimonia stands for – a meaningful life or well-being in the sense of actualization of human potentials through intrinsically motivated activities in a context of interpersonal relationships.

The idea that happiness is in essence relational offers a hint to a different explanation of the Easterlin paradox: higher income does not contribute to a happier life when more income involves a tendency to over-consume commodities – produced and purchased in the market economy – and to under-consume relational goods. See, for example, Lane (2000) and Putnam (2000) indicating that time devoted to interpersonal relations is diminishing, crowded out by the extension of markets and in particular of the market economy itself. The latter creates greater mobility between jobs and areas but erodes 'spaces' for interpersonal relations, shifting the care of children and elderly from family to market (compare Gui and Sugden 2005). Antoci et al. (2008) claim to explain the under-consumption of relational goods by focusing on relational goods as *public* goods: people in developed countries intentionally consume too little relational goods which ends in a sub-optimal equilibrium (as in a Prisoner's Dilemma game).

Scitovsky discussed this problem in *The Joyless Economy* (1976). Here he argues that people in affluent societies consume too much *comfort goods* and too little *stimulation goods*, such as relational goods, since the relative price of comfort goods is lower and even decreases more because of economies of scale and technologically induced increases in productivity absent with stimulation goods. Today Bruni and Stanca (2008), among others, point out complementary causes of comfort goods driving out relational goods, including the presentation of comfort goods as surrogate relational goods, such as a TV programme or the internet platform 'Second Life'.

Happiness, ethics and economics

Why are today's happiness studies important in discussions about economics and ethics? The paradox of happiness, or the 'Easterlin paradox', questions the ethical justification of economic science. Economics achieved as political economics – a branch of moral philosophy – an autonomous ethical status in relation to the theology of morality in the eighteenth century, when it became common sense that an increase in the 'wealth of nations' was synonymous with an increase in the 'welfare of nations' or even the 'public happiness'. This was the underlying ethical claim of political economy in the classical era, from Smith to Mill, but in a sense extending to John Maynard Keynes, Joseph Schumpeter and John Hicks. Even today this claim is present in economics when it focuses on the causes and nature of the wealth of nations because of wealth's supposed contribution to the amelioration of social well-being. Evidence from the paradox of happiness against this supposition, then, requires a reassessment of its ethical foundations. It perhaps also mandates contemporary economics to redefine its moral basis if it still intends to contribute to the well-being of people.

Rethinking economics' ethical foundations will have its effects on other parts of economists' frame of reference. The paradox of happiness affects the basic assumption of modern economics that the goods which contribute to an increase of both individual and social well-being are basically commodities. Maybe this assumption was adequate for societies of the first Industrial Revolution and Fordist societies, since the scarce resource then was actually material goods, commodities, physical and financial capital. But in contemporary or post-Fordist society, the goods becoming increasingly scarce are 'relational goods', non-instrumental relationships, as the paradox of happiness also indicates. Rethinking happiness in an eudaimonian way – by giving a more central place to relational goods and intrinsic motivation – could usher in a new era in the dialogue between economics and ethics.

Notes

1. Andrew J. Oswald, Robert H. Frank and Yew-Kwanh Ng.
2. On the history of happiness in economic tradition see Bruni (2006).
3. The choice (by Adam Smith) of the word 'wealth' (from 'weal') instead of 'riches' is also a sign of the profound nexus, in his thinking, of wealth with public happiness.
4. Cantril's data showed, for instance, that Cuba and Egypt were more satisfied than West Germany (1965, p. 258). He plotted satisfaction against the log of income and thus construed a lack of relationship.
5. For example, 'When we plot average happiness versus average income for clusters of people in a given country at a given time . . . rich people are in fact a lot happier than poor people. It's actually an astonishingly large difference. There's no one single change you can imagine that would make your life improve on the happiness scale as much as to move from the bottom 5 percent on the income scale to the top 5 percent' (Frank 2005, p. 67) and 'Of course within countries the rich are always happier than the poor' (Layard 2005, p. 148).
6. A similar criticism has been put forward by Oswald (1997, p. 1817) and others.
7. Among psychologists the relation between income and happiness is even more controversial. Some, on the basis of data different from those of the World Values Survey, challenge the correlations (also when other variables are controlled for) between income and happiness in general (*among* countries, *within* a country and *over time*). For a review, compare Diener et al. (2004).
8. In the World Values Survey questionnaires there is also the information about 'life satisfaction', measured on a numerical 1–10 scale.
9. For a critique of this theory see Lucas et al. (2002, p. 4).

References

Ahuvia, Aaron C. and Douglas C. Friedman (1998), 'Income, consumption, and subjective well-being: toward a composite macromarketing model', *Journal of Macromarketing*, **18**, 153–68.
Antoci, Angelo, Pier L. Sacco and Luca Zarri (2008), 'Social preferences and the private provision of public goods: a "double critical mass" model', *Public Choice*, **135**(3–4), 257–76.
Argyle, Michael (2001), *The Psychology of Happiness*, New York: Taylor & Francis.
Brickman, Philip and Donald T. Campbell (1971), 'Hedonic relativism and planning the good society', in M.H. Apley (ed.), *Adaptation-Level Theory: A Symposium*, New York: Academic Press, pp. 287–302.
Bruni, Luigino (2006), *Civil Happiness: Economics and Human Flourishing in Historical Perspective*, London: Routledge.
Bruni, Luigino and Luca Stanca (2008), 'Watching alone: relational goods, happiness and television', *Journal of Economic Behavior and Organization*, **65**, 506–28.
Cantril, Hadley (1965), *The Pattern of Human Concerns*, New Brunswick, NJ: Rutgers University Press.
Carlyle, Thomas ([1850] 1898), *Letter-Day Pamphlets*, London: Chapman and Hall.
Deci, Edward L. and Richard M. Ryan (2001), 'On happiness and human potentials: a review of research on hedonic and eudaimonic wellbeing', *Annual Review of Psychology*, **52**, 141–6.
Diener, Ed, Christi N. Scollon and Richard E. Lucas (2004), 'The evolving concept of subjective well-being: the multifaceted nature of happiness', *Advances in Cell Aging and Gerontology*, **15**, 187–219.
Dixon, Huw D. (1997), 'Controversy: economic and happiness. Editorial note', *Economic Journal*, **107**, 1812–14.
Duesenberry, James S. (1949), *Income, Saving and the Theory of Consumer Behaviour*, Cambridge: Harvard University Press.
Easterlin, Richard (1974), 'Does economic growth improve human lot? Some empirical evidence', in Paul A. Davis and Melvin W. Reder (eds), *Nation and Households in Economic Growth: Essays in Honor of Moses Abromowitz*, New York and London: Academic Press.
Easterlin, Richard (2001), 'Income and happiness: towards a unified theory', *Economic Journal*, **111**, 465–84.
Easterlin, Richard (2005a), 'Towards a better theory of happiness', in Luigino Bruni and Pier L. Porta (eds), *Economics and Happiness: Framings of Analysis*, Oxford: Oxford University Press.
Easterlin, Richard (2005b), 'Feeding the illusion of growth and happiness: a reply to Hagerty and Veenhoven', *Social Indicators Research*, **74** (3), December, 429–43.
Frank, Robert H. (1997), 'The frame of reference as a public good', *Economic Journal*, **107**, 1832–47.

Frank, Robert H. (1999), *Luxury Fever*, New York: Free Press.

Frank, Robert H. (2005), 'Does absolute income matter?' in Luigino Bruni and Pier L. Porta (eds), *Economics and Happiness: Framings of Analysis*, Oxford: Oxford University Press.

Frey, Bruno S. and Alois Stutzer (2002), *Happiness in Economics*, Princeton, NJ: Princeton University Press.

Frey, Bruno S. and Alois Stutzer (2005), 'Testing theories of happiness', in Luigino Bruni and Pier L. Porta (eds), *Economics and Happiness: Framings of Analysis*, Oxford: Oxford University Press.

Gui, Benedetto and Robert Sugden (2005), *Economics and Social Interactions*, Cambridge: Cambridge University Press.

Hagerty, Michael R. and Ruut Veenhoven (2003), 'Wealth and happiness revisited: growing national income does go with greater happiness', *Social Indicators Research*, **64**, 1–27.

Herrnstein, Richard J. and Charles Murray (1994), *The Bell Curve: Intelligence and Class Structure in American Life*, New York: Free Press.

Hirsch, Fred (1977), *Social Limits to Growth*, London: Routledge.

Höllander, Heinz (2001), 'On the validity of utility statements: standard theory versus Duesenberry's', *Journal of Economic Behaviour and Organization*, **45**, 227–49.

Kahneman, Daniel, Peter P. Wakker and Rakesh Sarin (1997), 'Back to Bentham? Explorations of experienced utility', *Quarterly Journal of Economics*, **112**, 375–405.

Kahneman, Daniel, Ed Diener and Norbert Schwartz (eds) (1999), *Well-Being: Foundations of Hedonic Psychology*, New York: Russell Sage Foundation.

Kahneman, Daniel, Alan Krueger, David Schkade, Norbert Schwarz and Arthur Stone (2004), 'A survey method for characterizing daily life experience: the Day Reconstruction Method (DRM)', *Science*, **306**, 1776–80.

Lane, Robert (2000), *The Loss of Happiness in the Market Democracies*, New Haven, CT: Yale University Press.

Layard, Richard (2005), 'Rethinking public economics: the implications of rivalry and habit', in Luigino Bruni and Pier L. Porta (eds), *Economics and Happiness: Framings of Analysis*, Oxford: Oxford University Press.

Lucas, Richard E., Andrew E. Clark, Yannis Georgellis and Ed Diener (2002), 'Unemployment alters the set-point for life satisfaction', Working Paper 17, Paris: Delta.

Lykken, David T. and Auke Tellegen (1996), 'Happiness is a stochastic phenomenon', *Psychological Science*, **7**, 186–9.

Ng, Yew-Kwang (1997), 'A case for happiness, cardinalism, and interpersonal comparability', *Economic Journal*, **107**, 1848–58.

Nickerson, Carol, Norbert Schwarz, Ed Diener and Daniel Kahneman (2003), 'Zeroing the dark side of the American dream: a closer look at the negative consequences of the goal for financial success', *Psychological Science*, **14**, 531–6.

Oswald, Andrew J. (1997), 'Happiness and economic performance', *Economic Journal*, **107**, 1815–31.

Putnam, Robert D. (2000), *Bowling Alone*, New York: Simon and Schuster.

Scitovsky, Tibor (1976), *The Joyless Economy: An Inquiry into Human Satisfaction and Consumer Dissatisfaction*, Oxford: Oxford University Press.

Veblen, Thorstein ([1899] 1998), *The Theory of the Leisure Class*, New York: Prometheus Books.

Veenhoven, Ruut (1991), 'Is happiness relative?', *Social Indicators Research*, **24**, 1–34.

World Values Survey, www.worldvaluessurvey.org/, accessed 1 October 2008.

See also the entries on: Aristotle; Hedonism; Virtue ethics.

28 Hedonism
Johannes Hirata

Hedonism, from the Greek word *hedone* or 'pleasure', refers to any theory stipulating that the experience of pleasure is the primary feature of a good life. In a wider sense, the term 'hedonism' is also used to refer to theories of behaviour (psychological hedonism) or to ethical theories (ethical hedonism) that give a central role to the experience of pleasure.

Hedonism as a school of thought is typically linked with Epicureanism, the Greek school named after its founder Epicurus (341–270 BC), who proclaimed pleasure and pain as the yardsticks for good and bad. However, in contrast to what Epicureanism means in today's colloquial use, for Epicurus 'pleasure' was essentially the absence of pain and fear rather than mindless physical delight; and the successful pursuit of pleasure required reflection and self-control rather than the impulsive execution of one's drives. Nevertheless, even the hedonism of Epicureanism stands out in its radical subsumption of all possible goods under one ultimate good.

An even earlier and more radical concept of hedonism can be ascribed to the Cyrenaic school headed by Aristippus (435–356 BC). The Cyrenaics explicitly believed that pleasure cannot vary in quality but only in intensity, and they embraced a material concept of pleasure as bodily pleasure and as the *presence* of pleasure rather than as the absence of pain (Drakopoulos 1991, p. 11). Aristippus also appears to have attempted to find a way to measure pleasure (ibid., p. 12), though little is known about his success in the venture.

Today, the terms 'hedonism' and 'hedonistic' are popularly used to describe a way of living that, on top of being egoistic, is aimed to maximize the experience of personal enjoyment and pre-reflective pleasure (rather than 'utility', 'well-being', 'happiness' or other more inclusive goods). Hedonism in this popular interpretation is often used with pejorative connotations, in particular, by advocates of traditional moral codes such as those of many religious communities which portray pleasure, in particular bodily pleasure, as morally suspect or as in itself objectionable.

In the scientific community, however, hedonism is not understood as a way of living but rather as a particular ethical or psychological concept which does not necessarily involve egoism.

The good life and the righteous life

In particular, hedonism can be construed as one of two distinct categories of ethical theory: as an evaluative (that is, teleological) theory, making statements about what constitutes a good life (an enjoyable life, a life worth living), or as a moral (that is, deontological) theory, making statements about what constitutes a righteous (legitimate, justifiable) life.

Evaluative hedonism holds that the goodness of a life is ultimately a matter of how much pleasure a person experiences. Living a good (enjoyable) life would thus require the maximization of the net balance of pleasure over pain. Other possible candidates for the content of a good life would then be merely instrumental to pleasure. For example, friendship would have no intrinsic value as such, but only because, and to the degree that, it furthers pleasure. Evaluative hedonism does not make any statement about whether a 'good life' in this sense would also be legitimate from a moral point of view. It merely states that such a life would be good from the individual's point of view when moral considerations are left out of the analysis.

Moral hedonism stipulates that morality is a matter of pleasure. This does not automatically follow from evaluative hedonism: subscribing to evaluative hedonism as a concept of the good life does not necessarily mean that one's conception of morality must be restricted to considerations of pleasure alone. This would only be the case if one believed that a life worth living is the same as a commendable life (that is, that a good life is the same as a righteous life), or if one believed that moral obligations can only be about directly furthering the good life (of oneself or of others).

Since neither of these premises is theoretically compelling, it is possible to combine evaluative hedonism as a concept of a good life with a moral theory that recognizes more reasons for moral obligations than just pleasure (for example, keeping a promise after the death of the person to whom it was given). Moral hedonism therefore is a substantive theory about the admitted scope of moral obligations rather than a mere theoretical extrapolation of evaluative hedonism. In particular, it is a *consequentialist* and a *welfarist* ethical theory: it holds that moral justifications must ultimately refer to consequences in terms of pleasure (and pain). For example, keeping a promise to a deceased person would be accepted as a morally relevant consideration only if and to the degree that this impacts upon the pleasure of living persons.

Moral hedonism can again be subdivided into two distinct theories: egoistic hedonism and universalistic hedonism. Egoistic hedonism holds that persons best fulfil their moral obligations by successfully pursuing their own pleasure. This perspective understands egoism not as a negative attribute (as in the colloquial use of the term), but rather as one (or the only) ethically commendable strategy that warrants legitimate behaviour. Egoism would typically be justified by one of two argumentative strategies. The first argues that demanding altruism (or rather non-egoism) from individuals would be asking too much of a sacrifice; only saints can be expected to act altruistically. In other words, demanding people to respect others' legitimate interests is deemed unjustifiable. The second argues that it is better for everybody if people act egoistically. Thus, even if altruism could be expected from people, altruism would not lead to a better overall outcome. 'Competition is more charitable than sharing', in the words of Homann and Blome-Drees (1992, p. 111). Thus, people's pursuit of pleasure without consideration of others' well-being not only enhances their own life, but also contributes to the pleasure of others thanks to societal mechanisms of one sort or another (perhaps an 'invisible hand' *à la* Adam Smith). Both argumentative strategies can be combined to form a doubly justified plea for egoism: it would be unreasonable (and unrealistic) to demand anything other than egoism, but – luckily – universal egoism leads to the better outcome anyway (compare Ulrich 2008 p. 113).

Egoistic hedonism thus effectively says that the good life is really the same as the righteous or virtuous life. By taking care of one's own pleasure, the pleasure of all others is optimally ensured.

Universalistic hedonism holds that the principle determining one's moral obligations is the duty to enhance, or maximize, total pleasure in society, construed as the net balance of one's own and all others' pleasure and pain. Universalistic hedonism can thus be considered a particular brand of utilitarianism that narrows the possible contents of utility down to pleasure, as in the original utilitarian formulation of Bentham.

By imposing heroic moral obligations on the individual, to wit, to give one's own well-being no more weight than that of any other person, universalistic hedonism has less in common with egoistic hedonism (for which moral obligations and personal pleasure maximization coincide) than their terminological proximity might suggest. In particular, universalistic hedonism does not endorse egoism, which is to say, it does not presuppose that universally egoistic behaviour leads to a desirable outcome. Rather, it requires people to take others' interests into account rather than blindly following their own selfish impulses.

A common problem of either variant of hedonism, evaluational or moral, is the malleability of the concept of pleasure. There appears to be no obvious or natural defining criteria by which to distinguish pleasure from other positive feelings. Linguistic research suggests that 'pleasure', as it is used in the (contemporary) English language, does not usually imply any cognitive scenario, unlike emotion words such as 'happiness' or 'contentment', and that 'pleasure' is only distantly related to 'pleased' so that inferences from one to the other are impossible (on that last see Wierzbicka 1999, p. 56). However, pleasure *can* be used to imply a cognitive evaluation (as in 'it was a pleasure meeting you'), opening the scope of pleasure to interpretation.

Depending on the scope attributed to pleasure, hedonism can therefore stand for an utterly selfish and short-sighted pursuit of unsophisticated pleasure or for a prudent and mindful way of life.

Psychological hedonism

Psychological hedonism is a descriptive theory of human behaviour with particular relevance to economic theory and its normative foundations. Since it is not an ethical theory, it is better considered a behavioural theory with analogies to hedonism, rather than a particular form of hedonism in the narrower sense described above. Hedonism proper, as most '-isms', is a theory with substantive ethical propositions of one kind or another.

Psychological hedonism basically states that, as a matter of fact, all human behaviour is ultimately motivated by the desire to maximize the experience of pleasure. Even apparently altruistic acts are reinterpreted in terms of the pursuit of pleasure. A classical example of such a reinterpretation was given by the English philosopher Thomas Hobbes (1588–1679), perhaps the most prominent (though not the earliest) spiritual father of psychological hedonism. When asked why he gave alms to a beggar outside St Paul's Cathedral despite his rejection of the possibility of altruism, he replied that he did so because it pleased himself to see the beggar pleased (*Encyclopaedia Britannica* 2003).

It is important to note that psychological hedonism does not raise any immediate ethical claims. Its propositions are about causal mechanisms of behaviour; that is, about matters of fact rather than about the distinction between good and bad (as evaluative hedonism) or right and wrong (as moral hedonism, see above).

It may still be argued, however, that psychological hedonism is not ethically neutral as long as ethical reasoning and debate are also considered a part of behaviour. In this case, any theory claiming to explain human behaviour in general will implicitly claim to also explain the 'true' nature of arguing in general and of ethical reasoning in particular. In the case of psychological hedonism, this would mean that rational arguing, too, would be governed – or rather supplanted – by the pleasure maximization principle. Defending psychological hedonism therefore leads to the problem of a performative contradiction: the possibility of arguing would be denied at the same time as it is being invoked.

Typically, however, psychological hedonism is combined with moral hedonism, making more explicit the link between the behavioural theory and ethics. Bentham, for example, not only stated that the 'two sovereign masters, pain and pleasure . . . govern us in all we do, in all we say, in all we think' but also that they 'point out what we ought to do' (Bentham [1789] 1907, Ch. 1.1). In fact, moral hedonism appears to follow logically from psychological hedonism as soon as it is assumed that only what is desired as an end can serve as a moral end: if pleasure alone is desired as an end, and if only what is desired as an end can be a moral end, then pleasure alone can be a moral end (compare Drakopoulos 1991, p. 8). Yet, while it is just a single step from psychological hedonism to moral hedonism, the combination of the two tends to conceal the fact that the theories are fundamentally different in nature – one being descriptive and the other prescriptive – and not just two ways of saying the same thing.

Keeping in mind the problem of the performative contradiction raised above, it appears doubtful that a defender of psychological hedonism could consistently defend any moral theory at all (including moral hedonism) or even that he/she could consistently participate in an argumentative discourse in the first place.

Psychological hedonism also suffers the problem of the malleability of the concept of pleasure described earlier. As the example of Thomas Hobbes shows, practically any behaviour can be explained in terms of the pursuit of pleasure. All it takes is the assumption that apparently 'non-hedonistic' behaviour is in fact instrumental for the experience of higher-order pleasure. For example, the fact that voters sacrifice time and effort to cast their ballot without any reasonable prospect of reward can be reinterpreted by claiming that casting their vote makes people feel good because they feel they fulfil a moral obligation and that people vote *in order to* experience this positive feeling (or to avoid a bad one).

This problem points to a more fundamental limitation of psychological hedonism. Since it makes propositions about the *motivation* underlying behaviour, and since motivation cannot be observed, psychological hedonism, as any theory on motivation, must remain a hypothesis that is impossible to empirically falsify. As such, psychological hedonism cannot be upheld as an empirically corroborated theory. At the most, it can play a role as an interesting or useful working hypothesis within confined limits.

Psychological hedonism should therefore be seen not so much as a specific behavioural theory but rather as a manifestation of a radically solipsistic concept of the person; that is, a concept that holds that a person cannot have any other reasons than own advantage and disadvantage. Such a concept contrasts with a self-transcendent concept of the person in which one is thought to also have reasons that cannot be reduced to the matter of personal advantage (even though advantage may play some role). For example, while a proponent of a solipsistic concept of the person would explain voting by construing a net personal benefit (for example, by means of 'the avoidance of a bad conscience'), an advocate of a self-transcendent concept of the person would also look for reasons outside the voter's psyche, arguing, for example, that a person has reached the conviction that it is right to vote and finds it important to do what is right.

Interestingly, it has been argued that a self-transcendent attitude ultimately results in more pleasure than pleasure's direct and solipsistic pursuit because lasting sources of pleasure – such as friendship, self-realization and integrity – do not lend themselves to being instrumentalized. Sidgwick, for example, argued that 'the principle of Egoistic Hedonism, when applied with a due knowledge of the laws of human nature, is practically self-limiting; i.e. . . . a rational method of attaining the end at which it aims requires that we should to some extent put it out of sight and not directly aim at it' (Sidgwick [1874] 1907, Book II, Ch. III; compare also Singer 1995, pp. 211ff.; Nietzsche 1988, p. 408).

Being concepts of the person rather than matter-of-fact hypotheses, neither concept – solipsism or self-transcendence – can of course be empirically falsified or corroborated, and one can always reinterpret observed behaviour in terms of one or the other.

Hedonism and economic theory

Psychological hedonism as a solipsistic concept of the person has become a central building block of economic theory in the form of the *homo economicus* model of human behaviour. In the course of the formalization of the economic method (from about the turn of the nineteenth century to the middle of the twentieth century), the hedonistic model of human behaviour went hand in glove with the project to derive an analytical and quantitative approach to economics. Featuring a single end, a perfectly consistent system of commeasurable preferences and a straightforward (at least in theory) decision algorithm (to wit, pleasure maximization), psychological hedonism was perfectly suited to the submission of human behaviour and rationality to rigid quantitative analysis. It may even be argued that the hedonistic *homo economicus* model was a crucial factor in the historical development of economics towards the rigidly analytical science it is today. However, whereas the pioneers of this approach emphasized the limited nature of the *homo economicus* model (compare Walras [1877] 1954, p. 256; and much less Edgeworth 1881, pp. 16, 61), modern economic literature largely takes the hedonistic *homo economicus* model at face value. The original ultimate end of psychological hedonism, pleasure, was replaced in the *homo economicus* model by 'utility' as the catch-all term for subjective valuation. This means that the ultimate motive of human behaviour is no longer assumed necessarily to be pleasure in the narrow sense (see above) but rather a malleable concept of advantage and well-being.

Hedonism today

At the beginning of the twenty-first century, hedonism is no longer a central topic of either philosophy or economics, even though implicit references to hedonism are frequent. While evaluational hedonism still has some advocates, moral hedonism has been all but marginalized. In particular, egoistic hedonism appears not to have a significant number of proponents, whereas the (potential) supporters of universalistic hedonism prefer the more generic brand of utilitarianism.

By contrast, psychological hedonism still appears to be the dominant concept of human behaviour in economic theory. Since the marriage of economics and psychological hedonism is a matter of methodological compatibility (see above), an end to this dominance seems a remote possibility since it would probably require a major paradigm shift of economic method. Nevertheless, the hedonistic model of human behaviour is criticized as reflecting an implausible and reductionist conception of rationality (compare

Sen [1977] 1983, 1987; Rawls [1971] 1999, p. 486). It has even been said to encourage egoistic behaviour among economics students (Frank et al. 1993).

References

Bentham, Jeremy ([1789] 1907), *An Introduction to the Principles of Morals and Legislation*, Oxford: Clarendon Press.
Drakopoulos, Stavros A. (1991), *Values and Economic Theory: The Case of Hedonism*, Aldershot: Avebury.
Edgeworth, Francis Y. (1881), *Mathematical Psychics: An Essay on the Application of Mathematics to the Moral Sciences*, London: Kegan Paul.
Encyclopaedia Britannica (2003), 'Ethics', www.britannica.com/eb/article-252536, 9 October 2006.
Frank, Robert H., Thomas Gilovich and Dennis T. Regan (1993), 'Does studying economics inhibit cooperation?' *Journal of Economic Perspectives*, **7** (2), 159–71.
Homann, Karl and Franz Blome-Drees (1992), *Wirtschafts- und Unternehmensethik*, Göttingen: Vandenhoeck & Ruprecht.
Nietzsche, Friedrich (1988), *Sämtliche Werke: Kritische Studienausgabe*, ed. Giorgio Colli and Mazzino Montinari, Berlin: Walter de Gruyter.
Rawls, John ([1971] 1999), *A Theory of Justice*, revised edition, Oxford: Oxford University Press.
Sen, Amartya ([1977] 1983), 'Rational fools: a critique of the behavioural foundations of economic theory', in *Choice, Welfare and Measurement*, Oxford: Basil Blackwell Publisher, pp. 84–106.
Sen, Amartya (1987), *On Ethics and Economics*, Oxford: Basil Blackwell.
Sidgwick, Henry ([1874] 1907), *The Methods of Ethics*, 7th edition, London: Macmillan.
Singer, Peter (1995), *How Are We to Live? Ethics in an Age of Self-Interest*, Amherst: Prometheus Books.
Ulrich, Peter (2008), *Integrative Economic Ethics: Foundations of a Civilized Market Economy*, Cambridge: Cambridge University Press.
Walras, Léon ([1877] 1954), *Elements of Pure Economics*, trans. William Jaffé, London: Allen and Unwin.
Wierzbicka, Anna (1999), *Emotions across Languages and Cultures: Diversity and Universals*, Cambridge: Cambridge University Press.

See also the entries on: Egoism; Homo economicus; Utilitarianism; Virtue ethics.

29 Hinduism
Narendar Pani

The influence of classical Hinduism on economic thought is as meagre as it is ancient. Nonetheless, Hindu thought lays claim to what is widely regarded as the first known economics text, Kautilya's Sanskrit work, *Arthashastra*. Roughly translated as *Instructions on Material Prosperity*, this text dates back to between the 4th century BC and 150 AD (Rangarajan 1992, pp. 18–21). *Arthashastra's* preoccupation with practical detail made it an important manuscript in its time, but inadequate elaboration of the thought underlying its prescriptions meant that it fell well short of becoming the foundation of an independent stream of Hindu economic thought. Indeed, the gap between Hinduism and economics is now so wide that where the religion is mentioned in modern economic literature, it is likely to take the form of a self-deprecatory Hindu economist using the term 'Hindu rate of growth' to refer to the low growth rates in which the Indian economy was once mired.[1] To delve into this relatively little explored territory we thus need to begin with a quick look at the nature of Hinduism and the ethics that derive from it, before exploring the implications of these ethical principles for economics.

The *Vedas*, which Indian tradition dates to about 4000 BC, are widely regarded as the foundation of Hinduism. These texts were initially passed on orally, and a great deal of emphasis was laid on it being remembered as well as on to whom it was to be passed. The *Upanishads*, the final portion of the *Vedas*, literally means 'secret teaching'. The *Upanishads* were originally considered to be the *Vedanta*, or the end of the *Vedas*. Over time *Vedanta* has come to mean the entire teaching of the *Vedas*, including later work that was seen to be developing Vedic thought. The *Upanishads*, the *Bhagavadgita* and the *Vedanta Sutras* are now considered the triple basis of *Vedanta*. Much of this work, particularly the *Vedanta Sutra*, is extremely cryptic and requires learned interpretation. This has resulted in the emergence of a number of schools of thought. These schools have been classified as Absolutistic or Theistic, 'the former representing *Brahman*, the ultimate reality, as an impersonal principle and the latter as a personal God' (Hiriyana 1995, p. 152).

Variations are reflected in perceptions of the relationship between *Brahman* and the self. The 'self' here goes beyond external attributes, like physical features or relationships, to mean the pure, objectless experience of consciousness; that is, the *atman*. The Absolutistic schools, like *Advaita* (non-dualism), see the *Brahman* and the *atman* as being one. The Theistic schools, on the other hand, believe there is a difference between the *Brahman* and the self. The perception of this difference in turn varies among Theistic schools. For instance, the *Visistadvaita* (qualified non-dualism) sees the *Brahman*, the self and the physical world as different though closely related, while the *Dvaita* (dualism) school sees a much sharper difference between the *Brahman* and the self.

Since our purpose here is to look at Hindu ethics in the context of a social science it may be useful to go with the choice made by Gandhi, who used Hindu thought to guide his social action. The influence of *Advaita* is evident in Gandhi's thought. The *Advaita* goes by the *Mundaka Upanisad's* description of *Brahman* as being 'without form, like ether . . . The Great One brings forth breath, mind, and all the senses' (Klostermaier 2006a, p. 91). It is a quality-less cosmic principle of all. According to *Advaita,* the self or the *atman* is the pure subject, pure consciousness. Perceptions of reality are distorted by the objects, senses and the mind. When realization removes these distortions, all that is left is the *atman*, which is identical to the *Brahman*. Realization of this truth is achieved by discerning what is false. Falsity is in turn recognized by first believing something to be true, then recognizing its contradictions, and moving on to a new set of what is believed to be true. This new set then throws up fresh contradictions leading to another perception of the truth. The process, which has been interpreted to be Hegelian in spirit, continues until there are no contradictions. This final point is not reached in a single lifetime. Individuals who have progressed to a better realization of the truth in this life continue the process in a next, higher, life, until they are ultimately liberated by direct experience of the ultimate truth and their *atman* becomes a part of *Brahman*.

Implicit in this process is recognition of the need to function in the real world with less than absolute truth. In the realm of religion, the Hindu thinker Sankara interprets this to mean there is a 'lower' *Saguna Brahman* and a 'higher' *Nirguna Brahman*. The *Saguna Brahman* is the God of religion who takes on various qualities and exists as long as the world exists. This allows for the many deities that Hindus worship – 330 million according to one count.[2] The *Nirguna Brahman* is the quality-less Ultimate that exists even after the world ends. Self-realization begins with worship of the 'lower' *Brahman* and moves on towards realization of the 'higher' *Brahman*.

On the journey towards the realization of the self, an individual must relate to the material world. This relation is determined by the three *gunas*, which can be taken to mean 'guiding principles'. The *Bhagavadgita* identifies the three *gunas* as the *satvik*, the *rajasik* and the *tamasik*, which have been translated as the pure, the passionate and the dark (Johnson 1994, p. 71). These traits are reflected not only in individuals' material desires, such as for food, but also in their approach to sacrifice and asceticism. When asceticism is practised without any desire for rewards it is pure. When practised for the sake of honour, respect or reverence, it is passionate. When asceticism is prasticed with deluded notions, with self-torture and with the idea of harming others, it is dark. The overall character of the individual depends on which of these three traits is dominant in one's personality.

Development of the right *gunas* helps in the realization of the self, but it is still not the realization itself; it is still not the absolute truth. As Gandhi argued, God alone is the absolute truth, while mortals function with relative truth (Gandhi 1972, pp. 478–9).

In a world of continuously changing relative truths it is imperative to distinguish between error and doubt. While what is known to be an error can be rejected, space must be provided for that which is not yet known to be true. This recognition extends to several systems of Hindu thought. As Mohanty pointed out, 'for the Nyaya, as for most systems of Indian philosophy, doubt is a species of knowledge, so that if I have a doubt of the form "Is S p or not?" most Indian logicians would say I have a knowledge – though not a valid one about S' (Mohanty 2002, p. 102). Thus, while reason is of primary importance, that which reason does not explain is not automatically false. The ability to operate in the realm of doubt, without falling prey to expediency, would once again be influenced, among other things, by the three *gunas* in the individual's character.

The ethic that derives from this thought is thus individual-centric. The *gunas* that are dominant within individuals determine their attitudes to ethics itself. The ethical principles an individual decides to follow depend on how far they have progressed towards the realization of the self. And acting on these principles depends on the perception of the ethical choices a situation throws up. An individual, thus, needs a great deal of freedom to make the right ethical choices, and this is reflected in the concept of *dharma*. Its literal translation, 'what holds together' (cited in Hiriyana 1995, p. 37), is an indication of the variety of dimensions of this concept. The concept is broad enough to allow individuals to identify and live up to their *dharma*. Individuals, however, do not live in isolation. The choices individuals make will be influenced by the society in which they live, as well as by the social group to which they belong within that society.

Hinduism defines the boundaries for these ethical choices by identifying two kinds of *dharma*. *Sadharana Dharma,* or common *dharma*, includes virtues like self-control, kindness and truthfulness which all are expected to follow. *Varnasrama dharmas* on the other hand are specific to certain groups. 'While the former are binding on *all*, irrespective of age or rank, the latter are so on particular classes or groups only' (Hiriyana 1995, p. 38). These social influences on an individual's *dharma* will necessarily depend on the nature of society. In India the caste system became a source of grave social inequalities between the four major castes and even more so in their relationship with those who were kept out of the system. The individual *dharmas* prescribed under the influence of such a reality would necessarily be iniquitous, if not exploitative. But these influences are themselves subject to the effects of social change. Gandhi believed that once those who were considered untouchable were brought on par with the other castes, the social influence on the *dharmas* of individuals of all castes would also change.

The pluralism built into the flexibility given to *dharmas* across individuals and situations is reflected in the *Niti Shastras*, which can be translated as the science of morals, and include the *Panchatantra* and the *Hitopdesha*. While the stories in the first four books of the *Panchatantra* each end with a specific moral, the stories in the fifth book emphasize that actions based on these morals could still go wrong. The emphasis is thus on the method that helps one to make the right ethical choices rather than on a prescribed set of ethical rules.

A key challenge in this method is to understand the relationship between consequences and duties. This is best reflected in the ethical dilemma that forms the basis of the *Bhagavadgita*, a part of the Hindu epic, *Mahabharata*. The epic tells the story of the Pandavas whose kingdom has been usurped by their cousins the Kauravas. While the cause of the Pandavas is righteous, the different perceptions of each of the individuals involved, influenced among other things by kinship ties, leads righteous individuals to choose different sides in the battle. As the two sides line up for battle, Arjuna, the most militarily acclaimed of the five Pandava brothers, begins to doubt the righteousness of the war. He knows it will mean the death of outstanding men on both sides along with widespread destruction. He cannot get himself to accept that victory in battle is worth these consequences. Time then stands still as the *Bhagavadgita* relates the debate between Arjuna and Lord Krishna, who has at that time taken on the role of Arjuna's charioteer. Arjuna presents the consequentialist dilemmas while Krishna meets them with deontological arguments. As Krishna reveals himself in the course of the *Gita* to be God, he represents the absolute truth and hence convinces Arjuna to do his duty and go to battle.

Interpreted entirely as a battle between consequential evaluation and deontology, the final result seems somewhat extreme. In fact, the willingness of prominent Hindus, who are otherwise sensitive to consequences, to accept the superiority of duties has surprised some modern analysts. Amartya Sen for one believes it is 'a tribute to the power of pure theory that even Mahatma Gandhi – no less – felt deeply inspired by Krishna's words on doing one's duty irrespective of consequences, even though the duty in this case was for Arjuna to fight a violent war (not in general a cause to which Gandhi could be expected to be warm)' (Sen 2000, p. 481).

But if we place the arguments between Arjuna and Krishna in the context of the belief in absolute and relative truth, the choice between consequentialism and deontology becomes less sharp. Since Arjuna can only function on the basis of relative truth, no matter how confident he is of his evaluation of the consequences, the truth could turn out to be different. Even if it appears quite obvious that a war in *Mahabharata* would kill brave and righteous warriors, Arjuna could not be certain that abandoning the battlefield would not lead to a worse situation. On the other hand, once Krishna is revealed as God, he is the absolute truth and can evaluate all the consequences with complete certainty. The duties he derives from this absolute truth must then be necessarily designed to prevent situations that are worse than the immediately apparent consequences. The appeal to Hindu thinkers of duty in the *Bhagavadgita* is then not an abandonment of consequential evaluation, but a faith that duties derive from a perfect knowledge of consequences. Duties and consequences cannot therefore be treated as if they were entirely independent of each other.

This precise relationship between duties and consequences in a specific situation will, of course, be completely beyond dispute only under conditions of absolute truth. Functioning as we do in the real world with relative truth, we cannot be sure that the process of deriving duties from consequences is without error. But the lack of a perfect understanding of the derivation of duties from consequences does not mean the link between the two ceases to exist. In other words, any desired consequence has a duty that goes along with it. And this duty can be identified subject to the constraints of knowledge available at a point of time. The acceptance of a relationship between duties and consequences that we can work with transforms the perception of rights.

From this perspective, rights can be seen as guaranteed consequences. To insist that there must be basic human rights, for instance, would imply that all actions are taken to protect these rights. If the duties are not done in the form of the appropriate actions, then the rights themselves will be difficult to protect. Human rights are then not something to be guaranteed by the state alone, but would be easier to achieve if society as a whole did its duty to protect these rights. It is for this reason that Gandhi advocated that the Indian Constitution be concerned with only fundamental duties rather than fundamental rights. As he insisted at that time, not entirely successfully, once fundamental duties were upheld, fundamental rights would automatically be protected (Gandhi 1983, p. 230).

Implications for economics

The focus of Hindu ethics on individuals makes economists' concept of rational individual behaviour a good place to begin looking for how Hindu ethics could influence economics. It has been pointed out 'that there are two predominant methods of defining rationality of behaviour in mainline economic theory. One is rationality as internal *consistency* of choice, and the other is to identify rationality with *maximization of self interest'* (Sen 1988, p. 12, emphasis in original).

Consistency, seen as making the same choices in identical situations, is not of the highest priority in Hindu ethics. It is not just because, as several economists have pointed out, in real life such perfectly identical situations are, at best, rare (for example, Basu 2005). Even in the extremely unlikely event of two situations being identical in every respect, it is still possible for an individual to make a different ethical choice, as the choice involves an element of judgement under imperfect knowledge. And the quality of this judgement could well change at different points in an individual's life.

In a general sense the Hindu ethical system is consistent with Edgeworth's contention, 'The first principle of economics is that every agent is actuated only by self-interest' (Edgeworth 1881, p. 16). If even the most selfless act can be traced to the interest of a person's soul, in the next life if not this one, it would be difficult for any action to escape the tag of being driven by self-interest. The Hindu ethical system would however emphasize that the choices made by individuals would not be uniform but would reflect their individual natures. It would develop models based on *satvik* behaviour, where a distinction is made between those who offer charity for personal prestige and those who offer it wanting nothing in return, not even having a fund that carries their name. It would consider most economic models based on the maximization of material self-interest as examples of *rajasik* personal choices. It would add in this category models of non-material moral choices made purely with the idea of gaining recognition. And it would recognize that economic rationality can also be found in a *tamasik* individual. The writer of a computer virus, for instance, does so, usually, for no direct personal gain, other than the satisfaction of destroying others. The Hindu ethical system would also recognize that in reality individual behaviour would be a combination of these traits rather than always completely explainable by any single model.

The view that models explain facets of reality rather than the entire reality has implications for macroeconomics as well. While there would be some general acceptance of models that explain specific relationships in macroeconomics, such as the one between money supply and price, there will be a recognition that, in reality, the precise working of this relationship would vary from situation to situation. A central bank may have to fix an interest rate without being certain whether its decision will have exactly the impact it has anticipated in each area. The judgement of the policymaker in such situations becomes critical. This judgement can be evaluated in terms of Nagel's distinction between 'characterizing value judgements' that evaluate evidence and 'appraising value judgements' that a particular state of affairs is worthy of approval or disapproval (Nagel 1984, pp. 492–3). Characterizing value judgements in the Hindu system reflect the need to deal with doubt. Appraising value judgements are based on the ethical choices built into an individual's *dharma*. The extent to which a policymaker goes by what is expedient alone is one such ethical choice.

A view of the economy as a whole then emerges by bringing together a series of models. The manner in which they are assembled is influenced by how the economist deals with doubt as well as his or her individual *dharma*. The degree of doubt is often linked to rigour. A high degree of rigour could reduce the doubt about the relationships in an economic model. But often this rigour is achieved by narrowing the focus of the model. The doubt is then transferred to identifying the role of each model when putting them together to arrive at the larger picture. The larger picture will also be influenced by the *dharma* of the economist. The choice of questions that the economist asks is influenced by personal individuality. Even when the questions raised are not the direct result of a moral position but based on, say, the availability of funding, it would still reflect the economist's idea of what is the right thing to do; which in turn derives from *dharma*.

This prominent role for individual judgements makes it difficult for the Hindu ethical system to be consistent with any large, all-explaining model. Indeed, in the early decades of the twentieth century when ideological models were the norm, Gandhi insisted that he could not accept any grand theory. This view rules out acceptance of a completely free market just as it rejects total state control. Instead it sees the economy as being the result of the actions of a variety of individuals. These individuals intervene in the economy either on their own, through institutions or as representatives of the state. It is the intentions and consequences of these interventions that determine their desirability. The state, institutions and market are then not mutually exclusive, but can work together. This would not rule out a model derived from neoclassical economics being used alongside one derived from post-Keynesian economics or, for that matter, even Marxist economics. The criteria for choosing the models to be put together would not be the intellectual tradition from which they come, but their ability to capture a specific reality in the economy.

The focus on individual actions also means the debate between the state and the market can never be completely independent of the morality of the persons involved. A corrupt, state-dominated economy would be as undesirable and inefficient as a market economy riddled with corruption. In a similar vein, combating corruption is not the responsibility of the state alone. Since it is believed that no rights can survive unless society as a whole carries out the duties that generate these rights, the state or regulatory authorities alone cannot guarantee the right to a corruption-free economy. Only the collective moral norms of all individuals in a society can effectively protect this right.

The Hindu view of the economy thus demands greater inclusiveness as well as pluralism. Its emphasis on the role of doubt ensures its rejection of the idea that economics can be completely value-free, but it would also be sensitive to the nature and degree of value judgements. While under relative truth there is always room for doubt, the degree of doubt could vary, with some statements having less doubt about them than others. And the judgements that are needed to deal with doubt are in turn very different from those required to make the ethical choices that form part of an economist's *dharma*.

Notes

1. Indian economist Raj Krishna coined the phrase 'Hindu rate of growth'.
2. This figure is cited by Klostermaier with the following elaboration: 'There is no record of the names of all of these, of course, and the figure serves to indicate that the number of higher powers is unimaginably high. There are lists of gods that go into the hundreds and there are litanies of names of major gods, such as Siva or Visnu, that enumerate a thousand names' (Klostermaier 2006b, p. 74).

References

Basu, Kaushik (2005), 'New empirical development economics: remarks on its philosophical foundations', *Economic and Political Weekly*, **40** (40/October 1), 4336–40.

Edgeworth, Francis Y. (1881), *Mathematical Psychics: An Essay on the Application of Mathematics to the Moral Sciences*, London: Kegan Paul.

Gandhi, Mahatma K. (1972), *Collected Works*, Vol. 49, New Delhi: The Publications Division.

Gandhi, Mahatma K. (1983), *Collected Works* Vol. 88, New Delhi: The Publications Division.

Hiriyana, Motilal (1995), *The Essentials of Indian Philosophy*, Delhi: Motilal Banarsidass Publishers Pvt Ltd.
Johnson, William J. (trans.) (1994), *The Bhagavad Gita*, Oxford: Oxford University Press.
Klostermaier, Klaus K. (2006a), *Hinduism: A Short Introduction*, Oxford: One World.
Klostermaier, Klaus K. (2006b), *A Concise Encyclopedia of Hinduism*, Oxford: One World.
Mohanty, Jitendra N. (2002), *Essays on Indian Philosophy*, New Delhi: Oxford University Press.
Nagel, Ernest (1984), *The Structure of Science: Problems in the Logic of Scientific Explanation*, New Delhi: Macmillan.
Rangarajan, L.N. (1992), *Kautilya: The Arthashastra*, edited, rearranged, translated and introduced by L.N. Rangarajan, New Delhi: Penguin.
Sen, Amartya (1988), *On Ethics and Economics*, New York: Basil Blackwell.
Sen, Amartya (2000), 'Consequential evaluation and practical reason', *Journal of Philosophy*, **97** (9) 477–502.

See also the entries on: Individualism; Pluralism; Religion.

30 Homo economicus
Carlos Rodriguez-Sickert

Homo economicus or *economic man* is a model of human agency in which the individual actor maximizes his own well-being given the constraints he faces. This approach has become the prevalent approach to human behaviour among economists, and has permeated other social sciences as well through so-called 'rational choice theory'. For instance, rational choice theory has been used to analyse crime, voting behaviour and educational choices (Becker, 1992).

Historical antecedents

The birth of *homo economicus* as we understand the concept nowadays is found in the work of John Stuart Mill. The concept was developed in his *Essays on Some Unsettled Questions of Political Economy* (1844) and full-fledged in his *Principles of Political Economy (1848). In his Essays, Mill wrote:*

> [Political economy] does not treat of the whole of man's nature as modified by the social state, nor of the whole conduct of man in society. It is concerned with him solely as a being who desires to possess wealth, and who is capable of judging of the comparative efficacy of means for obtaining that end. It predicts only such of the phenomena of the social state as take place in consequence of the pursuit of wealth. It makes entire abstraction of every other human passion or motive; except those which may be regarded as perpetually antagonizing principles to the desire of wealth, namely, aversion to labour, and desire of the present enjoyment of costly indulgences. (Mill 1844, Essay V, Ch. 3)

Mill's model of behaviour embodies a commitment to methodological individualism (that is, the basic unit of analysis is the individual and not the social system), and also to a set of assumptions regarding human nature. The assumptions embody (i) preferences that only consider the goods (or bads) consumed or experienced by the individual and (ii) rationality, meaning that the individual will anticipate the consequences of all his possible actions and choose the one that produces the most preferred results.

Although *homo economicus* was created by Mill, the term was coined by Mill's adversaries of the Historical School (Persky 1995), so from the outset the term carried a pejorative connotation. Mill's adversaries objected to both the moral lowliness and reductionist character of Mill's approach and the amoral character of his model of human nature. Ingram caricaturized *homo economicus* by demoting him from the *genus homo* and declaring it a 'money-making animal' (Ingram 1888, Ch. 6). Regarding the reductionism of Mill's approach, J. N. Keynes accused Mill 'of mistaking a part for the whole, and imagining political economy to end as well begin with mere abstractions' (Keynes 1891, Ch. I).

Methodological individualism and the assumption of a selfish human nature can be traced back to the so called 'selfish' school. The most prominent representatives of this school were Thomas Hobbes and Bernard Mandeville, who nonetheless differed radically on the social implications of selfishness. For Hobbes, as he argued in his *Leviathan (1651)*, selfish individuals in the absence of an entity which monopolizes power would be stuck in a war of all against all. In *Fable of the Bees* (1705), on the other hand, Mandeville argues that self-love can produce socially desirable outcomes. In this sense, Mandeville becomes an antecedent of Adam Smith's *Inquiry into the Nature and Causes of the Wealth of Nations* (1776) from which the coordination of individual courses of action oriented towards self-interest becomes an emergent property at the societal level: 'It is not from the benevolence of the butcher, the brewer, or the baker that we expect our dinner, but from their regard to their own interest' (Smith 1776, Book I, Ch. II, Section 1).

It is not the novelty (Mill himself situates his work on the *Principles* as a continuation of Smith's treatise) but the abstractness of Mill's *homo economicus* that made it one of the most influential paradigms in modern social sciences. It allowed the formalization of economics half a century later, though the inevitable trade-off between formality and generality gave grounds for lasting criticisms.

The model

In the late nineteenth century, marginalists like Stanley Jevons, Léon Walras and Carl Menger formalized Mill's ideas into a set of axioms. Axiomatization guaranteed the internal coherence of economic assumptions and allowed the use of mathematics to deduce testable implications from those assumptions. Formally (as presented in modern microeconomic textbooks), the agent's choice problem involves a set of possible actions A, a set of possible states of the world S, a probability distribution over the states in S, and a set of consequences C. Under incomplete information, an action's consequence depends on the state of the world that turns out to obtain; that is, for each pair formed by an action and a state of the world there is one consequence. Under complete information, there is a one-to-one relation between actions and consequences.

As economics developed as a discipline in its own right, increasing emphasis was placed on scarcity as the fundamental problem faced by *homo economicus*. This emphasis is captured by Lionel Robbins's widely accepted definition of economics: '[Economics is] the science which describes human behaviour as a relationship between [given] ends and scarce means which have alternative uses (Robbins 1935, Ch. 1).

In the axiomatization laid out above, scarcity is expressed by the finiteness of the space of consequences; that is to say, the actions *homo economicus* can choose do not exhaust all conceivable experiences in the world.

Each individual has a set of preferences P defined over 'consequences' C and rationality is taken to require that those preferences exhibit two characteristics:

- *Completeness.* All consequences can be ranked in an order of preference, that is, given any two alternative consequence c^0 and $c^1 \in C$, the individual either prefers c^0 to c^1, c^1 to c^0, or is indifferent between them.
- *Transitivity.* The order of preference is consistent; that is to say, given any three alternative experiences c^0, c^1 and c^2, if c^0 is preferred to c^1 and c^1 to c^2 then c^0 must be preferred to c^2.

Choice is assumed to be the outcome of rational deliberation. Namely, the decision-maker has in mind a preference relation P in the choice set faced. Also, given any choice problem, the decision-maker will choose an action which leads to an optimal consequence according to *P*.

An order of preferences *P* admits a utility representation if there exists a function *u:* $C \rightarrow IR$ such that if c^0 is preferred to c^1, then $u(c^0) > u(c^1)$ and vice-versa. In an environment characterized by scarcity, agents will maximize their utility subject to the constraints they face.[1]

The essence of rational choice (under both complete and incomplete information) is consistency, but the model is silent regarding the particular content of the preferences. De facto, mainstream neoclassical economics have worked on the basis of two additional assumptions:

- *Self-regardfulness of preferences.* The consequences evaluated by a set of self-regarding preferences are the consequences occurring to the individual that holds that preferences and not to others.
- *Exogeneity of preferences.* Preferences are unchanging and independent of the institutional environment in which choice is exercised.[2]

Assuming that scarcity is fully reflected in market and 'shadow' prices (the implicit prices applying to non-market decisions), the task of adherents to the *homo economicus* model is to search 'often long and frustratingly, for the subtle forms that prices and income take in explaining differences among men and periods' (Stigler and Becker 1977, p. 76).[3]

Criticism
Both internal criticisms (anomalies identified by experimental economists) and external criticisms coming from other social sciences have focused on the rationality assumption, and also on the auxiliary assumptions of self-regardfulness and exogeneity that neoclassical economists have incorporated in their toolbox. Here we focus on the auxiliary assumptions.[4]

Self-regardfulness
The self-regarding assumption has been challenged by experimental economists. Forsythe et al. (1994) show that, in a dictator game in which subjects freely choose how to divide a fixed amount of money between themselves and an anonymous receptor, subjects are willing to give away a significant portion of the pie. Simple models of unconditional altruism (for example, Collard 1978) explain such behaviour.

In collective action settings (for example, public good games or common pool resources games), agents express more complex forms of non-selfish behaviour. Specifically, a significant proportion of agents are willing to adhere to a cooperative norm conditionally (on others' cooperative behaviour), even when no future incentives are involved (Fischbacher et al. 2004). Furthermore, some agents are willing to spend resources to sanction uncooperative agents (Ostrom et al. 1992; Fehr and Gachter 2000, 2002). Bowles and Gintis (2002) refer to this form of behaviour – cooperate, and sanction those who do not, even if it is against one's self-interest – as strong reciprocity; and they highlight its central role within community governance mechanisms. It is noteworthy that although the prevalence of strong reciprocators might generate an environment in which cooperation becomes incentive-compatible for a self-regarding agent, costly sanctioning does not.[5,6] Hence, cooperation in these settings can only be explained beyond the *homo economicus* paradigm. Among the social preferences models which account for the behaviour of strong reciprocators are those based on distributional preferences (Fehr and Schmidt 1999; Bolton and Ockenfels 2000) and those based on intentions (Rabin 1993; Dufwenberg and Kirchsteiger 2004).[7]

Yet anything that passes for moral inclinations might be dismissed as irrational. Amartya Sen (1977) criticized the tendency to link rationality and self-regarding preferences, reminding us that it is consistency and transitivity that define rationality and not self-love. Providing an experimental test for this argument, Andreoni and Miller (2002) show that altruistic behaviour can also be described as rational. In their experiment, they examine how donating behaviour in a dictator game changes when the price of altruism varies. They show that most agents satisfy the 'generalized axiom of revealed preferences' (GARP).[8]

Exogeneity of preferences
The exogeneity of preferences neglects the possibility of preferences being determined by the social/institutional environment in which the individual is immersed. Cooperative dispositions depend not only on agents' intrinsic dispositions (that is, on their preferences), but also on the structure of the incentives they face. External enforcement of rules might change the intrinsic moral dispositions – as well as the behaviour – of an agent. In this scheme, Bowles warns:

> [If] preferences are affected by the policies or institutional arrangements we study, we can neither accurately predict nor coherently evaluate the likely consequences of new policies or institutions without taking account of preference endogeneity. (Bowles 1998, p. 77)

Changes in the structure of incentives associated with a new enforcement structure might eventually erode agents' moral dispositions in that particular context (see Falk and Kosfeld 2006; Gneezy and Rustichini 2000) or, conversely, might trigger the internalization of a social norm (Rodriguez-Sickert et al. 2007). Hwang and Bowles (2008) provide a detailed account of the empirical evidence on the interaction between cooperative dispositions and the institutional environment, and the policy implications of this interaction.

Henrich et al. (2001) provide consistent experimental evidence on deviations from the *homo economicus* model across fifteen traditional small-scale societies. Furthermore, they report notable differences in both cooperative and fairness dispositions among members of these societies. By dismissing any specific historical process which might explain current differences in preferences, the *homo economicus* model itself cannot account for these differences. Boyd and Richerson (2005) claim these differences can be maintained by cultural transmission in the form of conformist social learning. In this line of research, Henrich and Boyd (2001) and Guzmán et al. (2007) show how conformist transmission and strong reciprocity can co-evolve.

Discussion
It is important to stress that the criticisms of the *homo economicus* model described above must be understood in the context of the prevailing interpretation of the fathers of the model, Mill and Smith, by neoclassical economics. Indeed, the fathers of the model, Mill and Smith, were fully aware of the complexity of human nature.

In Mill's work, for instance, the importance of cultural transmission in the formation of preferences is recognized: the notion that more or less rational choices made by one generation predispose the tastes of subsequent generations to make similar choices (Persky 1995).

Smith, on the other hand, who is mainly known to economists for defending the virtues of self-love, describes human nature in *Theory of Moral Sentiments* (1759) as possessing moral dispositions opposed to selfish behaviour.[9] He opens his book with the following:

> How selfish soever man may be supposed, there are evidently some principles in his nature which interest him in the fortune of others, and render their happiness necessary to him though he derives nothing from it except the pleasure of feeling it. (Smith 1759, Part I, Section I, Chapter 1)

Furthermore, within Smith's framework, moral behaviour plays a key role in the adequate functioning of markets. This synergic interaction between markets and the community's moral structure is at the core of a more complex conception of social cohesion where, in addition to the state and the markets, morality becomes a third vertex of social order.

Richard Thaler (2000), in light of the accumulated experimental evidence, suggests a convergence route between the future of economic research and the original conception of the *homo economicus* model. Thaler maintains that *homo economicus* will eventually evolve into *homo sapiens*; or, more simply put, the economic model of man will hold close resemblance to actual human behaviour. We should embrace, however, the main lesson from Mill's methodological statement: understanding the mechanics of individual choice will always be an essential element in our understanding of social phenomena.

Notes

1. In Mill's interpretation of Smith's work, 'self-interest' lost the social aspect, explicitly discussed in the first part of the trilogy on moral philosophy, intended by Smith (see Smith's *The Theory of Moral Sentiments* and also the final section of this chapter).
2. Under incomplete information, following the approach of von Neumann and Morgenstern ([1944] 1963), agents will attach subjective probabilities to each consequence for each possible action and choose the action which maximizes expected utility
3. Stigler and Becker homologate preferences to the Rocky Mountains by asserting that both are there, will be there next year, and are the same for all men (Stigler and Becker 1977).
4. This 'logic of price' requires an additional assumption on the structure of preferences, namely that the preference relation P is convex. This is usually interpreted in terms of diminishing marginal rates of substitution: in order to compensate for successive losses of one commodity, increasingly larger amounts of an alternative commodity are required.
5. For cognitive anomalies, see Kahneman and Tversky (1979) on prospect theory, Schelling (1984) on intertemporal inconsistency and Simon (1976) on bounded rationality.
6. Boyd et al. (2003) and Bowles et al. (2003) explain how such pro-social norms might have evolved under the environmental conditions that characterized the early stages of human history.
7. In models of distributional preferences, besides their own material payoffs, agents also care about the distribution of payoffs. Alternatively, in intention-based models, people are willing to sacrifice resources in order to sanction or reward people according to the way in which they evaluate their actions towards them. Falk et al. (2003) report experimental evidence for the operation of both types of inclinations.
8. Satisfying GARP (developed by Afriat 1967) is an empirically testable necessary and sufficient condition for choices to be produced by a rational agent facing a linear budget constraint (Varian 1982).
9. In the history of economic thought the apparent contradiction between the two major pieces of work by Smith is known as Das Adam Smith Problem. See Sen (1995) for a discussion of this less well-known side of Smithian economics and its importance in understanding the way in which decentralized economies function.

References

Afriat, Sidney N. (1967), 'The construction of a utility function from expenditure data', *International Economic Review*, **8**, 67–77.

Andreoni, James and John H. Miller (2002), 'Giving according to GARP: an experimental test of the consistency of preferences for altruism', *Econometrica*, **70** (2), 737–53.

Becker, Gary S. (1981), 'Altruism in the family and selfishness in the market place', *Economica*, **48** (189), 1–15.

Becker, Gary S. (1992), 'The economic way of looking at life', Nobel Prize Lecture.

Bolton, Gary E. and Axel Ockenfels (2000), 'ERC: a theory of equity, reciprocity, and competition', *American Economic Review*, **90** (1), 166–93.

Bowles, Samuel (1998), 'Endogenous preferences: the cultural consequences of markets and other economic institutions', *Journal of Economic Literature*, **36** (1), 75–111.

Bowles, Samuel and Herbert Gintis (2002), 'Social capital and community governance', *Economic Journal*, **112** (483), 419–36.

Bowles, Samuel, Jung-Kyoo Choi and Astrid Hopfensitz (2003), 'The coevolution of individual behaviors and social institutions', *Journal of Theoretical Biology*, **223**, 135–47.

Boyd, Robert and Peter J. Richerson (2005), 'Solving the puzzle of human cooperation', in S. Levinson (ed.), *Evolution and Culture*, Cambridge, MA: MIT Press, pp. 105–32.

Boyd, Robert, Herbert Gintis, Samuel Bowles and Peter J. Richerson (2003), 'The evolution of altruistic punishment', *Proceedings of the National Academy of Science*, **100**, 3631–35.

Collard, David (1978), *Altruism and Economy: A Study in Non-selfish Economics*, Oxford: Martin Robertson.

Dufwenberg, Martin and Georg Kirchsteiger (2004), 'A theory of sequential reciprocity', *Games and Economic Behavior*, **47**, 268–98.

Falk, Armin and Michael Kosfeld (2006), 'Distrust: the hidden cost of control', *American Economic Review*, **96** (5), 1611–30.

Falk, Armin, Urs Fischbacher and Ernst Fehr (2003), 'On the nature of fair behavior', *Economic Enquiry*, **41** (1), 20–6.

Fehr, Ernst and Simon Gachter (2000), 'Cooperation and punishment in public good experiments', *American Economic Review*, **90** (4), 980–94.

Fehr, Ernst and Simon Gaechter (2002), 'Altruistic punishment in humans', *Nature*, **415**, 137–40.

Fehr, Ernst and Klaus Schmidt (1999), 'A theory of fairness, competition, and cooperation', *Quarterly Journal of Economics*, **118**, 817–68.

Fischbacher, Urs, Simon Gaechter and Ernst Fehr (2004), 'Are people conditionally cooperative? Evidence from a public goods experiment', *Economic Letters*, **71** (3), 397–404.

Forsythe, Robert, Joel L. Horowitz, N.E. Savin and Martin Sefton (1994), 'Fairness in simple bargaining experiments', *Games and Economic Behavior*, **7** (3), 346–80.

Gneezy, Uri and Aldo Rustichini (2000), 'A fine is a price', *Journal of Legal Studies*, **29** (1), 1–17.

Guzmán, Ricardo A., Carlos Rodriguez-Sickert and Robert Rowthorn (2007), 'When in Rome, do as the Romans: the coevolution of punishment, conformism and cooperation', *Evolution and Human Behavior*, **28** (2), 112–17.

Henrich, Joseph and Robert Boyd (2001), 'Why people punish defectors: weak conformist transmission can stabilise costly enforcement of norms in cooperative dilemmas', *Journal of Theoretical Biology*, **208**, 79–89.

Henrich, Joseph, Robert Boyd, Samuel Bowles, Colin Camerer, Ernst Fehr, Herbert Gintis and Richard McElreath (2001), 'Cooperation, reciprocity and punishment in fifteen small-scale societies', *American Economic Review*, **91** (2), 73–8.

Hobbes, Thomas (1651), *Leviathan*, online edition at Great Voyages, http://www.orst.edu/instruct/phl302/texts/hobbes/leviathan-contents.html, accessed 19 November, 2008.

Hwang, Sung-Ha and Samuel Bowles (2008), 'Social preferences and public economics: mechanism design when social preferences depend on incentives', *Journal of Public Economics*, **92** (8–9), August, 1811–20.

Ingram, John K. (1888), *A History of Political Economy*, online edition at McMaster University, http://socserv.mcmaster.ca/econ/ugcm/3ll3/ingram/contents.html, accessed 19 November, 2008.

Kahneman, Daniel and Amos Tversky (1979), 'Prospect theory: an analysis of decisions under risk', *Econometrica*, **47**, 313–27.

Keynes, John N. (1891), *The Scope and Method of Political Economy*, on-line edition at McMaster University, http://socserv2.mcmaster.ca/~econ/ugcm/3ll3/keynesjn/Scope.pdf, accessed 19 November, 2008.

Mandeville, Bernard ([1705] 1970), *Fable of the Bees*, Harmondsworth: Penguin Books.

Mill, John S. (1844), *Essays on Some Unsettled Questions of Political Economy*, online edition at Project Gutenberg, http://www.gutenberg.org/etext/12004, accessed 19 November, 2008.

Mill, John S. (1848), *Principles of Political Economy With Some of Their Applications to Social Philosophy*, online edition at Library of Economics and Liberty, http://www.econlib.org/library/Mill/mlPtoc.html, accessed 19 November, 2008.

Neumann, John von and Oskar Morgenstern ([1944] 1963), *Theory of Games and Economic Behavior*, Princeton, NJ: Princeton University Press.

Ostrom, Elinor, James Walker and Roy Gardner (1992), 'Covenants with and without a sword: self-governance is possible', *American Political Science Review*, **86**, 404–17.

Persky, Joseph (1995), 'The ethology of *homo economicus*', *Journal of Economic Perspectives*, **9** (2), 221–31.

Rabin, Matthew (1993), 'Incorporating fairness into game theory and economics', *American Economic Review*, **83**, 1281–302.

Robbins, Lionel (1935), *An Essay on the Nature and Significance of Economic Science*, 2nd edition, London: Macmillan.

Rodriguez-Sickert, Carlos, Ricardo Andrés Guzman and Juan Camilo Cárdenas (2008), 'Institutions influence preferences: evidence from a common pool resource experiment', *Journal of Economic Behavior and Organization*, **67** (1), July, 215–17.

Samuelson, Paul A. (1938), 'A note on the pure theory of consumer's behaviour', *Economica*, **1**, 61–71.

Schelling, Thomas (1984), 'Self-command in practice, in policy, and in a theory of rational choice', *American Economic Review*, **74** (2), 1–11.

Sen, Amartya (1977), 'Rational fools: a critique of the behavioural foundations of economic theory', *Philosophy and Public Affairs*, **6**, 317–44.

Sen, Amartya (1995), 'Moral codes and economic success', in Samuel Brittan, and Alan Hamlin (eds), *Market Capitalism and Moral Values*, Brookfield: Ashgate, pp. 23–34.

Simon, Herbert (1976), *Administrative Behavior*, New York: The Free Press.

Smith, Adam (1759), *The Theory of Moral Sentiments*, online edition at the Adam Smith Institute, http://www.adamsmith.org/smith/tms/tms-index.htm, accessed 19 November, 2008.

Smith, Adam (1776), *Inquiry into the Nature and Causes of the Wealth of Nations*, online edition at the Adam Smith Institute, http://www.adamsmith.org/smith/won-index.htm, accessed 19 November, 2008.

Stigler, George J. and Gary S. Becker (1977), 'De gustibus non est disputandum', *American Economic Review*, **67** (2), 76–90.

Thaler, Richard H. (2000), 'From *homo economicus* to *homo sapiens*', *Journal of Economic Perspectives*, **14** (1), 133–41.

Varian, Hal R. (1982), 'The nonparametric approach to demand analysis', *Econometrica*, **50** (4), 945–74.

See also the entries on: Rationality; Self-interest; Utilitarianism.

31 Human development
Des Gasper

'Human development' language and the UNDP

The language of 'human development' spread gradually within the circles of national and international development policy and planning from the 1970s onwards. It acquired its definitive form in the 1990s in the United Nations Development Programme's *Human Development Reports*. These publications defined human development as an extension of people's capabilities, the range of alternatives that they can attain and have reason to value.

The initiator of the *Human Development Reports* was the Pakistani development economist and planner Mahbub ul Haq (1934–98). Haq had been an apostle of overriding priority being given to economic growth and industrialization when he was a leading official in Pakistan's Planning Commission in the 1960s. He observed there, however, that despite economic growth of 6–7 per cent per annum throughout the decade priority aspects of human welfare went untouched. Social tensions in Pakistan brought the disintegration of the country in 1971, and hobbled its growth for the next decade. As director of the World Bank's Policy Planning Department through the 1970s, Haq gradually widened his conception of development, in consultation with a global network of academics and policymakers. Within the World Bank he promoted a focus on basic needs, viewed as food, water, clothing, shelter, health and education.

In retrospect that work on basic needs came to be seen as having at least six fundamental limitations. The first is its preoccupation with material inputs rather than more broadly with how people can live. The second is a further materialistic bias, in the sense of neglecting aspirations for freedom, equality, dignity, democracy and voice, including in determining what are basic priorities and how they should be pursued. Third is a technocratic bias towards central expert decision-making on priorities, marginalizing local knowledge and values. Fourth is an alleged downgrading of value differences, and the making of arbitrary universal standard prioritizations. Fifth is the deficiency style of thinking, focused on what people lack rather than on their assets and abilities. Sixth is its presentation in a condescending separate language for the poor, and its lack of a wider perspective to inspire and guide.

These criticisms do not apply to all basic needs approaches, for example, the 'Human Scale Development' of Manfred Max-Neef and his school (see Ekins and Max-Neef 1992). Rather, they apply to the type of needs-based development planning undertaken by many governments and international agencies from the 1950s to the 1980s. The criticisms were highlighted in the 1980s in decisions to downgrade such planning in favour of approaches which left prioritization to markets.

During the mid and late 1980s, Haq and associates considered and responded to these limitations and arrived at the formulation of 'human development' which was instituted in the first *Human Development Report* in 1990 (Gasper 2009). Its theoretical base includes the capability approach and a broader humanism, which lead to a style of policy analysis structured by human welfare concerns. The notion of a person's capability is comparable to the notion of a consumption possibility set, but with important differences. The alternatives in a capability set are not commodity bundles, but instead patterns of life, bundles of functionings; so the perspective is broader, covering far more than commodities, let alone only material goods, and it is also deeper, looking at being, not merely at having. This responds to the first and second limitations mentioned above. The main 'currency' of evaluation adopted is capability: the range of valued opportunities to function, leaving it to people themselves to choose from these opportunities. In response to the third and fourth objections above, there is an emphasis on reasoned valuation, not a priori specification. In emphasizing reasoned valuation and choice, the approach embodies a concern for human agency, rather than a donative orientation of top-down provision. In response to the fifth and sixth objections there is now a general perspective that, like humanist economics as a whole, is not restricted in scope to poor countries and poor groups. It offers a unifying vision centred on respecting freedom and giving real substance to it.

Haq (1999) summed up 'human development' as development for, by and of people. Thus it includes humane priorities, thoroughgoing participation and 'human resource development'. It is to be people-centred, rather than for a sub-group or of an abstraction. Its opposite, an 'inhuman development', excludes some or most people, even from fulfilment of their most basic needs, and measures performance by how much is bought and sold, regardless of its composition (for example, whether it is music or weaponry), or its distribution, use or relationship to people's particular requirements, and regardless too of its neglect of (and sometimes major negative impacts on) many of the important non-commodified goods and bads in life. Strong economic growth in a country is easily combined with lack of adequate nourishment and clean water for much of the population, including for young children, to the extent of permanently damaging their mental and physical capacity and life quantity and quality. Indeed the growing incomes of some groups often raise prices and reduce access for poor groups, and generate the physical displacement of the poor. By focusing on priority functionings, not money categories alone, Haq and others could show there was scope for enormous beneficial impact through reallocations within the budgets of low-income countries and international aid agencies. This was already clear from the experience of countries like Costa Rica and Sri Lanka (Drèze and Sen 1989), but the human development approach has given a general framework for such analysis and policy. It includes strong emphases on participation and empowerment, in their own right and as politically essential in order to initiate and sustain this sort of equitable strategy.

Overall, the UNDP approach refocuses development thinking on fundamental valued ends and valued means, and access thereto, not only monetized means. It reinstates development as a normative concept distinct from economic growth and social change, whose value content must be assessed and not presumed. The reconceptualization has broadened the range of objectives routinely considered in development debate and planning. The UNDP's standard definition of dimensions of human development has covered (i) empowerment, meaning the expansion of capabilities (ability to attain valued ends), valued functionings (attained valued ends) and participation (sharing in specifying priorities); (ii) equity in distribution of basic capabilities; and (iii) the sustainability and (iv) security of people's valued attainments and opportunities. The significance of the approach is that it embodies and institutionalizes a fundamental theme in earlier humanist economics and humanist thought: development means promotion of human values.

The emergence of 'human development' ideas
The language of 'human development', applied at societal and global levels and not only at the individual level, dates from at least the 1960s. Use of the term to describe the maturation and evolution of individual persons dates from much earlier in developmental and educational psychology. Writers like Donald Warwick (1968), a social psychologist, began to investigate the value content of the term 'development' when used as a normative category applied to local and national societies. In the 1950s and 1960s 'development' was typically equated to sustained economic growth and transformation, or to 'modernization', a series of arguably connected structural changes including urbanization, commercialization, industrialization, secularization and individualization. As people increasingly saw that there were choices around and in '(economic) development' and 'modernization' – that there existed no one sole path for progress and that no country offered an ideal model – they came to ask: development of what and towards what? Options exist concerning which goals societies develop towards and how societies develop towards given goals. Recognition of multiple distinct aspects of quality of life grew, leading to conclusions such as that of Roland Colin: 'There is no longer any country which can pretend to consider itself developed, that is, humanly developed' (1968, p. 4). This perception grew in part through the perspectives of Northerners returning home after periods of work in the global South, according to development ethicist Denis Goulet (1931–2006).

As early as 1960 Goulet wrote that 'development' means 'changes which allow human beings, both as individual persons and as members of groups, to move from one condition of life to one which is more human in some meaningful way' (1960, p. 14). Development concerns 'being more', not merely having more. In his view, given the competition between having and being, the only development that is 'worthy of man' (ibid., p. 15) includes self-restraint in having. To 'keep their liberty, people must know how to free themselves from excessive attachment to superfluous goods' (ibid.). Later such work holds that people's autonomy requires avoiding subjection to consumption standards and wants that are spread, intentionally or otherwise, from or by more affluent groups (Rahman 1992). Goulet made the question of 'human development' explicit, asking 'what kind of development can be considered "human"?' (Goulet 1971, p. 236). His seminal *The Cruel Choice* declared, 'The aim of this work is to thrust debates over economic and social development into the arena of ethical values . . . Is human development something more than a systemic combination of modern bureaucracy, efficient technology, and productive economy?' (ibid., p. vii). Development's 'ultimate goals are those of existence itself: to provide all men with the opportunity to lead full human lives' (ibid., p. x). He presented an ideal of 'full, comprehensive human development' (Goulet 1979, p. 105), and praised the Sri Lankan Sarvodaya movement's 'concept of human development . . . [based on] respect for all life and the concept of the well-being of all' (ibid., p. 109).

A concept of development as the improvement of people's life quality contains no *a priori* declaration about what are desirable means, unlike the equation of development to economic growth or social modernization or a supposed pre-industrial rural idyll. It neither romanticizes North or South, nor demonizes either. Rather it directs attention to the content of human lives and opens discussion of the range of criteria for assessing them.

The forerunners of such work lie in the traditions of humanistic economics and humanist critiques of mainstream economics. For Jean Sismondi (1773–1842), 'the increase in wealth is not the end in political economy, but its instrument in procuring the happiness of all' (cited by Lutz and Lux 1988, p. 65). John Ruskin (1819–1900) emphasized reasoned use values and the quality of work, and inspired Gandhi. Others in this line were J.A. Hobson (1855–1940) and E.F. Schumacher (1911–77). R.H. Tawney (1880–1962) summed up the humanistic tradition in terms of its treatment of material inputs and wealth 'as means to an end, and that this end is the growth towards perfection of individual human beings' (cited by Lutz 1992a, p. 98). Lutz called this 'a welfare standard explicitly expressed in terms of human welfare rather than "economic" or "social welfare"' (ibid., p. 103), in other words not in terms of a supposed 'utility' category imputed from market choices. The 'human welfare' notion uses a picture of a scale of human values, from basic material needs through a range of higher aspirations for expression, self-realization and dignity. In Lutz's formulation this welfare standard became 'material sufficiency and human dignity for all' (1992b, p. 166), further summarized as respect for basic human rights. He highlighted the corresponding '*a priori* ethical assumption of human equality' (1992a, p. 103) and the insistence on assuring the welfare of all.

The humanist economics tradition, together with the humanistic psychology of authors like Eric Fromm (1900–80), contributed to the milieu in which the ideas of Goulet, Warwick and similar authors appeared. These in turn provided the context for emergence of the contemporary 'human development' school in economics and development studies and policy.

A comprehensive, people-centred approach to analysis and policy

The UNDP's human development conception has had wide influence. It contains various elements: a form of open systems policy analysis, with a distinctive treatment of policy means and means-ends connections, not only of policy ends; a form of humanism with an agenda of mutual concern and public ethical discourse; and corresponding methodological and theoretical wings, in addition to those for measurement and modelling. Contrary to Srinivasan (1994), it involves far more than an extended list of objectives and a capability denominator (Gasper 2002).

The Indian economist Amartya Sen (b. 1933) gave the approach a conceptual basis. Between the two sets of concepts which were conventional in welfare economics – inputs to living, such as income and commodities, and subjective responses, often called 'utility' – a third set was introduced. This includes Lancaster's (1971) concept of characteristics of goods, the characteristics of people, people's capability to function and their functionings. A language is thus provided with which to discuss the contents of people's lives and the extent of their freedoms, not just the economic inputs to lives (owning, earning, spending) or the mental-state outputs of preference fulfilment or feeling good or bad. It encourages attention to far more types of information than did earlier economic work on welfare and policy. Which of the levels deserve priority as well-being measures? Not commodity acquisition, because different people have different needs; and not (solely) feelings of satisfaction, or the fact of preference fulfilment, because preferences may be formed under situations of deprivation of information and of options. Sen (1993) advocates that we stress instead functionings, how people actually live, and especially (in order to emphasize freedom) capability: the set of valued functionings-bundles they can attain, the life options they have.

The popular slogan that 'development is the enlargement of human capabilities' carries a danger, as not all capabilities are good. Which capabilities, why and to what end? Various authors speak of capability as ability to achieve what one wishes, but Sen speaks more cautiously of people's abilities to lead the lives they have reason to value. Obscurities remain in the terms 'people' and 'they', and the 'we' in 'we have reason to value'. For the public goods which are central in human development the associated reasoning must be group reasoning and prioritizations must be through group processes. The formulations also require that people are well equipped to reason. Further, not all widening of the range of options, even of desired options, improves well-being. The psychology literature (for example, Schwartz 2005) here supports the philosophical arguments of Goulet, Rahman and associates. A second slogan, 'development as freedom' (Sen 1999), carries similar dangers. Not all freedoms are good and not only freedoms are important (Gasper and van Staveren 2003). The slogan can be misused to defend a consumerist orientation of indiscriminate economic growth. Sen initially declared, 'freedom is the principal end and principal means of development' (1999, p. xii), but later modified this to say it is 'one of' the principal ends and principal means (Drèze and Sen 2002, p. 4). Haq used a safer formulation, that people are the key means as well as the valued end in development processes.

As an approach in policy analysis, for purposes both of explanation of the levels of fulfilment of valued ends and for design of policy responses, Haq and Sen stressed that the human development approach considers all relevant factors and means, without restriction in terms of disciplinary habits. It is a comprehensive and thereby potentially radical framework. It stresses, for example, popular empowerment as a method. In explanation too, Haq led a rejection of partitioned thinking: the analysis of processes and connections only within disciplinary and national boundaries. He espoused and illustrated 'joined-up thinking' not limited by those boundaries. National and international economic policies, for example, can have major impacts on conflict and violence (as in the case of the 1994 Rwanda genocide; Eriksson et al. 1996), the flow of arms and the creation or strengthening of international crime networks, disease, migration, international epidemics and more. Haq and the *Human Development Report* advised rich countries of their own need for structural adjustment programmes, by opening their markets and thereby promoting global social stability, rather than belatedly sending expensive and ineffective peacekeeping or punitive forces after crises have boiled over.

The human development approach involves not only wide-ranging specifications of values and causes – and thus of ends and means – it uses values of human welfare to structure and guide analysis. The broader range of values, focused on how people do and can live, guides choices of topics and boundaries of analysis, and some other matters, Priority is given to the socio-economic significance of findings, not merely their statistical significance. The approach has become a form of policy analysis that uses, and is guided by, human development values (Gasper 2008).

One aspect of this deserves underlining. As in human rights philosophy, the field of reference is all humans, wheresoever in the world. Unlike in market calculations, we do not focus only on those with purchasing power, let alone weighted according to their purchasing power. Global ethics arises as a topic of attention, for example, in the UNDP's work on global public goods, in the human development ethics of Martha Nussbaum, which stresses global responsibilities and solidarity, and in the growing connection of the human development approach to the human rights movement (for example, Nussbaum 2006).

Nussbaum (b. 1947), an American classicist, moral philosopher and social critic, connects the humanist strand in economics to older strands in philosophy and the humanities. While Sen rethought 'development' as concerning the increase of freedoms to do and to be, Nussbaum brings a closer attention to 'human', a focus on development as the promotion of human dignity, and a fuller conceptualization of capability (Nussbaum 2000). Sen's concept of capability modifies the notion of a consumption possibilities set. In contrast, Nussbaum, like for example Warwick, distinguishes (i) the person's inborn potential; (ii) the person's skills and attitudes, arising from his/her potential and experience; and (iii) the person's environment. The interaction of the last two generates (iv) capability in Sen's sense. The second category matches much everyday and professional usage of the term 'capability', and is essential since we need to identify and influence relevant skills and attitudes.

Nussbaum's form of human development theory is found useful by many analysts of education and empowerment. It involves close consideration of the contents of people's lives, looking at whole lives. This contributes to, she argues, seeing each person as distinct, and deserving of respect and concern; thinking hard about what is similar and what is different in their lives; and generating a picture of major aspects of life that deserve support and protection. Nussbaum's picture of human development thus uses a 'capabilities approach', that is more concrete than Sen's 'capability approach'. It is close in character to the human rights approach, and identifies a series of basic capabilities – including for a full lifespan, health, practical reason, affiliation and political participation – needed for a life with dignity.

Methodologically, authors like Nussbaum bring in methods from the humanities to add to those of more impersonal social sciences: studies of and testimony from the situations and life-stories of individuals (for example, Narayan et al. 2000), from novels (Nussbaum 1995), and from plays, films and reflective essays. These methods and sources support deeper understanding and also broader and stronger attention, sympathy and response. Nussbaum's work looks in depth at emotions and motivation (for example, Nussbaum 2001). Moreover, given the limits to how altruistic most people may become, and limits to how strong we may become as reasoners, negotiators and free agents, it looks at legal guarantees for some basic capabilities for everyone, rather than leaving everything open for decision in a supposedly democratic political process that can in reality be dominated by the rich and by the implications of wealth and poverty.

Finally, Nussbaum replies to objections that the 'human development' concept and approach over-generalize and (notwithstanding the South Asian background of its foremost progenitors) constitute a form of Western cultural imperialism. Cultural practices are not justified simply by existing, nor are cultures consensual and fixed; so discussion of values is appropriate. In such discussion, support for human development values appears widespread in all countries. The approach aims to provide the bases for competent choice by each person, including the choice to follow tradition. Rather than undermining diversity, she argues, it supports it.

The human development approach as a policy movement: in search of partners and priorities

The attempt to convert a humanist ethical orientation into an operational development policy approach that makes an impact on human development leads this stream of work in various directions. First is reporting and analysis, in the annual global reports, in human development indexes, in national and regional reports (http://hdr.undp.org/reports/) and in the work of the Human Development and Capability Association (www.capabilityapproach.com). The indexes make no claim to be comprehensive representations of human development. The plurality of diverse relevant values means no single index can suffice. The indexes' role is instead to show relevant contrasts. The Human Development Index, in particular, serves to vividly underline the unreliability of gross national product per capita as a well-being measure.

Second, to complement and prioritize across the vast landscape of human development objectives, Haq added the 'human security' theme. It is elaborated by Sen and others in the 2003 study *Human Security Now* (Commission on Human Security 2003). The stress is on stability of capabilities, and on truly basic functionings, to be guaranteed accessible to everyone as human rights. In particular, it gives high priority to 'freedom from fear', for intrinsic reasons and because physical violence and insecurity have such ramifying negative effects. The Millennium Development Goals (the topic of the *Human Development Report 2003*) are an attempt to commit governments worldwide to progress on these basic entitlements for all: by setting simple goals that can capture public attention and bring continuing pressure on governments, and by converting the goals into specific indicators and targets against which governments and agencies in poor and rich countries can be held accountable, while providing space for country variations. The Millennium Development Goals are only one of the possible ways of operationalizing and prioritizing a human development approach. It is technically crude but with a posited political rationale which is in the process of being tested.

Third, in seeking powerful policy instruments anchored in widespread strong feelings, human development work has had to ask how it relates to the longer instituted and larger stream of work on human rights. The *Human Development Report* did not originally promote guarantees for individuals, due to economists' common worries about human rights formulations as too absolutist and as too oriented to the state. But the approach sought an alliance with work on human rights, in the *Human Development Report 2000* and thereafter (see, for example, Andreassen and Marks 2006; Gasper 2007). Nussbaum (2000, 2006) argues that capabilities theory provides an intellectual basis for human rights. In response to the question 'Rights to what? What sorts of things and in what form?', it proposes capabilities rather than specific resources or guaranteed functionings. Human rights language provides in return suitably strong terms; and it supports personal independence, for typically one has both a right to a basic capability and a right not to use that capability. For the human development stream of thought and practice, working out its relationship to the field of human rights is a priority task, just as it is for the field of ethics and economics as a whole.

References

Andreassen, Bard and Stephen Marks (eds) (2006), *Development as a Human Right*, Nobel Symposium 125, Cambridge, MA: Harvard School of Public Health.

Colin, Roland (1968), 'Trois révolutions pour le développement', *Développement et Civilisations*, 36 (December).

Commission on Human Security (2003), *Human Security Now*, New York: UN Secretary General's Commission on Human Security, http://www.humansecurity-chs.org/finalreport/, accessed 15 October, 2008.

Drèze, Jean and Amartya Sen (1989), *Hunger and Public Action*, Oxford: Clarendon.

Drèze, Jean and Amartya Sen (2002), *India: Development and Participation*, Delhi: Oxford University Press.

Ekins, Paul and Manfred Max-Neef (eds) (1992), *Real Life Economics*, London: Routledge.

Eriksson, John et al. (1996), *The International Response to Conflict and Genocide: Lessons from the Rwanda Experience – Synthesis Report*, Copenhagen: Joint Evaluation of Emergency Assistance to Rwanda, http://www.um.dk/Publikationer/Danida/English/Evaluations/RwandaExperience/index.asp, accessed 15 October, 2008.

Gasper, Des (2002), 'Is Sen's capability approach an adequate basis for considering human development?' *Review of Political Economy*, **14** (4), 435–61.

Gasper, Des (2007), 'Human rights, human needs, human development, human security: relationships between four international "human" discourses', *Forum for Development Studies*, 2007 (1), 9–43.

Gasper, Des (2008), 'From "Hume's Law" to policy analysis for human development', *Review of Political Economy*, **20** (2), 233–56.

Gasper, Des (2009), 'Values, vision, proposals and networks: the approach of Mahbub ul Haq', in Charles Wilber and Amitava Dutt (eds), *New Directions in Development Ethics, Essays in Honor of Denis Goulet*, Notre Dame, IN: University of Notre Dame Press, forthcoming.

Gasper, Des and Irene van Staveren (2003), 'Development as freedom: and as what else?' *Feminist Economics*, **9** (2–3), 137–61.

Goulet, Denis (1960), 'Pour une éthique moderne du développement', *Développement et Civilisations*, **3** (September), 10–23; translated into English in Goulet (2006), *Development Ethics at Work: Explorations 1960–2002*, New York and London: Routledge, Ch. 1.

Goulet, Denis (1971), *The Cruel Choice: a New Concept in the Theory of Development*, New York: Athenaeum.

Goulet, Denis (1979), 'Development as liberation: policy lessons from case studies'; reprinted in Goulet (2006), *Development Ethics at Work: Explorations 1960–2002*, New York and London: Routledge, Ch. 9.

Haq, Mahbub ul (1999), *Reflections on Human Development*, 2nd edition. New York and Delhi: Oxford University Press.

Lancaster, K.J. (1971), *Consumer Demand*, New York: Colombia University Press.

Lutz, Mark (1992a), 'Humanistic economics: history and basic principles', in Paul Ekins and Manfred Max-Neef (eds), *Real Life Economics*, London: Routledge, pp. 90–112.

Lutz, Mark (1992b), 'A humanistic approach to socio-economic development', in Paul Ekins and Manfred Max-Neef (eds), *Real Life Economics*, London: Routledge, pp. 165–7.

Lutz, Mark, and Kenneth Lux (1988), *Humanistic Economics*, New York: Bootstrap Press.

Narayan, Deepa et al. (2000), *Voices of the Poor*, 2 vols, New York: Oxford University Press.

Nussbaum, Martha (1995), *Poetic Justice: The Literary Imagination and Public Life*, Boston, MA: Beacon Press.

Nussbaum, Martha (2000), *Women and Human Development: The Capabilities Approach*, Cambridge: Cambridge University Press.

Nussbaum, Martha (2001), *Upheavals of Thought: The Intelligence of Emotions*, Cambridge: Cambridge University Press.

Nussbaum, Martha (2006), *Frontiers of Justice*, Cambridge, MA: Harvard University Press.

Rahman, Anisur (1992), 'People's self-development', in Paul Ekins and Manfred Max-Neef (eds), *Real Life Economics*, London: Routledge, pp. 167–78.

Schwartz, Barry (2005), *The Paradox of Choice: Why More is Less*, New York: Harper Perennial.

Sen, Amartya (1993), 'Capability and well-being', in Martha Nussbaum and Amartya Sen (eds), *The Quality of Life*, Oxford: Clarendon, pp. 30–53.

Sen, Amartya (1999), *Development as Freedom*, New York: Oxford University Press.

Srinivasan, T.N. (1994), 'Human development: a new paradigm or reinvention of the wheel?' *American Economic Review, Papers and Proceedings*, **84**, 238–43.

UNDP (1990–), *Human Development Report* (annual), New York: Oxford University Press.

Warwick, Donald P. (1968), 'Human freedom and national development', *Cross Currents*, **XVIII** (4), 495–517.

See also the entries on: Capability approach; Humanism; Needs and well-being; Amartya Sen.

32 Humanism
Mark A. Lutz

Humanism through the ages

The concept of 'humanism' has, through the ages, defied easy specification. Where definitions, or even a clarifying description, have been attempted, they have quickly attracted controversy. Nevertheless, three meanings tend to be generally applied.

- First, humanism is the name given to the intellectual movement of the fourteenth to sixteenth centuries which characterized the culture of Renaissance Europe.
- Second, humanism is a particular worldview rooted in a distinctly human nature which emphasizes the person as capable of reason, autonomy and self-knowledge. As such, virtually all humanists share a belief in the possibility of man's perfectibility, which, regardless of whether they believe in the need for God's grace, they see as largely dependent upon man's own efforts. Moreover, everyone is viewed as having a rightful claim to be treated with dignity and to have an opportunity for a life of human flourishing and authenticity.
- Third, and most recently, humanism has been appropriated as a label by those who reject religion or spirituality of any kind, thereby giving the term a fully naturalistic and secular flavour.

Let us take a closer look at these three alternative meanings.

The humanism of the Renaissance

In the centuries following the first thousand years after the birth of Christ, the Church was seen as increasingly corrupt. Kingships were awarded for donated land, leading to the creation of a papal state with popes behaving more like lay princes than ecclesiastical rulers. In the fourteenth century, the ecclesiastical meddling in politics ended in the Great Schism (1378–1417), when rival popes simultaneously claimed the papacy in Rome and Avignon. Thus papal infallibility could no longer be taken as given, which contributed to depriving the Church of much of its monopoly on morality. As a result, the Church's traditional condemnation of greed and usury lost legitimacy and no longer inhibited commerce to the extent it had before.

The new vacuum set the stage for the humanism of the Renaissance. Often also referred to as 'classical humanism', it started in Italy, centred around the prosperous city of Florence. Francesco Petrarch initiated the movement. When studying law, he discovered the writings of Cicero and Virgil and declared them to be more interesting than the usual fare of endless inquiries into theological niceties. Petrarch soon started what was to become a lifelong quest to build an impressive private library of Roman and Greek books and documents. This tendency to seek truth and inspiration in the pagan writings of the classics soon spread to others, Giovanni Boccaccio being one of those better known.

Before long, a general revolt against religious limitations on knowledge took hold. Events were facilitated by a wave of refugee scholars from Constantinople who had fled the city before it fell to the Turks in 1453. They brought manuscripts from Byzantine libraries to Florence, as well as offering instruction in the Greek, Hebrew and Arabic languages.

One effect of the intense interest in this new scholarship which was fast replacing the monastic, God-centred worldview of the Middle Ages was to push Aristotelian scholastics off centre stage and into the shadow of Plato's rediscovered philosophy. In a short time, a Platonic academy under the leadership of Marsilio Ficino opened in Florence. There, Ficino's disciple, Pico della Mirandola, immersed himself in the neo-Platonic worldview and articulated his famous *Oration on the Dignity of Man*, published in 1486. This work is indicative of the philosophical sentiment prevailing at that time. In that slender masterpiece he has God say the following to Man:

> We have made you a creature neither of heaven nor of earth, neither mortal nor immortal, in order that you may, as the free and prouder shape of your own being, fashion yourself in the form you prefer. It will be in your power to descend to the lower brutish forms of life; [and] you will be able, through your own decision, to rise again to the superior orders whose life is divine. (Quoted in 'What is Humanism?', editorial essay in *Manas*, **XXXII** (5) (January 1980), 2)

The dignity of man, according to Pico, rests in human autonomy, the capacity to direct and shape one's own life. Above all, it is the freedom to raise oneself beyond the angels or reduce oneself below the level of the beasts. The human being 'as a creature of neither heaven nor the earth' is a way to picture the domain of humanism as lying somewhere between God and nature; that is, not fully contained in nature.

This early humanism, having sprung up in Florence and spread to other Italian cities, had more sympathy with pagan neo-Platonism than with dogmatic Christianity. But this does not mean there was a lack of belief in the existence of the divine. Rather, in the conflict with the Church the humanists were asserting the reality of a higher power or higher truth existing above the bureaucracy and conventionality of the ecclesiastical authority. In a sense, it was a quest for a spirituality that was more life-affirming and happiness-affirming than Christianity, especially in its medieval dress of otherworldly monasticism.

The humanist movement north of the Alps emerged in a more measured manner, being primarily of a practical and educational character. One of its main achievements was to reform and modernize universities by installing the first planks of a liberal educative curriculum, offering studies in Greek language and literature, poetry and rhetoric.

The overall flavour of the northern movement, in contrast to that of Italy, was more consistent with Christianity. Studying Cicero and the Stoics was not so much meant to provide a model for a more sophisticated secular life; rather it was a guide to a more sensible Christian way of living. Similarly, scholars used linguistic and textual skills developed by the Italian humanists for new and more 'true' Bible translations.

No doubt, the best-known representative of northern humanism was the Dutchman Desiderius Erasmus, born in 1467. After studying the classics in an Augustinian monastery and theology in Paris, he devoted his life to research, travel and writing. Almost half a century of rich cosmopolitan scholarship won him acclaim among his contemporaries as the 'prince of humanism'. He studied Greek not so much to understand pre-Christian secular culture as to learn more about the 'real' Christ. His acquired skills in Greek served him well in coming up with a new and more accessible translation of the New Testament. One of his best friends was the learned English chancellor and author of the visionary book *Utopia*, Thomas More, who is still celebrated today as a Catholic martyr because of his refusal to swear loyalty to King Henry VIII as the head of the English Church.

Erasmus and others, such as the Frankonian Knight Ulrich von Hutten, unintentionally paved the way for Martin Luther's Wittenburg rebellion of 1517, ushering in the Reformation and subsequently the next big phase in the history of Western civilization: the Enlightenment.

A worldview rooted in a distinctly human nature
The Commercial Revolution, which started with the decline of church influence and the growth of cities, and was further enhanced by the new cosmopolitan individualism of Renaissance thinking, created the 'new commercial man' primarily driven by self-interest. Throughout Europe the image of the bourgeois trader became the role model for the pursuit of wealth and power. The Reformation, itself an offspring of humanist inroads into Catholic Church social dominance, further contributed to a new capitalist ethic with its implicit glorification of individualistic wealth-seeking and pride. Generally, humanism, Protestantism and commerce went hand-in-hand, tending to reinforce one another along the way.

Humanist thought during the Age of Reason was diverse and also varied regionally. Much of its tone and force depended on the particular cultural context, whether in socially sanctioned Protestant universities or the less friendly territory of Catholic Church-supported monarchies, such as France. Not surprisingly, humanists in eighteenth-century England were more scientific, empirical, nominalist and sceptical, while in France they were more outspokenly materialist and aggressively atheistic. In both cases, the new humanism essentially became one with naturalism.

Not so in Germany, where the humanist tradition proceeded in a more philosophical, metaphysical, mind- (*geist*) affirming and religious direction, thereby allowing the concept to be somewhat distinct from its more naturalistic counterpart. The prime example, of course, is Kantian Enlightenment philosophy, with its human 'exceptionalism' and defining emphasis on human autonomy and dignity.

As a result there seem to be today, as one scholar aptly put it, as many different varieties of humanism as there are grades of wine and cheese. And as with wine and cheese, the absolutely latest vintages are not necessarily the best. From early on there has been a tension between the various types, particularly between the conceptions of humanism that are spiritually compatible and those that are not. Nevertheless, all of them, coming from the same Renaissance roots, find common ground in declaring,

> that they are *for man*, that they wish to actualize human potentialities, enhance human experience and contribute to happiness, social justice, democracy and a peaceful world. All say that they are opposed to authoritarian and totalitarian forces that dehumanize man. All profess compassion for human suffering and commitment to the unity of mankind. (Kurtz 1973, p. 6)

Similarly, Erich Fromm quotes Goethe in describing the essential: 'Man carries within himself not only his individuality but all of humanity, with all its potentialities, although he can realize these potentialities in only a limited way because of the external limitations of his individual existence' (Goethe in Fromm 1965, p. vi).

Modern humanism portrays man as multidimensional. It includes the intellectual, rational and scientific dimensions of being, as well as the emotional and spiritual elements contained in human relationships, such as affection, compassion and love. Unlike Renaissance humanism with its stress on education in making persons more fully human, modern humanism focuses more on social structure and institutions as catalysts for self-realization.

After the Council of Vienna (1815), the workings of the Industrial Revolution made the burgeoning capitalist system appear increasingly as a voraciously repressive and alienating force that if left unchecked would inhibit on a massive scale the full development of human personality. This led Sismondi in 1819 to call for a 'new' political economy. Karl Marx, going a step further, linked human emancipation to a new socialist economic system.

Similarly, in the twentieth century, it was the fear of man's enslavement by machine and technology, of being treated as a mere thing rather than respected as a person, that girded the more widespread revival of humanism. In spite of the basic agreement as to the very substance of the term, there continued to be a deep hidden fissure between spiritually compatible humanism and naturalistic, secular-leaning varieties whose more recent evolution is discussed in the next section.

To illustrate the divide, it may be helpful to enumerate five basic principles of the more traditional and spiritually compatible type, to show that from the naturalist viewpoint, some of these basic affirmations are more contentious than others.

- First, human nature is not static but developmental, meaning that as persons, we all are endowed with inherent goals for its unfolding. Within each of us is an inborn potential to grow, to flourish, to realize our 'true' or 'real' self. What is often observed as 'human nature' is but one of many of its manifestations – and often a pathological one.
- Second, human nature being universal implies basic normative standards that are not culturally relative. Entire cultures may be censured for the systematic stunting of human self-realization.
- Third, the normative image or ideal of actualizing 'real' and authentic personhood also opens the doors to problems of estrangement, or alienation from one's 'true nature'; witness the young Marx's indictment of capitalist employment and work. The situation is similar for other system-produced types of alienation, such as consumerism.
- Fourth, one of the most important focal points in a humanist conception of man centres on the distinctive capacity of free will, or autonomy. It entails the obligation to respect and cultivate the dignity and worth of human personality, in oneself and in all others. Human dignity, when seen as rooted in common human nature, is not conferred by society, but by something that transcends the merely social.
- Fifth, humanism has from the beginning been marked by confidence in the rational faculty of man. The Age of Reason further boosted this faith. It translates into a moral commitment to independent and free inquiry unhampered by ecclesiastical or secular authoritarian control.

Looking at these five principles from the point of view of naturalistic humanism reveals a certain unease. Although some of the points may be quite in harmony with that outlook, the talk of 'inherent nature', 'unfolding', 'free will', existence of a level that 'transcends the merely social' and 'real self', seems to clash with a naturalistic viewpoint. Similarly, it would indeed be ironic if an ideology anchored in free thought were also to profess that all things (and thoughts) have a natural cause and are therefore predetermined.

The late economist Walter Weisskopf provides a brief but excellent articulation of a basic distinction between philosophical humanism and its naturalist cousin:

> The naturalists and the humanists differ in the scope of their views on human reality. The humanists include elements that cannot be grasped by the purely logical and factual methods of the naturalists. The picture of man arrived at by the humanists with the help of introspection, intuition and empathy is all-inclusive, not partial, as the one of the naturalists . . .
> [It is recognized] that man is partly nature and partly more than nature. Through his memory, his imagination, his consciousness, self-awareness and reason, man transcends the conditioned, finite realm of nature, although he is part of this conditioned, finite realm . . . Their outlook is geared to *man in his totality*. (Weisskopf quoted from Maslow 1959, pp. 212–13, 214, emphasis in original)

Quite clearly, no scientific humanism can recognize the kind of reality that goes beyond the five senses to illuminate the many distinct aspects and capacities of humanity, such as consciousness, self-awareness, abstract thinking, free will, love, imagination and self-transcendence. These are really a matter of rather different epistemologies and ontologies.

Humanism as a naturalistic and secular label
As mentioned earlier, in the eighteenth century various thinkers, mostly in France (for example, O'Holbach, Lamettrie, Voltaire, Diderot), professed a materialistic atheism and took the position that only a complete break with any sort of religion would free man from the oppressions of churchly, as well as royal, authority. This philosophy became aggressively militant and laid the basis for widespread acceptance of philosophical materialism – the belief that there is no spirit, all is matter – in the nineteenth century.

Working in this context, and of great importance for the social sciences, was Auguste Comte (1798–1857), one of the founders of sociology and positivism, who also acted as a prophet of a new universal and secular 'religion of humanity'. But in the English-speaking world, it was Charles Darwin's theory of evolution (1859) that provided the main impetus for undermining any kind of theism and supernatural devotion. Strongly influenced by a small radical but militant 'free thought' movement, the kind of philosophical human-ism still adhered to by liberal Christianity was increasingly reduced to three bare-bone fundamentals: belief in a regnant God, belief in the validity of prayers and belief in the immortality of the soul. To this day, these three remnants summarize quite well what characterizes 'theistic humanism'.

Meanwhile, the strong secular current coming from Darwinism was soon to further reorient much of the modern humanist movement by increasingly identifying it with the negation of anything supernatural or divine. In the United States, Unitarians led by the theological thinking of the Harvard Divinity School turned increasingly rationalistic and naturalistic, eagerly subscribing to scientific methodology and secular ethics. It is prob-ably fair to say that these Unitarian ministers and their professors were pioneers, more than anybody else, in redefining contemporary humanism: a humanism naturalistic in philosophy, scientific in orientation and socially activist in sympathies.

Philosopher Corliss Lamont, the first recipient of the John Dewey Humanist Award, defines the concept in a nutshell: 'It [naturalistic humanism] rejects all forms of super-naturalism, pantheism and metaphysical idealism; it considers man's supreme ethical aim as working for the welfare of all humanity in this one and only life, using methods of reason, science and democracy for the solution of problems' (Corliss Lamont, quoted in Paul Kurtz 1973, p. 129).

Born from the convergence of free thought and religious liberalism, and nourished by the massive inhumane upheaval of World War I, the new naturalistic humanist move-ment started to organize in the 1920s. The Humanist Fellowship was founded in 1928 as a predecessor of what would later become the American Humanist Association. Under its auspices, this type of humanism came of age in 1933, with the proclamation of *A Humanist Manifesto*. Its three-dozen signatories, most of them Unitarian ministers or professors of higher education, including John Dewey, portrayed the new humanism as an anthropocentric religion. The term 'religion' here was to be understood in a most general and functional sense of being the means for realizing the highest values of life.

The document outlines a fifteen-point belief system containing the standard secular affirmations: the universe as self-existing, not created; man as a part of nature and a product of evolution; and a materialistic monism rejecting a body-mind dualism. But it also called for radical socio-economic change, replacing the acquisitive, profit-motivated economy with a more equitable and cooperative economic order.[1] The manifesto's general tone was optimistic, looking to science and technology as the putative saviours of a liberated humanity.

Shortly after the document's publication, a long series of disappointing events chal-lenged the humanist faith. The rise of Nazism demonstrated the extreme brutality of which humanity is capable. Then came deadly World War II, followed by the Cold War with its nuclear threat. The 1960s were marked by growing racial tension and a looming worldwide ecological crisis. The combination of all of these events and problems called for an updated version of the manifesto, which was formulated in 1973 and 2003.

Perhaps of greater significance today was the founding of the International Humanist and Ethical Union (IHEU) in Amsterdam in 1952. It represents more than 100 national organizations, akin to the American Humanist Association, and is spread over forty countries. For its fiftieth anniversary it issued the *Amsterdam Declaration of 2002*, meant to be an official statement of world humanism. It declares humanism to be ethical and rational, offering a life stance as well as an alternative to old-fashioned religion. It sup-ports democracy and human rights, it insists on socially responsible personal liberty and it values artistic creativity and an orientation of life aiming at maximum personal fulfil-ment. In order to promote a more unified humanist identity, the declaration recommends that the word 'Humanism' be written capitalized and used free of any further description, in particular, the adjective 'secular'.

The IHEU, as an umbrella organization, embraces atheist, rationalist, agnostic, sceptic, secular, ethical culture and free-thought groups, as well as the Gay and Lesbian Humanist Association. It stands for 'the building of a more humane society through an ethics based in human and other natural values in the spirit of reason and free inquiry through human capabilities'. In 2002, its International Humanist Award was given to economist Amartya Sen. This international flagship organization of (adjective-free) 'Humanism' has been closely aligned with the United Nations Educational, Scientific and Cultural Organization (UNESCO). The IHEU carefully discourages its member associations from portraying Humanism as a secular religion – a stance that may have been motivated by a still somewhat unsettled legal situation in America relating to whether Humanism qualifying as a religion would also make it subject to the US 'Establishment Clause', meaning that its doctrine and ethics could no longer be taught in public schools.[2]

Economics and humanism

Given this background, let us take a brief look at economics through the lens of humanist philosophy. It is true that today mainstream economics is taught on the model of physics and mathematics with precious little humanism. Workers, for example, are treated as mere inputs, not essentially different from units of capital equipment, heads of cattle or acres of land. Furthermore, contemporary welfare economics falls short of conforming to a humanist ethics – this, of course, contrasts sharply to Amartya Sen's proposed capability approach. Yet mainstream economics has not always been what it is now. In the early days, especially with Adam Smith and John Stuart Mill, political economy was regarded as a branch of moral philosophy with a human face, centred on the satisfaction of human needs.

Within the heterogeneous field of various alternative economics, it is not difficult to withhold any humanist credentials from economic thought that embraces postmodern philosophy with its explicit anti-humanist credo. In the postmodern category one also finds certain strands of institutionalist and feminist economics.

In contrast, perhaps the most outspoken embrace of a humanist point of view can be found in the almost two-century-old humanistic tradition of social economics. From Sismondi to the late E.F. Schumacher and Herman Daly's ecological economics, this strand can be understood as a variety of human welfare economics concerned particularly with poverty, unemployment, economic insecurity, the excesses of competition and unregulated trade, as well as the well-being of future generations.

Less explicit in name, but certainly no less humanist in substance, is the venerable Catholic social economics inspired by Pope Leo XIII's encyclical *Rerum Novarum* (1891) and the work of Heinrich Pesch. To this day, this type of economic thought is still very much alive under the name of solidarist social economics. It is significant to note that all of the here-mentioned proponents and humanistic schools of economic thought are incompatible with a naturalistic interpretation of humanism.

Conclusion

Western civilization has few concepts as integral as 'humanism'. Its history goes back at least six centuries. Until the last 150 years, the essential meaning of the term has been grounded in a theistic worldview. Today, thanks to both its secular sponsors and its fundamentalist Christian detractors confronting each other in a culture war, the concept now features two parallel and overlapping definitions.

Since the manifesto, humanism has increasingly seemed to carry an explicitly anti-God connotation. Clearly, this reductive shift in meaning has been the result of political organization and struggle rather than intellectual refinement. Moreover, this narrowing has been bought at the cost of excluding, or at least marginalizing, other contemporary and non-naturalistic conceptions of humanism – such as Martin Buber's 'believing humanism', and Jacques Maritain's 'integral humanism', as well as other contemporary strands of Catholic humanism.

Finally, one should keep in mind that naturalism's conquest of intelligentsia, as well as its demonstrated power in undermining theistic worship in church and temple, is the direct result of Darwinism's triumph in biology. Tomorrow's meanings of humanism, whatever they may be, will likely depend on future assessments of the intellectual power, scientific integrity and robustness of Darwinist-type evolutionary theories.

Notes

1. It was this last clause that provoked Chicago economist Frank Knight to abstain from signing the document.
2. This point became particularly important after the Supreme Court, in a 1961 case (*Torasco v. Watkins*), classified Secular Humanism, together with Taoism and Buddhism, as a religion.

References

Fromm, Erich (1965), 'Introduction', in Erich Fromm (ed.), *Socialist Humanism: An International Symposium*, Garden City, NY: Anchor Books.
Kurtz, Paul (ed.) (1973), *The Humanist Alternative: Some Definitions of Humanism*, Buffalo, NY: Prometheus Books.
Maslow, Abraham H. (ed.) (1959), *New Knowledge in Human Values*, South Bend, IN: Regnery/Gateway.

See also the entries on: Dignity; Freedom; Religion.

33 Identity
John B. Davis

Economics has only recently begun to employ and analyse the concept of 'identity' as applied to economic agents, and substantial differences still exist regarding its meaning and significance. The two main forms of the concept are 'social identity' and 'personal identity'. Social identity concerns an individual's identification with others, and personal identity concerns an individual's identity apart from others or their identity as a single individual through time. Social identity theory has been an important subject of investigation in social psychology since the 1970s (see Brown 2000), whereas personal identity has been investigated by philosophers in connection with the concept of the self throughout the history of the subject, especially in post-war analytic philosophy (see Martin and Barresi 2003).

Though social psychology is almost exclusively concerned with social identity, and philosophy is almost exclusively concerned with personal identity, the two are clearly related. When we ask who it is that has many social identities, we naturally raise the question of personal identity; when we ask how a single individual can have many selves over time, we often associate an individual's many selves with their different social identities. Nonetheless, social psychology and philosophy maintain a fairly sharp division of labour regarding the two forms, which has created problems for its adoption in economics. Indeed, economics has generally ignored the relation between the two concepts, often treating instead social identity *or* personal identity, whereas both forms can be seen to be part of what is involved in any complete account of the individual economic agent. Thus, assuming that economics will continue to emphasize individual economic behaviour in the future, the task it faces is to show how the two forms of the concept can be brought together in a single account of individual identity.

Two contributions to identity analysis in economics
The first influential appearance of the identity concept in economics is attributed to Amartya Sen, who introduced it in the form of social identity. Sen (1977) distinguished between sympathy and commitment, and later argued the importance of commitments made to social groups, where these are understood in terms of '*identifying* oneself with others of a particular group' (Sen 1999, p. 2, emphasis in the original). At the same time, in his critique of communitarian thinking, Sen emphasized that one's social identities are not something that one discovers, and about which one is powerless to decide, but something one may reason about and evaluate.

Indeed, individuals are generally able to engage in a process of reasoning and self-scrutiny, and this creates the 'problem' of 'the "identity" of a person, that is, how the person sees himself or herself', both as a whole and more specifically in regard to identification with others in social groups (Sen 2002, p. 215). Thus Sen recognizes that individuals having various social identities are somehow bound up with their having personal identities. He does not go further to explain just how individuals' social identities and personal identities are related, though it can be argued in connection with his capability framework that being able to engage in a process of reasoning and self-scrutiny is a special kind of capability for having a personal identity (Davis 2007).

In contrast to Sen's strategy of expanding the standard choice framework, Akerlof and Kranton (2000) introduced the concept of identity as social identity directly into a neoclassical utility maximizing framework (see Davis 2006). Individuals' utility depends on self-image, and self-image depends on how closely individuals' own characteristics correspond to established social categories (for example, race, gender, religion). When individuals' interactions with others threaten this correspondence – because they or others do not behave as their social categories prescribe – this creates anxiety which they seek to minimize, and this maximizes utility. Akerlof and Kranton draw explicitly on social psychology's 'social identity approach' and 'self-categorization theory' associated with the work of Tajfel (1972) and Turner (1985). Akerlof and Kranton do not employ the concept of personal identity, but for them, the utility function effectively constitutes an individual's personal identity, since in the standard framework utility functions identify individuals in terms of their own preferences. Nonetheless, there is little in the Akerlof-Kranton framework to explain how individuals' social identities and personal identities are related, since the analysis only explains how individuals maximize utility by making choices with respect to particular social identities, and not how they make choices across their different social identities. That is, Akerlof and Kranton essentially re-encounter the old, unresolved multiple selves problem associated with earlier work by Schelling (for example, 1984) and others (see Davis 2003, Ch. 4).

For Sen and also for Akerlof and Kranton, then, the main theoretical issue concerns how we are to understand individuals behaviourally in terms of their having both personal identities and social identities. But that individuals have both personal identities and social identities also raises important ethical and economic policy issues. Three such issues are (i) the normative significance of individuals having personal identities, (ii) the normative tension between personal identity and social identity, and (iii) the consequences for economic policy of taking personal identity and social identity seriously.

The normative significance of individuals having personal identities

Having a personal identity means that one somehow remains the same person despite change. From the point of view of the individual, this involves maintaining a unity to one's life whereby one is reasonably consistent in one's choices rather than constantly changing one's values and goals. Frankfurt (1971) saw this as a matter of having personal integrity, and being able to regulate first-order desires by higher-order desires, the latter reflecting the individual's deeper goals, values and commitments. But personal integrity is then close to moral integrity, as emphasized by Williams (1973, 1981) in understanding personal integrity as resulting from individuals' identity-conferring commitments to others and the values in which one believes. Indeed, moral integrity seems to presuppose personal integrity in that individuals need to maintain a unity to themselves throughout their lives in order to maintain consistent moral views and be moral persons.

An individual thus understood, however, is more than just a consistent moral actor. Being a consistent moral actor invests the individual with the status of being a moral being. Being a moral being, in turn, involves having moral respect for others and for oneself as well. This may be put in terms of the idea that the normative correlate of the notion of personal identity is the idea of individual dignity. Moral individuals thus have dignity by virtue of their consistent treatment of others and themselves as moral beings. Thus, the normative significance of individuals having personal identities is that they are thereby invested as individuals with moral importance, where this is understandable as the idea of individual dignity as a moral concept.

This concept, it should be noted, is altogether missing in standard economics, which treats individuals in a fully positive manner, and which restricts normative reasoning to Pareto judgements. Pareto judgements only require some improvement in preference satisfaction. But this ignores the individual as both a moral actor and the subject of moral action – the idea of individual dignity as a moral concern. The reason for this lies in the specific conception of the individual in standard economics as a preference (or utility) maximizer. This preference conception of the individual is unable to explain how individuals sustain personal identities (Davis 2003, Ch. 3). Thus, the standard preference conception of the individual is also unable to explain individuals as having dignity or moral value in and of themselves. This, in turn, has the effect of restricting the scope of normative reasoning in economics to Pareto judgements.

Enlarging the scope of normative reasoning in economics thus requires a broader conception of the individual as an economic and moral being. Avishai Margalit (1996) achieves this by drawing the consequences of there being a social basis for assuming individuals are objects of dignity. First, individuals have self-respect when society judges them to be worthy of being treated as beings with dignity. Having dignity with self-respect leads individuals to treat others morally and also to expect to be treated morally by others. Second, then, when does self-respect acquire a social basis, or when does society judge individuals as worthy of being treated with dignity? Following Immanuel Kant, Margalit answers that it is when society adopts the idea that individual human beings have human rights.

Similarly, the Universal Declaration of Human Rights (UN 1948) links dignity and human rights. Thus, in normative terms, an enlarged conception of the individual in economics can be grounded in individual dignity, self-respect and human rights. This goes considerably beyond the Pareto-based reasoning of standard economics, and helps to clarify the importance of the concept of personal identity in understanding individual economic agents.

Normative tensions between individuals having personal identities and social identities

Sen recently posed a set of questions concerning conflicting moral commitments that individuals may find they have when they consider their commitments and responsibilities to social groups of which they are members and to themselves. One issue concerns the basis for one's moral judgements. It is often argued that 'a person's moral judgments must be based on the values and norms of the community to which the person belongs, [and] also that these judgments can be ethically assessed *only within* those values and norms' (Sen 2006, pp. 33–4). It is certainly true that values and norms which people rely on to make moral judgements have social foundations. As Sen says, 'one cannot reason from nowhere' (ibid., p. 35). But, he adds, while our cultural attitudes and social beliefs may influence our choices, it goes too far to say that they determine them. Indeed, making moral judgements involves exercising practical reason rather than simply reciting the claims of others. Moreover, we are members of many social groups, so we often have conflicting sets of values and norms. This also makes it necessary for us to exercise practical reason in making moral judgements.

One issue here, then, is how individuals balance the conflicting claims of their different social identities. Family and workplace are two social identities with their own respective goals and time requirements. But because these two domains are so different in nature, it is not easy to decide how to compare their competing demands. In families, values and norms are tied to kin and household relationships that emphasize caring and emotional connection. In the workplace, values and norms are often tied to an impersonal meeting of one's assigned responsibilities and contributions to one's employer's commercial success. Thus, when conflicting claims arise, individuals find no common values and norms with which to adjudicate those claims. The problem is that one's social identities are usually highly compartmentalized.

Another issue involves the tension between individuals' needs and concerns and those of the social group(s) to which they belong. The former applies to the individual apart from others and the latter applies to the individual identifying with others. To go back and forth between these two vantage points often involves a substantial switch in perspective, since thinking of oneself as an independent individual and as a member of a group are quite different conditions. That they are often so incomparable means that individuals may not be able to decide what they owe themselves and the groups of which they are members.

Sen offers one way of addressing these issues in his emphasis on individuals being able to engage in reasoning and self-scrutiny. As he puts it, '[a] person is not only an entity that can enjoy one's own consumption, experience, and appreciate one's welfare, and have one's goals, but also an entity that can examine one's values and objectives and choose in the light of those values and objectives' (Sen 2002, p. 36). That is, individuals are reflective beings able to deliberate about their options and themselves rather than simply be impelled by their tastes to make certain 'choices'. Emphasizing individuals' capacity for deliberation may not provide a predictable basis for explaining how individuals solve problems of conflicting moral demands upon themselves, but it may offer a way of explaining how they address problematic choices – a subject which has gained increasing attention under the label of 'indeterminate rankings' or how individuals rank options that embody different values (compare Chang 1997).

Consequences for economic policy of taking personal identity and social identity seriously
Taking personal identity seriously requires changing the standard understanding of the individual economic agent. The standard view is short term in orientation, in that it focuses on individuals in relation to their decision-making at a certain point in time, and it does little to assess how the results of this decision-making influence their future decision-making. When individuals are assumed to have personal identities, they seek to sustain an identity through time that they understand prospectively – in terms of their goals, commitments and plans – and retrospectively – in terms of their evaluations of past outcomes and decisions in light of past intentions.

This long-term view of the individual is both more complex than the standard point-in-time view of the individual (involving as it does phenomena such as regret, value revision, feedback relationships and uncertainty) and also implies a higher degree of indeterminacy in predicted behaviour. Economic policy targeting individuals on this basis, then, needs to be more heuristic in nature and subject to multi-valued evaluation criteria.

Consider, for example, investment in training and education. According to the standard view, individuals make human capital investment decisions by comparing prospective benefits and opportunity costs. A long-term, personal identity understanding of the individual in the simplest before-and-after formulation looks at decision-making at time t_2 as an adjustment upon decision-making at time t_1, with the knowledge that that at t_1 was taken in anticipation of this future adjustment. One such model for training and education choices thus involves individuals making choices at t_1 that give a range of possible outcomes, as when one initially selects a general programme, so as to allow a comparison of further possible pathways at t_2. But this comparison when it occurs includes a retrospective component in that what possible outcomes actually materialize is unknown until t_2, so that t_1 is also re-evaluated at t_2. This interaction of prospective and retrospective thinking over many before-and-after episodes creates an identity for the decision-maker which is partly the result of the individual's decision and partly the result of the effects of the interactions between those decisions and the rest of the world.

Many individual lives exhibit coherence across their histories of decision-making, both from a personal perspective and that of others. But this is not the case for many others, whose life histories appear discontinuous and fragmented. One cannot conclude, however, that the former state of affairs is preferable to the latter, since well-being can be high with both continuity and discontinuity in life experience. With respect to the education and training example, increasingly focused pathways and pathways that involve significant reversals and redirections are both valuable. Thus, economic policy that takes personal identity seriously needs to accommodate both types of pathways. This conclusion runs counter to the standard, point-in-time human capital model which involves a highly determinate comparison of prospective benefits and opportunity costs. But that comparison is not a reliable basis for policy if the more complex account of individual decision-making is employed, and a higher degree of uncertainty regarding interaction of prospective and retrospective thinking is assumed.

Taking social identity seriously means recognizing that social groups play a role in determining social well-being, and that economic policy needs to target the well-being of social groups as well as the well-being of individuals. According to the standard view, social well-being is simply the aggregated well-being of all individuals in a society, and individuals are taken to be socially isolated. However, individuals are not socially isolated in that they depend on the many social groups to which they belong. For example, individuals live in households, and households permit economies that enhance individual well-being in ways not available to independent individuals. Thus economic policies that target households offer an indirect avenue for promoting individual well-being additional to policies that directly target individuals. This argument applies to all social groups that provide economic advantages to individuals, enhancing their well-being, such as local communities and neighbourhoods, racial and ethnic groups, gender groups, religious groups, and the like.

Designing policies that target social groups requires empirical analysis and evaluation of possible additional channels for promoting individual well-being, in order to determine effective policy instruments and the magnitudes with which they could be applied. For example, delivery of health-care services to individuals in communities where cultural values influence the use of such services requires that delivery be designed sensitive to those values, and set at levels consistent with what those communities can accommodate.

However, policy design may be complicated by the overlapping character of social groups and by individuals' memberships in different social groups. Two social groups may be strongly interconnected, but many of their members may also belong to other social groups to which these two groups are not connected.

In conclusion, the relatively recent introduction of the concept of identity into economics has left unaddressed important theoretical questions concerning its integration and significance. But the ethical and economic policy issues discussed here demonstrate the practical significance the concept of identity has in both of its main forms: social identity and personal identity. This practical significance is likely to motivate progress in explaining the role of identity in economics. As there are many ways of understanding social identity and personal identity, clearly much remains to be done to integrate the concept's theoretical and practical dimensions.

References
Akerlof, George A. and Rachel E. Kranton (2000), 'Economics and identity', *Quarterly Journal of Economics*, **115** (3), 715–53.
Brown, Rupert (2000), 'Social identity theory: past achievements, current problems and future challenges', *European Journal of Social Psychology*, **30**, 745–78.
Chang, Ruth (ed.) (1997), *Incommensurability, Incomparability and Practical Reason*, Cambridge: Cambridge University Press.
Davis, John (2003), *The Theory of the Individual in Economics*, London: Routledge.
Davis, John (2006), 'Akerlof and Kranton on identity in economics: inverting the analysis', *Cambridge Journal of Economics*, **31** (May 2007), 349–62.
Davis, John (2007) 'Identity and commitment: Sen's fourth aspect of the self', in Bernhard Schmid and Fabienne Peters (eds), *Rationality and Commitment*, Oxford: Oxford University Press.
Frankfurt, Harry G. (1971), 'Freedom of the will and the concept of a person', *Journal of Philosophy*, **68**, 5–20.
Margalit, Avishai (1996), *The Decent Society*, Cambridge, MA: Harvard University Press.
Martin, Raymond and John Barresi (2003), 'Introduction: personal identity and what matters in survival: a historical overview', in Raymond Martin and John Barresi (eds), *Personal Identity*, Oxford: Blackwell, pp. 1–74.
Schelling, Thomas C. (1984), 'Self-command in practice, in policy and in a theory of rational choice', *American Economic Review*, **74**, 1–11.
Sen, Amartya (1977) 'Rational fools: a critique of the behavioral foundations of economic theory', *Philosophy and Public Affairs*, **6**, 317–44.
Sen, Amartya (1999), *Reason before Identity*, New Delhi: Oxford University Press.
Sen, Amartya (2002), *Rationality and Freedom*, Cambridge, MA: Belknap Press.
Sen, Amartya (2006), *Identity and Violence: The Illusion of Destiny*, New York: Norton.
Tajfel, Henri (1972), 'Social categorization', in Serge Moscovici (ed.), *Introduction à la Psychologie Sociale*, Vol. 1, Paris: Larousse, pp. 272–302.
Turner, John C. (1985), 'Social categorization and the self-concept: a social cognitive theory of group behavior', in Edward J. Lawler (ed.), *Advances in Group Processes: Theory and Research*, Vol. 2, Greenwich, CT: JAI, pp. 77–122.
UN (1948), 'Universal Declaration of Human Rights', Geneva: The United Nations Office of the High Commissioner for Human Rights, www.unhchr.ch/udhr/, accessed 7 September, 2007.
Williams, Bernard (1973), 'Integrity', in J.J.C. Smart and Bernard Williams, *Utilitarianism: For and Against*, Cambridge: Cambridge University Press, pp. 108–18.
Williams, Bernard (1981), *Moral Luck: Philosophical Papers 1973–1980*, Cambridge: Cambridge University Press.

See also the entries on: Dignity; Individualism; Amartya Sen; Social economics.

34 Income distribution
Rolph van der Hoeven

Introduction

Of the many issues central to the development process, few have been characterized by the shifts, reversals and re-affirmations that have plagued analysis of the interaction between economic growth and poverty and income distribution. Evidence of worsening income distribution and poverty in many countries, including some in the industrialized West, in the 1980s and 1990s has rekindled ever-smouldering controversies (Cornia 2004; van der Hoeven 2002). One reason for the analytical shifts is the suggestion that income inequality and hence income distribution should not be a concern as long as poverty or deprivation is on the decline. Others argue, however, that there are moral reasons to be concerned with inequality. Cullity (2004) mentioned four of these:

- Inequality could be construed as domination, imposing hardships on other groups.
- Inequality of political and legal status could be a consequence of income inequality.
- Inequality represents callousness, as others cannot meet their basic needs.
- Brute inequality stands for a society's inability to include all groups in welfare enhancement.

An economic argument against excessive income inequality, which we will develop further on, is that income inequality in various circumstances hampers economic growth, slows poverty reduction and sustains deprivation.[1]

Inequality and growth

From the 1950s to the 1970s analyses emphasized the probable trade-offs between growth and income distribution. This derived in part from Kuznet's famous 'inverted-U hypothesis', which postulated that inequality would rise in the initial phases of development, then decline after some crucial level was reached and hence policy action to reduce inequality was unwarranted.

Growth theories were cited in support of the hypothesis, such as the Lewis model of 'economic development with unlimited supplies of labour'. Kaldor's growth model, in which capitalists have higher marginal propensity to save than workers, also implied that redistribution to profits raises economic growth rates. However, nowadays this model is acknowledged as being most appropriate for developed countries, in which the functional distribution of income largely consists of wages and profits, and less relevant to developing countries (Aghion et al. 1999).

After a brief period in the 1970s in which some policy attention was given to redistribution without hampering growth, the policy arena became dominated by neoliberalism, in particular, the Washington Consensus of the late 1980s. This held that growth itself would be the vehicle for poverty reduction, to be achieved through 'trickle-down' mechanisms, which themselves were not always clearly specified (van der Hoeven and Saget 2004).

Because poverty and inequality have a transitional component, induced by external shocks such as business cycles and price instability, they can be affected by short-term macro policies as well as by long-term growth. Particularly controversial are the possible adverse effects on poverty of stabilization and structural adjustment programmes. While the World Bank in some of its studies sought to deny the importance of such adverse effects, this sanguine view failed to establish itself.

In response to the controversy over the effects of adjustment on the poor, the World Bank and International Monetary Fund (IMF) proposed 'social safety nets' and 'social funds' in some countries, to target adjustment-induced poverty. These programmes were typically designed for a limited period. An evaluation of social safety nets suggests that these programmes, sometimes financed by multilateral lending, had some positive impact on what might be called 'adjustment losers', but did not reduce inequality or necessarily reach the poor.[2]

The perceived ineffectiveness of redistributive measures under the Washington Consensus led some to advocate targeting public expenditure to the poor, and judging effectiveness by the accuracy of that targeting. However, the targeting of expenditures in developing countries has been fraught with difficulty. Sen (1995) argued against targeting public spending for a number of reasons: (i) information asymmetries reduce the effectiveness of targeting in the presence of 'cheating', (ii) the prospect of losing targeted subsidies may reduce beneficiaries' economic activity, (iii) targeting may undermine the poor's self-respect, and (iv) the sustainability of targeted programmes is doubtful, as the potential beneficiaries are politically weak.

To Sen's list we can add the formidable measurement problem of identifying who qualifies. This problem, already serious in industrial countries, is virtually intractable in most developing contexts. Targeting public spending is more likely to be effective where the poor form a small proportion of the population; that is, if poverty is not a major problem. For countries in which poverty is widespread, the administrative costs of identification, monitoring and delivery of programmes may outweigh benefits.

In the early 1990s a strand of theory invoked so-called 'political economy arguments' in relation to inequality and, by implication, poverty (Alesina and Rodrik 1994). This analysis predicted a negative relationship between income inequality and growth on the grounds that higher initial inequality would (i) lead to increased public expenditure, because it prompts a demand for redistributive policies and (ii) incite political instability that undermines growth. This excursion into political science is nonetheless somewhat dubious. For example, it is not at all clear how a society with the power relationships to generate inequality would, at the same time, produce an underclass with the political clout to force redistributive policies upon a government.

On somewhat firmer analytical ground is the argument that inequality hinders growth through imperfect capital markets to which the poor have limited access (Aghion et al. 1999). In other words, if capital markets discriminate against the poor, potentially profitable activities by the poor are constrained by lack of credit. However, the imperfect capital markets argument has practical limitations in that it presumes the poor to be self-employed or to have the option to become so. While this may apply to a portion of

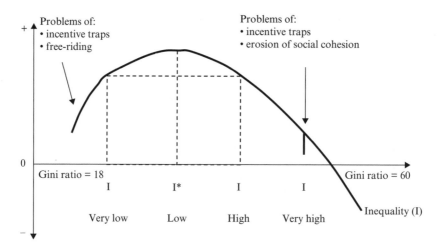

Source: Cornia (2004, p. 45).

Figure 34.1   Inequality and growth

the households in poverty, empirical evidence suggests that during the 1990s those in the lowest income quintile, in Latin America at least and perhaps elsewhere, were increasingly in wage employment. Indeed, the idea that most low-income wage earners could escape poverty through self-employment challenges the imagination as well as historical trends.

Towards the end of the 1990s, a number of studies challenged both the neoliberal analysis and the earlier view of a trade-off between growth and equity (Milanovic 1999; Ferreira 1999; van der Hoeven 2002; Weeks 1997). In particular, doubt fell upon the sanguine view that orthodox macro policies were, by their nature, inequality- and poverty-reducing. On the one hand, mainstream literature, with its emphasis on the efficiency of markets, tended to view inequality and poverty as accidental or occasional outcomes of a deregulated growth process. On the other hand, the persistence and severity of poverty in many, if not most, developing countries fuelled periodic arguments for poverty alleviation. The shifts in emphasis in the literature reflect the difficulty of reconciling these two perspectives.

Focusing on the effects of inequality and growth, Cornia (2004) found a distinct non-linear relationship between initial income inequality and economic growth in subsequent periods. Figure 34.1, based on these results, shows that too low inequality is bad for growth (leading to a proclivity for free-riding and high supervision costs), but that too high inequality levels can also have serious negative consequences. Income inequality in most developing countries is in the high range.

Birdsall (2005) therefore argues that income inequality in developing countries matters for at least three instrumental reasons:

- Where markets are underdeveloped, inequality inhibits growth through economic mechanisms.
- Where institutions of government are weak, inequality exacerbates problems in creating and maintaining accountable government, increasing the probability of economic and social policies that inhibit growth and poverty reduction.

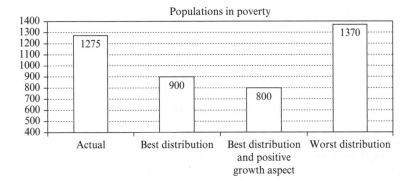

Source: Based on information in Luebker (2002).

Figure 34.2 *Population living on US$1/day or less under different distribution scenarios (millions)*

- Where social institutions are fragile, inequality further discourages the civic and social life that girds the effective collective decision-making necessary for the functioning of healthy societies.

The growing consensus is thus that countries with an 'initial condition' of relatively egalitarian distribution of assets and income tend to grow faster than countries with high initial inequality. This is an extremely important conclusion, because it means that reducing inequality strikes a double blow against poverty. On the one hand, a growth path characterized by greater equality at the margin directly benefits the poor in the short run. On the other hand, the resulting decrease in inequality creates in each period an 'initial condition' for a future that is growth-enhancing. Hence, any growth path that reduces inequality reduces poverty through redistribution and via 'trickle down'.

Poverty

Before considering issues of redistribution, we must still clarify one point. It is often argued that national redistribution is difficult to deal with, as historical and cultural factors determine to a large extent the magnitude of inequality in a given country, and policies of redistribution should therefore not be undertaken. This has often led to the policy stance that international organizations should not concern themselves with policies dealing with inequality.

To dismiss such a deterministic attitude, Luebker (2002) asked the question, 'How much lower, and respectively how much higher, would the World Bank's global estimate of people living in poverty be at the beginning of the 21st century, if each country at the start of the century had the lowest, or alternately the highest, level of inequality that each country had *itself* experienced since the 1960s?' (emphasis in original). As such, both historical and cultural characteristics of each country would be acknowledged. Figure 34.2 reproduces the results. Under the most equal scenario, the global estimate of the number of people in poverty would decrease from 1.275 billion to 900 million, while in the most unequal scenario it would increase to 1.370 billion.

These simulated numbers demonstrate two points:

- Inequality does matter, and even when respecting initial and historical trends, there is an important case to be made for lower inequality.
- Currently inequality is rather high compared to the last decades.

The latter point can be substantiated in more detail for both industrialized and developing countries.

Regarding income and earnings inequality in industrialized countries, Gottschalk and Smeeding (1997) observe that at any given time modern countries differ widely in their level of earnings, and nations with centralized bargaining (for example, Sweden and Germany) have greater equality than nations with less centralized bargaining (for example, the United States and Canada). They also observe in almost all industrialized countries some increase in wage inequality among prime-aged men during the 1980s. Wage inequality increased the most in the United States and United Kingdom and the least in the Nordic countries. The growing demand for skilled workers, coupled with differences between countries in growth in the supply of skilled workers, explains a large part of the difference. Furthermore (and important for policymaking) they observe that institutional constraints on wage determination seem to matter. The rise in relative unemployment rates among the least skilled in some, but not all, countries with centralized wage-setting institutions suggests that such institutional constraints were at least partially responsible for limiting the rise in inequality.

For the United States they explain the rapid rise in earnings inequality with reference to a variety of structural changes in the economy, such as changes in industrial structure, more foreign trade, more immigration, skill-based technical change and the weakening of labour-market institutions. These last limit the effects of the free market, for example, through minimum wage setting and unionization. Gottschalk and Smeeding (1997) cite studies confirming that the weakening of these two labour-market institutions explain a large part, possibly even 50 per cent, of the increase in the dispersion in wage earnings in the United States.

Looking for common features and differences between the United States and European countries, Gottschalk and Smeeding argue that differences in wage-setting institutions may well account for some of the differences in the growth in inequality: 'There is certainly a *prima facie* case that countries with high union coverage on centralized wage setting were able to limit the growth in inequality' (1997, p. 653).

Regarding developing countries, Cornia (2004) argues that the last two decades have witnessed a widespread and symmetric rise in within-country inequality in developing countries. There are three possible explanations for this. First, limited migration to the advanced nations did not help to equalize the distribution of income in the countries of origin. Second, international financial flows have become less stable and more disequalizing. And third, inequality was also significantly influenced by domestic policy and institutional reforms – such as those of the labour market, financial sector and taxes – which may have been introduced to facilitate the international integration of poor countries but which had unfavourable effects on labour income compared to profit income and wage differentials.

Finally, there are the inequality impacts of globalization. These contradict the predictions of standard theory, which is unable to capture the effect of other factors, such as domestic institutional weaknesses, the complexity of trade and finance in a multi-country multi-goods environment, persistent and rising protectionism in the North and the equity impact of the other domestic reforms that are often introduced to facilitate the drive towards globalization.

Redistribution

The argument made above is that inequality matters, that inequality has increased and that lower inequality is possible in most countries. The next question is then, 'What policies of growth and redistribution are best to consider?' Dagdeviren et al. (2004) show that policies for redistribution have often, especially in the short term, proven superior for reducing poverty than relying on growth alone, in 47 out of 50 developing countries for which robust data were available.

The major element required to introduce and effectively implement a redistributive strategy in any country is the construction of a broad political coalition for poverty reduction. The formidable task of this coalition would be to pressure governments for redistribution policies, while neutralizing opposition to those policies from groups whose self-interest rests with the status quo. In industrialized countries the policy solution depends mainly on political factors, as shown by the varied experiences of inequality in different industrialized countries. For this, little economic analysis is needed.

Perhaps the most important determinant of the effectiveness of the various measures and specifics of each redistribution strategy is the structure of an economy. This structure depends on the level of development, which to a great extent conditions the country's production mix, its endowments of socio-economic groups, remuneration to factors, direct and indirect taxes on income and assets, prices paid for goods and services and transfer payments.[3] The implementation requirements of redistributive policies can be summarized in a simple theoretical framework (see Hamner et al. 1997). Define the following terms:

Y denotes the income of a household, V is transfer payments, T is taxes, k is a vector of assets (including human capital), w is a vector of rates of return (including wages), p is the price vector of goods and services, q is the quantity vector of those goods and services, and S is household saving.

Then, by definition it follows:

$Y =$	$(V - T)$	$+ wk$	$=$	pq	$+ S$
	Transfer payments (unemployment compensation, pensions, child benefits, aid to disabled) (V); progressive taxes (on income and wealth) (T)	Minimum wages, low-wage subsidies, other labour-market regulations, public employment schemes (w); credit programmes for the poor, land reform, education (k)		Subsidies on goods for basic needs, public sector infrastructure investment (p); child nutrition programmes (q)	Facilitation of future asset acquisition, such as provision of village banks and other financial services for the poor (S)
	Effective in middle-income countries	Effective in middle-income and some low-income countries		Effective in most countries	Effective in most countries

The effectiveness of tax and expenditure policies (*T* and *V*) in generating secondary and tertiary distributions more equitable than the primary distribution depends upon the relative importance of the formal sector. This is for the obvious reason that governments can most effectively apply progressive income taxes to wage employees and corporations. All empirical evidence shows that the formal sector wage bill and profit shares increase with level of development. Working-poor urban households are more easily targeted than either the rural poor or urban informal sector households. This redistribution strategy is most appropriate for middle-income countries, because their per capita incomes are high relative to the absolute poverty line. These are also the countries whose economic structures make taxation and expenditure instruments effective redistribution tools.

For low-income countries dominated by petroleum or mineral production, a large portion of national income may be generated by modern sector corporations. This allows for effective taxation even though the administrative capacity of the public sector may be limited. Tax revenue can be redistributed through poverty-reduction programmes, though not through transfer payments if the labour force is predominantly rural. Examples of mineral-rich low-income countries with the (unrealized) potential to have done this are Nigeria, Liberia and Zambia.

Interventions to change the distribution of earned income (wk in the equation above), which alter market outcomes, will tend to be more effective in middle-income countries. The most common such intervention is a minimum wage, though there are many other policies to improve earnings from work (see van der Hoeven and Saget 2004). Further mechanisms include public employment schemes and tax subsidies to enterprises that hire low-wage labour.

Land reform might achieve poverty reduction for rural households, but the relationship between land redistribution and development level is a complex one. Low-income countries are predominantly rural, so if land ownership is concentrated, its redistribution could have a substantial impact on poverty. On the other hand, administrative weaknesses and so-called 'traditional tenure systems' represent substantial constraints to land redistribution in many low-income countries. For middle-income countries, experience in Latin America has shown that governments can effectively implement land redistribution. However, the relevance of land reform for inequality reduction tends to decline as countries develop and the rural population shrinks in relative and absolute terms.[4]

Interventions that directly affect the prices of and access to goods and services (*pq*) could be a powerful instrument for redistribution. Subsidies to lower prices of selected commodities have the administrative advantage of not requiring targeting, only identification of those items that weigh heavily in the expenditure patterns of the poor.[5] While multilateral adjustment programmes typically require an end to such subsidies on grounds of allocative efficiency or excessive budgetary cost, the rules of the World Trade Organization do not, as long as subsidies do not discriminate between domestic production and imports (FAO 1998). In low-income countries in which the majority of the poor live in the countryside, consumer subsidies are unlikely to have a significant impact outside urban areas. Basic goods provision in kind can be an effective instrument for poverty reduction even in very low-income countries, by delivering such items as milk to school children.

In all countries the poor suffer ill-health and inadequate education relatively more than the non-poor. Public expenditure on education and health has the practical advantage of helping the poor, who are easily identified, though the specifics of such efforts would vary by country. However, providing these services to the poor may in some countries be as politically difficult as more obviously controversial measures, such as asset redistribution. The same applies to infrastructure programmes directed at poverty reduction. Insofar as these would reduce public investment in projects favoured by the non-poor, especially the wealthy, such programmes may be no easier to implement than measures that at first appear more radical.

Conclusion

Though clearly numerous problems are involved in implementing an agenda of redistribution, the difficulties should not be exaggerated. In many countries they might prove no more intractable than the problems associated with implementation of other economic policies. An effective orthodox monetary policy is difficult to implement if a country is too small or underdeveloped to have a bond market. The absence of a bond market leaves monetary authorities unable to 'sterilize' foreign exchange flows. Similarly, replacing tariffs by a value-added tax constitutes a daunting task in countries where commerce is primarily through small traders. And lack of public sector capacity tends to limit the ability to execute a range of so-called 'supply-side policies': privatization, 'transparency mechanisms' and decentralization of central government service delivery (van der Hoeven and van der Geest 1999).

Multilateral agencies have recognized these constraints to adjustment programmes, typically deciding that constrained implementation is preferable to non-implementation. The same argument can be made for a redistributive growth strategy: to achieve poverty reduction, it might be preferable to redistribute growth imperfectly than to maintain the status quo imperfectly.

Notes

This contribution is based in part on Shorrocks and van der Hoeven (2004) and Dagdevieren, van der Hoeven and Weeks (2004).

1. There is also considerable evidence that the current process of globalization has widened inequality between countries in terms of gross national income (Gunther and van der Hoeven 2004). This is extremely important, and strong policy initiatives are required to reverse these trends (ILO 2004; UN 2005). However this chapter is concerned only with the equally important question of growing income inequality within countries.
2. Stewart (1995) argues that internally funded and locally designed anti-poverty programmes are more effective in reaching the poor than social funds.
3. There is considerable argument that current globalization is reducing the autonomy of the nation-state in economic and social matters. See Chang (2003) and Gunther and van der Hoeven (2004).
4. For example, at the end of the twentieth century in the five most populous Latin American countries, 20 per cent or less of the labour force was in agriculture.
5. This is preferred above a two-tier price system for basic consumer goods, which might stimulate corruption, though in some more advanced countries a two-tier price might achieve redistribution objectives.

References

Aghion, Philippe, Eve Caroli and Cecilia Garcia-Penalosa (1999), 'Inequality and economic growth: the perspective of the new growth theories', *Journal of Economic Literature*, **37** (December), 1615–60.
Alesina, Alberto and Dani Rodrik (1994), 'Distributive politics and economic growth', *Quarterly Journal of Economics*, **109** (2), 465–90.
Birdsall, Nancy (2005), 'The world is not flat: inequality and justice in our global economy', WIDER Lecture 9, World Institute for Development Economics Research, Helsinki.
Chang, Ha-Joon (2003), *Globalisation, Economic Development and the Role of the State*, London: Zed Books.

Cornia, Giovanni A. (ed.) (2004), *Inequality, Growth and Poverty in an Era of Liberalization and Globalization*, Oxford: Oxford University Press.

Cullity, Garrett (2004), 'Equality and globalization', in Keith Horton and Haig Patapan (eds), *Globalization and Inequality*, London: Routledge, pp. 6–22.

Dagdevieren, Hulya, Rolph van der Hoeven and John Weeks (2004), 'Redistribution does matter: growth and redistribution for poverty reduction', in Tony Shorrocks and Rolph van der Hoeven (eds), *Growth, Inequality, and Poverty: Prospects for Pro-poor Economic Development*, Oxford: Oxford University Press, pp. 125–53.

Fei, John C.H. and Gustav Ranis (1964), *Development of the Labour Surplus Economy*, New York: John Riley.

FAO (1998), 'The implications of the Uruguay Round Agreement on Agriculture for developing countries', Training Materials 41, Rome: Food and Agriculture Organization of the United Nations, Statistics Division.

Ferreira, Francisco H.G. (1999), *Inequality and Economic Performance*, Washington DC: World Bank.

Gottschalk, Peter and Timothy M. Smeeding (1997), 'Cross-national comparisons of earnings and income inequality', *Journal of Economic Literature*, **35** (June), 633–87.

Gunther, Bernhard and Rolph van der Hoeven (2004), 'The social dimension of globalization: a review of the literature', *International Labour Review*, **143** (1–2), 7–43.

Hamner, Lucia, Graham Pyatt and Howard White (1997), Poverty in Sub-Saharan Africa: What can be learnt from the World Bank's Poverty Assessments? Working Paper, The Hague: Institute of Social Studies.

Hoeven, Rolph van der (2002), 'Poverty and structural adjustment: some remarks on the trade-off between equity and growth', in Anne Booth and Paul Mosley (eds), *New Poverty Strategies: What Have They Achieved, What Have We Learned?* London: Macmillan, pp. 60–87.

Hoeven, Rolph van der and Willem van der Geest (1999), 'Africa's adjusted labour markets: can institutions perform?', in Willem van der Geest and Rolph van der Hoeven, *Adjustment, Employment and Missing Institutions in Africa*, London: James Currey, pp. 9–29.

Hoeven, Rolph van der and Catherine Saget (2004), 'Labour market institutions and income inequality: what are the new insights after the Washington Consensus? in Giovanni A. Cornia (ed.), *Inequality, Growth and Poverty in an Era of Liberalization and Globalization*, Oxford: Oxford University Press, pp. 197–220.

ILO (2004), *A Fair Globalization: Creating Opportunities for All*, Geneva: World Commission on the Social Dimension of Globalization.

Luebker, Malte (2002), 'Assessing the impact of past distributional shifts on global poverty levels', Employment Paper 2002–37, International Labour Organization, Geneva.

Milanovic, Branko (1999), 'Explaining the increase in inequality during the transition', World Bank Policy Research Department Paper, World Bank, Washington DC.

Sen, Amartya (1995), 'The political economy of targeting', in Dominique van de Walle and Kimberley Neat (eds), *Public Spending and the Poor*, Baltimore: Johns Hopkins University Press for the World Bank, pp. 11–24.

Shorrocks, Tony and Rolph van der Hoeven (eds) (2004), *Growth, Inequality, and Poverty: Prospects for Pro-poor Economic Development*, Oxford: Oxford University Press.

Stewart, Frances (1995), *Adjustment and Poverty, Options and Choices*, London: Routledge.

UN (2005), *The Inequality Predicament*, New York, NY: United Nations Department of Economic and Social Affairs.

Weeks, John (1997), 'Analysis of the Demery and Squire "adjustment and poverty" evidence', *Journal of International Development*, **9**, 827–36.

See also the entries on: Human development; Inequality; Poverty.

35 Individualism
John B. Davis

The term 'individualism' has functioned as one of the main organizing principles of economics for over a century. Yet despite this, considerable ambiguity still surrounds the discipline's use of the term. In particular, there is a lack of clarity on (i) its methodological interpretation and ultimate value as an organizing principle, (ii) the conception of the individual that is appropriate to reasoning in economics and (iii) the normative implications of the standard view of individuals in economics. These three issues are addressed in this chapter.

Competing views of individualism

Individualism in economics – often termed 'methodological individualism' – is the view that individuals should figure centrally in all economics-related explanations. In contrast, holism – or 'methodological holism' – is the view that social groups and other social aggregates should figure centrally in such explanations. Schumpeter coined the former term a century ago (Schumpeter 1908; and compare 1909), later defining it as an explanation that focused on the 'behavior of individuals without going into the factors that formed this behavior' (Schumpeter 1954, p. 889). He distinguished this from 'sociological individualism', the – in his view 'untenable' – idea that 'all social phenomena resolve themselves into decisions and actions of individuals that need not or cannot be further analyzed in terms of supraindividual factors' (ibid., p. 888). This last is what many economists and other social scientists today regard as the meaning of methodological individualism. For example, Elster defines methodological individualism as 'the doctrine that all social phenomena (their structure and their change) are in principle explicable only in terms of individuals – their properties, goals, and beliefs' (Elster 1982, p. 453). Schumpeter simply recommends that we take individual behaviour at face value, whereas Elster and others assert that all economic explanations are necessarily rooted in individual behaviour.

In this latter formulation, methodological individualism is sometimes associated with a strong form of ontological individualism. While general ontological individualism is the view that individuals are amongst the kinds of things that exist in the world, the strong form of this doctrine states that *only* individuals exist. Hayek (1955) was a leading proponent of this strong form of ontological individualism, arguing that supra-individual entities are not real things of the order of individuals but only concepts, where concepts are features of individuals. According to this view, methodological individualism implies a reductionist programme of explanation (compare Kincaid 1997). Following Elster's language above, this would seek to reduce all explanations framed in terms of social entities – such as institutions, classes and social groups, norms and conventions – to explanations framed in terms of individuals.

Much of contemporary rational choice theory operates on this programme, seeking to explain social institutions and other durable social arrangements as solely the outcome of the choices individuals make. Examples include the new institutional economics and classical game theory. The export of economic reasoning to other social sciences – known as 'economic imperialism' – is generally associated with the application of an individualist rational choice explanation to phenomena customarily believed to be inescapably social in nature in such fields as political science, sociology and law.

Agassi (1975), following Popper (1945), rejected this reductionist view. He argued that the correct form of individualism for economics and social science is what he termed 'institutional individualism'. If we suppose institutions and other supra-individual entities exist along with individuals, then we effectively combine individualism with holism by supposing neither can be reduced to the other (compare Boland 2003, Ch. 2). However, while this makes sense in principle, abandoning reductionism raises a new set of issues associated with explaining how individuals and institutions affect one another. Individual action is both influenced by its institutional environment, and also influences that institutional environment; similarly, institutions are the product of individual actions, and also condition individual actions. But if this is so, then why should we be speaking about any kind of individualism at all (Hodgson 2007)? Or, to turn this question around, why is the economics of Veblen, Commons and Ayers called 'institutionalism', since they also understood individuals and institutions to be mutually influencing? These questions suggest that focusing on methodological stances such as individualism and holism (institutionalism) may not be very helpful, and that if we are to better understand the significance of the individual in economics, we should begin by attending more closely to the conceptions of the individual used in economics.

Competing conceptions of the individual

Methodological individualism in the strong form identified above is associated with a particular conception of the nature of the individual. Since this conception strongly contrasts individuals with social institutions, individuals must by nature be non-social or socially isolated, atomistic beings. Thus, they can be defined only in terms of their own personal characteristics, which excludes any reference to individuals' social characteristics and social relationships. This particular conception originated in neoclassical economics in the late nineteenth century with the marginal utility theory. That theory described individuals subjectively in terms of their private psychological states. Later, the preference theory of neoclassical economics eliminated the concept of utility from the theory of choice, and post-war economics largely abandoned the earlier psychological interpretation of the individual. However, the individual remains an atomistic being in that individuals are still viewed strictly in terms of their own personal characteristics. Choices are explained simply in terms of the idea of individuals having their own separate objective functions, often still called 'utility functions', though without the original meaning of the term. Further, nothing is said regarding what factors, social or otherwise, might influence these objective functions.

Thus, individualism in this strong form simply reduces the individual to its most abstract conception possible. While this may be well suited to formal analysis in mathematical models, it tells us little about the behaviour of individuals in particular historical social settings. Indeed, there is nothing in this highly abstract conception of the individual that identifies what kind of individual is involved, since there is nothing in the idea of an objective function that prevents this formal tool from being applied to single human beings, groups of human beings (think of firms and countries), animals or even machines such as computerized stock trading programs. All can be understood as 'individuals'.

Alternatively, allowing that individuals have social characteristics as well as personal ones gives us a non-atomistic conception of the individual which may be termed the conception of the individual as 'socially embedded' (Davis 2003). Individuals who occupy locations in networks of social relationships are members of social groups and are influenced by social institutions. They are still individual by virtue of the distinct location they occupy in these social phenomena, but they also have social characteristics by virtue of their various relations to others. In this non-reductionist understanding, supra-individual entities also exist. Social networks, social groups, institutions and patterns of social relationships are all real entities alongside individuals. The challenge of this broader view, then, is to explain how individuals can be motivated by a combination of personal and social factors.

Sen offers one such account in his argument that commitment behaviour is fundamentally different from behaviour motivated by self-interest (Sen 1977). Commitment cannot be understood in terms of self-interest, since it is essentially other-oriented. At the same time, commitments to others are personal when they are made by one person to another (or to a number of others). Commitments, then, are made by individuals who are embedded in social relationships structured by commitments. Another example is the phenomenon of collective intentions or individual intentions expressed using the first-person plural 'we' language. When people make statements preceded by 'we', they bind themselves to others who fall within the scope of their use of the 'we' term. Their statement is thus essentially other-oriented. At the same time, expressing an intention is something one does individually. Consequently, individuals are socially embedded when using 'we' language, just as when they make commitments to others. A third example is the phenomenon of trust. When individuals trust one another they put aside their view of each other as different and separate. They are held by a bond that encompasses them as individuals. But they are still individuals in that trust holds between people. Thus, individuals are socially embedded when trust relationships prevail. A final example is associated with Smith's ([1759] 1976) concept of the impartial spectator. Smith believed that individuals could remove themselves from their own situation to judge the well-being of others from a disinterested, impartial perspective. In effect, they put themselves in the place of others, but since they are able to do this as individuals, they embed their own view in social understanding.

Individualism, therefore, need not imply either that individuals are socially isolated atoms or that they invariably act out of self-interest. When we substitute the conception of the individual as socially embedded for the conception of the individual as atomistic, we are still pre-eminently concerned with individuals, though individuals are then understood in terms of their social characteristics as well as their personal ones. This wider perspective is especially important when we turn from behavioural analysis to normative analysis in economics, since this perspective allows us to expand the array of normative considerations that we bring to bear on the evaluation of economic outcomes and states of affairs. That is, when individuals are seen to have social characteristics as well as personal ones, normative concerns that pertain to relationships between individuals come directly into the picture alongside normative concerns that pertain specifically to individual well-being.

The discussion that follows charts this expansion in normative concerns by first identifying those concerns that specifically target individual well-being, and then going on to
show how the wider perspective on the individual afforded by a conception of the individual as socially embedded raises additional normative concerns specifically associated
with relationships between individuals.

Expanding the scope of normative concern
The standard view of the individual as an atomistic being is also associated with normative evaluation by the standard of Pareto improvements. The Pareto criterion recommends changes that improve at least one individual's well-being without worsening that
of any other individual. An improvement in well-being for an isolated individual can be
measured only in terms of the individual's personal characteristics, which is a matter of
achieving a higher degree of 'preference' satisfaction, as understood in terms of the individual's objective function. There is a small space in which such improvements can also
concern the well-being of others when an individual feels sympathy for others. But such
well-being gains for others are only a by-product and not the determinant of a Pareto
improvement. Moreover, in the atomistic individual framework, individual advantage is
not comparable across individuals, so one cannot compare a collection of improvements
in well-being of others with whom an individual might sympathize with the individual's
own resulting improvement in well-being.

Pareto improvements, thus understood, are not a very good measure of what is
involved in improvements of an individual's well-being. Since the individual's objective
function represents the individual's own 'preferences', it is possible that what an expert
outside observer (such as a health professional) would regard as an improvement in the
individual's well-being would not be seen as such by the individual. The isolated individual framework, however, rules out outside observer evaluations. Therefore, this issue
cannot arise in Pareto evaluations, despite evidence from ordinary experience that others
do sometimes know what is to individuals' advantage better than they do themselves.

Thus, the first normative gain available in moving to the wider perspective of the
socially embedded conception of the individual is to allow for a broader evaluation of
individual advantage made possible by recognizing individuals' social characteristics.
For example, taking Sen's capability approach (Sen 1999) as providing one way of characterizing individuals as socially embedded (on the grounds that individual capabilities
are judged by social standards of attainment), individuals' social characteristics can be
evaluated to determine well-being improvements in a manner able to go substantially
beyond what the Pareto improvement measure tells us about individual well-being.

Another way of looking at an expanded understanding of individual well-being concerns the distinction between wants and needs. In the standard framework this distinction does not exist, because individuals' preferences are only associated with desires and
wants. However, in many instances social institutions, which involve relatively settled
networks of social relationships, effectively differentiate needs from wants by prioritizing some activities over others. For example, educational systems prioritize learning and
skill acquisition over other possible uses of individuals' time, and they justify doing so
by treating education as a need. Individuals are thus seen socially as having needs. This
identification of a need is often reinforced by emphasis in the practices of the relevant
institutions on the value of care. Taking care seriously as a value is equivalent to investing

intrinsic worth in its recipients. Thus institutions may not only redefine individual well-being in terms of a distinction between wants and needs, but also reshape the status of individuals as objects of well-being concern by establishing practices organized around the value of care.

What further normative concerns enter the picture, then, when we turn from seeing how individuals may be understood socially to individuals' own social characteristics, especially as reflected in the social relationships that arise between them? Here, Rawls's ([1971] 1999) influential thinking offers an excellent point of entry. Rawls emphasizes justice, freedom and equality, three fundamental social values that have long been a major part of the history of social ethics. Accordingly, his explanation of justice rests upon two principles. The first principle is that individuals are entitled to as much freedom as is compatible with all individuals having the same freedoms. This requires an equal distribution of what Rawls calls 'primary goods', namely, 'rights and liberties, powers and opportunities, income and wealth', and also 'self-respect' (ibid., p. 62). We may interpret this to mean that in a just society freedom requires a fundamental equality to exist between individuals. In contrast, in the atomistic view of the individual, freedom is only about subjective choice being constrained by one's resources and endowments, and has nothing to do with the existence of other people. Rawls's second principle of justice is the 'difference' principle, which modifies the extent of equality in a society by allowing for inequalities in access to opportunities in society only when they benefit the least well-off. That is, in a just society inequalities are only permitted when they do not infringe freedoms from the point of view of those at risk. In contrast, according to the atomistic view of the individual, inequality is socially unconditioned in that it simply reflects accidental differences in individuals' resources and endowments, and therefore lacks any foundation in normative principles.

Rawls's two principles of justice, then, implicitly require us to expand our understanding of the individual from the atomistic conception to a more normatively rich conception. More generally, it is fair to say that the narrowness of the atomistic conception significantly narrows the scope and quality of normative evaluation possible in economics, so that any serious engagement of economics with ethics depends on broadening the conception of the individual.

Rawls himself understood his thinking as a kind of Kantian constructivism (Rawls 1980, 1993). By this he meant a strategy of devising procedures for establishing legal and political arrangements that reasonable individuals would support given the opportunity for serious reflection (a 'reflective equilibrium'). While this does not tell us precisely how to handle cases in which apparently reasonable people disagree, it does serve to link the process of creating social arrangements with a particular view of individuals as being able to engage in civic dialogue framed by a general requirement of openness and willingness to revise one's thinking. Put in terms of the discussion here, individuals also have as one of their essential social characteristics the status of being citizens of a liberal society. They not only enter into social relationships with others that involve justice, freedom, and equality as underlying normative principles, but they also possess a special status as reasonable individuals by virtue of their capacity to reflectively engage with others in determining social and political arrangements for the societies of which they are members.

Kant himself ([1785] 1959) emphasized individuals' autonomy, arguing for the intrinsic value and moral dignity of individuals. Rawls ties individuals' autonomy to participation in society, and thus invests individuals with a value and dignity as social beings. Clearly the conception of the individual involved on either account is far removed from the narrow, socially isolated conception of the individual found in standard economics. We might conclude, then, by offering a final appraisal of what the concept of individualism can and ought to involve in social science and economics. An adequate concept of individualism, it seems fair to say, needs to comprehend individuals in the full range of aspects they exhibit and which concern them. This surely includes their natures as social and moral beings.

References

Agassi, Joseph (1975), 'Institutional individualism', *British Journal of Sociology*, **11** (3), 244–70.
Boland, Lawrence A. (2003), *The Foundations of Economic Method: A Popperian Perspective*, 2nd edition, London: Routledge.
Davis, John (2003), *The Theory of the Individual in Economics*, London: Routledge.
Elster, Jon (1982), 'Marxism, functionalism, and game theory', *Theory and Society*, **11** (4), 453–82.
Hayek, Friedrich (1955), *The Counter-Revolution in Science: Studies on the Abuse of Reason*, Glencoe, IL: Free Press.
Hodgson, Geoffrey (2007), 'Meanings of methodological individualism', *Journal of Economic Methodology*, **14** (2), 211–26.
Kant, Immanuel ([1785] 1959), *Grundlegung zur Metaphysik der Sitten* [Foundations of the Metaphysics of Morals], trans. Lewis White Beck, New York: Macmillan.
Kincaid, Harold (1997), *Individualism and the Unity of Science: Essays on Reduction, Explanation, and the Social Sciences*, Lanham, MD: Rowman and Littlefield.
Popper, Karl (1945), *The Open Society and its Enemies*, 2 vols, London: Routledge.
Rawls, John ([1971] 1999), *A Theory of Justice*, revised edition, Cambridge, MA: Harvard University Press.
Rawls, John (1980), 'Kantian constructivism in moral theory: the Dewey lectures 1980', *Journal of Philosophy*, **77** (September), 515–72.
Rawls, John (1993), *Political Liberalism*, New York: Columbia University Press.
Schumpeter, Joseph (1908), *Das Wesen und derHauptinhalt der theoretischen Nationalökonomie*, München and Leipzig: Duncker & Humblot.
Schumpeter, Joseph (1909), 'On the concept of social value', *Quarterly Journal of Economics*, **23** (2), 213–32.
Schumpeter, Joseph (1954), *History of Economic Analysis*, New York: Oxford University Press.
Sen, Amartya (1977), 'Rational fools: a critique of the behavioral foundations of economic theory', *Philosophy and Public Affairs*, **6**, 317–44.
Sen, Amartya (1999), *Development as Freedom*, New York: Knopf.
Smith, Adam ([1759] 1976), *The Theory of Moral Sentiments*, ed. D. Raphael and A. Macfie, Oxford: Clarendon Press.

See also the entries on: Homo economicus; Immanuel Kant; Rationality; John Rawls.

36   Inequality
Serge-Christophe Kolm

Introduction

When some people are treated more or less favourably than others without a seemingly valid reason, this inequality arouses a judgement of injustice which is conveyed in the term 'inequality'. Such inequalities are a major issue for judging societies or policies and are often compared across time or societies, in particular by the media and politicians. Such comparisons are a priori highly problematic, however, since given any two unequal distributions of some item, one can most of the time show that any one is more unequal than the other and the converse, with reasons, comparisons and measures which, a priori, may all seem convincing.

Does, for instance, growth tend to augment or diminish income inequality? Balanced growth followed by a fiscal partial redistribution of the gains diminishes inequality measured by ratios, but may augment inequality measured by differences. Inequality based on ratios is not changed when the pair 0.01 and 1 becomes the pair 0.1 and 10. Inequality based on differences is not changed when the pair 1 and 2 becomes the pair 11 and 12. Does a transfer from richer to poorer diminish inequality? It augments the pairwise inequalities between the richer and the still richer or equally rich and between the poorer and the still poorer and equally poor. One can pass from the income distribution of Australia to that of France (adjusted for population) by a sequence of such transfers, and yet Australia, with its large homogeneous middle class, seems a more egalitarian society.

During the first two-thirds of the twentieth century, scholars developed measures of inequality (Gini, Theil), and comparisons of distributions (Lorenz), and proposed reflections about the effects of transfers (Pigou, Dalton) and of variations in the same proportion (Dalton, Taussig), by the same amount (Dalton, Cannan, Loria), or in population size (Dalton).

After such considerations about dispersion with a vague feeling of injustice, a revolution in the rational ethical analysis of unjust inequality came with the last third of the twentieth century. It was opened by two remarks. First, *the effects of inequality and, notably, injustice are among the reasons for the overall ethical evaluation of a distribution, and they can be measured by the cost of inequality implied by this evaluation.* Second, *a number of important basic properties of the comparison of inequalities happen to be logically equivalent*, thus providing the basis of the modern ethico-logical analysis of economic inequalities.

The measures of economic inequality derived from overall ethical evaluations[1]

Overall ethical evaluation and inequality
The cost of inequality, notably of its injustice, is implicit in any overall ethical evaluation, and therefore its measure can be derived from this evaluation. However, the converse

view is also relevant. An overall ethical evaluation is the synthesis of moral judgements about the various relevant aspects and properties of a situation. One or some of these aspects or properties can concern inequality and in particular distributive injustice. Then, direct moral judgements about inequality matter. The overall judgement aggregates the various particular ones in a way that has to respect properties of consistency.

Consider the simplest and important case of the distribution of incomes – or any other desired quantity (other cases will be noted shortly). There are n individuals indexed by $i = 1, \ldots n$. Denote as x_i the income of individual i. A distribution is a set of n x_i, one for each individual i. Such a distribution is *equal* when all the x_i are equal. The sum $X = \Sigma x_i$ is the *total* or *social income*. The *average income* is $\bar{x} = X/n$. For an equal distribution, $x_i = \bar{x}$ for all i.

The overall ethical evaluation needs only be by judgements of better or worse. It is described by an ethical evaluation function $W(x_1, \ldots x_n)$ which takes a higher value when the distribution is considered to be better. The *nature* of this function is not further specified, and, hence, this function can be replaced by any increasing function of itself; that is, it is ordinal, and any increasing function of it is one of its specifications.

Moreover, we assume that the situation improves if one income increases while no other decreases, a property called the *benevolence* of the overall judgement. This translates as function W being an increasing function of the x_i.

Finally, the present concern about the ethics of inequality leads us to assume that all judgements relevant here about how to share a given total income X can be expressed through judgements about the inequality of the distribution.

The equal equivalent income
For the overall evaluation, a distribution can be replaced by any other that gives the same level to function W. In particular, it can be replaced by one such distribution which is also equal. The individual income of this latter distribution is called the *equal equivalent income* of the initial distribution, and it is classically denoted as $\bar{\bar{x}}$. It is therefore defined by the equality

$$W(x_1, \ldots x_n) = W(\bar{\bar{x}}, \ldots \bar{\bar{x}}). \tag{36.1}$$

This level $\bar{\bar{x}}$ is uniquely defined because function W is increasing (benevolence). Hence, the equal equivalent income of a distribution is the individual income of the equivalent equal distribution. It is the individual income such that, if all individuals had it, the resulting equal distribution would be as good as the distribution in question.

The equal equivalent income $\bar{\bar{x}}$ is a function of the distribution $(x_1, \ldots x_n)$ and of the function W (it is a 'functional' of function W). The expression $W = W(\bar{\bar{x}}, \ldots \bar{\bar{x}})$ shows that it is an increasing function of the value or level W. Hence, it is a particular specification of this ordinal evaluation function. Moreover, it has the nature of an individual income.

If the initial distribution $(x_1, \ldots x_n)$ is equal, $x_i = \bar{x}$ for all i, and hence, from equation (36.1), $\bar{\bar{x}} = \bar{x}$. If the evaluation function W has a specification of the form Σx_i, equation (36.1) writes $\Sigma x_i = n\bar{\bar{x}}$, and hence $\bar{\bar{x}} = \bar{x}$ again. This form of W implies that the ethical evaluation sees no injustice in any inequality resulting from the distribution of a total income $X = \Sigma x_i = n\bar{x}$.

The basic ethically derived indexes

If the inequality in the distribution $(x_1, \ldots x_n)$ is morally bad, in particular unjust, this implies that the equal sharing of the total income $X = \Sigma x_i$, the equal distribution $(\bar{x}, \ldots \bar{x})$, is better, that is

$$W(x_1, \ldots x_n) < W(\bar{x}, \ldots \bar{x}). \tag{36.2}$$

A discrepancy between these two values of function W measures a moral cost of inequality. Note that $\bar{x}$ is the equal equivalent income of the equal distribution $(\bar{x}, \ldots \bar{x})$. Inequality (36.2) also writes, given definition (36.1),

$$W(\bar{\bar{x}}, \ldots \bar{\bar{x}}) < W(\bar{x}, \ldots \bar{x}),$$

which implies $\bar{\bar{x}} < \bar{x}$. A cost is a difference between two values. Since function W is ordinal, a difference (or a ratio) in values of W is a priori not meaningful with respect to this property. However, the operation of difference (and ratio) is meaningful between quantities. It is, therefore, for the specification of W that is the equal equivalent $\bar{x}$. Hence, the difference $\bar{x} - \bar{\bar{x}}$ is a cost in income term of the inequality of distribution $(x_1, \ldots x_n)$. However, the cost can also be expressed in relative terms, by ratios, or for the whole population, as expressed by the following six classical meaningful indexes:

$I^a = \bar{x} - \bar{\bar{x}}$: *absolute* (per person) *inequality*;
$I^t = nI^a = X - n\bar{\bar{x}}$: *total inequality*;
$I^r = I^a/\bar{x} = I^t/X = 1 - (\bar{\bar{x}}/\bar{x})$: *income relative inequality*;
$I^e = I^a/\bar{\bar{x}} = I^t/n\bar{\bar{x}} = (\bar{x}/\bar{\bar{x}}) - 1$: *equal equivalent income relative inequality*;
$\eta = \bar{\bar{x}}/\bar{x} = 1 - I^r$: the *equal equivalent yield* of the distribution;
$\gamma = \bar{x}/\bar{\bar{x}} = 1 + I^e$: the *unit cost of the equal equivalent income*.

Each of these six indexes is a priori meaningful and it turns out to be the relevant one for specific questions met in the theoretical and applied analyses of inequality.

If the distribution is equal, or if Σx_i is a specification of the evaluation function W, $\bar{\bar{x}} = \bar{x}$, $I^a = I^t = I^r = I^e = 0$, and $\eta = \gamma = 1$. With an unequal distribution and a cost of inequality, $\bar{\bar{x}} < \bar{x}$, $I^a > 0$, $I^t > 0$, $I^r > 0$, $I^e > 0$, $\eta < 1$, $\gamma > 1$. With an extreme inequality-aversion, the smallest of the x_i, $\min_i x_i$, is a specification of function W, then $\bar{\bar{x}} = \min_i x_i$, and the six indexes have the corresponding values.[2] For the general function W, each index is between these two limiting values.[3,4]

Elementary properties

When the evaluation function W has a certain structure shortly noted – which is in particular satisfied if it has specifications of the form $\Sigma f(x_i)$ where function f is increasing and concave (it increases less and less when x_i increases by successive equal amounts) – the foregoing ethical evaluation-consistent measures of inequality classify distributions according to a comparison which has a number of other remarkable properties; for example, a transfer from a richer person to a poorer one of less than half the difference in their incomes diminishes inequality, the Lorenz curve of a distribution of a given total income is above that of another, and a number of other meaningful ways to compare inequalities. Before showing these properties, let us note a few more elementary properties that will be used.

A distribution to two persons ($n = 2$) (x'_1, x'_2) is *inclusion more equal* (more equal by inclusion) than another (x_1, x_2) if x'_1 and x'_2 are between x_1 and x_2, with the possibility that x'_1 or x'_2 is equal to x_1 or x_2 if the other is not also equal to the other x_1 or x_2 (a strict inclusion of the segments between the two incomes).

Comparisons are *constant-sum* when they compare distributions with the same total X or average $\bar{x}$ (for a given number n).

If, when only a subset of the x_i changes, a comparison of the distributions does not depend on the levels of the other, unchanging x_i, this comparison for $n > 2$ is said to be *independent* (or separable). Independence for the overall evaluation occurs if and only if a specification of the ordinal function W has the additive form $\Sigma f_i(x_i)$.[5]

If the incomes x_i are the only characteristics that relevantly differentiate the individuals for the problem at hand, the comparisons or measures are unchanged if the x_i are permuted (*invariance under permutations*). The corresponding functions – such as W – are *symmetrical* (by definition of the term). Note that this implies in particular that peoples' different specific tastes, needs, utilities, other possibilities and so on are found not to be relevant. In particular, such a W cannot be a classical social welfare function depending on individuals' utilities since individuals' utility functions are a priori different.[6] If it means 'welfare', this is welfare evaluated otherwise, by a judgement not following the individuals' evaluations of their own welfare, and the meaning of this concept has to be explained (which has not been done yet). However, we will consider a property that holds for all such judgements having some general properties. This symmetry is assumed in this simple presentation, but the cases in which it is not relevant have been studied. Symmetry plus independence of the function W hold if and only if it has a specification of the form $\Sigma f(x_i)$.

The core moral logic of economic inequalities

The basic ethical comparisons of economic inequalities

The transfer principle   A *progressive transfer* is a transfer from a higher income to a lower one of less than the difference (or not higher than half the difference). The *transfer principle* proposes that a progressive transfer diminishes inequality.

The transfer principle can be justified by the assumption that the unchanged incomes are irrelevant for the comparison and, given that the progressive transfer maintains the total sum constant, either the fact that it inclusion-reduces the inequality between the changing incomes, or the assumption that the increase in the poorer person's 'welfare' overcompensates the decrease in the richer's 'welfare', for amounts which are equal (concavity of the function f in an additive evaluation $\Sigma f(x_i)$).

'Social welfare'   If the overall evaluation of the distribution is both separable-independent and symmetrical, the ordinal function W has specifications of the form $\Sigma f(x_i)$. This cannot describe classical utilitarianism $\Sigma u_i(x_i)$ because the same function f applies to all x_i.[7] If this refers to 'welfare', this is a concept different from the individuals' evaluations of their own welfare. This raises two questions: what can this evaluation mean, and what

can it be? The second question is in part eschewed by the consideration of comparisons that holds for *all* functions f that are increasing (benevolence) and concave. This latter property means that an extra euro increases evaluation or 'welfare' more the lower the income to which it is added. It also is a property of 'satiation' in the evaluation or 'welfare' effect of individual income.

Concentration curve and Lorenz curve dominances   Denote as y_m the sum of the m lowest x_i. That is, if the numbering i of the x_i are rearranged in such a way that the new x_i are in a non-decreasing order ($x_1 \leq x_2 \leq \ldots \leq x_n$, that is, $i > j$ implies $x_i \geq x_j$), y_m is $y_m = \Sigma_{i=1}^{m} x_i$. Then, $y_n = \Sigma x_i = X$, the total amount.

Elementary textbooks of statistics call the curve of the y_m as function of m (or of m/n) the *concentration curve* of the distribution of the x_i.

The Lorenz curve of this distribution is y_m/X as a function of m/n.

When the x_i are all equal, these two curves are straight lines with these x_i and 1 as respective slopes.

A curve is said to be above another when it is somewhere above and nowhere below.

A distribution *concentration-dominates* another when its concentration curve is above that of the other, that is, for distributions $(x_1, \ldots x_n)$ and $(x'_1, \ldots x'_n)$, $y_m \geq y'_m$ for all m and $y_m > y'_m$ for at least one m. *Lorenz-domination* is similarly defined for Lorenz curves. Both comparisons coincide when comparing distributions with the same total $X = X'$, that is, in 'constant-sum comparisons'. Then, a preference for a higher concentration or Lorenz curve is called isophily (*isophilia* is the Greek term for inequality-aversion).

Averaging   A distribution is in a sense less dispersed than another if all its items are averages of those of the other. Distribution $(x'_1, \ldots x'_n)$ is a (linear convex) average of distribution $(x_1, \ldots x_n)$ when $x'_i = \Sigma_j a_{ij} x_j$ with $a_{ij} \geq 0$ for all i and j and $\Sigma_j a_{ij} = 1$ for all i. If the total sums are equal $X = X'$, notably for a redistribution, this implies the last equality of

$$\Sigma x'_i = \Sigma_{i,j} a_{ij} x_j = \Sigma_j (\Sigma_i a_{ij}) x_j = \Sigma_j x_j,$$

and therefore

$$\Sigma_j (1 - \Sigma_i a_{ij}) x_j = 0.$$

We consider such transformations that are independent of the initial distribution (the a_{ij} do not depend on the x_k), and applicable to all distributions. The foregoing identity then implies $\Sigma_i a_{ij} = 1$ for all j. Such a_{ij} constitute a *bistochastic matrix*, that is, a non-negative matrix whose sums of the elements in each row and in each column amount to 1. This transformation of x into x' is an *averaging*.

If $a_{ii} = 1$ for all i (hence $a_{ij} = 0$ if $i \neq j$), $x'_i = x_i$ for all i, nothing is changed, the transformation is an identity. If all a_{ij} are only zero or one, the transformation is a permutation of the x_i. If $a_{ij} = 1/n$ for all i, j, $x'_i = \bar{x}$ for all i (a 'complete averaging'). If, for $0 \leq \alpha \leq 1$, $a_{ij} = \alpha/n$ for all i, j with $i \neq j$ and $a_{ii} = 1 - \alpha + \alpha/n$ for all i, $x'_i = (1 - \alpha)x_i + \alpha\bar{x} = x_i + \alpha \cdot (\bar{x} - x_i)$ for all i. This is a *concentration* of the x_i (a uniform linear concentration towards the mean): each x'_i is an average between x_i and the mean $\bar{x}$, it goes the same fraction α

of the way towards the mean; the concentration amounts to an equal redistribution of the same fraction α of the x_i; it amounts to a decrease of all incomes in the same proportion followed by an increase of the same amount (which restores the total amount). A progressive transfer is a particular averaging: if $x_i > x_j$, $0 < t < 1$, $a_{ii} = a_{jj} = 1 - t$, $a_{ij} = a_{ji} = t$, $a_{kk} = 1$ for all $k \neq i, j$, and $a_{kl} = 0$ for the other entries, $x'_i = x_i - t \cdot (x_i - x_j)$, $x'_j = x_j + t \cdot (x_i - x_j)$, and $x'_k = x_k$ for all $k \neq i, j$. Of course, if all the x_i are equal, all the x'_i are also equal to them. Moreover, an averaging of an averaging is an averaging.

Share reshuffling   Divide each individual income into a series of shares, each share being the same fraction of the income for all incomes. Then, reshuffle the shares corresponding to the same proportion among the individuals, that is, perform a permutation of these shares among them. The permutations of the shares for the various fractions are unrelated. Formally, consider numbers $\lambda_k > 0$ with $\Sigma \lambda_k = 1$, and permute the shares of each k, $\lambda_k x_i$, among the individuals i, with independent permutations.

Mixtures   Denote as $x = \{x_i\}$ the vector of the incomes x_i. A permuted vector of x is x^π obtained by permuting the x_i of x by the n-permutation π (i.e., $x^\pi_i = x_{\pi(i)}$ for all i). The absence of relevant individual characteristics other than their incomes x_i implies that the x^π are equivalent. Then, a *mixture* of a distribution x is an average (a linear convex combination) of the x^π, $x' = \Sigma_\pi \lambda_\pi x^\pi$ with $\lambda_\pi \geq 0$ for all π and $\Sigma \lambda_\pi = 1$.

Since, in share reshuffling, if one writes π_k the permutation corresponding to share k, the result is $x' = \Sigma \lambda_k x^{\pi_k}$, mixtures and share reshuffling are clearly equivalent (each instance of one in an instance of the other). These transformations are not permutations when $\lambda_\pi \neq 1$ for all π for a mixture, and, for a share reshuffling, $\lambda_k \neq 1$ for all k (hence, there are at least two shares) and the permutations of the shares are not all identical.

A transformation that is not, in fact, a permutation is called *strict*.

The fundamental equivalences of ethical inequality comparisons
Each of these properties has a flavour of comparing more or less unequal distributions. Their meaning in this respect is very strongly reinforced by the fact that they are mathematically equivalent.

Indeed, when comparing 2 distributions $x = (x_1, \ldots x_n)$ and $x' = (x'_1, \ldots x'_n)$ with the same amount $X = X'$, the following properties are equivalent.

(1) x' can be obtained from x by a sequence of progressive transfers.
(2)   The concentration or Lorenz curve of x' is above that of x.
(3) $\Sigma f(x') > \Sigma f(x)$ for all increasing and strictly concave functions f.
(4) x' is a strict averaging of x.
(5) x' results from a strict share reshuffling of x.
(6) x' is a strict mixture of x.

Moreover, if the distributions can have different amounts, say $X' \geq X$, the following properties are equivalent.

(1) X' can be obtained from X by a sequence of progressive transfers or increases in incomes.

(2) $\Sigma f(x'_i) > \Sigma f(x_i)$ for all increasing strictly concave functions f.
(3) The concentration curve of distribution x' is above that of distribution x.

Clearly, these relations cannot be both ways between two distributions; if they hold from x to x' and from x' to x'', they hold from x to x'' (transitivity). They thus constitute an ordering of the distributions. For distributions with the same total amount, this is an important sense of comparisons by more or less unequal. Yet, they do not compare all distributions: they do not compare them when their concentration curves intersect. Other criteria can then be added.

An evaluation function $W(x)$, increasing, symmetrical and such that $W(x') > W(x)$ when x' relates to x as in the preceding relations, and the corresponding ethical evaluation-consistent inequality indexes, are called *rectifiant*, or, respectively, Schur-concave and Schur-convex[8] (the functions $\Sigma f(x_i)$ with increasing and concave f constitute a sub-class of such functions).

Finally, there are types of redistributions or transformations of distributions that are more inequality-reducing structures than the others. The two polar cases of the particularly inequality-reducing transformations are the *concentrations* in which all incomes diminish their distance to the mean in the same proportion, and *truncations* in which all incomes above a level are reduced to this level and all below a lower level are augmented to this level. Both have important applications in normative economics – this is notably the case for concentrations in the theory of optimum distribution, taxation and aid.

Inequality under co-variations of incomes
The foregoing mainly emphasizes the effects of transfers or redistributions on inequality, hence comparisons of the inequality of distributions with the same total amount. However, cases in which all incomes vary in the same direction are also important. Does general growth, or an equal distribution of a benefit or a charge, augment or diminish inequality? This depends on the relevant concept of inequality.

The two polar cases are those in which inequality does not change when all incomes vary in the same proportion and by the same amount, respectively. In the former case, inequality is what the sciences call an *intensive* property. In the latter case, inequality is said to be *equal-invariant*.

Measures of inequality derived from a separable evaluation that are *intensive* are the *relative* inequality with a *power* or a *logarithmic* individual welfare function ($f(x_i) = x_i^\alpha$ with $\alpha > 0$, or $\log x_i$), and those that are *equal-invariant* are the *absolute* inequality with an *exponential* individual welfare function ($f(x_i) = 1 - e^{-\beta x_i}$, $\beta > 0$). One consequence is that one cannot derive both an intensive and an equal-invariant measure of inequality from the same separable ethical evaluation.

Nevertheless, there is another class of measures of inequality, the *synthetic* measures, with an absolute form $I^a(x)$ and a relative form $I^r(x) = I^a(x)/\bar{x}$, such that the relative form is intensive and the absolute form is equal-invariant. One consequence is that the absolute form is also 'extensive', that is, multiplied by a scalar when all incomes are. These absolute forms are the linearly homogeneous functions of the differences $(x_i - \bar{x})$ or $(x_i - x_j)$. They include some of the most common measures of inequality such as the Gini index $\Sigma|x_i - x_j|$, $\Sigma|x_i - \bar{x}|$, or the standard deviation.

Moreover, one can derive, from a separable ethical evaluation, measures of inequality that are intermediate between the intensive and the equal-invariant measures. The simplest case is the 'income-augmented' intensive measures, which apply the intensive measures to new variables that are the incomes plus a non-negative constant. The measures are intensive when the constant is zero and equal-invariant when it tends to infinity.

For intensive or equal-invariant measures, one can reduce the comparison of the inequality of two distributions to constant-sum comparisons by respectively multiplying or increasing all the incomes of one of the distributions by the same number.

Conclusion

The foregoing properties constitute only the basics of the standard economic theory of unjust inequality. Many other properties are added. In particular, they describe the effects on this inequality of: transfers depending on the levels of or differences in incomes; the addition of several types of incomes to the same people; the aggregation of populations with intra-group and inter-group inequalities; growth; the income tax; characteristics which may relevantly differentiate the persons such as needs, size and type of family, labour provided, merit or desert, or various rights; judgements that violate the transfer principle, for instance because they attach importance to clusters of incomes (size of income classes); and so on.

The theory then considers the inequalities in other items than income or a single quantity, notably the multidimensional inequalities in a bundle of goods (to begin with in both income and labour or leisure, or in income, health, education and housing); inequalities in various types of freedom, power or opportunities; inequalities in ranks or status; and so on.

The nature of the items often implies particular properties of the comparison and measures of inequality. This happens even with the simplest case of quantities. For instance, if health is measured by the duration of life, it may be, on average, better to die at 35 rather than at 34 than to die not only at 95 rather than at 94 (concavity of the function f), but also at 5 rather than at 4 (non-concavity of f).

In other cases, the basic reference is not equality but some other particular distribution. For instance, it might be the outcome of markets, which has a possible moral justification from freedom of exchange (or self-ownership). In this case, the relevant concept is the degree of equalization achieved by redistributions from this state. For example, present-day redistributions at national levels are equivalent, in this respect, to fully equalizing the incomes from the labour of one to two days per week. Such durations turn out to be richly meaningful measures of the degree of equalization or solidarity in the community.

Finally, the issue of inequality is very closely related, both in fact and in analyses, to other very important economic and social phenomena such as poverty, polarization, segmentation, clusters, class or caste structure, exclusion, isolation, eliticism, envy, status, and so on.

The literature on economic inequality is very large and cannot be presented here. For interested readers, Silber (1999) offers an excellent bibliographical source.

Notes

1. The rest of this presentation of the basic properties of economic inequality consists of a simplified version of Kolm (1966, sections 6 and 7).

2. This particular W is no longer strictly increasing in all its arguments.
3. Further concepts have been defined when the overall evaluation is such that, for some distributions, $\bar{\bar{x}} >$ $\bar{x}$.
4. In a didactic and influential article, Atkinson (1970) also considered the equal equivalent income $\bar{\bar{x}}$ (the 'equally distributed equivalent income') and the relative measure I^r.
5. It suffices that the independence property holds when only a properly chosen set of subsets of the x_i changes, which can be reduced to $n - 1$ subsets, or to all pairs of x_i, or to $n - 1$ chosen pairs.
6. Justifying the symmetry of such a function by a lack of information about individual utilities is possible but analytically delicate (see Kolm in Silber 1999).
7. However, this additive form is the case where the remark of note 6 applies.
8. After I. Schur whose articles of 1922, 1923 and 1936 first considered the effects of the transfer principle and averaging on such functions (rectifiance means, more generally, the satisfaction of the transfer principle whether the functions are symmetrical or not).

References

Atkinson, Anthony B. (1970), 'On the measurement of inequality', *Journal of Economic Theory*, **2**, 224–63.
Kolm, Serge-Christophe (1966), 'The optimal production of social justice', in H. Guitton and J. Margolis (eds), *Proceedings of the International Economic Association Conference on Public Economics, Biarritz*; *Economie Publique*, Paris: CNRS, 1968, pp. 109–77; *Public Economics*, London: Macmillan, 1969, pp. 145–200.
Silber, Jacques (ed.) (1999), *Handbook on Income Inequality Measurement*, Boston, MA: Kluwer Academic Publishers.

See also the entries on: Income distribution; Justice.

37 Institutions
Anne Mayhew

Institutions are regular patterns of human activity and their attendant norms, folkviews, understandings and justifications. The original institutional approach to the study of economies followed from the observation that human activity varies, not idiosyncratically but rather in regular patterns across time and space. These patterns reflect inherited norms, which are themselves generated through time and by complex interactions between active human agents with cultural inheritances facing a variety of ecological systems. Human activity, as viewed by institutionalists, cannot be explained by simple recourse to human nature. While the biological nature of humans affects human activity in a variety of important ways, it does not determine it, for if it did, and granting a high degree of biological similarity across populations, there would be little variation. Nor can variation be accounted for by variation in exogenously determined constraints and incentives, for the important constraints and incentives are themselves largely institutional and therefore not exogenous to social systems.

This chapter considers how this original, and still very important, approach to the study of human institutions is related to ethics, or the science of morals. The focus is on the original institutional approach, which is closely related to the pragmatic approach in philosophy. As will be noted later, a variety of rather different approaches have come to be grouped under the rubric 'new institutional economics', sometimes identified as NIE as opposed to OIE or 'original institutional economics'. While the chapter gives some attention to NIE approaches, most is devoted to OIE.[1]

The study of institutions necessarily involves the study of both ethics and morals, though neither need be central to description. The institutions that concern economists are always embedded in a larger social system. For many analytical purposes it suffices to offer descriptions of patterns of behaviour without giving consideration to either the larger context or to the ethical systems involved. To illustrate, consider the case of an institutionalist approach to the study of changing patterns of expenditure for in-home entertainment. Such an approach could involve the simple observation that households spend a larger share of their entertainment outlays than they once did on leisure-time activities enjoyed within the household unit.

Such a simple observation could also lead to the conclusion that households value in-home entertainment more highly now than in the past or that in-home entertainment is more easily and cheaply available, which may lead to further conclusions about the cumulative effects of decreased extra-household social interaction. The analysis leading to such conclusions is complex and carries with it a variety of difficult issues. How do new patterns of behaviour emerge? At one level it may suffice to say that increased expenditures on in-home entertainment are a response to relative declines in prices of in-home equipment and the availability of movies, television and music of many kinds in combination with substantial improvements in the quality of such equipment. However, that leads to other questions: why did firms emphasize such improvements and cost reductions?

Did the values and norms that made stay-at-home movie and television watching and an emphasis on music as a source of entertainment for the young lead to product innovation and marketing, or vice versa? What is the role of human agency in the process? Did individuals, quite independently of one another, and of the effects of advertising and peer pressure, want to substitute in-home television watching for going out to live performances or group viewing? Did they, by similar individualistic process, want to reduce participation time in games of charades and amateur theatricals, in musical performances, or in group sports in order to watch more? These are questions that, when couched in more general terms, are fundamental to modern social science and about which much has been written.

For the purposes of this chapter, it suffices to repeat that the use of the institutional approach, an approach rooted in the broader traditions of modern social science, will lead in the case just cited to the conclusion that a combination of new technologies, themselves a product of social norms and technical discovery, plus changing patterns of human interaction and expectation, are involved in an ongoing process of social evolution. The institutional approach necessarily involves, therefore, the study of morals, of what it is right and wrong to do, of norms of behaviour and of the larger ethical systems of which the norms and morals are part. In our example, the observation that people spend more time and money on passive in-home entertainment than they once did may lead to conclusions about norms of human interaction and changing values given to face-to-face human interaction. This may lead, in turn, to analysis of a changing ethical system in which civic good is given relatively less importance, and individual and family-unit satisfaction becomes predominant.

Whether such conclusions about moral and ethical patterns and changes therein also and legitimately lead to ethical evaluation of these changes by the analyst is quite another question. Is more emphasis on individual and family-unit satisfaction, as opposed to a wider sharing of experience, a bad thing? Such valuations according to an ethical system that may or may not be the same as that of those being studied, and the choice of ethical system to be used, are highly controversial. It is to this topic that the remainder of this chapter is devoted.

Those who, in the late nineteenth and early twentieth centuries, adopted the institutionalist approach differentiated what they did from the work of other economists by their explicit commitment to both socioeconomic reform and to dispassionate study and description of human activities (Rutherford 2001, especially pp. 177–8; Mitchell 1924, p. 25). The apparent conflict between advocacy of reform and scientific description did not loom large for these institutionalists, largely because they worked primarily within one country, the United States, and on what were generally agreed by the broader public as well as academicians to be problems (Rutherford 2001, p. 183). There was also broad agreement on desired outcomes. Under these circumstances it seemed quite possible to be both a dispassionate social scientist describing, let us say, rate-setting by utilities, and at the same time an advocate for reform of public utility regulation.

The original institutional economists could also reconcile dispassionate study with advocacy of reform because the pervasive pragmatic and progressive ideas of the time treated reform always as a provisional solution to time and place-specific problems within a larger context of an ongoing and reiteratively defined ethical system. For example, trusts and business combinations were widely agreed to be a problem in early twentieth century America and 'social control' was a solution that could be explored by the institutional economists, acting as social scientists to understand price and output decisions and as reformers offering regulatory guidelines.[2] There was no need, and indeed it would have been foolish, to claim any proposed solution would be more than temporary. The ethical template that guided reform was ever changing.

With the collapse of the progressive and pragmatic framework within which they worked prior to World War II, the original institutional economists were faced with increasing moral and ethical certainty among non-institutional economists and the abandonment of a reform agenda by their social science colleagues. After the 1960s, the majority of economists came increasingly to accept a system of self-regulating markets as both natural to humankind and as productive of the best and most ethical solutions possible. Even though the ethical implications of accepting unregulated, or more accurately, self-regulated, markets as determining a wide variety of outcomes is a strong position, the assumption that markets are part of humankind's nature, and so beyond cultural variation, allowed these economists to assert markets as ethically neutral.

The most widely recognized loyal opposition to this neoclassical belief in the sanctity and efficiency of markets was some form of Marxian analysis, with either implicit or explicit acceptance of the idea of a definably just distribution, the attainment of which would lead to appropriately ethical consequences in all matters economic. For both the neoclassical and Marxian economists, the ethical systems that guided policy recommendations were fixed and certain. What could the increasingly marginalized progressive pragmatists offer that would measure up?

The lack of ethical certainty in their own approach led some who followed in the tradition of the original institutional economists to create a fixed ethical template of their own through reinterpretations of the work of Thorstein Veblen. Veblen had been heavily influenced by his study with the pragmatist philosopher, Charles Sanders Peirce. But in his own work he emphasized the role that enhanced understanding of how to manipulate the physical world had played and could play in enabling humankind to manage life more satisfactorily. Situated against the 'idle curiosity' that led humans to learn more and more about their world, there was an opposing tendency to structure life in inherited ways, ways that most often served to preserve differential status and hierarchy. Acquisition of knowledge of the physical could and did erode inherited socio-economic patterns, but the dualism between learning (via idle curiosity) and preservation of past ways was always present. Veblen returned over and over to this dualism and often used it in his harsh attacks on the world as it was. Despite that, and as Warren Samuels has argued most effectively, Veblen turned his own criticisms of the world in which he lived back onto his equally strong insistence that his understanding of humans and their systems gave him no basis for doing anything other than expressing an opinion derived from his own cultural context (Samuels 1990). In being self-referential in this manner, Veblen was, of course, a good pragmatist.

In the post-World War II era, as pragmatism was in decline, Veblen's self-referential approach was put into an eclipse of its own. The 'Veblenian dichotomy' was invoked to create a fixed ethical template, one based in many ways on the same ideas used by the technocratic movement of the 1920s and 1930s that also claimed Veblen as progenitor. The leading advocate of a fixed ethical standard was Marc Tool who offered a 'social value principle' that might stand as an alternative to Pareto optimality as a meta-systemic standard of value for economists (1986). Writing as what he called a neo-institutionalist,

Tool suggested that institutional patterns, and their suggested reform, should be judged by whether they served to ensure 'the continuity of human life and the noninvidious re-creation of community through the instrumental use of knowledge' (Tool 1986, p. 50).

The difficulty with this principle, as pointed out by many who considered themselves advocates of the original institutional approach, was that the meaning of 'noninvidious', 'community', and 'instrumental' varied with change of institutional context, so that the principle would amount, over time, or across different cultural settings, to little more than a requirement to 'do good'. In his discussion of the self-referential nature of Veblen's work, Samuels quotes Veblen's student, Wesley Mitchell: 'it is naïve to fancy that what is common sense to us will appeal as common sense to later generations. This is the most dazzlingly disconcerting of Veblen's insights – the hardest to live with, but also the most enlightening' (Samuels 1990, p. 714).

Many who have chosen the hard route and remained pragmatic in their approach to ethical standards have followed the example offered by John R. Commons. Commons came to the institutionalist approach by way of his interest in law and social reform. His focus was on conflict and its resolution. For Commons, the common good was to be found in resort to an agreed-upon system of dispute resolution, which is to say, reliance on a form of due process (Ramstad 1989). In this, Commons shared much with legal scholars of his era. Like Veblen, Commons offered no description of Utopian outcomes, nor did he see an end to recurring conflict between groups, but unlike Veblen he did suggest Western legal practice as a model for dispute resolution.

As noted earlier, over the past few decades a new institutional approach has surfaced and become important. This new approach combines aspects of the original institutional economics with neoclassicism. The definition of institutions is, on the surface at least, largely the same for both groups, but the new institutional economists have generally been marked by the claim of superiority over original institutional economics by virtue of a focus on intentionality. Rather than emphasizing the role of inheritance of norms, the new institutional economists describe the institutions of their focus as chosen by people via the same natural human process that is alleged to constitute the markets of a self-regulating market system. That is, individuals, and the organizations they create within a given set of institutions, act so as to achieve the highest 'payoff' (this is Douglass North's term) in a world of changing opportunities and constraints (see North 2005, Ch. 5; Jones 2006; Williamson 2000). The outcomes are like the outcomes of markets for products in that they are 'natural', and this in general allows new institutional economists to adopt the same stance of ethical neutrality adopted by the neoclassical economists, who content themselves with studying corn and hog markets. That is, in the absence of 'frictions' that prevent adaptation to changing circumstances, the results of the market process will be the best that can be reasonably achieved.[3]

An important difference between the new and original institutional traditions is precisely the ethical neutrality of the former and the continuing impulse to advocate for reform of the latter. Among those drawn to the new institutional economics there is a strong tendency to be suspicious of collective action (unless organized within business firms) as a way to achieve more ethical economic outcomes; among the original institutional economists the tendency was exactly the opposite. Recognition that institutions are made by humans meant that institutions could be changed by humans and the route to desirable (which is to say ethically sound) change was through collective action.

So among those institutionalists who persist in the OIE mission to develop and advocate for reform, the difficulty of establishing a secure ethical template is most troublesome. These economists share the dilemma of other social scientists, most particularly anthropologists. In fact, the programmatic and progressive context in which the original institutional economics developed was the same context in which the cultural relativism that is most often associated with the discipline of anthropology came into existence. Before World War II anthropologists studied relatively small and isolated groups of humans and came to see the 'cultures' of these groups, which is to say the entire set of interrelated institutional patterns, as understandable only within the framework of the society involved. The ideas and evaluative principles of the anthropologist came from a different society and could not be imported, via ethical judgement, into another culture without either excess hubris or recourse to a cross-culturally valid principle. Also, there was general scepticism about whether cross-culturally valid principles could stand the test of scientific scrutiny. This scepticism was born of and supported by the variety of human societies that anthropologists documented. The scepticism about cross-culturally valid principles was closely related to the same pragmatic attitude that original institutional economists had towards ethical principles across time in their own societies.

In the post-war world, and even among those who found it difficult to accept any of the available bases for absolute ethical standards, such scepticism has been difficult to justify. Truly isolated groups of humans are now extremely rare, and as individuals even in relatively isolated areas may have many contacts with groups in other parts of the world, functionalism and cultural relativism are harder to justify and indeed have come under fierce attack by those who accuse anthropologists of an earlier generation of idle indifference to human suffering and abuse. Indeed, murder, torture and mutilation have a cross-cultural reality that is hard to ignore.

The difficulty of defining appropriate boundaries for the ethical systems of analysts is made all the more complex by the fact that modern technology and science, which do offer solutions, if not perfect ones, to worldwide problems, have to date been most fully developed and associated with the West. How in the real world of medicine or hydrology or agronomy or any of the other practices that take Western scientists into communities not immediately their own, do these scientists ply their trade without trespassing into ethical areas without scientific warrant? Should a physician practising in a cultural context, whether in the United States or elsewhere, insist upon inoculations, transfusions or other practices condemned by some religious practice? Even as technology and science have enabled us to solve many of the world's problems, there is also growing recognition of the cultural embeddings of science and of the wide range of unexpected consequences of some solutions. Dams, such as the Aswan High Dam, built to control waterflow have done that but have also caused fish stocks to be depleted and soils to be damaged. Even as Western confidence in the wisdom of scientific and technological solutions has eroded, recognition that scientific knowledge is driven by differential power among Western groups has increased. Civil engineers, mid-western farmers, lobbies for some diseases all affect scientific effort and the development of solutions and their advocates.

In an important sense, the problem of finding appropriate ethical foundations for institutional reform go back to pre-World War II tension between those who looked to the experts (to the 'engineers' to use Veblen's phrase) for guidance and those who stressed the role of communal decision-making. For Commons, communal decision-making was crucial; Veblen often veered towards an emphasis on the role of the expert, and certainly his followers have done so. If you think that the greatest good is more likely to be achieved through community decision-making, then 'local' values and ethical systems have greater weight. If greater stress is put on the importance of expert knowledge in achieving the greatest good, then there is more ethical justification in overriding the local.

The quest for ethical standards by which to resolve this dilemma reveals a similar duality. Standards based on expertise may be derived from religious authority or from some form of analytical or scientific understanding that justifies authoritative answers to human problems. All have the advantage of giving definite answers, but the ethics of transporting such definite answers across cultural boundaries or through time can be seriously questioned. On the other hand, standards based on community acceptance have the advantage that they do not transgress local standards but they may exclude relevant and legitimate expert knowledge. Also, as the meaning of 'community' has become less clear with today's increased international communication and mobility, it is not at all clear what it means to say that 'community acceptance' should be a guide. What is the community of the young woman facing genital mutilation? Is it her tribal group? Or women everywhere who condemn the practice?

For those who work in the OIE tradition and who remain interested in both description and reform, the pragmatism of the early twentieth century seems to offer the best solution. That solution may now be restated explicitly: at any time and in every place institutions, which is to say the patterns of human activity and the set of ideas, symbols, norms and folkviews involved in those patterns, are those inherited from the past. People do, however, learn. They are curious and have opposable thumbs and the capacity for language. Over human history they have learned to manipulate the physical world and to transmit their knowledge. The experts in such manipulation, the scientists and engineers, can offer solutions to a variety of problems such as how to produce more things, how to prevent disease and how to grow more rice on one hectare. These scientists and engineers are also always part of a cultural context and carry with them cultural attitudes and values that are in addition to, and may even contradict, their scientific and engineering knowledge. For this reason and because change in any one part of the social fabric will produce additional change, some of which may be deemed desirable and some not, scientific and technological solutions to problems should be adopted with communal involvement. However, communities can no longer so easily be geographically defined and conflicts may arise. The only resolution for such conflicts that can be offered from the OIE perspective is the use of a mechanism (due process let us say) that allows all to be heard in the process of arriving at a decision.

To return to the example with which this chapter began, economists working from the OIE perspective would suggest that the combination of cheap in-house technologies for entertainment and the evolving individual and family-centred lives that such technologies have engendered raise serious ethical issues for modern societies. They would, however, resist the temptation to denounce these patterns and insist instead on the need for a wide conversation about both the effects and solutions to the changes produced.

The pragmatic answer to ethical dilemmas is, as Wesley Mitchell said, a hard one to live with, for it reduces the comfort of moral certainty. Yet, if one accepts the basic premise about institutions – that institutions are patterns of human activity that guide virtually all of what we do as humans, patterns that change over time and space – there seems no other answer possible. Institutional analysis necessarily involves the study of morals and of ethical systems, but those adopting the institutional approach will, and also necessarily, avoid becoming applied ethicists.

Notes

1. In OIE, institutions and a range of related concepts, such as mores, norms, habits, conventions and rules are defined largely through methods of study, which for OIE have been primarily descriptively statistical, ethnographic or historical. In NIE much attention has been given to definition of terms to allow their use in the largely deductive discourses of neoclassical economics, which has tended to be closely related to NIE, and now especially in game theory. In the OIE spirit in which this essay is written, I make no further effort at precise definition of terms.
2. James Kloppenberg (1986) presents this case in much fuller detail.
3. In his most recent book (2005), Douglass North, in a chapter entitled 'Getting it Right and Getting it Wrong', is not optimistic about the ability of humans to 'get it right' precisely because of frictions resulting from inadequate information and information processing and because 'dominant organizations' will try, usually effectively, to maintain the status quo. What is interesting is that 'getting it right', for North, is getting a relatively frictionless market system in place for institutional choice and change.

References

Jones, Eric L. (2006), *Cultures Merging: A Historical and Economic Critique of Culture*, Princeton, NJ and Oxford: Princeton University Press.

Kloppenberg, James T. (1986), *Uncertain Victory: Social Democracy and Progressivism in European and American Thought, 1870–1920*, New York: Oxford University Press.

Mitchell, Wesley C. (1924), 'The prospects of economics', in Rexford Guy Tugwell (ed.), *The Trend of Economics*, New York: Alfred A. Knopf.

North, Douglass C. (2005), *Understanding the Process of Economic Change*, Princeton, NJ and Oxford: Princeton University Press.

Ramstad, Yngve (1989), '"Reasonable value" vs. "instrumental value"', *Journal of Economic Issues*, **23** (3), 761–77.

Rutherford, Malcolm (2001), 'Institutional economics: then and now', *Journal of Economic Perspectives*, **15** (3), 173–94.

Samuels, Warren (1990), 'The self-referentiability of Thorstein Veblen's theory of the preconceptions of economic science', *Journal of Economic Issues*, **24** (3), 695–718.

Tool, Marc R. (1986), *Essay in Social Value Theory*, Armonk, NY: M.E. Sharpe.

Williamson, Oliver E. (2000), 'The new institutional economics: taking stock, looking ahead', *Journal of Economic Literature*, **38** (September), 595–613.

See also the entries on: Positive versus normative economics; Thorstein Veblen.

38 Islam
Rodney Wilson

Islamic economists are credited with taking an ethical approach to the subject of economics, emphasizing social justice and equality. These writers are producing a growing volume of literature, the emergence of which raises critical questions. First, what is distinctive about this literature, and to what extent does it represent a coherent body of ideas? Second, should Islamic economics be classified as a separate discipline, or as a separate school of economic thought? Third, to what extent can it be considered ethical? Or would it be more accurate to depict the approach as moralistic, indeed proscriptive, with a stress on right and wrong, *halal* and *haram*, rather than as pointing to ethical dilemmas that are arguably best dealt with by widespread debate? This chapter suggests some possible answers.

Approaching economics from an Islamic perspective

Most economists, including those who are Muslims, separate their religious beliefs from their teaching and writing. They view their professional and academic output as being of relevance to the material world, and quite distinct from the religious teachings that may shape their spiritual reflection and worship. In the Western world this separation tends to be taken for granted – though in the eighteenth century the founding father, Adam Smith, conceived economics as a branch of moral philosophy. Increasing disciplinary specialization for at least the past two hundred years has resulted in economists being deterred from involvement in moral or theological debate. At the same time the interventions and pronouncements of religious leaders, especially in relation to economic policy, have been viewed as amateurish meddling in matters beyond their professional competency.

Those self-designated Islamic economists whose writing is considered here attempt to bridge the gap between the material realm of concern to economists and the spiritual realm that is the focus for theologians. They are, in one sense, renaissance figures who do not belong solely to a single discipline. There are of course dangers in trying to be both economist and theologian, as it might be better to strive for the mastery of one subject rather than perhaps doing less well in two. Professional colleagues often regard those working inter-disciplinary as being at the margins of their discipline, rather than being central to any disciplinary debates. Indeed those least well equipped and technically competent often work at the disciplinary margins, almost as a type of disciplinary escape.

Two distinct groups of scholars identify themselves as 'Islamic economists'. The first group are theologians, moral philosophers and historians interested in economic subjects. This includes all of the pre-twentieth century scholars who are accorded respect by modern Islamic economists, from Abu Hamid al Ghazali, the moral philosopher of the twelfth century, to Taqi al Din Ahmad Ibn Taymiyah, the fourteenth-century scholar concerned with market governance and justice in transactions, and Abd al Rahman Ibn Khaldun, the late fourteenth-century and early fifteenth-century philosopher of history who developed a moral theory of the business cycle to explain the rise and fall of civilizations. In the twentieth century, Mohammad Baqir al Sadr, a leading theologian with an interest in economic systems whose work is reviewed here, provided a powerful critique from an Islamic perspective of the failings of communism and capitalism and the merits of an Islamic alternative. Baqir al Sadr, like his predecessors, was trained in *fiqh*, Islamic jurisprudence, although it would be a mistake to label him as a lawyer, as *fiqh* involves an understanding of divine law, the *shariah*, not the secular laws of states, including Muslim states, of which he had little knowledge. Muhammad Nejatullah Siddiqi is another *fiqh* scholar worthy of mention, perhaps the greatest living Islamic scholar with knowledge of economics and a concern for development issues.

The second group of Islamic economists have been educated, often up to doctoral level, in mainstream economics, but believe that some of the premises on which the subject is based conflict with Islamic values. While not disputing the remit of economics as a subject area, or indeed its methodology and techniques of analysis, these Islamic economists reject some of its policy implications. Amongst this group, Umer Chapra, Abbas Mirakhor and Syed Nawab Haider Naqvi are perhaps the most influential writers. But many others have made significant contributions to the literature, especially Taimur Kuran, who has adopted a critical approach towards these other writers, who he suggests have been too idealistic and Utopian in their vision of an Islamic economy (Kuran 1995, pp. 155–73).

Islamic economic doctrine

Al Sadr drew an important distinction between the science of economics, sometimes designated as 'positive economics', and economic doctrine or 'normative economics'. He had little dispute with economics as a science and the analytical tools developed over the past four centuries. For Al Sadr it was the economic doctrines of the West which were unacceptable in Muslim societies (Haneef 1995, p. 111). He believed that no coherent society could be devoid of an economic doctrine, and within each society, or nation, that doctrine determines how wealth is to be produced, the form that wealth will take and how it should be preserved and distributed. Economic doctrine will in turn be determined by the society's culture, history and experience.

In the case of Muslim society the values of Islam can, indeed arguably should, influence economic doctrine. Ultimately the teaching of the Koran shapes these values, as well as the *hadith*, the sayings and deeds of the Prophet Muhammad as recorded in the *Sunnah*. The Koran and the *Sunnah* form the basis of the *shariah*, the divinely inspired Islamic law that all Muslims are to follow. Also significant are the *fatwa* opinions of Islamic scholars concerning the interpretation and application of the *shariah*, but these can conflict, as humans inevitably have different opinions. Muslims are therefore not bound by the rulings of a particular *fatwa*, although they may choose to follow one if they value the opinions of the scholar or scholars involved.

An example is the prohibition of *riba,* meaning literally addition to a principal sum, which is spelt out in the Koran in several verses or *sura*, notably 2.275. Islamic scholars differ in their interpretation of the prohibition, some suggesting that it applies only to usury or exploitative interest, and others believing it to apply to all interest transactions, the view taken by all the Islamic economists cited here. The Koran itself is concerned with general principles, and there is an obvious problem facing the *shariah* scholars in defining the rate at which interest becomes usury. In any case, inflation complicates matters further, as even zero interest is problematic, as it might be unjust for lenders if prices are rising. Therefore the safest, and arguably the preferable reaction to the prohibition, is to use alternative methods of financing that do not involve any interest and which are more inherently just.

Social justice is at the heart of Islamic economic doctrine, as the central concern is *falāh*, the well-being of all, the aim being a balance between individual and collective interests so that the vision of Islam, *maqāsid al shariah*, can be realized. The material vision involves satisfaction of the basic needs of all in terms of food, clothing, shelter, education and security of life and property. The spiritual vision involves nearness to God, peace of mind and family and social harmony (Chapra 2000, p. 57). Economics is concerned with the allocation of scarce resources, but a central tenant of Islamic economic doctrine is that God has provided in abundance for humankind, and where shortages do arise these reflect individual greed and the misuse of resources. Just as Christianity emphasizes the importance of stewardship, in Islam the concept of *khalifah* or vice-regency applies, that is, the idea that men and women are responsible to God for how resources under their control are managed.

Ownership responsibilities and the distribution of wealth
Those responsible for the effective management of resources need to be able to exercise control, and the *shariah* recognizes that private ownership is normally the best way to ensure this. Ultimately, ownership is in the hands of God, but the legal owners, as God's trustees on earth, need to be able to buy and sell resources and have property rights that provide secure conditions for investment. There will inevitably be inequities in ownership of resources in a market economy based primarily on private property rights. But this is not necessarily unjust, as the rights of private property owners are matched by their obligations to God to manage the resources under their control in a socially responsible manner. Furthermore, society as a whole can benefit if the market is efficient, and those best qualified and most competent to manage property have the opportunity to do so.

Contemporary Islamic economists are nevertheless critical of the feudalistic inequities in land ownership that persist in many Muslim countries (Naqvi 2003, p. 105). Some urge land reform involving redistribution of holdings, but there is no explicit provision for this in *shariah* except through inheritance provisions. With inheritance, who gets what is determined by their relationship with the deceased, the number of children and their gender. Men are entitled to twice the share of women, this being justified by the provision that a husband is financially responsible for his wife and children, whereas a wife's earnings and inheritance do not have to be used to support her family, and she is financially autonomous (El-Ashker and Wilson 2006, pp. 78–9). As a person has discretion over one-third of their estate, it is of course possible to make an additional provision for a spouse from this proportion.

In Islam the poor have a right to a share in the wealth of the rich, this being provided for through *zakat*, an annual wealth tax levied on the basis of one-fortieth of total assets, although, not surprisingly there is much debate as to which assets should be included for liability to *zakat*. As *zakat* is one of the five pillars of wisdom in Islam, payment is a religious duty. Though faithful Muslims accept this obligation, the amount paid is self-assessed. In some jurisdictions, such as Malaysia, *zakat* receipts can be offset against income tax liabilities, but this is not the case in most of the Muslim world, including Saudi Arabia and the Gulf countries, where there is no income tax. *Zakat* can be regarded as a form of alms-giving rather than a tax, and the revenues are designated for eight categories of recipients, the foremost being the poor and needy (Al-Qardawi 1999, pp. 343–65). This means that where government departments administer collection and distribution, they cannot simply absorb *zakat* into general revenues. In many Muslim countries *zakat* is administered by religious charitable foundations, *waqf*, some of which enjoy considerable autonomy from the state, notably in Iran. Often in Muslim countries because of government failure to provide for basic needs, Islamic charities play a major role in helping the poor, and in recent decades the activity of the voluntary sector has increased as the state's role has declined (Siddiqi 1996, pp. 125–50).

Production and investment

Islam is concerned not only with how income and wealth should be produced, but also with the nature of that wealth and the income derived from it. For example, in an Islamic society, certain types of goods and services may not be produced or provided. Examples are alcohol and establishments such as casinos, bars and nightclubs. Resources are not allocated to such *haram* activities and thus are freed for other purposes, such as building mosques and religious study centres. *Shariah* is not excessively restrictive however, as all activities can be assumed to be permissible unless they are explicitly prohibited. Some activities are classified as being *haram* because of the harm they are believed to cause, with alcohol dulling the mind and making the believer unfit for religious worship, and gambling as a zero-sum game resulting in winners gaining at the expense of losers, with addicts spending recklessly and forgetting their family and social obligations.

To ensure that investment is not channelled into *haram* activities, screening for *shariah* compliance is necessary, this role usually being undertaken by the *shariah* board of a bank, which comprises specialists in Islamic jurisprudence or *fiqh*. There are parallels here with the screening of investments by so-called 'ethical funds' in the West which avoid investing in companies that exploit the environment in an unsustainable manner or that use suppliers with exploitative labour practices. For *shariah*-compliant investment, both sector and financial screening is used, with excluded sectors being, for example, companies involved in brewing, distilling or the distribution of alcohol, pork production and distribution, and entertainments such as betting shops, gaming clubs or media companies involved in the production or dissemination of pornographic print or video output.

Islamic banks and conventional banks offering *shariah*-compliant mutual funds can seek the advice of their own *shariah* boards concerning what company stock to exclude, though this vetting can also be outsourced to third parties such as the Dow Jones Islamic Indices, which provides a *shariah* screening service. They can also offer advice on financial screening, since although virtually all companies are involved in *riba* or interest through borrowings and treasury management, only excessive involvement is deemed to be *haram*. Specifically, if a company has a ratio of debt to capitalization exceeding one-third, it is excluded from a *shariah*-compliant investment portfolio, as are companies that derive more than one-third of their income from interest, which includes most conventional banks. Receivables are also an issue, as, if companies charge more for deferred payments, the increased charges usually reflect interest rates. Hence, if the ratio of receivables to capitalization exceeds 45 per cent, this precludes *shariah* compliance (Siddiqui 2004, p. 54).

These ratios are not of course specified in the Koran or the *Sunnah.* They are an attempt to apply *ijtihad*, or reasoning, to determine what the implications of these religious texts might be for permissible investment, the aim being to avoid dealing with companies excessively involved in or profiting from *riba.* Purists suggest that Muslims should not invest in any listed company or private equity enterprise, as they are all involved in *riba*, but this could put Muslims at a disadvantage in relation to non-Muslims in their financial dealings, and preclude them from investing in otherwise sound businesses that contribute to employment, including employment of Muslims. Furthermore as with ethical investors, it is arguably more important, perhaps even a duty, for Muslim investors to engage with businesses and change their practices in a more *shariah*-compliant direction, rather than remaining pure, ineffectual and marginalized. Admittedly, the ratios are a compromise, but any income that Muslims indirectly gain from the *riba* activities of the businesses can be donated to charity, thus purifying the dividends. It would be the responsibility of the *shariah* board to indicate how much should be donated (Usmani 2002, pp. 96–7).

Critique of Western economics and justice in rewards

Islamic economists are critical of both the assumptions on which much conventional economics is based and its policy prescriptions. While Islam stresses collective obligations and solidarity with the *ummah*, literally the Muslim nation or the entire Muslim community, the stress in the West is on individual rights in the absence of collective conscience. This individualistic approach manifests through the application to economics of utilitarianism, which assumes individuals are motivated by the desire to maximize their personal satisfaction rather than by a collective moral purpose (Chapra 1992, pp. 25–6).

Islamic economists associate utilitarianism with hedonism, which they see taking the place of moral values. That is not to deny the importance of material goods, but these are for human sustenance and the fulfilment of needs, including spiritual obligations, which cannot be properly satisfied if believers are preoccupied with mere survival. Also problematic is the concept of diminishing marginal utility and the notion that, for example, equilibrium occurs in a labour market when the utility from a level of wages equals the disutility from having to work, as sacrificing leisure is seen as amoral by Islamic economists. Humans should use their God-given talents and are meant to work, and remuneration is justified by social recognition of the dignity of the worker. The level of remuneration, in other words, is a moral issue, not simply a matter of an equation linking supply and demand in a labour market.

Unlike Marxist approaches to remuneration that see labour as the only source of value, Islamic economists recognize the legitimacy of rental income and profits. As already indicated, private property is viewed as legitimate under *shariah*, and owners who choose to rent buildings or equipment are entitled to a rental income. However a *shariah*-compliant leasing contract, referred to as *ijara*, corresponds to an operating rather than a financing lease. It is the owner's responsibilities for the maintenance of the leased asset that justify the rent, and if these were delegated to the tenant or lessee the contract would be unjust (Mannan 1986, pp. 114–15).

Profits are seen as a just reward for entrepreneurial effort involving risk-sharing. Muslims should not seek out speculative risks, as gambling or *masir* is prohibited under *shariah*, but it is recognized that everyday business activity involves operational and payment risks which cannot be totally eliminated. *Shariah* provides for specific forms of business organization to facilitate the sharing of these risks, notably *musharakah*, a form of partnership in which the investors share in the profits and losses in proportion to the capital that each partner provided (Siddiqi 1985, pp. 22–37). Where an entrepreneur has little or no capital, an alternative arrangement is a *mudarahah* contract, whereby investors and the entrepreneur share in the profits, but only the investors are liable for any losses. This is seen as a more just arrangement for entrepreneurs lacking capital, although they are unrewarded for their time in the case of business failure.

Interest, or *riba,* is regarded as an unjust reward, as it constitutes merely obtaining an income from a debt contract without engaging in effort or risk-taking. The only permissible debt contract is a *qard hasan* loan where there is no gain for the lender, although lenders are allowed to levy arrangement fees and management charges to cover costs. Charging interest for a bank loan is seen as unjust, as the bank obtains a return regardless of how the business performs. In the case of personal loans, encouraging clients to take on substantial amounts of debt, which they may struggle to repay, especially with the additional interest charges, is seen as immoral (Khan 1995, p. 244). Islamic banks are not, however, charities, and they can engage in leasing for a rental income, or finance inventories or other assets by buying the item and selling it on to the client who pays on a deferred basis, with the payments including a mark-up. Such *murabahah* transactions are viewed as legitimate, as banks assume ownership responsibilities with the initial purchase, hence taking the acquisition risks from the client (Wilson 1997, p. 153).

Moral governance and development
Acceptance of *shariah* does not mean the rejection of the tools of economic analysis. Rather, it implies the evaluation of economic policy from a moral perspective based on religious teaching. With the exception of oil- and gas-rich states, most Muslim economies are low- to middle-income developing countries, where all too often corruption is widespread, including in government, and exploitative conditions exist in industry, notably through the use of child labour. Islamic economists condemn these practices and indeed see corruption as a cause of development failures.

The great Muslim philosopher of the fourteenth century, Ibn Khaldun, developed a moral theory of long-term business cycles. Under just governance with rulers respecting the *shariah*, workers and artisans have the confidence to specialize and, like Adam Smith more than three centuries later, Ibn Khaldun believed that specialization and the division of labour were the drivers of wealth creation (Chapra 2000, pp. 146–59). However, the increasing wealth and rising income disparities that specialization often brought resulted in corruption and immoral governance. As a consequence law and order started to break down, artisans lacked the confidence to specialize, as they feared being cheated over payments, and civilizations went into decline.

There has been much debate amongst contemporary Islamic economists concerning the role of the state in the economy and the state's governance responsibilities. Most support on moral grounds the idea of the state guaranteeing a minimum living standard and undertaking redistributive policies. But there are disagreements over how far governments should go beyond the imposition of *zakat*, with some, such as Siddiqi (1996, p. 25), supporting the taxation of capital gains and economic rents, as well as levying indirect taxes on luxuries but not on necessities. Differences between Islamic economists over taxation and expenditure policies largely reflect political positions, and it is recognized that no one approach has a monopoly on morality. Sincere Muslims can legitimately differ on how God's will is best carried out on earth. This has been the case since the early years of Islam, when four major schools of Islamic jurisprudence emerged, the Hanafi, Hanbali, Maliki and Shafii, the last of which, dominant in Malaysia and Indonesia, is regarded as the most liberal.

Debates on the role of the state have also concerned the role of the private sector and the extent of public ownership. Private ownership, as indicated earlier, is considered moral and just as long as the owners are responsible to their creator for the resources they manage. There is disagreement about the merits of state ownership. Muhammad Baqir Al-Sadr (2000, p. 159) saw no virtue in nationalization by socialist states, as they were just as likely to abuse productive resources as the immoral landowners they sought to replace. But others are more sympathetic (Siddiqi 1996, p. 32; Chapra 1992, p. 267). Al-Sadr believes it to be legitimate, indeed a moral imperative, for an Islamic state to exercise control over natural resources such as oil and gas for the benefit of the wider community, and for services such as hospitals to be provided by the public sector for the benefit of the poor (Wilson 1998, pp. 46–59). However, he had no illusions about the misallocation of oil revenue by the regime under which he had the misfortune to live and indeed be martyred, that of Saddam Hussein.

Islamic economists have also debated development policy, and there have been attempts to define what development involves, especially in moral terms. An obvious question is whether richer countries are more moral, and devout, than poorer economies. Kurshid Ahmad (1980, p. 135) sees development in terms of the Islamic concept of *tazkiya*: purification plus growth linked with the concept of *falāh* discussed earlier, with prosperity defined in both material and spiritual terms. The notion is of a wider or comprehensive interpretation of development that involves the moral as well as the material, the social in addition to the economic and both the spiritual and the physical. The focus is on man, within and without, and development with justice, *adl*, rather than injustice, *zulm*. Development is desirable, and indeed imperative, as it equips believers to better carry out the will of Allah. At the same time, it brings an enhanced understanding of what serving Allah involves. In contrast to some Christian thinking, there is no virtue in poverty. After all, if Muslims are constantly thinking of ways to simply survive there is less space for the spiritual.

From an Islamic perspective the means of promoting development as well as the ends must be *shariah*-compliant. Government spending may be important for development, but deficit financing concerns Islamic economists, especially if it results in excessive state debt that becomes a burden for future generations. A persuasive critique of Third World debt problems is provided by Islamic economists who emphasize the unjust burden of *riba* for poor countries, especially when it is compounded as a result of payment failures. Conventional sovereign bond and note issues are condemned, as they involve interest payments. Muslim governments can raise finance however through the issuance of Islamic asset-backed *sukuk* securities, based on *shariah*-compliant methods of financing such as *ijara* or *murabahah* (Kahf 1997, pp. 35–9). These are seen as more just, as the investors hold real assets, which can be liquidated and sold in the event of a payments default, ending the indebtedness rather than having it perpetuated.

We may conclude that Islamic economics can be regarded as an approach to the subject of economics, not as a separate discipline. It is best depicted as a distinct school of thought, with a coherent set of ideas, both moralistic and proscriptive. The value of approaching economics from an Islamic perspective is that it highlights moral issues, challenges the assumptions on which conventional economics is based and encourages fresh thinking about policy issues. The approach is appealing not only for Muslims, but also for those of other faiths and no faith, who are nevertheless concerned with moral issues and ethical reflection.

References

Ahmad, Kurshid (1980), 'Some thoughts on a strategy for development under an Islamic aegis', in Mustapha Filali (ed.), *Islam and the New International Economic Order: The Social Dimension*, Geneva: International Institute for Labour Studies, pp. 134–6.
Al-Qardawi, Yusuf (1999), *Fiqh az-Zakat – A Comparative Study: The Rules, Regulations and Philosophy of Zakat in the Light of the Koran and Sunnah*, London: Dar Al Taqwa.
Al-Sadr, Muhammad Baqir (2000), *Our Economics (Iqtisaduna)*, London: Books Extra.
Chapra, M. Umer (1992), *Islam and the Economic Challenge*, Leicester: Islamic Foundation.
Chapra, M. Umer (2000), *The Future of Economics: An Islamic Perspective*, Leicester: Islamic Foundation.
El-Ashker, Ahmed and Rodney Wilson (2006), *Islamic Economics: A Short History*, Leiden: Brill Academic Publishers.
Haneef, Mohamed Aslam (1995), *Contemporary Islamic Economic Thought: A Selected Comparative Analysis*, Kuala Lumpur: Ikraq.
Kahf, Monzer (1997), 'Instruments of meeting budget deficits in an Islamic economy', Islamic Development Bank Research Paper No. 42, Islamic Research and Training Institute, Islamic Development Bank, Jeddah.
Khan, M. Fahim (1995), *Essays in Islamic Economics*, Leicester: Islamic Foundation.
Kuran, Taimur (1995), 'Islamic economics and the Islamic sub-economy', *Journal of Economic Perspectives*, **9** (4), 155–73.
Mannan, Muhammad Abdul (1986), *Islamic Economics: Theory and Practice*, Sevenoaks, Kent: Hodder and Stoughton.
Naqvi, Syed Nawab Haider (2003), *Perspectives on Morality and Human Well Being: A Contribution to Islamic Economics*, Leicester: Islamic Foundation.
Siddiqi, Mohammad Nejatullah (1985), *Partnership and Profit Sharing in Islamic Law*, Leicester: Islamic Foundation.
Siddiqi, Mohammad Nejatullah (1996), *Role of the State in the Economy: An Islamic Perspective*, Leicester: Islamic Foundation.
Siddiqui, Rushdi (2004), 'Islamic indices: the Dow Jones Islamic market framework', in *Islamic Asset Management, Forming the Future for Shariah Compliant Investment Strategies*, London: Euromoney Books, pp. 46–58.
Usmani, Muhammad Taqi (2002), *An Introduction to Islamic Finance*, The Hague: Kluwer Law International.
Wilson, Rodney (1997), *Economics, Ethics and Religion: Jewish, Christian and Muslim Economic Thought*, London: Palgrave Macmillan.
Wilson, Rodney (1998), 'The contribution of Muhammad Baqir Al-Sadr to contemporary Islamic economic thought', *Journal of Islamic Studies*, **9** (1), 46–59.

See also the entries on: Justice; Religion.

39 Justice
Serge-Christophe Kolm

Economics as ethics and economic justice

Economics is a moral and normative science. It always has been. A large part of economics is ethics, applied ethics and often pure ethics as with social choice, theories of
economic fairness or justice and concepts of economic inequality and poverty. Economics
is, indeed, almost the only normative social science (alongside social ethics or political
philosophy if this field is classified as a social science). The values economics classically
uses and analyses are liberty and welfare. Liberty can be an end value (notably concerning
basic rights, the free market and possibilities of choice) or a means to welfare. However,
recent 'normative economics' (of which 'welfare economics' is but a subfield) analyses
and applies a large variety of usual or new ethical concepts.

Since economics – *stricto sensu* – is the study of the allocation of goods to people, normative economics, and economic ethics, are practically co-extensive with the concepts of
economic, distributive and social justice. However, the direct evaluations bear not only
on end-state distributions of goods or satisfactions, but also often on the processes that
lead to them, in 'procedural justice', as with free exchange – a case of Aristotle's 'commutative justice' – or fair processes of numerous possible kinds and all types and scales
of application.

Economic justice is the answer to the question 'who should have what?' It draws the
moral boundaries between people's self-interests. Sentiments and claims of economic
injustice and the indignation they arouse are a main fuel of social and political life, and
of history through revolutions and wars. Justice is the condition for a free, peaceful and
efficiently cooperating society. It is the 'first virtue' of society (Aristotle) or of its institutions (Rawls).

The three basic distinctions

Understanding economic justice and, therefore, finding the proper policy for it, are based
on three crucial distinctions: people's actual judgements versus scholarly proposals,
macrojustice versus microjustice, and the types of human capacities and their possible
allocations.

People's actual judgements vs. scholars' proposals

Judgements, criteria and principles about the justice of economic situations originate
either in the actual opinions of people or in scholars' proposals. Applying, in given circumstances, a principle that goes against people's general view requires the use of dictato-
rial power. In most societies there is no such power, which may be morally valued in itself,
and there also may be no dictator not sharing the people's view. Hence, the principles of
economic justice that are useful to study are those that people share or can be persuaded
to endorse (by relying on rationality and moral feeling).

Macrojustice and microjustice
The common view makes a neat distinction between the question of *macrojustice* concerned with the allocation of the bulk of resources to everybody according to the general basic rules of society, and the multifarious issues of *microjustice* concerning allocations that are specific according to individuals, circumstances, goods or reasons. The income tax and the main income transfers belong to macrojustice. It is also sometimes fruitful to consider a field of *mesojustice* concerned with allocations of particular goods which are important and concern everybody (such as education and health).

People's capacities and the three basic principles
The largest part, by far, of the given resources to be allocated in society consists in human capacities. The contributions of factors of production to national income are commonly in the order of 80 for labour, 18 for capital, and 2 for non-human natural resources. However, in an intertemporal view, capital is itself produced. Hence, the shares of labour and of non-human natural resources are respectively in the order of 97.5 per cent and 2.5 per cent. Therefore, for the allocation of the bulk of the value of economic resources, the problem is the allocation of the value of productive capacities.

Moreover, in addition to their productive and earning capacities, individuals have capacities to enjoy, to be pleased or satisfied and to withstand hardship – their 'eudemonistic capacities' – represented in economics by their utility function.

The value of an individual's capacity can be allocated either to this individual, or to society as a whole and put into the common pool to be allocated according to other criteria, possibly by compensations. This gives three polar families of allocative criteria for respectful individualistic justice concerned with items valued by the individuals: full self-ownership, welfarism and income justice.

In the case of *full self-ownership*, each individual fully owns all her capacities. There is no forced transfer. This is 'classical liberalism', a widespread view of major historical importance (endorsed, for instance, in recent times, by Robert Nozick (1974), Friedrich Hayek or Milton Friedman).

In the opposite case, nothing is allocated a priori to the individuals, and the allocation can transfer incomes and compensate for individuals' different capacities to enjoy. It thus solely considers individuals' own final evaluations – their happiness or their 'welfare' – and derives its moral criterion from them alone. This is *welfarism* (Hicks 1959).

In the polar intermediate case, individuals own their capacities to enjoy – they are entitled to their beneficial effects and accountable for their shortcomings – but their production is submitted to the policy of a just distribution. The substance of this distributive justice can be taken to be *income*.

Both welfarism and income justice have to be further specified according to the way in which individuals' welfare (utilities) or incomes are used for determining the criterion. The standard way consists of maximizing an increasing function of individuals' utilities or incomes, respectively. The two polar forms in this respect are a *sum*, and an equality of the items which is replaced by a *maximin* (maximize the lowest) in order to face cases in which some possible states are better for everybody than the best equality. The sum of utilities is retained by utilitarianism. Maximin in comparable utility is implied by 'practical justice' (Kolm 1971). Maximin in income is John Rawls's (1971) 'difference principle' (he adds other, non-economic 'primary goods'). An ideal of income equality is also what

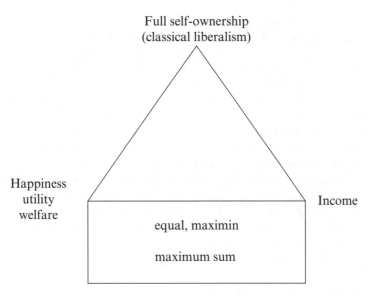

Figure 39.1   The triangle of economic justice

leads to the ethical theory of income inequalities. Various views advocate the highest sum of incomes, such as maximizing the growth of national product, Ronald Coase's (1960) opinion about the object of economists' advice, or Richard Posner's (1977, 1981) recommendation for judicial decisions. Figure 39.1 summarizes these polar principles of allocation.

Welfarism

The actual scope of welfarism
When people use concepts of welfare to evaluate or choose an interpersonal allocation, either the issue is individuals' pain or suffering, or the allocation is between people with some social proximity to one another (and who can have some empathy for the other).[1] The use of the utilities or welfares can have any of the above noted structures. Utilitarian judgements are manifested by comparisons of variations of individuals' utilities, and maximins by comparisons of individuals' total welfares. For instance, an organ for transplant or emergency care is allocated to the patient whom it relieves the most or who suffers the most. You allocate the toy to your daughter rather than to your son because she enjoys it more or because she is a little sadder at this moment. By contrast, the discussions about the income tax never refer to individuals' tastes or capacities to enjoy. These determinants of welfare are not deemed relevant for this type of redistribution.

The result is that welfarism is deemed irrelevant and is not actually used for choices of macrojustice in large societies which are not in an exceptional situation of disaster (war or natural) in which most people suffer, and where exceptional misfortunes are taken care of by particular insurance schemes or specific policies of microjustice. For example, no income tax administration has ever determined income tax liabilities by reference to individuals' lesser or greater capacities to enjoy.

Pareto efficiency does not imply welfarism

A possible state is said to be Pareto efficient if no other possible state makes one person better off and no one worse off, and in particular all better off. This is valuable both in itself and because it is a condition of democracy since, short of Pareto efficiency, some other possible states are preferred at unanimity.

A state that maximizes a social welfare function, that is, an increasing function of individuals' utilities (welfares), is clearly Pareto efficient. Conversely, for almost all Pareto-efficient states, there exist such social welfare functions that are maximal at this state. Does this imply that the requirement of Pareto efficiency implies that the best state can be defined as the maximum of a social welfare function – hence that the distribution it contains is determined by comparisons of levels or variations of individual utilities (welfares)? Not really. Indeed, a Pareto efficient state can be defined otherwise. In particular, a sharing of given resources followed by a perfect free market is Pareto efficient (as Pareto proved). Any of the social welfare functions that take their maximum at this state cannot be defined by intrinsic properties, without referring a priori to this state that it should determine, and to its definition, that is, tautologically.

Scholarly welfarisms and pseudo-utilitarianisms

Social welfare functions are very often considered in economics. They are applied sometimes for questions for which people's opinion would hold they can, and often otherwise. Arrow's (1963) 'social choice' is a quest for a way of defining a social welfare function (in the case in which what he calls 'individual values' represent welfare), with the conclusion that no one satisfies a number of interesting properties. Other scholars assume a priori such a function and add conditions that specify it in order to obtain utilitarianism. However, they obtain a sum of individual utilities that is not that of utilitarianism because these utilities and their variation cannot be said to refer to welfare or happiness (they are only increasing functions of them, which makes a difference for the interpersonal comparisons). One such theory (McKenzie) only adds conditions that amount to this additive form. Another (Harsanyi 1955) derives this structure from rational choice in uncertainty by both the individuals and the social ethical choice, and a particular assumption about the social ethics of risk (individuals' preferences should be respected both before and after the occurrence of the uncertain event).

Harsanyi (1953, 1976) also derives the same result from a theory of the 'original position': the social welfare function is the utility function of an individual who does not know which of the actual individuals he will become. However, the result depends on both this individual's own preferences about being the various actual individuals and his risk-aversion, and these elements have to be specified (they are a priori different for the various actual individuals). More basically, there is no reason why a self-interested choice in uncertainty would be identical to a choice of justice between several individuals – why prudence would mimic fairness – (this also affects Rawls's different original position theory). For instance, the individual in the original position may want to take a chance of being very rich by giving all income to only one actual individual (just as, in another context, he may bet all his money on a single horse for the same objective). The individual is accountable for his selfish choice in uncertainty towards himself and his own welfare, whereas the choice of justice is accountable towards others, society and morals. The items directly deemed relevant by the latter may not even be individuals' welfare.

Liberties

If the reference of an individualistic ethic is not welfare, it probably has to be liberty. In economics, if, in choice theory, one takes utility off, there remains the domain of free choice. Philosophical anthropology sees humans as sentient beings or as agents capable of free choice and action. However, there are two relevant kinds of economic freedom.

Social liberty means that individuals are free from forceful interference by others, individually, in groups or as institutions. People are only constrained not to impose force on others (there may also be particular constraints for safety or for the implementation of implicit contracts). Free exchange (without third-party interference) is possible and important. The respect extends to the effects of free acts – such as rights so created, in particular in exchange. Social liberty is the constitutional basis of our societies. It is the full theory of notions such as 'negative', 'civic' or 'formal' freedom (and the meaning of 'a free economy'). Social liberty is non-rival since that of an individual does not diminish that of another. Hence, people can all have it at satiety and, in this sense, equally. When people's intended actions are incompatible, this is due to the allocation of other means (notably rights), a result of the distribution.

Social liberty plus the other means (rights, incomes and so on) that people have determine their domains of choice.

Let us also remark here that justice refers a priori to an ideal or *prima facie* equality of something encompassing all that is morally assumed to be able to relevantly differentiate the individuals – including both allocations and pertinent characteristics – (insofar as this equality is possible and not overly costly in other respects), because the absence of other characteristics deemed relevant precludes proposing a reason for a different solution, justifying it ('justice is equality, as everybody thinks it is', in Aristotle's words). Various applications of this general remark constitute the essence of all theories of justice (main examples are shortly provided).

Macrojustice

From the above, macrojustice is achieved by an allocation of the values of the given productive capacities. The corresponding transfers should have an inelastic (given) base for respecting both social liberty and Pareto efficiency (a classical result of economics); these bases should not be individuals' utility functions (deemed irrelevant for a principle of macrojustice); hence they are these given productive capacities. Finally, these transfers should achieve equality in liberty.

Social liberty is non-rival and hence full, and it is equal for all in this sense. Productive capacities transform labour into income, and hence the relevant individual choice is that of labour and earned income. Social liberty precludes taxation based on the chosen labour or income (elastic). Hence, a possibility is social liberty from an equal allocation of income and leisure. Leisure is the complement of labour. Therefore, this equal basic allocation is obtained by equally redistributing the proceeds of the same given labour of all individuals (with their different productivities). There are other possible definitions of equality of liberty, which turn out to yield the same structure. Note that the identity of domains of choice is not possible for people with different productivities or wage rates (building up such a domain requires using individuals' utilities which are deemed irrelevant – and are not known). But a concept of equal liberty provided by non-identical domains gives the same result as above.[2] Moreover, the resulting distribution turns out to have a number of ethical meanings valuable in themselves.

Precisely, if the individuals i have wage rates w_i, the same labour k gives income kw_i to individual i, and an equalization of these incomes leads one to replace this income by the average $k\overline{w}$ where $\overline{w}$ is the average income. Hence each individual i is given the net transfer $t_i = k \cdot (\overline{w} - w_i)$, a subsidy if $t_i > 0$ (hence if $w_i < \overline{w}$ for $k > 0$) and a tax of $-t_i$ if $t_i < 0$ (hence $w_i > \overline{w}$ for $k > 0$). This is 'equal-labour income equalization' or ELIE. Each individual i then freely chooses to work ℓ_i and earns $w_i\ell_i$. Actual national fiscal redistributions diminish income inequalities as much as such a scheme with an equalization labour k between one and two days a week (from the United States to Scandinavia). For all normal full-time labour, $\ell_i > k$, and this is the case for macrojustice (other individuals are particular cases that may be the object of specific rules and policies of microjustice). Individual i's resulting disposable income is $y_i = w_i\ell_i + t_i = k\overline{w} + (\ell_i - k)w_i$. It consists of two parts, an egalitarian part $k\overline{w}$ for which all individuals earn the same income for the same labour, and a 'classical liberal' part $(\ell_i - k)w_i$ for which each individual keeps his earnings with his wage rate. These are the two basic ethics of overall distribution, and the coefficient k determines their relative proportion. The full macrojustice theory considers all dimensions of labour (duration, intensity, formation).

The property $\ell_i > k$ implies $y_i > k\overline{w}$. Hence, $k\overline{w}$ is a minimum income, and the social choice of a minimum income implies a choice of a coefficient k. The result also amounts to a universal basic income for all ($k\overline{w}$) financed by an equal labour of all (k); to each individual yielding to each other the product of the same labour in a general equal labour reciprocity (labour k/n where n is the number of individuals); and to two fiscal bonuses, a tax rebate or credit and an exemption of overtime labour, from a flat tax: $-t_i = (k/\ell)w_i\ell - k\overline{w}$, where ℓ is the official labour duration chosen at a moderate level, k/ℓ is the tax rate, and $k\overline{w}$ is the tax credit. This latter form shows the way of actual realization – these fiscal properties are achieved in some countries, including the tax exemption of overtime labour with de facto no cheating. Note that, by contrast, when the income tax is based on total earned income, 30 per cent of this base evades the tax in all countries where this is done.

Microjustice and mesojustice

If the overall income distribution is fair, with freedom of exchange implied by social liberty, the various goods are justly allocated by buying and the market. Non-marketable public goods can be financed by the distributively neutral 'benefit taxation' (or possibly, more precisely and fully, for these goods and for externalities, by a duplication of what free exchange would have achieved if the impediment to marketing did not exist – that is, a 'liberal social contract').[3] However, there still remain a number of allocative choices. The overall income distribution may be imperfect. Moreover, in any large society, there may remain a number of people out of the standard distributive system and in poverty. In addition, in a given society, overall productivity (hence the average $\overline{w}$) and the coefficient of redistribution (k) may not suffice for providing a minimum income $k\overline{w}$ that can cover all needs considered basic. This gives reasons for additional specific aid, possibly aiming at meeting specific needs.

The particular goods incorporated in humans raise specific issues of justice. Education and health can largely be allocated privately by spending fairly distributed income, with the appropriate loans and insurance. However, the effects of family on individuals are both a major externality and the main source of inequality through formation and educational choices and support, along with bequest and social position and relations. The general income policy compensates for part of the effects of education and formation. However, inequality of social origin can be seen as particularly objectionable, and the main one, nowadays, is that due to education, which depends not only on parents' support, but also, essentially, on their information and motivation (and hence is at work even where education is public and free). There should thus be a policy of educational mesojustice complementing the macrojustice of general income distribution. Health can be financed by private health insurance. However, a number of societies find that the basic health inequalities in propensities to be sick are a natural injustice which requires compensation. This is a main reason for health insurance being public, for instance in Europe.

Health-care and a basic education are parts of basic needs, and numerous studies have focused on the provision of basic needs. The satisfaction of these needs permits individuals' action, and emphasis is sometimes put on the liberty this provides. This is the case with the 'capabilities' that permit the choice of 'functionings' discussed by Nussbaum and Sen.[4] However, while the former demands securing minimum levels of capabilities (in the tradition of basic needs), the latter advocates that equal capabilities for all provide identical domains of free choice for all, and hence equal liberty. However, an equality in a bundle of produced goods, for individuals with different preferences, a priori entails Pareto inefficiency. But the principle can be generalized into a Pareto-efficient second-best multidimensional egalitarianism.[5] If all individuals have some amount of all the capabilities, the result is an equality in income for the production of capabilities.

The basic intention for focusing on capabilities was to find a material or substance of justice intermediate between those of welfarism and of Rawls's income justice (more involved with the person than income, and yet leaving a scope for free action). Cohen (1989) objected that the equalisandum (the 'currency of justice') should be what individuals are not responsible for. However, responsibility is one reason for accountability but not the only one, and people should sometimes be helped even when they are responsible for their fate.[6]

Moreover, societies face innumerable cases of microjustice that are considered not appropriately solved by exchange or auction even with legitimate incomes. The criteria used can generally be classified into three categories. They sometimes refer to merit, desert, responsibility or freedom of choice. In other cases, the reference is to needs or welfare. The other instances directly consider means or goods, with an ideally equal allocation. In fact, equality of some items is always present but depends on a number of choices: the specific nature of what should be equalized; the starting state from which the equality in question is defined; the characteristics that make the beneficiaries (or contributors for sharing a liability) relevantly identical or not; and one should add the choice of the second-best egalitarian criterion when the ideal equality is not possible, raises relevant costs of any kind or hurts other relevant values (possibly including the fact that some possible unequal state satisfies more all participants).

In still other cases, the objective is some social, non-individualistic one, the satisfaction of which determines the individual allocations. In fact, a social maximand function of individual items (such as goods, means, incomes or welfare) can be seen as either a particular overall social objective or a principle of inter-individual fairness. The linear forms of utilitarianism and of the highest social income are conspicuous in this respect: they seem to be social objectives, but they are also egalitarian objectives for local variations. Finally, allocative criteria often follow established traditions, sometimes for defining classes of people within which some equality should prevail.

The most important criteria of fairness associate various concerns and meanings. One of the most used ones demands that *no individual prefer any other's allocation to his own*. This associates an egalitarian intention (it amounts to equality if the allocation is of only one good) with the consideration of the less objectionable structures of individual preferences: ordinality and no interpersonal comparisons. However, this criterion also has a deep meaning of equal liberty, since it is satisfied if and only if there exists a domain of choice of individual allocation such that the given allocation of each individual could be his choice in this domain (such a domain includes all the given individual allocations plus any allocation that no individual prefers to his own). This criterion may be called 'equity-no-envy', although it does not exactly describe no-envy because an envious person's preferences are concerned *jointly* with his own allocation and that of others (however, the theory of envy nevertheless uses this criterion, but for fictive, 'envy-free' individual preferences).[7] This principle was suggested in passing by Tinbergen (1946) and Foley (1967), its properties were presented in works of Kolm (1971), Varian (1974, 1976), Schmeidler and Vind (1974), Pazner (1977), Baumol (1986) and Feldman (1987), it was extended into various principles in particular by Kolm (1973, 1991, 1996b, 1999), Feldman and Kirman (1974), Thomson (1983), Van Parijs (1995) and others, and applied to a number of issues of distributive policy as by Bös and Tillman (1985) and Fleurbaey and Maniquet (1996).

An important issue is the relation between equity-no-envy and Pareto efficiency. There exist allocations sharing a given bundle of ordinary goods that satisfy both properties, since this is the case of the allocation obtained by an equal sharing of these goods followed by a perfect market for the exchange of these goods between these individuals. However, when one of these goods is labour or leisure, whose price, the wage rate, may differ for different people, there may be no Pareto-efficient allocation that satisfies equity-no-envy. Nevertheless, when such an impossibility is met, an extension of the noted equivalent property of equal liberty into a comparison of being more or less free permits the definition of an efficient maximin in notional freedom.[8] This property of equity-no-envy has given rise to a large number of analyses, variants and proposals of neighbouring properties, and applications.

Many specific theoretical criteria of fairness have been studied, for allocating goods or costs and for collective choices such as voting rules. Their logical properties, their relations with other principles and properties, and their conceptual meaning and validity are analysed. Some use concepts of utility of various types (with a problem of meaning for cardinal utilities other than those relevant for risky choices). Some are defined in a framework of bargaining by proposing fair solutions. These solutions often refer to a disagreement state that prevails in the absence of agreement, sometimes to claims that are seen as legitimate but are not co-possible, and they use certain properties of equality or impartiality.[9] A general problem about criteria of justice consists of finding extensions of desired criteria when their strict satisfaction is too costly in any respect or impossible (for instance, the minimization of some measure of inequality).[10] One field of study focuses on the determination of the most elementary logical properties that imply the criteria, in a kind of moral axiomatics.[11]

The latest developments in the analysis of economic justice associate this study of the logical and mathematical properties of the criteria and principles with other dimensions of a psychological, social and philosophical nature. One is the analysis of the emotions that accompany the sentiments of justice and especially of injustice aroused by following or violating a principle. From this there develops both a phenomenology of economic justice trying to seize its purest and most basic 'intuitions', and a hermeneutics of economic justice analysing its history, its linguistic expressions and its insertion in the social and cultural ethos, alongside the analysis of the evolution and formation of its concepts in processes of social dialogue (with logical-mathematical models of these processes).[12]

Notes

1. A recent analysis of this evidence can be found in Kolm (2008, 2009).
2. For a full proof, see Kolm (2008, 2009).
3. See Kolm (1985, 1987, 1996a, 2004).
4. A. Sen (1985), Nussbaum (1992, 2000), Nussbaum and A. Sen (1993).
5. As in the more general presentation in Kolm (1996b).
6. The economics of responsibility is notably developed by Fleurbaey (2008).
7. Kolm (1995).
8. Kolm (1999). Other extensions of the concept of equity-no-envy provide sets of Pareto-efficient states that satisfy them that are too large to be interesting.
9. For presentations in book form see Binmore and Dasgupta (1987), Moulin (1988, 1995) and Thomson (1994).
10. Another solution consists of replacing the actual state by another, fictive state that all participants find as good as the actual one (it is 'equivalent' to it in this sense), and of applying the criterion to this state (the 'equivalence principle'). However, the actual possible state 'equivalent' to the best of the fictive states that have an equivalent possible state is not, a priori, the actual possible state that satisfies best any extension of the criterion. See, for instance, Kolm (1966, 2004), and Pazner and Schmeidler (1978).
11. Thomson (2001) and Moulin and Thomson (1997) present the method and the main results.
12. Kolm (2004, Part 4).

References

Space limitation precludes presenting a comprehensive bibliography of economic justice. The reader can find one in Kolm (1996a and 2004).

Arrow, Kenneth J. (1963), *Social Choice and Individual Values*, 2nd edition, New Haven, CT: Yale University Press.
Baumol, William J. (1986), *Superfairness*, Cambridge, MA: MIT Press.
Binmore, Ken and Partha Dasgupta (eds) (1987), *The Economics of Bargaining*, Oxford: Basil Blackwell.
Bös, Dieter and G. Tillman (1985), 'An "envy tax": theoretical principles and applications to the German surcharge on the rich', *Public Finance*, **40**, 35–63.
Coase, Ronald H. (1960), 'The Problem of Social Cost', *Journal of Law and Economics*, **3**, 1–44.
Cohen, G.A. (1989), 'On the currency of egalitarian justice', *Ethics*, **99**, 906–44.
Feldman, Allan M. (1987), 'Equity', in John Eatwell, Murray Milgate and Peter Newman (eds), *The New Palgrave Dictionary of Economics*, Vol. 2, London: Macmillan, pp. 182–4.
Feldman, Allan M. and Alan Kirman (1974), 'Fairness and Envy', *American Economic Review*, **64** (6), 995–1005.
Fleurbaey, Marc (2008), *Fairness, Responsibility and Welfare*, Oxford: Oxford University Press.
Fleurbaey, Marc and Francois Maniquet (1996), 'Fair allocation with unequal production skills: the no-envy approach to compensation', *Mathematical Social Sciences*, **32**, 71–93.
Foley, Duncan K. (1967), 'Resource allocation and the public sector', *Yale Economic Essays*, **7**, 45–98.
Harsanyi, John C. (1953), 'Cardinal utility in welfare economics and in the theory of risk-taking', *Journal of Political Economy*, **61**, 434–5.

Harsanyi, John C. (1955), 'Cardinal welfare, individualistic ethics and interpersonal comparisons of utility', *Journal of Poltical Economy*, **XLIII**, 309–21.
Harsanyi, John C. (1976), *Essays in Ethics, Social Behaviour and Scientific Explanation*, Dordrecht: Reidel.
Hayek, Friedrich A. (1976a), *The Mirage of Social Justice, Law, Legislation and Liberty*, London: Routledge and Kegan Paul.
Hicks, John (1959), *Essays in World Economy*, Oxford: Basil Blackwell.
Kolm, Serge-Christophe (1966), 'The optimal production of social justice', in H. Guitton and J. Margolis (eds), *Proceedings of the International Economic Association Conference on Public Economics, Biarritz*; *Economie Publique*, Paris: CNRS, 1968, pp. 109–77; *Public Economics*, London: Macmillan, 1969, pp. 145–200.
Kolm, Serge-Christophe (1971), *Justice et équité*, Paris: CEPREMAP; Reprinted (1972), Paris: CNRS; English translation by H. See (1998), *Justice and Equity*, Cambridge, MA: MIT Press.
Kolm, Serge-Christophe (1973), 'Super-équité', *Kyklos*, **XXVI**, 441–3.
Kolm, Serge-Christophe (1985), *Le Contrat social libéral (Théorie et pratique du libéralisme)*, Paris: Presses Universitaires de France.
Kolm, Serge-Christophe (1987), 'Public Economics', in John Eatwell et al. (eds), *New Palgrave Dictionary in Economics*, London: Macmillan, pp. 1047–55.
Kolm, Serge-Christophe (1991), 'The normative economics of unanimity and equality: equity, adequacy and fundamental dominance', in Kenneth J. Arrow (ed.), *Markets and Welfare*, London: Macmillan, pp. 243–86.
Kolm, Serge-Christophe (1995), 'The economics of social sentiments: the case of envy', *Japanese Economic Review*, **46**, 63–87.
Kolm, Serge-Christophe (1996a), *Modern Theories of Justice*, Cambridge, MA: MIT Press.
Kolm, Serge-Christophe (1996b), 'The theory of justice', *Social Choice and Welfare*, **13**, 151–82.
Kolm, Serge-Christophe (1998), 'Chance and justice: social policy and the Harsanyi-Vickrey-Rawls problem', *European Economic Review*, **42**, 1393–416.
Kolm, Serge-Christophe (1999), *Freedom Justice*, University of Caen: CREME.
Kolm, Serge-Christophe (2004), *Macrojustice: The Political Economy of Fairness*, Cambridge: Cambridge University Press.
Kolm, Serge-Christophe (2008a), 'Equal liberties and the resulting optimum income distribution and taxation', in J. Bishop and B. Zheng (eds), *Inequality and Opportunity*, Emerald.
Kolm, Serge-Christophe (2008b), 'Economic macrojustice: fair optimum income distribution, taxation and transfers', in C. Gamel and M. Lubrano (eds), *Macrojustice*, Berlin: Springer Verlag.
Moulin, Hervé (1988), *Axioms of Cooperative Decision Making*, Cambridge: Cambridge University Press.
Moulin, Hervé (1995), *Cooperative Microeconomics*, Princeton, NJ: Princeton University Press.
Moulin, Hervé and William Thomson (1997), 'Axiomatic analysis of resource allocation problems', in Kenneth J. Arrow, Amartya Sen and Kotaro Suzumura (eds), *Social Choice Re-examined*, Vol.1, London: Macmillan and New York: St Martin's Press.
Nozick, Robert (1974), *Anarchy, State and Utopia*, New York: Basic Books.
Nussbaum, Martha (1992), 'Human functioning and social justice: in defense of Aristotelian Essentialism', *Political Theory*, **20** (2), 202–46.
Nussbaum, Martha (2000), 'Aristotle, politics and human capabilities', *Ethics*, **111**, 102–40.
Nussbaum, Martha and Amartya Sen (eds) (1993), *The Quality of Life*, Oxford: Oxford University Press.
Parijs, Philippe van (1995), *Real Freedom for All: What (if Anything) Can Justify Capitalism?* Oxford: Oxford University Press.
Pazner, Elisha A. (1977), 'Pitfalls in the theory of fairness', *Journal of Economic Theory*, **14**, 458–66.
Pazner, Elisha and David Schmeidler (1978), 'Egalitarian-equivalent allocations: a new concept of economic equity', *Quarterly Journal of Economics*, **92**, 671–87.
Posner, Richard (1977), *The Economic Analysis of Law*, 2nd edition, Boston, MA: Little Brown.
Posner, Richard (1981), *The Economics of Justice*, Cambridge, MA: Harvard University Press.
Rawls, John (1971), *A Theory of Justice*, Cambridge, MA: Harvard University Press.
Schmeidler, David and Karl Vind (1974), 'Fair net trades', *Econometrica*, **40**, 637–42.
Sen, Amartya (1985), *Commodities and Capabilities*, Amsterdam: North-Holland.
Thomson, William (1983), 'Equity in exchange economies', *Journal of Economic Theory*, **19**, 217–44.
Thomson, William (1994), *Bargaining Theory: The Axiomatic Approach*, San Diego, CA: Academic Press.
Thomson, William (2001), 'On the axiomatic method and its recent applications to game theory and resource allocation', *Social Choice and Welfare*, **18**, 327–87.
Tinbergen, Jan (1946), *Redelijke Inkomensverdeling*, Haarlem: De Gulden Pers.
Varian, Hal (1974), 'Equity, envy, and efficiency', *Journal of Economic Theory*, **19**, 63–91.
Varian, Hal (1976), 'Two problems in the theory of fairness', *Journal of Public Economics*, **5**, 249–60.

See also the entries on: Efficiency; Equity; Freedom; Inequality; Utilitarianism.

40 Immanuel Kant
Mark D. White

Mainstream economics and Immanuel Kant's duty-based ethics might at first seem odd bedfellows, given the utilitarian roots of the former. Models of individual choice in economics are based on maximizing an index of utility based on preference-satisfaction, while Kant's deontological ethics deal with immeasurable right and wrong. Modern welfare economics assesses policies based on their effects on the sum of these utilities, with no judgement on procedure, while Kantians would focus on the possible violations of human dignity in pursuit of this goal. Most broadly, Kantian moral theory is fundamentally individualistic, while maintaining an emphasis on the social. Economics, in contrast, is schizophrenic on this score, claiming firm support of individuals' rights while actually subordinating them to utilitarian calculus.

This chapter briefly introduces Kant's ethics, after which it discusses two areas of economics particularly affected by Kantian considerations. The first area is that comprising work done by economists incorporating Kantian ethics into the standard model of choice. The second is the much more limited area of work on the implications of a Kantian welfare economics.

Introduction to Kantian ethics

Immanuel Kant (1724–1804) spent his entire life in Königsberg, East Prussia, most of it as a professor at the University of Königsberg. Kant was renowned not only for his published works, but also for his vibrant lecturing style and frequent dinner parties with friends, neighbours and students. His seminal contributions spanned many fields of philosophy, including metaphysics, logic, aesthetics and, of course, moral philosophy. His ethical system is laid out chiefly in three books: *Grounding for the Metaphysics of Morals* (1785), *Critique of Practical Reason* (1788) and *The Metaphysics of Morals* (1797); additional insights are scattered throughout his other writings.[1] While explicit discussion of economics is rare in his work, he was known to be quite fond of Adam Smith's writings in particular; in fact, several near-quotes from *The Wealth of Nations* appear in his later work (see Fleischacker 1996).

Kant based his ethics on his belief in human beings' ability to use reason to motivate choices, independent of the pull of both external influences and internal desires. (This was in direct opposition to David Hume's contention that reason is 'slave to the passions' and can never itself initiate any action.) Kant used the terms 'autonomy' and 'freedom' to represent this power, and because of it, he attributed to every person an inherent and incomparable dignity. This dignity, and the respect for persons that it requires, is at the heart of Kant's ethics, although the technical details of the various formulae of the categorical imperative often obscures its importance.[2]

Kant considered his famous categorical imperative to be merely a formalization of the moral intuition of the average person. It is usually stated in one of three different formulae, which are ideally identical, but which emphasize different aspects of what Kant called the 'moral law'. The most well-known version, possibly due to its emphasis on universalization and its applicability as a formal test, is the *Formula of Autonomy or of Universal Law*: 'act only according to that maxim whereby you can at the same time will that it should become a universal law' (1785, p. 421).

A more directly humanistic version of the moral law is the *Formula of Respect for the Dignity of Persons*: 'act in such a way that you treat humanity, whether in your own person or in the person of another, always at the same time as an end and never simply as a means' (1785, p. 429).

The third version, the *Formula of Legislation for a Moral Community*, combines elements of the first two, while emphasizing the autonomous self-legislation integral to Kant's ethics: 'every rational being must act as if by his maxims he were at all times a legislative member of the universal kingdom of ends' (1785, p. 438). This invokes a utopian society in which all persons respect the moral law and can therefore consistently pursue their own ultimate good of happiness.

Each formula can be applied to an agent's plan of action, or *maxim*, to arrive at duties which govern their moral behaviour. Duties resulting from the categorical imperative can be divided into two types, perfect and imperfect. *Perfect duties* (also called narrow duties) are those that admit no exception; they are mostly negative in nature (do not kill, do not steal and so on). The moral agent has no choice or latitude when it comes to executing perfect duties. *Imperfect duties* (or wide duties) require no specific action, but rather an attitude that must be adopted. An example is the duty of beneficence, which does not dictate how one must be kind to others, but only that one must do kind things when it does not conflict strongly with other duties, including duties to oneself. (This contradicts a common perception that Kant demands extreme altruistic sacrifice, for this would contravene the basic duties to maintain one's health and well-being, as well as a due level of happiness.) Accordingly, perfect duties are sometimes called duties of *action*, while imperfect duties are called duties of *ends*.

In Kant's view, however, it is not enough to follow the dictates of duty; one must do so for the *sake* of duty. If a person acts simply in accordance with duty, but is motivated by inclinations or desires – no matter how altruistic they may be – that person is not regarded as moral in so doing (regardless of the goodness of the act itself):

> There are many persons who are so sympathetically constituted that, without any further motive of vanity of self-interest, they find an inner pleasure in spreading joy around them and can rejoice in the satisfaction of others as their own work. But I maintain that in such a case an action of this kind, however dutiful and amiable it may be, has nevertheless no true moral worth. (1785, p. 398)

Only if a dutiful act is performed for the sake of duty can it be judged to derive from reason alone, and not inclination or preference, and therefore to reflect the agent's autonomy.[3]

Kant's moral theory may seem excessively demanding at times, but he was quite realistic regarding actual persons' ability to follow the categorical imperative and the duties derived from its application. Human beings are not perfectly rational or moral (only God is), and that is why the moral law presents itself as a categorical imperative: we must compel ourselves, through force of will or character, to act morally (or autonomously) and resist the pull of inclinations or desires (or of acting heteronomously). Moral lapses in this sense reflect weakness of will or deficiency of character, and do not imply that the agent is evil (as would deliberate violations of duty).

Kantian models of economic choice

The literature incorporating Kantian ethics into economic theories of choice is modest, but nonetheless quite diverse.[4] The groundwork for this body of work is perhaps traceable to Amartya Sen, who included Kantian ideas explicitly or implicitly in several of his papers from the 1970s. Sen (1974) argued that prisoners' dilemma outcomes could be avoided if players follow the categorical imperative, specifically the Formula of Universal Law. However, he writes 'certainly neither prisoner would *like* that confessing becomes a universal practice, and the only universal law that each prisoner would *like* is that everyone should refuse to confess' (ibid., p. 76, emphasis added). This misinterprets the categorical imperative as relying on agents' preferences about the results of applying the universalization test, rather than the inconsistency of universalizing the maxim as judged by an impartial and autonomous will.[5]

Without mentioning Kant explicitly (except in a passing reference to the prisoners' dilemma analysis in the earlier paper), Sen's famous 1977 paper 'Rational Fools' did popularize the concept of commitment in economics, one interpretation of which is duty in the Kantian sense. Sen defines 'commitment' as an instance of a person 'choosing an act that he believes will yield a lower level of personal welfare to him than an alternative that is also available' (1977, p. 92). This is, in other words, acting against one's own self-interested preferences, which can be understood as a reflection of Kantian autonomy.

More recently, Lanse Minkler (1999) built on Sen's foundation, developing a formal model of economic choice that includes commitment and identifies Kantian ethics as one source of that commitment. In Minkler's model, agents follow a two-stage thought process, first considering their commitments before turning to the standard preference-satisfaction, thus granting commitment lexical priority over preferences, consistent with Kantian ethics.

Amitai Etzioni argued forcefully for a more elaborate choice framework in economics that can incorporate ethical values, including those drawn from Kantian ethics. In the 1987 article 'Towards a Kantian socio-economics', Etzioni recommends a 'bi-utility conception' to represent ethical decision-making, which he elaborates in his book *The Moral Dimension* (1988). He ascribes to Kantians the view that 'the self is divided, one part standing over the other, judging it and deciding whether or not to yield to any particular desire' (ibid., p. 140). This bears some similarity to the two-stage choice process that Minkler describes, but if taken too literally, the idea of a 'divided self' contradicts Kant's arguments for a unified will (Beck 1960, p. 180). From a broader perspective, Etzioni emphasizes the ability to judge one's own preferences, an important aspect of moral decision-making identified above, as representing true autonomy.

Another problematic aspect of Etzioni's conceptualization of Kantian ethics is that he models ethical motivation as a type of satisfaction or utility, parallel to but qualitatively different from the standard sense of utility in economics. Etzioni writes, 'acting in line with one's moral values produces a kind of satisfaction, a sense of moral worth, but it is more the kind one achieves when a hard day's work is done than the pleasure of getting off work early with full pay', and 'one has a sense of affirmation' from behaving morally (1988, p. 45, emphasis removed). This method of depicting ethical decision-making certainly has its virtues, and certainly it seems to be a realistic portrayal of the moral deliberation of many individuals. But in terms of modelling Kantian ethics it falls short; for acting solely in pursuit of satisfaction, no matter how noble the basis of that satisfaction or how good the act, is heteronomous, as detailed above.

Nonetheless, Kant did recognize 'moral feeling . . . the susceptibility to feel pleasure or displeasure merely from being aware that our actions are consistent with or contrary to the law of duty', and he even called its cultivation a duty, since it reflects dedication to the moral law (1797, pp. 399–400). But 'the moral law is valid for us not because it interests us . . . but, rather, the moral law interests us because . . . it has sprung from our will as intelligence and hence from our proper self' (1785, pp. 460–61). This indicates that we should feel good because we do good, not the other way around.

More recently, White (2004) outlined a model of economic choice that incorporates Kantian ethics based on the distinction between perfect and imperfect duties, as well as character and will. Relying on the standard economic choice framework of preference-maximization within constraints (and a formal understanding of preferences as rankings with no specific psychological basis), he models perfect duties as constraints, and includes imperfect duties among self- and other-interested preferences. Agents then maximize among their preferences (including imperfect duties) as always, recognizing their constraints (including perfect duties), resulting in actions that correspond (ideally) with the demands of Kantian ethics (provided that their duties are adopted for the sake of duty).

White's model also incorporates Kant's conception of character, allowing for moral imperfection and weakness of will in the economic model of choice.[6] He does this with a binary probability distribution which represents the uncaused nature of free, autonomous choice. Since free or autonomous choice in a Kantian context is a true act of will, impossible to explain based on any influence from within or without the agent, it would appear random to the outside observer, and must therefore be represented by a probability distribution. In this framework, the character of an agent is represented by the probability of her following duties rather than inclinations or preferences. A person with a 75 per cent likelihood of following the dictates of duty has a stronger character (and will) than a person with only a 60 per cent likelihood of doing the same. This aspect of the model allows for moral imperfection (without implying evil nature on the part of the agent). It also allows for different degrees of moral imperfection in different persons (or even within a single person at different times or under different circumstances).

Kantian ethics and welfare economics

Kant's ethics, or more precisely, his political theory, has drastic implications for social choice or welfare economics, but much less has been written on this than on individual choice models involving Kantian ideas. This section briefly outlines Kant's political theory, and then summarizes several strands of work criticizing welfare economics using these concepts.[7]

Put simply, Kant's political theory was a straightforward application of his moral theory. Like Hobbes, Kant wrote that the state develops as an escape from the state of nature. But unlike Hobbes, Kant thought that the ultimate justification for the existence of the state rests in its ability to ensure the maximum freedom of action for each person that is consistent with the same for all. Therefore, the institutions of a just government, including its laws, have to conform to the *Universal Principle of Right*, a generalized version of the categorical imperative: 'any action is *right* if it can coexist with everyone's freedom in accordance with a universal law, or if on its maxim the freedom of choice of each can coexist with everyone's freedom in accordance with a universal law' (1797, p. 230). This principle justifies state coercion, but only in a negative sense, to limit individuals' coercion of one another and to allow maximum mutually compatible external freedom.[8]

In a series of books, Timothy P. Roth (1999, 2002, 2004) outlines a critique of welfare economics and interventionist politics based on Kantian ethical and political theory and its close modern analogue, John Rawls's (1971) theory of justice. Roth emphasizes the moral equivalence of persons, which is embodied in Kant's Universal Principle of Right (as well as the categorical imperative), and which the state must acknowledge as a check on consequentialist policy. But as Roth explains, consequentialist welfare economics cannot give the necessary priority to the basic rights implied by individuals' dignity. It thereby violates the Kantian imperative to respect each person's freedom equally.

The ethical problems with the consequentialist orientation of welfare economics are perhaps most evident in the economic analysis of law (or 'law and economics'), which explicitly deals with the 'optimal' assignment and enforcement of rights. Normative law and economics evaluates changes in laws or legal institutions according to their effects on efficiency, most often according to the Kaldor-Hicks criterion. By this, a policy is approved if its benefits (to some) outweigh its cost (to others). But even though, by implication, the 'winners' benefit enough to compensate the 'losers' and still benefit from the change, making possible a Pareto improvement, the Kaldor-Hicks test requires no actual compensation. It is therefore often referred to as a 'potential Pareto improvement'.

As White (2006b) points out, this clearly violates the Formula of Respect for the Dignity of Persons by using some persons merely as a means to benefit others. Even if compensation were given, but the consent of those affected was not secured, the Kaldor-Hicks test would still fall short of the Kantian imperative to respect the dignity of persons by not coercing them except to prevent coercion of others. Finally, the Pareto test itself seems to accord the proper respect to persons by requiring that no persons be harmed as a condition of benefiting others.

Even the Pareto criterion may conflict with Kantian ethics if it relies on implicit rather than actual consent, because implicit consent is usually inferred based on individuals' self-interest, whereas actual consent may not have been similarly based, given that agents would make their choices based on a principle or duty. Once again, Sen laid the foundation for this when he wrote that commitment 'drives a wedge between personal choice and personal welfare, and much of traditional economic theory relies on the identity of the two . . . The basic link between choice behaviour and welfare achievements in the traditional models is severed as soon as commitment is admitted as an ingredient of choice' (1974, p. 94).

Conclusion

As we have seen, the essentially consequentialist nature of mainstream economics is in stark contrast to central Kantian ideals such as duty and human dignity. If Kantian ethics is to be taken seriously by economists, at least two methodological changes must be made. First, economists' models of choice must be modified to allow factors other than preferences to influence decisions, as emphasized by Sen and others. Economists (and many philosophers) remain resistant to the suggestion that choices might be based on desire-independent reasons, so they attempt to account for any other-regarding behaviour by including such motivations in preferences. But duties cannot always be modelled as preferences. Even when they can, care must be taken to understand the exact nature of duty-based preferences, which cannot be motivated by any type of satisfaction or sense of affirmation. More generally, economists must recognize that choices do not flow deterministically from preferences, but that human beings have true free choice to make decisions independent of their preferences (as well as of their duties).

Second, policy-oriented economists must realize that governments are not exempt from the moral constraints binding their citizens. Policy instruments must be re-evaluated in light of the Universal Principle of Justice, and the procedures used to find the optimal values for the instruments or their targets must be redesigned to take into account respect for human dignity and essential rights. Evaluative criteria such as Kaldor-Hicks efficiency must be reconsidered, and actual consent must be required for any consideration of a Pareto improvement. In the extreme, welfarist evaluation would be abandoned altogether in favour of the deontological standard of procedural justice, by which the rightness of policies and institutions has priority over the goodness of outcomes.

Notes

1. Sullivan (1989) provides a comprehensive review of Kantian ethics.
2. Social economists have a strong affinity for Kant's sense of dignity; see Lutz and Lux (1988, pp. 146–50), Lutz (1999, pp. 132–6), Etzioni (1987) and Ellerman (1988). For a critique of the use of Kantian dignity in social economics, see White (2003).
3. Kant realized, however, that we never know our true motivations, and that often we have several motivations to act as we do, so our moral self-assessment can never be perfect.
4. Space considerations prohibit discussion of *every* mention of Kant in the economic literature, which are surprisingly many. The focus here, instead, is on the most substantive and explicit uses of Kantian ethics in economics.
5. This mistake is repeated often in the literature on altruism and public good financing, but is sometimes recognized as such. For instance, Bilodeau and Gravel (2004) understand 'Kantian' to mean 'compelling an individual to undertake any action which we would *want* everyone else to undertake' (p. 646, emphasis added). They cite many papers that share this conception, including Laffont (1975), which was one of the earliest attempts to integrate Kantian concepts into mainstream economics. But they also cite Wolfelsperger (1999), who points out that this conception is not truly Kantian. See also Ballet and Jolivet (2003), who provide a critical overview of this literature that makes the same point.
6. See White (2006a) for an elaboration of this aspect of the model, and White (2005) for an application of the model to the economics of crime.
7. Many important points regarding Kant and welfare economics derive more generally from Kant's deontological stance, and less from his specific moral theory. These are therefore included in the deontology chapter; only the specifically Kantian contributions to this topic are discussed here.
8. For more on Kant's political theory, see Murphy ([1970] 1994) and Sullivan (1989, Ch.16).

References

Ballet, Jerome and Patrick Jolivet (2003), 'A propos de l'économie kantienne', *Social Science Information*, **42**, 185–208.

Beck, Lewis White (1960), *A Commentary of Kant's Critique of Practical Reason*, Chicago: University of Chicago Press.

Bilodeau, Marc and Nicolas Gravel (2004), 'Voluntary provision of a public good and individual morality', *Journal of Public Economics*, **88**, 645–66.

Ellerman, David P. (1988), 'The Kantian person/thing principle in political economy', reprinted in David P. Ellerman (1995), *Intellectual Trespassing as a Way of Life*, Lanham, MD: Rowman and Littlefield.

Etzioni, Amitai (1987), 'Toward a Kantian socio-economics', *Review of Social Economy*, **45**, 37–47.

Etzioni, Amitai (1988), *The Moral Dimension: Toward a New Economics*, New York: The Free Press.

Fleischacker, Samuel (1996), 'Values behind the market: Kant's response to *The Wealth of Nations*', *History of Political Thought*, **17**, 397–407.

Kant, Immanuel (1785), *Grounding for the Metaphysics of Morals*, trans. James W. Ellington, Indianapolis, IN: Hackett Publishing Company.

Kant, Immanuel (1788), *Critique of Practical Reason*, trans. and ed. Lewis White Beck, Upper Saddle River, NJ: Prentice-Hall.

Kant, Immanuel (1797), *The Metaphysics of Morals*, trans. and ed. Mary Gregor, Cambridge: Cambridge University Press.

Laffont, Jean-Jacques (1975), 'Macroeconomic constraints, economic efficiency and ethics: an introduction to Kantian economics', *Economica*, (n.s.) **42**, 430–7.

Lutz, Mark A. (1999), *Economics for the Common Good: Two Centuries of Social Economic Thought in the Humanistic Tradition*, London: Routledge.

Lutz, Mark A. and Kenneth Lux (1988), *Humanistic Economics: The New Challenge*, New York: The Bootstrap Press.

Minkler, Lanse (1999), 'The problem with utility: toward a non-consequentialist/utility theory synthesis', *Review of Social Economy*, **57**, 4–24.

Murphy, Jeffrie G. ([1970] 1994), *Kant: The Philosophy of Right*, Macon, GA: Mercer University Press.

Rawls, John (1971), *A Theory of Justice*, Cambridge, MA: Harvard University Press.

Roth, Timothy P. (1999), *Ethics, Economics and Freedom: The Failure of Consequentialist Social Welfare Theory*, Aldershot: Ashgate.

Roth, Timothy P. (2002), *The Ethics and Economics of Minimalist Government*, Cheltenham, UK and Northampton, MA, USA: Edward Elgar.

Roth, Timothy P. (2004), *Equality, Rights and the Autonomous Self: Toward a Conservative Economics*, Cheltenham, UK and Northampton, MA, USA: Edward Elgar.

Sen, Amartya (1974), 'Choice, orderings and morality', reprinted (1982) in *Choice, Welfare and Measurement*, Cambridge, MA: Harvard University Press, pp. 74–83.

Sen, Amartya (1977), 'Rational fools: a critique of the behavioural foundations of economic theory', reprinted (1982) in *Choice, Welfare and Measurement*, Cambridge, MA: Harvard University Press, pp. 84–106.

Sullivan, Roger J. (1989), *Immanuel Kant's Moral Theory*, Cambridge: Cambridge University Press.

White, Mark D. (2003), 'Kantian dignity and social economics', *Forum for Social Economics*, **32** (2), 1–11.

White, Mark D. (2004), 'Can *homo economicus* follow Kant's categorical imperative?' *Journal of Socio-Economics*, **33**, 89–106.

White, Mark D. (2005), 'A social economics of crime (based on Kantian ethics)', in Margaret Oppenheimer and Nicholas Mercuro (eds), *Law & Economics: Alternative Economic Approaches to Legal and Regulatory Issues*, Armonk, NY: M.E. Sharpe, pp. 351–73.

White, Mark D. (2006a), 'Multiple utilities and weakness of will: a Kantian perspective', *Review of Social Economy*, **64**, 1–20.

White, Mark D. (2006b), 'A Kantian critique of neoclassical law and economics', *Review of Political Economy*, **18**, 235–52.

Wolfelsperger, Alain (1999), '*Sur l'existence d'une solution 'kantienne' du problème des biens collectifs*', Revue Économique, **50**, 879–901.

See also the entries on: Deontology; Efficiency; John Rawls.

41 Labour standards
Günseli Berik

Background

'Labour standards' refer to rules, norms, rights, processes and outcomes associated with working conditions. The conventions of the International Labour Office (ILO), 188 of them as of early 2008, come closest to representing benchmarks of strong labour standards towards which countries could strive (ILO 2007a). However, ILO conventions and its non-binding recommendations also cover a range of issues that go beyond worker protections, rights and administrative capacity regarding work and employment, to include social security, social policy and related human rights (ILO [2005] 2007).

Concern about poor labour standards of trading partners and interest in linking trade policy with labour standards have a long history (Heintz 2003; Burda 2007; Berg and Kucera 2008). Nonetheless, poor labour standards in developing countries have received increasing attention since the early 1980s, when global commodity and capital flows began a robust expansion. During this period the ascendancy of arguments on the benefits of free trade and markets led to a weakening of national regulatory systems, and international treaties and institutions were established to safeguard unfettered trade relations. These developments have made it difficult to address weak labour standards in developing countries and to defend labour standards in industrialized countries. As a result, since the early 1990s – the period leading up to and following the establishment of the World Trade Organization (WTO) and the ratification of the North American Free Trade Agreement (NAFTA) and other regional free trade agreements – these concerns have led to calls for stronger enforcement of labour standards by incorporating them into the rules governing international trade.

The ILO's 1998 *Declaration on Fundamental Principles and Rights at Work* represents an important step in delineating the basic labour market norms to be upheld universally regardless of level of economic development (ILO 2007b). This declaration identifies four workplace rights, enshrined in eight ILO conventions, known as the 'core' labour standards: freedom from forced labour, nondiscrimination, abolition of child labour, freedom of association and collective bargaining rights. The ILO plays an important role in advocacy, guidance and monitoring of international labour standards (Berg and Kucera 2008). However, a country's membership in the ILO does not require it to ratify ILO conventions, including any that are part of the core. Furthermore, ratification of ILO conventions does not guarantee their implementation, as the ILO has limited power to enforce conventions, relying on moral suasion and embarrassment to remedy breach of obligations by countries and to bring about voluntary compliance.

The main governing body of world trade since 1994, the WTO, on the other hand, has kept labour standards outside its purview and has not sought close collaboration with the ILO on labour standards matters. WTO rules stipulate that, with few exceptions, production processes of goods cannot be taken into consideration in regulating trade, effectively barring a member country from using trade restrictions as a mechanism for addressing violations of core labour standards and other ILO conventions by another member. The exceptions – set out in the articles of the General Agreement on Tariffs and Trade (GATT) – permit use of trade restrictions when production processes endanger the health and safety of human, plant and animal life; violate public morals; or use forced labour (narrowly defined as prison labour) (Burda 2007). While other forms of linking trade with labour standards exist (for example, the use of market access as an incentive for improvement of labour standards under the Generalized System of Preferences (GSP) or in bilateral trade agreements), such linkage has become synonymous with the application of trade sanctions.

As of 2008, no multilateral enforceable mechanism for ensuring progress toward stronger labour standards globally had as yet emerged. Responses to demands for stronger enforcement of labour standards have instead taken three forms: (i) incorporation of labour standards conditionality into bilateral and regional trade agreements (for an innovative approach see Polaski 2006); (ii) proliferation of nongovernmental labour regulation initiatives to negotiate and monitor compliance with voluntary codes of conduct of companies and (O'Rourke 2005) (iii) ILO's decent work agenda that promotes objectives beyond worker protections and the 'core' conventions, but continues to rely on the moral suasion approach (ILO 1999).

The labour standards debate

The labour standards debate centres on the desirability, feasibility and effectiveness of using trade policy as an instrument to improve labour rights around the world (hereafter called 'linkage' for short). It is part of the discussions on the relative merits of the global integration of the late twentieth century. The arguments on either side echo those in the long-standing debate on the benefits and shortcomings of the market system (Freeman 1994). The emphasis of much of the labour standards debate has been on a global institutional arrangement for monitoring and improving working conditions that is linked to rights to international trade and, to a lesser degree, on bilateral or regional free trade agreements as a vehicle for improving labour standards (Sengenberger and Campbell 1994; Compa and Diamond 1996; Basu et al. 2003; Alston 2005).

The economic arguments

Proponents of linkage are mostly institutionalist economists who argue that labour standards are inputs to development, promote high-wage and more stable growth, and enable well-functioning markets (Marshall 1994; Palley 2004). Accordingly, higher labour standards are a means for shifting the pattern of incentives facing firms and governments to bring about productivity-enhancing investment and higher labour productivity (via healthier, more educated workers and greater worker cooperation) and improved economic and political stability (Agell 1999; Piore 2004; Palley 2004). These micro and macro level effects are thus likely to offset the higher labour costs associated with improved working conditions.

Institutionalist arguments and evidence also show that labour or social protection measures enable interaction and functioning of markets and serve as mechanisms to reduce risks associated with the market economy, such as increased vulnerability to income loss associated with rising trade openness (Rodrik 1997b; Agell 1999; Amable 2003).

Proponents of linkage also argue that in the absence of an international enforcement mechanism, there will be downward pressure on labour standards as firms compete on the basis of labour costs. The economic mechanism that facilitates this erosion or race-to-the-bottom is the increasing opportunities for firms to substitute foreign for domestic labour in production. The search for lower labour costs (for a given level of labour productivity) increases the bargaining power of corporations vis-à-vis workers and governments and allows them to dictate the terms of employment as a condition for their stay (Rodrik 1997a). To prevent this process of downward harmonization, a multilateral system to enforce stronger standards everywhere is argued to be more effective than a unilateral one (Rodrik 1996; Palley 2004).

Those who oppose linkage hail from diverse perspectives in economics. The opposition is united, however, on the undesirability and the ineffective, even counterproductive nature of any linkage. The main opponents of linkage are trade economists who view labour standards as solely a cost factor and as outputs of development. They argue that imposition of minimum international labour standards on poor countries would undermine their comparative advantage in producing goods that utilize their relatively abundant and low-cost labour and would stifle their growth prospects (Bhagwati 1995, 2004; Flanagan 2006). Similar arguments are made by proponents of poverty elimination and decent work in low-income economies (Singh and Zammit 2003; Kabeer 2004). Given the mobility of capital, higher costs associated with improved working conditions in export production are likely to trigger corporate flight, result in loss of formal jobs and movement of work toward informal units, out of the sight and reach of enforcement.

Institutionalist economists, who otherwise emphasize the benefits of labour market regulation, view improvement in labour standards as the outcome of a long-term process of changing economic incentives and social norms, rather than the product of legal reforms (Agell 1999; Brown and Stern 2007). Accordingly, linkage is said to be unlikely to bring about improvements unless the enforced labour standards are consistent with social norms and failure to comply with them is met with widespread social disapproval. Moreover, linkage arrangements must be attentive to the economic structures and conditions of developing countries.

Opponents of linkage question the race-to-the-bottom argument on theoretical and empirical grounds (Bhagwati 2004; Flanagan 2006). Cross-country statistical analyses on the relationship between labour standards and comparative advantage or export success generally find either no relationship or a positive relationship and do not find higher labour standards to be a deterrent to foreign direct investment (Brown 2000; Kucera 2002; Neumayer and de Soysa 2005; Kucera and Sarna 2006). Yet, there is evidence that elasticity of labour demand has been on the rise in the United States in recent decades (Rodrik 1997a). Case studies indicate that the threat of corporate flight exerts downward pressure on labour standards (Bronfenbrenner 2000; Palley 2004), and export-oriented foreign-invested firms are more likely to violate wage- and hours-related labour standards (Liu et al. 2004).

Questions of feasibility are also debated. Proponents of linkage pursue an institutional design and process that addresses the common objections to linkage (Barry and Reddy 2006), while opponents are sceptical that problems of implementation (in agreeing on standards beyond the general ILO principles and ensuring compliance with them) could be overcome (Bhagwati 2004; Flanagan 2006; Brown and Stern 2007).

Moral considerations

The moral *premises* of arguments or moral *consequences* of policy choices are mostly implicit in the debate. When moral issues are explicit they tend to be presented as separate from economic arguments in a manner typical of the economics discipline (Hausman and McPherson 1996). The moral premises involve arguments about the worth of persons and what is permissible in the treatment of individuals. The arguments in favour of linkage generally draw upon the centrality of labour for human beings, for example, exploitation and capabilities arguments, while those against linkage are generally based on libertarian premises.

Proponents of linkage focus on the morally objectionable conditions of production of some goods that enter international trade and the need to redress these conditions. Moral premises concerning the nature of human labour underlie concern about poor labour standards. Many theories of justice share the premise that work is a distinguishing characteristic of human beings. They view coercive contractual work arrangements, and, more generally, situations in which workers' dignity and rights are violated, as exploitative, unjust and as defining an unjust society (for example, see Elster 1983; Cohen 1988; John Paul II [1981] 2007). Proponents of linkage utilize varieties of (mostly implicit) notions of exploitation. In some formulations, exploitation and injustice are the outcome of economic coercion of workers to sell their labour power in the capitalist system, while in others the implied meaning is some combination of excessive hours of work and low wages.

Similarly, the capabilities approach grants that the right to gainful employment is a fundamental entitlement of human beings, and that it also helps people to expand capabilities such as life, bodily health and bodily integrity, which are the goals of development (Chen 1995; Sen 1999; Nussbaum 2003). In order to promote individual capabilities, however, conditions of gainful employment must be just. They must not involve 'exploitative conditions and low wages' (Chen 1995, p. 54); 'one must be able to work as a human being, exercising practical reason, and entering into meaningful relationships of mutual recognition with other workers' (Nussbaum 2003, p. 42). As such, improvement in working conditions is constitutive of as well as a means for a just society.

According to these perspectives, the prevalence of weak labour standards – for example, hazardous working conditions, forced labour, child labour, discrimination against women and ethnic minority workers, unpaid back wages, excessive hours of work, payment of wages inadequate to support workers and their family – is intrinsically wrong and must be remedied by social arrangements. Respect for workers' rights must shape the economic organization of society (John Paul II [1981] 2007) and improvements in conditions of work should not be left to the forces of supply and demand (Polanyi 1944). Unregulated markets will not generate just employment conditions, given that firms benefit from exploitative conditions both directly, as employers of such labour, and indirectly, as consumers of products made by this labour (inputs to their production), and desperation might force workers to consent to exploitative conditions.

Besides degradation of human labour, leaving labour markets unregulated creates other adverse moral consequences, such as health problems and a decline in family and community life (Polanyi 1944). These consequences follow from the unique nature of labour power, that it is not produced for sale and therefore is not a commodity, and that the conditions of employers' use of labour power have moral, psychological and physical effects on the human being to which it is attached. Based on these ethico-political considerations pursuing reforms that make trade rights conditional on promotion of labour standards would be one means of promoting a just society.

Consideration of moral consequences of unfettered international trade (for example, under the rules of the WTO) supports the argument that labour standards are a matter of concern for trade policy. Focusing on the process through which comparative advantage comes about, Rodrik (1996, 1997a) makes explicit the moral considerations that are absent in the arguments put forward by opponents of linkage. Within the framework of conventional international trade theory, weak worker protections and rights in developing countries strengthen their labour cost advantage in labour-intensive products and expand their market access in industrialized economies. Industrialized countries, in turn, reap the benefits of trade with these countries in the form of lower priced goods for consumers, greater average real income and a smaller import bill. This process, seen by international trade theory as mutually beneficial for trading partners, raises questions of distributive justice, fairness and legitimacy.

First, import competition causes job losses and slows wage growth for workers who produce goods that compete with the lower priced imports. Together with increasing mobility of capital, import competition threatens to erode working conditions in industrialized economies and increasingly in developing countries that compete with dominant producers such as China (Ross and Chan 2002). Case study evidence indicates the validity of these concerns about the spread of objectionable working conditions (Bronfenbrenner 2000; Palley 2004; Liu et al. 2004).

A second moral consequence of unfettered international trade is the unfairness of the process of job competition for industrial country workers. These workers have to compete with workers in distant lands who work under poor conditions. They bear the cost of a rise in the average real income and lower priced consumer goods (albeit they also benefit from the latter).

Third, through consumption, consumers in industrialized economies come into contact with goods produced under objectionable conditions, which raises the question of the legitimacy of such trade (Rodrik 1997a). If we grant that consumers are not narrowly self-interested and that societies can form values through public discussion (Sen 1995), then it is reasonable to assume that consumers may have preferences not only for products but also for types of production processes (Rodrik 1996). Indeed, there is evidence that consumers are willing to pay higher prices for ethical products (Elliott and Freeman 2003; Pollin et al. 2004) and that they have an aversion to inequity which includes consideration of workers in distant, poor countries (Becchetti and Rosati 2007). Satisfaction of importing-country consumer preferences for good labour standards then promotes the well-being of consumers.

The nature of the processes of producing goods that underlies trade is thus a relevant consideration for national trade policy. Further, linkage is argued to be the more effective instrument for addressing these moral considerations compared to the product labelling approach (Rodrik 1996). Linkage is also consistent with the established national practice of placing restrictions on market transactions that violate a widely held moral principle (for example, use of slave labour or product development based on human and animal experiments) (Rodrik 1996). This argument for linkage, however, does not address other moral consequences that potentially arise from successful implementation of a linkage scheme:

loss of employment for poor workers in developing countries and degradation of labour conditions as jobs move to less visible, informal, non-traded sectors. These are the likely unintended adverse consequences of linkage which are primarily raised by its opponents.

Some of the opposition to linkage is premised on libertarian notions of the right of individuals and, by extension, countries to pursue any goals that they see fit or to uphold a moral code of their own (Bhagwati 1995). By implication, individuals should be able to choose the jobs they wish to work at, and countries ought to be able to maintain the labour standards that accord with their cultural values and traditions, and trading partners should have the freedom to trade. Thus, it is immoral to prevent individuals from being able to work (if a trade sanction causes loss of jobs) or to impose one's values about good labour standards on another country. Accordingly, the very idea of universal labour standards is suspect (Bhagwati 1995). This argument for global diversity of labour standards and self-determination overlooks the extent to which the objectionable conditions of sweatshop labour are the product of internationalization of production itself, which transplants production processes and degrades existing labour conditions (Piore 2004).

Many opponents of linkage dispute that production for the global market in developing countries, often located in export-processing zones (EPZs) which are recipients of foreign direct investment, entails poor labour standards relative to local alternatives (Bhagwati 2004; Kabeer 2004; Flanagan 2006). Even when they grant that the working conditions in export production may be poor, these opponents argue that such jobs are superior to the available alternatives. As for the non-EPZ working conditions, recognition of poor working conditions sometimes accompanies implicit libertarian claims. According to this view, prevailing labour standards represent the informed choice of workers and firms, made in the context of abundant labour supplies and the resource constraints typical of developing countries.

Opponents of linkage also tend to minimize or dismiss industrial country workers' concern about their wage levels and job losses to developing countries with poor labour standards as 'egotistical and self-serving' (Bhagwati 2004, p. 244). Characterization of these concerns as 'protectionist' or as 'competitiveness considerations' implies that workers' anxiety about making a living is devoid of any legitimacy or moral basis.

Compared to the moral premises of their arguments, opponents of linkage are more explicit and united about the moral consequences of having labour standards conditionality on trade. They argue that poor working conditions are preferable to the likely harm that will befall these workers if their labour is made more costly by forcing upon developing countries improvements in labour standards. Thus, any linkage will harm precisely the group that it was intended to help. This argument, widely read in the popular press as well as in academic literature, sets up a dilemma for those concerned about the well-being of the poor in developing countries (Reddy and Barry 2006). Accordingly, there is a trade-off between two moral bads and we must settle for the lesser evil. The dilemma is a false one, however, as it does not consider ways of overcoming the trade-off.

Another variant of this trade-off argument tips the scales further against linkage. Jobs in the export sector are argued to promote greater personal freedom for women workers as well as offering them better pay than available alternatives and a path out of extreme poverty (Kabeer 2004; Sachs 2005). Women workers are argued to have greater say in marriage, fertility and household decisions. Thus, the risk of losing jobs by introducing linkage is unacceptably high.

A third variant further strengthens the moral claim against linkage: 'For these young women, these factories offer not only opportunities for personal freedom, but also the first rung on the ladder of rising skills and income for themselves and, within a few years, for their children' (Sachs 2005, p. 12). The implication is that intergenerational benefits should offset any moral bads associated with the sweatshop employment experienced by the current generation. Furthermore, Sachs seeks to assure that these are historically specific transitory conditions, which today's industrialized economies also experienced but successfully left behind. For this intergenerational trade-off argument to be sound, however, a moral bad experienced by the current generation has to be both *inevitable* and *necessary* for the next generation to be better off. Both are questionable. There is no inevitability that there will be an intergenerational improvement in well-being or that poor labour standards will be left behind in each and every case of industrialization. Historical evidence indicates that long-term growth does not bear a straightforward relationship with labour standards (Brown and Stern 2007). As regards the necessity of the current bad, one could argue that there are available means for overcoming any current trade-off between employment and better labour standards that would make the next generation unequivocally better off. There is also evidence that where enforcement of labour legislation is limited there has been little change in sweatshop conditions in an intergenerational sense (Berik and Rodgers forthcoming).

In conclusion, for most opponents of linkage the best means for promoting labour standards are the removal of trade barriers and economic growth together with continued reliance on the ILO's moral suasion approach (Bhagwati 2004; Sachs 2005; Flanagan 2006). Others emphasize tackling poverty in order to eliminate a major source of poor working conditions (Kabeer 2004). Proponents of linkage support overcoming the trade-off between jobs and labour standards by reforming international trade rules, incorporating incentives in global linkage arrangements (Barry and Reddy 2006) and pursuing complementary policies to achieve success based on these schemes (Berik and Rodgers forthcoming).

Acknowledgement

I am grateful to David Kucera and Cynthia Stark for comments on this chapter, though I alone am responsible for the final version.

References

Agell, Jonas (1999), 'On the benefits from rigid labour markets: norms, market failures, and social insurance', *Economic Journal*, **109**, F143–64.
Alston, Philip (2005), *Labor Rights as Human Rights*, Oxford: Oxford University Press.
Amable, Bruno (2003), *The Diversity of Modern Capitalism*, New York: Oxford University Press.
Barry, Christian and Sanjay Reddy (2006), 'International trade and labor standards: a proposal for linkage', *Cornell International Law Journal*, **39** (3), 545–639.
Basu, Kaushik, Henrik Horn, Lisa Roman and Judith Shapiro (2003), *International Labor Standards: History, Theory and Policy Options*, Oxford: Blackwell Publishing.
Becchetti, Leonardo and Furio Camillo Rosati (2007), 'Global social preferences and the demand for socially responsible products: empirical evidence from a pilot study on fair trade consumers', *World Economy*, **30** (5), 807–36.
Berg, Janine and David Kucera (2008), 'Labour institutions in the developing world: historical and theoretical perspectives', in Janine Berg and David Kucera (eds), *In Defence of Labor Market Institutions: Cultivating Justice in the Developing World*, Basingstoke: Palgrave Macmillan, pp. 9–31.
Berik, Günseli and Yana Rodgers (forthcoming), 'Options for enforcing labour standards: lessons from Bangladesh and Cambodia', *Journal of International Development*.

Bhagwati, Jagdish (1995), 'Trade liberalisation and "fair trade" demands: addressing the environmental and labour standards issues', *World Economy*, **18** (6), 745–59.

Bhagwati, Jagdish (2004), *In Defense of Globalization*, New York: Oxford University Press.

Bronfenbrenner, Kate (2000), 'Uneasy terrain: the impact of capital mobility on workers, Wages, and Union Organizing', report submitted to the US TDRC, 6 September, Trade Deficit Review Commission, Washington DC.

Brown, Andrew G. and Robert M. Stern (2007), 'What are the issues in using trade agreements for improving international labour standards?' Research Seminar in International Economics Discussion Paper No. 558, www.fordschool.umich.edu/rsie/workingpapers/wp.html, accessed 21 December, 2007.

Brown, Drusilla (2000), 'International trade and core labour standards: a survey of the recent literature', OECD Labour Market and Social Policy, Occasional Papers No. 43, Organisation for Economic Co-operation and Development, Paris.

Burda, Julien (2007), 'Chinese women after the accession to the World Trade Organization: a legal perspective on women's labor rights', *Feminist Economics*, **13** (4), 259–85.

Chen, Martha (1995), 'A matter of survival: women's right to employment in India and Bangladesh', in Martha Nussbaum and Jonathan Glover (eds), *Women, Culture and Development*, Oxford: Clarendon Press, pp. 37–57

Cohen, Gerald A. (1988), *History, Labour, and Freedom*, Oxford: Clarendon Press, pp. 239–54.

Compa, Lance A. and Stanley F. Diamond (eds) (1996), *Human Rights, Labor Rights, and International Trade*, Philadelphia, PA: University of Pennsylvania Press.

Elliott, Kimberly Ann and Richard B. Freeman (2003), *Can Labor Standards Improve under Globalization?* Washington DC: Institute for International Economics.

Elster, Jon (1983), 'Exploitation, freedom, and justice', in J. Roland Pennock and John W. Chapman (eds), *Marxism, Nomos XXVI*, New York and London: New York University Press, pp. 277–304.

Flanagan, Robert (2006), *Globalization and Labor Conditions*, New York: Oxford University Press.

Freeman, Richard B. (1994), 'A hard-headed look at labour standards', in Werner Sengenberger and Duncan Campbell (eds), *International Labour Standards and Economic Interdependence*, Geneva: International Institute for Labour Studies, International Labour Office, pp. 79–92.

Hausman, Daniel M. and Michael S. McPherson (1996), *Economic Analysis and Moral Philosophy*, Cambridge: Cambridge University Press.

Heintz, James (2003), 'Global labour standards: their impact and implementation', in Jonathan Michie (ed.), *The Handbook of Globalisation*, Cheltenham, UK and Northampton, MA, USA: Edward Elgar, pp. 216–33.

ILO (1999), *Decent Work*, Report of the Director General, International Labour Conference, 87th Session, Geneva: International Labor Office.

ILO ([2005] 2007), *Rules of the Game: A Brief Introduction to International Labor Standards*, ILO, Geneva, www.ilo.org/public/english/standards/norm/download/resources/rulesofthegame.pdf, 15 June, 2007.

ILO (2007a), 'ILO conventions', www.ilo.org/ilolex/english/convdisp2.htm, ILO, Geneva, 19 May, 2007.

ILO (2007b), 'Declaration on fundamental principles and rights at work', ILO, Geneva, www.ilo.org/dyn/declaris/DECLARATIONWEB.INDEXPAGE, 19 May, 2007.

John Paul II ([1981] 2007), *Laborem Exercens*, www.vatican.va/holy_father/john_paul_ii/encyclicals/documents/hf_jp-ii_enc_14091981_laborem-exercens_en.html#-8, 11 June, 2007.

Kabeer, Naila (2004), 'Globalization, labor standards, and women's rights: dilemmas of collective (in)action in an interdependent world', *Feminist Economics*, **10** (1), 3–35.

Kucera, David (2002), 'Core labour standards and foreign direct investment', *International Labour Review*, **141** (1–2), 31–69.

Kucera, David and Ritash Sarna (2006), 'Trade union rights and exports: a gravity model approach', *Review of International Economics*, **14** (5), 859–82.

Liu, Minquan, Luodan Xu and Liu Liu (2004), 'Wage-related labour standards and FDI in China: some survey findings from Guangdong province', *Pacific Economic Review*, **9** (3), 225–43.

Marshall, Ray (1994), 'The importance of international labour standards in a more competitive global economy', in Werner Sengenberger and Duncan Campbell (eds), *International Labour Standards and Economic Interdependence*, Geneva: International Institute for Labour Studies, International Labour Office, pp. 65–78.

Neumayer, Eric and Indra de Soysa (2005), 'Trade openness, foreign direct investment, and child labor', *World Development*, **33** (1), 43–63.

Nussbaum, Martha (2003), 'Capabilities as fundamental entitlements: Sen and social justice', *Feminist Economics*, **9** (2–3), 33–59.

O'Rourke, Dara (2005), 'Multi-stakeholder regulation: privatizing or socializing global labor standards?', *World Development*, **34** (5), 899–918.

Palley, Thomas (2004), 'The economic case for international labour standards', *Cambridge Journal of Economics*, **28**, 21–36.
Piore, Michael (2004), 'Rethinking international labor standards', in William Milberg (ed.), *Labor and the Globalization of Production: Causes and Consequences of Industrial Upgrading*, Basingstoke: Palgrave Macmillan, pp. 249–65.
Polanyi, Karl (1944), *The Great Transformation*, Boston, MA: Beacon Press.
Polaski, Sandra (2006), 'Combining global and local forces: the case of labor rights in Cambodia,' *World Development*, **34** (5), 919–32.
Pollin, Robert, Justine Burns and James Heintz (2004), 'Global apparel production and sweatshop labour: can raising retail prices finance living wages?' *Cambridge Journal of Economics*, **28** (2), 153–71.
Reddy, Sanjay and Christian Barry (2006), 'The false dilemma of the sweatshop', *Financial Times*, 24 July, www.policyinnovations.org/ideas/policy_library/data/01334, accessed 25 April, 2007.
Rodrik, Dani (1996), 'Labor standards in international trade: do they matter and what do we do about them?', in Robert Lawrence, Dani Rodrik and John Whalley (eds), *Emerging Agenda for Global Trade: High Stakes for Developing Countries*, Washington, DC: Overseas Development Council, pp. 35–79.
Rodrik, Dani (1997a), *Has Globalization Gone Too Far?* Washington, DC: Institute for International Economics.
Rodrik, Dani (1997b), 'The "paradoxes" of the successful state', *European Economic Review*, **41**, 411–42.
Ross, Robert and Anita Chan (2002), 'From North-South to South-South: the true face of global competition', *Foreign Affairs*, **81** (5), 8–13.
Sachs, Jeffrey D. (2005), *The End of Poverty*, New York: The Penguin Press.
Sen, Amartya (1995), 'Rationality and social choice', *American Economic Review*, **85** (1), 1–24.
Sen, Amartya (1999), *Development as Freedom*, New York: Alfred Knopf.
Sengenberger, Werner and Duncan Campbell (1994), *International Labour Standards and Economic Interdependence*, Geneva: International Institute for Labour Studies, International Labour Office.
Singh, Ajit and Ann Zammit (2003), 'Globalization, labor standards and economic development', in Jonathan Michie (ed.), *The Handbook of Globalisation*, Cheltenham, UK and Northampton, MA, USA: Edward Elgar, pp. 191–215.

See also the entries on: Globalization; Minimum wages.

42 Market
John O'Neill

Markets and ethics

In a market economy goods are produced for, distributed by and subject to contractual forms of exchange in which money and property rights are transferred between agents (O'Neill 1998, Ch. 1). Decisions about the production and distribution of goods are made by agents responding independently to changing relative prices of different goods. The resulting pattern of production and distribution is generally viewed as an unintended consequence of those individual responses. As such, it has long been subject to a particular form of ethical criticism. Patterns of production and distribution are not the result of any individually or socially determined ethical ends. In that sense, market economies are ethically disembedded economies (Polanyi 1957) and seem to face special problems concerning their ethical justifiability. Exchange relations are entered into not with the aim of realizing some good, but to accumulate further means of exchange. This critical line of argument can be traced back to Aristotle's distinction between the form of acquisition characteristic of the household and polis in which goods are produced and acquired directly to meet some human need, and forms of chrematistic acquisition characteristic of the market which aim at the accumulation of the means of exchange. The first form of acquisition has limits given by the needs it satisfies; the second knows no limits (Aristotle 1948, Book 1, Chs 8–9). Aristotle's influence is apparent in Marx (1970, Ch. 4) and in Polanyi (1957, pp. 53–4).

The critic's argument could be stated in a simplified form something as follows:

1. In market economies, economic transactions are not oriented by ethical considerations.
2. For any economic system, if transactions are not oriented by ethical considerations then that system is ethically indefensible.
3. Hence, market economies are ethically indefensible.

The first premise of this argument requires some clarification. It would be difficult to sustain the claim that market economics lack any ethical dimension. Market economics have certain ethical prerequisites if they are to exist at all. Property relies on the mutual recognition of rights. Contracts, if they are not always to be backed by the sword, require mutual trust between agents. Adam Smith argues that while positive beneficence may not be necessary for commercial society, the rules and sentiments of justice governing negative responsibilities to avoid harming others are a necessary condition (Smith 1982a, II.ii 3.2).

This line of argument can be stated more strongly. Markets form an ethical sphere in which free agents enter into voluntary contractual relations with each other that involve mutual recognition and respect of each other as free, independent and autonomous beings. Versions of this line of thought are found in Smith's defence of markets in terms of their developing the Stoic virtues of independence (Smith 1982b, vi.6), in Hegel's account of contract as a relation in which individuals 'recognise each other as persons and property owners' (Hegel 1967, 71R), and in libertarian defences of markets that appeal to the Lockean concept of self-ownership (Nozick 1980).

These stronger claims are themselves subject to debate in social theory. However, even if they are accepted they do not yet show that the first premise of the critic's argument should be rejected. What they do point to is the need for a more careful specification of the kinds of ethical orientation to which the critic is appealing. Market exchanges are not oriented by a direct regard for justice in the overall distribution of goods, the satisfaction of human needs or the realization of human goods and virtues. It is the absence of ethical orientation in these more specific senses that is central to the critic's argument. The critical argument might be restated thus:

1. In market economies, economic transactions are not directly oriented by distributive, welfarist or perfectionist ethical considerations.
2. For any economic system, if transactions are not directly oriented by distributive, welfarist or perfectionist ethical ends then that system is ethically indefensible.
3. Hence, markets are ethically indefensible.

Given this formulation of argument, the standard move of the defender of the unconstrained market economy has been to reject the second assumption. There are two standard moves for doing so. One is to question whether distributive or perfectionist ethical considerations should directly orient economic choices. The second is to defend an indirect form of welfarist justification according to which ethics-free zones can produce ethically optimal outcomes.

Should distributive or perfectionist ethical consideration orient economic choices and institutions?

Distributive justice
One standard move in defending market economies against the charge of issuing in unjust distributions is to reject the supposition of the critic that justice requires that a distribution of goods meets some patterned outcome. Such patterned end-state conceptions of justice are criticised by Nozick for being incompatible with liberty – liberty upsets patterns (Nozick 1980, pp.160–4). Hayek takes the application of the concept of justice to the outcome of market transactions to involve a mistake about the proper object of justice. Injustice can result only from actions that are the responsibility of some individual agent, that is, that are foreseen and intended by an agent. There are no natural injustices. In market societies, distributions of goods are the result of the unintended consequences of individual transactions. Hence, provided that no individual transactions are unjust, the resulting distribution cannot be unjust: 'what is called "social" or "distributive" justice . . . is meaningless within a spontaneous order' (Hayek 1973, Ch. 8). Both Nozick and Hayek defend versions of a procedural account of justice according to which justice is a property of procedures, not outcomes.

The defensibility of these claims opens large debates in political philosophy. Two brief critical comments are in order here. First, any distribution of private property itself already enhances the liberty of some and restricts the liberty of others. Hence the enforcement of such rights already limits liberty. Second, restricting responsibility to the results of intentional action does not offer a defensible account of legal justice where an individual can be assigned responsibility for foreseeable but unintended consequences of an act. It is difficult to see why such a strict account of justice should be extended to social justice in conditions in which an unequal distribution between groups is a foreseeable consequence of market exchanges.

Neutrality and perfectionism
A standard liberal justification of the market economy is to reverse the Aristotelian objection. It is not a vice but a merit of market economies that they do not promote human goods and virtues. In modern pluralistic societies, public institutional arrangements should be neutral between different conceptions of the good, and the market offers such an institutional arrangement. It allows individuals with quite different ends and beliefs about the good to cooperate with one another (Hayek 1976, p. 109). This argument from neutrality depends on the assumption that perfectionism is inconsistent with pluralism. There are reasons to question that assumption (O'Neill 1998, Ch. 2). Indeed, classical liberalism of the kind developed by Mill and defended more recently by Raz (1986) appeals to a particular perfectionist account of the good life centring on the virtues of the autonomous character which presupposes pluralism.

Indirect ethical justifications of markets
The second premise presupposes that an economic institution is ethically defensible only if transactions within it are directly oriented by ethical considerations. Another defence that can be offered of the market is to suggest that human goods are best realized by institutions that do not make the realization of those goods the end of economic acts. Consider the well-known paradox of hedonism – that if one wants a life of pleasure then one should not make pleasure one's aim. Similarly there may simply be a paradox that the goods of human life develop in societies that do not make their realization the aim of economic and political life. This argument finds an unlikely ally in Marx (1973, pp. 487–8):

> [T]he old view, in which the human being appears as the aim of production . . . seems to be very lofty when contrasted to the modern world, where production appears as the aim of mankind and wealth as the aim of production. In fact, however, what is wealth other than the universality of human needs, capacities, pleasures and productive capacities etc., created through universal exchange.

For Marx the argument shows only that commercial society is a prerequisite for a post-capitalist society that fully realizes human capacities. However, the defender of the market might attempt to employ a version of the argument to show that markets better realize the goods of human life than other feasible economic arrangements.

One version of the indirect argument is found in some standard welfarist justifications of the market. The paradox that some ends are best achieved by forbearance from their active pursuit is a basic thought behind indirect utilitarianism, for which this paradoxical pattern holds for the realization of the greatest welfare: if you make the realization of total welfare the aim of particular decisions, it will not be realized. Standard welfare arguments for the market in economic theory can be understood as following something like this indirect utilitarian route. Total human welfare is best improved through a market society in which individuals pursue their own interests and do not aim at improving total welfare. The argument is developed in different versions in both neoclassical and Austrian traditions (see also the chapter on Egoism).

In both traditions this argument normally appeals to a preference satisfaction theory of welfare according to which well-being consists in the satisfaction of preferences, the stronger the preference, the greater the improvement in well-being. A consumer's willingness to pay for some good is a measure of the strength of their preference for the good at the margin. In responding to price signals, producers and providers of services are guided to meet the preferences of consumers given their budget. Hence, the market is an institution that best realizes the satisfaction of consumer preferences and thereby best improves overall welfare. The view is taken to receive empirical support in the long-term growth of income, which allows consumers to satisfy a larger array of preferences, supplied by producers who, in order to compete, must successfully identify and satisfy those preferences.

This argument has been subject to scepticism from both hedonic and eudaimonic approaches to well-being which question the direct identification of welfare with preference satisfaction. Such scepticism receives its own empirical support in the finding that the growth in total aggregate income has not been correlated with a growth in reported life satisfaction (Lane 2001). At least one reason, sceptics suggest, is that individuals in market societies pursue comparative status and positional goods whose worth to any particular person is affected by the consumption of the same goods by others. In markets each individual independently makes a choice for a good that is affected by the same choice made by others. The promise to each individual that a good will make them better off is not realized, since collective consumption of that good means that no one is better off. Hence, increased income and consumption are not matched with any increase in welfare (Hirsch 1977).

While this objection may have power against recent welfarist defences of the market, at least some classical defences of the market may not be subject to this criticism. For example, Adam Smith argues that the concern for social appearance that fosters the 'vain and insatiable desires' that drive the growth of commerce is inimical to human happiness and founded upon a mistake as to its constituents. However, while the pursuit of 'the gratification of . . . vain and insatiable desires' in commercial society corrupts the character, at the same time it creates the conditions for the development and wide distribution of goods required for human welfare and promotes mankind 'to cultivate the ground, to build houses, to found cities and commonwealth, and to invent and improve all the sciences and arts which ennoble and embellish human life' (Smith 1982a, IV.1.10). The theme reappears in *The Wealth of Nations*:

> A revolution of the greatest importance to the publick happiness [commerce], was . . . brought about by two different orders of people, who had not the least intention to serve the publick. To gratify the most childish vanity was the sole motive of the great proprietors. The merchants and artificers . . . acted merely from a view to their own interests. (Smith 1981, III.iv.17)

This argument is not subject to the criticisms of recent welfarist defences of market economies outlined above. Smith allows that in market economies, the material and cultural means of proper happiness and the development of human virtue are the result of the behaviour of agents who not only do not aim at well-being but are moved by the vices of vanity. However, even granted the assumption that markets have these beneficial consequences, Smith's argument entails the existence of an internally corrosive tendency within market economics to foster forms of character that are incompatible with the flourishing of the practices and virtues which markets are taken to engender.

The ethical limits of markets

The indirect justification of the market relies on the claim that the goods of human life develop in societies that do not make their realization the aim of economic life. An economic framework may be ethically justifiable according to certain ethical considerations, for example, in the case of Smith, certain perfectionist considerations, even if exchanges within that framework are not directly oriented by those considerations. However, even if those arguments were successful, it is not clear that such indirect justifications are generalizable to all goods. It may be that there are certain goods that can only be realized if they are the direct object of proper normative consideration. This argument can be stated thus:

1. In market economies, economic transactions are not oriented by a particular set of significant ethical considerations.
2. For any economic system, there are some goods such that, if transactions about those goods are not oriented by that set of significant ethical considerations, then the system is ethically indefensible as an institution for distributing those goods.
3. Hence, there are goods for which markets are an ethically indefensible institution for their distribution.

This argument rejects the market not as a general economic institutional arrangement, but rather as an arrangement that is appropriate for the distribution of a particular set of goods. There are certain goods that ought not to be the object of market exchange, either directly by being rendered commodities for sale or indirectly by being made subject to the norms of market exchange (Walzer 1983).

The arguments for ethical boundaries in markets are diverse. One set of arguments can be developed from the claim noted earlier that markets have moral prerequisites and hence an ethical dimension. If it is granted that markets themselves are insufficient to generate the norms and character required for market contracts, that 'a contract is not sufficient unto itself' (Durkheim 1964, p. 215), then markets presuppose non-market spheres of kinship, education, association and community in which those norms and character themselves are fostered. Hence, there are internal ethical limits to the expansion of markets into those spheres. A second class of arguments for market boundaries is political. It is a constitutive condition of democratic political procedures that votes and political office are not objects of market exchange. The ability to buy political influence is not consistent with equality of citizenship in democratic societies. A third class of arguments is distributive: universal provision of goods according to need in spheres such as health or education is often justified on distributive grounds as a condition of the development of basic human capacities.

Another set of arguments for ethical boundaries for markets that is influential in the Kantian tradition appeals to the conditions for dignity.

> In the kingdom of ends everything has either a *price* or a *dignity*. If it has a price, something else can be put in its place as an *equivalent*; if it is exalted above all price and so admits of no equivalent, then it has dignity. That which is relative to universal human inclinations and needs has a *market price*; but that which constitutes the sole condition under which anything can be an end in itself has not merely a relative value – that is, a price – but has an intrinsic value – that is, *dignity*. (Kant 1948, p. 77, emphasis in original)

Treating persons as objects of exchange is incompatible with respect for their dignity. This argument of itself immediately rules out buying and selling persons. However, it might be extended to other goods if further conditions of human dignity can be specified in more detail. Thus, for example, it is sometimes argued that respect for bodily integrity is central to human dignity and as such this rules out the sale of bodily parts.

Another related thought is that markets are not appropriate where they result in the loss of self-command over significant activities. Traditional socialist criticism of wage labour often appealed to the claim that in selling their labour power workers give over the command of central activities. Versions of this form of argument have been revived with respect to commercial surrogacy:

> The worker contracts out right of command over the use of his body, and the prostitute contracts out right of direct sexual use of her body. The selves of the worker and the prostitute are, in different ways, both put out for hire. The self of the 'surrogate' mother is at stake in a more profound sense still. The 'surrogate' mother contracts out the right over the unique physiological, emotional and creative capacity of her body, that is to say, of herself as a woman. (Pateman 1988, p. 215)

Liberal critics of such arguments have claimed that they stray onto perfectionist ground. The normative asymmetry between reproductive labour and other forms of labour and service relies on perfectionist presuppositions about the significance of different activities for a good human life (Arneson 1992). However, it is open to the defender of market boundaries to simply accept and defend those perfectionist presuppositions.

A shift to perfectionist arguments moves the debate from Kantian to more Aristotelian considerations around the nature of the kinds of goods and social relations that are conditions of a flourishing human life. One important line of argument has appealed to the way incommensurabilities with market exchange are constitutive of certain relations and commitments. A variety of social relations and evaluative commitments that are central to the possibility of a good human life are constituted by a refusal to treat them as commodities which can have a price put on them (Raz 1986; compare Anderson 1993). Love and friendship are obvious examples. Someone who could put a price on friendship would simply not understand the loyalties that are constitutive of that relationship. Similarly, moral commitments are such that they are not open to being subject to market exchange. For this reason they fall within the domain of application of the concepts of bribery, corruption and betrayal: to offer money for someone to break a moral commitment is to offer a bribe, to accept the money is to betray the commitment. Constitutive incommensurabilities rule out the very possibility of market exchange in particular goods.

There exist other goods which can be bought and sold in markets, but which it is often argued ought not to be. Consider for example Richard Titmuss's influential defence of a non-market sphere of gift relationships in blood. Blood can be bought and sold, but in defining a sphere of gift relationships one is able to foster a set of relations of care between strangers which market relations undermine (Titmuss 1970). The potentially corrosive nature of market relations is invoked not just with respect to general care for strangers, but also with respect to more particular relationships that define specific roles in social practices, such as science and education. The spread of attitudes, norms and relations characteristic of the market in these cases may be possible, but they transform the nature of relationships that are central to human flourishing. For example, in education to treat students as 'consumers' is to potentially transform the nature of the relation of teacher and student in contractual terms.

An influential argument for the view that market relations potentially corrode particular social practices that are central to human flourishing is implicit in the work of Alasdair MacIntyre (1985). MacIntyre characterizes practices in terms of the pursuit of goods which are internal to a practice in the sense of being constitutive of the practice and such that they 'can only be identified and recognized by the experience of participating in the practice in question'(MacIntyre 1985, pp. 188–9). Typical examples of practices that have such internal goods are farming, architecture, chess, the arts and the sciences. Practices are contrasted with 'institutions' – those organizational arrangements which are concerned with the acquisition and distribution of external goods, such as wealth and power, that can be identified independently of any particular practice. 'Institutions' in MacIntyre's sense are both a necessary condition for practices but also potentially corrupting of them where the desire for external goods displaces and undermines the pursuit of internal goods. This claim about the potentially corrosive character of institutions is made quite generally, but MacIntyre's examples point to particular problems with market institutions in their potential to undermine practices. Where an organization, such as a fishing enterprise, develops the aim to 'only or overridingly satisfy as profitably as possible some market's demand', then that organization will no longer be primarily concerned with 'the respect of skills, the achievement of goods and the acquisition of virtues' that are internal to the practice (MacIntyre 1994, p. 285). This argument can be interpreted as offering reasons for the protection of specific practices from the incursion of market norms and institutions (Keat 2000). However its central point is also a version of the more general Aristotelian criticism of markets with which we began and can be understood as such. It illustrates the continuing significance of the Aristotelian tradition in criticism of market economies.

References

Anderson, Elizabeth (1993), *Value in Ethics and Economics*, Cambridge, MA: Harvard University Press.

Aristotle (1948), *Politics*, trans. Ernest Barker, Clarendon Press, Oxford.

Arneson, Richard J. (1992), 'Commodification and commercial surrogacy', *Philosophy and Public Affairs*, **21**, 132–64.

Durkheim, Emile (1964), *The Division of Labor in Society*, trans. George Simpson, New York: The Free Press.

Hayek, Friedrich A. (1973), *Law Legislation and Liberty: Volume 1*, London: Routledge and Kegan Paul.

Hayek, Friedrich A. (1976), *Law, Legislation and Liberty: Volume 2*, London: Routledge and Kegan Paul.

Hegel, Georg W. F. (1967), *Philosophy of Right*, trans. T. Knox, Oxford: Oxford University Press.

Hirsch, Fred (1977), *Social Limits to Growth*, London: Routledge and Kegan Paul.

Kant, Immanuel (1948), *Groundwork of the Metaphysics of Morals*, trans. H. Paton, London: Hutchinson.

Keat, Russell (2000), *Cultural Goods and the Limits of the Market*, London: Palgrave.

Lane, Robert E. (2001), *The Loss of Happiness in Market Democracies*, New Haven, CT: Yale University Press.

MacIntyre, Alasdair (1985), *After Virtue*, 2nd edition, London: Duckworth.

MacIntyre, Alasdair (1994), 'A partial response to my critics', in John Horton and Susan Mendus (eds), *After MacIntyre*, Cambridge: Polity Press.
Marx, Karl (1970), *Capital I*, London: Lawrence and Wishart.
Marx, Karl (1973), *Grundrisse*, Harmondsworth: Penguin.
Nozick, Robert (1980), *Anarchy, State and Utopia*, Oxford: Blackwell
O'Neill, John (1998), *The Market: Ethics, Knowledge and Politics*, London: Routledge.
Pateman, Carole (1988), *The Sexual Contract*, Cambridge: Polity Press.
Polanyi, Karl (1957), *The Great Transformation*, Boston, MA: Beacon Press
Raz, Joseph (1986), *The Morality of Freedom*, Oxford: Clarendon.
Smith, Adam (1981), *An Inquiry into the Nature and Causes of the Wealth of Nations*, Indianapolis, IL: Liberty Press.
Smith, Adam (1982a), *The Theory of Moral Sentiments*, Indianapolis, IL: Liberty Press.
Smith, Adam (1982b), *Lectures on Jurisprudence*, Indianapolis, IL: Liberty Press.
Titmuss, Richard M. (1970), *The Gift Relationship*, London: Allen and Unwin.
Walzer, Michael (1983), *Spheres of Justice*, Oxford: Blackwell.

See also the entries on: Karl Marx; Adam Smith.

43 Karl Marx

Jack Amariglio and Yahya M. Madra

Karl Marx (1818–83) is an unusual figure in the history of ethical and economic thought. Perhaps few such internationally influential thinkers have been so (apparently) contradictorily understood. He is variously interpreted as a trenchant moral critic of the exploitation and alienation of the existing industrial capitalist social order (Buchanan 1982; Geras 1985, 1992); as an amoral historicist who relegated ethics to the realm of 'false consciousness'; as a broadly conceived moralist who rejected 'the moral point of view' (Miller 1984); as a moral relativist who regarded ethical norms as incommensurable, culturally and locationally specific and constantly changing along with transformations in concrete economic conditions; as an ethical visionary who proposed one of the more enduring conceptions of economic and distributive justice of the past two centuries (DiQuattro 1998); as a strict economic determinist who assigned to ethics a not-so-privileged place in the 'superstructure' of politics, law, religion and ideology; as a pre-Nietzschean nihilist who saw 'values' as a blind for humans living fully (Ruccio and Amariglio 2003); as a one-sided ethical partisan who reserved for the working classes an objective position within morality worth its historical weight; as a transcendental humanist who believed that shared, communal ethical standards would triumph over the course of humanity's long haul (Kain 1988); and as much else besides. In addition, Marx is thought to have held, unsatisfactorily, several, if not many, of these positions simultaneously (see Lukes 1985), thus adding to the confusion and debate over his relation to existing ethical discourse.

According to some interpretations (Resnick and Wolff 1987), Marx makes the issue of class exploitation the central economic element of his critique of capitalism. While Marx's focus on class exploitation has been defended as the cornerstone of his 'scientific' analysis of market capitalism, this focus is also propounded as decisive in adjudicating debates concerning the continuity of a strong moral element in Marx's writings over the course of his life. In this latter view, Marx goes beyond a 'mere' formal definition of economic exploitation, according to which the capitalist's profit is the surplus value that the capitalist appropriates after having paid labourers a wage that only recompenses them for their 'necessary labor' (Roemer 1988, pp. 52–71), Marx periodically decries this surplus value, this unpaid labour, as robbery or theft, since capitalists use their substantial economic, political and cultural power in and through the wage-labour contract to take away from workers that which the capitalists neither produced nor won through a fair agreement with these workers. Marx's characterization of this appropriation as social theft constitutes, for many, the main ethical outlook from which Marx excoriated capitalism and promulgated an alternative, non-exploitative communism (see Geras 1985, 1992; Bensaïd 2002, pp. 122–62). Marx's detailed investigation in *Capital* of the effects of capital accumulation – as capitalists exploit workers both intensively and extensively in their fevered drive to stay ahead of their competitors – includes descriptions of the possible and actual 'immiseration of the proletariat' (1976, pp. 781–870).

Historically, these descriptions of worker suffering have pulled on readers' heartstrings and tugged at their sense of justice (Wilde 1998, p. 2). Marx provides wrenching images of how capitalists must periodically throw workers out of work, creating a reserve army of the unemployed, a 'surplus population' that ebbs and flows with the needs of capitalist accumulation. This imagery has been a primary rhetorical source for a labour-based 'philosophy of liberation' (Dussel 1985) and an ethics of the oppressed. These days, the working 'victims' have been propelled, at least in descriptions, to the post-colonial margins of a previously well-formed central capitalism by the ever more voracious and seemingly interminable process of capitalist globalization (Amin 2001; see Bergeron 2001 for the impact of such descriptions upon left and feminist counter-discourses).

The dictum from *Critique of the Gotha Programme*, 'from each according to his ability, to each according to his needs' (1938, p. 10), regarding contribution according to ability and distribution according to need provides a thread linking Marx's early notion in *The Economic and Philosophic Manuscripts* that communal productive activity principally defines the species nature of human beings – thereby initiating a generalized ethics based upon valuing labour-in-common – to his discussions in *Grundrisse* and *Capital* of the origin and distribution of surplus under capitalism. *Critique of the Gotha Programme* announces this dictum, as George DeMartino (2003) points out, as a two-part moral position: the first, 'from each according to his ability', establishes a principle of 'productive' justice, and the second, 'to each according to his needs', demarcates a principle of distributive justice.

In his writings, Marx occasionally muses upon a social division of labour in which the burdens (or pleasures, depending on the viewpoint) of production might be equally divided and shared within a community (see, for example, the contrast Marx draws in *Capital* (1976, pp. 477–9) between the 'spontaneous' development of 'the organization of the labour of society in accordance with an approved and authoritative plan' that characterized 'ancient Indian communities' and the hierarchical, despotic division of labour he finds in capitalist manufacturing). Thus, justice initially could be served by a community's intentional decision to disperse 'equitably' the responsibility of productive activity needed to sustain and expand the community's material standard of living.

In communism, though, this formal equality can be surpassed by a fully attainable, higher principle, one based on the real contributions that productive labourers could and would be willing to make to each other and to the community as a whole. The justice of this arrangement consists of the non-coerced differential that could contribute to a socially valued norm (such as economic growth). In Marx's eyes, the distributive justice of social allocation by need stood in sharp contrast to the injustice of distribution in capitalism according to sheer class power, class position and the reproductive needs of capital accumulation. Thus, one of Marx's main contributions to ethical theory is considered to be his recurring concern for distributive justice, that is, the question of what principle does or should determine how a society's productive resources and the income generated by those resources are divided (DiQuattro 1998; Fleischacker 2004, pp. 96–103). In that light, followers of Marx emphasize the second part of the so-called 'communist axiom' ('to each . . .') as the more useful but also controversial element of a Marx-derived ethics (Madra 2006). It is controversial because it does not seem to square with a different notion of class justice – one based upon what DeMartino identifies as 'appropriative justice' – which also can be found in Marx. This is the Lockean-tinged idea that reward should be tied to productive contribution (this tension is adeptly discussed by Burczak 2006, pp. 98–121). This principle takes shape in Marx's claim that workers are entitled to appropriate that which they have produced, especially 'their' surplus: non-productive claimants have few if any grounds for a different initial appropriation and subsequent distribution of that economic surplus.

A broader debate apropos the absence or presence of any moral element in Marx's writings opens upon the considerations stemming from exploitation as social theft in *Capital* and the communist axiom in *Critique of the Gotha Programme*. Probably less successfully argued today is that the entirety of Marx's work is devoid of universalist moral stances (Peffer 1990, pp. 35–79). There appears to be wide agreement at present that Marx's earliest writings did, in fact, proceed from a premise of an essential human nature whose obfuscation in stage after historical stage of human alienation and class-based mystification must be negated into an ethical imperative for liberating this essence. This early Marx is highly concerned, or so say his defenders, with the specification of 'the good life', which is elaborated from his uncovering the qualities of human essence (Brudney 2001). Marx's so-called 'eudaimonism' (Gilbert 1984) places him closer to Aristotle than his contemporary socialist comrades in his pursuit to stipulate this good life.

The claim that Marx adopted this transcendental perspective in his subsequent writings is more contested. This claim has been contrasted with Marx's 'mature' and supposedly more scientific stance that the process of delivering humans from alienation in the capitalist-organized production process and the exchange of commodities via markets is 'immanent' in the real conditions of production and consumption within capitalism. Some, like George Brenkert (1983), find no necessary contradiction between the morally inclined 'meta-ethics' of Marx and his scientific theories. Yet, other Marxist critics frequently link the first position – the emphasis on universalism and the moral stance to which it gives rise – to an overarching 'humanism'. As John Roche (2005) notes, the liberation of humans from their self- and other-imposed alienation was a measure with which Marx took his distance from capitalism and all other class-based societies. As long as humans, workers in particular, found themselves subordinated to and positioned 'under' capital in production, they were not the subject of their own history, but, rather, were forced to attend capital in the same way that religion had made humans subservient to God.

For this humanist Marx, the immorality of subordination would be challenged and replaced by a liberatory ethics that signals the final freeing of a suppressed, immanent human nature. The self-realization of humans would lead them to understand that their attributions of creative powers to supra-human beings and forces were nothing more than alienated and mystified ideology brought about and maintained by the castes and classes (other humans) who mostly benefited from this kind of self-serving misspecification. The humanist struggle to liberate humans in thought and practice from anything that 'stands above' them and exercises domination over their economic production, consumption and distribution cuts across historical epochs and, hence, gives rise to a universal moral position and goal according to which all ethical claims may be judged.

There is at least one other way in which Marx's critique of capitalism and class exploitation can be said to be morally humanist. This is the claim that Marx held the view, first presented in *The Economic and Philosophic Manuscripts*, that there is a transhistorical human essence, expressed best in and through the free, creative and non-alienating labour that people, when liberated, are capable of performing (Wilde 1998, p. 5). This essence defines human potentiality and, in Marx's opinion, was concretely realizable in the communist forms of social production that were emerging in his time as real possibilities out of the socializing of the labour process brought about by rapacious capital accumulation. Ever looking to reduce costs and increase surplus/profit, capitalists, as Marx describes them in *Capital*, are driven to bring together under one roof a mostly undifferentiated labour force, one that now has as its objective conditions a commonality hitherto proscribed by the division of labour and specialization of task and by the fragmenting stratagems of capitalist owners and their managerial proxies in the labour process. The possibility that workers could self-consciously overcome their alienation and exploitation by recognizing these objective conditions – the possibility, in this case, that workers now comprised a fully socialized and confederated proletariat, capable of running the most advanced production processes on their own behalf – led Marx (according to some views) to a moral claim about the superiority of the proletariat in the dialectical sweep of human history.

Not only does this self-conscious proletariat serve as the gravedigger for the capitalist mode of production (as Marx and Friedrich Engels expressed in the Communist Manifesto), in so doing, it relieves humankind of this particularly odious aberration in human essence. But this class also acts as a singularly affirmative moral force by putting an end to alienation and by bringing to fruition the full expression of this human essence through communal production. It is only on the basis of this a priori moral humanism, or so it is claimed, that Marx is capable in his historical materialism of privileging the struggles of the working class in the fight against capitalism and its many alienations.

The ultimate emergence and victory of a self-conscious, morally heroic proletariat may rely partly on this humanist transcendence and, therefore, on an a priori ethics that inscribes within it a universalist and eternalist view of a human essence. But the historic role of the proletariat is also defended in Marx's writings by a non-moralist notion of immanence, that is, a putatively scientific description of the true potential within, and the factually-based trajectory of, real historical movement. In this 'scientific' tradition, Marx is even decidedly anti-moralist, as his discussions of historical change within capitalism, leading to its eventual supersession by communism, disapprove of the notion that morality could ever be the prime motivating force of socio-economic transformation. In *The German Ideology*, Marx and Engels emphasize the superstructural role of morals and ethics, and consign these to the category of ideology. It is not that ideology lacks historical force; rather, its force is determined and mediated by the play in the economic base between the forces and relations of production. So, in Marx's terms, historical change is the result of human action, but not according to conscious plan or intention. If the proletariat steps into the sunlight as the subject that brings humans closer to living according to ideals of productive, appropriative and distributive justice, it is not the consequence of workers necessarily holding these ideals (although they may). Rather, it is the outcome of an unfolding process of incessant change set off by determinations that are real/material and that can never be reduced to the effects of any subject's consciousness, moral or otherwise. As Marx puts it in 'The civil war in France', workers 'have no ideals to realise, but to set free elements of the new society with which old collapsing bourgeois society is pregnant' (1978b, p. 636).

An important implication of this 'historicist' reading of Marx (even though this position may not always be held by those who embrace 'scientific' Marxism) is that the norms of each social formation are thought to be produced within those formations and, therefore, do not transcend the historical conditions that are necessary for their existence (West 1991). This is the position that Marx puts forward both in *The German Ideology* and in *A Contribution to the Critique of Political Economy*. The historical conditions also describe the limits or boundaries of the applicability of such norms. Thus, moral positions and ethical stances are 'relative' to their historical context, and they can never escape these constraints in order to comprise a god's eye perspective from which to judge alternative economic and social arrangements of the production and distribution of economic surplus. Transcendence is forsaken and replaced by the concrete, historical conjuncture, and it is only in terms of this conjuncture that morals may arise, but now as secondary effects of the primary forces driving socio-economic change. This Marx – a radically historicist and anti-moralist Marx – is the Marx to which many postmodern Marxists are drawn since they share a suspicion of transhistorical and transdiscursive moral norms, and they find the rough equality of moral positions, determined in their relative weight of persuasiveness and influence by extra-discursive forces, as far more palatable than an a priori moral balance sheet of universal rights and duties covering all historical formations.

Indeed, history itself can be seen as Marx's moral standpoint (Elliott 1986). Several dimensions of this stance are worth noting. First, it is unnecessary to see Marx as a strict determinist in the realm of causation. Marx's writings also enable a reading that emphasizes the complex 'many-sidedness' of every event (as described in *Grundrisse*), including moral discourse and its activation. In this way, Marx embraces the 'overdetermination' and possibly the indeterminacy of morality, as the conditions of existence of morality, and its effects, are multiple and frequently subject to historical change. This is the aleatory aspect of Marx's ethics (Althusser 2006; Callari and Ruccio 1996). From Marx's vital intervention in value theory in volume one of *Capital*, which leads him to invent the concept of 'commodity fetishism', to his influential discussion of the various 'forms of the commune' that precede capitalism in *Grundrisse*, there is always an element of uncertainty and chance. This indeterminate element often takes the form of a conceptual 'inversion' in which subjectivity and consciousness are not simple reflections of the modes of production, but, instead, are the uncertain productions of a complicated overplus of determinants, none of which can hegemonize the field of causation. (In Bertolt Brecht's famous words, cited in Benjamin (2003), 'you never know where you are with production: production is the unforseeable'.)

By this aleatory logic, morals may always be included in the set of multiple determinations since they can be (but need not be) a feature of a particular concrete social formation. But morality likewise is overdetermined, and, as an outcome, moral principles are not generally predictable from a given set of material conditions. In this reading, Marx rejects viewing morality as an unyielding set of principles impervious to fortuitous changes in both content and form. Future socialism would not be exempt from changes in moral standards (Wilde 2001, p. 5).

Further, Marx's position is consistent with the 'amoral' view that morals may even disappear because they change shape to such an extent that they are no longer recognizable or usable as morality – this is a more 'nihilistic' reading of Marx that places him in close relation to Nietzsche and the latter's 'transvaluation of values' (see Ruccio and Amariglio 2003). This position is amoral only in the sense that it holds to no specific definition of morals across all moments of history.

From the aleatory standpoint, it follows that Marx's commitment to communism is not to an actual economic model, nor to a stable and definite social order nor to a system of morality that reflects or accommodates a presumed human essence. Instead, Marx's commitment takes the form of a deliberate ethical axiom ('from each . . . to each') to be sustained each time society faces the question of how to produce, appropriate and share the social surplus. Understanding it as an axiom subtracts from communism the teleological dimension characteristic of nineteenth-century visions of socialism and renders it vulnerable to the test of experimentation and political action (see Özselçuk and Madra 2005). Marx's defence of communism, in this aleatory tradition, is not a matter of his reversion to a morally preferable 'Utopian socialism' that he and Engels in the Communist Manifesto had already absorbed and then dispensed with. But, rather, this defence is a risky intervention into the unfolding life of the capitalist social formation.

In his 1843 letter 'For a ruthless criticism of everything existing' (1978a, pp. 12–15), Marx announces his revulsion toward bourgeois ethics and, in particular, religious morality (Collier 2001). Neither could serve as the basis for a critical appraisal of capitalist exploitation or alienation, nor could a radical politics be constructed upon their edifice.

But, Marx also brutally disparages the counter-discursive 'dogma' which appears as the reaction against these universalizing ethical discourses. For his followers, Marx advises a never-ending 'ruthless criticism', which includes the will to criticize one's own pet moral positions and political truisms. Marx's commitment to communism is always/ already uncertain and fragile, in that the moral basis for communism and its perceived content are for him prime objects of such ruthless criticism and should be expected to change, perhaps in surprising ways. He posits the transitory nature of concepts of 'rights' and 'equality' within the horizon of the communist struggle. In *Critique of the Gotha Programme*, Marx belittles

> the attempt . . . to force on our party again, as dogmas, ideas which in a certain period had some meaning but have now become obsolete rubbishy phrases . . . perverting the realistic outlook, which has cost so much to instill into the party, but which now has taken root in it, by means of ideological nonsense about 'right' and other trash common among the democrats and French socialists. (1938, p. 10)

This suggests the very impossibility of having a stable relationship with ethics. We can view Marx's adherence to a 'ruthless criticism' as an ethical maxim. His support for a non-dogmatic communism permits us to see sometimes contradictory positions in his critique of capitalism and to accept as understandable his very fragmentary and changing formulations of communism.

In this reading of Marx, ethics is not about having answers to regulate the order of things or 'being' (this is morality), but rather to be in fidelity with the 'event' or the revolutionary moment (this idea is the main contribution of Alain Badiou's Marx-inflected *Ethics*; see also Gibson-Graham 2006). The revolutionary moment could be a theoretical as well as a political one. The Marxist commitment to communism is a by-product of the evolving analysis of capitalism, the study of the history and diversity of forms of social organization of surplus production, appropriation and distribution, and the account of commodity fetishism as the emergent subjectivity associated with a particular kind of capitalism. Marx's ethics of communism is located in his fidelity to sustaining this project of imagining and even enacting 'another way' of relating to the question of social and economic reproduction (for example, Marx's late-in-life unforeseen comments on Russian communes, see Shanin 1984). The ethical is embodied in Marx's enduring faithfulness to sustaining a critical position toward the existing state of affairs, not in his particular and changing dismissals of capitalism or in his obscure, partial formulations of the shape that communism might take. The lesson of Marx is that, facing the abyss of an unknown communism, the ethical is the will to risk a different social organization of surplus.

References

Althusser, Louis (2006), *Philosophy of the Encounter: Later Writings, 1978–1987*, ed. François Matheron and Olivier Corpet, trans. G.M. Goshgarian, New York: Verso.

Amin, Samir (2001), 'Imperialism and globalization', *Monthly Review*, **53** (2), 7–24.

Badiou, Alain (2001), *Ethics: An Essay on the Understanding of Evil*, trans. Peter Hallward, New York: Verso.

Benjamin, Walter (2003), *Understanding Brecht*, trans. Anna Bostock, New York: Verso.

Bensaïd, Daniel (2002), *Marx for Our Times: Adventures and Misadventures of a Critique*, trans. Gregory Elliott, London and New York: Verso.

Bergeron, Suzanne (2001), 'Political economy discourses of globalization and feminist politics', *Signs: Journal of Women in Culture and Society*, **26** (4), 983–1006.

Brenkert, George G. (1983), *Marx's Ethics of Freedom*, London: Routledge & Kegan Paul.

Brudney, Dan (2001), 'Justifying a conception of the good life: the problem of the 1844 Marx', *Political Theory*, **29** (3), 364–94.

Buchanan, Allen E. (1982), *Marx and Justice*, Totowa, NJ: Rowman & Allenheld.

Burczak, Theodore A. (2006), *Socialism after Hayek*, Ann Arbor, MI: University of Michigan Press.

Callari, Antonio and David F. Ruccio (eds) (1996), *Postmodern Materialism and the Future of Marxian Theory: Essays in the Althusserian Tradition*, Middletown, CT: Wesleyan University Press.

Collier, Andrew (2001), *Christianity and Marxism: A Philosophical Contribution to their Reconciliation*, London and New York: Routledge.

DeMartino, George (2003), 'Realizing class justice', *Rethinking Marxism*, **15** (1), 1–31.

DiQuattro, Arthur (1998), 'Liberal theory and the idea of communist justice', *American Political Science Review*, **92** (1), 83–96.

Dussel, Enrique (1985), *Philosophy of Liberation*, trans. Aquilina Martinez and Christine Morkovsky, Maryknoll, NY: Orbis Books.

Elliott, John E. (1986), 'On the possibility of Marx's moral critique of capitalism', *Review of Social Economy*, **44** (2), 130–45.

Fleischacker, Samuel (2004), *A Short History of Distributive Justice*, Cambridge, MA: Harvard University Press.

Geras, Norman (1985), 'The controversy about Marx and justice', *New Left Review*, **150**, 47–85.

Geras, Norman (1992), 'Bringing Marx to justice: an addendum and rejoinder', *New Left Review*, **195**, 37–69.

Gibson-Graham, J.K. (2006), *A Postcapitalist Politics*, Minneapolis, MN, and London: University of Minnesota Press.

Gilbert, Alan (1984), 'Marx's moral realism: eudaimonism and moral progress', in Terence Ball and James Farr (eds), *After Marx*, Cambridge: Cambridge University Press.

Kain, Philip J. (1988), *Marx and Ethics*, Oxford: Oxford University Press.

Lukes, Steven (1985), *Marxism and Morality*, Oxford: Oxford University Press.

Madra, Yahya M. (2006), 'Questions of communism: ethics, ontology, subjectivity', *Rethinking Marxism*, **18** (2), 205–24.

Marx, Karl (1938), *Critique of the Gotha Programme*, New York: International Publishers.

Marx, Karl (1964), *The Economic and Philosophic Manuscripts of 1844*, New York: International Publishers.

Marx, Karl (1973), *Grundrisse*, New York: Vintage.

Marx, Karl (1976), *Capital, Volume 1*, trans. Ben Fowkes, New York: Penguin Books.

Marx, Karl (1977), *A Contribution to the Critique of Political Economy*, ed. Maurice Dobb, trans. S. W. Ryazanskaya, Moscow: Progress Publishers.

Marx, Karl (1978a), 'For a ruthless criticism of everything existing', in Robert C. Tucker (ed.), *The Marx-Engels Reader*, New York: W.W. Norton & Company, Inc., pp. 12–15.

Marx, Karl (1978b), 'The civil war in France', in Robert C. Tucker (ed.), *The Marx-Engels Reader*, New York: W.W. Norton & Company, Inc., pp. 618–52.

Marx, Karl and Frederick Engels (1970), *The German Ideology*, ed. C.J. Arthur, New York: International Publishers.

Marx, Karl and Frederick Engels (1978), 'Manifesto of the Communist Party', in Robert C. Tucker (ed.), *The Marx-Engels Reader*, New York: W.W. Norton & Company, Inc., pp. 469–500.

Miller, Richard W. (1984), *Analyzing Marx*, Princeton, NJ: Princeton University Press.

Özselçuk, Ceren and Yahya M. Madra (2005), 'Psychoanalysis and Marxism: from capitalist-all to communist non-all', *Psychoanalysis, Culture and Society*, **10** (1), 79–97.

Peffer, Rodney G. (1990), *Marxism, Morality, and Social Justice*, Princeton, NJ: Princeton University Press.

Resnick, Stephen A. and Richard D. Wolff (1987), *Knowledge and Class: A Marxian Critique of Political Economy*, Chicago, IL: University of Chicago Press.

Roche, John (2005), 'Marx and Humanism', *Rethinking Marxism*, **17** (3), 335–48.

Roemer, John E. (1988), *Free to Lose: An Introduction to Marxist Economic Philosophy*, Cambridge, MA: Harvard University Press.

Ruccio, David F. and Jack Amariglio (2003), *Postmodern Moments in Modern Economics*, Princeton, NJ: Princeton University Press.

Shanin, Teodor (ed.) (1984), *Late Marx and the Russian Road: Marx and the Peripheries of Capitalism*, New York: Monthly Review Press.

Tucker, Robert C. (ed.) (1978), *The Marx-Engels Reader*, New York: W.W. Norton & Company, Inc.

West, Cornel (1991), *The Ethical Dimensions of Marxist Thought*, New York: Monthly Review Press.

Wilde, Lawrence (1998), *Ethical Marxism and its Radical Critics*, Basingstoke: Macmillan.

Wilde, Lawrence (ed.) (2001), *Marxism's Ethical Thinkers*, Basingstoke: Palgrave Macmillan.

See also the entries on: Justice; Labour standards.

44 Minimum wages
Ellen Mutari

Minimum wages are labour market regulations setting pay level standards. Minimum wage regulations may involve legislated wage floors or the establishment of wage boards that set minimum standards per industry or occupation. The idea of a minimum wage is closely linked to the concept of *living wages*, that is, the idea that wages should ensure a socially determined, sustainable living standard for workers and their families.

Advocacy of minimum wage regulations in industrialized countries took root at the end of the nineteenth century. At that time, minimum wage regulations were one of a number of policies established to protect workers from the vicissitudes of market forces, laying the groundwork for the modern welfare state. New Zealand passed the first country-wide minimum wage law in 1894. Australia, Great Britain and Ireland soon passed similar regulations: Australia in 1904 and the other two countries in 1909. These early minimum wage systems utilized industrial wage boards that set minimum standards for particular industries (Leonard 2000; Waltman 2000). This was the model recommended by an international network of social reformers advocating policies to improve working conditions in sweatshops (small, competitive manufacturing firms, frequently located in apartment buildings in urban areas, where employees worked long hours in crowded, unhealthy and dangerous conditions).

The regulatory approach was soon adopted by labour and social reformers in the United States, especially the National Consumers' League (NCL). In that country, however, the first minimum wage laws applied only to women workers, the primary labour force in sweatshop industries. Between 1912 and 1923, fifteen states, the District of Columbia and Puerto Rico passed minimum wage laws. The US Supreme Court overturned all but the weakest state regulations in 1923. In the wake of the Great Depression, however, the United States passed a gender-neutral federal minimum wage law in 1938. That law established a legislated wage floor enforced by complaint-driven litigation rather than proactive investigation by industrial councils (Figart et al. 2002, Chs 5–6).

Minimum wage laws did not become prevalent in continental Europe until the later twentieth century. They then became a norm of industrial relations systems. Today, the International Labour Office (ILO) estimates that more than 90 per cent of the world's nations have some form of minimum wage standards, most of which set a nationwide wage floor. In only 10 per cent of countries is the minimum wage set by government alone; most systems involve some kind of consultation with social partners or a tripartite body (ILO 2006).

Recent policy debates in the United States and other industrialized countries have centred less on the ethical dimensions of minimum wages and more on empirical debates over their impact. The ethical underpinnings of wage floors are frequently masked by economic modelling.

Ethical arguments for minimum wages
Arguments on both sides of the minimum wage debate reflect differing assumptions about the process of wage setting, specifically the relative importance of market-based processes. Critics of minimum wage policies tend to emphasize the primacy of market forces over other processes, arguing that unregulated labour markets will lead to efficient allocation of resources. Minimum wage policies, according to Thomas Leonard, arouse fierce debates because 'the core of modern economics – neoclassical price theory – is seen to be at stake. In particular, minimum-wage research has come to be seen as a test of the applicability of neoclassical price theory to the determination of wages and employment' (Leonard 2000, p. 118). For this reason, one's position on minimum wages has become a 'disciplinary litmus test' (ibid.)

Unilateral faith in market forces, grounded in neoclassical economics, is relatively recent. Classical economic theory in the eighteenth and nineteenth centuries was broader, viewing wages as the result of multiple institutions and processes. Specifically, classical political economics drew upon the analogous concept of living wages and the idea that the wage paid to labour must be sufficient to guarantee the continuing health and productivity of the worker. Wages also maintain the reproduction of the labour force and macroeconomic growth. These analytic arguments, in which systemic needs for social reproduction and sustainable growth are linked to adequate living standards, are inextricably intertwined with value-based arguments derived from socially constructed norms and definitions of fairness (Figart et al. 2002).

Adam Smith, for example, noted in *The Wealth of Nations* that employers ('masters'), because they are fewer in number and less economically vulnerable, have more bargaining power than the workers they hire ([1776] 1937). This greater bargaining power puts a downward pressure on wages. Wages, however, cannot fall below a socially necessary minimum. Further, he viewed high wages as advantageous to society, not only because they are an indicator of economic growth but because they enable working families to raise healthy children (ibid., p. 81). Smith's position, however, is based on ethics as well as the preconditions for prosperity:

> No society can surely be flourishing and happy, of which the far greater part of the members are poor and miserable. It is but equity, besides, that they who feed, cloath and lodge the whole body of the people, should have such a share of the produce of their own labour as to be themselves tolerably well fed, cloathed and lodged. (Smith [1776] 1937, p. 79)

Smith, like Karl Marx and other classical political economists, endorsed a labour theory of value, and this is reflected in his view that workers deserve a fair share of society's output. Even some of the early proponents of neoclassical economics, notably John Bates Clark, pragmatically endorsed minimum wage policies because of the unequal bargaining power between individual workers and large firms (Prasch 1999, 2000).

Unless it is viewed as a biological minimum below which survival is unlikely, the living wage is a social construct, based on the historically specific, accepted standard of living for workers and their families. When wages define appropriate living standards, they circumscribe not only someone's material standard of living, but also the ability to choose with whom to live and how to allocate one's time. Appropriate living standards have been based upon family structure, gender, race-ethnicity, segments within classes and many other social categories. Thus, the notion of a living wage has been gendered and racialized, as social understanding of what is an appropriate wage varies according to the context and sex and race of the worker (Figart et al. 2002).

Ethical arguments on behalf of living wage policies and practices advance three positions. First, echoing Adam Smith, many proponents view living wages as a just reward for the productive contributions of workers. As summarized in the book *Raise the Floor*, 'Work should pay enough to support workers and their families. If you work full time, you should not be poor. It's as simple as that' (Sklar et al. 2001, p. 1). Pollin and Luce similarly note, 'The primary argument the early supporters gave for establishing minimum wage laws, identical to that of living wage proponents today, was simple: people working at full-time jobs should be able to provide a decent life for themselves and their families' (Pollin and Luce 1998, p. 27). Economic justice, in this view, is predicated upon distributive justice – a concept articulated a century ago by social economist John Ryan (Figart 2004, p. 4). Work provides individuals (and their dependents) with the right to access a fair portion of the social product. Wilkinson (2004) suggests that such arguments treat poverty-level wages as a form of exploitation. He maintains, however, that exploitation arguments do not consider why it is the responsibility of employers, rather than government-provided social welfare programmes, to raise income levels.

The response to Wilkinson's objection, according to living wage advocates, constitutes a second ethical defence of minimum wage regulations; that is, employers who pay less than a living wage are portrayed as 'parasitic' or 'social parasites'. The parasitic industries argument dates back to the Progressive Era, the period in which minimum wage laws were first formulated. Living wage advocates such as Beatrice and Sidney Webb asserted that when market wages are insufficient for social reproduction, workers and their families are forced to rely upon charities and public assistance. This amounts to an indirect subsidy to employers (Power 1999; Prasch and Sheth 1999; Robinson 2004). Such arguments are currently being resurrected in contemporary living wage campaigns (Leonard 2000; Figart 2004; Robinson 2004; Luce 2005).

Third, productivity is determined by structural factors associated with industrial organization and technology rather than the qualities of individual workers. Basing wages on productivity is therefore unfair. It is also inefficient from a macroeconomic perspective. Low-wage industries are less dynamic and less beneficial for the macroeconomy than industries in which higher wages generate incentives to improve productivity and efficiency (Acemoglu and Pischke 2003). Further, substandard wages under sweatshop conditions may generate low levels of productivity. Since private sector employers make decisions based upon short-run profit maximization, government intervention is necessary to promote the social good (Power 1999; Figart 2004). Such productivity-based arguments are closely linked with efficiency wage theory (Prasch and Sheth 1999).

Wages, as is true more generally of prices in a market economy, are also a marker of value. Minimum wages and other policies to ensure adequate living standards affect more than material living standards; they also impact less tangible aspects of well-being. For example, Guy Standing has argued that during the twentieth century, 'Measures such as minimum wages were meant as instruments for social solidarity, for integrating the vulnerable into a society of common human dignity, as instruments for citizenship' (Standing 1995, p. 12). Setting standards for wages (and hours of work) marks an important aspect of the transition from a feudal to a market economy. Under feudal traditions, labourers are akin to property under the nearly unilateral control of lords and masters.

Such systems of labour relations did not automatically disappear with the transition to capitalism. However, government-imposed labour standards in a market economy limit the power of employers to impose their will, and they provide employees with a set of rights and entitlements (Levin-Waldman 2001, pp. 82–4).

Market mechanisms under challenge

In contrast to living wage advocates, mainstream economists have viewed market mechanisms as a means of guaranteeing fair wage-setting practices. Fairness, from this standpoint, is based upon the equality of exchange. As the price of an input to the production process, wages are a cost that must be offset by an at least equal benefit to the individual employer purchasing labour services. This benefit is the revenue gained by selling labour's product. Market mechanisms, specifically adjustments in the quantity of labour supplied and demanded, are hypothesized to regulate wages until marginal costs and benefits are equalized, particularly when both the product and factor markets are competitive.

Ethical objections to minimum wage regulations also cite alleged disemployment effects. An increase in wages above equilibrium levels, according to supply and demand models, supposedly creates a surplus; in the case of labour, this surplus is unemployment. Minimum wage opponents maintain that the unemployment generated by minimum wage regulations generally impacts the least skilled members of the labour force, especially teenagers, making it inefficient as a transfer programme (Deere et al. 1996; Neumark 2004). Therefore, losses in efficiency are not balanced by equity gains.

As noted by Jerold Waltman, for free market opponents of minimum wage laws, 'the market and justice are synonymous'. He continues:

> If the market assigns a certain value to a good or service, then it has that value, objectively and morally . . . Manifestly, when it comes to labor – people selling their services for a wage – they see absolutely no difference between a labor market and markets for pizzas, shoes, hammers, or automobiles. If an employer is willing to pay me a given amount for eight hours and I accept, we must both be better off than we were before the transaction. (Waltman 2000, p. 18)

Robert Prasch (2004) notes that those who favour minimum wage legislation contradict neoclassical labour market theory by arguing that labour is not morally equivalent to other commodities. In fact, labour is characterized by three distinguishing characteristics:

- Labour cannot be separated from its providers.
- Labour cannot be stored.
- Labour embodies the quality of self-consciousness.

Prasch traces the view that labour is 'different in form and ethical status from a bag of concrete' to the work of Karl Polanyi, who termed labour a 'fictitious commodity' (ibid., p. 155).

Real-life violations of the assumptions of perfect competition also challenge the ethical presumption that market wages reflect relative productivity. Labour markets are not competitive. In their landmark study *Myth and Measurement*, David Card and Alan B. Krueger (1995) note that the standard competitive model is only a theoretical model of how labour markets operate. Card and Krueger pioneered what they term the 'new economics of the minimum wage'. Using three US case studies of federal and state minimum wage increases, they challenge the deductive conclusion that mandated increases in wage floors lead to job losses. Relying upon 'natural experiments', they found either minimum disemployment effects or even a positive demand elasticity for labour in certain markets.

In sorting through alternative explanations for their findings, Card and Krueger suggest that low-wage employers (such as fast-food franchises) operate with some monopsony power, rather than as price-takers in labour markets. Such firms face high employee turnover and constant job vacancies. Therefore, mandated but moderate increases in wage levels may actually have a positive impact on employment – a hypothesis supported by their empirical findings. Firms with market power in output markets and heterogeneous labour, along with monopsony power in labour markets, modify the anticipated results of relying upon market forces to set wages.

Catherine Saget supports Card and Krueger's analysis in her study of developing countries, asserting that the impact of the minimum wage cannot be determined a priori when the assumptions of perfect competition are waived, even in the presence of an informal sector (Saget 2001, p. 21). Minimum wage opponents have conceded that monopsony power in labour markets obviates the free market argument (see, for example, Kennan 1995; Neumark 2004).

Card and Krueger's (1995) work has generated a multitude of empirical studies about the economic impact of minimum wage laws (see, for example, Kennan 1995; Kosters 1996; Jones 1997; Dolado et al. 2000; Levin-Waldman 2001; Saget 2001; Fiscal Policy Institute 2006; Fox 2006; Wicks-Lim 2006). Critics allege that their data are unreliable and their results may only reveal short-run responses (Leonard 2000, p. 135). Wilkinson contends that these empirical arguments are at the heart of ethical considerations regarding minimum wages. He proposes a 'consequentialist criterion' for assessing the policy, focused on the impact of wage regulations on the 'jobs and incomes of the worst off' (Wilkinson 2004, pp. 351–2). Because empirical research remains unclear on this issue, Wilkinson maintains that it is premature to evaluate the ethics of minimum wages.

Are minimum wages still relevant?

Some analysts have questioned the continued relevance of minimum wage regulations. More than 60 per cent of countries do not specify regular adjustments of minimum wage rates, according to the ILO. This has been a particular problem in recent decades, as legislated and negotiated minimum wage standards in industrialized countries have not kept pace with inflation (Standing 1995; Pollin and Luce 1998; Sklar et al. 2001; Figart 2004). Standing (1995) has argued that flexibilization of labour markets has diminished the coverage and positive impact of such regulations, which are better suited for a social economy of full-time workers in regular employment. The diminished power of organized labour, a key constituency advocating minimum wage increases, is a key factor as well (Levin-Waldman 2001). All of these factors indicate decreased bargaining power for workers.

Developing countries have faced similar pressures to abandon wage regulations as they strive to compete in global markets. Export-oriented growth has been at the heart of development strategies. Further, structural adjustment policies linked to debt servicing have pressured developing countries to deregulate labour markets and reduce public sector programmes. Liberalization advocates are particularly concerned that wage floors will shift employment into the informal sector (Jones 1997).

Yet, according to Saget (2001), the real values of minimum wages in developing countries have not uniformly declined in response to these political and economic forces. Further, her cross-national empirical study of 31 countries indicates that strong minimum wages have no significant disemployment effects or impact on the relative size of the informal sector, while having a significant impact on poverty. In fact, workers in the informal sector may find their bargaining power enhanced by minimum wage laws covering formal sector workers, since such laws establish social norms (Saget 2006).

Many analysts therefore continue to view minimum wage policies, and a broader living wage movement, as a crucial response to the politics of deregulation. Saget (2001) argues that labour market regulations may, in fact, be making a comeback. Labour market institutions and regulations, according to Jonas Agell (1999), serve as a remedy for market failures and reflect basic social norms and customs. If we account for the real behaviour of socially embedded actors, market forces may actually generate inefficiencies, as workers respond to perceived unfairness.

Such responses pave the way for a return to the 'political economy of citizenship' that characterized living wage movements a century ago (Waltman 2000). One hopeful sign is the movement for 'decent work'. Decent work is a concept that originated in a 1999 report by the director-general of the ILO (Ghai 2003). It focuses on the social and regulatory context necessary to ensure that work is performed in accordance with human dignity.

References

Acemoglu, Daron and Jörn-Steffen Pischke (2003), 'Minimum wages and on-the-job training', *Research in Labor Economics*, **22**, 159–202.
Agell, Jonas (1999), 'On the benefits from rigid labour markets: norms, market failures, and social insurance', *Economic Journal*, **109** (453, Features), F143–64.
Card, David and Alan B. Krueger (1995), *Myth and Measurement: The New Economics of the Minimum Wage*, Princeton, NJ: Princeton University Press.
Deere, Donald R., Kevin M. Murphy and Finis R. Welch (1996), 'Examining the evidence on minimum wages and employment', in Marvin H. Kosters (ed.), *The Effects of the Minimum Wage on Employment*, Washington, DC: AEI Press, pp. 26–54.
Dolado, Juan J., Florentino Felgueroso and Juan F. Jimeno (2000), 'The role of the minimum wage in the welfare state: an appraisal', Discussion Paper Series, Institute for the Study of Labour (Forschungsinstitut zur Zukunft der Arbeit), Bonn.
Figart, Deborah M. (2004), *Living Wage Movements: Global Perspectives*, London: Routledge.
Figart, Deborah M., Ellen Mutari and Marilyn Power (2002), *Living Wages, Equal Wages: Gender and Labor Market Policies in the United States*, London: Routledge.
Fiscal Policy Institute (2006), *States with Minimum Wages above the Federal Level have had Faster Small Business and Retail Job Growth*, New York: Fiscal Policy Institute, www.fiscalpolicy.org/minimumwage_01. html, accessed 29 October, 2008.
Fox, Liana (2006), 'Minimum wage trends: understanding past and contemporary research', EPI Briefing Paper, Economic Policy Institute, Washington DC.
Ghai, Dharam (2003), 'Decent work: concept and indicators', *International Labour Review*, **142** (2), 113–45.
ILO (2006), 'Minimum wages policy, Information Sheet No. W-1', International Labour Office, Geneva.
Jones, Patricia (1997), *The Impact of Minimum Wage Legislation in Developing Countries where Coverage is Incomplete*, Working Paper, Oxford: Centre for the Study of African Economies, University of Oxford, www. csae.ox.ac.uk/workingpapers/pdfs/9802text.pdf, accessed 29 October, 2008.
Kennan, John (1995), 'The elusive effects of minimum wages', *Journal of Economic Literature*, **33** (4), 1950–60.
Kosters, Marvin H. (ed.) (1996), *The Effects of the Minimum Wage on Employment*, Washington DC: AEI Press.

Leonard, Thomas C. (2000), 'The very idea of applying economics: the modern minimum-wage controversy and its antecedents', *History of Political Economy*, **32** (4, supplement), 117–44.

Levin-Waldman, Oren M. (2001), *The Case of the Minimum Wage: Competing Policy Models*, Albany, NY: SUNY Press.

Luce, Stephanie (2005), 'Lessons from living-wage campaigns', *Work and Occupations*, **32** (4), 423–40.

Neumark, David (2004), 'Minimum wages and living wages: raising incomes by mandating wage floors', in Deborah M. Figart (ed.), *Living Wage Movements: Global Perspectives*, London: Routledge, pp. 171–87.

Pollin, Robert and Stephanie Luce (1998), *The Living Wage: Building a Fair Economy*, New York: New Press.

Power, Marilyn (1999), 'Parasitic-industries analysis and arguments for a living wage for women in the early twentieth century United States', *Feminist Economics*, **5** (1), 61–78.

Prasch, Robert E. (1999), 'The economics and ethics of minimum wage legislation', *Review of Social Economy*, **57** (4), 466–87.

Prasch, Robert E. (2000), 'John Bates Clark's defense of mandatory arbitration and minimum wage legislation', *Journal of the History of Economic Thought*, **22** (2), 251–63.

Prasch, Robert E. (2004), 'How is labor distinct from broccoli? Unique characteristics of labor and their importance for economic analysis and policy', in Dell P. Champlin and Janet T. Knoedler (eds), *The Institutionalist Tradition in Labor Economics*, Armonk, NY: M.E. Sharpe, pp. 146–58.

Robinson, Tony (2004), 'Hunger discipline and social parasites: the political economy of the living wage', *Urban Affairs Review*, **40** (2), 246–68.

Saget, Catherine (2001), 'Is the minimum wage an effective tool to promote decent work and reduce poverty? The experience of selected developing countries', Employment Paper 2001/13, International Labour Office, Geneva.

Saget, Catherine (2006), 'Wage fixing in the informal economy: evidence from Brazil, India, Indonesia and South Africa', Conditions of Work and Employment Series No. 16, International Labour Office, Geneva.

Sklar, Holly, Laryssa Mykyta and Susan Wefald (2001), *Raise the Floor: Wages and Policies that Work for All of Us*, New York: Ms. Foundation for Women.

Smith, Adam ([1776] 1937), *The Wealth of Nations*, New York: Modern Library.

Standing, Guy (1995), 'What role for the minimum wage in the flexible labour markets of the 21st century?' in Guy Standing and Daniel Vaughan-Whitehead (eds), *Minimum Wages in Central and Eastern Europe: From Protection to Destitution*, Geneva: International Labour Office, pp. 7–14.

Waltman, Jerold (2000), *The Politics of the Minimum Wage*, Urbana, IL: University of Illinois Press.

Wicks-Lim, Jeannette (2006), 'Mandated wage floors and the wage structure: new estimates of the ripple effects of minimum wage laws', Working Paper No. 116, Political Economy Research Institute, Amherst, MA.

Wilkinson, T.M. (2004), 'The ethics and economics of the minimum wage', *Economics and Philosophy*, **20** (2), 351–74.

See also the entries on: Discrimination; Income distribution; Labour standards.

45 Needs and agency
Lawrence Hamilton

The concept of 'human needs' is conspicuous by its absence in modern economics. This is especially true of neoclassical economics, ever since Marshall criticized Smith's and Ricardo's distinction between 'necessaries' and 'luxuries' (Marshall [1920] 1964, pp. 56–7). However, most forms of mainstream economic analysis in fact are neglectful of the concept, as exemplified by the omission of an entry for 'needs' in the four-volume *New Palgrave Dictionary of Economics* (Eatwell et al. 1998).

This is odd but not difficult to explain. It is odd because, at least in part, economics is about understanding human agency and motivation, and human needs constitute one very important component of human motivation to act. Moreover, as exemplified in the work of, amongst others, Aristotle (1980, 1988), Smith ([1776] 1975, [1790] 1976), Marx ([1932] 1992, [1847] 1976, [1939–41] 1973, [1867] 1976–78, [1890–91] 1996) and Sen (1985a, 1985b, [1997] 1987a, 1987b, 1993a, 1993b; Hamilton 1999), economic and political discourses and institutions have always been characterized by constant recourse to the idea of 'need' (Wiggins 1998, p. 4n; Hamilton 2003, p. 9). Thus, mainstream economics excludes a central component of human motivation in general and of economic and political discourse in particular. It does so as a consequence of the triumph of utilitarianism within economics and the concomitant reduction of human agency to utility maximization.

The focus of this chapter is on how this omission impairs our understanding of the social, economic and political practices and goods that determine how we act – love, produce, consume, judge, rule – and why the concept of 'human needs' constitutes a fruitful basis for understanding economic and political agency. This involves outlining the provenance of the depleted state of conceptual affairs and clarifying the conception of 'human needs' that does exist, if often only implicitly, within economics.

The concept of 'human needs' is rare because an economics or politics of needs has over the past two centuries become *doctrina non grata*. This is mainly due to the hallowed position of utilitarianism within the tradition of mainstream economics. The legacy of utilitarianism provides justification for purely preference-based economics and politics (Bentham [1781] 1970; Becker and Stigler 1977; compare Menger [1871] 1981; Arrow [1952] 1963; Sen 1970, 1973, 1976–77; Sen and Williams 1982). Utilitarianism's subject-relative approach to morality, which treats pleasure or desire-satisfaction as the sole element in human good, has provided constant support for the reduction of economics and politics to the aggregation of individual preferences (or avowed wants).

Utilitarianism offers justification for the evaluation of individual actions or social achievement in terms of their consequences on individual or social utility, as determined by individual preference alone. The concept of preference thus has come to be prioritized because of its alleged epistemological importance in calculating individual welfare and as a consequence of the moral imperative to respect the judgement of individuals as regards their own welfare.

These matters of epistemology and sovereign judgement are vital in any form of individual or social evaluation, but the utilitarian framework for understanding and safeguarding them is counterproductive. In its quest for a universal 'calculus', it has excluded most of the real world that it purports to understand. This is exemplified by the ethical impoverishment of mainstream economics, the demise of both the concept of 'human needs' and objective ethical analysis, and in the fact that it fails to provide a coherent understanding of preference formation and human agency.

Utilitarianism generates the *unconditional* prioritization of subjective preferences despite the acknowledged fact that preferences are determined (at least in part) by sources beyond the individuals who avow them, and despite the potential effects of satisfying these preferences on other individuals. This principled priority excludes any systematic understanding and evaluation of how preferences are and ought to be transformed. In other words, it impoverishes our understanding of and control over the institutions and practices that do in fact determine, influence and transform our preferences, for example, existing state institutions, legal practices, welfare provision, production and consumption practices and so on (Hamilton 2003, pp. 7–8).

Thus, not only does the priority of preference leave little room for the more ethically capacious concept of 'human needs', the eschewal of the idea of needs has occurred hand-in-hand with the complete disassociation of ethics and economics. Utilitarian preferences fit perfectly the 'non-ethical character of modern economics' (Sen 1987b, p. 2) because their principled inviolability does not admit of any objective moral analysis.

The dissociation between ethics and economics is unfortunate for a whole raft of reasons, but the most significant is that it impoverishes our understanding of human motivation. By reducing human choice, judgement and well-being to self-interested satisfaction of desire, modern preference-based economic analysis artificially reduces human motivation to the single dimension of utility maximization. Although economics is (or at least ought to be) concerned with real people and their actions, the reductive character of the prevailing discourse is unable to explain many actual motivations for action, most of which directly impact upon economic agency.

In the market and elsewhere, real people are motivated to act by a range of forces and drives: self-interest, self-hate, habit, prudence, ethical principles, ethical ideals, altruism, manipulation, coercion and so on. If the evaluation of these actions and achievements is confined solely to the calculus of utility maximization (or, indeed, solely to objective ethical considerations), the result is likely to be misunderstanding. The origins and political and economic significance of these actions and achievements are therefore also likely to be misplaced or underestimated.

Preference-based economics, it is argued, liberates policy from convoluted and paternalistic analyses of objective well-being and human needs. But this reduction of human agents to utility-maximizers is achieved at the cost of understanding human well-being and motivation. Properly conceived, the idea of human need constitutes a normatively and historically rich tool for understanding most human goods and motivations for actions as well as a practicable mechanism around which to organize policy. It thus provides a fruitful tool with which to understand some of the perennial problems within economics, for example, the problem of demand in microeconomics, as illustrated by the famous 'water-diamond' paradox. Most mainstream positions claim that this paradox was explained by Marshall upon the introduction of supply-demand analysis (for example, Nicholson 2002, pp. 9, 11, 78–9; Marshall [1920] 1964). However, this only shifts the problem by arguing that the relative price of diamonds is high because the supply of diamonds is limited and the demand for diamonds is high, without explaining *why* the demand for diamonds is high.

A needs-based approach to this question can provide an explanation, because it does not take avowed preference as given, but interrogates the source of the avowed need or want for diamonds. In other words, as will be explained below, one of its functions is to identify the determinants of demand, that is, to understand and evaluate the institutions and practices that generate avowed needs. But, in order to see how this may be achieved, it is necessary, first, to grasp the nature of human needs.

Human needs are the necessary conditions and aspirations of full human functioning. They manifest in three forms: (i) vital needs, (ii) agency needs and (iii) particular social needs.

Vital needs are the necessary conditions for minimal human functioning. These include the need for water, shelter, adequate nutrition, mobility, social entertainment and so on. They are termed 'vital needs' because their satisfaction is a necessary condition for *vita*, or life. This is more obvious with regard to needs such as oxygen and water than for others, such as adequate shelter. But the lack of satisfaction of any of these needs tends to impair healthy human functioning (Hamilton 2003, pp. 23, 27–31; Braybrooke 1987; Doyal and Gough 1991).

Agency needs are the necessary conditions and aspirations for individual and political agency characteristic of full human functioning. These include autonomy (or freedom), recognition and active and creative expression. They are termed 'agency needs' because they are ongoing aspirations whose development increases an agent's causal power to carry out intended actions and to satisfy and evaluate needs. Developed and satisfied agency needs supply feelings of safety, self-esteem and confidence, enabling individuals to function fully, individually and politically (Hamilton 2003, pp. 24, 35–47; compare Doyal and Gough 1991).

Needs are normally felt not as abstract vital and agency needs, but as particular drives or goals, for example, the desire to drink apple juice or the felt need to work. Manifest in this concrete form, these are what have been called particular social needs, and include a broad spectrum of largely uncontested needs which are either the focus of public policy or are seen to be of private concern. These needs are brought to light in one of several ways: by bald need-claims, for example, the need for an efficient train service; by the content of public – state or otherwise – provision, for example, the need for basic income support; and by patterns of production and consumption, for example, the need for a car, as elaborated below (Hamilton 2003, pp. 23–4, 31–5, 63–102).

Particular social needs are the most common form of needs. In fact, their normal usage seems to inspire modern analytical philosophy to treat 'need' solely as a verb and confine it to the logical or analytical form of '*A* needs *X* in order to *Y*'. This is an instrumental understanding that conceives of needs as means to other acts, or states of being or becoming. All need statements, it maintains, are triadic. This distinguishes needs from other drives and highlights one aspect of their normativity. Need-claims demand justification. When we say we need *X*, the force of the claim rests on the fact that what *X* is needed for is justifiable. The need-claim is evaluated in light of this, making *Y* the crucial normative variable (Connolly 1983, p. 62; Thomson 1987). For example, my claim 'I need a house' cannot be evaluated until we know why I need a house. 'I need a house so as to have shelter' is a different kind of claim from 'I need a house for weekend trips in the country.' The former holds greater normative weight because it makes reference to the objective vital human need for shelter.

However, this focus on the triadic nature of some need-claims is not the entire story. It does not cover all needs and need-claims. Some needs, particularly vital and agency needs, are ends in themselves. Nothing lies beyond them. They cannot be justified by reference to any other need or normative claim. Moreover, because these kinds of needs are themselves ends or states of being or becoming, they are not normally expressed in the triadic form characteristic of instrumental needs. Normally they are understood and articulated in dyadic form: 'I need to be mobile'; 'I need to be free'; 'I need to express myself.' This is reinforced by the fact that when they are part of a triadic analytical form, they are normally not the X but the Y. They are not the need itself but the normative variable used to justify the need or need-claim: '*A* needs meaningful work in order *to express herself.*' The fact that not all needs are instrumental provides the clue to the special role played by vital and agency needs: they are simultaneously needs themselves and the normative basis for the evaluation of all other needs – or 'particular social needs'.

These three characteristics, or forms of needs, help to explain common usage. We use the notion of need, often in contrast to want, to denote a degree of seriousness, priority and objectivity. Needs are not simply strong wants. Needs are objective and normative (Wiggins 1998; Thomson 1987), and their state of development and satisfaction has a direct effect on human functioning (Hamilton 2003). In contrast, wants are subjectively felt desires or second-order desires for a specific object or state of being. Moreover, wants normally depend on conditions in the world.

However, it is possible to overstate the objectivity of needs in two different but equally problematic ways. First, some theorists have argued that needs are *universal*, basic, material requirements of continued human existence. In so doing, they focus exclusively on the first form of needs, 'vital needs'. This is most apparent in the 'basic needs' approach within development discourse on inequality (for example, Stewart 1985). One important exception to this rule is the work on 'inequality' and 'capability' developed by Amartya Sen. As conceived by Sen, 'capabilities' constitutes an ample category that includes an individual's objective well-being and 'agency freedoms'. In other words, Sen's 'capability approach' can be understood as a theory of true interests or needs (Sen 1985a, 1985b, [1979] 1987a, 1987b, 1993a, 1993b; Hamilton 1999).

Other theorists shift the emphasis towards the second, 'agency' component of needs, and conceive of needs as universal ethical goals, the lack of which creates objective harm (Braybrooke 1987; Doyal and Gough 1991; compare Wiggins 1998).

In either case, emphasis on an unchanging list of universal needs enables theorists to draw a clear, strict distinction between needs and wants. This is reinforced by the fact that 'wanting something does not entail needing it, and vice versa . . . [S]omeone may have a need without having a desire *for what he needs* and . . . he may have a desire without having a need *for what he wants*' (Frankfurt 1998, p. 30, emphasis in original). For example, someone can have a need for periodic exercise without ever desiring exercise in any way, and one may have a strong desire to smoke cigarettes without needing to.

However, this clear analytical distinction between needs and wants rests on an oversimplification of the nature of needs that belies a more complicated causal reality. First, particular wants over time can become interpreted as needs. Think of how easily the desire for refrigerators and televisions has become a legitimate need for these commodities. Second, new satisfiers and commodities generate new wants, which affect our ability to satisfy our needs. For example, the car produces both the desire for a car and a need for more motorways. Subsequent economic and political decisions that shift investment from the upkeep of an efficient public transportation system to the construction of more motorways ensure that, in order for me to be able to satisfy my need for mobility, I need a car.

The three forms of needs underscore the fact that in order to grasp the full nature of human needs, they must be understood in normative, ethical, historical and political terms. While the normativity and objectivity of needs is of utmost importance, needs are not simply normative and objective. They are historical, social and political as well. Their objectivity is not universal; they are also affected by wants and institutions, and they change as human nature changes. Thus, the normativity of needs is best captured via an analysis of the history of the institutional environment within which particular social needs were generated.

To understand this we must move beyond the accepted wisdom that there exist only two senses of normativity: a broad sense and a narrow one. In the broad sense a normative claim or theory is understood as being an evaluative claim or theory as opposed to a descriptive one, in which the evaluative component requires no further analysis concerning obligation or enforcement. In other words, it encompasses a wide range of 'oughts' and 'shoulds' (even those applicable to the evaluation of things like apples, as in 'apples should be round, sweet . . .'). The narrow sense maintains that the normativity of a claim or theory is determined by whether it incorporates a claim that there is an absolute moral obligation (often on some particular agent) that X should come about, for example, 'children should respect their parents'. This is the Kantian and Christian moral usage.

There is also, however, a large and fruitful area of normativity that lies between these two extremes. One aspect of this area is vital for understanding the ethical nature of needs: in short, this deals with what ought to be done in any specific context to ensure individuals' full human functioning (Hamilton 2003, p. 15). This involves the political imperative to choose between a set of possible economic paths or trajectories down which the needs of a state's citizens could develop.

The narrow, normally Kantian, sense of normativity does have a role to play: it can be argued that individuals have a moral responsibility to meet the needs of others (Brock 1998; Reader 2005). So too does the broad sense, especially in light of the tendency in mainstream economics to conceive of needs in purely descriptive terms, which is a consequence of the obstinacy of positivism. However, it follows from the socially determined nature of needs – the fact that needs are not only objective human goods but also historically and politically determined feelings of desire, lack and want – that their normativity is historical and ethical (as well as natural and moral). They must therefore be evaluated in a manner that provides true understanding of this nature, furnishing individuals with the necessary means to reflect on their own and others' needs and thus to participate in the collective choice (judgement) over how to proceed.

In other words, the nature of needs calls for objective and subjective input into the determination of the contemporary state of need development and satisfaction. And this input will ultimately involve ethical reflection and judgement on the part of individuals.

Full participation in the determination of needs is vital because any ethical and material decisions that follow from it must be made with as much information as possible (Dunn 2005, pp. 94–7).

This is achieved via the idea of 'true interest' in the context of evaluating needs and institutions. A true interest is an individual's role- and context-specific post-reflective vital or agency need or a satisfier thereof (Hamilton 2003, pp. 16–7, 88–102). As Sen argues with regard to 'capabilities' and the 'quality of life', this kind of reflection must involve subjective and objective evaluation (Sen 1985a, [1979] 1987a, 1993a, 1993b; Hamilton 2003, pp. 91–102). This is only possible under political and economic conditions that allow individuals the time and institutional means to undertake both forms of evaluation. In order for individuals to undertake an evaluation of their true interests, existing particular social needs and economic and political institutions must enable citizens to satisfy and develop their vital and agency needs and perceive their true interests. Thus the existing complex of needs, institutions, practices and roles can be evaluated in the light of the effects they have on the satisfaction and development of vital and agency needs and the perception of true interests.

An evaluation of this kind would be rooted in an analysis of the histories of particular need formations understood in terms of the roles, practices and institutions that generate and justify them and the effects that these have on the perception and satisfaction of needs and interests. Take again the example of the water-diamond paradox: a needs-based approach can provide an explanation for the high demand for diamonds without having to refer to use values, scarcity or marginal utility. It would explain it via an analysis of the institutions that generate the need for diamonds. As symbols of luxury, diamonds satisfy a strongly felt need to display achieved wealth.

Which institutions justify this special role for diamonds? Which institutions lead people to feel the need to display their wealth? These questions help to identify the institutions that generate the need and thus demand for diamonds, which would explain what motivates the high demand for diamonds. But it would also enable an evaluation of this demand. The identified institutions can be assessed in terms of their effects on the development or satisfaction of vital and agency needs and the perception of true interests. (Even if one were to exclude the problem of 'conflict diamonds', the institutions that generate the felt need for diamonds and justify the diamond industry are unlikely to score very highly in these terms.)

Vital and agency needs are not free-standing, a priori moral standards or principles. They are affected and changed by history. Yet, with sufficient historical purview and abstraction, vital and agency needs can be used as standards for ethical and political evaluation. Met vital and agency needs are not only necessary conditions for the perception of true interests, they also provide a means of evaluating the effects of institutions on an individual's quality of life. In this way value is determined not by pleasure (or happiness or desire) alone but by the positive and negative effects of a specific act, claim or institution on the meeting of vital needs, the development and satisfaction of agency needs and the perception of true interests. This avoids utilitarianism without abandoning consequentialism, and has thus been called 'institutional consequentialism'.

The goal of institutional consequentialism is not the maximization of the valued objectives – vital and agency needs. It is concerned with an ethical evaluation that takes at least the maximization of agency needs and the evaluation of true interests to be the concern of individuals; it evaluates the provision of the conditions for these and the rectification of power imbalances in the everyday evaluation of true interests. The most important subset of conditions is that of the meeting of vital needs (Hamilton 2003, p. 122).

Like most forms of decision-making, the evaluation of institutions, needs and true interests involves collective choice under conditions of moral and material disagreement. In other words, subjective involvement in the determination and evaluation of needs is vital, and agreement or consensus in this process is highly unlikely. Under these conditions a state (or other kind of coercive authority) would be legitimate if it produced and maintained conditions in which citizens could effectively evaluate their needs, institutions and true interests and representatives could act on the outcome of these evaluations despite disagreement.

In particular, the state would have a fourfold function (Hamilton 2003, pp. 148–61), the first part of which is to ensure the satisfaction of vital needs. The second part is to use frequent census and consequentialist evaluations of institutions to provide some of the objective data necessary for individuals to evaluate their true interests; the individuals themselves would provide the rest.

Third, the state would institutionalize two mechanisms by which to safeguard individual participation and power: an annual true interest evaluation and a decennial plebiscite. In the annual true interest evaluation individuals would evaluate and avow their true interests. Rotating local level representatives (who could be chosen at random) could then defend these interests within local government. The aim would be to reach a decision as to the exact nature of local true interests and thus enable local government administration and market-related institutions to respond to post-evaluation needs and interests. The outcome would not affect the standing of the existing government. The decennial plebiscite would assess the actual and possible paths or trajectories down which the development of needs could progress. In contrast to the short-term and local concerns of the true interest evaluation, the decennial plebiscite would involve a relatively protracted evaluation of broader policy matters and structural features of the polity and economy. This might be a month-long assessment of existing and possible policy – fiscal, environmental, transport – and kinds of production, property ownership, and so on. In other words, it would assess the kinds of concerns, goals and institutions that one finds established within constitutions. The outcomes of the plebiscite would then be used to reformulate the relevant sections of the state's constitution. Consultative referenda could be used to supplement both the annual true interest evaluation and the decennial plebiscite.

Fourth and finally, following each evaluation, the state would transform institutions that have been identified as acting against the satisfaction of post-evaluation vital and agency needs and the perception of true interests.

Together these state functions and procedural requirements and safeguards would provide citizens with participative control over the local level evaluation of needs as well as the legal framework that determines the parameters of representative democracy, that is, the constitution (Hamilton 2003, 2009). They would also provide the state with the authority to implement and maintain a politics and economics of needs.

References

Aristotle (1980), *The Nicomachean Ethics*, trans. and intro. D. Ross, Oxford: Oxford University Press.
Aristotle (1988), *The Politics*, ed. S. Everson, Cambridge: Cambridge University Press.

Arrow, Kenneth J. ([1952] 1963), *Social Choice and Individual Values*, 2nd edition, New Haven: Yale University Press.

Becker, Gary S. and George J. Stigler (1977), 'De gustibus non est disputandum', *American Economic Review*, **67** (2), 76–90.

Bentham, Jeremy ([1781] 1970), *Introduction to the Principles of Morals and Legislation*, London: Athlone.

Braybrooke, David (1987), *Meeting Needs*, Princeton, NJ: Princeton University Press.

Brock, Gillian (ed.) (1998), *Necessary Goods: Our Responsibilities to Meet Others' Needs*, Oxford: Rowman and Littlefield.

Connolly, William E. (1983), *The Terms of Political Discourse*, Oxford: Martin Robertson.

Doyal, Len and Ian Gough (1991), *A Theory of Human Need*, London: Macmillan.

Dunn, John (2005), *Setting the People Free: The Story of Democracy*, London: Atlantic Books.

Eatwell, John, Murray Milgate and Peter Newman (1998), *New Palgrave Dictionary of Economics*, Basingstoke: Palgrave.

Frankfurt, Harry (1998), 'Necessity and desire', in Gillian Brock (ed.), *Necessary Goods: Our Responsibilities to Meet Others' Needs*, Oxford: Rowman and Littlefield, pp. 19–32.

Hamilton, Lawrence (1999), 'A theory of true interests in the work of Amartya Sen', *Government and Opposition*, **34**, 4.

Hamilton, Lawrence (2003), *The Political Philosophy of Needs*, Cambridge: Cambridge University Press.

Hamilton, Lawrence (2009), '"(I've never met) a nice South African": popular sovereignty and virtuous citizenship', *Theoria*, 119, June.

Marshall, Alfred ([1920] 1964), *Principles of Economics*, 8th edition, London: Macmillan.

Marx, Karl (1932), 'Economic and philosophic manuscripts', in L. Colletti (ed.) (1992), *Karl Marx: Early Writings*, Harmondsworth: Penguin.

Marx, Karl ([1847] 1976), *The Poverty of Philosophy*, in *Karl Marx Frederick Engels Collected Works Vol. 6* (1976), London: Lawrence & Wishart.

Marx, Karl ([1939–41] 1973), *Grundrisse*, trans. M. Nicolaus, Harmondsworth: Penguin.

Marx, Karl ([1867] 1967–68), *Capital*, 3 vols, intro. E. Mandel, trans. D. Fernbach, Harmondsworth: Penguin.

Marx, Karl ([1890–91] 1996), 'Critique of the Gotha programme', in Terrell Carver (ed.), *Marx: Later Political Writings*, Cambridge: Cambridge University Press.

Menger, Carl ([1871] 1981), *Principles of Economics*, trans. James Dingwall and Bert F. Hoselitz, intro. Friedrich A. Hayek, New York and London: New York University Press.

Nicholson, Walter (2002), *Microeconomic Theory: Basic Principles and Extensions*, Mason, OH: Southwestern.

Reader, Soran (ed.) (2005), *The Philosophy of Need*, Cambridge: Cambridge University Press.

Sen, Amartya (1970), *Collective Choice and Social Welfare*, San Francisco: Holden-Day.

Sen, Amartya (1973), 'Behaviour and the concept of preference', *Economica*, **40** (159), 241–59.

Sen, Amartya (1976–77), 'Rational fools: a critique of the behavioral foundations of economic theory', *Philosophy and Public Affairs*, **6**, 317–44.

Sen, Amartya (1985a), 'Well-being, agency and freedom: the Dewey lectures 1984', *Journal of Philosophy*, **82** (4), 169–221.

Sen, Amartya (1985b), *Commodities and Capabilities*, Amsterdam and Oxford: North-Holland.

Sen, Amartya ([1979] 1987a), 'The equality of what', in Sterling M. McMurrin (ed.), *Liberty, Equality and Law*, Cambridge: Cambridge University Press.

Sen, Amartya (1987b), *On Ethics and Economics*, Oxford: Basil Blackwell.

Sen, Amartya (1993a), 'Capability and well-being', in Martha Nussbaum and Amartya Sen, *The Quality of Life*, Oxford: Clarendon Press.

Sen, Amartya (1993b), 'Positional objectivity', *Philosophy and Public Affairs*, **22** (2), 126–45.

Sen, Amartya and Bernard Williams (1982), *Utilitarianism and Beyond*, Cambridge: Cambridge University Press.

Smith, Adam ([1776] 1975), *An Inquiry into the Nature and Causes of the Wealth of Nations*, 2 vols, reprinted in R.H. Campbell, A.S. Skinner and W.B. Todd (eds), Oxford: Clarendon Press.

Smith, Adam ([1790] 1976), *The Theory of Moral Sentiments*, reprinted in D.D. Raphael and A.A. Mackie (eds), Oxford: Clarendon Press.

Stewart, Frances (1985), *Basic Needs in Developing Countries*, Baltimore: Johns Hopkins University Press.

Thomson, Garrett (1987), *Needs*, London and New York: Routledge.

Wiggins, David (1998), *Needs, Values, Truth*, Oxford: Clarendon.

See also the entry on: Needs and well-being.

46 Needs and well-being
Des Gasper

Needs language has three central functions. The first is to make analyses of motivation richer and more realistic, extending our explanatory repertoire beyond 'economic man'. The second is to elucidate instrumental roles and connections in means-ends analyses. The third is to help to structure and humanize policy prioritization and extend our evaluative repertoire beyond measures such as per capita income. In all of this, needs language attempts a communicative function too: to support explanatory, elucidatory and normative work by providing frames that are simple but robust enough to be widely usable yet not too misleading in routine professional and political discourse.

The concepts of 'need' and 'needs' are correspondingly pervasive: in everyday discourse, in public policy, especially social policy (see, for example, Witkin and Altschuld 1995; Brazelton and Greenspan 2000), in management and marketing (see, for example, Jackson et al. 2004) and in international policy areas such as humanitarian aid and the Millennium Development Goals. They have a long history in humanistic economics (Lutz and Lux 1988) and parts of welfare economics (for example, Pigou 1920), even if different words have sometimes been used for the same concepts (Amartya Sen, interviewed in Weiss et al. 2005, p. 240).

Needs language is hard to order, because its roles are major, widespread and varied. Pervasive use has been frequently accompanied by casualness and obscurity. That misuse, together with currents opposed to any notion of publicly determined priorities rather than only market-determined ones, has led to frequent opposition to the category of 'needs' in economics. In response, work in the past generation has strengthened the structures of needs language, reinforcing it as a central medium in policy and administration and connecting it to the languages of well-being and human rights.

This chapter looks at the variety and nature of needs concepts and at their relationship to research on human well-being as well as to ideas of human rights.

Three modes of needs discourse
We must distinguish descriptive, instrumental and normative modes in needs discourse, and several levels within each of these (Taylor 1959; Gasper 1996). Since the labels 'descriptive', 'instrumental' and 'normative' are imperfect and open to misunderstanding, we refer here to modes A, B and C (Douglas et al. 1998; Gasper 2004).

In mode A, 'need' covers various categories used in evaluatively neutral description or explanation: a strong want or drive; a commodity with low income elasticity of demand (both when income rises and falls); or a potential whose non-fulfilment brings dissatisfaction, for example, a motivational force instigated by a particular lack: 'a drive or some inner state that initiates a drive' (Doyal and Gough 1991, p. 35). 'Need' typically figures in mode A as a noun, a presence.

In mode B, a 'need' is a requisite for achieving an objective, for example, the various types of nutrition required for survival, health and working capacity (see, for example,

Dasgupta 1993). The term 'need', unfortunately, tends to be used both for the objective and the implied requisite. 'Need' often also appears here as a verb, of lacking ('these people need more food in order to survive'). The requisite's instrumental necessity depends on how far it really is needed and not substitutable, in order to reach the objective; its normative necessity depends in addition on the status of the objective.

Mode C concerns requisites for normatively endorsed priority objectives. It is a subset of mode B. In mode C, a 'need' establishes a strong normative claim since the objective is a normative priority, and the requisite is indeed essential. Doyal and Gough, for example, propose that normative needs are 'a particular category of goals which are believed to be universalisable' (1991, p. 39) because they are necessary conditions for avoidance of serious harm to persons. Their theory's main variant concerns needs that derive from the required objective of being a competent member of one's society.

Within these three modes are dozens of different specific concepts of need (Gasper 1996, 2004).

Much usage is careless of the modal distinctions. In one and the same text 'need' may be treated sometimes as an in-built (whether inborn or inculcated) drive, sometimes as the implied requirement of a given objective, sometimes as a normative priority and sometimes as presumptively all three together. Mode memberships are indeed not mutually exclusive. Often, fulfilment of some want, drive or potential is necessary for achievement of a specified objective which is in turn a normative priority. However, unless we distinguish modes we cannot consider clearly such cases of proposed coincidence and the different intellectual traditions and activities involved.

Mode A usage and mode B usage slide into each other too easily, since both are normatively neutral; and mode B and mode C usages are also easily fused, since they employ the same instrumental logic and there is often ambiguity over the normative status of the objectives referred to (for example, 'the policy's objectives', 'society's objectives'). Mode A and mode C usages can then merge too and usage overall can approach incoherence. The essential distinction between a mode-A notion of species-wide behavioural potentials and propensities and a concept of instrumental linkages towards priority objectives (Doyal and Gough 1991) has also been obscured by optimistic evolutionary ideology.

Needs theory and well-being research

The Venn diagram in Figure 46.1 shows five possible types of 'need'. Only in case 3 does a need fit all three modes. The uppermost rectangle represents needs which are wants and/or behavioural drives (mode A needs); it consists of zones 1 + 2 + 3. The middle rectangle represents needs which are requirements for a given objective (mode B needs); it consists of zones 2 + 3 + 4 + 5. The third rectangle is a subset of the middle one and covers needs which are normative priority requirements (mode C needs); it consists of zones 3 + 4. This normative concept of needs links, despite the terms in standard use, to the concept of objective well-being.

Zone/case 3 indicates behavioural drives or wants whose fulfilment satisfies normative priority requirements. A presumption that all drives are of this type lies behind much misuse of the term 'need'. It rests on a rosy theory of human nature that evolution or providence have selected for us solely those drives which lead to the promotion of normative priorities; zones 1 and 2 – drives which lead elsewhere – are presumed empty. A mistaken sister presumption holds that we have no normative priorities which are not

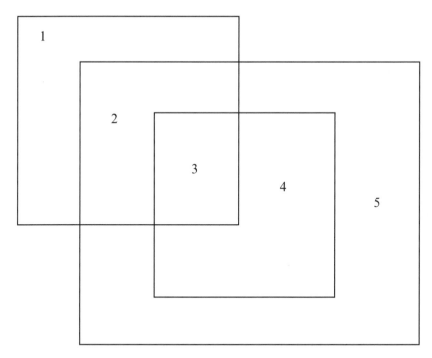

Figure 46.1   Venn diagram of the three modal usages of 'needs'

targeted by behavioural drives; in other words, that zone 4 is empty. In reality, some drives fulfil no objective (see zone 1); they are non-functional, perhaps relics from pre-history. Some drives fulfil an objective but not one that is a normative priority (case 2). This could be the case for drives that promote subjective well-being in forms that are not endorsed after reflection or by authorized decision-makers; the drives of the addict exemplify dysfunctional drives leading to undesirable outcomes. The drives in case 2 might also be evolutionary experiments that failed but have not been eliminated, or that were once helpful but became outmoded (for example a drive to eat heavily whenever the opportunity arises). Many of the requisites for particular objectives are not drive-based (cases 4 and 5), but only some of them concern normative priority objectives (case 4). In case 5 a requisite serves some function, but one that is not of normative priority and that, fortunately, has no behavioural drive behind it.

So while case 3 is ideal, it is far from the only case. Cases 1, 2 and 4 are all important but do not match the rosy classical conception of needs. Some drives do not promote normative priorities, and some are even dangerous; some functional requirements and normative priorities lack a behavioural motor behind them (Jackson et al. 2004); and drives that fulfil no objective only divert us. This modal analysis implies a research agenda on well-being. Can, for example, space 4, the sphere of priority needs that are divorced from wants, be diminished – by promoting wants corresponding to those needs or finding functional substitutes for their fulfilment? Hamilton (2003) considers also the social dynamics of generation and transformation of mode A needs, from pure wants to felt needs in the sense of drives, and how this may affect what are instrumental requirements and agreed priorities. Drives are not only instinctual in origin, but are continually newly generated and also sometimes dissipated; sometimes what were approved felt needs decline into mere wants.

Economics and needs language

To judge from social science dictionaries, perhaps no social science discipline refers both clearly and regularly to all three modes (Gasper 2007); but whereas sociology, psychology, politics and philosophy do regularly distinguish and use more than one, mainstream modern economics has often tried to avoid the 'need' term altogether (Jackson et al. 2004). This may be partly due to confusion about modes. Resistance to engaging in mode C discourse on publicly reasoned priorities, as opposed to relying on individual preferences alone, and objection further to claims that the state should provide some priority items have contributed to a neglect in economics of all modes of needs discourse. Much of economics has been deficient in engaging with a mode-A explanation of wants (Scitovsky 1992 was one important exception) and a mode-B investigation of human requisites. Economic theory has, for example, typically assumed, rather than checked, that market wages will suffice for subsistence. Partha Dasgupta (1993) showed this assumption is often invalid in low-income countries, where many wage-earners must be cross-subsidized by others, or survive thanks to access to common property resources. Many exist in a state of destitution and vulnerability that reduces their lifespan.

Mainstream economics has worked with a very limited, descriptive needs concept in mode A, namely goods for which the income elasticity of demand is low. Such goods are more often called 'necessities'; they may also be subject to low price elasticity of demand. Demand for 'inferior goods' even falls as income rises. Conversely, 'luxuries' are deemed to be those goods for which income elasticity of demand is high. What are 'necessities' and 'luxuries' in this sense varies greatly across time and place. Demand elasticities are of strong interest to businesses for planning and marketing, including for targeting international markets, and to economists for drawing implications for the structural transformations of economies as incomes rise. In particular, the limits on growth of long-run demand for food and fibres imply the necessary relative decline of agriculture (Tomich et al. 1995). The US Department of Agriculture compiles price and income elasticity data for many countries for basic commodities, such as food, clothing and footwear, fuel and power and medical care (USDA n.d.).

The concept of 'needs' or 'necessities' in this conventional economics sense has no basis of underlying theory about what motivates demand or what are the results of consumption of different goods, and hence about what claims they might have for priority status in public policy. Cigarettes, for example, have often had low income- (and price-) elasticities of demand. 'Need' here has become merely a synonym for strong preference. As a result, modern mainstream economics often no longer uses the term at all; and similarly its classical forerunner 'necessities' became seen as archaic or dangerous. Yet in reality people not only have preferences but also views about which preferences they would like to have, especially which strong preferences. Many people wish, for example, not arbitrarily but for powerful reasons, that they did not have a strong preference for smoking.

Normative needs language allows us to discuss the ranking of preferences other than merely in terms of their intensity. In policy work some economists employ normative notions of 'needs', but typically wish to emphasize that '[t]here is an inherent subjectivity and social specificity to any notion of "basic needs", including nutritional requirements' (Ravallion 2008). They then leave to politics, philosophy and other disciplines the discussion of that social specificity and of the criteria and processes for social specification and for the ordering of subjectivity. Let us look at some of the central ideas with which any policy economist should be familiar.

Needs and satisfiers

A second fundamental distinction, one highlighted by the Chilean economist Manfred Max-Neef (1991), concerns not mode but level: the contrast between needs, meaning target outcomes, and satisfiers, meaning things which allow achievement of those outcomes. The need-satisfier distinction obviously arises within the instrumental mode B, and thus also within the normative mode C. But it applies too within mode A, when needs are seen as drives or urges, and satisfiers as things which allow their fulfilment.

Satisfiers vary enormously (for example, the types of food that are acceptable vary according to place), whereas the needs they serve might be common and stable (in this example, needs for nutrition, pleasure and affiliation). A satisfier is a way of fulfilling a requirement. It has in turn its own requirements, which too have their requirements, and so on. A satisfier can contribute to fulfilling several needs; and a need/lack can often be met by many alternative satisfiers. Darcy and Hofmann (2003) warn that failure to use the need-satisfier distinction causes conflation of needs assessment with formulation of responses. If the need for nutrition becomes conflated with the need for a particular satisfier, namely relief food supplies ('they need relief supplies'), this forecloses attention to other and possibly more appropriate satisfiers, for example, direct monetary payments or employment. Normative needs analysis tries to establish reasoned priorities; it does not have a fixed commitment to any particular form of action, such as the use of any particular set of satisfiers or direct provision by a public authority.

Elements of normative needs analysis

Mode C discourse contains further elements. Several are captured in a 'relational formula' (Barry 1990; Wiggins 1985): Entity E needs S if S is a necessary condition, in the given context, for E to achieve N, and N is either directly an approved priority or is a necessary condition for achievement of P, an accepted approved priority. Braybrooke (1987) and Doyal and Gough (1991) highlight that the chains of instrumental linkage can be long. More elaborately, Braybrooke identifies the following elements in normative needs analysis: (i) implicitly, a decision-making group deciding for a particular target population within a particular political community (the three can be identical but can also differ); (ii) a criterion, such as a target objective [P] which one uses to determine need, for example, survival (for a normal human lifespan) or health or autonomy or a conception of human flourishing; (iii) a set of types of need [N], derived as proposed necessary implications of that criterion; (iv) a chain of levels, such as illustrated in Table 46.1, at each level of which we identify satisfiers [S] that contribute towards the chosen criterion; and (v) at each level, for each of the types of need/satisfier (where relevant) a specified indicator and perhaps an achievement target. The focus can be on actual attainment (functioning) or on ability to attain (capability).

The first row in Table 46.1 presents the criterion, the types of normative basic need and the set of levels in Doyal and Gough's influential *A Theory of Human Need* (1991). It should be read from left to right. It shows too how the structure of their theory is

Table 46.1   Levels in normative needs analysis

	Basic Criterion	Requirements in order to fulfil the basic criterion (Needs level 1)	Required satisfier characteristics (Needs level 2/Satisfier level 1)	Specific required satisfiers (Needs level 3/Satisfier level 2)	Required preconditions (Needs level 4)
Doyal and Gough's (1991) main formulation of human need	Avoidance of serious harm	Health, autonomy of agency	Nourishment, housing, secure environment, work, childhood, health-care, education, etc.	The satisfiers required to provide those 'characteristics' vary according to geographical, socio-economic and cultural setting	Conditions concerning production, reproduction, cultural transmission and political authority
In the categories of Sen's capability approach and UNDP's 'human development'	Priority functionings	Capabilities that are required to achieve the priority functionings	'Characteristics' of goods that are required to achieve those capabilities	The goods and 'commodities' that are required to provide those characteristics	The societal conditions that are required to sustain the supply of those goods
From Klein Goldewijk and Fortman's (1999) formulation of human rights	Dignity and non-humiliation, self-respect	Equality and freedom or equality and agency	Implications of needs level 1 in this row	Implications of needs level 2 in this row; they vary according to . . .	. . .

Source: Gasper (2005).

paralleled in Sen's capability approach and in contemporary formulations of human rights. Penz (1991) shows these three perspectives to be closely connected and complementary. Within normative needs analysis, each particular criterion of priority generates a particular specification of implied requirements, the proposed normatively fundamental needs. From an understanding of mode C needs as the requisites for well-being, we see how different conceptions of well-being can lead to different specifications of need. In addition, each choice of a particular level as the main focus in needs discourse matches a particular type of conception of well-being (Gasper 2007).

Doyal and Gough's approach helps one to think clearly about choices of public action priorities, including through its use of available positive theory and evidence from many fields. It illustrates too how, contrary to the arguments of some earlier authors (for example, Fitzgerald 1977; Springborg 1981), needs discourse does not inherently treat persons as passive or materialistic and ignore them as active, rights-claiming, choice-making agents. Promotion of autonomy of agency, together with health, stands as the central principle in Doyal and Gough's formulation. Like other modern theorizations of needs discourse for public policy, such as Braybrooke's, it is explicitly dynamic and dia-logical, is not restricted to physical requirements alone and makes no presumption that goods will be accessed through the state rather than markets, or that a needs framework displaces politics rather than structures policy debate. Still, why should it be adopted to structure debate, besides merely its lack of some previously argued defects? Frohlich and Oppenheimer (1992) found from repeated experiments in different cultural contexts that a basic needs floor was overwhelmingly the principle of justice that people chose from behind a Rawlsian veil of ignorance, not Rawls's own difference principle nor some other alternatives. (See also Brock 2005.)

Ideas of basic need
The adjective 'basic' is often applied to normative needs in order to emphasize high pri-ority; for example, perhaps needs whose non-fulfilment will produce great suffering. It is also used for those derived needs which are proposed as essential for a great range of, or even all, posited priority concerns; for example, nutrition and water and the capacities for effective agency, practical reasoning and interaction with others. 'Basic' is also used to describe cases having special significance in mode A discourse: impulses that suppos-edly exist universally or underlie all surface manifestations. The early version of the basic needs theory of Abraham Maslow (1943) is a famous example of such claims.

Maslow's own later work, and subsequent such work by humanistic psychologists (for example, Deci and Ryan 2000; Ryan and Deci 2000; Sheldon and Elliot 1999), has partly a predictive thrust. It aims to explain and better forecast behaviour in terms of underly-ing needs. But much of their work falls into zones 2 and 3, aiming to predict mental (and physical) states rather than behaviour, and notes that behaviour and well-being are not necessarily well linked. Such work posits various requirements for personal physical and mental health and well-being, but does not assert that behaviour necessarily follows those requirements. It hopes to influence behaviour through changing awareness and influenc-ing motives.

Max-Neef's widely used work on 'fundamental human needs' (1991) has a similar character. The posited fundamental needs are subsistence, protection, affection, under-standing, participation, recreation, creation, identity and freedom. Each is examined with reference to existential categories of being, having, doing and interacting, thus generating a 36-cell matrix. People and groups can consider possible satisfiers for each cell. Such analysis is not a fixed predictive theory for complex human agents, but deepens consid-eration of motives, requirements, options and priorities. Max-Neef elaborates how not all mode-A need fulfilment leads to well-being, except perhaps if we interpret well-being as sheer activity. He identifies as 'pseudo-needs' those behavioural drives whose fulfilment fails to bring maturely reflective satisfaction. 'Pseudo-satisfiers' give only fleeting fulfil-ment; 'violators' completely fail to satisfy, yet one can be habituated to them; 'inhibiting satisfiers' satisfy one need (often a short-term one) but at the cost of reducing satisfaction of other needs; whereas 'synergistic satisfiers' fulfil several needs at once. Max-Neef's framework is found useful in many organizational development and community development initiatives. It extends the agenda for well-being research relevant for economic and social policy, especially for socially and environmentally sustainable consumption (for example, Raskin et al. 2002; Jackson 2006).

Very distant from these forms of 'basic human needs' theory, which treat persons in terms of assets and capacities and not only of lacks and deficiencies, is the 'basic material needs' approach to policy priorities. (Hettne (1990), amongst others, contrasts these two basic needs approaches.) The latter approach was adopted by various development planning agencies throughout the twentieth century. Examples include work by Indian government agencies from the 1950s on, and programmes led by the World Bank in the 1970s and early 1980s. Material needs work centred on provision of quantified target amounts of food, water, clothing, shelter, health and education. The approach came to be seen as having several fundamental shortcomings, including materialistic and technocratic biases and an overly generalizing, top-down, donative perspective. Its critique laid a basis for the growth of the 'human development' and 'capability' approaches (see chapters on these subjects in this volume). Current work towards the Millennium Development Goals intends to take into account those earlier shortcomings (UNDP 2003).

Needs and rights

Prior to the World Bank, but lacking the financial power to propagate its message as forcefully, the International Labour Office enunciated a basic needs approach (ILO 1976) that it situated 'within a broader framework – namely the fulfilment of basic human rights' (cited by Jolly et al. 2004, p. 114). Connection between conceptions of needs and human rights was slowed by their primary locations in different disciplines and professions. Added to this was the confusion around modes of needs discourse and the attacks on it by some libertarians and free-market advocates, and the antagonism by some socialists and economists to rights formulations. More recently, these obstacles have diminished and the connection of the two bodies of thought has become more evident, in work by, for example, Johan Galtung (1994), Alan Gewirth (1996) and Bas de Gaay Fortman (Klein Goldewijk and Fortman 1999).

Human rights can be seen as rights to the fulfilment of, or ability to fulfil, normative basic human needs. Basic human needs are whatever people require to be able to achieve a level of functioning that satisfies a given ethical conception of the acceptable minimum. Such conceptions include, as we saw in Table 46.1, human dignity and the avoidance of serious harm. The needs implied by all of these conceptions typically include, in particular, basic levels of physical and mental health. These normative needs provide a grounding for human rights (Klein Goldewijk and Fortman 1999). Galtung (1994) adds that even if not all needs imply rights, and not all rights correspond to needs, a central set of human rights rests on basic needs. Nussbaum (2000) proposes similarly that many human rights are best seen as rights to fulfilment of basic needs, in turn best seen as basic capabilities to function, in other words real access to those priority functionings. Human rights language gives to normative needs theory an insistence on the value of each person and a vivid, widely accepted, mobilizing idiom. Rights that are instituted as social norms or legal instruments form essential tools in struggles to claim fulfilment of basic needs.

References

Barry, Brian (1990), *Political Argument*, 2nd edition, London: Harvester Wheatsheaf.
Braybrooke, David (1987), *Meeting Needs*, Princeton, NJ: Princeton University Press.
Brazelton, T. Berry and Stanley I. Greenspan (2000), *The Irreducible Needs of Children*, Cambridge, MA: Perseus.
Brock, G. (2005), 'Needs and global justice', in Soran Reader (ed.), *The Philosophy of Need*, Cambridge: Cambridge University Press, pp. 51–72.
Darcy, James and Charles-Antoine Hofmann (2003), 'According to need? Needs assessment and decision-making in the humanitarian sector', HPG Report 15, Overseas Development Institute, London.
Dasgupta, Partha (1993), *An Inquiry into Well-Being and Destitution*, Oxford: Clarendon Press.
Deci, Edward L. and Richard M. Ryan (2000), 'The "what" and "why" of goal pursuits: human needs and the self-determination of behavior', *Psychological Inquiry*, **11**, 227–68.
Douglas, Mary, Des Gasper, Steven Ney and Michael Thompson (1998), 'Human needs and wants', in Steve Rayner and Elizabeth L. Malone (eds), *Human Choice and Climate Change, Vol. 1: The Societal Framework*, Columbus, OH: Battelle Press, pp. 195–263.
Doyal, Len and Ian Gough (1991), *A Theory of Human Need*, London: Macmillan.
Fitzgerald, Ross (1977), *Human Needs and Politics*, Rushcutters Bay, Australia: Pergamon Press.
Frohlich, Norman and Joe A. Oppenheimer (1992), *Choosing Justice: An Empirical Approach to Ethical Theory*, Berkeley, CA: University of California Press.
Galtung, Johan (1994), *Human Rights in Another Key*, Cambridge: Polity Press.
Gasper, Des (1996), 'Needs and basic needs', in Gabriele Köhler, Charles Gore, Utz-Peter Reich and Thomas Ziesemer (eds), *Questioning Development*, Marburg: Metropolis Verlag, pp. 71–101.
Gasper, Des (2004), *The Ethics of Development: From Economism to Human Development*, Edinburgh: Edinburgh University Press.
Gasper, Des (2005), 'Securing humanity: situating "human security" as concept and discourse', *Journal of Human Development*, **6** (2), 221–45.
Gasper, Des (2007), 'Conceptualising human needs and wellbeing', in Ian Gough and J. Allister McGregor (eds), *Wellbeing in Developing Countries: New Approaches and Research Strategies*, Cambridge: Cambridge University Press, pp. 47–70.
Gewirth, Alan (1996). *The Community of Rights*, Chicago: University of Chicago Press.
Hamilton, Lawrence (2003), *The Political Philosophy of Needs*, Cambridge: Cambridge University Press.
Hettne, Bjorn (1990), *Development Theory and the Three Worlds*, Harlow: Longman.
ILO (1976), *Employment, Growth and Basic Needs*, Geneva: International Labour Office.
Jackson, Tim (ed.) (2006), *The Earthscan Reader in Sustainable Consumption*, London: Earthscan.
Jackson, Tim, Wander Jager and Sigrid Stagl (2004), 'Beyond insatiability: needs theory, consumption and sustainability', in Lucia Reisch and Inge Røpke (eds), *Consumption: Perspectives from Ecological Economics*, Cheltenham, UK and Northampton, MA, USA: Edward Elgar.
Jolly, Richard, Louis Emmerij, Dharam Ghai and Frederic Lapeyre (2004), *UN Contributions to Development Thinking and Practice*, Bloomington, IN: Indiana University Press.
Klein Goldewijk, Berma and Bastiaan de Gaay Fortman (1999), *Where Needs Meet Rights*, Geneva: WCC Publications.
Lutz, Mark and Kenneth Lux (1988), *Humanistic Economics*, New York: Bootstrap Press.
Maslow, Abraham (1943), 'A theory of human motivation', *Psychology Review*, **50**, 370–96.
Max-Neef, Manfred (1991), *Human-scale Development*, New York and London: Apex Press.
Nussbaum, Martha (2000), *Women and Human Development: The Capabilities Approach*, Cambridge: Cambridge University Press.
Penz, Peter (1991), 'The priority of basic needs', in K. Aman (ed.), *Ethical Principles for Development: Needs, Capacities or Rights*, Upper Montclair, NJ: Montclair State University, pp. 35–73.
Pigou, Arthur C. (1920), *The Economics of Welfare*, London: Macmillan.
Raskin, Paul, Tariq Banuri, Gilberto Gallopin, Pablo Gutman, Al Hammond, Robert Kates and Rob Swart (2002), *Great Transition*, Stockholm Environment Institute, Boston, MA, http://www.gtinitiative.org/documents/Great_Transitions.pdf, accessed 15 October, 2008.
Ravallion, Martin (2008), 'Poverty Lines', in Steven N. Durlauf and Lawrence E. Blume (eds), *The New Palgrave Dictionary of Economics*, 2nd edition, Basingstoke and London: Palgrave, www.dictionaryofeconomics.com/article?id=pde2008_p000349>doi:10.1057/9780230226203.1319, accessed 15 October, 2008.
Ryan, Richard M. and Edward L. Deci (2000), 'The darker and brighter sides of human existence: basic psychological needs as a unifying concept', *Psychological Inquiry*, **11**, 319–38.
Scitovsky, Tibor (1992), *The Joyless Economy: The Psychology of Human Satisfaction*, revised edition, New York: Oxford University Press.

Sheldon, K.M. and A.J. Elliot (1999), 'Goal striving, need-satisfaction, and longitudinal well-being: the self-concordance model', *Journal of Personality and Social Psychology*, **76**, 482–97.

Springborg, Patricia (1981), *The Problem of Human Needs and the Critique of Civilization*, London: Allen and Unwin.

Taylor, Paul W. (1959), '"Need" statements', *Analysis*, **19** (5), 106–11.

Tomich, Thomas P., Peter Kilby and Bruce F. Johnston (1995), *Transforming Agricultural Economies*, Ithaca, NY: Cornell University Press.

UNDP (2003), *Human Development Report 2003: Millennium Development Goals*, New York: Oxford University Press for United Nations Development Programme.

USDA (n.d.), 'Data sets: International food consumption patterns', US Department of Agriculture, Washington DC, www.ers.usda.gov/data/InternationalFoodDemand/, accessed 15 October 2008.

Weiss, Thomas G., Tatiana Carayannis, Louis Emmerij and Richard Jolly (2005), *UN Voices: The Struggle for Development and Social Justice*, Bloomington, IN: Indiana University Press.

Wiggins, David (1985), 'Claims of need', in Ted Honderich (ed.), *Morality and Objectivity*, London: Routledge.

Witkin, Belle Ruth and James W. Altschuld (1995), *Planning and Conducting Needs Assessments*, Thousand Oaks, CA: Sage.

See also the entries on: Capability approach; Human development; Needs and agency.

47 Pluralism
Esther-Mirjam Sent

Introduction
Calls for pluralism in economics date from the publication of 'Plea for a Pluralistic and Rigorous Economics', issued in 1992 by a group of economists in the form of an advertisement in the *American Economic Review* calling for

> a new spirit of pluralism in economics, involving critical conversation and tolerant communication between different approaches. Such pluralism should not undermine the standards of rigor; an economics that requires itself to face all the arguments will be a more, not a less, rigorous science.

The 'Plea' was organized by Geoffrey Hodgson, Uskali Mäki and D. McCloskey and signed by 44 illustrious names including Nobel laureates Franco Modigliani, Paul Samuelson, Herbert Simon and Jan Tinbergen. The following year, the call for pluralism was institutionalized with the establishment of the International Confederation of Associations for Pluralism in Economics (ICAPE). This organization's commitment to a 'new pluralism' was renewed recently in a series of petitions by students and professors in France, Italy, the United Kingdom and the United States, leading to the creation of the Post-Autistic Economics Network.

Implicit in these appeals is the observation that economics lacks pluralism. The pleas for pluralism are defended with an assortment of arguments, such as the complexity of the economy, the restrictions inherent in modelling and cognitive limitations on the part of economists. The advertisement in the *American Economic Review* employed a reflexive strategy as well: 'Economists today enforce a monopoly of method or core assumptions, often defended on no better ground [than] that it constitutes the "mainstream". Economists will advocate free competition, but will not practice it in the marketplace of ideas.'

This chapter interprets pluralism as the view that some phenomena observed in science require multiple explanations to account for their nature. This 'scientific pluralism' is closely associated with, for example, 'value pluralism' (also known as 'ethical pluralism' or 'moral pluralism'), which is the idea that several values may be equally correct and fundamental, and yet conflict with one another. Indeed, one of the strong arguments for pluralism in terms of tolerance for a variety of approaches is the ethical one. After all, pluralism is the advocacy of plurality. This ethical dimension is implicit in much of the remaining discussion.

Starting from the definition of scientific pluralism, several concerns may arise when using pluralism as an organizing principle. First, the nature of 'pluralism' often differs. In fact, distinctions should be made amongst theories, methods, methodologies, approaches, perspectives, models, explanations and so on (see, for example, Salanti and Screpanti 1997). For instance, pluralism about methodologies concerns the methodologists' understanding of the multifaceted enterprise of economics, which may be inspired by a plurality of 'shelves', including history, literary criticism, philosophy and sociology (see, for example, Hands 2001). Pluralism about methods, on the other hand, involves types of models, reasoning and so on upon which economists rely (for example, Dow 1997, 2002). Note that a practising economist employing one method may still be pluralist by being tolerant of economists adopting other methods.

Second, the source of pluralism varies. It could be ontological, epistemological, pragmatic, historical, sociological, heuristical, political and so on (for example, Salanti and Screpanti 1997). With some of these sources, one quickly returns to monism. Consider pluralism about theories. Then, the argument that theories vary across different scientific contexts (domains, times, interests and so on) raises the question whether for every phenomenon, query and so on there would be a single, best account. If so, then this view seems to reduce to monism, which foreshadows the arguments of the subsequent sections. Before proceeding there, we make one more observation concerning pluralism.

Third, the classification of pluralism must be taken into consideration. The various objects of pluralism could be translatable or not and might be compatible or not. Reflexivity concerns should keep one from casting the classification in terms of complements and substitutes. As Uskali Mäki (1999) argues, 'some of the fundamental economic concepts applied to the study of science are in need of critical scrutiny. If economists themselves are not fully clear about these concepts, this should alert philosophers and sociologists considering their employment as well' (p. 505). Returning to translatability and compatibility, suppose heterodox and neoclassical economics are considered to be neither translatable nor compatible; then one, again, introduces the possibility of a reduction to monism for reasons much like those noted above.

The remainder of this chapter develops a historical understanding of various forms of pluralism, or the lack thereof, in economics. In particular, it argues that pluralism in economics is recurring, but often denied. Instead of locating the source in epistemology, metaphysics and the like, the analysis proposes that the lack of success of the monist movement in economics strengthens the case for pluralism. The next section offers an overview of movements towards monism about theories, showing that repeated efforts at securing a single theory have failed. These developments have extended towards the level of economies, as suggested by the subsequent section, which shows that attempts to treat economic agents monistically have failed. The lack of success of these efforts to achieve monism has paved the way for a return to pluralism, as elaborated in the final section of the chapter.

While pleas for pluralism on the part of heterodox economists come as no surprise, pluralism within mainstream economics is often unacknowledged. This explains the focus on the mainstream in the subsequent sections and is a point to which we return in the conclusion. Indeed, heterodox economists might argue that there are limits to the present pluralism even so.

Monism about theories
As evidenced by the various calls for pluralism, economics has until recently been characterized by efforts to achieve monism at the theoretical level. However, this has not always been the case. Before World War I and in the inter-war period, pluralism was the dominant force in economics (Morgan and Rutherford 1998a). Yet World War II stimulated

the move in economics towards monism about beliefs, ideology, theories, models and policy advice. During the war, heavy demands were placed on economists to develop tools for solving policy problems. Economists thus emerged from the war period with a firm belief in the formalism that characterized neoclassical economics. While economics became associated with a certain tool-kit as opposed to a particular area of study, the formalism further supported economists' efforts to gain identity as a 'national science' and thus to achieve professional status.

Complicating our observations and foreshadowing our claim that pluralism in economics is recurring, though often denied, some have suggested that neoclassical economics owes its strength to its persistent inability to enforce any monolithic orthodoxy. For instance, Wade Hands and Philip Mirowski (Hands and Mirowski 1998; Mirowksi and Hands 1998) outline various approaches to neoclassical demand theory. Perry Mehrling (1998, p. 295) suggests that 'although the neoclassical language might have become hegemonic, what economists wanted to say with that language remained as pluralist as in the interwar years'. In addition, our observations concern developments in the United States, as justified by that country's 'predominant influence on the expansion and internationalization of economics during the past half century' (Coats 1996b, p. 4). The result is that the trends outlined here are spreading, with some lag, to Europe and Japan.

It should also be acknowledged that our observations up until now concern microeconomics. Pluralism re-emerged during efforts to reduce other fields to microeconomics. To start, microeconomics has come under attack for not having a notion of 'the social' other than summing 'the individual' (Hands 1994, 1995, 1997a). Even if one accepts the exclusive focus on 'the individual' in economics, problems occur. As neoclassical economists themselves have acknowledged (for example, Arrow 1959), 'competitive' markets require something beyond an 'individualistic' explanation. Basically, individual agents in a competitive market take prices as a given in their individual choice problem. This raises the question, then, from where these prices come (Hands 1995).

Accepting the stress on 'the individual' and ignoring some of its limitations, efforts to achieve monism about theories in microeconomics inspired efforts to reduce other fields to it, especially macroeconomics. Attempts to develop neoclassical microfoundations for macroeconomics date back to the years just after World War II, when the problem of aggregation received prominent attention (Klein 1946; also see Janssen 1993; Nelson 1984; Weintraub 1977, 1979). This problem has two components. The first is whether there exist functional relationships among macroquantities obtained by aggregating relevant microquantities. The second is whether the functions obtained by aggregating microfunctions are the same as macrofunctions independently derived. In the process of examining these questions, neoclassical economics was modified in a variety of ways to provide a conceptual base for the formulation of macroeconomic concerns, and 'by say 1960 the microfoundations problem appeared, on the surface, to be "settled"' (Weintraub 1977, p. 4).

Matters changed during the 1960s, when non-neoclassical economists uncovered difficulties with aggregating from 'the individual' (Harcourt 1969, 1972; Kurz and Salvadori 1995; Robinson 1953). This was evidenced by what came to be known as the 'Cambridge controversies in the theory of capital', indicating the critics in Cambridge, England, and the defenders in Cambridge, Massachusetts. The target of attack was the aggregate production function. In the course of investigating the meaning of this production function for total output, Joan Robinson (1953) found the construct to be incoherent, due to the fuzzy nature of the capital variable. In particular, the British side of the controversy outlined two problems with the aggregate production function, namely, reswitching and reverse capital deepening. Neoclassical economist Joseph Stiglitz (1974, p. 898) drew the following conclusion from these insights: '[T]he restrictions embodied in neoclassical macroeconomic models do not necessarily follow from the microeconomic (disaggregative) models from which they should be derived.'

In the late 1960s, the rise of rational expectations economics at the macro level gave new impetus to the microfoundations project and the associated efforts to achieve monism about theories (Sent 1998). In particular, rational expectations economists argued that the suboptimal use of available information under adaptive expectations was hard to reconcile with the idea of optimization that forms the foundation of neoclassical economic analysis. Instead, rational expectations economists claimed that since agents were posited as optimizers, it was only natural to presume that they would also form their expectations optimally. In other words, the rational expectations hypothesis was a direct derivation from the neoclassical optimization principle extended to the problem of expectations of future events.

Yet again, stumbling blocks arose in including macroeconomics in the efforts towards monism about theories, as illustrated by the so-called Sonnenschein-Debreu-Mantel result, which concerns the restrictions imposed on the structure of aggregate demand functions (Sonnenschein 1972; Debreu 1974; Mantel 1976; Kirman 1989, 1992; Rizvi 1994a). According to this result, the weak axiom of revealed preference (WARP) may not be satisfied at the aggregate level. Yet, if we are to obtain uniqueness and stability of equilibria, some such restrictions must be imposed. Hands (1995, p. 617) succinctly summarizes the problem: 'In other words, the standard micro model has almost no implications for macrobehavior.'

As a result of the difficulties in achieving monism about theories, the present situation in (mainstream) economics might be characterized as one of moderate pluralism. Recent years have witnessed, for instance, efforts to incorporate bounded rationality approaches, behavioural insights, chaos theory, complexity approaches and experimental methods, some of which are discussed in the concluding section of this chapter. First, however, a discussion of further responses to the failed attempts at monism about theories leads us to a look at monism about economies.

Monism about economies

Whereas pluralism about theories is a familiar concept, pluralism with economies as its object is perhaps less so. Yet it has an interesting ethical dimension. It concerns an economy in which people (or groups) value things differently and in which this diversity is valued (Hargreaves Heap 1997). There is not just plurality, but there is also a political commitment to pluralism. Economics, however, does not respect a diversity of views concerning the agents populating its models. Indeed, economics has always had difficulty dealing with distinctly different agents (Sent 1998), as illustrated by the cloning argument Francis Ysidro Edgeworth (1881) developed in the course of analysing exchange, and the fact that general equilibrium theory does not successfully apply to an economy that is fully specialized and in which the possibility of self-sufficiency is the exception rather than the rule (Rizvi 1991).

Monism about economies is also a consequence of the Sonnenschein-Debreu-Mantel result. For, if the behaviour of the economy could be represented as that of a representative agent or a number of identical agents, aggregate excess demand functions would have unique and stable equilibria, much like individual excess demand functions (Kirman 1992). With one representative agent there clearly can be no difference of opinion, which we call a situation of monism in economies.

Much like efforts to achieve monism about theories, endeavours towards monism in economies encountered major stumbling blocks. Some of these concern the relationship between the representative individual and the group she supposedly embodies (Kirman 1992). In addition, representative agent analysis has encountered other problems (Sent 1998). First, a representative agent is ill-suited for the study of macroeconomic problems that are coordination failures, such as unemployment. Second, a representative individual cannot exhibit the complicated dynamics witnessed at the macroeconomic level. Third, how can there be trade if there is only one representative agent? Or, suppose there are several representative agents who are alike in several dimensions, how can there be trade among these? (Lucas 1972; see also Varian 1987.)

Overall, the response to the Sonnenschein-Debreu-Mantel result and the problems associated with the resulting embrace of representative agent analysis has been for neoclassical microeconomics to move towards game theory (Kirman 1992; Rizvi 1994b). Yet, much like its predecessors, game theory does not accommodate a diversity of views concerning the agents populating its models. Briefly, game theory relies on a whole range of common knowledge assumptions (Brandenburger 1992; Geneakoplos 1992; Rizvi 1994b), thereby reducing pluralism in the sense of diversity of views. Much like the efforts to use representative agent analysis to achieve monism regarding economies, the common knowledge assumption encountered major hurdles, such as the agreement theorem and the non-speculation theorem. Similar to the failure of monism about theories, then, monism about economies encountered significant stumbling blocks, which brings us to the conclusion of this chapter.

Conclusion

In light of the efforts to establish monism on the part of neoclassical economists, it comes as no surprise that outsiders to the mainstream appear to be supporting pluralisms and criticizing monisms, as evidenced by the pleas with which this chapter started. However, upon closer scrutiny, heterodox economists are frequently monists about theories. In the opinion of John Davis, the motivation of heterodox economists 'is not that their own theoretical approaches are *also* correct – a theoretical pluralist view – but rather that neoclassical economics is mistaken and misguided in its most basic assumptions, and that their own approaches remedy the deficiencies of neoclassicism – a theoretical monist view' (1997, p. 209, original emphasis). Indeed, appeals to pluralism on the part of heterodox economics may be seen as an instance of strategic pluralism (Davis and Sent 2007). Though their advocacy of pluralism may be couched in metaphysical or epistemological terms, it is often inspired by efforts to achieve professional power and dominance.

If heterodox economists are serious about their advocacy of pluralism, as we hope they are, they need to consider carefully the nature, source and classification of pluralism. And they need to confront the charge that pluralism inevitably leads to an 'anything goes' view. They must also beware of sliding into monism. For instance, an ontological perspective that stresses the patchiness of the world risks being reduced to monism because it might be consistent with the idea that for every phenomenon there is a single, best account. An epistemological view that involves the hedging of bets may reduce to monism if the long-term goal is a single comprehensive account. An epistemological view that relies on the cognitive limitations of economists may reduce to monism if the limitations merely delay the development of a single, complete and correct theory. If heterodox economists desire pluralism, they should honour its spirit when offering interpretations of the mainstream. If heterodox economists employ appeals to pluralism strategically in an effort to achieve monism, they leave themselves vulnerable to criticism. Finally, they should ensure that the material and social conditions for the flourishing of pluralism are met.

Returning to mainstream economics, despite the apparent acceptance of monism, this chapter illustrates economics' failure to achieve monism. Indeed, it shows that pluralism is recurring, though often denied. The breakdown of the microfoundations project suggests that phenomena at the micro and macro levels in economics are so complex that one theoretical approach, for instance, microeconomics, lacks the resources to provide a complete explanation or description. For economists, these failures have led in the direction of exploring cognitive limitations on the part of the agents populating their models. Ironically, when economists made the agents in their models more bounded in their rationality, they had to be smarter, because the models then became larger and more demanding econometrically. This, in turn, gives additional plausibility to the suspicion that pluralism further results from cognitive limitations on the part of human inquirers. The main focus of this chapter, however, was to strengthen the case for pluralism by offering an overview of the lack of success of several monist movements in economics.

References and other further reading

Arrow, Kenneth J. (1959), 'Toward a theory of price adjustment', in Moses Abramovitz (ed.), *The Allocation of Economic Resources*, Stanford, CA: Stanford University Press, pp. 41–51.
Brandenburger, Adam (1992), 'Knowledge and equilibrium in games', *Journal of Economic Perspectives*, **6** (4), 83–101.
Caldwell, Bruce J. (1988), 'The case for pluralism', in Neil De Marchi (ed.), *The Popperian Legacy in Economics*, Cambridge: Cambridge University Press, pp. 231–44.
Coats, A.W. (ed.) (1996a), *The Post-1945 Internationalization of Economics*, Annual Supplement to Volume 28, History of Political Economy, Durham: Duke University Press.
Coats, A.W. (ed.) (1996b), 'Introduction', in A.W. Coats (ed.), *The Post-1945 Internationalization of Economics*, Annual Supplement to Volume 28, History of Political Economy, Durham: Duke University Press, pp. 3–11.
Davis, John B. (1997), 'Comment', in Andrea Salanti and Ernesto Screpanti (eds), *Pluralism in Economics: New Perspectives in History and Methodology*, Cheltenham, UK and Lyme, USA: Edward Elgar, pp. 207–11.
Davis, John B. (1999), 'Postmodernism and identity conditions for discourses', in Robert F. Garnett, Jr (ed.), *What Do Economists Know? New Economics of Knowledge*, London: Routledge, pp. 155–68.
Davis, John B. and Esther-Mirjam Sent (2007), *Heterodoxy's Strategic Pluralism*, working paper, available from authors.
Debreu, Gerard (1974), 'Excess demand functions', *Journal of Mathematical Economics*, **1** (1), 15–23.
Dow, Sheila C. (1997), 'Methodological pluralism and pluralism of method', in Andrea Salanti and Ernesto Screpanti (eds), *Pluralism in Economics: New Perspectives in History and Methodology*, Cheltenham, UK and Lyme, USA: Edward Elgar, pp. 89–99.
Dow, Sheila C. (2002), 'Pluralism in economics', paper presented at the Annual Conference of the Association of Institutional and Political Economics, 29 November.
Edgeworth, Francis Ysidro (1881), *Mathematical Physics: An Essay on the Application of Mathematics to the Moral Sciences*, London: C. Kegan Paul & Co.
Geanakoplos, John (1992), 'Common Knowledge', *Journal of Economic Perspectives*, **6** (4), 53–82.
Green, H.A. John (1964), *Aggregation in Economic Analysis*, Princeton, NJ: Princeton University Press.

Hands, D. Wade (1994), 'Blurred boundaries: recent changes in the relationship between economics and the philosophy of natural science', *Studies in History and Philosophy of Science*, **25** (5), 751–72.

Hands, D. Wade (1995), 'Social epistemology meets the invisible hand: Kitcher on the advancement of science', *Dialogue*, **34**, 605–21.

Hands, D. Wade (1997a), 'Caveat emptor: economics and contemporary philosophy of science', *Philosophy of Science*, **64** (Proceedings), S107–16.

Hands, D. Wade (1997b), 'Frank Knight's pluralism', in Andrea Salanti and Ernesto Screpanti (eds), *Pluralism in Economics: New Perspectives in History and Methodology*, Cheltenham, UK and Lyme, USA: Edward Elgar, pp. 194–206.

Hands, D. Wade (2001), *Reflection without Rules: Economic Methodology and Contemporary Science Theory*, Cambridge: Cambridge University Press.

Hands, D. Wade and Philip Mirowski (1998), 'Harold Hotelling and the neoclassical dream', in Roger Backhouse, Daniel Hausman, Uskali Mäki, and Andrea Salanti (eds), *Economics and Methodology: Crossing Boundaries*, London: Macmillan, pp. 322–97.

Harcourt, Geoffrey C. (1969), 'Some Cambridge controversies in the theory of capital', *Journal of Economic Literature*, **7** (2), 369–405.

Harcourt, Geoffrey C. (1972), *Some Cambridge Controversies in the Theory of Capital*, Cambridge: Cambridge University Press.

Hargreaves Heap, Shaun (1997), 'The economic consequences of pluralism', in Andrea Salanti and Ernesto Screpanti (eds), *Pluralism in Economics: New Perspectives in History and Methodology,* Cheltenham, UK and Lyme, USA: Edward Elgar, pp. 282–94.

Hodgson, Geoffrey M. (1998), 'The approach of institutional economics', *Journal of Economic Literature*, **36** (1), 166–92.

Janssen, Maarten C.W. (1993), *Microfoundations: A Critical Inquiry*, London: Routledge.

Kirman, Alan P. (1989), 'The intrinsic limits of modern economic theory: the emperor has no clothes', *Economic Journal*, **99** (395), 126–39.

Kirman, Alan P. (1992), 'Whom or what does the representative individual represent?', *Journal of Economic Perspectives*, **6** (2), 117–36.

Klein, Lawrence (1946), 'Macroeconomics and the theory of rational behavior', *Econometrics*, **14** (2), 93–108.

Kurz, Heinz D. and Neri Salvadori (1995), '*Theory of Production: A Long-Period Analysis*', Cambridge: Cambridge University Press.

Lucas Robert E. (1972), 'Expectations and the neutrality of money', *Journal of Economic Theory*, **4** (2), 103–24.

Mäki, Uskali (1999), 'Science as a free market: a reflexivity test in an economics of economics', *Perspectives on Science*, **7** (4), 486–509.

Mantel, Rolf R. (1976), 'Homothetic preferences and community excess demand functions', *Journal of Economic Theory*, **12** (2), 197–201.

Mehrling, Perry (1998), 'The money muddle: the transformation of American monetary thought, 1920–1970', in Mary S. Morgan and Malcolm Rutherford (eds), *From Interwar Pluralism to Postwar Neoclassicism*, Annual Supplement to Volume 30, History of Political Economy, Durham, NC: Duke University Press, pp. 293–306.

Mirowski, Philip (1989), *More Heat than Light*, Cambridge: Cambridge University Press.

Mirowski, Philip and D. Wade Hands (1998), 'A paradox of budgets: the postwar stabilization of American neoclassical demand theory', in Mary S. Morgan and Malcolm Rutherford (eds), *From Interwar Pluralism to Postwar Neoclassicism*, Annual Supplement to Volume 30, History of Political Economy, Durham, NC: Duke University Press, pp. 260–92.

Morgan, Mary S. and Malcolm Rutherford (eds) (1998a), *From Interwar Pluralism to Postwar Neoclassicism*, Annual Supplement to Volume 30, History of Political Economy, Durham, NC: Duke University Press.

Morgan, Mary S. and Malcolm Rutherford (1998b), 'American economics: the character of the transformation', in Mary S. Morgan and Malcolm Rutherford (eds), *From Interwar Pluralism to Postwar Neoclassicism*, Annual Supplement to Volume 30, History of Political Economy, Durham, NC: Duke University Press, pp. 1–26.

Nelson, Alan (1984), 'Some issues surrounding the reduction of macroeconomics to microeconomics', *Philosophy of Science*, **51** (4), 573–94.

Rizvi, S. Abu Turab (1991), 'Specialization and the existence problem in general equilibrium theory', *Contributions to Political Economy*, **10**, 1–20.

Rizvi, S. Abu Turab (1994a), 'The microfoundations project in general equilibrium theory', *Cambridge Journal of Economics*, **18** (4), 357–77.

Rizvi, S. Abu Turab (1994b), 'Game theory to the rescue?', *Contributions to Political Economy*, **13**, 1–28.

Robinson, Joan V. (1953), 'The production function and the theory of capital', *Review of Economic Studies*, **21**, 81–106.

Rubinstein, Ariel (1998), *Modelling Bounded Rationality*, Cambridge, MA: MIT Press.

Salanti, Andrea, and Ernesto Screpanti (eds) (1997), *Pluralism in Economics: New Perspectives in History and Methodology*, Cheltenham, UK and Lyme, USA: Edward Elgar.

Sargent, Thomas J. (1993), *Bounded Rationality in Macroeconomics*, Oxford: Oxford University Press.

Sent, Esther-Mirjam (1998), *The Evolving Rationality of Rational Expectations: An Assessment of Thomas Sargent's Achievements*, Cambridge: Cambridge University Press.

Sonnenschein, Hugo (1972), 'Market excess demand functions', *Econometrica*, **40** (3), 549–63.

Stiglitz, Joseph E. (1974), 'The Cambridge-Cambridge controversy in the theory of capital; a view from New Haven. A review article', *Journal of Political Economy*, **82** (4), 893–903.

Theil, Henry (1954), *Linear Aggregation of Economic Relations*, Amsterdam: North-Holland.

Varian, Hal R. (1987), 'Differences of opinion in financial markets', in *Financial Risk: Theory, Evidence, and Implications*, Proceedings of the 11th Annual Economic Policy Conference of the Federal Reserve Bank of St. Louis, pp. 3–37.

Weintraub, E. Roy (1977), 'The microfoundations of macroeconomics', *Journal of Economic Literature*, **15** (1), 1–23.

Weintraub, E. Roy (1979), *Microfoundations: The Compatibility of Microeconomics and Macroeconomics*, Cambridge: Cambridge University Press.

See also the entries on: Epistemology; Individualism; Positive versus normative economics; Rationality.

48 Positive-normative distinction in British history of economic thought
Samuel Weston

Economics has more often than not been motivated by moral concerns. Broadly, economics is a product of the revolution in thinking that followed in the wake of Francis Bacon's *Novum Organum*, which, among other things, decreed that the purpose of knowledge is to improve human lives.[1] More specifically, Adam Smith held increasing national wealth to be morally important, because much behaviour that we regard as evil results from harsh material circumstances. In his 'Introduction and Plan of the Work' to *The Wealth of Nations* ([1776] 1937), Smith describes 'savage nations of hunters and fishers' who are

> so miserably poor, that from mere want, they are frequently reduced, or, at least, think themselves reduced, to the necessity sometimes of directly destroying and sometimes of abandoning their infants, their old people and those affected with lingering diseases, to perish with hunger, or to be devoured by wild beasts. (pp. lvii–lviii)

This idea comes directly from Smith's *Theory of Moral Sentiments* ([1759] 1790). In this earlier work he presents his idea that people make moral judgements according to whether they think an 'impartial spectator' would be in sympathy with an act. The specific content of one's impartial spectator is culturally determined. Section V of Chapter 2 of *Theory of Moral Sentiments* provides numerous examples similar to the one above from *The Wealth of Nations*.

In addition to its account of why some nations are materially richer than others, *The Wealth of Nations* makes an important contribution to classical liberal political philosophy. It argues that a high degree of individual freedom is compatible with national material prosperity. Economics has a long history of being widely regarded as a body of apologetics for laissez-faire. Economists have often given policy advice, and the public perception of particular economists as being left-leaning or right-leaning is usually accurate. Such perceptions are reinforced by the fact that economists tend to be better known to the general public for their policy positions than for their professional work.

So how and why did a discipline motivated by normative concerns come widely to accept a line drawn between normative and positive economics? In British economics this acceptance occurred in the nineteenth century. In the early part of the century, Nassau Senior and Richard Whately, while delivering the first economics lectures at Oxford, expressed the root ideas underlying this distinction in response to real and anticipated criticisms of economics.

Toward the end of the nineteenth century, John Neville Keynes, while acting as a lieutenant in Alfred Marshall's campaign to gain acceptance for economics as an academic subject and as a profession, articulated a three-way distinction between positive, normative and the art of economics. By the time Keynes did this, various writers, including J.S. Mill, Henry Sidgwick and J.E. Cairnes, had distinguished either normative from positive economics or the science from the art of economics.[2] Thus, Keynes was to a significant extent codifying a tradition. He was also asserting the desirability of that tradition against those, including the British and German historicists, who would require economists to be moralists. Because of the role that Keynes played in establishing economics at Cambridge, and because Cambridge economics came to define economic professionalism in the English-speaking world, what began as a defensive move on the part of Senior and Whately became part of economics' disciplinary and professional delineation.

The first economics lectures at Oxford

Economics was widely read and discussed in Britain in the early nineteenth century, but it was slow to gain acceptance into universities. The first economics lectures at Cambridge occurred in 1816 (Rashid 1980, p. 283). The Drummond Professorship of Political Economy was established at Oxford in 1825 (Mitchell 1967, p. 425).

Nassau Senior (1790–1864) was the first holder of the Drummond Chair and delivered the first economics lectures at Oxford in 1826. He was succeeded in 1830 by his Oxford tutor and close friend Richard Whately (1787–1863) (Levy [1943] 1970, p. 34). In 1831, Whately was named the Anglican Archbishop of Dublin. In that capacity he established, in 1832, the Whately Chair in Political Economy at Trinity College. While there is insufficient evidence to establish decisively the direction of influence between the two, Senior and Whately were personally and intellectually close. Bowley ([1937] 1967, pp.106–7) judges that Whately got his economics from Senior while Senior turned to Whately for help with logic.

Nassau Senior

The climate at Oxford was not especially receptive to economics (see Oslington 2001, p. 3; Rashid 1977, pp. 148–52; Schumacher 1973, pp. 38–9). In the opening remarks of their lectures both Senior and Whately exhibit a degree of defensiveness. Both carefully articulate what economics is and is not in order to avert criticisms based on misunderstanding. Senior begins by expressing fears that the imperfect state of development of economics 'offers the fairest scope to the objections of an idle or interested adversary. When I consider how numerous those adversaries are, and how widely diffused are the prejudices which they excite and propagate . . . the failings of the professor may be imputed to the subject' ([1826] 1966, pp. 2–3).

As part of his effort to clarify the intentions of economists, Senior divides economics into 'theoretic' and 'practical' branches (ibid., pp. 7–10). The theoretic branch rests on a few general propositions resulting from observation or consciousness, which allows the inference of general conclusions about the nature, production and distribution of wealth. The practical branch has the job of determining which institutions are most favourable to wealth. This task is more difficult, since it uses induction from specific cases in addition to the results of theory. Senior thinks that failure to distinguish theoretical from practical economics is responsible for disagreements about the certainty of economic conclusions. Some people may mistakenly attribute certainty to conclusions which are in fact contingent on particular circumstances; while others may use the uncertainty of practical economics to wrongly dismiss all economic conclusions as uncertain.

In *An Outline of the Science of Political Economy*, Senior begins by defining economics as 'the Science which treats of the Nature, the Production, and the Distribution of Wealth'

([1836] 2003, pp. 1–3). As in his inaugural lecture, he defines the science of political economy as consisting of a few general propositions and the inferences from these propositions. 'But his conclusions, whatever be their generality and their truth, do not authorize him in adding a single syllable of advice' (ibid.) That privilege is reserved for those who have 'considered all the causes which may promote or impede the general welfare of those whom he addresses . . . The business of a Political Economist is neither to recommend nor to dissuade, but to state general principles which it is fatal to neglect' (ibid.) Senior thinks that confusing the science of political economy with the sciences and arts, such as government, to which it is subservient, interfered with the development of economic science by exciting unfavourable prejudices and misleading economists as to their objectives.

In his later lectures, delivered in 1847–48, Senior (1966, pp. 39–48) elaborates on the science of economics versus the art of economics. He provides numerous examples of economists who proposed to do science, but in fact practised the art. He expresses concern that the lack of specialization necessitated by someone trying to perform a broad science of government would result in incomplete treatment. Bowley ([1937] 1967, pp. 49–52) interprets Senior's 1836 position as restricting economics to the science and not allowing for an art of economics. She sees this as a major shift from his earlier 'theoretic/practical' distinction, which he then reverses in his 1847–48 lectures. Schumpeter (1954, p. 540) reads Senior's 1836 position as being merely a recognition that policy questions involve many elements, and that such questions should not be answered with economic reasoning alone.

Richard Whately

As a clergyman with an enthusiasm for economics, Whately was especially bothered by economics' poor reputation among his fellow clergymen. The first three of his nine lectures are devoted to defending economics against fallacious criticisms. He considers a number of objections to the discipline: (i) that economics confines its attention exclusively to wealth; (ii) that economics should not be studied because it is inimical to religion; (iii) that focusing on wealth confuses the means to happiness with happiness itself; (iv) that economics is better dealt with using common sense; and (v) that making economics scientific removes the role of judgement (see Whately 1832, Lectures I–III; Whately's arguments are summarized in Rashid 1977, pp. 149–52).

In the course of refuting the objection that economics is narrowly concerned with wealth, Whately (1832, p. 19) says,

> When a physician tells his patient, 'you ought to go to sea'; or, 'you ought to abstain from secondary employments', he is always understood to be speaking in reference to *health* alone. He is not supposed to imply by the use of the word 'ought', that his patient is *morally* bound to follow his prescription. (Italics in the original)

To use Kantian language, Whately is saying that economists' advice is in the form of hypothetical imperatives, not categorical imperatives. Economics provides knowledge about the means to certain ends; it does not provide moral judgements of those ends.

The beginning of a tradition

Even if Senior had never delivered his Drummond Lectures, it is possible that the science/art distinction in economics would have become established because of the enormous influence of John Stuart Mill (1806–73). Mill's *A System of Logic Ratiocinative and*

Inductive ([1843] 1872) was a leading influence on British intellectuals of the 1850s and 1860s, and was widely read and admired by the general public.

Mill distinguished the science of economics from the art of economics in *A System of Logic* (Book VI, Chapter 12, Section 6), and also in *Essays on Some Unsettled Questions of Political Economy* (Essay V). In articulating this distinction, Mill associates science with the language of 'is or will be', while the art is expressed in terms of 'ought or should be'. This is Hume's language (1739–40; Hume [1888] 1896, pp. 469–70). This usage lends some support to the idea that the normative/positive distinction in economics originates with Hume. Schumpeter (1954, p. 450) asserts that Mill relied heavily on Whately for his logical fundamentals. If so, this could provide an indirect link from Mill to Senior.

Among Mill's followers were J.E. Cairnes (1823–75) and Henry Sidgwick (1838–1900). Cairnes held the Whately Chair at Trinity College and was considered by his contemporaries to be a leading British economist of his day. In *The Character and Logical Method of Political Economy* (1857; Cairnes [1888] 2001, pp. 17–9), Cairnes argues that political economy is a science like physics. It is neutral with regard to competing social schemes, just as mechanics is neutral between competing plans for building a railway.

Sidgwick was Marshall's colleague and Neville Keynes's teacher at Cambridge. Sidgwick (1883, pp. 14–29) sees a problem with applying the science/art distinction that is rooted in political economy's origins as a practical guide to increasing national prosperity. Smith and the physiocrats introduced scientific methods to this problem without fully realizing the extent to which they had changed the nature of the discipline. While clarity can be gained by distinguishing scientific problems from political or ethical ones, the scientific problem is generally only a small part, and often not even the most important, of the question that people are trying to answer.

Crisis in economics in the late nineteenth century

In the late nineteenth century economics faced a more complicated situation than had been the case in the first decades of the century. What appears here is only a brief sketch of this period, to describe the context in which John Neville Keynes wrote *The Scope and Method of Political Economy* (1917). The era has been ably described by other writers.[3]

The major points are as follows. Alfred Marshall (1842–1924), a would-be man of the cloth who lost his religious faith, transferred his missionary zeal to the promulgation of economics. Marshall was not a fiery preacher but a calm deliberate strategist. His main objectives were two: to restore the prestige that economics had lost and to overcome institutional forces at Cambridge in order to move economics out of the moral sciences and into a department of its own. John Neville Keynes (1883–1946), once Marshall's student and now his colleague, was Marshall's most trusted and competent ally in this campaign.[4] His *Scope and Method of Political Economy* was intended to serve a tactical purpose in achieving Marshall's goals. It was an attempt to forge a peace among many factions that were in conflict at the time by showing how they fit together in a classificatory scheme. One part of this scheme is Keynes's three-way distinction between positive economics, normative economics and the art of economics. Marshall's campaign was successful. This success translated into influence over the shape of economic curricula and the self-understanding of what it is to be an economist in the English-speaking world.

Diminished status of economics c. 1870–90
In 1877 a formal proposal was made to drop Section F (economics and statistics) from the British Association for the Advancement of Science 'because its proceedings and subject matter were unscientific' (Coats 1954, p. 143).

Several factors contributed to the low standing of economics during this period. First, traditional British classical economics had peaked around 1848 with the publication of J.S. Mill's *Principles*. Foxwell (1887, p. 85) writes that Mill had perceptively grasped the importance of the rise of the working class, and this allowed him to animate 'the dry bones of the old theory', but not to enable them grow.

Second, creative ferment was rising within economics. German and British historical economists challenged the abstract deductive method and the narrow scope of traditional British economics. The development of marginal utility analysis by Stanley Jevons, Carl Menger and Leon Walras in the early 1870s challenged the classical theory of value and offered a tool that promised further development. Thus new ideas were now challenging older ideas that the general public had believed to be 'established'. To those who understood science as a body of 'truths', rather than an ongoing process of improving knowledge, the challenging of hitherto accepted ideas demonstrated the weakness, not the strength, of economic science.

Third, there existed no formal credential to distinguish economists from non-economists. Hence, Coats (1954, p. 143) writes, 'No clear line can be drawn between the scientific and popular writings of this period, and many persons identified the teachings of the economists with policy recommendations.'

Fourth, in addition to the traditional religious, humanistic and ethical concerns about economics, such as Whately had faced, there were new developments in these areas. For one, there was a strong tendency to identify economics with laissez-faire policies, and these had fallen out of favour over the course of the nineteenth century. For another, as Skidelsky (1983, pp. 26–7) tells us, Marshall was part of the generation of Cambridge men (around 1860) who had lost their religious faith. A religion-centred education had long served as part of the training of clergy and government. The loss of traditional faith posed a problem for the inherited social order. There were three main responses to this. One was to aggressively reassert the place of traditional religious values in higher education, including economics. This approach is seen in John Henry Newman's *The Idea of a University*. Another response, typified by Henry Sidgwick, was to find a philosophical non-religious basis for morality, though Sidgwick is widely viewed as having failed in this endeavour (Skidelsky 1983, p. 32). Finally, thinkers such as Marshall never lost faith in these economists' morality, even though their religious faith had collapsed (Skidelsky 1983, p. 40). Yet having witnessed Sidgwick's failure, Marshall concluded that such efforts were unlikely to be successful anytime soon; hence, economics would do better to focus on problems that it could solve (Skidelsky 1983, p. 32).

Establishing economics at Cambridge
George Pryme had been delivering economics lectures at Cambridge since 1816. He became the first professor of political economy there in 1828 (Rashid 1980, p. 283). The Moral Sciences Tripos was established in 1848. It consisted of moral philosophy, political philosophy, logic, psychology and economics (Skidelsky 1983, p. 10). Marshall grew increasingly dissatisfied with the position of economics as one element in the

moral sciences. He believed that the 'metaphysics' in the moral sciences interfered with his ability to recruit top-notch students into economics. After a prolonged campaign, Marshall finally succeeded in establishing the Economics and Political Tripos in 1903 (Skidelsky 1983, pp. 44–5). Marshall's leadership in this fight transformed economics from a gifted amateur's pursuit which had fallen on hard times into a profession.

The role of John Neville Keynes

John Neville Keynes's *Scope and Method of Political Economy* ([1917] 1963, first published in 1890) was a tactical move in Marshall's strategy to restore to economics its rightful prestige, and to establish a separate economics department at Cambridge. The book was intended to bring peace among traditional classical economists, marginalists, historicists and moralists. The idea was to show how all these pieces fit together into a larger coherent scheme (Coats 1996, p. 81; Skidelsky 1983, pp. 61–3). Today we call the economics that Marshall succeeded in establishing at Cambridge 'neoclassical'. This usage accurately reflects the fact that Marshall integrated what he thought was worthwhile from the newer work with a core inherited from traditional British classical economics. The roots of the normative/positive/art distinction were part of that inheritance. The reassertion of this distinction was aimed at British and German historical economists. It allowed economists to morally evaluate economic ends, while keeping such evaluations conceptually separate from economic science.

In Chapter II of *The Scope and Method of Political Economy*, entitled 'On the Relation of Political Economy to Morality and Practice', Keynes ([1917] 1963, p. 34) defines *positive science* as a 'body of systematized knowledge concerning what is'; he defines *normative or regulative science* as '[a] body of systematized knowledge relating to criteria of what ought to be, and concerned therefore with the ideal as distinguished from the actual'; and the *art* as '[a] system of rules for attainment of a given end'. Keynes also restates these definitions in terms of goals: 'the object of positive science is the establishment of *uniformities*; of a normative science the determination of *ideals*; of an art the formulation of *precepts*' ([1917] 1963, p. 35, italics in the original).

Keynes's three-way distinction involved no neologisms. The *Oxford English Dictionary* shows 'normative' being used to mean 'prescriptive' in 1852 and 'art' as 'applied science' as early as 1489. 'Positive' presents more of a problem. The relevant definition, 'having relation only to matters of fact', is recorded as early as 1594. Whether economics is a positive science in this sense or hypothetical was a point of controversy. Senior (1966) devoted a lecture to challenging Mill on this point. The question of how to interpret economic theory continues to this day, for example, in controversies regarding the role that Milton Friedman (1953) assigns to theory in *Methodology of Positive Economics*. Keynes ([1917] 1963, p. 34) recognizes these difficulties, and he admits having considered using 'theoretical' and 'speculative' before deciding on 'positive'.

Keynes intended to make a conceptual distinction between different aspects of economic thought, not a behavioural rule banning economists from some of them. He argues that to claim the logical possibility of separating the positive science of economics from the ethical and practical aspects does not imply that this is desirable. Moreover,

> No one desires to stop short at a purely theoretical enquiry. It is universally agreed that in economics the positive investigation of facts is not an end in itself, but it is to be used as a basis for a practical enquiry, in which ethical considerations are allowed their due weight. ([1917] 1963, pp. 46–8)

The reason for conceptually separating the two is that, 'the attempt to fuse together enquiries as to what is, and enquiries as to what ought to be, is likely to stand in the way of our giving clear and unbiased answers to either set of questions' (ibid.) Yet this conceptual distinction does not imply that economists must adopt a position of value neutrality or suppress their own views.

Although *The Scope and Method of Political Economy* received favourable reviews, it appears not to have been widely read in its day because the peace that Keynes was trying to make had largely been attained before the book was published (Skidelsky 1983, p. 61). Denis Robertson, a Cambridge undergraduate in 1910, said that the book was on the reading list, but he doubted 'if many of us read it' (cited in Coats 1967, p. 708). The book's reputation seems to have grown with the passage of time. *Scope and Method* received renewed attention by virtue of being a primary source for Friedman's *Methodology of Positive Economics* (1953). Daniel Hausman included an excerpt in *The Philosophy of Economics* (1984) in a section of 'classic discussions' of economic methodology.

Conclusion and further thoughts

Keynes's three-way distinction is an articulation of ideas that had been developing in British economics for more than half a century. It gained prominence because Keynes allied himself with a school of economic thought that became one of the most successful and influential in the history of the discipline.

Keynes was quite clear that his distinction was conceptual. It was not his intention to ban normative concerns from economics. While there is room for doubt about how to interpret Senior's 1836 remarks, in practice nineteenth-century economists did not avoid policy issues or normative pronouncements. Keynes's understanding was echoed forty years later by Lionel Robbins (1935, pp. 149–50) who said, 'Nor is it implied that economists should not deliver themselves on ethical questions, any more than an argument that botany is not aesthetics is to say that botanists should not have views of their own on the lay-out of gardens.' If there is a widespread perception among economists and others that the normative/positive distinction implies a ban on normative economics, the next job would be to find out how this came to be.

Notes

1. Bacon ([1620] 1955, Aphorism 81, p. 44) says, 'Now the true and lawful goal of the sciences is none other than this: that human life be endowed with new discoveries and powers.'
2. Due to space limitations I focus on Senior, Whately and Keynes. See Coats (1996) and Yuengart (2000) for descriptive surveys of economists' treatment of 'the art versus the science' or 'normative versus positive' in the years between Senior and Keynes.
3. See Coats (1954, 1967, 1996); Maloney (1976); Rashid (1980); and Skidelsky (1983, Chs 1–3). This section draws heavily on these works.
4. According to Maloney (1976, p. 445), Marshall considered Keynes to be 'his one real ally in England with the required combination of ability, enthusiasm, and reliability to do battle with real effect for professional standards'.

References

Bacon, Francis ([1620] 1955), *Novum Organum*, Book I, Chicago, IL: The Great Books Foundation.
Bowley, Marian ([1937] 1967), *Nassau Senior and Classical Economics*, New York: Octagon Books, Inc.
Cairnes, John E. ([1888] 2001), *The Character and Logical Method of Political Economy*, 2nd edition, Kitchener (Canada): Batoche Books.
Coats, A.W. (1954), 'The historist reaction in English political economy 1870–90', *Economica*, n.s., **21** (82), 145–53.

Coats, A.W. (1967), 'Sociological aspects of British economic thought (ca. 1880–1930)', *Journal of Political Economy*, **75** (5), 706–29.

Coats, A.W (1996), 'Utilitarianism, Oxford idealism, and Cambridge economics', in Peter Groenwegen (ed.), *Economics and Ethics?* London and New York: Routledge.

Foxwell, Herbert S. (1887), 'The economic movement in England', *Quarterly Journal of Economics*, **2** (1), 84–103.

Friedman, Milton (1953), *Essays in Positive Economics*, Chicago, IL and London: University of Chicago Press.

Hausman, Daniel M. (1984), *The Philosophy of Economics: An Anthology*, Cambridge and New York: Cambridge University Press.

Hume David ([1888] 1896), *Treatise of Human Nature*, Oxford: Clarendon Press.

Keynes, John Neville ([1917] 1963), *The Scope and Method of Political Economy*, 4th edition, New York: Augustus M. Kelley.

Levy, S. Leon ([1943] 1970), *Nassau W. Senior 1790–1864: Critical Essayist, Classical Economist and Advisor of Governments*, New York: Augustus M. Kelley.

Maloney, John (1976), 'Marshall, Cunningham, and the emerging economics profession', *Economic History Review*, n.s., **29** (3), 440–51.

Mitchell, Wesley C. (1967), *Types of Economic Theory*, Vol. 1, New York: Augustus M. Kelley.

Mill, John Stuart ([1843] 1872), *A System of Ratiocinative and Inductive, Being a Connected View of the Principles of Evidence, and the Methods of Scientific Investigation*, London: Longmans, Green and Co.

Mill, John Stuart ([1848] 1987), *Principles of Political Economy*, Augustus M. Kelly.

Mill, John Stuart ([1874] 2000), *Essays on Some Unsettled Questions of Political Economy*, 2nd edition, Kitchener, Canada: Batoche Books.

Oslington, Paul (2001), 'John Henry Newman, Nassau Senior, and the separation of political economy from theology in the nineteenth century', *History of Political Economy*, **33** (4), 825–42.

Rashid, Salim (1977), 'Richard Whately and Christian Political Economy at Oxford and Dublin', *Journal of the History of Ideas*, **38** (1), 147–55.

Rashid, Salim (1980), 'The growth of economics studies at Cambridge: 1776–1860', *History of Education Quarterly*, **20** (3), 281–94.

Robbins, Lionel (1935), *An Essay on the Nature and Sigificance of Political Economy*, London: Macmillan.

Schumacher, Ernst F. (1973), *Small is Beautiful: Economics as if People Mattered*, New York and London: Harper Colophon Books.

Schumpeter, Joseph A. (1954), *History of Economic Analysis*, New York: Oxford University Press.

Senior, Nassau W. ([1826] 1966), 'An introductory lecture on political economy', in *Selected Writings on Economics by Nassau W. Senior*, New York: Augustus M. Kelley.

Senior, Nassau W. ([1836] 2003), *An Outline of the Science of Political Economy*, Honolulu, HI: University Press of the Pacific.

Senior, Nassau W. (1966), 'That political economy is a positive, not an hypothetical science', in *Selected Writings on Economics: A Volume of Pamphlets 1827–1852*, New York: Augustus M. Kelley.

Sidgwick, Henry (1883), *The Principles of Political Economy*, London: Macmillan.

Skidelsky, Robert (1983), *John Maynard Keynes, Volume I: Hopes Betrayed*, New York: Penguin Books.

Smith Adam ([1759] 1790), *The Theory of Moral Sentiments*, 6th edition, London: A. Millar, www.econlib.org/library/Smith/smMS0.html, accessed 30 July, 2006.

Smith Adam ([1776] 1937), *The Wealth of Nations*, ed. Edwin Cannan, New York: The Modern Library.

Whately, Richard (1832), *Introductory Lectures on Political Economy*, New York: Augustus M. Kelley.

Yuengert, Andrew M. (2000), 'The positive-normative distinction before the fact-value distinction', www.gordon.edu/ace/pdf/Yuengert_PosNorm.pdf, accessed 15 May, 2006.

See also the entries on: Positive versus normative economics; Adam Smith.

49 Positive versus normative economics
Eric van de Laar and Jan Peil

Introduction
Since its beginnings economics has been criticized for intermingling science with ethico-political discourses. Substitution of the worldview of modern science for the moral philosophical perspective made obsolete the old unifying approach to understanding economic life. This change in perspective raised questions about how to draw a demarcation line between science – that is, the search for positive knowledge of the world out there – and non-science – that is, discourses about politics and opinions, values and beliefs.

How economics accommodated the criticism in the nineteenth century is illustrated by John Stuart Mill's reinterpretation of Adam Smith, after Ricardo's twist towards an abstract-deductive approach. Smith discussed problems of production and distribution of wealth in a unifying framework of moral philosophy, while Ricardo understood the economy as governed by fixed, immutable laws. Mill tried to disentangle these parts, referring to the distinction between positive economic analysis – science – and normative judgements. Mill ([1844] 1874) shared Ricardo's view that science was about universal laws, but he opposed the idea that both production and distribution of wealth were determined by rigid laws. Mill did conceive the production of wealth as law-governed, but he understood the distribution of wealth as governed by rules embedded in customs and institutions. So, in his approach the production of wealth became the domain of positive economic analysis, while discussions about the distribution of wealth were conceived as exchanges of normative judgements, labelled 'normative economics'.[1] Mill saw no problem in economists dealing with both wealth production and distribution, as long as they distinguished between the context of economic science – that is, positive economics – and that of normative judgements – that is, normative economics.[2]

In the second half of the nineteenth century the distinction between positive economic analysis and normative judgements became part of the hard core of mainstream economics. It was canonized in John Neville Keynes's methodological publication *The Scope and Method of Political Economy* (London, 1890). In addition to positive economics, defined as analysis and theory about the economic world, and normative economics, understood as discourses about economic order, policy goals and aims, John Neville Keynes introduced a third label, the art of economics, to indicate the context of application of theory to policy.[3]

The final step in the process of accommodating the criticism of intermingling science with non-science was the segregation of positive and normative economics in the first half of the twentieth century. Important in this final stage was the reorientation in economic methodology by authors including Terence Hutchison, Lionel Robbins and Thomas Nagel on developments in the philosophy of science after the positivistic turn in 1920s and 1930s. This new methodological stance viewed it as no longer sufficient for economists to be aware of what kind of discourse they were involved in – a scientific or ethico-political one. Serious economic science, instead, demanded that economists confine themselves to what *is* and leave questions about what *ought to be* to ethics and politics. Introductory textbooks reproduce this rule to this day. Referring to a presupposed dichotomy between fact and value, economics is conceived as a modern science, to be separated from other – ethico-political – discourses. According to Lionel Robbins's formal definition, 'Economics is the science which studies human behaviour as a relationship between ends and scarce means which have alternative uses' (1932, p. 57). In mainstream economics the segregation of positive and normative economics had settled the dispute at last.

A revival of the debate in the 1960s and 1970s indicated, however, the inadequacy of the way the problem of intermingling science with ethico-political discourses had been addressed so far. The tables even seemed to be turned. Backed by rival views of science, fuelled by authors such as Pierre Duhem, Willard van Quine and Thomas Kuhn, heterodox economists argued for a conception of economics as a normative science. From the perspective of mainstream positive economics this appeared to be a plea to negate the distinction between fact and value, between science and politics, from which would follow naturally a return to the times in which philosophy was bound to politics. Viewed from some distance, however, this was clearly not the objective of the adversaries of mainstream positive economics. The plea for a new normative economics, rather, stemmed from a drive to get rid of an economics that concealed its value-ladenness by pretending that referring to facts ensured value-freedom. The argument was that theories and facts must be discussed in relation to their frames of reference, including values and worldviews. Different views of science clashed. The debate was not very fruitful; it was more heat than light, using an expression of Mirowski (1989) typifying a similar dispute about principles of economic thought.

Looking at more recent literature on the positive-normative dichotomy, discussions aiming to clarify the nature of economics as a science and to improve its methodology still too often end in an impasse. As before, discussions are handicapped especially by Babylonian confusions of tongues. Authors use the same words and terms, but interpret and apply them differently. Two problems in this regard are discussed in the following sections. The first concerns the distinction between 'value judgements' and 'facts'. What exactly are authors talking about when they use these terms? Is it possible to claim a strict separation? What alternatives have been proposed? The second, related problem concerns the ontological aspect of science. What is ontology? What is the relation between scientists' worldviews and their work? The sections below address these questions, first taking a linguistic approach and then a hermeneutic approach, thus widening the scope towards the ontological aspect of economics.

Linguistic approach

Misunderstandings are fuelled mostly by unawareness of rivalries between interpretations. Discussants often have different interpretations of the distinction between positive and normative statements.

Producing and diffusing knowledge is a linguistic operation. Words and concepts are anything but pure representations of states of affairs from the outside world, as we have known since Immanuel Kant debunked this understanding. After the breakthrough of logical empiricism/positivism in early twentieth-century philosophy of science, fact and value became separated. Elaborating on the linguistic aspect of knowledge may help to clear up some of the confusion. Two questions may be asked in particular: how do proponents of a value-free science perceive and ground their claim? Can value judgements actually be radically separated from statements about facts, as adherents of positive economics claim with dichotomous interpretations of positive and normative economics?

A well-known proponent of the positivistic stance in economics is Mark Blaug (for example, [1980] 1992, 1998, p. 370). Being aware of the critiques of positivism and later also expressing reservations towards a too naive view of the distinction between positive and normative economics, Blaug nevertheless holds that economics *in principle* can be value-free and should be so, in order to prevent economics from relativism or ideological bias. The separation of positive and normative economics, according to Blaug, is a valid one which should be maintained in research, 'as far as it can be maintained' (1980, p. 373). Scientists have to investigate facts, have to develop theories about their findings, and have to confront their theoretical statements with new facts in order to test their validity. Thus runs the positivist credo since Popper. Consequently as scientists, economists should refrain from value judgements and not interfere in normative affairs.

Blaug's (1998) recent prudence – recall expressions like 'in principle' and 'as far as it can be maintained' (p. 373) – addresses exceptional situations where values penetrate the economics discourse. The exceptions are situated at the borders of regular science and mark the transition from science into non-science, in Blaug's view. One such exception concerns the issue of methodological values and methodological value judgements. Blaug acknowledges that economics is value-laden in the choice of both methods and the subject of investigation. But these value issues are pre-scientific; they must be dealt with before the actual scientific work starts. Another exception concerns policy advice. In this view policy advice is post-scientific, at least when it takes place, as it should do, after the scientific work has been done. When economists observe some discipline as scientists and live up to these rules, the positivistic – that is, the scientific – core of economics is salvaged, according to Blaug.

The question is whether the way Blaug (1998) addresses these so-called exceptional situations is adequate. Do values penetrate science only at the borders? Is it just a matter of discipline, or of more or less difficulty, to separate values and value judgements from science? When do reservations such as 'in principle' or 'as far as it can be maintained', which are apparently needed to safeguard this stance, come into play, and what exactly do they mean? Neither Blaug nor congenial economists have answered these questions satisfactorily to date. Obviously, one might reply that these reservations refer to the positivistic legacy, to their ideal of science, the status of (scientific) knowledge and the implicit view of what reality ultimately is like. But that is not much of an answer.

Outside economics, especially in philosophical discourses, the positivistic view on facts, theory, and more generally (scientific) knowledge has been criticized since the 1930s. Think of the path-breaking work on meaning and understanding by philosophers such as Martin Heidegger and Ludwig Wittgenstein. Heidegger's elaborations on ontology stimulated continental philosophers to view understanding and knowledge as interpretations embedded in worldviews. In Anglo-Saxon philosophy Wittgenstein, himself a former adept of positivism, provoked the so-called 'linguistic turn', investigating the forms and functions of linguistic expressions.[4] He dismissed the positivists' idea of a scientific language directly covering bare facts, and replaced it with his notion of 'language games', being a broad range of divergent forms of language, expressing the view that the meaning of concepts, theories and even statements of facts is discourse-related.

Meanwhile, a linguistic approach was also introduced in economics discussions on the positive-normative separation.[5] Hilary Putnam (2002, 2003) elaborated a critique from a linguistic perspective of the dichotomous interpretation of the positive-normative distinction in economics.[6] A positive-normative dichotomy is indefensible, according to him. The idea that it is possible to separate value judgements from statements of facts conflicts with established findings from linguistic research and the philosophy of language. It appears – rather remarkably for scientists with a positivist point of view – to be based on an incorrect understanding of language. This is the more remarkable when one brings to mind that this understanding is of an idealized, even metaphysical stance, which positivists – in fields other than economics – abandoned as soon as they became aware of its metaphysical nature during the philosophical debates of the 1930s.

In linguistics and the philosophy of language it became apparent that the range of evaluative language is much wider than usually assumed (Putnam 2003, p. 399; Mongin 2006). Not all value judgements are ethical judgements, and neither can all ethical statements be equated with prescriptions. So a divide between positive and normative economics cannot be legitimized with an appeal that economists as scientists should not interfere at all in ethico-political affairs. Since the philosopher Quine, with his critique of the positivist perception of the language of science, demonstrated that all knowledge consists of a mix of experience and convention, it has no longer been possible to deny that science is inherently value-laden, or that values permeate science as a whole.

The argument against the positive-normative dichotomy becomes particularly convincing when we look at the phenomenon which Putnam (2003, p. 396; 2002, p. 34) calls *'the entanglement of facts and values'* (emphasis in original). When historians, for example, ascribe a rebellion to the cruelty of a regime, they are not in the first place judging the situation; rather, they are giving an explanation wherein the evaluative terms are an indispensable aspect of the description. Leaving out the evaluative terms would make the explanation senseless. These 'virtue terms' (2003, p. 396) or 'thick ethical concepts' (2002, p. 35) are simultaneously descriptive and evaluative. They cannot be divided into a purely descriptive and a purely evaluative part, simply because they make sense only due to the mutual reference to the factual and the valuable. Separating them would be an artificial act that destroys the semantic function of these concepts.

An example from the field of economics is found in Putnam's (2003, p. 372) discussion of Sen's capability approach: 'Just about every one of the terms that Sen and his co-workers and followers use when they talk about capabilities – "valuable functioning", "functioning a person has reason to value", "well nourished", "premature mortality", "self-respect", "able to take part in the life of the community" – is an entangled term.' From the linguistic perspective it is clear that economists cannot leave aside value-laden questions. With Putnam, we must even conclude that interfering with normative issues requires economists to conduct responsible evaluations in which valuation and 'ascertaining' of facts are interdependent activities.

Hermeneutic approach

As said before, critics of the positive-normative dichotomy pleaded for a new normative economics in the 1960s and 1970s. They wanted to be rid of an economics that concealed its value-ladenness by pretending that referring to facts ensured value-freedom. From a hermeneutical perspective, it could be argued that positivists have misunderstood a reference to facts as a reference to reality as such or to the world out there. Presentations of facts or confrontations with facts are not presentations or confrontations with reality as such but with interpretations of it.

When a positivist economist like Blaug (1998, p. 372) argues that it is possible to separate methodological choices and values from economic research, he presumes that methodological considerations are only instrumental and relate merely to the question of which approach is most suitable in the sense of offering an undistorted view on the economic world. With hindsight this methodological position is hardly defensible. Empiricists of the seventeenth century argued – in contrast to the rationalists – that the human mind is a *tabula rasa*, an unwritten leaf ready to be imprinted by 'impressions' of the outside world.[7] According to this view, humans are capable of acquiring positive – that is, certain – knowledge of reality.

Kant's critique that the human mind is all but an empty and passive receiver is widely accepted today. Research on the mind as a receptive framework has shown that its influence in the formation of knowledge is complex and multilayered. The influences vary from basic neurological and linguistic features (processes) of the brain to accumulated historical and social knowledge of the world we live in (Chomsky 1967; Lenneberg 1967; Bourdieu 1980, p. 51; 1987, p. 147). Together they constitute our worldviews or, more formally spoken, our frames of reference. From this perspective, knowledge evolves as a linguistic appropriation of the world from a commutative process between our frames of reference and the world. Science is in this view a multi-voiced discourse aiming at acquiring knowledge through an intersubjective exchange of explanations and views of the world.

This understanding of knowledge and science found support among heterodox economists in the second half of the twentieth century. They criticized the positive economic approach. Referring to concepts like 'paradigm', 'language game' and 'worldview' they reconstructed economics as a plurality of rival schools of economic thought. In contrast to the first years of this reinterpretation of the principles of economics, today rivalry is understood less as a period of transition leading to a new period of normal science; instead of a Kuhnian interpretation of the plurality of schools, nowadays the view gaining ground could be characterized as 'hermeneutic'. In this approach, acquiring knowledge is in essence an interpretation of experience, of observations, against horizons expressed in the very same processes of knowing. 'Plurality' and rivalry are in this hermeneutic view the inevitable result of differences in interpretation.

Authors involved in discussions about the hermeneutic approach include Don Lavoie (1990), Uskali Mäki (2001) and Sheila Dow (2002a and b). Using concepts such as *worldview, modes of thought, belief systems, visions of reality* and *frames of reference* they argue that what is conceived of as *the world, reality* or *facts* is always an interpretation of the world, of reality, of what happened, happens or will happen. When we let 'facts speak for themselves', it is always through the interference of our interpreting selves. Thus, the content of observation and understanding always differ in accordance with the variety of the frames of reference. Neglecting that theories, discussions of theories and tests of theories are contextually framed, easily gives way to bias and Babel-like confusion, because of its accompanying illusion of being objective, that is, free of distorting values of any kind.

For an appraisal of recent discussions about understanding economics it is important to note that the turn to a hermeneutical approach is all but finished. It is even doubtful whether all of the authors involved in these discussions would consent to the qualification of hermeneutic, because of its association with specific trends in philosophy.[8] To be clear, 'hermeneutic' as used here expresses the trend in understanding the rivalry of approaches in economics as a phenomenon characteristic of a scientific discourse about the economic world, not as a sign of weakness, of being a science still immature or a science in a revolutionary stage. An impression of the state of the art in this regard is provided by Mäki's 'one world principle' view on pluralism and his use of 'the way the world works' as a criterion to assess (or understand assessments of) theories.

Mäki's view on pluralism is based on the distinction between plurality and pluralism. Plurality with respect to economic theory, for example, means that there is, or there might be, a multitude of rival or complementary theories. Pluralism addresses the assessment of a situation of plurality. Someone is called a 'pluralist' – for example, a theoretical pluralist – if and only if that person contends to have good reasons to accept – temporarily or permanently – the plurality of theories as appropriate.[9] Mäki explains that scientists may have good reasons to adhere to pluralism in many fields with regard to theory, methods or language. While accepting the possibility of many sorts of pluralism, he opposes ontological pluralism (2001, p. 124). This refusal seems to suggest that though he accepts the idea that the world is complex and appears in many ways according to the perspectives used (2001, p. 127), in the end he does not accept the hermeneutic approach.

According to Mäki, ontological pluralism implies the claim that a plurality or multitude of worlds exists or can exist.[10] He opposes this claim with his 'one world' principle, meaning that 'the world is one in the sense that the many theories we hold do not create worlds of their own; plurality of theories does not imply plurality of worlds, but rather the many theories about one world' (2002, p. 127). The idea of a plurality of worlds makes science with its aim of intersubjective knowledge of the world impossible. Acknowledging the very existence of scientific discourses we have good reasons to accept Mäki's 'one world' principle. But does this imply the rejection of ontological pluralism? The answer has to be negative. Ontology strictly speaking is logic of the ontic, that is, of the basic features of reality. It is a linguistic articulation and appropriation of the ontic, and as such it belongs to the category of views. 'Ontology' is not another word for 'the world' or 'reality', as seems to be the case in Mäki (2002). Reinterpreting ontological plurality as a plurality of ontologies – that is, worldviews – makes clear that ontological and theoretical pluralism are not radically different, and – more important – that ontological pluralism does not contradict the 'one world principle'. So accepting ontological plurality in the sense of 'a plurality of ontologies' does not implicate a conformation to the perspective of every person their own world, meaning isolated individuals encapsulated in their own, idiosyncratic worlds.

While Mäki's plea for theoretical pluralism contradicts the framework of positive economics, we argue that the acceptance of pluralism can be enlarged to ontological pluralism without opposing one of the prerequisites for science, that is, the reference to a shared world. Also relevant to this chapter on positive versus normative economics, is Mäki's suggestion of introducing the notion of the so-called 'www constraint' to the understanding of economists' choice and assessment of theories ('www' is short for 'the way the world works').

In contrast to the conception in positive economics of worldviews as pre-science, Mäki's discussion of the 'www constraint' (Mäki 2001) seems to suggest that these views are an essential part of economic science. According to him, the aim of economics is to understand and explain the economic realm. Theories must be relevant and reliable. He argues that in addition to empirical and social criteria, a third class of criteria 'should be invoked both in descriptive and normative considerations of theory choice in economics' (ibid., p. 370). Mäki argues, '[R]esearch has led to the discovery that empirical criteria play only a limited role in theory development and in discriminating between rival fundamental theories' (ibid.). He mentions the trend in economic methodology to add 'social factors' as a second class of criteria. Social factors (such as, rhetoric, path dependence and gender bias) are suggested to play a role as 'determinants, complementing or replacing or shaping the conventional empirical criteria' (ibid.) Unconvinced of the sufficiency of adding social factors as a second class of criteria, Mäki suggests adding a third class in accordance with his observation that many economists refer to 'the way the world works' as a constraint on theorizing. He calls this new class of criteria 'ontological criteria' because 'consistency with conceptions of the structure and functioning of the world serves as a criterion of, or a constraint on, theory choice' besides empirical and social criteria (ibid.)

Referring to economists' discussions of the model of perfect competition Mäki demonstrates that in economics realisticness (see this volume, chapter 56, note 1) as such is not a criterion in selecting theories. The problem is not simply that the model does not present a complete picture of the subject matter. Economists like Richardson, Coase and Buchanan reject the model of perfect competition because it abstracts from essential aspects (for example, imperfection), elements (for example, transactions and transaction costs) and causes (for example, rules embedded in institutions). Because of these harmful abstractions the model cannot live up to what it is expected to deliver: understanding – that is, explaining the essential structure and processes – of a competitive economy.

For the discussion of the positive-normative distinction it is important to note that the criteria used in critics' assessment of the model of perfect competition do not concur with the positivist's methodology of facts and nothing but facts. Not every failure in realisticness appears decisive in theory choice. Some are considered to be harmful and others are not. Mäki calls the criteria the critics use 'ontological constraints', since they refer in their assessments to ontological views of how the world works. This way of evaluating and adjusting models in relation to worldviews seems to resemble the methodological device used in interpreting texts: the hermeneutic circle, extended with notions of double hermeneutics and fusion of horizons.[11] The device of the hermeneutic circle reflects the idea that the interpretation of a text has to be conceived as a never-ending dialectic process between the text and its contexts (the frames of reference of both author and interpreter). Notions of double hermeneutics and fusion of horizons address the problem of older interpretation models to leave out the influence of the hermeneutical context of the interpreter or to proceed as though the hermeneutics of the horizon of the author can be separated from the horizon of the interpreter. Interpreting a text has to be conceived as a process in which through the fusing of the horizons of the author and the interpreter, the meaning of the content is produced.

By analogy, the assessment by the competitive model's critics looks like a dialogical process in which the critics reassess the received model in the context of today's renewed discussions about competitive models. According to Mäki, the critics address the model against the background of what they conceive as the way the world works. Using expressions like 'conception' and 'view', Mäki suggests that he understands ontological criteria as criteria based on ontology – that is, worldview; but elaborating on what makes an abstraction harmful or not, he appears to adhere to an interpretation criticized earlier in this chapter related to his rejection of ontological pluralism. Similar to his apparent understanding of ontology as reality 'as such', discussing ontological pluralism, he argues in his essay on the 'www constraint' that for an adequate understanding of this constraint '[a]n element of ontic necessity – necessity *de re* rather than just *de dicto* – appears to be involved' (2001, p. 379).

Drawing on Mäki's discussion of pluralism and the 'www constraint' and Putnam's elaboration on fact and value as examples of today's state of the art in economic methodology, this chapter concludes that the positivistic interpretation of the positive-normative distinction is losing ground, but that alternative approaches are still in need of elaboration, especially when it comes to questions about the relation between knowledge, language and ontology.

Notes

1. See for a short introduction to John Stuart Mill's contribution to economic thought Landreth and Colander (2002, pp. 156–86).
2. Mill's economics was not always in line with his methodological reflections. He was criticized, for instance, for intermingling science and art in his *Principles of Political Economy* in a similar way to Smith's approach in economics, which he had criticized before (Alvey 2000, p. 1239; Hutchison [1964] 1992, p. 29).
3. For an extended discussion of the emergence of the normative/positive distinction in nineteenth century British economics, see Samuel C. Weston's chapter([1994] 1998) by the same name.
4. Compare Hanefling (1996 pp, 193 ff.)
5. The worldview perspective is discussed below in the section on the hermeneutic approach.
6. Weston ([1994] 1998) mentions linguistic and ontological aspects but leaves problems related to these aspects undiscussed. His approach to why economists have to acknowledge the difference between 'positive propositions' and 'ethical evaluations' resembles the conventional view.
7. Compare Bonevac (1993, pp. 44 ff.) and Jimack (1996).
8. An example is Mäki (2001, p. 15), who associates hermeneutics with opposition to quantitive, formal and causal modelling in the human realm.
9. Mäki (2001, p. 130) distinguishes relative, absolute, temporary and permanent pluralism.
10. Dow (2002a, pp. 155–6; 2002b) seems to have a different interpretation of ontological pluralism. She accepts ontological pluralism, albeit a moderate kind of pluralism, since in the extreme case of no shared context of meaning any communication (discourse) would be impossible.
11. Compare Madison (1994,pp. 290 ff.) and Peil (1999, pp. 10–20).

References

Alvey, James E. (2000), 'An introduction to economics as a moral science', *International Journal of Social Economics*, **27** (12), 1231–51.
Blaug, Mark ([1980] 1992), *The Methodology of Economics or How Economists Explain*, Cambridge: Cambridge University Press.
Blaug, Mark (1998), 'The positive-normative distinction', in John B. Davis, Wade Hands and Uskali Mäki (eds), *The Handbook of Economic Methodology*, Cheltenham, UK and Lyme, MA, USA: Edward Elgar.
Bonevac, Daniel (1993), 'Kant's Copernican revolution', in Robert C. Solomon and Kathleen M. Higgins (eds), *The Age of German Idealism: Routledge History of Philosophy*, Vol. VI, London: Routledge, pp. 44–6.
Bourdieu, Pierre F. (1980), *Le Sens Pratique*, Paris: Minuit.
Bourdieu, Pierre F. (1987), 'Espace social et pouvoir symbolique', in *Choses Dites*, Paris: Minuit.
Chomsky, Noam (1967), 'General properties of language', in Clark L. Millikan and J.L. Darly (eds), *Brain Mechanisms Underlying Speech and Language*, New York and London: Grune & Stratton, pp. 73–88.
Dow, Sheila C. (2002a), *Economic Methodology: An Inquiry*, Oxford: Oxford University Press.
Dow, Sheila C. (2002b), 'Methodological pluralism and pluralism of methods', in Geoffrey M. Hodgson, *A*

Modern Reader in Institutional and Evolutionary Economics, Cheltenham, UK and Northampton, MA, USA: Edward Elgar, pp. 136–46.

Hanefling, Oswald (1996), 'Logical positivism', in Stuart G. Shanker (ed.), *Philosophy of Science, Logic and Mathematics in the 20th Century: Routledge History of Philosophy*, Vol. IX, London: Routledge.

Hutchison, Terence W. ([1964] 1992), *Positive Economics and Policy Objectives*, Aldershot: Gregg Revivals.

Jimack, Peter (1996), 'The French Enlightenment I: science, materialism and determinism', in Stuart Brown (ed.), *British Philosophy and the Age of Enlightenment: Routledge History of Philosophy*, Vol. V, London: Routledge, pp. 238–9.

Keynes, John Neville (1890), *The Scope and Method of Political Economy*, London: Macmillan.

Landreth, Harry and David C. Colander (2002), *History of Economic Thought*, Boston, MA: Houghton Mifflin.

Lavoie, Don (ed.) (1990), *Economics and Hermeneutics*, London: Routledge.

Lenneberg, Eric H. (1967), *Biological Foundations of Language*, New York: Wiley.

Madison, Gary B. (1994), 'Hermeneutics: Gadamer and Ricoeur', in Richard Kearny (ed.), *Continental Philosophy in the 20th Century: Routledge History of Philosophy*, Vol. VIII, London: Routledge.

Mäki, Uskali (2001), *The Economic World View: Studies in the Ontology of Economics*, Cambridge: Cambridge University Press.

Mäki, Uskali (2002), 'The one world and the many theories', in Geoffrey M. Hodgson, *A Modern Reader in Institutional and Evolutionary Economics*, Cheltenham, UK and Northampton, MA, USA: Edward Elgar, pp. 124–35.

Mill, John S. ([1844]1874), *Essays on Some Unsettled Questions of Political Economy*, London: Longmans.

Mirowski, Philip (1989), *More Heat than Light: Economics as Social Physics*, Cambridge: Cambridge University Press.

Mongin, Philippe (2006), 'Value judgements and value neutrality in economics', *Economica*, **73**, 270.

Peil, Jan (1999), *Adam Smith and Economic Science*, Cheltenham, UK and Northampton, MA, USA: Edward Elgar.

Putnam, Hilary (2002), *The Collapse of the Fact/Value Dichotomy, and other Essays*, Cambridge, MA: Harvard University Press.

Putnam, Hilary (2003), 'For ethics and economics without dichotomies', *Review of Political Economy*, **15** (3) (July), 395–412.

Robbins, Lionel (1932), *An Essay on the Nature and Significance of Economic Science*, London: Macmillan.

Weston, Samuel C. ([1994] 1998), 'Towards a better understanding of the positive/normative distinction in economics', *Economics and Philosophy*, **10** (1), 1–17; reprinted in Charles K. Wilber (ed.), *Economics, Ethics, and Public Policy*, Lanham: Rowan and Littlefield, pp. 33–49.

See also the entries on: Fact/value dichotomy; Positive-normative distinction in British history of economic thought; Pluralism; Realism.

50 Postmodernism
David F. Ruccio

Introduction

Common belief holds postmodernism not only to be incompatible with ethics but also to undermine any attempt to create a viable or vibrant ethical framework. This is because relativism, with which postmodernism is often conflated, and to which it is often reduced, calls into question universal foundational values. Therefore, modernist critics argue, since one or another set of such values is considered a necessary basis for an ethics, it is incumbent upon philosophers and social theorists (including economists) interested in elaborating an ethical framework to reject postmodernism.

From a postmodern perspective, however, quite the opposite may be the case. Whereas modernism has endeavoured to push ethics into the margin, postmodernism creates spaces or moments that highlight or call for ethical decisions. Thus, while there may be no such thing as a 'postmodern ethics' – a single ethical stance or framework that can be derived from the writings of postmodern thinkers – the various ideas and approaches grouped under the rubric of postmodernism do establish the terms for a renewed, albeit changed and transformed, conversation about ethics within economics.

Postmodernism and modernist ethics

There is more than a grain of truth in the modernist proposition asserting that post-modernism makes existing ethical stances difficult if not impossible. Three main theories are generally associated with postmodernism: poststructuralism, especially the work of Michel Foucault; deconstruction, pioneered by Jacques Derrida; and postmodernism proper, associated with Jean-François Lyotard. These have each formulated criticisms of the key premises on which many modernist approaches to ethics have rested. Let us briefly consider each of them in turn.

Poststructuralism involves, among other elements, 'a strong anti-humanism, culminating in the rejection of all notions of subjectivity in which the existence of a universal and unified "I" is presumed, and its replacement with a "decentred" subject' (Amariglio 1998, p. 384). The poststructuralist critique of the universal, centred subject not only deprives ethics of the rational or reasonable agents by and for whom ethical judgements are made, but it also shows that attempts to universalize moral claims represent an exercise of power that constitutes human beings as subjects.

Deconstruction, for its part, focuses on the fundamental undecidability and uncertainty of meaning, emphasizing the 'relations of difference and deferral which create the interpretative contexts within which meanings are produced and disseminated' (Ruccio 1998, p. 91). Insofar as ethical discourses presume generally acknowledged ways of conceptualizing or codifying human welfare and of appraising the rules that govern moral reasoning, deconstruction undermines such efforts by emphasizing both the 'play' of meaning attendant upon attempts to fix the interpretation of standards and rules and the idea that all such attempts merely serve to marginalize or repress (however unsuccessfully) other interpretations.

Finally, the 'postmodern condition' is characterized by an incredulity with respect to totalizing 'grand metanarratives', especially those that 'hold out the hope for a total change in society through advocacy of particular principles and perspectives' (Ruccio and Amariglio 2003, p. 10). Postmodernists not only refuse ethical narratives that presume or promise overall progress in the human condition; they also argue that attempts to justify other practices (for example, science or politics) by such ethical principles are illusory or dangerous or both. It is not surprising, therefore, that modernist philosophers and social thinkers perceive key postmodern notions – the decentred subject, the deconstruction of meaning and suspicion toward master narratives of human progress or liberation – as destabilizing and thus as unsuitable as the foundations of ethical discourses.

Postmodernists look at matters quite differently. First, they see modernism as having pushed ethical issues to the margins, thereby narrowing the space within which ethical discourses can be elaborated and have any consequence. Second, the issues highlighted by postmodernists – the critique of the subject, the play of meaning and the focus on discontinuous, local narratives – are precisely those that allow for the possibility (perhaps even the necessity) of ethical deliberation and decision-making. Therefore, postmodernism serves both to make ethical issues of key concern within human inquiry and endeavour and to lead to new ethical discourses and practices.

Modernism: ethics out of economics?
What is it about modernism that undermines the significance and relevance of ethics? According to Zygmunt Bauman (1993), the modernist attempt to eliminate moral uncertainty and to secure a universal moral code through reason (rather than, for example, through tradition or faith), in order to ensure that 'individual freedom could have morally positive consequences', results in the creation of coercive institutions. This means ceding to 'socially approved agencies the right to decide what is good and submit[ting] to their verdicts' (ibid., p. 29). The result is to 'replace morality with legal code, and to shape ethics after the pattern of the Law'. Thus, individual responsibility is reduced to 'following or breaching the socially endorsed, ethical-legal rules' (ibid.), thereby narrowing (or perhaps eliminating entirely) the ambit of moral judgement and ethical decision-making.

The modernist distancing of ethics from economics (or, alternatively, economics from ethics) registers in several ways. First, when economic scientists are viewed as merely positive theorists and analysts of economic reality, when they are seen (and see themselves) as detached observers who can objectively arrive at conclusions about the economy while avoiding all normative attachments and commitments, there is no room for explicit consideration of moral judgements.

Second, according to modernist conceptions of economic theory, the decisions made in the course of economic theorizing and empirical analysis – the choice of topics and methods, the steps taken to move from one concept to another in formulating a model, the decision to focus on one subset of causes and effects during the course of investigation to the exclusion of other causes and effects, the elaboration of conclusions or findings, the formulation of policy recommendations – are governed by a purely scientific logic. Therefore, these decisions are understood to be dictated by the protocols of scientific procedure and epistemological veracity. They are thus seen as absent of ethical considerations or ethical implications.[1]

Finally, if the object of economic inquiry is conceptualized as a closed, homogeneous space, governed by structural laws and rule-driven agents, then the realm of economic activity can be treated as an external object constituted independently of the ethical commitments on the part of either economic observers or economic agents. That is, modernism treats economic reality as available for rational inquiry and accurate representation (by both economists and agents) but not as a terrain that is constructed (and, thus, which can be reproduced or transformed) by ethical decisions or commitments (again, by either economic scientists or economic agents). The effect, therefore, of modernist approaches to economics is to relegate ethical issues to (or beyond) the margins of inquiry.

The conception of disciplinarity associated with modernism is that economic inquiry can and should take place far from ethical commitments and values. However, according to George DeMartino (2000, p. 77), in the case of neoclassical economics, 'the decision to banish values to intellectual regions beyond economics (such as philosophy) is itself fully normative'. In DeMartino's view, neoclassical 'welfarism', the idea that the evaluation of economic policy and economic outcomes can be conducted solely in terms of individual preferences, and therefore independently of normative values and ethical stances, actually undoes itself. In the end, the presumed ethical neutrality of neoclassical economics involves a firm ethical commitment to the market, to the idea that market-based forms of economic organization are 'optimal for all human communities for all time' (ibid., p. 76).[2]

Antonio Callari (2002) presents and elaborates another way in which modernist discourse unsuccessfully closes the space of ethics: through the gift. For Callari, the modernist conception of economics as a 'science of exchange' is based on the presumption that (i) the economy is a 'world of goods' and (ii) the world of goods is a 'homogeneous field' (ibid., p. 252). The result is a conception of the economy (and of the larger social order) governed by individual calculations over a homogeneous field of goods, in which altruism and generosity are reduced to self-interest and ethical judgements and decisions play no role. The anthropological legacy of the gift, however, threatens to destabilize this notion of economics, by presenting both an aporia (for example, the uncertainty attendant upon the 'return', the reciprocity occasioned by the debt caused by the gift) and a state of excess (because it combines desire and responsibility, and therefore exceeds the world of homogeneous goods). The gift, therefore, disrupts the 'circle of value' that separates economy from non-economy (including, perhaps especially, ethics): it serves to create a moment of undecidability within both economic discourse (because it undermines the idea that there is a single value principle, thus occasioning an ethical choice between different theories of value) and within the economic and social order (which, because the structures of calculable exchange are rendered impossible, suggests an independent or 'suturing' role for ethics). In Callari's view, the event of the gift offers something more than a set of practices oriented around generosity or sharing. It represents the very impossibility of a discourse of economics and an economic order devoid of and separate from ethics.

From postmodernism to ethics
Postmodernism not only serves to identify the ethical gap or silence created by modernism; it also calls forth an ethical stance – that is, the possibility of a set of ethical

commitments and decision-making practices on the part of economic and social subjects. Again, let us examine each theory of postmodernism in turn.

The poststructuralist approach to ethics stems directly from the critique of the subject: since the subject is neither a given (natural or universal) entity nor a necessary condition for meaning or experience, it becomes possible to analyse modern discourses and apparatuses as operating to impose particular forms of identity on individuals, to constitute them as subjects. Therefore, the task of ethics is to problematize or denaturalize these identities (along with the modes of knowledge and power in and through which they are created) and to open a space for the fashioning of new identities.

According to Timothy O'Leary (2002), Foucault (1985, 1988, 1997) followed up his inquiry into the modes of operation of and the costs incurred by modern techniques of 'subjectivation' (especially through the production of scientific knowledges about and governmental regulation of sexuality, but also of madness, criminality and much else) by retrieving from ancient Greece the idea of cultivating 'a relation of self to self in which the self is neither given nor produced, but is continuously worked on in a labour of care (*epimeleia*) and skill (*techne*)' (O'Leary 2002, p. 2). The goal of this 'aesthetics of existence' is to serve as an alternative to traditional ethics, either following a moral code or fostering one's virtues. It is an aesthetics of self-care rather than an asceticism of self-sacrifice, a process of self-fashioning rather than a matter of self-discovery. O'Leary explains that, by aesthetics, Foucault means both a particular relation to the self – a certain attitude towards the self 'not unlike that of an artist faced with his or her material' (O'Leary 2002, p. 14), a way of giving form to one's life and one's relationships with others – and a general goal – the kind of self one might create during the course of the work of self-transformation, oriented around and toward the idea of beauty (ibid.) However, there is no general model or necessary agreement with respect to either what is a beautiful result or the method one might follow to achieve such a result. Therefore, the ethics that Foucault offers is less a finished procedure or state than a process of creating new forms of life, an infinite labour 'which knows no completion' (ibid., p. 170).

The ethical implications of deconstruction are, not surprisingly, bound up with the undecidability of meaning that characterizes the reading and interpretation of texts. Both Simon Critchley (1999) and Geoffrey Bennington (2000) argue that Derrida's thought (1976, 1988, 1992, 1994) comprises an ethics – an 'ethical demand' (Critchley, p. 12) or 'a new way of thinking about some of [the] problems traditionally posed by ethics' (Bennington, p. 64). This is to the extent that ethics is understood in a new way, along the lines traced by Emmanuel Levinas (1969, 1981). That is, while deconstruction can be identified with neither a set of consensual values nor with a procedure guaranteed to produce ethical decisions, and therefore not with an ethics in the traditional meaning of that term, the logic of deconstruction entails a particular response to the Other. And it is this relation of alterity – a practice of language based on a recognition that the other (for example, a text) is not absolutely other (because, if it were, no reading would be possible) and, at the same time, that this otherness is irreducible (that is, that the act of reading does not involve a mere deciphering of the text but something more) – which creates a responsibility with respect to the other. The undecidability of meaning therefore creates an act of inventiveness, an opening toward the other that refuses to reduce that alterity to sameness.

Finally, to eliminate all doubt that this responsibility to the other cannot induce a 'consensual euphoria', a traditional moralism, deconstruction entails recognition that ethics is always contaminated by the non-ethical: the chance of ethics is both created and compromised by an other, the introduction of a third party, the idea that ethics can be perverted and so on. Ethics, then, is ethical only insofar as it registers the undecidability of the responsibility with respect to the singular other.

The notion of ethics that emerges from the postmodern suspicion of grand narratives is informed by a 'justice of multiplicity'. In the work of Lyotard (1988), universal narratives (for example, of the subject, language, history and so on) are replaced by a radical heterogeneity, a set of multiple and incommensurable 'phrase regimens' and 'genres of discourse'. Thus, for example, phrases from different regimens (such as reasoning, knowing and describing) can be linked one onto the other according to the goals appropriate to the particular genre (for example, to know, to teach, to justify). However, a 'differend' arises when, in the case of a conflict between two or more parties, the absence of a rule of judgement applicable to both arguments prevents equitable resolution. In other words, since a universal rule of judgement between heterogeneous genres is lacking, 'a wrong results from the fact that the rules of the genre of discourse by which one judges are not those of the judged genre or genres of discourse' (ibid., p. xi).

Lyotard considers such dilemmas to be without resolution (instead of assuming that there is some 'conversation of humankind' able to cut across or encompass all local narratives or discursive genres). He argues that what is at stake 'is to bear witness to differends by finding idioms for them' (Lyotard 1988, p. 13), to formulate idioms that do not yet exist. The ethical universe is precisely that which occurs when one is called to bear witness not by a somebody but rather by a 'phrase in abeyance' (ibid., p. 136), conditioned by the feeling that victimization is (or has been or will be) taking place. It involves an 'ethical hesitation', which leads to suspicion regarding the unity of the subject as well as any specific phrasing of justice, and an 'ongoing and in principle interminable deliberation over the manner in which the phrasing of language is to proceed' (Hatley 2002, p. 80).

Clearly, none of the three theories of postmodernism offers what is traditionally understood as an ethics – whether a conception of the ethical subject, a set of consensual moral values or a procedure for guaranteeing the making of ethical choices or decisions. The major themes of postmodernism – the critique of the subject, the undecidability of meaning and suspicion toward grand narratives – prevent elaboration of such a universalist or foundationalist ethics. In this sense, the search for a 'postmodern ethics' cannot but be frustrated.

Postmodernism, ethics and economics

However, it is equally clear that 'some sense of ethics or the ethical' (Bennington 2000, p. 64) survives the postmodern critique and, perhaps, emerges as its source or consequence.[3] That is, postmodernism cannot be simply dismissed (by those interested in ethics) as an amoral or anti-ethical approach to philosophy and social theory. The theories that together comprise postmodernism serve to problematize both non-ethical thought (it is simply not possible to operate as if ethical issues and questions could be ignored) and traditional conceptions of ethics (whether of moral subjects, ethical procedures or narratives of justice).

They also pose a way of thinking about ethical issues (at least in the sense of identifying when and where ethical choices are called for or can be made). And no important dimension of economics is immune from the contaminating features of these ethical moments. Not the economists: once they are confronted by the possibility of inventing new identities, for themselves and for the subjects who populate the academic and everyday worlds. Not economic theory: since it cannot finally fix the meaning of concepts, and therefore is faced by its theoretical other. And not the economy itself: because it is characterized by irresolvable conflicts, both inside (within the economy) and outside (between economy and non-economy). In each case, economics perforce encounters – by explicitly engaging or remaining silent (which, of course, is another form of engagement) – the ethical of ethics.

Postmodern approaches to ethics therefore complicate or problematize modernist economic discourse, by showing that it is impossible to remain content with, to merely follow, to justify in some absolute sense, the rules of the existing language. But they also enable other moves, other ways of doing economics. An example is the pointedly non-modernist ethical universalism that guides the work of postcolonial scholars in economics. According to S. Charusheela (2004), postcolonial theory involves a critique of modernist attempts to ground ethics, which also refuses to endorse its presumed opposite, ethical relativism. The goal of a postcolonial approach to economics is to analyse the discursive field in which marginalized and subaltern subjectivities (as well as marginality and subalternity themselves) are constructed and to create a variety of critical strategies to reshape the field, in order to wrest agency for such subjects. Therefore, the postcolonial position in economics is guided by an ethical orientation based on 'identification with the pain of someone who is, literally, a not-Us in the current maps organizing material and discursive access to power and authority' (ibid., p. 55).[4]

Another example can be found in the recent work of Gibson-Graham (2006).[5] Their project calls for, and is an attempt to produce, 'new ethical *practices of thinking* economy and becoming different kinds of economic beings' (ibid., p. xxviii, emphasis original). By ethics, they understand 'the continual exercising, in the face of the need to decide, of a choice to be/act/think a certain way' (ibid.), which not only takes place on an ultimately undecidable terrain of different possibilities but explicitly seeks to proliferate new identities, modes of intervention and ways of thinking. As thinkers, Gibson-Graham seek to connect affects and emotions to the practice of thinking, and thus to cultivate for themselves (and, by extension, for others) a new identity as subjects who, rather than gazing at the world critically and dispassionately, 'can imagine and enact a new economic politics' (ibid.) In terms of theorizing, they propose new techniques – of 'ontological reframing' (for example, conceptualizing contingent, rather than stable or invariant, relations), rereading (uncovering what is possible but obscured from view) and creativity (of encountering and being open to the unexpected) – in order to imagine and create economic concepts and systems that existing modes of thought (in the name of seeing the world 'as it is') render invisible or impossible. Finally, they view the economy not as something 'out there', a stable set of relations and institutions that can be known and controlled, but as a terrain of possibility that can be brought into being, a becoming that can occur through language, subjectivity and collective action.

If the result of J.K. Gibson-Graham's project is to turn economic theory and the economy itself into spaces of ethical deliberations and decisions, they offer no guarantees

– no blueprint, no hidden structure waiting to be recognized and liberated, no consensus. Instead, they invent a theoretical and social 'emptiness' that they can only hope will be filled (through the new beings, thinkings and actings pursued by them and others). In the ethical language of Alain Badiou (2001), what they propose is an 'event', and the 'truth' that emerges from 'fidelity' to the event. For Badiou, the ethic of a truth is precisely the 'principle that enables the continuation of a truth-process' (ibid., p. 44). It is the injunction to 'Keep going!'

Notes

I want to thank the editors for inviting me to prepare this essay, various colleagues and friends for their encouraging reaction to the first draft, and two anonymous reviewers for their helpful comments and suggestions in preparing the final draft.

1. Indeed, continual references to the 'economic method' may serve to close off any attempt to see the decisions taken during the course of economic research as involving anything that pertains to or is affected by moral judgement or ethical concerns. The master narrative of human progress, which serves to justify the following of scientific rules without intrusion of other considerations, represents a thin link to ethics.
2. Some of these issues are raised, although without an explicit link to ethics, within the literature on the role of ideology in economics. In Roger Backhouse's (2005) language, DeMartino refers both to intellectual and political value judgements. Vivian Walsh (2003) argues that the fact/value dichotomy often invoked by neoclassical economists leads to an impoverished conception of rationality, and prefers instead to emphasize the 'entanglement' of fact, value and convention. Both approaches stop far short of the postmodern critique.
3. There is a certain parallel between a postmodern approach to ethics and contemporary contextual or pragmatist ethics, in that both involve a suspicion of universalism and foundationalism. See, for example, Hilary Putnam's (2004) discussion of the possibility of ethics without metaphysics or a modernist ontology. Putnam also invokes the work of Levinas, which figures prominently in at least some postmodern approaches to ethics. Still, while Putnam might endorse the first part of this claim – that some sense of ethics survives the postmodern critique – it is doubtful he would agree with the second part – that the postmodern critique calls for or is based on an ethical stance.
4. Charusheela conceives this ethical orientation to be universal in the sense that it 'simply *is* the ontological moment defining the origin of analysis' (2004, p. 55), but not modernist, since it derives 'from no particular moment of mapping the body, the mind, the being, the culture, the identity' (ibid.) of what it means to be human.
5. Gibson-Graham is the pseudonym of a pair of authors, Julie Graham and Katherine Gibson. Hence, my use of the plural in the text.

References

Amariglio, Jack (1998), 'Poststructuralism', in John B. Davis, Wade Hands and Uskali Maki (eds), *The Handbook of Economic Methodology*, Cheltenham, UK and Lyme, USA: Edward Elgar, pp. 382–8.

Backhouse, Roger E. (2005), 'Economists, values, and ideology: a neglected agenda', *Revue de Philosophie Économique*, **11**, 31–55.

Badiou, Alain (2001), *Ethics: An Essay on the Understanding of Evil*, trans. P. Hallward, New York: Verso.

Bauman, Zygmunt (1993), *Postmodern Ethics*, Cambridge, MA: Blackwell.

Bennington, Geoffrey (2000), 'Deconstruction and ethics', in Nicholas Royle (ed.), *Deconstructions: A User's Guide*, New York: Palgrave, pp. 64–82.

Callari, Antonio (2002), 'The ghost of the gift: the unlikelihood of economics', in Mark Osteen (ed.), *The Question of the Gift: Essays across the Disciplines*, New York: Routledge, pp. 248–65.

Charusheela, S. (2004), 'Postcolonial thought, postmodernism, and economics: questions of ontology and ethics', in Eiman O. Zein-Elabdin and S. Charusheela (eds), *Postcolonialism Meets Economics*, New York: Routledge, pp. 40–58.

Critchley, Simon (1999), *The Ethics of Deconstruction: Derrida and Levinas*, 2nd edition, West Lafayette, IN: Purdue University Press.

DeMartino, George F. (2000), *Global Economy, Global Justice: Theoretical Objections and Policy Alternatives to Neoliberalism*, New York: Routledge.

Derrida, Jacques (1976), *De la grammatologie*, trans. Gayatri C. Spivak, Baltimore, MD: Johns Hopkins University Press.

Derrida, Jacques (1988), *Limited Inc*, trans. Jeffrey Mehlman and Samuel Weber, Evanston, IL: Northwestern University Press.

Derrida, Jacques (1992), *Derrida: A Critical Reader*, ed. David Wood, Oxford: Blackwell.

Derrida, Jacques (1994), *Politics of Friendship*, trans. George Collins, New York: Verso.

Foucault, Michel (1985), *The History of Sexuality, Vol. 2: The Uses of Pleasure*, New York: Pantheon.

Foucault, Michel (1988), 'The ethic of care for the self as a practice of freedom', in James Bernauer and David Rasmussen (eds), *The Final Foucault*, Boston, MA: MIT Press, pp. 1–20.

Foucault, Michel (1997), *Ethics: Subjectivity and Truth*, ed. Paul Rabinow, New York: New Press.

Gibson-Graham, J.K. (2006), *A Postcapitalist Politics*, Minneapolis, MN: University of Minnesota Press.

Hatley, James (2002), 'Lyotard, Levinas, and the phrasing of the ethical', in Hugh J. Silverman (ed.), *Lyotard: Philosophy, Politics, and the Sublime*, New York: Routledge, pp. 75–83.

Levinas, Emmanuel (1969), *Totality and Infinity*, trans. Alphonso Lingis, Pittsburgh, PA: Duquesne University Press.

Levinas, Emmanuel (1981), *Otherwise than Being, or Beyond Essence*, trans. Alphonso Lingis, The Hague: Martinus Nijhoff.

Lyotard, Jean-Francois (1988), *The Differend: Phrases in Dispute*, trans. Georges van den Abbeele, Minneapolis, MN: University of Minnesota Press.

O'Leary, Timothy (2002), *Foucault and the Art of Ethics*, New York: Continuum.

Putnam, Hilary (2004), *Ethics without Ontology*, Cambridge, MA: Harvard University Press.

Ruccio, David F. (1998), 'Deconstruction', in John B. Davis, Wade Hands and Uskali Maki (eds), *The Handbook of Economic Methodology*, Cheltenham, UK and Lyme, USA: Edward Elgar, pp. 89–92.

Ruccio, David F. and Jack Amariglio (2003), *Postmodern Moments in Modern Economics*, Princeton, NJ: Princeton University Press.

Walsh, Vivian (2003), 'Sen after Putnam', *Review of Political Economy*, **15** (3), 315–94.

See also the entries on: Epistemology; Identity; Pluralism.

51 Poverty
Andy Sumner

Introduction

Poverty has long been a concern of economists. It drove not only the 'founding fathers' of quantitative economics, such as Petty and Quesnay, but also the 'pioneers' of political economy – Malthus, Marx, Mill, Ricardo and Smith. Many contemporary academics might place poverty at the heart of development economics.

Definitions and conceptualizations of poverty

Poverty is about deprivation, but deprivation of what? In this regard, considerable ground has been covered since World War II. For much of the earlier part of the period, poverty was viewed as economic in nature, with deprivation measured in terms of income. Since the late 1960s other dimensions have been added, notably deprivation of education and health. More recently, political dimensions, under the label of 'participation', have also been added to objective or universal understandings of poverty. Emphasis has, in fact, shifted from universal definitions of poverty towards recognition of the heterogeneity of location-specific meanings of poverty, such as those elicited via participatory poverty assessments. Further, definitions based purely on physiological conditions (that is, the objective *condition* of the individual) have given way to interest in the psychological experiences of poverty (the subjective *experience* of the individual).

Dudley Seers (1963) launched the paradigm shift to broader understandings of poverty when he expanded the meaning of development beyond gross domestic product (GDP) per capita and into 'basic needs'. These 'basic needs' include not only income and employment but also the physical necessities for a basic standard of living, such as food, shelter and public goods (see for greater detail, ILO 1977; Streeten 1984; Stewart 1985). Much of the research was led by the International Labour Office, particularly through its World Employment Programme (see, for example, ILO 1977). This coincided with the emergence in the 1960s and 1970s of 'levels of living indicators' in response to dissatisfaction with the use of income per capita as a measure of welfare and of development. The culmination of all these efforts was the first composite measure of standard of living – Morris's (1979) physical quality of life index (PQLI).

In the early 1980s, the publication of Chambers's (1983) work on non-monetary poverty (in particular isolation and empowerment) and the 1980 *World Development Report* (WDR) appeared, in the first instance, to be shifting the debate further away from economic determinism. The WDR characterized poverty as beyond income and encapsulating nutrition, education and health (World Bank 1980, p. 32). However, the debt crisis, structural adjustment and conditionality policies pushed non-economic concerns off the agenda. Despite this, towards the end of the decade there was a renewed interest in poverty, as the human costs of adjustment programmes became more evident (see Cornia et al. 1987). What emerged was a definition of poverty that synthesized the economic and non-economic components of poverty.

The UNDP *Human Development Report* (HDR) was established in 1990. It provided a new framework known as 'human development' or, in Amartya Sen's terms, 'capabilities approach', and a related set of composite indicators led by the UNDP's own Human Development Index. For Sen the capabilities approach provided an 'evaluative space', consisting of the means, opportunities or substantive freedoms which permit the achievement of a set of 'functionings' – things which we value 'being' and 'doing'. This, according to Sen, is the essence of human development. However, because capabilities are difficult to measure, many of the components of the Human Development Index are actually based on functionings. Further, human development is confused by some as being synonymous with human capital formation.

Sen (in particular 1999), Nussbaum (in particular 2000) and the UNDP (1990–2007) have argued that development is not, as previously conceived, based on desire fulfilment (utility or consumption measured by a proxy for income, such as GDP per capita). After all, this takes insufficient evaluative account of the physical condition of the individual and of a person's capabilities. Income is *only* an instrumental freedom – it helps to achieve other constitutive freedoms. Sen does not ignore income, rather he argues that too much emphasis can be placed on this dimension of development:

> Development consists of the removal of various types of unfreedom that leave people with little opportunity of exercising their reasoned agency . . . Development can be seen . . . as a process of expanding the real freedoms that people enjoy . . . the expansion of the 'capabilities' of persons to lead the kind of lives they value – and have reason to value. (Sen 1999, pp. xii, 1, 18)

Thus, poverty is a lack of freedom or opportunities to achieve the 'beings' and 'doings' individuals value. Sen has argued that there is a broad set of conditions (including being fed, healthy, clothed and educated) that together constitute well-being. Individuals have a set of entitlements (command over commodities), which are created through a set of endowments (financial, human, natural, social and productive capital) and exchange (production and trade by the individual). These entitlements are transformed into a set of opportunities (capabilities) in order to achieve a set of functionings (outcomes of well-being). Sen resolutely refused to name the capabilities. However, he (1999, p. 38) did identify five basic freedoms:

- political/participative freedom or civil rights, such as freedom of speech and free elections;
- economic facilities, for instance, opportunities to participate in trade and production and sell one's labour and product on fair, competitive terms;
- social opportunities, such as adequate education and health facilities;
- transparency guarantees, including openness in government and business and social trust;
- protective security, for instance, law and order, social safety nets for the unemployed.

Further, there have been numerous attempts to construct sets of capabilities (Alkire 2002 presents a discussion).

The related UNDP indices are the Human Development Index, the Gender Development Index and the Human Poverty Index. In the case of the Human Poverty

Index, two separate versions are provided: one for the South and the other for the North. The Human Development Index and Gender Development Index use life expectancy, knowledge and education and adjusted income per capita as a proxy for the range of economic choices available. The Human Poverty Index is a measure of deprivation, calculated on the basis of the proportion of a country's population living below some minimum level of human development indicators. There is also a gender empowerment measure which gauges gender equality in politics and the labour market.

The launch of the HDR and Human Development Index in 1990 played a role in what was to become known as the decade in which poverty and social development rose to prominence in academic and policy arenas. That same year, the World Bank also issued a new, albeit money-metric or economic, measure of poverty, the dollar-a-day poverty indicator. Throughout the decade, numerous United Nations conferences dealt directly or closely with poverty and human development.

The 2000/1 *World Development Report* played a role in solidifying developed country support for poverty reduction in the development discourse and promoted a multidimensional model of poverty. However, of far greater significance was the UN Millennium Assembly in New York. On 18 September 2000 all countries signed the Millennium Declaration, from which the 'Millennium Development Goals' or poverty reduction targets for 2015 were derived.

The Millennium Declaration is based on six 'fundamental values': freedom, equality, solidarity, tolerance, respect for nature and shared responsibility. The Millennium Goals are in fact a collation of goals previously agreed at various UN conferences. There are eight Millennium Development Goals, and these are accompanied by 18 targets and 48 indicators. These constitute a mandate for combating extreme income poverty and poor nutrition (MDG 1), providing universal primary education (MDG 2), promoting gender equality and empowerment of women (MDG 3), reducing child mortality (MDG 4), improving maternal health (MDG 5), combating HIV/AIDS and malaria (MDG 6), ensuring environmental sustainability (MDG 7) and forming global partnerships for development (MDG 8).

Other approaches to conceptualizing poverty make reference to livelihoods, rights and exclusion. These different frameworks identify different people as 'poor' and also imply different responses. A 'livelihoods' approach is concerned with the evaluative space of a 'livelihoods strategy' which is shaped by household assets, the context, the institutional rules, norms and the like, as well as the policy regime that mediates capital accumulation across those assets. The approach has been defined as follows:

> [T]he process of identifying the resources and strategies of the poor, the context within which they operate, the institutions and organisations with which they interact and the sustainability of the livelihood outcomes which they achieve, providing a way of picking a path through this complexity at micro level. (Shankland 2000, p. 6)

The so-called 'sustainable livelihoods approach' is associated with the seminal paper by Chambers and Conway (1992).

A 'rights-based approach' is concerned with achieved 'rights'. These 'rights' are universal and objectively defined by various UN agreements, in particular the Universal Declaration of Human Rights. They include the right to food, shelter, education and health-care. Thus, there is much resonance with the human development and capability approach. The rights-based approach provides a set of indicators or 'goals' of develop-ment accepted by all countries party to the Universal Declaration of Human Rights. The rights-based approach shifts the focus to the largest deprivations. The approach defines 'the achievement of human rights as an objective of development [and invokes] the inter-national apparatus [of] rights accountability in support of development action' (Maxwell 1999, p. 1).

The rights-based approach is associated with various UN declarations and conven-tions. In addition to the Universal Declaration of Human Rights, there is also the Convention on the Rights of the Child and the Convention on the Elimination of Discrimination against Women.

Our final approach, the 'social exclusion approach' pushes concern for the most deprived further by focusing on specific groups. It investigates the structural processes and agency factors that lead to exclusion through the dynamics facing certain groups (such as ethnic minorities, lower caste members, the disabled). The approach explores the evaluative space of processes leading to exclusion and seeks to expose relative depriva-tion. It is an approach that has been popular in the 'North' but is increasingly also used in southern contexts (for details see Maxwell 1998).

In recent years a relatively new fault line has emerged – that between universal or 'objective' conceptualizations of poverty (such as those discussed above) and 'subjec-tive' or local experiences of well-being. These subjective approaches are associated in particular with Chambers (1983, 1997, 2006), who argues that the perceptions of poor people (rather than of rich people or members of the development community) should be the point of departure because top-down understandings of poverty may not correspond with how poor people themselves conceptualize changes in their well-being. For them, security, dignity, voice and vulnerability may be more important than consumption. For example, Kingdon and Knight (2004, p. 1) argue, '[A]n approach which examines the individual's own perception of well-being is less imperfect, or more quantifiable, or both, as a guide to forming that value judgment than are the other potential approaches.'

These psychological elements of development indicators have shifted discussion from objective well-being to subjective well-being and from physiological conditions (namely the objective physical condition of the individual) to happiness and psychological experi-ences (the subjective psychological experience of the individual). In short, this concerns 'what a person has, what a person can do with what they have, and how they think about what they have and can do' (McGregor 2006, p. 1).

Participatory methods such as rapid rural appraisal and participatory poverty assess-ments have been utilized as techniques to elicit poor households' perspectives on well-being (albeit with the contradiction of having to use some definition of poverty to identify the poor sample beforehand). Chambers (1994, p. 1253) defines these as a family of approaches and methods to enable local (rural and urban) people to express, enhance, share and analyse their knowledge of life and conditions, to plan and to act.

The largest such study to date is the World Bank's *Voices of the Poor* (Narayan et al. 1999) which included 60 000 people in more than 60 countries. *Voices of the Poor* concluded that the poor define poverty as multidimensional and beyond material well-being (though food security and employment were mentioned). The poor also highlight participation and voice as well as risk and vulnerability as acute aspects of poverty.

The meaning of 'participation' has however become contentious. Chambers himself (2001) identified several connotations. Participation is used to describe an empowering process, or it may merely refer to a cosmetic label or co-opting practice. Due in part to their conceptual ambiguity, both 'participation' as an overall approach and 'participatory' methods and techniques have faced significant criticism, despite their rise to the mainstream. Arguments against participatory approaches tend to focus on their limited attention to wider structures of injustice, power and social relations.

In short, the emergence of 'participatory' techniques and talk of 'participation' in the politics of poverty remains contentious. Harriss (2006) argues that it is the politics of poverty that are actually missing. Research focuses on explaining individual deprivation, not the study of social relations and inequality in power and wealth. Studying poverty is not the same as studying the poor: '[T]he way in which poverty is conceptualised separates it from the social processes of the accumulation and distribution of wealth, which depoliticises it – and depoliticisation is of course a profoundly political intellectual act' (ibid., p. 5).

The growth of interest in participatory approaches and the politics of poverty is at least a partial response to the postmodern critique of 'development'. The postmodern approach suggests that conceptualizations of poverty and development imply that some people and countries are 'inferior' to those who constructed the concept or the 'discourse'. Indeed, central to the 'postmodern' critique is that development has been defined as synonymous with modernity, which is presented in the discourse as a superior condition. This goes to the heart of the postmodern condemnation of development as a discourse constructed in the North as 'modernity' and applied to the South. The 'discourse' is socially constructed and values certain assets which the South does not have. Thus the South is viewed as 'inferior'. For example, 'traditional' or non-modern/non-Western approaches to agriculture or medicine or other aspects of society are perceived as 'inferior':

> Post-modern approaches [to] poverty see it as socially constructed and embedded within certain economic epistemes which value some assets over others. By revealing the situatedness of such interpretations of economy and poverty, post-modern approaches look for alternative value systems so that the poor are not stigmatised and their spiritual and cultural 'assets' are recognized. (Hickey and Mohan 2003, p. 38)

Critiques of the postmodern conceptualization of development typically focus on its perceived nihilism, its celebration of severe deprivation as a form of cultural autonomy, its romanticized notion of the 'noble savage' and the assumption that all Southern social movements are emancipatory (for further discussion see Kiely 1999).

Inequality and poverty
One important question is that of inequality and its relationship with poverty, not only overall, but also in terms of inequality amongst the poor. First, aggregate measures of poverty, such as those detailed above, take limited or no account of the difference between the average (for example, life expectancy or primary school enrolment) and the experience of those in the bottom quintile of say, education, nutrition or health expenditure. Further, it is much easier to improve the aggregate or average data than the data amongst the poorest, and when growth does benefit the poor it is more likely to benefit

those near the poverty line than those most deprived. The fact is that poverty is more severe in a household that is 30 per cent below the poverty line than in a household that is only 5 per cent below the poverty line (this is reflected the indices of Foster et al. 1984). Yet no headcount measurement would differentiate between these two households. An alternative is the poverty gap index which shows the intensity of poverty by measuring the difference between the average income of all poor households and the poverty line.

Second, and very much related, the intra-household allocation of income, consumption and resources is an important dimension of poverty. Much poverty analysis and data is at the household level, and assumes income and other resources are equally shared. In reality this assumption often does not hold. For example, malnutrition, illiteracy and other dimensions of poverty may be significantly worse amongst women. Children and girls in particular may suffer a greater depth of deprivation. This may remain hidden in 'traditional' proxy monetary measures of poverty. Data sources such as income and consumption are deeply problematic for women and children for several reasons:

- data is not collected from women and children themselves but from male heads of households and from carers in the case of children;
- women and children's employment is often in the informal economy;
- non-market channels may be more important in shaping gender dimensions of poverty and childhood poverty;
- women and children's access to and control of income may be extremely marginal, with resources and power distributed unequally within the household.

Finally, for various reasons, such as seasonality, some people and households move in and out of poverty over time. For others, the experience of poverty (whatever its dimension) may be a long-term phenomena that is even inter-generationally transferred (for a discussion see Hulme et al. 2001). Sen (1999, p. 4) notes, '[C]apabilities that adults enjoy are deeply conditional on their experiences as children'. For example, the priority period for nutrition is while a child is in the womb up to 18 months of age. Malnutrition losses in this period are irreversible – they represent losses the child will carry throughout life. Of the female babies that survive, those that remain malnourished in adolescence are more likely, in turn, to give birth to malnourished babies.

Strategies for poverty reduction

It has been assumed that economic growth would eventually diminish poverty by a mechanistic 'trickle-down' effect. If this is true and growth is good for the poor (either in relative or absolute terms), there is no need for government policy to depart from a focus on growth strategy. However, if growth is not necessarily good for the poor, then quite different policies may be required. If economic development, in the early stages at least, leads to an increase in inequality then the implication is that poverty may take many years to be reduced, as the benefits of growth to the poor are diminished by the increase in inequality. Consistent with the 1970s studies that supported the so-called Kuznets trade-off between growth and inequity, a series of studies conducted as new data became available argued that economic growth did not benefit the poor. Chenery et al. (1974, p. xiii) asserted that a decade of growth had bypassed with 'little or no benefit' a third of the population in developing countries. Adelman and Morris (1973, pp. 189–93) wrote of hundreds of millions 'hurt' by economic development. An old idea packaged anew then became one of the most pervasive and widespread phrases in development policy: 'pro-poor growth' emerged as a synthesis of 'growth with redistribution', 'broad-based growth' and 'growth with equity'. Though 'pro-poor growth' has been defined in numerous ways, two groupings can be distinguished according to outcomes: that based on whether the poor have benefited in an absolute way – the headcount falls or the incomes of the poor rise – and that based on the poor benefiting in a relative sense that implicitly entails reductions in inequality.

Conclusions

In their review of the evolution of thinking on poverty, Kanbur and Squire (2001) concluded by asking what Rowntree would have to say if he were alive today. They suggested he might be surprised, one hundred years on, that income was still a proxy for poverty, but he would have been likely to agree that health and education were important factors in well-being. What might some of the founding fathers of quantitative economics or classical political economy have to say were they alive today? All would likely emphasize the essential link between poverty and economic welfare. However, Marx might add that any overemphasis on economic welfare would deny the broader aspects of the human condition. Smith, for his part, might point to the corrupting influence on moral sentiments of overemphasis on money and income. One might speculate that Quesnay, Ricardo and Malthus would take a close interest in the role of malnutrition, given their shared interest in agricultural output, and Petty might well have focused on the provision of public goods such as health and education given his work on public finance and fiscal policy. However, it might well be John Stuart Mill who would have the most to say about the current poverty debates, given his focus on the importance of economic, political and social freedoms.

References

Adelman, Irma and Cynthia Morris (1973), *Economic Growth and Social Equity in Developing Countries*, Stanford, CA: Stanford University Press.
Alkire, Sabina (2002), *Valuing Freedoms*, Oxford: Oxford University Press.
Chambers, Robert (1983), *Rural Development: Putting the First Last*, London: Intermediate Technology Development Group.
Chambers, Robert (1994), 'Participatory rural appraisal: challenges, potentials, and paradigm', *World Development*, **22** (10), 1437–51.
Chambers, Robert (1997), *Whose Reality Counts? Putting the First Last*, London: Intermediate Technology Development Group.
Chambers, Robert (2001), 'The best of both worlds?' in Ravi Kanbur (ed.), *Q-Squared: Qualitative and Quantitative Methods of Poverty Appraisal*, Washington DC: Permanent Black.
Chambers, Robert (2006), 'Poverty unperceived: traps, biases and agenda', IDS Working Paper 270, Institute of Development Studies, Brighton.
Chambers, Robert and Gordon Conway (1992), 'Sustainable rural livelihoods: practical concepts for the 21st century', IDS Discussion Paper No. 296, Institute of Development Studies, Brighton.
Chenery, Hollis, Montek Ahluwalia, Clive Bell, John Duloy and Richard Jolly (1974), *Redistribution with Growth*, Oxford: Oxford University Press for the World Bank.
Cornia, Giovanni A., Richard Jolly and Frances Stewart (eds) (1987), *Adjustment with a Human Face, Volume I: Protecting the Vulnerable and Promoting Growth*, Oxford: Clarendon Press.
Dollar, David and Aart Kraay (2002), 'Growth is good for the poor', *Journal of Economic Growth*, **7** 195–225.
Foster, James, Joel Greer and Eric Thorbecke (1984), 'A class of decomposable poverty measures', *Econometrica*, **52**, 761–6.

Harriss, John (2006), *Why Understanding of Social Relations Matters More for Policy on Chronic Poverty than Measurement*, London and Manchester: Chronic Poverty Research Centre.

Hickey, Sam and Giles Mohan (2003), 'Relocating participation within a radical politics of development: citizenship and critical modernism', draft working paper prepared for the conference 'Participation: From Tyranny to Transformation? Exploring new approaches to participation in development', University of Manchester, 27–28 February.

Hulme, David, Karen Moore and Andrew Shepherd (2001), 'Chronic poverty: meanings and analytical frameworks', CPRC Working Paper No. 2, Chronic Poverty Research Centre, Manchester and London.

ILO (1977), *Meeting Basic Needs: Strategies for Eradicating Mass Poverty and Unemployment*, Geneva: International Labour Office.

Kanbur, Ravi and Lyn Squire (2001), 'The evolution of thinking about poverty: exploring the contradictions', in Gerald M. Meier and Joseph E. Stiglitz (eds), *Frontiers of Development Economics*, Oxford: Oxford University Press.

Kiely, Ray (1999), 'The last refuge of the noble savage? A critical assessment of post-development theory', *European Journal of Development Research*, **11**, 30–55.

Kingdon, Geeta G. and John Knight (2004), 'Do people mean what they say? Implications for subjective survey data', GPRG Working Paper No. 3, Global Poverty Research Group, Oxford.

Maxwell, Simon (1998), 'Comparisons, convergence and connections: development studies in North and South', *IDS Bulletin*, **29** (1), 20–31.

Maxwell, Simon (1999), 'What can we do with a rights-based approach to development?' ODI Briefing Paper 3, Overseas Development Institute, London.

McGregor, J. Allister (2006), 'Researching well-being: from concepts to methodology', Working Paper No. 20, Well-Being in Developing Countries (WeD) Research Group, Bath.

Morris, David (1979), *Measuring the Condition of the World's Poor: The Physical Quality of Life Index*, London: Cass.

Narayan, Deepa, Raj Patel, Kai Schafft, Anne Rachemacher and Sarah Koch-Schulte (1999), *Voices of the Poor: Can Anyone Hear Us?* Washington DC: World Bank.

Nussbaum, Martha (2000), *Women and Human Development: The Capabilities Approach*, Cambridge: Cambridge University Press.

Seers, Dudley (1963), 'The limitations of the special case', *Bulletin of the Oxford Institute of Economics and Statistics*, **25** (2), 77–98.

Sen, Amartya (1999), *Development as Freedom*, Oxford: Oxford University Press.

Shankland, Alex (2000), 'Analysing policy for sustainable livelihoods', IDS Research Report No. 49 (September), Institute of Development Studies, Brighton.

Streeten, Paul (1984), 'Basic needs: some unsettled questions', *World Development*, **12** (9), 973–80.

Stewart, Frances (1985), *Basic Needs in Developing Countries*, Baltimore, MA: Johns Hopkins University Press.

UNDP (1990–2007), *Human Development Report*, Geneva: United Nations Development Programme.

World Bank (various years), *World Development Report*, Washington DC: World Bank.

See also the entries on: Capability approach; Human development; Income distribution; Inequality; Needs and well-being; Amartya Sen.

52 Prices
Paul Downward

Introduction

This chapter explores the links between various accounts of prices and their normative character. Classical, neoclassical and heterodox analyses of prices are examined. Three key features of the discussion should be noted at the outset. First, unlike classical and neoclassical economics, the normative content of heterodox analysis is unclear, commensurate with its emergent nature. For heterodox analysis, only suggested lines of enquiry exist.[1] In this regard, this chapter notes some issues for future deliberation rather than providing an *account* of prices and ethics per se. Second, the discussion draws freely upon a variety of ethical perspectives, including virtue ethics, deontological ethics and consequentialist ethics (see, for example, Norman 1983; Vardy and Grosch 1999). This is because elements of these ethical theories are maintained as having greater or lesser relevance to understanding and evaluating particular theories. Moreover, the various traditions of thought each contain different, if implicit, conceptions of 'just' or 'fair' prices.[2] Finally, drawing upon Downward (1999, 2000, 2004) and a critical-realist methodological framework, the chapter maintains a distinction in heterodox analysis between theories of *price* and theories of *pricing*. The different methodological characteristics implied by this distinction have implications for ethical analysis.

Normative diagnosis: relationships between fact and value

Classical economics

The classical economic analysis of prices was derived from a focus on calibrating the value and distribution of production in terms of social classes. 'Use value' thus resided in the objective conditions of production, and was measured by prices of production. Market prices, reflecting conditions of exchange, or 'exchange value' could deviate from these prices. In this regard the classical economic schema embraced elements of more ancient thinking rooted in Aristotle and Aquinas that 'just prices' were inevitably associated with economic creation and it was this that laid the foundations of intrinsic value or worth. Consequently, prices of production governed the ability of the economy to either reproduce or to grow and were the essential numeraire of economic well-being.

This is not to deny differences in nuance or fundamental theoretical interpretation within the classical schema. For example, both Sen (1987) and Walsh (2000, 2003) attribute to Smith the explicit ethical concern that the most relevant *motivation* for economic activity reflected the virtue of prudence, that is, reason and understanding, in combination with self-interest. Such prudence, moreover, could be sacrificed for the common good, by embracing other virtues, such as humanity, justice and generosity. This suggests that the economic values captured by the calculation of prices of production according to, say, models of intersectoral production do not necessarily reflect well-being.

This point was made all the more starkly by Marx, who focused on the exploitation implied by the division of surplus in capitalism. In contrast, however, Putnam (2002), Walsh (1998, 2003) and Sen (1987) identify Ricardo's analysis as focusing primarily upon technical rather than ethical issues. Ricardo's emphasis finds its logical conclusion in Sraffa (1960) and potentially other neo-Ricardian analyses of intersectoral prices in which ethics are not directly discussed.

Neoclassical economics
Ethics has nonetheless always played a central role in discussions of neoclassical prices, but the relationship is a convoluted one. To begin with, Jevons (1871) integrated mathematics into 'moral science' through the use of calculus, drawing upon the 'concrete deductive method' of J.S. Mill.[3] Moral science was identified with Bentham's utilitarianism, and subsequently individual *self-interest* was presented as the predominant motivation in economic agency. Market exchange, rather than the conditions of production, was said to derive prices, thus reconciling the differential subjective valuations placed on resources by individual agents. Prices were viewed as automatically 'fair'. It was proposed, moreover, that such individual valuations could be added together to generate a collective statistic for economic well-being.

In contrast, subsequent developments in consumer and producer theory, culminating in Walrasian general equilibrium theory, focused explicitly on establishing the technical possibility of a set of prices through which market exchange could allocate all resources. The technicalities involved suggested a shift of emphasis away from concern about the normative character of prices, as elaborated by Bergson (1938); and flaws in the additive form of a social welfare function were established as a result of this theoretical work. Subsequent contributions by Hicks (1939) and Kaldor (1939), drawing upon the work of Pareto (1896) and Barone ([1908] 1935) and under the banner of the 'New Welfare Economics', consequently rejected the calibration of social welfare through the addition of cardinally measurable utilities. These contributors established the view that utility is an ordinal measurement and that optimal economic 'efficiency' is established when any subsequent reallocation of resources leaves at least one individual worse off.

The first and second fundamental theorems of welfare economics provide the links between normative issues and the technical analysis of Walrasian general equilibrium. These theorems maintain that a Walrasian competitive equilibrium is Pareto efficient, and that Pareto efficient equilibria can be achieved via the Walrasian competitive mechanism.[4] It is important to recognize that a number of alternative prices may achieve this efficiency criterion equally well. A further explicit and arbitrary ethical judgement is thus required to specify a social welfare function that establishes a unique social optimum. One either has to aggregate utilities or use prices to derive an aggregate value of output, but prices will depend on the distribution of income. However, this would involve an appropriate weighting of different income endowments and, to a degree, interpersonal comparisons of utility. The same can be said of attempts to consider any policy initiative that seeks to redistribute resources, as discussed by Kaldor (1939), Hicks (1939) and Scitovsky (1941).

An uneasy link is therefore clearly evident in neoclassical economics between its analytical and normative content. This linkage has helped to sustain the traditional view that there should be a duality between positive and normative economics. This position is summarized in Friedman (1953), which advocates a focus on the 'positive' aspect of economics concerned with a body of systematized knowledge regarding what 'is' as opposed to what 'ought to be' such that 'Positive economics is in principle independent of any particular ethical position' (ibid., p. 24). Walrasian perfect competition is recommended as an exemplar because it yields clear and unambiguous testable predictions.

A further complication is that recent contributions to neoclassical economics by Becker (1974, 1976, 1992) emphasize the possibility of applying the rational choice framework of optimizing behaviour to social interactions and of incorporating alternative motivations for economic agents, including those of an explicitly ethical or moral character. In this sense virtuous or envious behaviour is treated as a specific case of a broader utilitarian approach, because these specific motivations for behaviour will incur opportunity costs implied in the shadow prices that govern the resource allocation involved to meet the objectives. For example, opportunity costs are evident if expenditures are required to accrue a good reputation or to undermine that of someone else, or one might purchase 'ethical' products at a higher price than alternatives or make charitable donations. In this respect, utility maximization becomes generalized to the trading of moral values *which in themselves have prices* and this is primarily driven through 'self-interest' being defined differentially by the self. Values, however, remain fundamentally entangled in the analysis. After all, utilitarianism is presupposed. Putnam (2002), and of course others, thus argue that facts and values are 'entangled', and this entanglement is said to have specific features.

Heterodox economics
A major issue in the neoclassical approach is that prices, from whichever specific theoretical contribution is discussed, reflect subjective utilities, and their determination rests on a concept of rationality that espouses the optimization of a goal. Sen (1987) has argued that this conflates notions of economic agency and economic well-being, because one must necessarily lead to the other in a logically tight mapping. This is problematic for a number of reasons, as exemplified in discussions of prices.

In the 1930s, empirical analyses of industry revealed that growing monopoly power could lead prices to be set consistently above costs, and with potentially persistent profits. The degree of monopoly (Lerner 1934) that this reflected might then well reflect an unfair price inasmuch as it is connected with the exercise of power. These ideas have, of course, become the central focus of the industrial organization literature, much of which shares the concerns of heterodox economics insofar as predicting price behaviour is concerned (see Downward 1999, 2000, 2004).

Yet, as Sen (1987) also argues, agency may well reflect a different character of choice, for example, one in which incomplete information exists. Well-being may also be judged in terms of the achievements of and opportunities available to an individual in specific contexts, and these are, of course, tied to agents' freedom to act *even if* failing to achieve valued outcomes. Such issues are implied, if not by Sen, in heterodox accounts of pricing processes, the normative characters of which are not always fully transparent. On one hand, norms, routines and administrative organizational procedures find a rationale in coping with uncertainty in which the possibility of optimizing is not accepted by the agents themselves, though it may remain an aspiration. On the other hand, there are hints at an explicit moral dimension to price-setting by the economic agents themselves.

In studying actual business behaviour, Means (1936) distinguished between prices set by large corporations as being either administered or monopoly prices. Whilst the latter would be unfair, correspondent with industrial organization concepts, the former reflects the realities of pricing policies, perhaps born of technical requirements, in large-scale production. Even if such prices were set by government and fair in the sense of not exceeding costs, then their inevitable inflexibility would make them an unsuitable base for government policy in coordinating the economy. The implication is that prices cannot perform the coordinating function implied in neoclassical theory.

The idea that prices that reflect costs are fair, of course, echoes classical economics. Significantly, other studies of the actual behaviour of firms surveyed by Downward (1999) express similar sentiments. These recognize firms' common practice of defending goodwill and long-run reputation and achieving long-term objectives by setting 'fair prices' and following procedures so as not to 'antagonize' customers. The upshot is that adjusting prices in line with costs is seen as acceptable business practice, as a means of earning a justifiable long-run return. Short-run price adjustments to capitalize on movements in market demand are less so. It is noteworthy that these findings apply most to smaller firms, for which business networks are probably most transparent. So too, these studies recognize that competition often embraces 'known rivalry'. In such a context, personal contact and attitudes are likely to shape behaviour such that, particularly with smaller scale organizations, prices are also set to meet concerns regarding the firm's prestige and to avoid personal worries such as financial embarrassment. Finally, popular movements such as 'fair trade' build on such notions, championing higher prices where they reflect the 'true' cost of production, in this case defined as guaranteeing an acceptable return for farmers in developing countries.

It is clear that neoclassical economics would interpret such concepts differently as implied earlier. Explanations would draw upon 'competitive' pressure or the rational individual cost-benefit calculation of reputational investment. However, it follows that an alternative perspective would be to recognize that a whole series of value judgements, some of which are ethical, can be seen to underpin pricing decisions, at least from the agents' perspective. Some resonance with the classical economic perspective is also implied, in the agent balancing self-interest against other values. However, this insight emerges from a focus upon the distribution of resources, through appropriate pricing of resources at the level of specific agents and organizations rather than social class and the broader economy.

Ethics and heterodox pricing and prices

The above discussion raises two important issues, both of which are relevant to producing a more logical account of how values and price/pricing theory are related if one seeks to reject the utilitarian account, which is implied in heterodox economics, and upon which one can build a fuller ethical account. The first concerns the nature of the broader ethical perspective from which agent behaviour, to which a theory of prices or pricing refers, is understood and evaluated from outside the context of the research without drawing upon utilitarianism. The second, related, issue is the legitimacy of the role of norms and implied obligations in theories of prices and pricing. This is important, because these seem to be features of agent activity and are stressed in heterodox theories.

Regarding the first, both Putnam (2002, 2003) and Walsh (2003) identify Sen's (1993,

1999) capability approach as a potential framework in which to reintegrate moral discussion into economic evaluation, but rejecting utilitarianism. They seek to develop this perspective in the context of rebuilding an 'enriched' classical economic approach drawing upon Smith. Sen (1993, 1999) argues that entitlements and access to commodities, rooted in the virtue of freedom, structure capabilities to achieve outcomes, the latter of which become realized as 'functionings'. In this regard, distinctions made by classical economists between the necessities of life and other goods could be modified to account for differential advantages in life. Prices in this respect would be indices of some socially relative set of values, based on distinctions between commodities.

Notwithstanding earlier comments, it is not entirely clear that this 'structural' and price-focused interpretation of Sen helps to make a sufficient break with neoclassical economics and an overtly consequentialist orientation. This is because potentially the focus could be on outcomes of processes. Moreover, Becker (1973) clearly identifies how utilitarianism can account for the consumption of a good that is used in the production of a more basic commodity and also reminds readers that Bentham's and Marshall's concepts of utility were *inventories* of a set of 'pleasures' or 'pains', which as Mill suggested, could have a hierarchical content. A richer account is clearly required.

Sen emphasizes that there will be differential access to entitlements, that is, to freedom, and that agents and structures *combine* to transform these differential entitlements into capabilities, from which choice produces functionings or outcomes. There is therefore clearly an element of process connected to outcomes as implied in Sen's account, but this should be emphasized. It is here that a richer account might be developed, but this requires an elaboration of structure and agency.

Critical realism offers such an account of the relationship of structure and agency *as a process*. However, there are clear consequences of adopting this approach, which is to shift some of the focus away from freedom and entitlements as virtues *per se*, towards the importance of structures, and their moral character, from which actions jointly emerge through their interaction with agency. For example, critical realism maintains that voluntary human action, or efficient cause, combines with involuntary pre-existing social structures, or material cause. Price-setting can be thus understood. In methodological terms there is a subjective/objective dialectic that produces prices as outcomes that are historically relative but also partially independent of the actions of the individuals that set them, reflecting enduring decision-making structures.

Consequently a critical-realist approach might be important to maintain the logical distinction between individual agency and well-being as argued by Sen. It would also provide a logical foundation for an external – to the research context or specific agents – moral evaluation of choices, as it does not draw upon pure subjectivity, in either utilitarian or social constructivist terms. This would help in rationalizing policy activism.

These issues are important to address not only in terms of providing a logically consistent framework for examining ethical issues but, as Nussbaum (2003) argues, because Sen seems reluctant to specify the content of any moral improvement, that is, contribution to well-being, other than to focus upon the concept of freedom. This seems insufficient for evaluating well-being in an Aristotelian-virtue sense and, consequently, one over which political consensus can be built. For example political and decision-making processes will hinge upon and produce space- and time-relative valuations of resource transfer. It is accepted, as discussed earlier, that in practical terms, these will not be the product of the aggregation of the complete set of individual preference/value orderings. In contrast, as the outcome of a less restrictive rule, or set of criteria, this aggregation may at best indicate what functionings are currently viewed as contributing to a good life. They will also rely upon the freedoms that agents have to achieve them according to current social arrangements. Given a historically enduring set of decision-making criteria, comparable orderings of alternative outcomes are possible. Over time, however, such criteria shift and thus evaluations differ. Whilst the key message of Sen's analysis is that well-being can be said to have been enhanced when agents seeking particular capabilities now have the freedom to obtain and exercise them, problems arise, as with Paretian criteria, when some agents' freedoms to act need to be constrained in order to facilitate such options; in other words, when redistribution of resources is required. This might manifest with respect to taxation being required to subsidize the price of health-care. There is nothing inherent in political systems that ensures this could be the case if desired, or indeed that establishes this as a desirable case. Concrete discussion of alternatives needs to be aired and political will established to pursue relevant options.

That said, an important element of the critical-realist view of decision-making is that agency necessarily implies elements of moral obligation, echoing MacIntyre's (1981) argument that practices and virtues interact and reinforce themselves. Moral content thus becomes *objective* in recognizing the relational context of specific agents, which transcends them as specific individuals. The moral content, however, remains *relative* to the prevailing contingent social relationships and the values which underpin them.

The upshot of this discussion is that as far as pricing and prices are concerned, both the decision-making apparatuses and the criteria of choice that exist within and surrounding the firm, for example, in public policy agencies and consumer representation, as well as the consequences of such decision-making, manifest as prices, must logically and separately represent potential foci over which discussions about the 'rightness' or 'wrongness' of prices can take place. Significantly this implies not treating pricing processes, or prices, as outcomes and their impact upon citizens' well-being as synonymously related – as implied in the taut logic of rational choice theory and utilitarianism. Different processes might yield the same outcomes and well-being, or the same process might yield differential well-being. Rather, evaluations and recommendations need to examine specific arrangements instead of drawing upon universal claims. This scenario is implied because it reflects a particular array of capabilities producing a set of particular functionings from an agent-structure interaction that is necessarily embedded in moral content. The justness of prices then is automatically evaluated. This is done either implicitly, through agents conforming to current norms and behaviour, or explicitly, through formal representation and expressed concerns.

Significantly, the competition regulation bodies currently in existence are an implicit recognition of the necessity and practicality of this latter process of evaluation. Clearly, however, in today's context, utilitarian universal epistemic values as embedded in the industrial organization literature dominate concepts of appropriate prices and the organizational arrangements to achieve them. The focus is primarily upon fairness as being the inverse of the degree of monopoly. To change this set of values would require a shift in political discourse. In turn, it is argued here that this would require a shift towards the emphasis and methodological character of pricing theories of the sort developed by heterodox analysis.

Notes

This chapter has benefited from the comments received at the SCHEME workshop, held at the University of Stirling, 19 May 2007.

1. See Downward (1999) for a discussion of what I understand by the neoclassical paradigm in the context of pricing. I essentially define this in terms of the methodological characteristics of analysis rather than a specific subject matter.
2. This implies the prior recognition that, despite claims to the contrary, economic theory cannot be understood as value-free, not withstanding allusions to the contrary in elements of neoclassical thought.
3. This is not to imply that mathematical relations were not employed in political economy before then. The difference here is that it is identified as *the* appropriate method of analysis.
4. Consequently Walrasian competition is sufficient but not necessary for Pareto efficiency.

References

Barone, Enrico ([1908] 1935), *Il Ministro della Produzione nello Stato Collettivista, Giornale degli Economisti*, first translated and printed as 'The ministry of production in the collectivist state', in Friedrich A. Hayek (ed.), *Collectivist Economic Planning*, London: Routledge and Kegan Paul, pp. 245–90.

Becker, Gary (1973), 'On the new theory of consumer behaviour', *Swedish Journal of Economics*, **75**, 378–95.

Becker, Gary (1974), 'A theory of social interactions', *Journal of Political Economy*, **82** (6), 1063–91.

Becker, Gary (1976), *The Economic Approach to Human Behaviour*, Chicago, IL: University of Chicago Press.

Becker, Gary (1992), 'The economic way of looking at life', *Journal of Political Economy*, **101** (3), 385–409.

Bergson, Abram (1938), 'A reformulation of certain aspects of welfare economics', *Quarterly Journal of Economics*, **52**, 310–34.

Downward, Paul M. (1999), *Pricing Theory in Post Keynesian Economics: A Realist Approach*, Cheltenham, UK and Northampton, MA, USA: Edward Elgar.

Downward, Paul M. (2000), 'A realist appraisal of post Keynesian pricing theory', *Cambridge Journal of Economics*, **24** (2), 211–24.

Downward, Paul M. (2004), 'Post Keynesian pricing theory: alternative foundations and prospects for future research', *Journal of Economic Psychology*, **25** (5), 661–70.

Friedman, Milton (1953), 'The methodology of positive economics', in *Essays in Positive Economics*, Chicago, IL: Chicago University Press, pp. 3–43.

Hicks, John R. (1939), *Value and Capital*, Oxford: Clarendon Press.

Jevons, William S. (1871), *Theory of Political Economy*, London: Macmillan and Company.

Kaldor, Nicholas (1939), 'Welfare propositions of economics and interpersonal comparisons of utility', *Economic Journal*, **49**, 549–52.

Lerner, Abba (1934), 'The concept of monopoly and the measurement of monopoly power', *Review of Economic Studies*, **1**, 157–75.

MacIntyre, Alasdair (1981), *After Virtue: A Study in Moral Theory*, Notre Dame: University of Notre Dame Press.

Means, Gardiner C. (1936), 'Notes on inflexible prices', *American Economic Review*, **26** (1), Supplement, Papers and Proceedings of the Forty-eighth Annual Meeting of the American Economic Association, 23–35.

Norman, Richard (1983), *The Moral Philosophers: An Introduction to Ethics*, Oxford: Clarendon Press.

Nussbaum, Martha (2003), 'Tragedy and human capabilities: a response to Vivian Walsh', *Review of Political Economy*, **15** (3), 413–18.

Pareto, Vilfredo (1896), *Cours d'Economie Politique*, Lausanne: F. Rouge.

Putnam, Hilary (2002), *The Collapse of the Fact/Value Dichotomy and Other Essays*, Cambridge, MA: Harvard University Press.

Putnam, Hilary (2003), 'For ethics and economics without the dichotomies', *Review of Political Economy*, **15** (3), 395–412.

Scitovsky, Tibor (1941), 'A note on welfare propositions in economics', *Review of Economic Studies*, **9**, 77–88.

Sen, Amartya (1987), *On Ethics and Economics*, Oxford: Blackwell Publishing.

Sen, Amartya (1993), 'Capability and well being', in Martha Nussbaum and Amartya Sen (eds), *The Quality of Life*, Oxford: Clarendon Press.

Sen, Amartya (1999), *Development as Freedom*, Oxford: Oxford University Press.

Sraffa, Piero (1960), *Production of Commodities by Means of Commodities: Prelude to a Critique of Economic Theory*, Cambridge: Cambridge University Press.

Walsh, Vivian C. (1998), 'Normative and positive classical economics', in H.D. Kurz and N. Salvadori (eds), *The Elgar Companion to Classical Economics*, Vol. 2, Cheltenham, UK and Lyme, USA: Edward Elgar.
Walsh, Vivian C. (2000), 'Smith after Sen', *Review of Political Economy*, **5** (1), 1–25.
Walsh, Vivian C. (2003), 'Sen after Putnam', *Review of Political Economy*, **15** (3), 315–94.
Vardy, Peter and Paul Grosch (1999), *The Puzzle of Ethics*, London: Fount.

See also the entries on: Fact/value dichotomy; Market; Needs and well-being; Positive versus normative economics; Amartya Sen.

53 Protestant ethics
William Schweiker

Introduction

Foreshadowed by reform movements throughout Europe, the Protestant 'Reformation' broke onto the world scene in the early sixteenth century.[1] Protestant ethics is difficult to describe definitively, as it takes many forms. Moreover, diversity of expression makes it near impossible to isolate unifying themes. Nevertheless, Protestants have always insisted that the core of the Gospel, the Christian message, is the reality of God's free act of grace in Jesus Christ, accepted in faith and lived in love for the neighbour. In the words of Martin Luther, a central originating figure, in *The Freedom of the Christian*,

> [A] Christian lives not in himself, but in Christ and in his neighbor. Otherwise he is not a Christian. He lives in Christ by faith, in his neighbor through love. By faith he is caught up beyond himself into God. By love he descends beneath himself into his neighbor. (Luther [1520] 1961, p. 80)

The connection between faith and love is at the centre of Protestant ethics, although this is variously expressed by different Protestant churches.

This chapter explores the core aspects of Protestantism – faith and love, callings and spheres of life and ideas about the Church – in order to isolate the distinctiveness of Protestant ethics but also to note the most salient differences between Protestant communities. Insofar as this handbook examines the connection between economics and ethics, the following pages explain some of the ways in which Protestants conceive of economic life. For many reasons, some of which have little to do with faith, Protestants helped to advance modern democratic political forms as well as the spread of capitalist economies. So, our initial account of Protestant ethics will later be linked to economic life. The chapter concludes with comments on the future of Protestant ethics.

Features of Protestant ethics

This chapter cannot explain all of the differences between Protestant Christians on moral matters (see Gustafson 1978; Meilaender and Werpehowski 2005). Happily, there are shared basic convictions. Christianity has been called a religion of love. Of course, Christians have engaged in wars, crusades and complicity with unjust secular powers. Nevertheless, the message of Christianity is, first, God's love in creating reality and also God's redeeming love for the world embodied in Jesus Christ. Conjoined to the belief in divine love, the second fulcrum around which Christian life revolves is the double command to love God and to love one's neighbour as one's self. Jesus even bid his disciples to love the enemy. As John Wesley, the founder of Methodism put it, Christian perfection is love of God and every neighbour and in this love is found the bond between true happiness and holiness.

Every Christian accepts these beliefs about God's love in creation and redemption and also the freedom and responsibility to love God and others. Nevertheless, differences between Christian communities are important for understanding Protestant ethics. Medieval Roman Catholic moral thought is typically seen in the writings of St Thomas Aquinas. He held that faith, hope and love are 'theological' virtues (Aquinas *Summa Theologiae* I–II, qq. 62). The theological virtues, like all virtues, are the perfection of human capacities. However, the theological virtues are given by God and received through the sacraments. The Christian must cooperate with God's action in order to grow in holiness, and salvation is attained only through becoming perfectly holy as God is holy. Furthermore, 'love' is the 'mother of the virtues'. This is because God is love and the end of human happiness is union with God. The emphasis on growth in love and eternal blessedness has meant that the moral life and taking sacraments are essential to salvation.

The so-called 'magisterial reformers' of the sixteenth century (for example, Martin Luther, Ulrich Zwingli and John Calvin) saw the Roman Catholic scheme of salvation as 'works righteousness', meaning that an individual must somehow work for and merit salvation. That scheme of salvation seemed to displace God's grace in redemption with human moral effort. Following St Paul's letter to the Galatians, these Protestants insisted that we are 'saved while yet sinners' and, therefore, no cooperation between God's grace and human effort is needed for salvation. Faith is central in one's relation to God; the trust of the heart alone gives God glory and clings to God's trustworthiness. One is justified by grace through faith in Christ alone, as Luther would put it. This means, importantly, that Protestants rejected any notion that faith, love or hope could be defined as 'virtues', that is, as human excellences. With these insights about faith and salvation many things change in the Christian conception of existence. The sacraments are no longer the main means to receive grace; it is received through the scriptures and the proclamation within the Church of God's saving action in Christ. Every Christian is a 'priest'; each can proclaim the Word and minister to others, just as Christ gave of himself. Every sphere of life is an appropriate place for Christian existence, including marriage and political office; there is no division between those seeking perfection (for example, monks and nuns) and ordinary Christians. Correlatively, the commands of the Bible apply to every Christian; there is no distinction between precepts and the so-called 'counsels of perfection'. Emphasis is on personal responsibility (which some commentators believe leads to modern individualism). Finally, the relation of love and faith are decisively changed. Insofar as one is saved through faith in Christ, then love is not the mother and perfection of faith, but, rather, love is the way in which faith becomes active in the world for the sake of others. This last point and its connection to various spheres of life and 'callings' are essential to a grasp of most, if not all, Protestant ethics, especially for economic matters.

At the core of Protestant ethics, as generally described, is the essential connection between faith, freedom and love. Through faith in God's redeeming action in Christ, the Christian is free from sin, damnation and the demands of moral perfectionism. That freedom to exist in grace before God manifests itself in the freedom to love others. Early Protestants worried that the Roman Catholic scheme of salvation meant, practically speaking, that a Christian must do works of love for others but ultimately for her or his own sanctification. If Christian love is a 'virtue' and the point of the Christian life is to attain sufficient holiness to merit heaven, then it is too easy for the neighbour to be made a means to the end of the believer's salvation. To forestall that possibility, Protestants have always insisted that justification presupposes nothing in the believer and that salvation is not contingent on virtuous action. Faith and its distinctive form of freedom become active through love of the neighbour without prudential calculation of merit or virtue.[2] This is true even of the 'Radical Reformers', or Anabaptists, who emphasized an understanding of the Church as a voluntary association of believers. The act of faith is marked by the decision to join the Church through baptism and enter into a life of discipleship to Jesus and love of others.

This schematic relation of faith and love means that Protestants conceive of human existence as transpiring in two realms, or under two governments as John Calvin (1966, BK 4, 20) put it. One exists in the Kingdom of Christ through faith and simultaneously in the worldly kingdom through one's calling or vocation. While the Christian should live in the world and do acts of love, it is plain that neither Christians nor others always do. The kingdom of the World is under the domination of sin and evil; Christians are not only saved but they are also always sinners (Luther [1535] 1963). However, Protestants have responded differently to the 'world'. For Luther and his followers, one needs various means to restrain human wickedness, ranging from coercive political power to the commands of the natural moral law, revealed anew in scripture. While Christians are 'free' in faith before God, in temporal life one remains under the moral law and within the structures of the social order. According to John Calvin and the 'Reformed Protestants', God is to be honoured in all areas of life; all human activity – family, politics, economics – should be in the service of God who is sovereign over all existence. To this end, various Radical Reformers and their communities have sought to separate themselves from the world, forming alternative communities. Later, we will trace the importance of these differences for economic life.

For Calvin and Luther a Christian has a 'calling' or 'vocation' within the social order and must abide by the goods and duties required of a specific social sphere or what was also called an 'order of creation'. One might be (say) a mother or pastor or teacher with the joys and responsibilities that flow from the natural, created shape of human associations. The requirements of right motherhood, for instance, might be to discern rationally the demands of home and family and the raising of children. The good teacher has to meet requirements of education and formation. One might be called to be a magistrate and thus, if necessary, to wield the 'sword', that is, to use coercive, even lethal, force for the sake of restraining evil and promoting the common social good. And according to Calvin, the 'state' must even protect the right worship of God. These duties or responsibilities of one's calling can be acts of love in which faith is active. They might also bring one a good name, genuine joy and social honours, forms of what Luther called 'civil righteousness'. One might be called a good mother, a wonderful teacher or a just magistrate. The moral predicates assigned to individuals fulfilling their calling (for example, 'good', 'wonderful', 'just') arise from the praise of others for one's conduct and therefore signal the social nature of human existence and the moral life. Yet because one is saved by faith and not works, those forms of honour and righteousness have no value for salvation. They might be ways to honour God, as Calvin taught, but they do not merit redeeming grace. Social spheres and callings are, rather, the context for works of Christian love and moral responsibilities. Interestingly, Protestantism has in some situations been socially conservative when stress is placed on the unchangeable nature of callings and orders. If God has ordained the state or family order or the nature of the religious community, then those orders cannot and should not be changed despite historical pressure. In other circumstances, when Protestants have insisted on freedom of conscience and the lordship of Christ, they have been a force for the historical transformation of social structures.

This broad framework for understanding the Christian life provides the means by which Protestants specify the details of political, economic, personal and social ethics. It is also the point at which Protestants differ among themselves insofar as the connection between the Kingdom of Christ and the Earthly Kingdom can be variously construed (see Niebuhr 1951). These differences between Protestants provide the background for explaining options in economic ethics. One can explore these differences by focusing on the relation between self-interested economic striving and the demand on Christians to labour in love for the common good.

Varieties of economic ethics
Within the Western Christian tradition, distinct but related options have aimed at the resolution of conflict between self-interest and the common good. In the Middle Ages, Thomas Aquinas annunciated the theological and metaphysical backing to Roman Catholic economic ethics. 'Now it should be borne in mind', he wrote, 'that the common good is, accordingly to right reason, to be preferred to one's proper good. As a result, each member of the body is directed to the good of the whole by natural instinct' (Aquinas 1960, p. 250; see also Aquinas *Summa Theologiae* I–II, qq. 90–92; Augustine 1984, BK 19). Christians may use private property but always within the context of a commitment to the common good. The priority of the whole over the parts does not mean a denial of an individual's good. Right reason discerns in God the *summum bonum* (the highest good). It thus recognizes no ultimate conflict between self-interest and the common good. This metaphysical vision has continued to dominate Roman Catholic ethics up to today. The social good is envisioned as a solidarity or social commitment to identify a common vision of the good life as well as to protect the individual and the poor (see Holland 2003).

Protestant ethics in its various forms offers a different account. These have taken manifold expressions ranging from the primitive communism of some Anabaptist communities to the famous, or infamous, contribution of Calvinism to what Max Weber called the 'spirit of capitalism'. As noted before, for many Protestants in the Radical Reformation the relation between Church and world is defined by a separation. The Christian community is to remove itself from the world and witness to a form of life beyond greed and violence. From Menno Simons to the Swiss Anabaptists, these movements sought to reclaim a vision of discipleship to Jesus. Their moral reasoning followed a simple if demanding logic: since Jesus did not bear the sword or hold political office or take vows, Christians ought to forgo political obligations in the civil order. Because Christ bid his followers to give to the poor and not accumulate wealth, the Christian community should live in bonds of mutual care and support around economic needs. Christians are called to be in the world but not of the world. A Christian ethic requires rejection of earthly goods, values and social responsibilities. The task of the Church is to bear witness to the world as a community of common service and peace.

Other Protestants, mainly those influenced by Luther, insist on a tension between Church and world and therefore consent to worldly power with respect to political and economic matters. Reformed Protestants following John Calvin and some English Protestants believe that the Church is charged to transform the world in order to help to realize the Kingdom of God on earth. All spheres of life are to be put to the service and honour of God. Not surprisingly, many thinkers, both inside and outside theological circles, agreed with Max Weber's famous thesis advanced in his *The Protestant Ethic and the Spirit of Capitalism* ([1904–05] 1958). His contention was that the faith of various Protestant groups, mainly Calvinists, was a crucial, maybe the crucial, motivation for the rise of modern capitalism. He reasoned that insecurity among Calvinists about predestination, the idea that God has predetermined who will be saved and who will be damned, led to a quest for signs that one was elected by God to salvation. Success from labour was seen as the favour of God. When one is willing to work and accumulate and save money in quest of assurance of election, then capital grows as it did among those Protestants. Weber called 'inner worldly asceticism' the attitude of those who acted morally but with self-interest in the marketplace while having assurance of salvation. Reformed Protestants combined the idea of God blessing people for their right conduct with a specific attitude and moral commitment conducive to the rise of capitalism.

While Protestants did not intend to create modern capitalism, the result of their piety was to foster the view of life, an inner-worldly asceticism, needed for capitalism to arise. According to theologian Ernst Troeltsch (1986, p. 73), this faith 'becomes the parent of a tireless systematically disciplined laboriousness'. Especially among the Calvinists, this ethics provided, as one scholar notes, '[a] set of values in society that offer[s] vigorous encouragement to self-interest in the market and yet maintain[s] powerful normative inhibitions on the expression of self-interest in many other less socially acceptable areas' (Nelson 2001, p. 6). Of course, Troeltsch, like Max Weber, thought capitalistic striving had turned into an iron cage: 'In the breaking down of the motives of ease and enjoyment, asceticism lays the foundations of the tyranny of work over men' (Troelstch 1986, p. 73).[3]

The Calvinistic resolution did not rely solely on the inducements and inhibitions of self-interest. Later Reformed theologians, including Abraham Kuyper of the Netherlands, articulated a social theory built on the idea of 'sphere sovereignty'. Social subsystems, such as politics, education, media and also economy, are here said to function appropriately to their own norms and purposes within a covenantal structure. A similar argument is found in Troeltsch's more Lutheran 'departments' or 'callings of life'.[4] Covenants, or implicit contracts, provide the normative perimeters for action within a social domain without demanding that all social subsystems be ordered by one system, as held by Roman Catholic thought. Asceticism in motives was matched to covenantal obligations in social action or Luther's idea of 'callings'; that is, these forms of Protestantism linked the desire for esteem before God to trust among people and thereby resolved the relation between self-interest and the common good.

Another variation of Protestant thought should be noted. English divines took a different tactic from Calvinism. In the famous sermon *The Use of Money*, John Wesley, drawing on the Anglican tradition, argued for the right use of money. He cited an ancient distinction, drawn from Clement of Alexandria and St Augustine, between those things that are to be used (*uti*) and those things that are to be enjoyed (*frui*). Confusion and vice arise when we enjoy or treasure things that only have use value. Granting that money can be used for ill, Wesley insisted that it 'is of unspeakable service to all civilized nations, in all common affairs of life: it is a most compendious instrument of transacting all manner of business, and (if we use it according to Christian wisdom) of doing all manner of good' (1975, p. 578).[5] Wesley even argued that one must 'gain all you can', 'save all you can' and 'give all you can'. The limits on acquisition and the orientation of economic action are the health and betterment of body and soul, one's own and one's neighbour. But Christians certainly are not enjoined to luxury or ease! A certain asceticism remains, as well as the awareness that social systems function by distinctive means, like markets and money. Still, the resolution of self-interest and the common good is found in the right love of God, self and neighbour. This makes the moral life, 'scriptural holiness' as Wesley called it, basic to social existence. The focus on love and Christian perfection is different from Roman Catholic ideas about the common good or the Calvinist 'sphere sovereignty' in response to conflicts of self-interest and common good or the kind of communism found among the Radical Reformers.

One can see, then, that differences between Protestants on economic ethics arise from alternative conceptions of the relation of Church and world. Earthly callings and works of love are not the means to salvation, but, rather, domains in which faith can be active in love for others. In the terms of moral theory, ultimate human good, one's relation to the divine, is linked to but distinct from obedience to norms of moral rightness and justice.

Given the modern expansion of capitalist systems, the growth of the nation-state and the general differentiation of Western societies into interlocking subsystems, it is not surprising, historically speaking, that there was a close connection between the spread of Protestant Christianity around the world and the flourishing of market capitalism. This is seen in the easy relations between free-market capitalism, mass consumption and American-style evangelicalism. In a different way, in the early twentieth century there was the co-called 'Social Gospel' movement in the United States and 'religious social- ism', largely Protestant, in Europe. For the followers of Social Gospel, the task was to Christianize the social order, meaning to combat various social ills including poverty and unjust wages. The religious socialists used biblical ideas of justice to challenge economic systems and insist on the priority of the poor in the struggle for the common good.

Protestantism alone did not bring about capitalism. Nevertheless, in nations perme- ated with Protestant freedom and activism vibrant market economies developed and advanced. This was especially the case during the age of colonialism and global evange- lism in the nineteenth and twentieth centuries. Often the market and the Gospel moved together, carried along by the forces of national policy, aspirations to empire, global evangelism and world wars. Importantly, in the twentieth century there was the birth and flowering of the ecumenical movement among Protestants which found institutional form in the World Council of Churches (WCC). Drawing on Christians around the world, the WCC has advocated tirelessly for economic and social justice. Anglican theologians from the Church of England, such as William Temple, and the various forms of liberation, black, feminist and Third World theologies, have all worked to raise the question of the justice of the economic system in light of the Christian message and the plight of the poor. These developments have sought social justice in the face of economic inequality and have found parallels in concerns expressed by modern popes and Roman Catholic bishop conferences around the world. Even today, some Protestants eagerly embrace capitalism while others seek to redress what they see as its moral and social failures.

It is against this backdrop that we speculate about the future of Protestant ethics in the age of global dynamics.

What future for Protestant ethics?
Globalization has been called 'modernity at large', 'high modernity' and even 'reflective modernity' (see Schweiker 2005; Steger 2003; Stackhouse et al. 2000–05). Whatever the designation, the current age has many features of 'modernity' (the dignity of the individual, differentiated societies, pluralistic cultures, democratic processes, rationalized social systems, capitalist markets and sovereignty of the nation-state) even as these features are in the process of readjustment and revision under the pressure of global forces: the break-up of colonial powers, media and communications technology, migrations of peoples, growth of international cities, worldwide spread of disease (for example, HIV), environmental crises and so on.

Insofar as this is the case, one would expect to see the globalization of Protestantism as well. This is true of the explosive growth in various forms of Protestantism throughout Latin America, Africa and parts of Asia, despite the retreat of the Protestant and Roman Catholic churches throughout Europe and other First World countries. Yet it is unclear what will be the form of Protestantism in an age of globally interdependent, post-colonial dynamics, shaped, moreover, by global capitalism. This is all the more true insofar as diversity within Protestantism itself is developing on the global scene.

While the actual future of Protestantism in its many forms is hard to determine, one can note features of its core ethical outlook that might and ought to contribute to a sustainable, humane and responsible future. First, Protestant communities might work with other political forces and religious communities to transform unjust and oppressive social structures. While the Kingdom of God will never be realized by human effort alone, the vibrancy of active love can and ought to become a power on the world scene. Second, with its distinctive understanding of callings and social spheres, Protestants have the ethical outlook needed to affirm the dignity of human labour and creativity and also to struggle for just economic conditions. Third, as a message of freedom through faith, the Protestant understanding of the Gospel provides a bulwark against the kinds of oppression and dehumanization that characterize the lives of many people. Fourth, because of the relation between faith and love, Protestants can and ought to join forces with religious and non-religious people in works of love; that is, in shared ethical projects aimed at the responsible respect for and enhancement of the integrity of life, human and non-human. Precisely because Protestants distinguish but do not separate faith from the moral life, shared moral projects between peoples need not be encumbered by religious differences. Fifth, given the profound entanglement between the global economy and the natural environment, we should expect to see Christians around the world care for the earth in ways that have distinctive economic implications. Ideas about stewardship, ownership and distribution of goods, as well as ecological burdens, can be applied to that end, along with other ideas. When it is the poor of the earth who suffer most from ecological degradation, it is clear that economic ethics must be linked to environmental concerns. Finally, the Protestant insistence that one is saved by grace and not works places strict limits on the continual maximization of human power through technology aimed at saving the human race and the planet. In a time in which all forms of life are increasingly endangered by the tremendous expansion of human power, the simple but pointed message of freedom from works through free grace has profound and enduring ethical meaning (see Klemm and Schweiker 2008).

It remains to be seen whether Protestant communities will make a unique contribution to the current global age, marked as it is by economic and ecological interdependence. Yet if the history of Protestantism is any indication, the future of the present age will also be shaped in some measure by the message of freedom and faith active in love. Certainly Protestant ethics will find new meaning within the whirl of global dynamics.

Notes

1. For helpful supplementary discussions see Sptize (2003), Hillerbrand (2007) and Lange (1992).
2. It is not surprising that ethics, like that of Immanuel Kant, which insist on treating human beings never only as means but also as ends find their roots in the Protestant outlook.
3. For more recent examinations of the place of asceticism in Christian ethics see Schweiker and Mathewes (2004).
4. For analogous arguments see Gramsci (2000), Walzer ([1983] 1990) and Stackhouse (1987).
5. While traditional Roman Catholic ethics looked to natural law and the virtues and Protestant Reformers to the Decalogue, Wesley found the heart and soul of the Christian life in the Sermon on the Mount.

References

Aquinas, Thomas (1960), 'On the perfection of the spiritual life', in Vernon J. Bourke (ed.), *The Pocket Aquinas*, New York: Pocket Books.

Aquinas, Thomas (1981), *Summa Theologiae II*, 5 vols, translated by the English Dominican Province, Westminster: Christian Classics.

Augustine, (1984) *City of God*, trans. Henry Bettenson, New York: Penguin Books.

Calvin, John (1966), *Institutes of the Christian Religion*, 2 vols, ed. John T. McNeill, Philadelphia: Westminister Press.

Gramsci, Antonio (2000), *The Antonio Gramsci Reader*, ed. Douglas Forgacs, New York: New York University Press.

Gustafson, James M. (1978), *Protestant and Roman Catholic Ethics: Prospects for Rapprochement*, Chicago, IL: University of Chicago Press.

Hillerbrand, Hans J. (2007), *The Protestant Reformation*, New York: Harper Perenial.

Holland, Joe (2003), *Modern Catholic Social Teaching: The Popes Confront the Industrial Age 1740–1958*, New York: Paulist.

Klemm, David E. and William Schweiker (2008), *Religion and the Human Future: An Essay on Theological Humanism*, Oxford: Blackwell.

Lange, Dietz (1992), *Ethik in Evangelischer Perspektive*, Göttingen: Vandenhoeck & Ruprecht.

Luther, Martin ([1520] 1961), 'The freedom of a Christian', in John Dillenberger (ed.), *Martin Luther: Selections from his Writings*, Garden City, NY: Anchor Books.

Luther, Martin ([1535] 1963), 'Commentary on Galatians', in *Luther's Works*, Vols 26–7, ed. Jaroslav Pelikan, Minneapolis, MN: Concordia Press.

Meilaender, Gilbert and William J. Werpehowski (eds) (2005), *The Oxford Handbook of Theological Ethics*, Oxford: Oxford University Press.

Nelson, Robert (2001), *Economics as Religion: From Samuelson to Chicago and Beyond*, University Park, PA: Pennsylvania State University Press.

Niebuhr, H. Richard (1951), *Christ and Culture*, New York: Harper and Row.

Schweiker, William (2005), *Theological Ethics and Global Dynamics: In the Time of Many Worlds*, Oxford: Blackwell Publishing.

Schweiker, William and Charles Mathewes (eds) (2004), *Having: Property and Possession in Social and Religious Life*, Grand Rapids, MI: Eerdmans.

Sptize, Lewis William (2003), *The Protestant Reformation, 1519–1559*, Minneapolis, MN: Concordia Publishing.

Stackhouse, Max L. (1987), *Public Theology and Political Economy: Christian Stewardship in Modern Society*, Grand Rapids, MI: Eerdmans.

Stackhouse, Max L. (ed) (2000–5), *God and Globalization*, 4 vols, Harrisburg, PA: Trinity Press International.

Steger, Manfred B. (2003), *Globalization: A Very Short Introduction*, Oxford: Oxford University Press.

Troelstch, Ernst (1986), *Protestantism and Progress: The Significance of Protestantism for the Rise of the Modern World*, Philadelphia, PA: Fortress Press.

Walzer, Michael ([1983] 1990), *Spheres of Justice: A Defense of Pluralism and Equality*, New York: Basic Books.

Weber, Max ([1904–05] 1958), *The Protestant Ethic and the Spirit of Capitalism*, trans. T. Parsons, New York: Charles Scribner's Sons.

Wesley, John (1975), 'The use of money', in *Sermon on Several Occasions*, First Series, London: Epworth Press.

See also the entries on: Thomas Aquinas; Religion; Max Weber and the Protestant work ethic.

54 Rationality
Shaun P. Hargreaves Heap

I

The dominant model of individual rationality in economics, sometimes known as the rational choice model, identifies individuals with their preferences and casts reason in the role of deciding how best to satisfy them. This is a calculative, instrumental sense of reason. Its task, much as David Hume suggested when famously averring reason as 'slave of the passions', is to work out the means to given ends.

A person's preferences are often represented in this tradition by a mathematical device called a 'utility' function. Some care is required with the term 'utility'. It reflects the historical association of this model with the moral philosophy of utilitarianism, yet that connection has long been lost. The utility function now simply assigns numbers to outcomes such that the highest number goes to the outcome that best satisfies a person's preferences, the second highest number goes to the next best, and so on until the least valued outcome gets the lowest number. This mapping enables simple mathematics to be used in the analysis of choice, because acting so as to best satisfy preferences is now the equivalent of choosing to maximize utility. To re-create the connection with the moral philosophy of utilitarianism would require in addition that these 'utility' numbers be interpersonally comparable, whereas they are entirely personal devices for representing preferences (and so by themselves are only likely to license a condition like Pareto optimality).

Little is said about a person's preferences on this account. They must satisfy certain conditions, like transitivity, otherwise one cannot sensibly talk about a person having a preference ordering, but their character is usefully unrestricted.[1] As a result, a person might have preferences that are ethically or morally oriented and, in such cases, it becomes rational to behave ethically because this is what is entailed in acting so as to satisfy one's preferences. Section II, below, supplies some examples of the kinds of ethical preferences that have been hypothesized in economics.

Since, in this view, ethics affect actions because they are embedded in people's preferences, this conception of rationality fits well with emotivist theories regarding the origins of ethics. It is not, however, the only relation between this model and theories of ethics. This is, in part, because the introduction of ethical preferences into the rational choice model is not always unproblematic. In particular, when the satisfaction of ethical preferences is conditional upon reciprocation by others, the associated requirement that an ethical view/preference be shared can qualify the underlying model of rational choice in ways that are more familiar to versions of institutional economics rooted in the philosophy of pragmatism: behaviour on this account is often better understood as governed by 'rules' and 'norms' and can spawn an alternative conception of 'expressive' rationality. This too is explained in section II.

An obvious question arises when ethical preferences have this reciprocal character. Where do the shared ethical views come from? The emotivist view makes sharing of this kind entirely serendipitous. At first, this seems unlikely to account for the prevalence of moral norms for behaviour in most societies. An alternative explanation centres on a weaker version of the rational choice model, where people are assumed to be boundedly rational. Rather than making precise calculations, people now use rules of thumb to decide what is the best thing to do. When these rules or heuristics get updated with experience, there emerges a powerful reason for individuals to converge on shared rules: it aids coordination. Thus, whenever the interaction has multiple Nash equilibria, the sharing of a rule for decision-making can help with the problem of equilibrium selection. If these shared practices acquire normative force (as well as the pragmatic value that comes from facilitating coordination), then this evolving type of bounded rationality has an obvious ally in naturalist accounts of the origins of ethics (for example, see Hume [1740] 1978). This possibility is briefly discussed in section III, but note again that the acquisition of normative force may well necessitate a shift in the model of rationality in the 'expressive' direction.

Both the rational choice model and the weaker boundedly rational version (so long as it does not turn into a full blown account of rule- or norm-governed behaviour) make the relation between rationality and ethics contingent. That is, rational behaviour *may* but need not entail any moral or ethical orientation. Section IV considers two ways in which the relation between rationality and morality might become necessary rather than contingent (that is, it becomes rational to be ethical or moral). One way accepts the rational choice model and argues that it entails ethical behaviour. The other shifts to a Kantian model of rationality. The reason for this shift can be seen in a sense from the other way round. Kant's moral system is deontological and this is difficult to align with the consequential account of rationality found in the rational choice model. For the same reason it might be argued that virtue ethics sits uneasily within the dominant model.

In other words, just as some kinds of ethical behaviour would seem to require an expanded notion of rationality (the argument in sections II and III), we also find in section IV that some ethical systems also require a different model of individual rationality. Section V concludes, therefore, that while the concept of a preference is famously elastic and much recent work in economics has been concerned with plotting and understanding the influence of 'other-regarding' preferences on individual behaviour, it is not obvious that the rational choice model can properly account for many varieties of ethical behaviour. To do this would seem to require a notion of rationality where reason does more than calculate the best means to an end; and in doing more it is liable to be necessarily rather than contingently connected with ethics.

II

Economics provides considerable evidence that people do not always behave selfishly. Experiments with what seem, under an assumption of selfishness, to be prisoner's dilemmas supply some illustrations (Dawes and Thaler 1988). Table 54.1 reproduces the dilemma when each person's preferences are concerned only with the dollars that they will receive through their action, and each prefers more dollars to fewer. In this case, the dollar value becomes an index of each person's utility payoff and 'defect' is the best action for each person (whatever they might expect the other person to do). Between 30 and 70 percent of people, however, do not defect when playing the game, and economists

Table 54.1 Payoff table for Prisoner's Dilemma game

		B	
		Cooperate	Defect
A	Cooperate	$3, $3	0, $4
	Defect	$4, 0	$1, $1

Table 54.2   Payoff table in Prisoner's Dilemma game incorporating participants' dislike of inequality

		B	
		Cooperate	Defect
A	Cooperate	3, 3	−2, 2
	Defect	2, −2	1, 1

have often sought to explain why by appealing to the idea that people's preferences are frequently unselfish, having an 'other-regarding' ethical dimension. That is, people care not only about how any outcome affects themselves, but also about how other persons are affected, with the result being that cooperation can become rational.

Various models of altruistic behaviour have a long history in this respect (and it will be apparent that a utilitarian would also likely favour cooperation in this example). A recent line of argument in this vein posits more specifically that individuals dislike inequality (Fehr and Schmidt 1999). Individual i's utility function representation of their preferences in an interaction with j now takes the form of (1), where $\$_i$ refers to the financial return to i. Thus person i would like to have dollars for him or herself, in the first term, but dislikes *any* difference between his or her own dollars and those enjoyed by j; in the second/third term, c is the parameter capturing the weight attached to this dislike for inequality:

$$U_i = \$_i - c.\max (0, \$_i - \$_j) - c.\max (0, \$_j - \$_i). \qquad (54.1)$$

In particular, suppose c has the value 0.5. The game in Table 54.1 is now transformed into that in Table 54.2.

There are two Nash equilibria in this transformed game: [cooperate, cooperate] and [defect, defect]. Hence if acting rationally on one's preferences (with common knowledge of this rationality and common priors) licenses actions that are in a Nash equilibrium, it would no longer be surprising to find that people sometimes choose to cooperate in the interaction depicted in Table 54.1.

The economics literature presents another broad category of ethical preference which is distinguished by its conditional nature; that is, a person is motivated by an ethical concern for another but only when they expect this concern to be reciprocated by that other person. There is experimental evidence of this conditional behaviour as well as examples from history, like the 'live and let live' norm at the start of World War I (see, respectively, Clark and Sefton 2001 and Axelrod 1984). It is also an idea with a long pedigree in economics.

Adam Smith ([1759] 1976), for example, famously argued that people obtain a very special pleasure from sharing judgements regarding what is appropriate (moral) behaviour. The origin of such shared judgements in Smith is the 'sympathy' that we feel for others, which he treats as a psychological fact and which he suggests is the basis for our moral judgements. Such 'sympathy' is, in effect, no different from the kind of feeling that the altruist has. What makes Smith's account different from the mere addition of altruistic preferences is his further argument that people enjoy a special pleasure from 'mutual sympathy': 'nothing pleases us more than to observe in men a fellow feeling with all the emotions of our own breast'. So when Simone acts and Joe sympathizes or approves and Simone knows that Joe sympathizes in this way, she gets a very special pleasure. This is quite different from the reflective effect among altruists, because this takes its character from the initial experience: if this is good then others feel it as good, if it is bad then others feel it as bad. With mutual sympathy, when Simone experiences something bad, Joe's initial sympathy will also experience the badness, but when Simone knows that Joe has sympathized, she derives a pleasure (Sugden 2002). Since moral ideas encode feelings of sympathy, the sharing of these ideas (so that they become moral norms) becomes a guide to the actions that will generate the special pleasure of mutual sympathy. Or to put this slightly differently, shared rules of moral conduct create an expectation that one should act in a particular way and acting in accord with this expectation creates the special pleasure of mutual sympathy.

The first formal, 'modern' model of decision-making where preferences have this reciprocal quality is Geanakoplos et al. (1989). It is probably best known through Rabin (1993) and is set out in (54.2) and (54.3) below. Equation (54.2) is similar in form to (54.1) in the sense that it comprises two parts. The first is the 'material' payoff that i receives from some outcome O: that is, the utility value of whatever are the material aspects of the outcome for i $(=M(O))$. So in the game depicted in our first table above, this would be the utility value of the dollar outcome. The second part is the 'psychological' payoff associated with this outcome $(=P(O))$. This is akin to the element in (54.1) that comes from people valuing equality, but it now has a more complicated form which is set out in (54.3).

$$U_i(O) = (1 - v) M_i(O) + vP_i(O) \qquad (54.2)$$

where v is a parameter that weights the 'material' and 'psychological' aspects of an outcome.

$$P_i(O) = f_i(O)[1 + f_j(O)] \qquad (54.3)$$

where f is a function that identifies the fairness $(f > 0)$ or unfairness $(f < 0)$ of each person's action.

Here i enjoys positive 'psychological' payoffs when the outcome involves either *both* people acting 'fairly' $(f > 0)$ or *both* acting 'unfairly' $(f < 0)$. In other words, it depends on reciprocation. The positive effect of both behaving badly is sometimes controversial but can account for why people punish each other when each expects the other to breach whatever is the reigning norm of fairness. It is not an essential part of this theory. Equally, Rabin's original expression for how 'fairness' might be judged is controversial, but can be easily amended.

Such amendments may change some of the character of the behaviour that is predicted in such models, but they are unlikely to change a feature that is worth bringing out and which has already been hinted at in the discussion of Adam Smith. To judge the 'fairness' or 'rightness' of someone's action, you typically need to know what they were expecting you to do. Thus 'cooperate' may be the 'right' action in a prisoner's dilemma when the other person expects you to 'cooperate', but if they expect you to 'defect', then 'defect' might be the 'right' action in the sense that this is what the prevailing norm within that group dictates. This dependence of the psychological payoffs on expectations potentially complicates the usual chain of causation in game theory whereby beliefs about what others will do are to be derived from knowledge of the payoffs and the assumptions of rationality, common knowledge of rationality and common priors. Instead, in this case one would need to fix beliefs about what people will do before the payoffs can be determined. To place some restriction on the admissible beliefs for this purpose and so bring some determinacy to the analysis, it is natural to require that beliefs are equilibrium ones. But once this is done, there is a sense in which the whole apparatus of game theory becomes strangely irrelevant.

After all, once one knows equilibrium beliefs, one knows the actions that are to be undertaken. In that case, there is no real need to calibrate payoffs in order to show that the actions are, indeed, in equilibrium relative to these payoffs (Hargreaves Heap and Varoufakis 2005). One might as well say that people followed the norm that is captured by these equilibrium beliefs and in this way the rational choice model gives way to a model of rule- or norm-governed behaviour. This is a 'modern' game theoretic route to a conclusion that has long distinguished the tradition of institutional economics that came from the North American philosophy of pragmatism. Since the 'rules' or 'norms' also often encode shared beliefs about why an action is appropriate, behaviour of this kind is assimilable to a model of 'expressive' rationality (Hargreaves Heap 2006). When the currency of 'appropriateness' is ethical in character, this would tie ethics to this 'expressive' form of rationality.

Another example of a conditional preference that can have an ethical flavour comes from the work on 'we' or 'collective' intentionality in economics (Sugden 2000; Tuomela 1995; Davis 2003). When a central defender in a soccer match tackles and wins the ball in the penalty area and decides to pass the ball promptly to a colleague in midfield, there is a natural question. Why didn't he or she try to beat a few of the opposing players before passing or shooting at the opposition goal? Anyone who has played football knows that the six-metre pass is humdrum, whereas the pleasure of taking the ball past an opponent is second only to scoring a goal. One explanation is that the defender discounts this pleasure by the risk of failure and the attendant threat of, for example, being dropped from the team or transferred. Alternatively, when the player puts on a number 5 shirt, it could be said that he or she becomes a member of a team and so now decides what to do with reference to the team's interests and not their own. This is the idea behind 'collective' or 'we' intentionality: when we belong to a team we reason using a different set of collective preferences. This reasoning is sometimes called 'team reasoning'.

Table 54.3   Payoff table in Prisoner's Dilemma game incorporating team reasoning

		B	
		Cooperate	Defect
A	Cooperate	3, 3	2, 2
	Defect	2, 2	1, 1

To see how it might work, consider again the dilemma in Table 54.1 above. When A and B belong to the same team, the team's interests might be defined by the average payoff, with the result that the payoffs become those in table 54.3.

A team thinker then considers what action each member of the team should take in order to maximize the average payoff; the result is that, in this case, each team member decides to cooperate. Reciprocation is crucial in this account because the transformation from our first table to our third occurs only when team members play with each other (this is explicit in Bacharach 1999). A team player interacting with a non-team player would have no reason to use 'team reasoning' because they are not in a team in these circumstances.

These reciprocal theories of ethical behaviour, while working with a rational choice or maximizing model, introduce two difficult and related issues concerning how particular norms arise and how groups or teams are formed. Section III says more about this.

III

The rational choice model often seems to make impossible informational demands upon an individual. Models of bounded rationality, where people use simple rules of thumb or heuristics to make decisions, are a response to this criticism (Simon 1978). When these decision rules apply to interactive decision problems and they evolve through learning, there is the interesting possibility that a social convention may arise (Sugden 1986). To see this, consider a version of the crossroads game where two motorists converge from different roads on the same intersection. If some people start to use a rule that assigns priority to one of the parties when they meet, then those using the rule will achieve a mutually superior outcome, with one person speeding up and the other slowing down, as compared to the free-for-all without a rule where there will always be some crashes or delays as both stop. This advantage encourages others to use the same rule until it spreads within a population.

Since the shared rule is, in effect, a coordinating device, there is no reason to expect any particular rule to emerge. 'Give way to traffic coming from the right' works just as well, in principle, as 'give way to traffic coming from the left' or 'give way to the major road' or any of a number of others, provided they are shared. This has the interesting effect of making the details of history matter because 'who' chose 'what' and 'when' influences the actual selection of a rule and typically the character of the rule affects the distribution of the gains from coordination in society. Thus, in the 'crossroads of life', one is as likely to find rules like 'give way to the man/woman' or 'give way to the old/young' emerging with consequent effects on social stratification.

It is apparent that the same evolutionary line of argument could be used to explain the hardwiring of these conventional behaviours into individuals' underlying preferences; and this is the move made by evolutionary psychology.

In both versions of this evolutionary argument, it is sometimes suggested that these historical processes can account for the emergence of shared moral views. The difficulty, however, with this is that the evolutionary learning model explains the emergence of a convention, a simple shared rule; it does not explain how such a rule comes to have normative appeal. That is to say, it says nothing about how such a rule comes to be seen not just as the sensible thing to do, but also as the 'right' thing. It is tempting to rely on some psychological mechanism that turns an 'is' into an 'ought' for this purpose. Hume ([1740] 1978) supplies a famous example of this line of argument, and modern theories on removal of cognitive dissonance supply others (for an application which explicitly makes preferences endogenous see, for example, Festinger 1957; Deci 1975; Frey 1997). Whichever is preferred, the bridge has now been opened between a rational choice model (albeit one adumbrated by evolutionary processes and whatever this projecting psychological mechanism is) and a naturalistic account of ethics and morality. The addition of this 'projecting psychological mechanism' may not, however, be innocuous. It clearly adds to the psychology apparatus of the rational choice agent; and this could move the model in the direction of 'expressive' rationality for the reasons that were sketched in the previous section.

IV

Whether a person's preferences just happen to exhibit ethical properties or they come to do so through one version of evolution or another, the connection between ethics and rationality in the rational choice model looks merely contingent. One might argue that conventions are bound to arise, and so given the psychological propensity to turn an 'is' into an 'ought', people will necessarily have *some* ethical views that guide behaviour. But even in this case, the substance of those views will depend on the peculiarities of the history through which those conventions evolved. In contrast, there are arguments that necessarily relate ethics and rationality; that is, it is a condition of being rational that one acts ethically and not an accident of history.

One such argument that preserves the rational choice sense of rationality comes from Gauthier (1986). Specifically, he argues that it is rational to cooperate in the prisoner's dilemma game. His argument rests on two points. First, people choose dispositions on rational choice grounds. Second, it is better to have the disposition of a 'constrained maximizer' than that of a 'straightforward maximizer'. The difference with the constrained maximizer is that such an individual cooperates in prisoner's dilemma interactions with fellow constrained maximizers while defecting with straightforward maximizers. This wrinkle for constrained maximizers produces superior payoffs, because they achieve the cooperative result in their mutual interactions and suffer no loss when coming across the straightforward maximizers. Thus, since the payoffs from being a constrained maximizer are better than those from being a straightforward one, one decides on rational choice grounds to adopt the disposition of a constrained maximizer (and so to cooperate with fellow constrained maximizers).

There is one significant difficulty with this argument. The best payoffs will be obtained by the person who chooses to be a constrained maximizer and then defects when interacting with another constrained maximizer. This is because, whatever the other person does, defecting always produces a better payoff than cooperating in the prisoner's dilemma. The difficulty is that if the only thing that secures a person's choice of disposition is a rational choice calculation with respect to payoffs, then the rational choice is to declare constrained maximization and sucker anyone who believes the claim by defecting like a straightforward maximizer. In other words, there is no mechanism for making a rational choice person live up to their chosen disposition. Of course if the interaction is repeated in the knowledge of how one has behaved in the past, there are good reputational reasons for wanting to be seen as a *bona fide* constrained maximizer. It is well known that cooperation can emerge in a repeated prisoner's dilemma game for these sorts of reasons. The puzzle of cooperation occurs in the one-shot version of the game and this is what Gauthier is addressing. To solve it, it seems, he too must add some psychological mechanism that can explain commitment not ordinarily present in the rational choice model.

Reason has a restricted role in the rational choice model. Some find this curious on another but related ground. People can reflect rationally on the best means to achieve their ends, but not apparently on the ends themselves. Why should reason stop at this point?

In a limited way, one could gesture to a more ambitious role by allowing that people are motivated by a concern for self-worth that comes from pursuing the kinds of projects in life that are worthy. The desire for self-worth could then be turned into a preference, and the complaint would thereby be neutralized without doing much damage to the rational choice model. Yet, although the concept of preference is famously elastic, this move does not quite work. Once it is acknowledged that judgements of worth are liable to be social in character, we return to the argument regarding the indispensability of norms and their problematic place in the motivational structure of the rational choice individual. It is precisely this reasoning that has underpinned arguments in favour of an 'expressive' conception of rationality (Hargreaves Heap 2006).

Immanuel Kant, of course, offers something more than a limited response to the question. He assigns reason the pre-eminent role of deliberating on what objectives one should pursue. It is only by taking one's objectives to be one's own in this sense that one can achieve a state of autonomy. What does reason tell us in this regard? Famously, Kant observes that if an action results from reason in this sense, then, since reason is a universal human characteristic, only those actions that are universalizable could possibly be candidates for what reason dictates. This requirement, the categorical imperative, has an evident moral character and so would seem to fuse the moral with the rational. There are, however, some doubts over whether this imperative will ever deliver much concrete advice (although see O'Neill 1989 for a counter view), but it would plainly point in the direction of cooperation in the prisoner's dilemma. Sen (1977) also famously seeks to expand the notion of rationality in his argument about 'rational fools' and he has developed this into a distinctive form of ethics (Sen 1985).

One famous line of argument inspired by Kant has been fused with a version of the rational choice model to produce some specific advice about the kinds of ends that one should pursue. It is found in Rawls's *Theory of Justice*. One of Rawls's arguments, drawing on Kant, is that justice requires impartiality, and to discover concretely what justice demands he suggests we cloak ourselves in a 'veil of ignorance'; that is, we consider what states of the world we would prefer when we do not know what position we ourselves are to occupy. This is the Kantian part. The rational choice element enters through an argument that we will or should be risk averse in these circumstances and select the state of the world that yields the best payoff for the person who is worst off. This is the 'maximin' rule, and it yields Rawls's 'difference principle' for selecting between different states of the world on grounds of justice. Harsanyi (1955) in an earlier and similar argument suggested that we should respond to the uncertainty of the 'veil of ignorance' by attaching an equal probability to occupying each possible position in each state and then as expected utility maximizers, we would rank on grounds of justice states of the world according to the sum of the payoffs. In other words, in a curious turn of the wheel, a type of utilitarianism is commended.

The departure from the rational choice model is evident in the case of Kantian morality, even when it is allied with the model in the 'veil of ignorance' arguments sketched above; and it arises because the rational choice model is consequentialist, while Kant's morality is deontological. For related reasons, the position of virtue ethics is liable to rest uneasily with the rational choice model (for example, see MacIntyre 1987). The difficulty here is that the pursuit of virtue is in part understood as being different from the pursuit of individual happiness. Indeed, happiness on some accounts is essentially a by-product of the virtuous life (that is, a life given over to virtue and not happiness). This tension between happiness and virtue is liable both to undercut any attempt to assimilate virtue ethics within the rational choice model (van Staveren 2001) and to return us again to questions surrounding characterization of the influence that norms have on behaviour.

V

This last observation supplies a useful way to summarize the argument of this chapter. The rational choice model takes preferences as given, gives reason a restricted role and rests well with an emotivist account of the origin of ethics and with substantive ethical systems that are consequentialist. This is because taking individual preferences as given allows the operation of reason to be pinned down as merely calculative. Preferences give a source for how ethics enter the world and the ethical assessment of any outcome can be calibrated in terms of how well these individual preferences are satisfied. The moment a person's preferences become social, or conditional on the behaviour of others, the glue that holds this triad together begins to dissolve. The result is an opening to a more expanded, 'expressive' notion of rationality and other accounts of the origins of ethics and their substantive content.

Note

1. There are versions of the rational choice model that dispense with the psychology of preference satisfaction and make rational choices simply those that satisfy these axioms. Since it is not obvious what would make these axioms constitutive of rationality unless they were connected with some motivational psychology, this is a problematic interpretation. More particularly in this context, without a motivational account of rationality, it would be difficult to see how any relation might exist between rationality and ethics.

References

Axelrod, Robert (1984), *The Evolution of Cooperation*, New York: Basic Books.
Bacharach, Michael (1999), 'Interactive team reasoning: a contribution to the theory of cooperation', *Research in Economics*, **53**, 117–47.
Clark, Kenneth and Martin Sefton (2001), 'The sequential prisoner's dilemma: evidence on reciprocation', *Economic Journal*, **111**, 51–68.
Davis, John (2003), *The Theory of the Individual in Economics: Identity and Value*, London: Routledge.
Dawes Robyn M. and Richard H. Thaler (1988), 'Anomalies: cooperation', *Journal of Economic Perspectives*, **2**, 187–97.
Deci, Edward L. (1975), *Intrinsic Motivation*, New York: Plenum Press.

Fehr, Ernst and Klaus M. Schmidt (1999), 'A theory of fairness, competition and cooperation', *Quarterly Journal of Economics*, **114**, 817–68.

Festinger, Leon (1957), *A Theory of Cognitive Dissonance*, Stanford, CA: Stanford University Press.

Frey, Bruno S. (1997), *Not Just for the Money*, Cheltenham, UK and Lyme, USA: Edward Elgar.

Gauthier, David (1986), *Morals by Agreement*, Oxford: Clarendon Press.

Geanakoplos, John, David Pearce and Ennio Stacchetti (1989), 'Psychological games and sequential rationality', *Games and Economic Behaviour*, **1**, 60–79.

Hargreaves Heap, Shaun (2006), 'The mutual validation of ends', in Benedetto Gui and Robert Sugden (eds), *Economics and Social Interactions*, Cambridge: Cambridge University Press.

Hargreaves Heap, Shaun and Yanis Varoufakis (2005), *Game Theory*, London: Routledge.

Harsanyi, John (1955), 'Cardinal welfare, individualistic ethics and interpersonal comparisons of utility', *Journal of Political Economy*, **63**, 309–21.

Hume, David ([1740], 1978), *A Treatise of Human Nature*, ed. L.A. Selby-Bigge, Oxford: Clarendon Press.

O'Neill, Onora (1989), *Construction of Reason*, Cambridge: Cambridge University Press.

MacIntyre, Alasdair (1987), *After Virtue*, London: Duckworth.

Rabin, Matthew (1993), 'Incorporating fairness into economics and game theory', *American Economic Review*, **83**, 1281–302.

Sen, Amartya (1977), 'Rational fools', *Philosophy and Public Affairs*, **6**, 317–44.

Sen, Amartya (1985), *Commodities and Capabilities*, Amsterdam: North Holland.

Simon, Herbert A. (1978), 'Rationality as process and as product of thought', *American Economic Review*, **68**, 1–16.

Smith, Adam ([1759] 1976) *The Theory of Moral Sentiments*, Oxford: Clarendon Press.

Staveren, Irene van (2001), *The Values of Economics: An Aristotelian Perspective*, London: Routledge.

Sugden, Robert (1986), *The Economics of Rights, Cooperation and Welfare*, Oxford: Basil Blackwell.

Sugden, Robert (2000), 'Team preferences', *Economics and Philosophy*, **16**, 175–204.

Sugden, Robert (2002), 'Beyond sympathy and empathy: Adam Smith's concept of fellow feeling', *Economics and Philosophy*, **18**, 63–87.

Tuomela, Raimo (1995), *The Importance of Us: A Philosophical Study of Basic Social Notions*, Stanford, CA: Stanford University Press.

See also the entries on: Egoism; Game theory; Immanuel Kant; Self-interest.

55 John Rawls
Hilde Bojer

Introduction

John Rawls (1921–2002) is the most influential moral and political philosopher of the last 100 years. His major book, *A Theory of Justice*, first appeared in 1971 and has since been translated into 27 languages. A bibliography of articles on Rawls published in 1981 listed more than 2500 entries (Freeman 2003, p. 1).

Rawls is the founding father of contemporary debates on social justice. He is also one of the very few moral philosophers taken notice of by economists. Economic literature speaks of him mainly as the inspiration for the maximin social welfare function, which is also – and somewhat mistakenly – called the Rawlsian social welfare function. The name is a misnomer, because Rawls argues most decisively against utility, or individual welfare, as the distribuendum of distributive justice. In fact, one reason for his great impact is his pioneering opposition to utilitarianism and to welfarism in general.

Rawls wrote widely and in depth about all aspects of the just society. Among the many subjects he discussed, his analysis of distributive justice has the most relevance to economic thought. That will be discussed here.

As a method for studying questions of social justice, Rawls proposed what he called 'reflective equilibrium'. Reflective equilibrium is achieved when our abstract principles and our concrete intuitions are in harmony. For example, the abstract principle may be that people should be rewarded according to their contribution to production. But this principle leaves those unable to work, like children and the disabled, with no income. If we accept this result, we are in reflective equilibrium. If not, the principle must be modified, for instance, by adding that disabled adults should be provided for by taxing the working population.

Rawls is clear that his intention is not to study distribution in the short term or to specific persons. He writes:

> [These principles] are meant to regulate basic institutional arrangements. We must not assume that there is much similarity from the standpoint of justice between an administrative allotment of goods to specific persons and the appropriate design of society. Our common sense intuitions of the former may be a poor guide to the latter. (Rawls 1999a, p. 64)

Fundamental to Rawls's thought is that the common ground of a society, what creates its cohesion, should be an agreement on what institutions and arrangements are just. Such a basis of society is different from a society built on common ethnicity, religion or language, which are factors more commonly assumed to create the nation-state. Rawls defines a liberal society as 'a society that allows for a plurality of different and even incommensurable conceptions of the good' (Rawls 1982, p. 160). The Rawlsian society, hence, is a liberal one.

But a society is also a community of citizens, a place of social cooperation, where everyone depends on everyone else:

> The intuitive idea is that since everyone's well-being depends upon a scheme of co-operation without which no one could have a satisfactory life, the division of advantages should be such as to draw forth the willing co-operation of everyone taking part in it, including those less well situated. (Rawls 1999a, p. 13)

It is often thought important that society be organized so as to retain the voluntary cooperation of its most resourceful and gifted members. But when we put the question as Rawls does above, we see that the most successful members of any given society are the ones with the most to lose from general non-cooperation, while the poorest are those with the least to give up. Therefore, the important point is indeed to secure the voluntary cooperation of the least successful.

The social contract

Rawls bases his theory of the just society on a version of the social contract. The Rawlsian social contract is the hypothetical contract which free and equal human beings would agree should regulate the 'basic institutional arrangements' of society if they were able to free themselves from the prejudices and self-interest that arise from knowing what is to their own immediate advantage or disadvantage. Since it is a voluntary act, agreement to the contract must be unanimous. Rawls argues that we can deduce the contents of this contract by a thought experiment.

Imagine an original position, where all members of society meet to negotiate a social contract. In this original position, the participants are ignorant of their own position in society. A veil of ignorance hides from them their sex, talents and other genetic endowments, their place in the distribution of economic and other resources, their place of birth, the economic and social positions of their parents, even their tastes and preferences (their conception of the good).

From behind this thick veil of ignorance, the contracting parties are to decide what the just distribution of goods and burdens should be in a society in which they themselves would want to live. The choice is to be made by rational persons in enlightened self-interest. The veil of ignorance must not be taken, however, to mean that the parties are generally ignorant. On the contrary, 'It is taken for granted . . . that they know the general facts about human society . . . Indeed, the parties are presumed to know whatever general facts affect the choice of principles of justice' (Rawls 1999a, p. 137).

The choice of social contract, or basic social arrangements, is thus in Rawls's imagined original position the solution to a problem of choice under uncertainty. The uncertainty concerns where in the distribution of goods and burdens each particular individual will end up as well as what kind of life they would prefer to live. The choice concerns, among other features, which form of distribution of economic goods the rational individual would then prefer.

Rawls argues that rational parties in the original position would unanimously agree on a social contract based on the following two principles:

> First: each person is to have an equal right to the most extensive basic liberties compatible with similar liberties for others. Second: social and economic inequalities are to be arranged so that

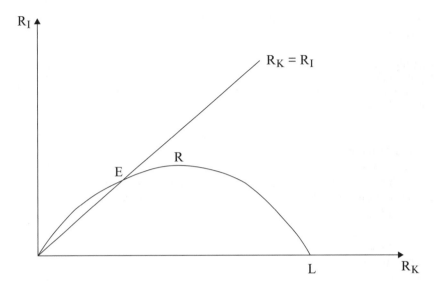

Figure 55.1   The difference principle

they are both (a) reasonably expected to be to everyone's advantage, and (b) attached to positions and offices open to all. (Rawls 1999a, p. 60)

Rawls maintains moreover that the principle of equal rights to extensive liberty takes lexical priority over the second principle. The priority follows from the fact that the parties are ignorant of which life plans they will prefer. They will therefore choose to allow any life plan, except life plans that limit the liberty of others.

The second principle, 'reasonably expected to be to everyone's advantage', is Rawls's first version of what he calls the 'difference principle'. It is better known in another version in which point (a) in the quotation above reads, 'to the greatest benefit of the least advantaged' (Rawls 1999a, p. 82). Here, for practical reasons, the least advantaged is understood to be the least advantaged group, not individual, since the least advantaged group is easier to identify. This last version is also called the 'maximin principle' by many commentators, though not by Rawls himself.

The difference principle
The difference principle is an egalitarian one, but it represents an egalitarianism which accepts that the way the pie is distributed may influence how much there is of it to distribute. It is the outcome of a trade-off between equality and wealth, and accepts certain, but not all, inequalities.

Figure 55.1 illustrates one aspect of how it works. For simplicity, it assumes that there is only one good to be distributed, called income. This figure is based on figures 6 and 8 in *A Theory of Justice*.

Assume there are two persons in the economy, K is economically active and I is a pensioner, dependent on transfers. The curve shows all possible distributions of income (R) between I and K, L being the income produced when K is allowed to retain the whole for him or herself. Increasing taxation makes K produce less. As taxes increase, K's income decreases while I's income increases up to the point R. Here, the greatest possible income for I is obtained. Beyond R, both I's and K's incomes decrease in absolute terms while I's share increases. The point E is that of absolute equality. Here both I and K receive less than at R. By the difference principle, the distribution chosen will be R. The distribution preferred by a utilitarian social welfare function will be somewhere between R and L, depending on the shape of the respective utility functions. Figure 55.1 shows that the difference principle produces shares that are unequal, but less unequal than a utilitarian distribution.

To reveal another aspect of the difference principle, we need an economy with more than two persons, say four. Now compare two distributions (5, 5, 5, 5) and (4, 8, 9, 10). By the difference principle, the first, equal, distribution is the preferred one, even though the majority is better off in the second. This result has bothered many critics of Rawls. It would not be the outcome of, say, a utilitarian evaluation. On the other hand, it is a consequence of Rawls's interpretation of the Kantian principle that a person should never be used as the means to an end of other persons. The principle is violated, according to Rawls, when a person is forced to lose something, even if very little, in order to advantage someone who is better off than him or herself. In the distribution (4, 8, 9, 10), the situation of the majority is improved at the cost of one person.

The difference principle is not a complete ordering of distributions. Rawls applies it only in comparing unequal distributions with full equality, not to compare two distributions that are both unequal. The social welfare functions maximin and leximin give complete orderings. They are generalizations of the difference principle frequently used to represent egalitarianism, especially welfarist egalitarianism. The maximin function uses the welfare of the least well-off person as the sole criterion when ordering distributions: W = min[U1, U2, .. Un]. It is the standard representation of Rawls's theory in economic textbooks, even though, as noted above, Rawls himself was emphatically not a welfarist. Leximin considers first the least well-off. If they are equal, it compares the second worst off and so on. For a thorough discussion of the relationship of maximin and leximin to egalitarianism and the Pareto principle, see Tungodden and Valentyne (2005).

On the use of the difference principle in welfare analyses, Rawls argued that it should not be applied to justice between generations. But this is exactly how several economists have applied it, among them Arrow (1973), Solow (1974) and Asheim (1988).

Primary goods

Rawls rejects individual welfare as the good to be equally distributed. There are several reasons for this rejection. But the most basic reason for Rawls is probably that for him, social justice must be compatible with a society that allows for a plurality of different and possibly opposing conceptions of the good. Social justice cannot, then, build on the assumption that individual welfare in the sense of personal happiness is the one, final good for all persons.

Rawls postulates that there exist what he calls 'primary goods' which every individual wants more of, whatever their life plan, and that these goods also determine social and economic inequalities in lifetime prospects. The first edition of *A Theory of Justice* can be read as if primary goods are biologically determined and common to all human beings whatever their social circumstances. In other words, in order to learn which goods are primary ones, we have to know something about human nature. Later, particularly in Rawls (1982, 1997), he explains that his theory is not connected to any particular view of human nature, and that the concept of primary goods should be understood as social primary goods. The qualifier 'social' means that primary goods are what every adult person needs in order to participate fully in society as a citizen. Primary goods are therefore also to be understood as connected to the public sphere of life, not the private.

In 'Social unity and primary goods' (1982, p. 162), Rawls provides a list of primary goods:

(a)   First, the basic liberties as given by a list, for example: freedom of thought and liberty of conscience; freedom of association; and the freedom defined by the liberty and integrity of the person, as well as by the rule of laws; and finally the political liberties;

(b)   Second, freedom of movement and choice of occupation against a background of diverse opportunities;

(c)   Third, powers and prerogatives of offices and positions of responsibility, particularly those in the main political and economic institutions;

(d)   Fourth, income and wealth.

(e)   Finally, the social bases of self-respect.

In the paper, Rawls makes clear that he thinks of the social contract as regulating rights and duties in public life only. This means inter alia that he does not visualize children as being parties to the contract. The boundary Rawls draws between public and private life is the conventional one, with the family belonging to the private sphere.

Social primary goods are meant to be those of use to normal, healthy adults. Although they are supposed to serve a person's life-prospects, that is, throughout life, they are not meant to cover periods of sickness, the period of childhood or the possibility of disabling accidents. Many commentators feel that this makes the concept too narrow. In particular, it does not sufficiently take into account that people are different and have different needs. There is a sense in which a disabled person needs a higher income in order to function in society than an able-bodied person. Rawls (1982) defends 'income and wealth' against this criticism by stating, for example, that health is not a social primary good, being what he calls 'a natural good' and therefore not subject to government distribution.

Rawls acknowledges that, since there are several primary goods, there is an index problem when weighting them together for purposes of comparison. However, several of the goods on the list are to be equally distributed separately; this is in particular true of all political rights and liberties and the social bases of self-respect. In the final account, only the goods 'powers and prerogatives of position' and 'income and wealth' need to be weighted together in an index. Rawls also points out that the index problem is considerably eased by the difference principle. Applying the difference principle, we need only somehow to identify the least advantaged group, which may well be possible without the exactness of a numerical index, and then construct an index for this one group in order to measure the consequences of basic policies. Apart from these comments, Rawls does not indicate how an index should be constructed.

In several papers Rawls underlines the importance of having political objectives that are open to public debate, and therefore in some sense observable and understandable, 'a practical and limited list of things (primary goods) which free and equal moral persons . . . can accept as what they in general need as citizens in a just society' (Rawls 1982, p. 183). This is probably the reason why he has income and wealth on his list of primary goods, in spite of the objection that equal incomes may give very different life prospects if people have different objective needs for reasons that are beyond their own control.

But there are difficulties with 'income and wealth' as a primary good, also by Rawls's own definition of, and intention with, social primary goods. Rawls, like many other philosophers, underestimates the difficulties connected not only with the practical measuring, but also with the theoretical definition of income and wealth. In 'Reply to Musgrave and Alexander' (1974), Rawls adds leisure to his list of primary goods. The implication must be that income is to be understood as full income as defined by Gary Becker. Full income is not, however, a well-known or easily understood concept.

Some criticisms of Rawls

Rawls's concept of the original position has been criticized by several thinkers, among them Habermas (1995), as being 'monological'. The basis of the criticism seems to be that no plurality of voices and viewpoints is represented; essentially, the parties in the original position are several copies of one single human being. Feminist critics point out that, in particular, no women are present. Neither do the parties in the original position engage in conversation or exchange points of view.

The criticism is correct in a sense, since the parties are without individual traits or characteristics beyond being human. But the original position is not a description of human behaviour nor of any situation that has actually occurred. It is a model or metaphor used to define impartial social justice. Every conceivable kind of human being is a party to the Rawlsian social contract because the contracting parties have to take into account the possibility of turning out to be of this kind. When choosing a society that they themselves would want to live in, it is clear to the contracting parties that they must choose a society they would want to live in whatever their place in that society turns out to be. Women are represented in the original position by the fact that the contracting parties have a probability of 50 per cent of turning out to be women, which should ensure a contract with equal rights and opportunities for women and men.

As Okin (1989) and Nussbaum (2003) point out, Rawls never worked out the consequences of women's equality with men. He discussed some feminist criticisms of his thought in a later paper, 'The idea of public reason revisited' (Rawls 1997). In it, however, he did not consider including the organization of the family in the social contract, but stuck to the traditional liberal view that the family is part of the private, not the public sphere. On the other hand, both Okin and Nussbaum maintain that in other respects, Rawls's social contract is well suited as the foundation of a feminist theory of justice. Bojer (forthcoming) looks into some aspects of a feminist application of Rawlsian justice to the organization of the family.

The assumption that the parties are 'mutually disinterested' has also been criticized as giving a too narrow view of human nature. But, again, this assumption is not an assumption about actual human beings. In several papers, Rawls explains that his theory of justice is not, and does not imply, a specific theory of human nature. The purpose of making the contracting parties 'mutually disinterested' is to ensure a social contract that guarantees impartial justice.

Many commentators, for instance, Barry (1989), Kolm (1996) and Roemer (1996), claim that the difference principle is not the correct solution to the Rawlsian problem of choice under uncertainty. Rawls himself writes that his theory of justice is part of the general theory of rational choice. The choice to be made by the parties in Rawls's original position can be stated in a way similar to conventional analysis of choice under uncertainty. But then, the individual maximizes expected utility. The corresponding choice for parties in the original position would be a social contract based on a utilitarian social welfare function (Harsanyi 1982). Roemer (1996, p. 181) showed that the difference principle corresponds to the maximization of expected utility only in the special case in which the person concerned is infinitely risk averse. Unless we assume that all human beings are infinitely risk averse, there would not be agreement on the choice of distribution. Rawls thus seems to appeal to the theory of rational choice under uncertainty without being willing to accept the results of that theory.

On the other hand, the choice of distribution of lifetime prospects, as in the social contract, would seem to be of far greater import, and to call for a far greater degree of caution (risk aversion) than a single investment project affecting only part of one's life. It seems plausible that such a choice would imply a special concern for the worst possible thing that could happen.

References

Arrow, Kenneth J. (1973), 'Rawls's principle of just saving', *Swedish Journal of Economics*, **75**, 323–35.
Asheim, Geir B. (1988), 'Rawlsian intergenerational justice as a Markov-perfect equilibrium in a resource technology', *Review of Economic Studies*, **55** (3), 469–83.
Barry, Brian (1989), *Theories of Social Justice*, London: Harvester Wheatsheaf.
Bojer, Hilde (forthcoming), 'The social contract, child care and women's economic capability', in Flavio Comin and Martha Nussbaum (eds), *Capabilitites, Gender, Equality: Toward Fundamental Entitlements*, Cambridge: Cambridge University Press.
Freeman, Samuel (2003), 'Introduction: John Rawls, an overview', in Samuel Freeman (ed.), *The Cambridge Companion to Rawls*, Cambridge: Cambridge University Press, pp. 1–61.
Habermas, Jurgen (1995), 'Reconciliation through the public use of reason: remarks on John Rawls's political liberali', *Journal of Philosophy*, **92** (3), 109–31.
Harsanyi, John C. (1982), 'Morality and the theory of rational behaviour', in Amartya Sen and Bernard Williams (eds), *Utilitarianism and Beyond*, Cambridge: Cambridge University Press, pp. 39–62.
Kolm, Serge-Christophe (1996), *Modern Theories of Justice*, Cambridge, MA: The MIT Press.
Nussbaum, Martha (2003), 'Rawls and feminism', in Samuel Freeman (ed.), *The Cambridge Companion to Rawls*, Cambridge: Cambridge University Press, pp. 488–520.
Okin, S.M. (1989), *Justice, Gender and the Family*, New York: Basic Books.
Rawls, John (1971), *A Theory of Justice*, Cambridge, MA: Harvard University Press.
Rawls, John (1974), 'Reply to Alexander and Musgrave', *Quarterly Journal of Economics*, **88**, 633–55. Reprinted in Rawls (1999b), pp. 232–53.
Rawls, John (1982), 'Social unity and primary goods', in Amartya Sen and Bernard Williams (eds), *Utilitarianism and Beyond*, Cambridge: Cambridge University Press, pp. 159–85. Reprinted in Rawls (1999b), pp. 359–87.
Rawls, John (1997), 'The idea of public reason revisited', *University of Chicago Law Review*, **64**, 765–807, Reprinted in Rawls (1999b), pp. 573–615.
Rawls, John (1999a), *A Theory of Justice*, revised edition, Cambridge, MA: Harvard University Press.
Rawls, John (1999b), *Collected Papers*, Cambridge, MA: Harvard University Press.
Roemer, John E. (1996), *Theories of Distributive Justice*, Cambridge, MA: Harvard University Press.
Solow, Robert M. (1974), 'Intergenerational equity and exhaustible resources', *Review of Economic Studies*, **41**, 29–45.
Tungodden, Bertil and Peter Valentyne (2005), 'On the possibility of Paretian egalitarianism', *Journal of Philosophy*, **102**, 126–54.

See also the entries on: Feminism; Income distribution; Inequality; Justice; Utilitarianism.

56 Realism
Andrew Mearman

Introduction

This chapter examines the relation between realism and ethics in economics. As this volume attests, ethical positions are implicit in much of what economists do and say. Also clear is that often what economists advocate as right or good partly depends on what they believe exists; that is, what the world is like. Realism, which in simple terms is the belief in the existence of a world independent of what we know or think, bolsters such arguments. As Gasper (2007) implied, there can be no well-being without being.

The question of realism and ethics in economics is examined here principally through a focus on two key interventions in the recent debates on realism in economics. First, Uskali Mäki made an excellent recent contribution to the methodology of economics on the question of realism. Mäki offered a number of distinctions in realism which attempt to clarify a number of debates in economics, particularly related to neoclassical economics and key figures within it. One point made by Mäki is that realism is a varied concept, and no single definition of realism can describe economics completely accurately.

The second key intervention relates to critical realism, a variant of realism which has recently been extremely influential in economics, associated particularly with Tony Lawson. Specific features of critical realism are relevant to ethics, as are its specific ethical claims. Before we look at these contributions, it is first necessary to clarify the meaning of realism.

Realism

As a project, realism in economics has taken particular forms: (i) clarification of what is meant by realism; (ii) advocacy of certain types of realism, particularly critical realism; and (iii) claims that schools of thought or meta-schools have adopted, albeit implicitly, one or another variant of realism. To do justice to realism as a philosophical position, it is necessary to recognize its nuances and variety. That is because realism has many opponents and often suffers from oversimplification.

For Mäki (1989),[1] 'simple realism' (also known as 'ontological realism') is a philosophical position which makes a claim about the existence of objects outside the human mind. Realism can be stronger: things *do* exist; or weaker: things *might* exist. Stronger realism engages in what Mäki calls 'truth ascription', whereas weaker realism attempts only 'truth nomination'; but both are realist (Mäki 2005). These distinctions are important, because criticisms of realism often attack the strength of its claims, or even its perceived claims of infallibility. Mäki (ibid.) argues that the weaker truth nomination definition of realism refutes a series of arguments against realism.

The nature of existence is important in this context. Mäki (1996) differentiates *independent* existence (existing independently of the human mind); *external* existence (existing externally or independently of any individual human mind); and *objective* existence (existing unconstituted by any representation of it). Realism tends to favour that last definition, since it is clear that although theories and other conceptions of objects can causally affect them, objects can be conceived independently. There can be a temporal referential detachment between the person's identification of an object and the object itself (Mäki 2005).

For example, one can examine one's own *past* consumption choices as an object of analysis. In fact, economics has a preponderance of concepts, such as equilibrium, for which it is difficult to claim strongly that they exist. However, while the exact measurement of unemployment is obviously relative to some agreed standard, an idle machine or worker remains idle irrespective of our conception of them.

According to Mäki, the crucial distinction is between *common sense* realism and *scientific* realism. In the former, objects exist and are identifiable through common sense. In many ways, economics rests on common sense realism, since its objects, such as firms, households and other economic agents, may be said to exist simply by looking around. This is unlike, for example, the way in which quarks exist, although the same cannot be said for equilibrium or utility. Economics is populated by 'folk' objects and indeed folk theories, including that of *homo economicus* (Mäki 1992). In some ways, therefore, the project of everyday economics (see Ruccio and Amariglio 2003, Ch. 7) is, if not redundant, not as radical a departure from conventional economics as might be supposed. Mäki (1992) argues that theory from the Austrian School, for example, accepts the existence of the entrepreneur from simple common sense. In other ways, however, economics represents scientific realism. Scientific realism depicts entities lying beyond the realm of common sense, identifiable by some set of 'scientific' procedures. The entities exist independently of investigations into them, which succeed in referring to entities and describing them approximately correctly; this explains the uncontroversial success of science (Mäki 1996). (Though economics is not uncontroversially successful like some branches of physics or chemistry.) Clearly economics is also populated by scientific theories about scientific objects. For example, those of the Austrian School regard the market process, and post-Keynesians regard uncertainty, as objects requiring scientific investigation.

Certain tenets of scientific realism are commonly held (albeit certainly not universally). For example, a central notion is that scientific objects are entities which possess causal powers. Often the metaphor of depth is used to communicate the notion of causal powers. Powers may be said to reside 'beneath' their effects. Mäki (1990, 1992) uses such concepts to discuss Austrian theory. He argues that some economists in the Austrian School (for example, Kirzner 1979) regard entrepreneurial alertness as one such power.

Critical realism

One example of a version of scientific realism is critical realism, which developed from the philosophical work of Roy Bhaskar (1978, 1979, 1986). There are several distinct stages of critical realism, but most of the work in economics has been developed from Bhaskar's early work on transcendental realism and critical naturalism. Critical realism in economics has been developed mainly by Tony Lawson (1997, 2003) based primarily on Bhaskar's earlier work and does not explicitly engage with the later dialectical critical realism phase. Rather, critical realism is taken to be already dialectical. Critical realism is based on the transcendental deduction of reality from objects of experience. Bhaskar (1978) uses scientific experiment as the canonical explanandum, and Bhaskar (1979) generalizes this to any intentional act. Critical realism argues that for those acts to be possible, the world must be stratified, differentiated and open. Here, 'stratified' implies the metaphor of depth, as discussed above. 'Lower levels' contain causal mechanisms which generate actualities (particularly events) and experiences of them at 'higher levels'. Critical realism also stresses the importance of properties at one level rooted in, but irreducible to and emergent from, lower levels. 'Differentiated' implies that the world is not uniform. 'Open' refers to the fact that event regularities of the sort 'if *x* then *y*' will not occur. This definition is buttressed by notions that mechanisms interact with one another, are sometimes not activated and therefore that their effects are not always manifest.

Critical realism has been criticized for engaging only in philosophical ontology; that is, in identifying real objects very abstractly and abdicating the identification of actually existing objects to science. Nonetheless, it has been influential in social science and to some extent in economics in affecting the practice of research. Critical realism has been particularly effective in refocusing practitioners on ontology, in raising questions about mathematics and quantitative methods, in resisting anti-realist positions and in clarifying bases for truth claims. Like Mäki, critical realist authors have made claims about various schools of thought being implicitly critical realist. Such claims tend to focus on the so-called 'heterodox' traditions, including post-Keynesianism, Marxism, Austrianism, institutionalism and feminism.

Several key features of critical realism are worthy of note. First, its transformational model of social activity provides a lens through which one can understand the independent existence but causal interdependence of agency and social structure. Thus, social structure, which might include morality, conditions agency, but is also conditional on it. A moral dimension therefore pre-exists agents' actions based on it, but is also transformed and reproduced by those agents' actions. As such, specific societies can have their own historically specific ethics without abandoning the concept of moral realism.

Critical realism attempts to be critical in a number of ways, including of itself. First, theories are considered fallible, reality being the arbiter of the value of a theory. Thus, the claims of critical realism must be regarded as less strident than some anti-realists might presuppose. Second, Bhaskar (1979, 1986) developed an explanatory critique, discussed below, which aims to expose false beliefs and identify structures which cause them. A third key element is the recent stress on absence.

Mäki criticizes some realisms as being too global; that is, being too top-down. He prefers bottom-up realism, arguing that global approaches cannot adequately describe economics, and that economics thus displays multiple realisms. One could also take the view that there are no grounds a priori for holding one realism to be inherently superior to another. Implicitly he is arguing against critical realism, which can be interpreted as adopting a top-down approach in economics. In its defence, by adopting a position which involves some prescription, critical realism is able to comment on inconsistencies between theory and practice, as well as on methodological incoherence and the like. Further, it could be argued that all practitioners have an implicit methodology and thereby philosophical approach. In effect, although imposing a realism on a discipline can be an oversimplification, positing a specific realist position may describe very well the practice of many economists, allow one to identify significant movements in economics and permit injunctions into practice. Indeed, arguably current practice is partly the consequence of past methodological injunctions.

Critical realism offers its own specific view on ethics, which is discussed further below. First, though, it is useful to examine whether realism in general has ethical implications.

Realism and ethics
Examining the relation between realism and ethics is not straightforward. One might begin by asking, 'Realism about what?' The implications of realism for ethics (and by extension, for economics) follow from two types of argument: (i) realism *about* ethics and (ii) specific ontological claims about the real world which lead to ethical claims and implications for ethical theories.

In the second category of argument come ethical claims which implicitly accept realism about ethics and are based on specific ontologies, such as that people's well-being is based on their objective needs, for example, to eat and get shelter, but also on non-physical needs, such as conditional and unconditional recognition, mutual recognition among equals and equality of moral worth (see Sayer 2005). These have direct implications for economics. In the first category of argument, if one holds a *moral realism* – the existence of moral properties irreducible to people's beliefs and attitudes or judgements as to what is right or wrong; the positing of an independently existing morality – then morality is a cause, independent of one's understanding of it, which can in principle be identified and perhaps modified. Morality can then be treated like any other causal mechanism. Such a position is one of *ethical naturalism* (see Calder 2007). Of course, as that example shows, the two types of argument can be combined.

The first type of argument is a broad philosophical one and perhaps has fewer implications for economics than the second; it will be considered first. Gasper (2007) offers a simple direct implication of realism for ethics, which is the basic argument that without being, there can be no well-being. However, Gasper's argument also acknowledges that 'well-being' has a normative component in the definition of 'well', which still begs the question of what status the normative dimension has.

Putnam (2004) in *Ethics without Ontology* offers several arguments against realism about ethics. His arguments are against Ontology generally; that is, against theories which a priori make universal claims about existence. Putnam questions the bases of such claims in a variety of ways. For example, referring to the above discussion of existence, Putnam might claim that a single definition of existence is assumed. Yet he argues that the word 'exist' has multiple meanings. Which meaning is used is a question of convention. Putnam adopts a Deweyan pragmatism, which states that ethics concerns the solution of practical problems and that ethical positions emerge from people attempting to resolve these problems. Ethics, in this view, do not pre-exist practice, they emerge from it. Putnam seems to be rejecting moral realism. Indeed, Putnam rejects *apriorism* generally, which suggests he could be read as opposing scientific realist philosophical ontological claims about causal powers.

In other ways, though, Putnam's position is similar to recent, more sophisticated treatments of realism offered by, for example, Mäki and critical realism. There is agreement that what is moral is contestable and varies with context, being sorted out through practical problems and action. Ethical judgements are recognized as being highly complex (see Sayer 2000) and fallible. They are held to be based on intelligence, without reverting to a strict rationalism, which disallows the role of inclination or emotion (compare Collier 2000; Putnam 2004, p. 104). Furthermore, the moral dimension is agreed as being pervasive and as affecting action. In sum, although there is an 'interminable' (Kourany 2000, p. S98) debate about realism about ethics (as there is about realism generally), it is unclear that realism per se has direct implications for ethics.

The second category of argument about realism concerns ethical claims that implicitly accept some ontology. Traditionally, treatments of ethics deal with the three schools: virtue ethics, deontology and utilitarianism. Some positions are consistent with more than one school (perhaps even all three) in different ways. For Gasper (2007), 'well-being' varies with the ontological perspective taken, because it refers to having (needs met), doing (capacity to do activities) and feeling. Thus, well-being as 'living well' fits more with virtue ethics, whereas well-being as 'feeling good' is consistent with utilitarianism. Fleetwood (1997) argues that utilitarianism is based on an empiricist ontology, in which reality is exhausted by experiences, and therefore in which human capacities or *telos* are irrelevant. That position contrasts with ontologies in which humans are purposeful and use their capacities to propel them towards ends. Ethical positions which stress activity and living deny implicitly a Cartesian dualism of mind and body (Brown et al. 2007). The critical realist approach is also a combination of different approaches. It is a consequentialism (in terms of self-realization and freedom), a deontology entailing that humans possess an expanded range of rights and a virtue ethics including, for example, solidarity and care and sensitivity.

More generally, ontological claims have ethical implications. For example, critical realism argues for a specific morality, one in which good actions are those which encourage human flourishing. Thus, critical realism provides an ethics of removing or transforming structures which preclude flourishing and the institution of structures which promote it. This claim is in turn based on the claim that although humans do have a more culturally dependent nature in different contexts, there is a common human nature (although this must be empirically established) and an (albeit fallibly) identifiable species being: humans have generalized capacities (see also Lawson 1997, 2003). This is the *alethic truth* of humans. Further, we have needs to realize these capacities. Our needs contribute to our survival and flourishing. We then engage in *explanatory critique* of structures which preclude human flourishing. Once identified, we pass automatically from an explanatory account of that structure to a value judgement on it; specifically, to a negative evaluation of those structures. This is to say that in our actions we 'effectively accept the goal of the good or eudemonistic society as a goal already' (Lawson 2000, p. 55). We rationally act in keeping with our real natures and towards our own flourishing; we are true to ourselves.

Realism, ethics and economics

Thus far the discussion has been fairly abstract, dealing with general implications for ethics of realisms and their associated ontologies. However, at a more concrete level, it should be clear that specific scientific findings, for example, may have ethical implications.

Furthermore, specific ontological claims have their own implications for economics in terms of the ethical content of economic theory and policy. One area of application is the literature on well-being and happiness. This has developed in response to dissatisfaction with measures of national income as proxies for well-being which can be identified as empiricist and utilitarian.[2] The argument implicit in the well-being and happiness literature is whether humans are fulfilled by material consumption. That, in turn, contains an implicit ontological claim about humans and their nature, capacities, needs and so on. The implication of that, in turn, is the claim that humans have real essences. Building on these notions, Fleetwood (1997), drawing on Aristotle and relating to Marx (and implicitly critical realism) argues that humans have *telos* directed towards a 'good life' and take actions towards that end. To do so requires they (partly) create conditions which allow their capacity to flourish. Modern techniques of production and marketing, such as built-in obsolescence, driven by the need to secure *exchange* value, are then considered bad, because they prevent people from acquiring the *use* values which they require to meet their essential needs. Thus, he argues, modern societies which stress such activities are bad.

Sayer (2004) tries to demonstrate how the moral dimension affects economic activities. For example, he notes that ideas of natural rights underpin exchanges; claims about exploitation clearly rest on a judgement that natural rights have been violated. The same applies to perceptions of unjust production relations. Sayer takes the position that moral positions are essential to humans and are rooted in human psychology and nature: they are not merely social constructs. This is an example of how realism about ethics might make a difference. For instance, he argues that economic responsibility for others is a transhistorical necessity of any economy, because economies by their nature make individual agents dependent on others. Thus, economic activities require trust (see also Lawson 2000).

Fleetwood (2008) applies Sayer's analysis to the issue of consumer sovereignty and simultaneously illustrates some of the points made earlier. He argues that the concept of consumer sovereignty is one which is continually reinforced by the practice of agents. Consumer sovereignty itself contains a normative dimension that consumers ought to drive production and its conditions. Further, that position is supported by an ontology of individualism. In turn, individualism supports an ethic of selfishness. However, Fleetwood argues that in fact a strict consumer-focused approach to production may well be ethically unsound because it leads to detrimental effects on workers. Specifically, consumer sovereignty leads to the domination of workers and a lack of recognition of their needs as workers and humans. This lack of recognition prevents their flourishing and thus their essential needs are not met. Therefore, consumers buying a 'bargain' are ignoring the conditions of its production and the detrimental effects on workers producing it. Similar arguments could be made with regard to cheap goods and the effects of their production on ecosystems and other species.

Ontological claims about the nature of humans as complex (see, for example, van Staveren 2001) suggest that human decision-making is a multifaceted activity, including ethical judgements. Moreover, for Sayer (2004), the economy is moral in an even deeper sense, that all economic practices have implicit ethical bases. For example, labour relations (and for instance wage levels) 'presuppos[e] the establishment of moral economic norms' (Sayer 2004, p. 5). The same could be said of property rights, including intellectual property. Thus, as Tomer (2001) suggests, even if humans may at some point resemble the self-interested, separate, non-reflexive and unchanging nature of *homo economicus*, at other, perhaps more mature points in their lives, they exhibit different ethical positions. Thus, a consumption decision may include ethical judgements on what purchases may aid pursuance of the good life; whereas under the utilitarianism which may be implicit in neoclassical economics, the consumption decision is based purely on whether utility is maximized.

Conclusions

Realism remains highly influential. Realism is simply the view that there is (or may be) a world existing independently (in some sense) of our conception of it. However, realism is highly variegated. In economics, Mäki and critical realism have tried to add clarity to realism in different ways. Mäki has attempted to categorize realism(s) via analyses of the practices within economics. Critical realism has also examined the practice of economists, but from the perspective of a philosophy of science. Specific realist positions usually accompany ontological claims, which in turn lead to ethical positions. Both are employed, most often implicitly, by economists in their formulation of theory and policy analysis.

Notes

This Chapter benefited from comments by Andrew Brown, Steve Fleetwood, Irene van Staveren and two referees. The usual disclaimer applies.

1. An important element of Mäki's contribution is to (*passim*) clarify the distinction between realism and realisticness. While realism is a philosophical position (such as those discussed above), realisticness is an attribute of representations. If realism is to say that the vocabulary of true and false may be applied to a theory T, realisticness is to say that theory T is true (Mäki 1998a). Mäki holds that this is an important distinction because many of the debates in economics over realism (for example, realism of assumptions) actually confuse realism and realisticness. Mäki (1998b) applies this distinction to the work of Coase (1937, 1960) on transaction costs.
2. That is not to conflate literatures on well-being and happiness. Brown et al. (forthcoming) argue that the concept of happiness employed in that literature is an attempt to reinstate cardinal utility, and is based on individualism. They stress that well-being may have an alternative, objective basis. See also Gasper (2007).

References

Bhaskar, Roy (1978), *A Realist Theory of Science*, Hemel Hempstead: Harvester.
Bhaskar, Roy (1979), *The Possibility of Naturalism: A Philosophical Critique of the Contemporary Human Sciences*, London: Verso.
Bhaskar, Roy (1986), *Scientific Realism and Human Emancipation*, London: Verso.
Brown, Andrew, Andy Charlwood, Cristopher Forde and David Spencer (2007), 'Job quality and the economics of New Labour: a critical appraisal', *Cambridge Journal of Economics*, **31**, 941–71.
Calder, Gideon (2007), 'Ethics', in Mervyn Hartwig (ed.), *Dictionary of Critical Realism*, London: Routledge.
Coase, Ronald (1937), 'The nature of the firm', *Economica*, **4**, 386–405.
Coase, Ronald (1960), 'The problem of social cost', *Journal of Law and Economics*, **3**, 1–44.
Collier, Andrew (2000), *Being and Worth*, London: Routledge.
Fleetwood, Steve (1997), 'Aristotle in the 21st century', *Cambridge Journal of Economics*, **21**, 729–44.
Fleetwood, Steve (2008), 'Workers and their alter ego as consumers', *Capital and Class*, **94**, Spring, 31–47
Gasper, Des (2007), 'Uncounted or illusory blessings? Competing responses to the Easterlin, Easterbrook and Schwartz paradoxes of well-being', *Journal of International Development*, **19** (4), 473–92.
Kirzner, Israel (1979), *Perception, Opportunity and Profit*, Chicago, IL: Chicago University Press.
Kourany, Janet (2000), 'A successor to the realism/anti-realism question', *Philosophy of Science*, **67** (Supplement), S87–101.
Lawson, Tony (1997), *Economics and Reality*, London: Routledge.
Lawson, Tony (2000), 'Evaluating trust, competition and co-operation', in Yuichi Shionoya and Kiichiro Yagi (eds), *Competition, Trust and Co-operation: A Comparative Study*, Berlin: Springer.
Lawson, Tony (2003), *Reorienting Economics*, London: Routledge.
Mäki, Uskali (1989), 'On the problem of realism in economics', *Richerche Economics*, **63** (1–2), 176–98.
Mäki, Uskali (1990), 'Scientific realism and Austrian explanation', *Review of Political Economy*, **2** (3), 310–44.
Mäki, Uskali (1992), 'The market as an isolated causal process: a metaphysical ground for realism', in Bruce Caldwell and Stephan Boehm (eds), *Austrian Economics: Tensions and New Developments*, Boston, MA: Kluwer.
Mäki, Uskali (1996), 'Scientific realism and some peculiarities of economics', in Robert Cohen, Risto Hilpinen and Qiu Renzong (eds), *Realism and Anti-Realism in the Philosophy of Science, Boston Studies in the Philosophy of Science*, Boston, MA: Kluwer.

Mäki, Uskali (1998a), 'Aspects of realism about economics', *Theoria*, **13** (2), 301–19.
Mäki, Uskali (1998b), 'Is Coase a realist?' *Philosophy of the Social Sciences*, **28** (1), 5–31.
Mäki, Uskali (2005), 'Reglobalizing realism by going local, or (how) should our formulations of scientific realism be informed about the sciences?', *Erkenntnis*, **63**, 231–51.
Putnam, Hilary (2004), *Ethics without Ontology*, Cambridge, MA: Harvard University Press.
Ruccio, David and Jack Amariglio (2003), *Postmodern Moments in Economics*, Princeton, NJ: Princeton University Press.
Sayer, Andrew (2000), *Realism and Social Science*, London: Sage.
Sayer, Andrew (2004), *Moral Economy*, mimeo Department of Sociology, Lancaster University, www.lancs. ac.uk/fass/sociology/papers/sayer-moral-economy, accessed 27 October, 2008.
Sayer, Andrew (2005), *The Moral Significance of Class*, Cambridge: Cambridge University Press.
Staveren, Irene van (2001), *The Values of Economics: An Aristotelian Perspective*, London: Routledge.
Tomer, John (2001), 'Economic man versus heterodox men: the concepts of human nature in schools of economic thought', *Journal of Socio-Economics*, **30** (4), 281–93.

See also the entries on: Epistemology; Positive versus normative economics.

57 Religion
Robert H. Nelson

After long neglect, the subject of religion has received growing attention in the economics profession over the past two decades. One of the reasons is that it has proven difficult to explain the levels of economic development of many nations around the world without reference to a national culture, and many of these cultures have been significantly influenced by religion. Contrary to a wide expectation in the modern era that the role of religion would gradually diminish, and perhaps eventually disappear, in many parts of the world various forms of religious fundamentalism have instead been growing, both in numbers of followers and in political and economic impact. In economic terms, individual consumers can be said to demand a variety of forms of religious activity as part of their maximization of utility, and producers of religion have emerged to supply religious services in an overall market for religion.

There is also increasing understanding that secular religions, such as Marxism and the American progressive 'gospel of efficiency', incorporate economic arguments while borrowing heavily from traditional Christian sources, which is one of the reasons for their success. In the intellectual sphere in general, there has been a blurring of the lines between secular religion and traditional religion, reflecting that the category of religion can legitimately include fundamental belief systems that may or may not include a God in the hereafter. A religion of economics may be one in that category.

The subject of religion and economics is large and diverse. This chapter reviews three important elements of the new attention to religion among economists: (i) the role of religion in national economic development, (ii) the economic behaviour of consumers and producers in the market for religion, and (iii) the religious side of economics itself as a professional discipline.

Max Weber revisited
One hundred years ago, Max Weber looked to religion as a root explanation for the rise of capitalism, and the subsequent economic success of the West, arguing that certain tenets of the Calvinist theology of salvation encouraged an ascetic commitment to a worldly calling. Weber's thesis was subsequently strongly criticized, partly because important features of capitalism had first arisen in Italy. Yet, though the debate continues, Weber's thinking is experiencing a revival. Many economic and other historians continue to consider the rise of capitalism as closely linked to the Protestant Reformation.

The reasons, however, extend well beyond Weber's original focus on Calvinist theology. Protestantism encouraged the individual reading of the Bible and thus higher rates of literacy and the development of human capital. Also, Protestant confiscations of large Catholic properties opened them for commercial use in the market. Protestantism abolished the Catholic separation between the priesthood and the laity – creating a new 'priesthood of all believers'. The perfection of all of society – including its economic elements – became a religious obligation, as seen in the American Puritans' belief that they were a chosen people, with a divine mission to create God's Kingdom in Massachusetts. This Protestant sense of a divine responsibility here on earth reappeared in the American social gospel movement, which played a significant role in the founding of the American Economic Association in 1885. Leading economists such as Richard Ely argued that a valid Christian religion was now about curing the ills of this world and that scientific knowledge of the workings of society – and especially of the economy – would be essential to fulfilling this religious task.

Many of the most important economic impacts of Protestantism were thus unintended; the rise of capitalism almost certainly would have been regretted by John Calvin and other Protestants of his time. Furthermore, the greatest economic impacts of Protestantism often came long after the Reformation, and indeed many of them became evident only in the modern era when the specific character of Protestant theology had been significantly altered. The economic importance of Protestantism may reflect its competitive organizational structure as a religion as much as its specific doctrines. Because Protestantism had many denominations and greater religious fluidity, it had a greater ability to accommodate its theology and its practices to rapid social change. If one Protestant denomination was not filling the economic bill, so to speak, another Protestant competitor could rapidly arise in its place. Protestantism sustains a 'free market' of religion and thus is more adaptable than the hierarchical religious organization of the Roman Catholic Church with its elaborate centralized system of religious regulations.

Barro and McCleary (2003) include religious variables among the explanatory variables in their models of national economic growth, finding some statistical significance. La Porta et al. (1998) find specifically that a Catholic national religious history and national economic growth are negatively correlated. Latin America has attracted growing interest because its long-time poor economic performance is difficult to explain in conventional economic terms. Lawrence Harrison (1985) argued that the economic failures of the region were due to a Latin American cultural 'state of mind' that was significantly attributable to the legacy of the long Spanish Catholic colonial period. Timur Kuran (2004) finds that the relative economic backwardness of Muslim nations has reflected in part specific features of Islamic religion.

Drawing on the work of Ronald Coase and Oliver Williamson, a 'new institutional economics' has focused since the 1970s on transaction costs as a determinant of economic organization and efficiency. Among many factors, transaction costs might be higher or lower, according to the ethical system in society. Religious beliefs might be particularly important economically – whatever the ultimate validity of its message, a religion might be more or less economically 'efficient' – because religion could foster trust and higher ethical standards of behaviour, thus significantly reducing transaction costs. Douglass North and other economic historians have sought to explore the impact of 'social capital' – often the product of religious influences – on economic outcomes. In Italy, Robert Putnam (1993, p. 107) found that devout Catholics showed less trust and fewer other behavioural characteristics that enhanced the level of social capital, thus contributing to the large economic disparities between the north and the south of the country.

There has been growing recognition that economic development is more than just a process of making necessary capital investments, or of creating a system of property rights and other appropriate economic institutions. It involves major changes in beliefs and indeed a wholesale process of social transformation that encompasses change in almost every dimension, including religion. Other than warfare, the free market is the greatest instrument for social change in the history of the world. It sweeps aside not only inefficient businesses, but much else of the old order. Religion, however, often resists such rapid change. Future economic research should examine not only the relative ability of Protestantism versus Catholicism to accommodate the transformative forces of modernization in the West but also the receptivity to such change of Buddhism, Islam, Hinduism and Eastern Orthodox Christianity in other parts of the world. Economists should be leading contributors to this research, but its inherent interdisciplinary character will necessarily involve significant contributions from political scientists, historians, sociologists, cultural anthropologists, theologians and other fields.

Weber and other economists began this effort 100 years ago, but the contemporary process of exploring the cultural – and thus often religious – roots of economic development is yet at an early stage. Any grand theory to explain the role of ethics and religion in economic growth and development is unlikely at this time. It will be important first to conduct a number of analyses of specific nations and particular episodes in economic history.

The microeconomics of religion

Asking a different set of questions, a second new area of economic study is the microeconomics of religion (Iannaccone 1998). For example, are individuals with higher incomes more likely to go to church? What is the relationship between church attendance and the size of individual donations? Economically, membership of a religion can be understood as a way of maximizing individual utility and thus be placed under the same economic lens as other acts of individual consumption. For those who believe in life after death, long-run consumption – and thus the total long-run individual level of utility – might be conceived to include even events in the hereafter (Azzi and Ehrenberg 1975).

Iannaccone (1995) analyses religious activity within an economic framework of rational choice theory. One chooses a religion (Roman Catholic, Anglican, Southern Baptist, Lutheran and so on.) and a particular church and clergy in order to maximize one's future advantage. Some churches require strictly observant behaviour as a condition of membership, thus raising the individual costs of religion, while others make little effort to oversee the religious practices of their membership. Religions have varying requirements – in Judaism, for example, following kosher rules may be mandated – and thus widely varying opportunity costs are created to full religious participation. In matters of achieving salvation, Roman Catholicism gives a greater importance to positive actions in this world according to well-defined church rules, while Protestantism preaches salvation 'by faith alone'. Among other consequences, rational consumers with different risk preferences will factor the alternative theologies of salvation into their religious choices.

Areas of religious activity will involve different prices – in terms of both money and time, with the value of time varying substantially among individuals, normally closely correlated with incomes and marginal wage rates. Given both an income and a time constraint, the choice among religious commitments and actions will then be embedded in a larger framework of individual consumer choice to maximize overall utility, subject to these constraints. Some people will therefore rationally choose to watch or play football on Sundays instead of going to church, possibly making different choices in this regard in the course of their lifetime, reflecting changing relative 'prices'. Others will choose to hike in the wilderness, perhaps finding greater spiritual inspiration there than in attending official church services indoors. Various forms of spirituality compete along the many potential dimensions of religious satisfaction to maximize individual benefits minus costs.

As in other areas of consumer choice, increasing income is likely to have significant consequences for religious activities. With more feasible choices, the opportunity cost of direct religious participation will rise, perhaps causing individuals with higher incomes to attend fewer church services. If individuals wish to maintain a high degree of religious involvement, they may instead rationally substitute higher monetary donations and other financial contributions for the commitment of their own time and effort to church affairs. Alternatively, once people have satisfied their core material needs for food, clothing and shelter, religion may become a higher need that attracts greater direct involvement of those with more income, making religion a 'luxury good'. Christianity in the medieval period was largely the province of the wealthier segments of society. Today, surveys show that religious commitment – if not total time spent in church – increases at least modestly with rising income. Contemporary environmentalism can be seen as a secular form of contemporary religion that may be similarly income elastic. More definitive answers to such microeconomic issues of religion require further research.

On the supply side of religion, a church is a special form of 'business' and the 'market for churches' offers a potentially interesting case study in the field of industrial organization. In this new area of research, economists assume that the leaders of religious organizations act according to the economic motives of the marketplace. Contrary to the usual assumptions of the past, a religion and a church may not be distinguished by an ethical or altruistic set of motives but by the unusual setting in which private profit-making takes place. A religion can be good business, including the economic 'monopoly' that the Catholic Church long asserted as a matter of a divine command. According to economists such as Ekelund et al. (1996), historic Vatican assertions are not to be taken at face value but should be seen as business strategies for discouraging the rise of religious competitors.

In Protestantism, by contrast, widespread religious competition is the norm. The denominations within Protestantism partially serve as brand names with the same informational purposes as say 'Toyota' and 'Ford' among automobile makers. Just as free markets outperform monopolies in the production of ordinary goods and services, Stark and Iannaccone (1994) argue that nations with wide religious freedom and competition – more likely historically to have a large Protestant influence – encourage greater devotion and stronger religious attachments. From this perspective, the notably high degree of religious belief and observance in the United States – unusual for such a high-income nation, and in contrast to Europe – is due to the fierce religious competition which better serves 'customers'. In religion as well as ordinary goods and services, the unregulated free market often yields greater total product at less cost.

Because many churches depend for their operation on voluntary contributions of time and money, they face a major free-rider problem. Some churches function less as profit-maximizing businesses than as self-organized clubs of individuals. As Mancur Olson described for such collective action in general, one strategy is to offer individual benefits to members of the group (a church in this case) that exceed the individual costs of membership. Historically, until the rise of the welfare state, churches took care of the poor. Churches today provide not only activities designed to inspire religious knowledge and faith but also child-care, Sunday potluck dinners, personal counselling, weddings and funerals and other social activities and services. For many people, the church has become not only their place of worship but also the focal point of their community life.

Some churches place much higher demands on members than others. This may be seen as creating a particular type of 'hostage' commitment that helps to address the free-rider problem. Once individuals have invested a large amount of time and effort in a particular church, they will be reluctant to leave because they would then forgo this significant past investment. It is therefore more difficult to free-ride on the actions of others in the church because this may result in a costly expulsion from the group. Thus, members of demanding religious sects do not have to rely on idealistic motives alone; they can reliably trust others in the group for economic reasons. In an extreme case, acts of terrorism may create particularly strong hostage effects, establishing powerful economic incentives to maintain support and cooperation within the group without threat of free-rider defections.

Religion can play an important role in understanding the economic workings of non-religious organizations as well. Gary Richardson (2005) argues that, in the functioning of medieval guilds, Christianity played an important practical role by threatening defectors with loss of religious benefits, thereby helping to resolve the free-rider problems of the guilds. Within the modern business corporation, as in the wider society, it is important to foster a cultural environment of trust and mutual cooperation. In some businesses, a shared religion may play an important role in this respect.

Until recently, most economists neglected the impact of religion on consumer and producer behaviour. But this was rapidly changing by the end of the twentieth century, as evidence was increasing of the large influence religion has in the affairs of society. The microeconomics of religion is still at an early stage of research, leaving a wide range of economic issues for study in the future.

Economics as religion

From one perspective, analysing religious behaviour as a case study in individual rational choice and in industrial organization is an exercise in achieving greater scientific understanding of the social phenomenon of religion. From another perspective, however, it is a symbolic statement of the higher religious authority of the economic way of thinking – of an 'economic religion'. In the broadest sense, religion consists of the framing process by which events in the world are understood, interpreted and given an ultimate meaning. In Marxism, the laws of economic history took the place of the Christian God in controlling and ordering events in the world (economics was 'omnipotent'). Reflecting an underlying Christian eschatology, the end of economic history in Marxism is a new heaven on earth.

Neoclassical economics can also become a religion in this sense (Nelson 1991, 2001). When former Princeton University economist William Baumol was asked to explain why he had entered the economics profession, his response was that he had hoped to cure poverty which was the 'root of all evil'. In the Bible, original sin in the Garden of Eden is the 'root of all evil'. In Baumol's alternative theology, there is a new explanation for the presence of sin in the world. Severe economic deprivation – the dire poverty in which human beings have lived for almost all of human history – has driven people to lie, cheat, steal and commit other sinful acts.

If poverty is the true explanation for the presence of sin in the world, then the economic successes of the modern age have created a radical new possibility for humanity. If economic shortages could be entirely eliminated, it would be possible to 'save the world' through human economic actions alone. The biblical God would no longer be necessary. Economic progress would eliminate the old divisions between human beings grounded in resource scarcities, thus leading us to a new heaven on earth. Indeed, John Maynard Keynes wrote in the essay 'Economic possibilities for our grandchildren', ([1930] 1963) that rapid economic growth would soon lead to a condition of general and total abundance and thereby to a new and far better era in human history.

When religion is understood as an economic act of rational choice, it amounts to an assertion that traditional religion should be viewed within the framing lens of economic analysis – and not vice versa. The highest order of understanding, the genuine route of access to the highest truths, is achieved through processes of economic reasoning. Thus, the past indifference of social scientists to traditional religion partly reflected a disdain for a religious competitor. The social sciences – with economics leading the way – challenged traditional Judaism and Christianity, in effect claiming through their methods of analysis to be the highest religious authority of our time. With the rise of the microeconomic study of religion, they have reasserted that dominance by seeking to 'explain' religion in economic terms – religion is merely an alternative form of consumer good. Economists do not speak, by contrast, of the exercise of such rational choice in their individual decision to become an economist or in their choice of economic school (economic 'denomination') with which to affiliate. Apparently for them, the practice of economics, unlike traditional religion, is above all that, not a matter simply of individual consumption of a good or service, but involving a higher order of understanding and existence – entering into the true religious domain of life.

When economics and other social sciences are seen in a theological light, new questions of fundamental values emerge. How does economic religion understand (sometimes explicitly but more often implicitly) traditional religious questions, such as the relationship between human beings and nature? Is it appropriate that 'the Creation' of traditional Christianity has become the materially productive 'natural resource' of economic religion? Is the course of history leading us to a new heaven on earth, as many economic prophets have said, or perhaps to a new hell on earth, as many environmental critics of the 'worship' of economic growth more recently warn? What distinguishes 'good' from 'evil' in economic religion? Were 'efficient' and 'inefficient' the most important categories of ethical approval in the twentieth century?

In the past century, belief in economic progress has appeared to be the most powerful religion of the age. Professional economists did not create this belief, nor were they principally responsible for the deep modern conviction of the saving powers of 'progress'. However, given that a faith in economic progress was (and still is) the religion of such large numbers of people around the world, the twentieth-century profession of economics can itself be viewed as a priesthood in the following sense. As the technical experts in the workings of economic growth and development, it was the economists' teachings that provided an operational content to the modern faith in earthly salvation by economic progress. By assuring the world that economic knowledge can reveal the inner workings of economic advance, moreover, economists have helped to sustain hopes for continuing rapid economic growth. If society follows the policy recommendations of the economic priesthood, the wonderful result – and it will not be far in the future – will be a new heaven on earth reached by economic means.

Whether or not current professional economists explicitly make any such statements is unimportant to this argument. In fact, few do so today, although more did in the past. Nonetheless, this economic theology remains implicit in the thinking of perhaps the majority of current economists. Indeed, part of the attraction of the idea of economic progress as a religion is that it seemingly leaves behind the old wars within Christianity and other fierce religious disagreements of the past.

Conclusion

Religion is partly about changing preferences – as in being 'born again' – and in this respect it fits awkwardly with the standard assumption of economics that takes preferences as given. Economists have previously addressed such matters in a limited way, as in the study of advertising, but the power of religion to change individual behaviour through a greater sense of guilt, higher hopes for salvation and many other psychological mechanisms is of an altogether different magnitude. Study of the role of religion in shaping national culture, and thus influencing the level of social capital in society, will require greater attention to past historical events than economists have been accustomed to giving.

Religion is ultimately more than an element of the individual utility function or an object of market production. In the most profound sense, religion is about the very act of framing our understanding of our existence in the world. It is in this sense that economics may for many individuals even become their own religion. To ask the question, how does the choice of a basic way of framing human existence influence subsequent economic outcomes, individually and collectively, would have fallen outside the scope of most economic thought in the twentieth century. Research into the economic impact of religion may therefore require that current economists learn to think more broadly about the essential character of human beings and the historical and cultural workings of society. In the end, the complexities introduced by the full study of religion and economics in all of its dimensions may add to the pressures for a wider rethinking of economics in the twenty-first century.

References

Azzi, Corry and Ronald Ehrenberg (1975), 'Household allocation of time and church attendance', *Journal of Political Economy*, **83** (1) February, 27–56.

Barro, Robert J. and Rachael M. McCleary (2003), 'Religion and economic growth across countries', *American Sociological Review*, **68** (5), 760–81.

Ekelund, Robert B., Robert F. Hebert, Robert D. Tollison, Gary M. Anderson and Audrey B. Davidson (1996), *Sacred Trust: The Medieval Church as an Economic Firm*, New York: Oxford University Press.

Harrison, Lawerence E. (1985), *Under-development is a State of mind: The Latin American Case*, Lanham, MA: Madison Books.

Iannaccone, Laurence R. (1995), 'Vodoo economics? Defending the rational choice approach to religion', *Journal for the Scientific Study of Religion*, **34** (March), 76–89.

Iannaccone, Laurence R. (1998), 'Introduction to the economics of religion', *Journal of Economic Literature*, **36** (3) September, 1465–96.

Keynes, John Maynard ([1930] 1963), *Essay's in persuasion*, New York: W.W. Norton.

Kuran, Timur (2004), 'Why the Middle East is economically underdeveloped: historical mechanisms of institutional stagnation', *Journal of Economic Perspectives*, **18** (3) Summer, 71–90.

La Porta, Rafael, Florencio Lopez-De-Silanes, Andrei Shleifer and Robert W. Vishny (1998), 'The quality of government', NBER Working Paper 6727, September, National Bureau of Economic Research, Cambridge, MA.

Nelson, Robert H. (1991), *Reaching for Heaven on Earth: The Theological Meaning of Economics*, Lanham, MD: Rowman & Littlefield.
Nelson, Robert H. (2001), *Economics as Religion: From Samuelson to Chicago and Beyond,* University Park, PA: Penn State University Press.
Putnam, Robert D. (1993), *Making Democracy Work: Civic Tradition in Modern Italy*, Princeton, NJ: Princeton University press.
Richardson, Gary (2005) 'Christianity and craft guilds in late medieval England: a rational choice analysis', *Rationality and Society*, **17** (2), May, 139–89.
Stark, Rodney and Laurence R. Iannaccone (1994), 'A supply-side reinterpretation of the "secularization" of Europe', *Journal for the Scientific Study of Religion*, **33** (3), September, 230–52.

See also the entries on: Catholic social thought; Islam; Protestant ethics; Sin; Max Weber and the Protestant work ethic.

58 Rhetoric
Arjo Klamer

Rhetoric is an ancient discipline. It lost interest over the past century but has more recently made a comeback. This chapter explores the discipline of rhetoric as it is currently understood, in connection with the ethical life. The objective is to show how conventional wisdom on both rhetorical and ethical practices can be turned on its head by connecting rhetoric and ethics. The conclusions are twofold. First, if rhetoric is understood as sophistry, as the art of finding the right words to convince people of anything, rhetoric would lend itself to any purpose, ethical and unethical. If rhetoric is defined as the art of persuading others of the right thing or the right idea, rhetoric could be understood as the midwife of ethical ideas and practice. Second, if ethics is believed to be a subject of rational thought leading to principles to which any reasonable person would adhere, ethical reasoning would be non-rhetorical. If we follow Alasdair MacIntyre, Stuart Hampshire and, for that matter, Aristotle and Adam Smith, we would quickly acknowledge the rhetorical characteristics of ethical reasoning and practice.

On rhetoric
In order to connect rhetoric with ethics in an economic context we do well to first address the implications of perceiving rhetorical practices in all communication, including the communication of ethical ideas and values.

Aristotle wrote *On Rhetoric* with a sharp rejection of rhetoric by his teacher Plato in mind. He had to carve out a role for rhetoric avoiding the reasons for which Socrates and Plato dismissed rhetoric as unethical. In his dialogue *Gorgias*, Plato has the main protagonist Gorgias, a rhetorician himself, define the rhetorician as follows:

> The rhetorician is competent to speak against anybody on any subject, and to prove himself more convincing before a crowd on practically every topic he wishes, but he should not any the more rob the doctors – or any craftsmen either – of their reputation, merely because he has his power. (1991, section 457)

Gorgias portrays the rhetorician as we would now the contemporary public relations person, communication specialist and arguably lawyer, all of whom would make a convincing case for any claim or position, for or against the death penalty, for or against smoking, for or against any. Socrates argues that people should strive to speak the truth and only those who know the truth can do so honestly. Rhetoricians like Gorgias may have no inkling of the truth but just connect the proper words to any position. That makes them unethical by the logic of Plato and Socrates.

Aristotle, therefore, limits rhetoric as pertinent to just three types of speech: that in the political arena (deliberative), that in the court of law (forensic) and that at special occasions like weddings and funerals (eipideictic). In all of these cases, so he argues, the speaker must convey a message that is only probable, and therefore has to rely on an arsenal of rhetorical figures, like enthymemes (incomplete syllogisms), metaphors and all kinds of topoi (commonplaces).

Interest in rhetoric subsided and all but disappeared in the middle of the nineteenth century, when science took over and the endless possibilities of scientific reasoning captured the collective imagination. The subject was revived by the failure of logic and science to live up to the high expectations, as awareness grew that science has serious shortcomings and that uncertainty remains a fact of life. Philosophers achieved the insight that we humans not only have to deal with the divide between our mind and the world out there, but also with the divide that separates us from others (see Klamer 2007, Ch. 5). Even when I think I know something, I still face the challenge of persuading others that I do. How do I get you, the reader, to understand of this topic what I understand of it? This is the question all of us face all of the time, in some form or another, as teachers, as colleagues, as employees, as customers, as traders, as friends, as spouses and as parents. Accordingly, contemporary rhetoricians see cause to be attentive to rhetorical practices in all of human communication, including communication in scientific communities. This would mean science is rhetorical, as is economics (Nelson et al. 1986; McCloskey [1984] 1998).

To argue that economics is rhetorical implies arguing that economists use various rhetorical strategies and rhetorical figures to make their case. It also implies an awareness that the persuasiveness of an economic argument depends on the three major means of persuasion that Aristotle distinguished in his *Retorica*: (i) the ethos or reputation of the speaker or writer, (ii) the pathos or emotions of the audience and (iii) the logos or the arguments.

Ethos stands for the quality of the person making the case. It matters whether this person is a freshman at university or a full professor. The ethos of a Nobel prize winner is such that almost anything they say demands attention. Ethos is something people who want to persuade can work on. *Pathos* concerns the audience. The emotions of an academic audience are unlike those of the members of a family. When academic economists are not challenged by a paper or talk, they tend to get bored and sometimes even angry. When family members are challenged with the latest development in cooperative games, they may get bored and perhaps angry as well. The emotions of students are again of another order. *Logos* comprises the invention and composition of a range of arguments, and includes the choice of appropriate metaphors, topoi (commonplaces), anecdotes, narratives and arguments.

Arguments can be theoretical and empirical. In accordance with the terminology of Toulmin ([1958] 1994), they include claims (what the argument is about), grounds (first indications), warrants (theories), backings (empirical tests), modals (qualifications), rebuttals (refutation of possible criticisms) and conclusions (with the possible consequences of the argument). The warrants generally include the application of *metaphors*. Economists use metaphors whenever they draw elements from a domain that is more or less known and apply them to a phenomenon they want to account for. So when economists call education an 'investment' they draw from the domain of finance the concept investment and apply this to the domain of education. Such a metaphor has a heuristic purpose, as it gets listeners to think of education in terms of capital, and the returns it will yield. 'Education is a market' is another metaphor that gets economists thinking in terms of demand, supply, price and product (see also Klamer 2007, Ch. 6).

People who are skilled in the rhetoric of economics know the appropriate topoi, or commonplaces. That means in conversation or in writing they can draw on all kinds of topics. When a student complains that the rationality assumption is unrealistic, they may reach for the topos 'the realism of assumptions does not matter'. When a student exclaims that trade is unfair for developing countries, they may appeal to the topos 'positive statements versus normative statements'. They may not know the ins and outs of these topoi, but that is unnecessary; they are commonly understood and accepted (until someone is able to persuade economists to the contrary). The *narrative* in scientific arguments is usually somewhat hidden. Even so, in seminars the presenter of an essay will often begin by telling the basic story that drives the argument. In everyday discourse narratives tend to be dramatic; they have heroes and villains who win or lose. An academic paper usually narrates the experience of the researcher who faces a problem and in the quest for truth overcomes various obstacles in order to reach a surprising answer (result) with some ingenuity. Academic economics is about academic economists and is for that reason usually not all that persuasive for non-academic audiences: they do not share the academic pathos and do not identify with the narrative.

The conclusion is that a science like economics is rhetorical for the simple reason that arguments that rely on mere logic and facts do not suffice to bridge the divide between people. Science depends on the ability to communicate and communication relies on the use of rhetorical means. Ethical discourse is no different.

Ethics

If ethics is believed to be a subject of rational thought leading to principles that any reasonable person would adhere to, ethical reasoning would be non-rhetorical. At least, that is what one might believe. The reasoning that establishes an ethical principle, however, is inevitably rhetorical itself even where it denies or ignores the rhetorical aspects of ethical life. When economists take up the subject of ethics they usually do so in the terms of rational decision-making. In the light of the preceding we can say that the metaphor of choice is the heuristic. The metaphor borrows from the domain of physics and engineering (Mirowski 1989); it poses an objective function, one or more equations that express the constraints, and it calls for a maximization calculation.

This metaphor directs the exploration of ethics into two directions. Norms could be considered constraints that need to be taken into account in the maximization calculation; alternatively the theorists can postulate ethical preferences as elements of the objective function. Exemplary is the approach that economist Amartya Sen took in order to include ethics in economic reasoning (for example, Sen 1982). Sen argued that there are metapreferences that somehow limit or influence the preferences in the utility function of an individual. Another possibility he explores is that the utility function of an individual is partly dependent upon the welfare of others. There is an extensive literature that investigates all possible variations on this theme. (Later Sen would abandon this approach and proposed to focus on capabilities instead.)

All of this work is in no need of rhetoric in the sense that it does not address the communicative gap between the agent and others. (As we already established, the articulation of the argument is rhetorical, as each presentation of scientific ideas inevitably is.) Agents presumably make up their mind as they form their (meta)preferences, they make the appropriate calculations using the right algorithm, maybe do some risk analysis in case of uncertainty, and there they are, ready to make a rational choice. If they adhere to norms and values then these are parameters in the decision process. In such an analysis the theorist abstracts, for example, from all the talk that decision taking involves. The rhetorical perspective calls attention to the deliberation that usually accompanies decision processes.

A reason to focus on the talking is the instability of the ethical categories. When agents value honesty, they find themselves deliberating on what honesty means, what they have to do in order to be honest, whether they can be too honest, and when they are being dishonest. Values are subject to interpretation, and their enactment usually depends on the circumstances. Would we even consider being honest to an intruder and revealing our daughter's hiding place? Are we to go around and tell everybody exactly what we think? If we do not reflect on all of these options, others may compel us to do so. They would bring in arguments, tell anecdotes, appeal to certain values and discuss the effects of our honesty. We would defend ourselves, trying to neutralize the arguments, appealing to some of our heroes, telling different anecdotes and calling upon other values. Such talk inevitably involves more than logic and facts; no one sorts out all of the variables, draws up a formula or two and does the calculation. Everyone makes assertions that are plausible at best and often merely suggestive ('Her honesty only got your mother in trouble'; 'Where did your mother's honesty take her? Eh?'). The deliberation is all about persuasion, saying the things that may change other people's minds. Since such a deliberation is rhetorical, we can say that ethics is rhetorical.

Such a rhetorical process also characterizes moral discussions in economic settings. When diamond traders identify honesty as an important value in their business, new participants in the trade have to find out what exactly that means. How much do you need to tell in order to qualify as honest? Do you have to go around telling who you like and don't like? That would be honest, but it is probably not what the other traders want to hear. Is it dishonest to forget to mention something? If you are expected to adhere to oral agreements, how far are you to go? What if the situation changes dramatically – war breaks out, whatever? Accordingly, knowing what is the right thing to do, requires what Clifford Geertz calls a thick description of particular situations in order to know the meaning of a value like honesty (Geertz 1973).

Virtue ethics is about deliberation
Contemporary moral philosophy pays plenty of attention to the contingent and deliberative character of moral reasoning. An important strand in this line of research is virtue ethics.

Virtue ethics harks back to an ancient tradition with sources such as the *Nichomachean Ethics* by Aristotle – yes, the same philosopher who defined the subject of rhetoric for us. According to this philosopher, moral behaviour is mainly a matter of attitude (a *habitus* Foucault would say). If I am a soldier, to use an often cited example, the attitude I should strive for is that of courage. Courage is the primary virtue that befits a soldier, and not, for example, a nun, whom we expect to have 'piety' as her primary virtue. What courage means concretely, what I am supposed to do in battle, cannot be determined from the outside, and certainly not from an armchair. When I run alone towards the enemy I am probably being reckless, too courageous, in the assessment of other soldiers. I would have done better to seek cover. In another situation, seeking cover signals cowardice, a lack of courage. A good soldier, according to Aristotle, knows how to negotiate the middle ground between cowardice and recklessness. That ability constitutes the excellence of the soldier. The emotion that comes with that he calls *eudaimonia*, which is often translated as happiness but is rather the emotion of someone who knows they are doing good, being courageous in the case of the soldier.

The example highlights three characteristics of virtue ethics. One is that virtue is a value that someone has internalized and enacts. The second is that virtuous action aims at the middle ground between two extremes, and the third is that judging virtuous behaviour requires situational knowledge.

Although Aristotle presumed that the good is somehow known to the agent, contemporary virtue ethicists stress the uncertainties involved. Alasdair MacIntyre (1981) emphasizes the practice of acting in accordance with virtues. We negotiate our way trying to act in accordance with the appropriate virtues, being often confused about what those virtues are or what they mean. The quest for the good life, which characterizes all human life, relates to the circumstances, to what others do and say.

An economic example is the discussion about remuneration. Although economists may evoke the forces of the market that determine remuneration and would like to settle the issue with a formal analysis, in daily practice people argue about what amount is deserved or not. What is an appropriate earning or compensation for services rendered? Note the moral language in which the discussion is couched: 'earnings', 'compensation', 'reward'. Is the pay I receive for a lecture deserved? A great variety of topoi is available such as the topos 'what others get paid', or the topoi 'hard work' and 'responsibility'. Discussants may evoke notions of greed or suggest that the money distracts me from the good towards which I should be striving. The example could be Socrates, who refused payment for his quest for the truth and who condemned the sophists for demanding pay for their services. I could reply by pointing out my needs. How am I to live if I do not ask any compensation? Or the changing times calling for different responses. What then makes remuneration just right? An executive may see a multimillion bonus as evidence of doing well. Others may perceive it as a manifestation of greed. The argument may include a family or tribal metaphor invoking the notion of solidarity and suggesting that such a payment is anti-social and hence immoral. The CEO's self-defence may bring in the topos of the market – this is apparently the going market price for the kind of services rendered. The argument would thicken with more detail and particulars. The discussion is a sign of the unsettledness of what is appropriate pay, of disagreements as to what constitutes the good. Nobody knows for sure. That is why people argue, deliberate, evoke values, give examples and anecdotes; in other words, they practice rhetoric.

This deliberative character of moral reasoning is also stressed by Stuart Hampshire (1983). 'Our everyday and raw experience', so he writes, 'is of a conflict between contrary requirements at every stage of almost anyone's life; why then should moral theorists – Kantians, utilitarians, deontologists, contractarians – look for an underlying harmony and unity behind the facts of moral experience?' (1983, p. 151). In daily life we have to negotiate between the various values to which we adhere, not all of them point in the same direction, as we are to find out; we must live with competing demands and conflicting interests. Take the case of my friend who faced a great offer for his firm. His wife was very much in favour of taking the offer, as she saw the advantage of the money and the free time; but he worried about his associate, who preferred remaining independent, and his employees, who faced a less generous employer. I offered him a heuristic device of Stuart Hampshire and suggested he convene a council with all values and interests at the table. He would hear them all out, have a good night's sleep and see how he felt when he awoke. The moral quality of his decision was not so much determined by a reasoned justification (which would be nothing more than a rationalization anyway), but by the quality of the deliberative process that preceded it. Did he invite all important values, interests and needs to the table. Did he allow the devil's advocate to speak out? Had he heard out everyone at the table? Did he allow sufficient time to process everything he heard? (He decided to sell the company and retired a few years later; the employees and his associate did lose from the deal and his wife was pleased, as was he in the end.)

As the examples indicate, as soon as we acknowledge the rhetorical character of ethical life, our investigation has to turn to a study of discursive practices. Mere blackboard reasoning does not suffice if we want to understand and cope with conflicting values and interests. The first instances of such work by economists are Irene van Staveren (2001), Benjamin Friedman (2005) and Deirdre McCloskey (2006).

References

Aristotle (1976), *Ethics*, trans. J.A.K. Thomson and Hugh Tredenick, New York: Penguin Books.
Aristotle (1991), *On Rhetoric: A Theory of Civic Discourse*, trans. George A. Kennedy, Oxford: Oxford University Press.
Friedman, Benjamin (2005), *The Moral Consequences of Economic Growth*, New York: Albert Knopf.
Geertz, Clifford (1973), *The Interpretation of Cultures: Selected Essays*, New York: Basic Books.
Hampshire, Stuart (1983), *Morality and Conflict*, Cambridge, MA: Harvard University Press.
Klamer, Arjo (2007), *Speaking of Economics*, London: Routledge.
MacIntyre, Alasdair (1981), *After Virtue*, Notre Dame, IN: University of Notre Dame Press.
McCloskey, Deirdre ([1984] 1998), *Rhetoric of Economics*, Madison, WI: University of Wisconsin Press.
McCloskey, Deirdre (2006), *Bourgeois Virtues,* Chicago, IL: University of Chicago Press.
Mirowski, Philip (1989), *More Heat Than Light: Economics as Social Physics; Physics as Nature's Economics*, Cambridge: Cambridge University Press.
Nelson, John, Alan Megill and Deirdre McCloskey (eds) (1986), *The Rhetoric of Human Inquiry*, Madison WI: University of Wisconsin Press.
Plato (1961), *The Collected Dialogues of Plato*, ed. Edith Hamilton and Huntington Cairns, Princeton, NJ: Princeton University Press.
Sen, Amartya (1982), *Choice, Welfare and Measurement*, Oxford: Basil Blackwell.
Staveren, Irene van (2001), *The Values of Economics: An Aristotelian Perspective*, London: Routledge.
Toulmin, Stephen E. ([1958] 1994), *The Uses of Argument*, Cambridge: Cambridge University Press.

See also the entries on: Aristotle; Code of ethics for economists; Teaching economics; Virtue ethics.

59 Rights
Stephen D. Parsons

A considerable variety of discourses today appeal to the idea of rights. However, such appeals are as problematic as they are ubiquitous. Examples of humankind's recourse to the idea of rights are the 1789 document called the *Declaration of the Rights of Man* produced following the French Revolution, the series of amendments added to the US Constitution in 1791 known as the *Bill of Rights*, and the *Universal Declaration of Human Rights* adopted by the United Nations in 1948. Alluding to the problematic status rights can have, MacIntyre asserts 'there are no (human) rights and belief in them is one with belief in unicorns and witches' (MacIntyre 1981, p. 67).

Hausman and McPherson (2006, p. 165) offer three reasons why rights are important in economics. First, clear definitions and demarcations of rights, especially property rights, promotes economic efficiency. For example, North and Thomas (1973) argued that the assignment of clearly defined property rights to intellectual inventions stimulates intellectual innovation. Second, rights, again especially property rights, are frequently taken as a 'starting point' in economic analyses. Hence, investigations into the distributional properties of different economic arrangements often begin from a given allocation of property rights. Third, rights are frequently invoked in order to limit the pursuit of economic goals. For example, even if child labour were economically efficient, it is widely regarded as contravening the rights of children.

One consequence of the particular significance of property rights in economics is that certain authors distinguish between these rights and human rights, referring to the former as 'economic rights' concerned with the 'rights to use, possess, exchange, and otherwise dispose of property' (Paul et al. 1992, p. vii). Indeed, it has been claimed that the distinction between economic and human rights, in the United States at least, 'has been a cornerstone of constitutional law for the past sixty years' (Macey 1992, p. 141). Particularly significant here are the different ways in which these rights are justified and defended. In the case of human rights, appeals are frequently made to the idea of the dignity of the individual, with rights defended to preserve this dignity. However, economic rights are frequently justified on utilitarian or instrumental grounds, in terms of their claimed efficiency.

This has led to the charge that, in the United States again, 'federal courts consistently have taken the position that Congress is free to abuse citizens' economic liberties but is not permitted to interfere with other, non-economic, "rights"' (ibid., p. 141). For example, redistribution through the taxation system is frequently justified on efficiency grounds, even though it can be viewed as an unnecessary interference with property rights. Consequently, Macey (1992) argues that all rights should be given an equivalent status. This rejection of a valid distinction between economic and other rights has led some writers, following Locke, to argue that all rights are essentially property rights. Nozick argues that as the taxation of earnings from labour violates property rights, it is equivalent to forced labour (Nozick 1974, p. 169).

An alternative procedure would be to justify human rights from an efficiency perspective. However, rights-based theories are normally contrasted with the utilitarian-based theories that tend to inform economic discourses. Rights are thus introduced as some form of 'side constraints upon action' (Nozick 1974, p. 30). Hence if an individual has a right to X this right cannot be set aside in order to satisfy aggregate utility considerations. Similarly, if freedom of expression is a right, it cannot be set aside, even if doing so could be justified by considerations of aggregate welfare. Indeed, certain rights are regarded as inviolable. Hence, they cannot be set aside even by the rights-holder. For example, in many countries an individual cannot give up their right to life even if they would choose to. Of course, this partly explains why MacIntyre and others are sceptical: if rights are both fundamental and universal, why do they differ across cultures? What, exactly, is the status of 'a right'?

Attempts to clarify the relevant issues often invoke the juridical positions developed by legal theorist Hohfeld. According to Hohfeld (1923), to have a right is to have a claim whereby if, say, individual A has a right or claim to $10 from individual B, B has a duty to pay A the $10. Rights and duties are thus correlative, with a right, or claim, being a legal position created by imposing a duty on someone else. Hohfeld distinguished this 'claim right' from a liberty, which involves an individual not having a duty not to do an act. Thus, if A has a right to be free from interference by B, B has a duty not to interfere. However, if A has no such right, B does not have a duty not to interfere.

In everyday discourse, the terms 'right' and 'liberty' are frequently conflated. For example, an individual may claim a right to wear odd socks, when in Hohfeld's scheme this is a liberty, not a right. Similarly, under English law, an individual may claim the right to look over the fence at their neighbour. However, this 'right' means they do not have duty not to look, and the neighbour has no duty to be so observed, and hence may erect a high fence (Hart 1982, pp. 166–7). A professional football player has the liberty to score points, but no right, as opponents do not have a duty to allow points to be scored against them.

Given this framework, it can be appreciated that duties may extend beyond rights, and an individual may feel a duty to aid A even if A has no corresponding right. An individual may feel a duty to help a neighbour push start their car, although the neighbour has no right to this assistance. However, Hohfeld is offering a definition of legal rights, where such rights are legally enforceable, although this enforcement is not necessarily at the discretion of the individual with the rights claim. 'Human rights', however, are not justified in terms of legal norms, but as those rights possessed by every person simply by virtue of being human. The rights enshrined in the UN Declaration apply to all individuals, even individuals who inhabit countries which neither legally recognize nor uphold these rights.

At this stage it is useful to briefly compare the observations made here so far with a highly influential appeal to the idea of rights in economics; that appeal is Sen's investigation of the impossibility of a Paretian liberal (Sen 1970). The investigation assumes that individuals have 'nosey preferences', that is, they have preferences regarding outcomes involving others. Sen argues that there is no social decision function that satisfies an unrestricted domain (any individual preference ordering can feature), the Pareto principle and what he terms 'minimal liberalism'. By minimal liberalism Sen assumes a 'liberal sphere' for each individual whereby each has a recognized personal sphere in which his or her preferences alone are significant. Hence here each individual can decide, for example, whether or not to read a certain book. From the previous discussion, we can appreciate that this personal sphere can only be protected in terms of rights, not liberties, hence each has a right to decide whether or not to read the book. Sen is thus arguing that individual rights can conflict with the Pareto principle (see below).

In his initial formulation, Sen considered two individuals, prude (A) and lewd (B), and the act of reading a copy of Lawrence's *Lady Chatterley's Lover*. Sen's argument can be understood in terms of three social states:

a. Neither reads the book.
b. Prude (A) reads the book and lewd (B) does not.
c. Lewd (B) reads the book and prude (A) does not.

Prude (A) is assumed to prefer that no one read the book, but would rather read it herself than have the lewd read it (worried presumably about the further debilitating effect the book might have on lewd). Hence, for A, $a>b>c$.

In contrast, lewd (B) would prefer it if prude (A) read the book, either from enjoyment at the thought of prude's embarrassment, or because of the belief that it would enlighten prude. Further, lewd would prefer prude to read the book than if no one read it. Hence, for B, $b>c>a$.

Sen then introduces the minimal liberalism condition, by which prude prefers that no one read the book rather than that she read it, hence A here has $a>b$. By the same condition, the lewd B has $c>a$. That is, lewd would rather read the book than that no one read it. Introducing the Pareto principle (P), whereby if every individual prefers social state X to social state Y, then X must be socially preferred over Y, then as both individuals rank $b>c$, social state b must be ranked above c. Consequently, prude A has $a>b$, the lewd B has $c>a$, yet the Pareto principle gives $b>c$. Thus, a cycle results.

If the minimal liberalism condition is understood as involving rights claims – and it is difficult to appreciate how the required level of protection can be offered unless rights are involved – there are considerable differences between Sen's analysis and the investigation thus far. First, according to Sen's view, rights are conditional, as preferring no one to read the book, to one's self reading the book, to the lewd reading the book is conditional upon the lewd not reading the book. Hence if the lewd does read the book, the prude's preference becomes irrelevant in the example. However, the earlier discussion assumes rights to be unconditional: if an individual has a right to life, this right is not conditional upon the actions of others. Second, in Sen's example, choices are defined over states of the world, where each chooses their preferred states. However, the previous discussion assumes that rights refer to choices over actions, not social states. Given this, then if an individual has a right to do x – say, sell some property – they may or may not choose to exercise this right. Hence both the prude and the lewd can have a right to read the book, but not rights over social states.

These two differences are indicative of a more fundamental difference. Given the minimal liberalism condition, each has a protected sphere and within this sphere it is assumed that the prude would prefer no one read the book to reading it herself. Sen's 'solution' is to grant priority to the liberalism principle, where, in Mueller's characterization, 'Sen's own preferred solution is to require that the Pareto principle defer to liberal rights' (Mueller 2003, p. 644). However, if 'no one reads the book' entails a right, then all others have a duty not to read the book, and it is far from clear how prude's preference ordering can entail this form of duty. According to Sen, minimal liberalism entails that whatever one thinks is better must be taken to be better for society as a whole (ibid., p. 664). Sen's argument thus does not appear to rest upon issues of rights.

Assisting us in further exploring this idea are two competing theories concerning the conditions necessary for a right to exist (Kramer et al. 1998). According to the first, the benefit or interest theory, a necessary and sufficient condition to have a right is being capable of having, or actually having, an interest or benefit that the right protects. Hence, constraints on conduct can be imposed or relaxed depending upon the individual's interest. According to the second theory, the choice theory, a necessary and sufficient condition for a right to exist is that constraints on conduct can be imposed and relaxed through the choice of another. If individual A has a right to $10 from individual B, then A can choose to claim the money or forgo the claim.

These two accounts do not necessarily conflict. However, as the interest theory is more concerned with the justification of rights and the choice theory with the identification of a right, they frequently do conflict (Freeman 1995). The theories are compatible only in cases where imposing or relaxing constraints on the conduct of A is compatible with the interests of A. Two major problems have been proposed regarding the interest theory. The first concerns third-party claims, where, for example, individual A pays individual B to care for A's sick mother C. In this case, although individual A holds the right, the interest involved is that of individual C.

Consequently it is argued that 'this fact, that the beneficiaries of a claim/duty relation can be rightless third parties poses a considerable difficulty for Benefit Theory' (Steiner 1994, p. 62). The second problem is that interests may conflict, and thus rights will conflict (ibid., pp. 80–1).

However, the claim that the choice theory is hence logically superior is somewhat at odds with our intuition that rights claims can compete. Furthermore, the choice theory is not without problems. It must, for example, indicate how there can be some rights that are regarded as inalienable. It also appears to deny that individuals who cannot exercise choices in the required manner can have rights. As such, animals, children and the mentally impaired would appear incapable of being rights-holders.

Given these competing theories, it is difficult to appreciate how Sen's argument is compatible with either. According to the interest theory, rights protect interests. However, although the prude may prefer that no one read the book, it is far from obvious that no one reading the book is in prude's interest. The prude's interests thus do not appear to give grounds here for granting a right. However, justifying the prude's preferences in rights terms appears to fare no better from the choice perspective, as the preference structure does not appear to permit the prude to allow or not allow anyone else to read the book.

Another way that is found in the literature to distinguish between different forms of rights is in terms of the different stages in the evolution of individual rights, although again controversy reigns. First, there are civil rights or rights to liberty, which grant individuals or groups an area of freedom from the state, for example, the right not to be subject to arbitrary arrest. Second, there are political rights which grant liberties within the state, such as the right to vote in elections or stand for office. Third, there are social, economic and cultural rights, which involve liberties available through, or by means of, the state, such as the right to education. The UN Declaration refers to all three types of rights. However, this third type of right is identified by many as being problematic.

For example, the UN Declaration refers to the 'right to work'. However, if this is a right, who possesses the correlative duty? In most societies, individuals are not able to claim that firms have a duty to offer them employment. Consequently, the possessor of the corresponding duty would appear to be the state. However, in most countries again, although governments may be committed to the idea of full employment, they would invariably refer to 'market conditions' in explaining why they do not possess a duty to employ all unemployed individuals. However, if there is no duty, how can there be a right? The consequent fear is that including such rights will result in a proliferation of possible 'rights claims', where it is difficult to establish the bearers of corresponding duties.

Even a less demanding right, such as the right to an elementary education, if imposing duties on states, would appear to invoke heavy financial burdens on less affluent countries. Advocates of social and economic rights have therefore argued that all rights require extensive financial expenditure by states. Shue (1980), for example, argued that all rights require three kinds of duty in order that the right be effective. These are the duty to avoid depriving a person of a right, the duty to protect them from deprivation of the right and the duty to assist them when deprived. All these duties are ultimately the responsibility of the state. Hence, even the right to liberty and political rights require the state to provide, for example, a judicial system and a police force.

Although the majority of rights advocates would defend civil and political rights, there is no such consensus concerning social and economic rights. Hence even if the state is required to enforce and prevent abuses of rights to liberty and political rights, and this enforcement is expensive, is it necessary to include additional rights that the state must also enforce? Moreover, whilst an individual might be prepared to contribute towards the maintenance of liberty and political rights, it is unclear why the individual should have to contribute goods to provide for the rights of others in cases where they are capable of providing the required goods for themselves. Economic and social rights would thus seem to entail a redistribution of resources between individuals in a manner that the other two forms of right do not (Beetham 1995).

It is useful to return now to the question of the status of rights. Theorists such as Hobbes and Locke defended rights as being 'natural', hence ultimately in theological terms. Such a justification is unlikely to find widespread support today. However, once this metaphysical belief structure is relinquished, the status of rights becomes problematic. The subsequent claim that we have rights because we are human would appear to anchor the possession of rights in the appeal to some transhistorical idea of 'human nature'. This idea appears rather questionable, hence McIntyre's equating the belief in human rights with a belief in witches. The problem is that of justifying the idea of human rights without appealing to some form of 'foundational' discourse.

Marx raises a further issue for rights claims. The common assumption is that rights are located at the level of the individual. Hence the appeal to rights appears to enshrine a commitment to some form of individualism, and moreover assumes a tension between the individual and the collective. Marx objects that 'none of the so-called rights of man goes beyond egoistic man . . . an individual withdrawn behind his private interests and whims and separated from the community' (Marx [1844] 1975, p. 230).

This objection to the 'individual versus the community' perspective was recently taken up from a communitarian perspective (Mulhall and Swift 1996). An important argument here is that rights claims can appear not to be open to negotiation, hence embodying a strident, individualistic perspective. Thus, if an individual claims a 'right' to something, this claim appears non-negotiable: the appeal to rights does not appear to leave open any possibility of compromise. An individual claiming a 'right' to free speech does not appear to leave open the possibility of not speaking freely although free speech may, on some occasion, cause offence to others in the community.

This introduces a further issue: although the tendency is to regard individuals as rights-holders, can there be, say, group rights, or collective rights? For some, any such rights could only be derived from individual rights, and hence have no privileged status. However, for others 'collective rights have important features that distinguish them from individual human rights' (Freeman 1995, p. 39). For example, it might be argued that certain communities have suffered historically from injustices, and hence should be granted collective rights that are unavailable to others. However, this granting of a priority to collective rights over individual rights can be problematic. What, for instance, if the collective being granted the right does not recognize certain individual rights within the community, yet these are regarded as important from a 'universal' standpoint?

This leads to possibly the most radical claim against human rights theories: that they represent the imposition of particular Western values on others who do not subscribe to these values. For example, societies may value and invoke duties rather than rights, group identities over individual autonomy, or collective values over individual claims. If the appeal to rights is thereby abandoned, are there any other discourses that can be appealed to in offering individuals protection against arbitrary claims by states? The idea of rights may be problematic, but it is not clear what could both replace it and yet offer individual protection.

References

Beetham, David (1995), 'What future for economic and social rights?', *Political Studies*, **43**, Special Issue: Politics and Human Rights, 41–60.
Freeman, Michael (1995), 'Are there collective rights', *Political Studies*, **43**, Special Issue: Politics and Human Rights, 25–40.
Hart, Herbert L.A. (1982), *Essays on Bentham*, Oxford: Clarendon.
Hausman, Daniel M. and Michael S. McPherson (2006), *Economic Analysis, Moral Philosophy, and Public Policy*, 2nd edition, Cambridge: Cambridge University Press.
Hohfeld, Wesley (1923), *Some Fundamental Legal Concepts as Applied in Judicial Reasoning*, New Haven, CT: Yale.
Kramer, Matthew H., N.E. Simmons and Hillel Steiner (1998), *A Debate over Rights: Philosophical Inquiries*, Oxford: Clarendon.
MacIntyre, Alasdair (1981), *After Virtue*, London: Duckworth.
Macey, J.R. (1992), 'Some causes and consequences of the bifurcated treatment of economic rights and "other" rights under the United States constitution', in Ellen Paul, Fred Miller and Jeffrey Paul (eds), *Economic Rights*, Cambridge: Cambridge University Press, pp. 141–70.
Marx, Karl ([1844] 1975), 'On the Jewish question', in Karl Marx, *Early Writings*, Harmondsworth: Penguin.
Mueller, Dennis C. (2003), *Public Choice III*, Cambridge: Cambridge University Press.
Mulhall, Stephen and Adam Swift (1996), *Liberals and Communitarians*, Oxford: Blackwell.
North, Douglass C. and Robert P. Thomas (1973), *The Rise of the Western World: A New Economic History*, Cambridge: Cambridge University Press.
Nozick, Robert (1974), *Anarchy, State & Utopia*, Oxford: Blackwell.

Paul, Ellen, Fred Miller and Jeffrey Paul (eds) (1992), 'Introduction', in Ellen Paul, Fred Miller and Jeffrey Paul (eds), *Economic Rights*, Cambridge: Cambridge University Press, pp. vii–xi.
Sen, Amartya (1970), 'The impossibility of a Paretian liberal', *Journal of Political Economy*, **78**, 152–7.
Shue, Henry (1980) *Basic Rights*, Princeton, NJ: Princeton University Press
Steiner, Hillel (1994), *An Essay on Rights*, Oxford: Blackwell.

See also the entries on: Deontology; Amartya Sen.

60 Joan Robinson
Prue Kerr

Joan Robinson (1903–83) was passionate about social justice. Her topics of study ranged from unemployment and poverty in the United Kingdom in the 1930s to the arms race as an entrenched feature of capitalism in both rich and poor nations in the post-World War II era. Robinson was also concerned with the relationship between values and economic theory, drawing upon her economic theory to argue her moral position.

In 1932, at the outset of her long career, Robinson undertook a methodological introspection which culminated in two pieces of writing. One was published as *Economics is a Serious Subject: The Apologia of an Economist to the Mathematician, the Scientist, and the Plain Man* (see Harcourt [1990] 2001). The other, 'A passage from the autobiography of an analytical economist', was for more limited exposure (see Aslanbeigui and Oakes 2006). Both documents reveal Robinson's absorption of the pervasive language and structure of the local logical positivists. Sharply distinguishing between 'values' and 'facts', she declared 'the subject matter of economics is neither more nor less than its own technique' (Robinson 1932, p. 4). Hence, the method pre-empts the problems with which it deals. She saw economics as a 'box of tools'.

Robinson initially required axiomatic assumptions. It was perhaps her acquaintance with Sraffa, Kahn and Keynes that soon led her to favour 'realistic' assumptions (Robinson [1933] 2002). The adequacy of a theory, for her, then became a matter of the realism of its assumptions and the logical coherence of its arguments. Her main methodological issue was the choice between the opposing forces of tractable and realistic assumptions. For many years she maintained her view of economics as a body of techniques. In 1937, in her *Essays in the Theory of Employment*, she wrote 'An economist's sermon', in which she shows how orthodox economic theory had been used to justify certain moral positions. Her dispute was with the logic of those theories, and she took a position in support of the poor and the unemployed based on the alternative Keynesian theory. This was perhaps one of her first polemical pieces. In the same collection another essay, 'Indeterminacy', observes that an economic theory may be indeterminate because factors 'which cannot easily be fitted into the existing structure of pure economic analysis', such as the position of trade unions and political disturbances, 'have to be brought into the story' ([1937] 2002, p. 171). The answer to this methodological problem, she asserts, is 'to discover determinate problems on which to work' (ibid.) This is necessary for economics to become a science.

The economist must dutifully separate out the values inherent in assumptions and theoretical propositions for the unsuspecting reader. In 1955, Robinson delivered a series of lectures entitled 'Marx, Marshall and Keynes: three views on capitalism'. Here, she compared analyses of the three authors, noting that each addressed a different stage of capitalism and each author held a different political attitude towards capitalism, '[b]ut each has significance for other times, for insofar as each theory is valid it throws light upon essential characteristics of the capitalist system which have always been present in it' ([1955] 1960, p. 3). Her strict duality of fact and value, however, seemed to be weakening:

> Economic doctrines always come to us as propaganda. This is bound up with the very nature of the subject and to pretend that it is not so in the name of 'pure science' is a very unscientific refusal to accept the facts . . . The element of propaganda is inherent in the subject because it is concerned with policy'. (Ibid., pp. 3–4)

A questioning of her earlier approach is also evident:

> Economic theory, in its scientific aspect, is concerned with showing how a particular set of rules of the game operates, but in doing so it cannot help but make them appear in a favourable or an unfavourable light to the people who are playing the game . . . This element of propaganda enters into even the most severely technical details of the subject . . . to pretend that we are not interested in the evaluation is mere self-deception. (Ibid., pp. 4–5)

She continued to argue that while 'every economic doctrine that is not trivial formalism contains political judgements . . . it is folly to reject a piece of analysis because we do not agree with the political judgement of the economist who puts it forward' (Ibid., p. 6). One implication of this view is that laissez-faire economics can be dismissed as trivial. Indeed, Robinson used such a criterion of relevance to accept or reject a theory. But she subsequently proposed that '[t]o learn from the economists regarded as scientists it is necessary to separate what is valid in their description of the system from the propaganda that they make, overtly or unconsciously, each for his own ideology' (ibid., p. 12). And, ultimately, 'An economic theory at best is only a hypothesis . . . It suggests a possible explanation of some phenomenon and it cannot be accepted as correct until it has been tested by an appeal to the facts' (ibid.) But the role of the economist extends to policy: 'To make good use of an economic theory we must first sort out the relations of the propagandist and the scientific elements in it, then by checking with experience, see how far the scientific element appears convincing, and finally recombine it with our own political views' (ibid., p. 17). Although still within a positivist framework, with this, she now allowed the economist to take a stance.

Robinson continued to present this view. In 'Marxism: religion and science' ([1962c] 1965) she differentiates between ideology and science, the latter of which can be proven true or false. Science may, however, fall short of adequately describing an actual situation. Here, Robinson tries to reject the proposition that 'Marxism is a scientific ideology', but she lacks the philosophical insight to examine the meanings of such a proposition. Her confusion is apparent:

> It is perfectly legitimate to have schools of thought in a developing subject. A school of thought is distinguished by its method, not by its tenets. Science itself, in a certain sense, is based on faith and on a confident belief that all phenomena will yield to investigation and will turn out to fit into a scheme of natural law. (Ibid., pp. 155–6)

With this she returns to her early view of the unity of science extending to the epistemological space of economic theory. Her translation of Marx's concepts into 'operational' terms perhaps begs the question of by which criteria she compares the different writers' interpretations of the development of capitalism ([1961] 1965, pp. 167–72). In fact, she concentrated on the conclusions drawn by the respective writers about twentieth-century capitalism, commenting on the relationships they proposed and the selection and interpretation of particular features of that history. By this time she had adopted the classical framework and developed a theory of growth which integrated Keynes's principle of effective demand, using class categories and aggregate social relationships (for example, [1956] 2002, 1962d).

In 1973, she again broached the subject of morality and its relationship to theory:

> The flow of production taking place in an industrial economy is an extremely complex entity that cannot be represented in any simple measure. It is something which exists. It is *there* in reality. It is not affected by the way we chose to represent it, but various ways of representing it are connected with the various alternative ways of diagnosing its behaviour through time, its distribution between classes and so forth. ([1973] 1979, p. 255)

Through her discussion of the institutions of modern capitalism, the dominant social relationships and political forces, Robinson, although still entrapped in positivism, nevertheless 'enriched' her basic concepts and what she had to say about economies. She both broadened her scope of what economists should comment upon and gave her own concepts more depth.

Vivian Walsh notes, 'we constantly add to the ways in which language can be responsible to reality' (2003, p. 342). He continues, 'The responsible use of the net product, or surplus, has been the deepest moral issue for classical political economy from its beginnings' (ibid., p. 346). This issue represents a large segment of Robinson's life's work. She focused her concern for the poor in developing countries, particularly India and China, on an attempt to direct the surplus both to immediately improving the conditions of the poorest and to sustainable investment in projects which would return benefits to them. Robinson did not see this body of work as involving a moral choice for her; in her role as economist, she saw it as her responsibility. Walsh also discussed the nature of 'entanglements', as representing the interrelationships between facts, values or conventions and analysis. In the 1977 essay 'What are the questions?' ([1977] 1979, pp. 1–31), Robinson again addressed the issue of what constitutes economics:

> Discussion of an actual problem cannot avoid the question of what should be done about it; questions of policy involve politics . . . Politics involve ideology; there is no such thing as a 'purely economic' problem that can be settled by purely economic logic; political interests and political prejudice are involved in every discussion of actual questions. (ibid., p. 1)

Here, she seems to differentiate 'pure' economics, the logical structure and sequence of the analysis, from the broader scope, which includes the questions asked or issues raised and the nature of the intervention. She refers to the economist's need to defer to historical evidence which, she says, 'can always be read both ways' (ibid., p. 2). But once again, the comparison with the natural sciences leads her first to focus her theoretical attention on getting the logic right and then to accept the limits to the 'scientific' status of economics, due to the ambiguously interpretable nature of its facts. Her commitment to demonstrating the errors in neoclassical theory illustrates the former domain and her prolific work on China and development issues illustrates the latter.

Hence, although she questioned the scope and nature of economic reasoning, she remained trapped by a positivist methodology. While in her later writings she tried to integrate values into the body of her argument she lacked the philosophical instruments to guide her thinking and lend her viewpoints philosophical validity. Her positivism seriously interfered with and limited her theoretical developments, denying her passionately held views on social justice a status equivalent to the 'scientific' element of political economy.

Robinson viewed the arms race as immoral and saw war as shameful but possibly inevitable. She perceived the domain of economics as closely related to morality and both as being integral to understanding. Knowledge in science, according to Robinson, is reached through observation, experimentation and refutation, as well as rational debate. In contrast, she defined 'ethics', one's morality, as a pattern of beliefs about appropriate behaviour in a range of situations; it was constituent of one's ideology. She argued that a person comes to develop these beliefs usually early in their life through a psychological process analogous to language acquisition. Herewith, people learn through the complexity of social interaction and observation within their daily context. The content of this conscience then reflects individuals' interpretations of the beliefs, values and practices of that society in which they were brought up. These beliefs refer to the interests of the self both as individual and in relation to others:

> The biological necessity for morality arises because, for the species to survive [there must be egoism and this should be extended to the family . . . [T]he pursuit of self interest is mitigated by respect and compassion for others . . . [and] there must be a set of rules to reconcile them. Moreover, there must be some mechanism to make the individual keep the rules when they conflict with his immediate advantage . . . Since the egoistic impulses are stronger than the altruistic, the claims of others have to be imposed upon us. The mechanism by which they are imposed is the moral sense or conscience of the individual. (1962a, pp. 10–1)

The implication for the social group is, 'A society cannot exist unless its members have common feelings about what is the proper way of conducting its affairs, and these common feelings are expressed in ideology' (ibid., p. 9).

More particularly:

> In the general mass of notions and sentiments that make up an ideology, those concerned with economic life play a large part, and economics itself . . . has always been partly a vehicle for the ruling ideology of each period as well as partly a method of scientific investigation. (Ibid., p. 7)

According to Robinson, economics addresses partly moral problems with partly 'scientific' methods. Economics can, in the formulation of its propositions and theories, represent an ideology and can also provide a means for investigating the implications of that ideology. 'Any economic system requires a set of rules, an ideology to justify them, and a conscience in the individual which makes him strive to carry them out', she wrote (ibid., p. 18). 'It is the business of the economists, not to tell us what to do, but to show why what we are doing anyway is in accord with proper principles' (ibid., p. 25). That is, the economist provides a rational basis for pursuing ideologically-determined objectives in ideologically correct ways. Robinson takes this responsibility one step further, arguing, 'The task of social science now is to raise selfconsciousness to the second degree, to find out the causes, the mode of functioning and the consequences of the adoption of ideologies, so as to submit them to rational criticism' (1970, p. 122).

Robinson made incidental remarks about the immense wastage of war and armaments production. In 1981, she delivered the Tanner Lectures on Human Values on the subject of the arms race. While her lecture referred to the Cold War, her argument was more general, addressing the dynamic of the military-industrial complex and the economic justifications for arms expenditure. The lectures elaborated ideas and arguments about military expenditure which, up to that point, had been scattered throughout her work. In her Tanner lectures, she proposed three factors which, she said, contributed weight to the continuance and escalation of the arms race.

The first factor was the Cold War, or 'the clash of ideologies'. Such an ideological confrontation makes the positioning of an 'enemy' simple to represent in binary terms; one is either for or against what it represents. It also makes it easy to represent the 'enemy' as irrational, evil and fanatic, as the United States represented the Soviet Union in the 1950s and as it represents the Arab world in the early twenty-first century.

According to Robinson, conflict can be resolved by other means than warfare. Though, even if participants could attain some dialogue, she cautions, 'Nor do I think that purely economic argument can ever finally settle any questions[,] for political and human considerations are always involved in every question and are usually decisive' ([1957] 1960, p. 113). She further notes, 'Political aims require economic planning to carry them out. It is equally true that economic planning require[s] political aims' ([1964] 1965, p. 145). While she understands rationality as extending beyond economic theory, the scope of her notion of economic theory is not entirely confined by rationality; it has a moral dimension. Where rivalry is represented as ideological differences, the scope for negotiation is more limited. After World War II, she notes, the role of military expenditure changed from 'defence' to 'deterrence'. Moreover, deterrence expenditure became, effectively, 'aggressive' expenditure. She classified the (1981) state of the arms race as a 'balance of terror' in which the outcome was meant to be deterrence.

The second factor she considered as contributing to the momentum of the arms race was the force built up, first, by the process of research and development, and then, by the evolution and consolidation of the structures making up the defence industry. The very establishment of the military-industrial complex, she said, propagates its own dynamic. Science in progress, according to Robinson, is difficult to stop, and the domestic armaments industry is indisposed to contain its own competitive forces and rivalries. There is also the weight of vested interests. Incomes earned from the military industry, including salaries, profits and consultancy fees, rely on the continuation of research. Some scientists may construct new problems to accommodate their particular line of research. The complexity of the modern armaments industry, she argued, gives the military authority for its singular competence in its own direction and in the nature of national security. Robinson cited several cases of compromise by scientists who were continually frustrated in their attempts to call a halt to development of arms by the momentum of research. This momentum was said to be assisted by exaggerations of the threat posed by 'the enemy'. Robinson cited Herbert York, a former director of defence research at the Pentagon, who refers to a steady flow of 'phony intelligence' which, due to secrecy, is never disputed (Robinson 1981, p. 270). It is a culture of competition, secrecy and status that is difficult to opt out of, let alone to speak out against. With a national climate of vaguely focused fear, objecting scientists are hardly heard.

Alva Myrdal takes the momentum argument further, beyond the personally competitive. Myrdal places the rationale of the defence industry outside the forces of laissez-faire capitalism. Robinson quotes Myrdal on the perpetuation of the arms race:

> 'The arms race has become politically connected with the vested interests [of] "the military-industrial complex". In military matters, no limit is set by market forces, by competitive demand or by prices. Every new plant for military production, every new production contract, increases the weight of these vested interests. In democratic countries these interests, both labour and business, often become rooted in the parliaments and provincial assemblies, whose representatives are expected to defend local interests'. (Myrdal in Robinson 1981, p. 288)

Robinson adds, 'The vested interest of all who depend for profit or employment on the arms industry (including a large proportion of the universities and research institutes) gave it a solid backing, and the crusade for "freedom" gave it a noble aim' (1970, pp. 85–6).

The third force said by Robinson to sustain the arms race emerges from the connection between military expenditure and employment policy. Robinson proposed an argument that is an economic alternative to laissez-faire. Keynes introduced the possibility of policy intervention to achieve full employment, and in much of the post-World War II environment this was successfully implemented. '[I]t is precisely the economic success of the military-industrial complex (though it has over-reached itself in Vietnam) that puts the greatest obstacle in the way of any such attempt [to resolve conflict peacefully]' (ibid., p. 86). It is the rationality of the economic principle of laissez-faire which dominates over that of a more humane set of values (though Robinson would not go as far as to argue that war is a necessary outcome of laissez-faire).

Robinson explains:

> State expenditure has provided a balancing element in demand to preserve near-stability and continuous growth in the market for goods. The easiest line of expenditure for the state to undertake is for so-called defence . . .
>
> Whatever its causes, the consequence of the Cold War was to provide an outlet for government expenditure which did not compete with private enterprise and which did not saturate demand by producing anything that the public could consume. (Ibid., pp. 84–6)

Here, she is arguing that arms expenditure is justified by ideological factors as well as by the economic factors of preserving certain industries and jobs. Neither is necessary for the economic survival of Western capitalism. The economic factors can be changed. She sees no rational problem in transforming the military sector by structural adjustment programmes: armaments per se are not necessary as a source of government spending. 'It has not been proved that recessions can be avoided, except by armament expenditure, and, since to justify armaments, international tension has to be kept up, it appears that the cure is a good deal worse than the disease' ([1962b] 1965, p. 123).

There is a further consideration. In 1961 she wrote about the United States in 1958:

> [I]t is estimated that expenditure on what is euphemistically called 'defence' was running at more than 11 per cent of the gross national product and in the UK at nearly 8 per cent, which is about equal in each country to the volume of productive industrial investment. This means that without any extra sacrifice or any greater inflationary pressure than has been experienced, the annual increment of industrial productive capacity could have been about doubled if the arms race had been halted. ([1961] 1965, p. 109)

Robinson distinguished between short-run and long-run aspects of the economy. In the short run, the level of employment and the degree of utilization of capital goods vary in association with a given stock of capital; in the long run, this stock of capital changes and new technologies are introduced. The major influences on costs in the short run are in terms of wages and material costs. But in a prosperous economy capital accumulation and technical progress together raise productivity faster than money wages and prices.

In Robinson (1981), she argued that if a certain flow of finance is diverted from civilian to military expenditure, employment falls and costs per unit of employment rise. She then extrapolates to argue that a switch the other way should see correspondingly favourable effects from a short-period position. 'From a long-period point of view the loss due to the arms race is literally incalculable' (ibid., p. 284). She points to the examples of Germany and Japan which developed after World War II with no military industry and experienced 'miracle' growth rates. In the long run, high military budgets, she says, hold back public investment and so inhibit the productivity growth associated with high levels of social investment and, furthermore, incur additional social and economic costs associated with the absence of such investments.

Robinson suggested redirecting arms expenditure into research into energy production. But to redirect resources away from armaments and into energy or social infrastructure for example 'would involve drastic political changes' ([1962b] 1965, p. 115). Military expenditure, she said, depends for its rationale on the Cold War, the 'missile gap' and 'the crusade against Communism in Asia' ([1967] 1979, p. 183).

In the twenty-first century, similar economic arguments are still relevant. It is clear that the military budget is not necessary to maintain full employment. It is also clear that the same resources currently used for military expenditure, if diverted to civilian purposes, would in the short term increase employment and in the long term contribute to greater productivity and higher real wages. Yet exaggerated intelligence reports still sustain public pressure for a military industry. At the same time, the weapons have become increasingly dangerous, deterrence has become damage limitation or, even worse, a pre-emptive strike. Robinson's suggestion that instead of using funds for arms, they be diverted to investment in energy resources and economic development, could contribute to lessening international tension.

All of this goes against the laissez-faire ideology. Robinson rejects the pursuit of self-interest as the fundamental basis for organizing social behaviour and as the singular road to 'freedom'. In 1970, she wrote, '[T]he shadow of the Cold War still hangs over the scene. On the one side this allows the authorities to override objections to the arms race and on the other side allows the authorities to stifle free discussion for fear that criticism may turn into disloyalty' (1970, p. 99). The culture of fear was thus still being nurtured, with the enemy too disparate to target.

Robinson concluded, 'Rationality requires that the prime aim of policy should be to make war obsolete and to find alternative ways of dealing with the problems that gave rise to it' (1970, p. 122), including the denial of aid for arms to developing countries. Her moral stand is against the arms race and, indeed, war. The rationale of her economic arguments is one contribution to the larger moral issue of the arms race post-World War II. With her classical approach to political economy and embrace of a moral issue, she was struggling towards an 'entanglement'.

Acknowledgement

Comments from Stephanie Blankenberg and Geoff Harcourt are gratefully acknowledged.

References

Aslanbeigui, Nahid and Guy Oakes (2006), 'Joan Robinson's "secret document": a passage from the autobiography of an analytical economist', *Journal of the History of Economic Thought*, **28** (4), 413–26.

Harcourt, Geoff C. ([1990] 2001), 'Joan Robinson's early views on method', *History of Political Economy*, **22** (3), 411–27; reprinted in Prue Kerr with Geoff C. Harcourt (eds), *Joan Robinson: Critical Assessments of Leading Economists*, Vol. V, London: Routledge, pp. 24–40.

Robinson, Joan (1932), *Economics is a Serious Subject: The Apologia of the Economist to the Mathematician, the Scientist and the Plain Man*, Cambridge: Heffers.

Robinson, Joan ([1933] 2002), *The Economics of Imperfect Competition*, London: Macmillan.

Robinson, Joan ([1937] 2002), *Essays in the Theory of Employment*, London: Macmillan.

Robinson, Joan ([1955] 1960), 'Marx, Marshall and Keynes', Delhi School of Economics Occasional Paper No. 9; reprinted in Joan Robinson, *Collected Economic Papers*, Vol. II, Oxford: Basil Blackwell, pp. 1–17.

Robinson Joan ([1956, 1969] 2002), *The Accumulation of Capital*, London: Palgrave.

Robinson, Joan ([1957] 1960), 'Population and development'; reprinted in Joan Robinson, *Collected Economic Papers*, Vol. II, Oxford: Basil Blackwell, pp. 107–13.

Robinson, Joan ([1961] 1965), 'Beyond full employment', *Annals of Collective Economy* (Liege), April–June; reprinted in Joan Robinson, *Collected Economic Papers*, Vol. III, Oxford: Basil Blackwell, pp. 103–12.

Robinson, Joan (1962a), *Economic Philosophy*, Harmondsworth: Penguin.

Robinson, Joan ([1962b] 1965), 'Latter-day capitalism', *New Left Review*, July–August; reprinted in Joan Robinson, *Collected Economic Papers*, Vol. III, Oxford: Basil Blackwell, pp. 113–24.

Robinson, Joan ([1962c] 1965), 'Marxism: religion and science', *Monthly Review*; reprinted in Joan Robinson, *Collected Economic Papers*, Vol. III, Oxford: Basil Blackwell, pp. 148–57.

Robinson, Joan (1962d), *Essays in the Theory of Economic Growth*, London: Macmillan.

Robinson, Joan ([1964] 1965), 'The final end of laissez-faire', *New Left Review*; reprinted in Joan Robinson, *Collected Economic Papers*, Vol. III, Oxford: Basil Blackwell, pp. 139–47.

Robinson, Joan ([1967] 1979) 'Smoothing out Keynes', a review of *The Age of Keynes* by Robert Lekachman, *The New York Review of Books,* 26 January; reprinted in *Collected Economic Papers,* Vol. V, Oxford: Basil Blackwell, pp. 178–83.

Robinson, Joan (1970), *Freedom and Necessity: An Introduction to the Study of Society*, London: George Allen and Unwin.

Robinson, Joan ([1973] 1979), 'Ideology and analysis', in *Collected Economic Papers*, Vol. V, Oxford: Basil Blackwell, pp. 254–61.

Robinson, Joan ([1977] 1979), 'What are the questions?' *Journal of Economic Literature*; reprinted in *Collected Economic Papers*, Vol. V, Oxford: Basil Blackwell, pp. 1–31.

Robinson, Joan (1979), *Collected Economic Papers*, Vol. V, Oxford: Basil Blackwell.

Robinson, Joan (1981), 'The Tanner Lectures on Human Values: the arms race', in S.M. McMurrin (ed.) (1982), *The Tanner Lectures on Human Values,* Boulder, CO: Westview Press, www.tannerlectures.utah.edu/lectures/documents/robinson82.pdf, accessed 29 October, 2008.

Walsh, Vivian (2003), 'Sen after Putnam', *Review of Political Economy*, **15** (3), 315–94.

See also the entries on: Market; Fact/value dichotomy.

61   Scarcity
Rutger Claassen

The postulate of scarcity in economic science

The scarcity postulate delineates the object field of modern economic theory.[1] Although it was already implicit in theories of marginal utility of the 1870s (Xenos 1989, p. 67), its most authoritative statement is found in Lionel Robbins's essay on the nature and significance of economic science. Robbins contrasted the 'materialist definition', which maintains that economics is the study of the causes of material welfare, with the 'scarcity definition', which maintains that economics studies the allocation of scarce means between competing ends (Robbins [1932] 1984, pp. 12–15). According to the latter definition, both ends and means can be of a material or a non-material nature. For example, the need for aesthetic beauty or religious inspiration is no less potentially subject to scarcity of means than the need for bread and butter. The satisfaction of all of these different types of needs under conditions of scarcity marks the 'economic aspect' of action. Since every action has such an economic aspect, every action is a legitimate subject of economic analysis. Thus the domain of economics is principally unlimited.[2]

For Robbins, and most economists after him, scarcity is characteristic of the human condition.[3] It arises from the unavoidable opposition of endless wants and limited means to satisfy these wants. The concept of 'opportunity costs' explains why means (time and resources) are always limited in supply: every choice for one course of action implies the costly sacrifice of alternative courses of action. Under these conditions, the 'economic problem' is how to use these limited means as efficiently as possible, that is, how to raise productivity to enable the satisfaction of as many wants as possible. This implies that wants, or 'preferences' for the purpose of economic analysis, are to be treated as given or 'exogenous'. Their endlessness is formalized in standard microeconomic theory as the axiom of non-satiation: every consumer prefers to possess more rather than less of any available bundle of commodities (Hodgson 2001, pp. 7, 51).[4]

The postulate has not gone uncontested. Here a sharp distinction needs to be drawn between the scarcity condition itself and its prescribed 'treatment'. It is one thing to say that an individual is always confronted with endless wants and limited available means (a descriptive claim). It is quite another thing to propose that people should respond by maximizing the satisfaction of their preferences (a normative claim). On the descriptive side, critics have questioned the 'fact' of scarcity, disputing that it represents a universal predicament and claiming it to be the historical product of modernity. On the normative side, criticism has focused on the fact that economics' prescribed response leaves no room for the mirror strategy of reducing scarcity by limiting wants or criticizing preferences. At both the descriptive and the normative level, economic theory has some arguments available in its defence against these criticisms.

The 'fact' of scarcity as a social construction

The argument that scarcity is not a natural fact is inspired by anthropological interpretations of primitive tribal societies as 'societies of affluence', despite their low level of material want satisfaction. Low levels of consumption in these societies of hunters and gatherers result from low levels of time spent working and correspondingly low levels of wants. The experience of scarcity would therefore be largely absent in these societies (Sahlins 1972, pp. 1–39).[5] Absolute levels of production and consumption (imagine them forming a scale from great wealth to extreme poverty) should not be confused with levels of our subjective experience of them, measured against our needs and desires. 'Scarcity' and 'abundance' denote these experiences, and as we all know, wealthy persons can experience scarcity just as poor persons can experience abundance. The anthropological evidence suggests that modern societies are like the wealthy person experiencing scarcity, while primitive societies are like the poor person experiencing abundance.

This raises the question why *modern* societies – as an apparent exception to the historical rule – experience scarcity despite high levels of want satisfaction (wealth). Here, a distinction between scarcity as a temporary or concrete experience and scarcity as a permanent or general condition may be useful (Claassen 2004, pp. 41–4). Primitive societies knew periods of scarcity, when droughts or other natural conditions cut them off from their supply of basic necessities, but such experiences were passing in that as soon as natural conditions improved scarcity was over. The experience of such specific forms of scarcity did not influence the level of wants. Xenos (1989, p. 3) calls this form of scarcity 'insufficiency of supply'. By contrast, 'permanent scarcity' refers to scarcity as a dynamic process of both increasing productivity and increasing wants, with the latter ever remaining one step ahead. Several hypotheses have been put forward to explain this dynamic, all pointing to some kind of social construction of scarcity.

Some claim that the production side of the economic circle is causally responsible: higher levels of production necessitate higher levels of want creation. Advertising and 'salesmanship' become necessary to sell the fruits of higher productivity and are largely successful in doing so. In this way, preference formation is endogenous to the economic system – this has been coined the 'dependence effect' (Galbraith [1958] 1998, pp. 124–31). Emphasis on the production side is shared by some in the Marxist tradition, who give a similar explanation. The increases in productivity and wealth made possible by capitalism allow either extra leisure or higher levels of production and consumption. 'Now, capitalism inherently tends to promote just one of the options – output expansion – since the other, toil reduction, threatens a sacrifice of the profit associated with increased output and sales, and hence a loss of competitive strength' (Cohen 1977, p. 118; similarly Booth 1989). Increased consumption is treated as a mere consequence of this autonomous process.

For others the consumption side is primary in explaining scarcity. The upward spiral of production and consumption levels is said to be due to people's quest for status in careers and consumption choices. This hypothesis is associated with the work of economists such as Thorstein Veblen, Fred Hirsch and Robert Frank.[6] Veblen maintained that individuals strive to emulate relevant others with their superior consumption patterns (Veblen [1899] 1998). This is the phenomenon of 'conspicuous consumption', familiarly known as 'keeping up with the Joneses'. Hirsch distinguished a 'material economy' and a 'positional economy'. The latter consists of all those goods that are scarce in a social sense ('positional goods'), scarce because their supply is limited by definition. Hirsch distinguished two categories of such goods: goods people want because of their being scarce, that is, as a sign of distinction (snob and luxury goods) and goods that are scarce because others' use of them limits one's own opportunities to use them (congestion goods). The crux of his argument is that with economic growth, more people are able to join the race for these socially scarce goods. As a consequence, the proportion of the positional economy, relative to the material economy, grows. This explains the frustration that comes with economic growth – contrary to popular expectations it does not become easier but instead harder to purchase socially scarce goods (Hirsch 1976).

The most recent elaboration of the status hypothesis comes from Robert Frank, who emphasizes the contextual nature of most human preferences and formalizes this in interdependent utility functions. Insofar as preferences concern positional goods, he characterizes the ensuing form of competition as identical to an arms race: both parties have to invest ever more resources in the race without gaining a better chance of winning the good. The problem is therefore structurally similar to a prisoner's dilemma (Frank 1985, p. 122). For Frank, the desire for status is a 'universal' of human nature. It occurs because of the evolutionary advantage that comes with a superior position within a group (Frank 1999, p. 146). Nonetheless, its realization depends upon the existence of favourable social institutions. In modern society the decline of fixed status hierarchies opens an arena of ubiquitous status competition with permanent scarcity as a result.[7]

Ethical evaluations of scarcity
For convenience sake I will divide the normative approaches into two ideal-typical categories, the 'ascetic' and the 'collective action' approaches. Both are critical of scarcity-generating processes and propose to mitigate or eliminate them. Schematically, the difference lies in two interrelated propositions that are affirmed by the ascetic approach and rejected by the collective action approach: (i) the content of individual preferences is the legitimate and appropriate target of normative evaluation and (ii) the responsibility to revise one's preferences – if that is the recommendation resulting from such an evaluation – belongs to the individual.

The evaluation under (i) in *ascetic approaches* leads to a critical or even outright negative view of human desires. Its origins can be traced to several philosophical theories from classical antiquity. For instance, it is visible in Plato's rejection of the unruly desires of democratic man and in Aristotle's condemnation of *chrèmatistikè* as an unnatural form of wealth seeking that knows no boundaries and prevents people from experiencing the good life in activities outside of the economic domain. Furthermore, Stoic, Epicurean and Christian thought all – in one way or another – urge a stance of disapproval toward indulgence in wealth, luxury and avarice. In contemporary Western societies the idea that scarcity must be combated by individually renouncing the fulfilment of (certain of) one's preferences is promulgated by the so-called 'voluntary simplicity' movement, which promotes downscaling consumption patterns.

Ascetic positions do not rely on any specific *explanation* of the scarcity condition. They are compatible with the idea that people come to desire goods for their intrinsic characteristics, but also with explanations based on social construction. If they endorse the first kind of explanation, they must explain why possession of or attachment to goods is intrinsically wrong. Here the range of options is wide: an attachment to possessions might distract one from concentrating on preparation for the afterlife (as in Christianity), or it might disturb one's personal peace of the soul (as in Stoic ethics). When relying on social construction explanations, ascetic theories must critically relate to the motive of status seeking, instead of the goods sought. This sits somewhat uneasily with the idea that individuals should voluntarily restrain themselves: it requires that the drive for status be depicted as both malleable – individual effort may soften if not completely suppress it – and reproachable, something to be morally condemned (see, for an example of this combination, consumer critic Juliet Schor 1998).

The *collective action approach* rejects the appropriateness of evaluating the content of individual preferences because such an evaluation is bound to be perfectionist or even paternalist. Any such evaluation must rely on a hierarchy of values that is always 'extremely controversial' (Heath 2005, p. 211). An assessment of needs reveals as much about the value orientation of the observer as about the value of the preferences of the observed. The reason for rejecting individualist strategies of preference suppression as a solution lies in an adherence to the explanation of scarcity as socially conditioned by status seeking. Since the problem has the structure of a prisoner's dilemma, it cannot and should not be solved by individual restraint but rather by social-institutional arrangements that mitigate status consumption. The collective action approach considers a voluntary withdrawal from an arms race for income or consumption goods 'too much to ask for'. Since the possession of many status goods enhances one's chances of survival and reproduction, it is an innate drive that people cannot be expected to give up (Frank 1999, p. 187). Thus, the solution should come from a structural adjustment of the rules that create status games. Different proposals have been made, such as a tax on consumption, a (more) progressive income tax and schemes for restricting specific status struggles, such as those for leadership positions and educational positions in prestigious institutions (ibid., p. 194 ff.)

The normative ground is found in efficiency considerations. Status games create negative externalities, hence they are inefficient. More resources are used to combat contestants for status than would be necessary if the 'arms race' was curbed by an 'arms control agreement' – a form of waste. So it is not that wants at higher levels of wealth production and consumption are less urgent (as Galbraith would maintain), or that they are morally reprehensible (as the ascetic would say); the point is that their satisfaction comes at an unnecessarily high cost (for a different normative foundation see Claassen 2008). Recent empirical research on happiness is sometimes used to support these conclusions. In rich countries (those with average per capita annual incomes greater than US$15,000) subjective well-being does not increase when national income rises. By contrast, people do become happier when their income rises relative to others in their society (but the extra happiness enjoyed by the upwardly mobile is offset by those going down in relative terms). Some conclude that this makes striving for economic growth useless – or even harmful, in that it distracts resources (such as people's time and energy) from activities that research has shown to actually make people happier, such as family life and spending time with friends (Lane 2000; Layard 2005).

Economics' defence and a mixed conclusion

The scarcity condition as adhered to in mainstream economics can be defended at two levels, corresponding to the descriptive and normative levels of criticism. The descriptive defence is that scarcity is a universal feature of human action after all, while the normative strategy is to value the recurrence of scarcity positively.

David Gauthier defends economics' *theory of action*. He argues that a utopian world without scarcity is unthinkable: 'Paradise is gained when all obstacles to fulfilment are overcome, but when all obstacles are overcome, instrumental activities lose their point and cease to afford fulfilment' (Gauthier 1986, p. 333). What is of intrinsic value in human life is engaging in instrumental activities; that is, activities in which obstacles must be overcome. Scarcity is therefore a precondition for human fulfilment, the 'humanly necessary evil' (ibid., p. 335). According to this argument, wants are endless in one specific sense: as long as we are alive, we act and so we have to have some ends in view. On the other hand, *what* ends there should be, remains an open question. So this defence of the scarcity condition does not commit one to endorse economics' attitude of treating preferences as authoritative at the normative level. Rejecting some ends does not imply being without ends, for such a thing is impossible; it merely implies preferring the attainment of some types of ends over others. From this perspective, economic theory strictly speaking can accommodate preferences with any kind of content.

Nonetheless, in practice economics seems to favour an interpretation of the end of human action as the attempt to satisfy individual preferences for goods that can be *privately appropriated* (allegedly contrary to interpretations of action by members of premodern societies). In this interpretation of action certain institutions are presupposed: private property, freedom of contract and exchange in a market context. Only this focus on individual preferences for private goods can explain the occurrence of constant increases in preferences. Dynamic preferences are to be observed where action is interpreted as a quest for individual appropriation by persons who exchange and consume under the pressure of producers or try to get ahead of other persons in terms of status. This reconciles the universal and the socio-historical explanations of the scarcity condition (to a certain extent[8]). Within this framework scarcity is universal, but the framework itself is a social construct, supported by a set of specific social institutions (Claassen 2007). Correspondingly, the limit of such a framework lies where the reach of the presupposed institutions stops. The relevant question therefore is which goods should (not) be subject to private appropriation in a market context. Providing an answer requires engaging with the essentially normative challenge of boundary setting.

The classical *normative defence* of scarcity is utilitarian: the satisfaction of individual preferences increases overall utility.[9] Such an endorsement of the positive value of preference satisfaction stands in noteworthy contrast to other (for example, Kantian) theories, which ascribe moral value to the capacity of practical reason to critically scrutinize one's preferences. Given modern economics' utilitarian background, its reluctance to consider the problem of how to value the formation of new preferences is understandable, as well as its neglect of the alternative option of increasing overall utility by reducing preferences.[10] It is thus unsurprising that there is hardly any explicit engagement with the scarcity problem from a utilitarian point of view. A more explicit answer to the critics is delivered by several writers who acknowledge scarcity's social construction but maintain that it creates positive external effects, such as making people enrich their culture and refine their talents. The roots of such a positive evaluation go back to the endorsements of the rise of commerce by eighteenth-century authors such as Mandeville, Smith and Hume.

A more contemporary example is Friedrich Hayek's rejection of Galbraith's dependence effect. According to Galbraith, the law of diminishing marginal utility, routinely applied to the demands for individual goods, should also be applied to preference satisfaction itself. Wants at a higher level of economic development are not innate but created within the economic system and therefore are less important or urgent. Preference satisfaction is itself subject to diminishing utility (Galbraith [1958] 1998, pp. 118–23). According to Hayek, it makes no sense that only innate wants be important or urgent. Desires for art and literature, for example, have been developed in a social context – but we never protest as to their origins; so why should we protest against attempts by advertising and marketing to induce wants for standard market goods? Furthermore, there would only be reason for protest when producers could causally determine these wants, but this is something Galbraith cannot prove. Producers' attempts to instil wants in consumers are only one among many influences upon consumers, who in the end make a free choice (Hayek 1961, pp. 346–48).

This argument implies that different types of activities have to be evaluated on their merits. Whether private consumption creates more or less 'positive externalities' compared to activities such as art, cannot be determined a priori. Both types of activity can be framed as a struggle for status, and both can have positive as well as negative externalities. The battle between those judging the overall balance to be positive and those perceiving the contrary, will probably continue for a long time.

Notes

1. I thank Thomas Fossen, Pieter Pekelharing and two anonymous referees for their comments.
2. The only exceptions, according to Robbins, are those 'free commodities' whose acquisition requires no effort, such as the air we breathe (quite an ironic example nowadays, since air pollution has rendered air quality all but free).
3. The treatment of scarcity as part of the human condition also found its way into liberal normative theory. Rawls, following Hume, maintained that 'moderate scarcity' is one of the two 'circumstances of justice' that necessitate and render possible social cooperation. Cooperation is necessary because there is scarcity rather than abundance; cooperation is possible because scarcity is moderate rather than extreme (Rawls [1971] 1999, p. 110; Hume [1739] 2000, p. 312).
4. Technically, economic analysis acknowledges the existence of 'satiated preferences', but these are considered to be less interesting from the point of view of economic choice than those choices that concern unfulfilled preferences (Varian 2003, p. 43).
5. For the debates in anthropology between formalists and substantivists over the applicability of the scarcity condition to primitive societies, see Prattis (1982) and references therein.
6. A closely related hypothesis points to the imitation of others' desires (so-called 'mimetic desire'), which was largely suppressed in premodern societies by religious and moral teachings and practices. Scarcity only gets free reign when these are removed – which happened in Western societies from the eighteenth century onward. The concept of mimetic desire, originally developed by René Girard, was applied to scarcity by Dumouchel (1979) and Achterhuis (1988).
7. For an evolutionary explanation of the birth of modern societies in terms of a struggle for status, see Coelho (1985).
8. Economists may still object that their theory also has application outside of this framework. This carries the discussion into the problem of 'economic imperialism'. The question then becomes whether the rational choice methodology can and should also be applied outside of 'traditionally economic' fields of action, such as the family or the courtroom.
9. I leave aside the political view that preference satisfaction is a legitimate part of the private sphere protected from interference (which has to explain what should belong to the private sphere and what not – so that the issues re-appear). I also leave aside the Romantics' attitude toward scarcity. Although they were often highly critical of the emerging capitalist economy, they also advocated endless desires as a realm of imagination and refuge from reality (thanks to Pieter Pekelharing for this suggestion).

10.   See McPherson (1983) for a critique of economics' treatment of preferences as given; Bowles (1998) attempts to recover the idea of endogenous preferences.

References

Achterhuis, Hans (1988), *Het Rijk van de Schaarste: Van Thomas Hobbes tot Michel Foucault* [*The Reign of Scarcity: From Thomas Hobbes to Michel Foucault*], 4th edition, Baarn: Ambo.

Booth, William James (1989), 'Economies of time: on the idea of time in Marx's political economy', *Political Theory*, **19** (1), 7–27.

Bowles, Samuel (1998), 'Endogenous preferences: the cultural consequences of markets and other economic institutions', *Journal of Economic Literature*, **36**, 75–111.

Claassen, Rutger (2004), *Het Eeuwig Tekort: Een Filosofie van de Schaarste* [*The Eternal Shortage: A Philosophy of Scarcity*], Amsterdam: Ambo.

Claassen, Rutger (2007), 'Schaarste en overvloed: Een strijd tussen twee interpretaties van de menselijke conditie' [Scarcity and abundance: a contest between two interpretations of the human condition], *Tijdschrift voor Filosofie*, **69** (1), 3–34.

Claassen, Rutger (2008), 'The status struggle: a recognition-based interpretation of the positional economy', *Philosophy and Social Criticism*, **34** (9), 1021–49.

Coelho, Philip R.P. (1985), 'An examination into the causes of economic growth: status as an economic good', *Research in Law and Economics*, **7**, 89–116.

Cohen, Gerald A. (1977), 'Labor, leisure, and a distinctive contradiction of advanced capitalism', in Gerald Dworkin, Gordon Bermant and Peter G. Brown (eds), *Markets and Morals*, Washington DC: Hemisphere Publishing Corporation, pp. 107–36.

Dumouchel, Paul (1979), 'L'ambivalence de la rareté' [The ambivalence of scarcity], in P. Dumouchel and J.P. Dupuy, *L'enfer des choses: René Girard et la logique de l'économie*, Paris: Editions du Seuil, pp. 135–254.

Frank, Robert H. (1985), *Choosing the Right Pond: Human Behavior and the Quest for Status,* Oxford: Oxford University Press.

Frank, Robert H. (1999), *Luxury Fever: Money and Happiness in an Era of Excess*, Princeton, NJ: Princeton University Press.

Galbraith, John Kenneth ([1958] 1998), *The Affluent Society*, Harmondsworth: Penguin.

Gauthier, David (1986), *Morals by Agreement*, Oxford: Clarendon Press.

Hayek, Friedrich A. (1961), 'The non sequitur of the "dependence effect"', *Southern Economic Journal*, **27** (4), 346–48.

Heath, Joseph (2005), 'Liberal autonomy and consumer sovereignty', in John Christman and Joel Anderson (eds), *Autonomy and the Challenges to Liberalism: New Essays*, Cambridge: Cambridge University Press, pp. 204–25.

Hirsch, Fred (1976), *Social Limits to Growth*, London: Routledge & Kegan Paul.

Hodgson, Bernard (2001), *Economics as a Moral Science*, Berlin/Heidelberg: Springer Verlag.

Hume, David ([1739] 2000), *A Treatise of Human Nature*, New York: Oxford University Press.

Layard, Richard (2005), *Happiness. Lessons from a New Science*, New York: Penguin Press.

Lane, Robert (2000), *The Loss of Happiness in Market Democracies*, New Haven, CT: Yale University Press.

McPherson, Michael S. (1983), 'Want formation, morality, and some "interpretative" aspects of economic inquiry', in Norma Haan et al. (eds), *Social Science as Moral Inquiry*, New York: Columbia University Press, pp. 96–124.

Prattis, J.I. (1982), 'Synthesis, or a new problematic in economic anthropology', *Theory and Society*, **11** (2), 205–28.

Rawls, John ([1971] 1999), *A Theory of Justice*, Oxford: Oxford University Press.

Robbins, Lionel ([1932] 1984), *An Essay on the Nature and Significance of Economic Science*, 3rd edition, London: Macmillan.

Sahlins, Marshall (1972), *Stone Age Economics*, New York: Aldine de Gruyter.

Schor, Juliet B. (1998), *The Overspent American: Why We Want What We Don't Need*, New York: Harper Perennial.

Varian, Hal. R. (2003), *Intermediate Microeconomics: A Modern Approach*, 6th edition, New York: W.W. Norton & Company.

Veblen, Thorstein ([1899] 1998), *The Theory of the Leisure Class*, Amherst, NY: Prometheus Books.

Xenos, Nicholas (1989), *Scarcity and Modernity*, London and New York: Routledge.

See also the entries on: Consumerism; Market.

62 Self-interest
Johan J. Graafland

Introduction

Self-interest is an extraordinarily powerful assumption in economics. The reasons for its dominance have been partly positive and partly normative. On positive grounds, the assumption is defended because it leads to reasonable empirical predictions. Economists tend to believe that societal processes can be explained and predicted by assuming that people act out of self-interest. Members of the so-called public choice school, such as Gary Becker, believe that self-interest can explain all behaviour. In their view, individuals will not allot resources to public goods, will free-ride whenever they can get away with it and will lie, cheat and violate other moral precepts and laws when the penalty is smaller than the gain.

Self-interest, however, is not only a descriptive assumption in economics. It is also defended on moral grounds. In his famous *Wealth of Nations* Adam Smith (1776) argues that self-interested behaviour facilitates efficient operation of the economy. This view remains more or less intact in modern economic theory. As K.J. Arrow and F.H. Hahn state:

> There is by now a long and fairly imposing line of economists from Adam Smith to the present who have sought to show that a decentralized economy motivated by self-interest and guided by price signals would be compatible with a coherent disposition of economic resources that could be regarded, in a well-defined sense, as superior to a large class of possible alternative dispositions. (1971, p. vi, cited in Sen 1977, p. 321)

Whereas we might expect chaos in a situation where self-interest prevails, economists believe that an economy in which people are so motivated and in which behaviour is coordinated by a price system produces harmony and coherence.

This chapter discusses the descriptive and moral meaning of self-interest. First, we define the concept of self-interest. Next, we discuss the empirical validity of the assumption of self-interest. Are people indeed mainly driven by self-interest? Third, we consider the moral validity of self-interest, discussing its relationship with virtues such as prudence, justice and benevolence and analysing the influences of such virtues on the efficiency of market operations.

Self-interest defined

Self-interest is similar to several concepts, such as egoism (or selfishness) and enlightened self-interest. Like self-interest, egoism may refer to a descriptive view of human nature that holds that individuals are always motivated by self-interest (psychological egoism) or to a normative view that holds that individuals ought to do what is in their self-interest (ethical egoism).

Yet egoism must be distinguished from enlightened self-interest or self-interest rightly understood. 'Enlightened self-interest' means that persons acting to further the interests of others (or the interests of the group or groups to which they belong) ultimately serve their own self-interest. In that case, self-interest is often closely linked to the virtue of prudence, as defined by Adam Smith. Whereas egoism has a narrow short-term focus, enlightened self-interest considers the long term, taking into account all possible relations between furthering certain goals and one's own interest. When an individual pursues enlightened self-interest that person may have to sacrifice short-term interests in order to maximize long-term interests.

In addition to short-term and long-term, one can also distinguish between the types of goals to which self-interest relates. In the usual economic theory of consumer choice, individuals are assumed to prefer a bundle of commodities that they will consume themselves. This is a rather narrow goal. Normally, the utility of a person also depends on other goals. For example, people may have internalized certain social goals, such as the standard of distributive justice, meaning that their own happiness or utility will increase if income distribution is more in line with their own social preference.

However, broadening the definition of self-interest to the extent that social preferences are included reduces its conceptual clarity and prevents differentiation between various goals. Once a concept is defined so broadly that it encompasses all motives for all human activities, it ceases to enhance the ability to explain.

For that purpose, goals can be usefully distinguished as follows (Sen 1987, p. 80):

- *Self-centred welfare.* A person's welfare depends only on his or her own consumption.
- *Self-welfare goals.* A person's utility depends on his or her own welfare (and not directly on the welfare of others), but his/her welfare may not depend only on individual consumption but also include values like the admiration of others.
- *Self-goal choice.* An individual's every act of choice is guided directly by the pursuit of his/her own goals, but these goals may involve objectives other than maximizing individual welfare, including moral goals such as compensatory and distributive justice.

The following discussion assumes that departures from self-interested behaviour should be interpreted in terms of violations of the first and second interpretation of self-interest and not in terms of violations of self-goal choices.[1]

The descriptive value of self-interest: outcomes of experimental research

In order to identify the empirical relevance of self-interest, we have to define motives that depart from self-interest and look for research that tests for both types of motives.

The most obvious departure from self-interest is altruism. Altruism is a selfless concern for the welfare of others. It is closely related to the virtue of benevolence, charity or generosity. As reflected in the subtitle of Section II of Part VI of *The Theory of Moral Sentiments* by Adam Smith, the virtue of benevolence affects the happiness of other people. Adam Smith distinguishes several degrees of benevolence. After the care for oneself, one is naturally most concerned with the happiness of one's own family: children, parents, brothers and sisters are the objects of the warmest affections. Second come friends, colleagues and people living in the same neighbourhood. Smith explains this affection as nothing but habitual sympathy for the sake of convenience and accommodation. There is a great deal of mutuality or reciprocity in these kinds of relations.

Third comes the benevolence to the persons who receive our benevolent attention by their great fortunate position. We are fascinated by their greatness and respect them for their fortune. Finally comes universal benevolence to the greatly unfortunate, the poor and the wretched. This kind of noble and generous benevolence plays a relatively small role, according to Adam Smith. Because of the imperfection of humanity, we are unable to act according to the motive of universal benevolence.

People do exhibit behaviour that is seemingly not motivated by self-interest, such as donations of money and time given voluntarily to other people or social organizations (Rose-Ackerman 1996). Nonetheless, economists are often sceptical about motives other than self-interest. Alternative explanations can also be provided for this kind of behaviour in terms of self-interest (Collard 1978). One set of explanations draws on enlightened self-interest. My apparently social behaviour will rebound to my advantage indirectly or in the future. I give to a beggar so that the beggar and others will think well of me. Gifts may also be based on implicit exchange. An economist would see these as simple barter transactions, which can be easily handled within the framework of self-interest. In that case, the gift is an investment (with uncertain benefits) rather than a truly altruistic action. Furthermore, acts of giving may be associated with the reinforcement or confirmation of status. Parents' gifts to their children may be of this kind, in the sense that in accepting the gift, recipients confirm their status vis-à-vis the donor. Lastly, acts of giving or self-abnegation may be due not to love or benevolence, but to their opposite: fear.

In the past decades, much experimental research has been conducted to test the empirical relevance of altruism. Economics integrates this type of social preferences in its mono-utility approach by assuming that persons act as if they are maximizing preferences of the form $U(x) = (1-r) Y(x) + r Z(x)$, where $Y(x)$ is the person's own material well-being obtained from a choice x, and Z is the well-being of another person obtained from x, for whom the agent has altruistic feelings. If r is zero, people are self-interested. If $r>0$, people also have a concern for others (Rabin 1998). Experiments show this kind of pure altruism to be rare.

A more common attitude is reciprocity (sometimes also called reciprocal altruism, see Rabin 1998, p. 21). Social preferences often depend on the behaviour, motivations and intentions of those other people to whom we have altruistic feelings. If someone is nice to you or to others, you are inclined to be nice to them. If someone is mean to you or to others, you are inclined to be mean to them. Reciprocity has been documented in many so-called 'trust games' or 'gift exchange games' (Gächter and Fehr 1999). It is much more common than altruism. One experiment showed reciprocal behaviour as five times more common than pure altruistic behaviour (Rabin 1998).

Reciprocity seems to be much more in line with the assumption of self-interest than altruism, because it focuses upon how one is treated and regarded by others, whereas the focal point for altruism is how one wishes to treat and regard others. Still, the dominance of reciprocal behaviour does not completely confirm the economist's view that self-interest is the basic motive of human behaviour. In particular, reciprocity departs from self-interest because it also includes an element of compensatory justice, meaning, restoring to persons that which they have done wrong or good to you (Velasquez 1998). Just as people support some kind of rectification if some person B is unfairly treated by another person A, they also demand rectification if they happen to be person B. Many experiments show that people are willing to hurt others who have harmed them, even if this will also harm their own welfare. A consumer may refuse to buy a product sold by a monopolist at an unfair price, even if that consumer is hurt by forgoing the product. Members of a striking labour union may strike longer than is in their material interests, because they want to punish a firm for being unfair. The *homo economicus*, the opportunistic self-interested agent, would choose instead to try to forget the unfair treatment so as to salvage some of the personal material benefits. Experiments show that the fraction of subjects behaving reciprocally is high (never below 40 per cent), but there is also a non-negligible fraction of subjects (between 20 and 30 per cent) who behave completely selfishly (Fehr and Gächter 1999).

As altruism relates to a certain distribution (between one's own interest and the interests of others), it is also connected to sentiments of distributive justice. Sentiments of distributive justice also depart from pure self-interest. Distributive justice concerns the fair distribution of society's benefits and burdens. Very roughly, distributional fairness can be modelled by taking a person's utility function as $U(x) = (1-r) Y(x) + r W(Y(x), Z(x))$, where W is the person's view of the proper allocation, $Y(x)$ is that person's self-interested payoff (as above) and $Z(x)$ is the payoff for another person. The parameter r measures the weight the person puts on a fair distribution and $1-r$ is the weight of self-interest. Experiments which subject individuals to self-interested choices and fair choices, show that about half of all subjects behave in a way significantly inconsistent with pure self-interest (Rabin 1998).

The moral value of self-interest and the virtue of prudence
One of the great but paradoxical strengths of the assumption of self-interest is that it can be worked out into a social harmony doctrine. Even before Smith, Bernard Mandeville (1714) had argued in his famous allegory *The Fable of the Bees* that the hive prospered under egotism but flagged under moral restraint. His argument can be summarized by the slogan 'Private vices, public benefits!' In Mandeville's view, pride and vanity have built more hospitals than all the virtues put together.

Also, Adam Smith stressed the favourable outcomes of the pursuit of self-interest in his *Wealth of Nations,* which argues that the pursuit of self-interest contributes to the common good. In particular, by supplying goods in order to earn profits, a producer fosters the total supply of the good on the market. As a result, the price of the good declines and this enables people to buy the good at the lowest possible price. Although such producers only intend to serve their own interest, the unintended consequence is that the common good is served. This is realized by the 'invisible hand', which is Smith's metaphor for the idea that if people interact freely on the market, the pursuit of their self-interest is not incompatible with and rather serves the common good (Peil 1995). Seen from the perspective of the system of natural liberty, self interest is the driving force – *causa efficiens* – behind the (common) wealth of the nation – *causa finalis.*

The Smithian argument about the merits of self-interest can also be defended by another important notion concerning the informational role of self-interest. Self-interested behaviour not only gives all people the role of protecting and pursuing their own interests, but also it allocates this role to the one best informed of what these interests are, namely the persons themselves. If another person or the government were to pursue your interest, they would do a worse job than if you were to look after your interests yourself. The person who knows an individual best is that very individual, and this signalling function may well be lost if rather than acting on the basis of personal self-interest one pursues other goals (Sen 1984).

Because of its favourable effects, self-interest well understood can be considered a virtue. In *The Theory of Moral Sentiments* Smith distinguishes four virtues: prudence, justice, benevolence and self-command. The virtue of prudence aims at the pursuit of self-interest. It is the central virtue of the *homo economicus*. Prudence is highly regarded in society and is beautiful in itself: 'Although the prudent man is in most cases motivated by the pursuit of his own interest, we not only approve in some measure of the conduct of the homo economicus, but also admire it and think it worthy of a considerable degree of applause' (Smith 1759, p. 273).

Prudence is superior reasoning and understanding, by which one is capable of discerning the remote consequences of all of one's actions (Smith 1759, p. 271). People, as they grow up, soon learn that care and foresight are necessary to provide the means of procuring pleasure and avoiding pain. According to Smith, people's happiness depends on the fulfilment of three basic needs: health, fortune and status. In order to obtain these goals, prudent individuals improve their skills, value assiduity and industry in their work and exercise soberness and parsimony in their expenditure. Prudent individuals always study seriously and earnestly to understand things. They are cautious and do not expose their health, fortune or reputation to any sort of hazard. Persons who live in this way, according to Smith, will be contented with their situation, which, by continual though small accumulations, grows better every day. As they grow richer, they are enabled gradually to relax, both in the rigour of their soberness and in the severity of their application. From producer they gradually change into consumer.

The *homo economicus* combines prudence with self-command by which one is able to abstain from present pleasures or to endure present pain, in order to obtain greater pleasures or to avoid a greater pain at some future time. Without self-command a person is unable to act in accordance with the rule of prudence. Together with self-command prudence comprises several lower virtues, such as alertness, cautiousness, temperance, firmness, industry, entrepreneurship and efficiency.

Is prudence sufficient for efficient market operation?

Economists often assume that prudence is the only virtue that is required to make markets work. If economic subjects are prudent, they will watch their reputation and serve others. Non-prudent virtues, such as benevolence, are not needed. According to this 'prudence only' ethic, the reason to be just or loving or temperate is precisely that it is prudent.

McCloskey (2006) argues, however, that a well-functioning economy also requires other virtues. If the conditions for a good reputation mechanism – transparent information about past performance, long-term horizon and willingness of market parties to punish bad performance (Bovenberg 2002) – are not fulfilled, the reputation mechanism works insufficiently. In that case, virtues such as justice, integrity, trustworthiness and benevolence are of great importance for the trust required for overcoming market imperfections (Graafland 2007). Integrity and trustworthiness are not motivated by rational calculation, but by other virtues. The motivation comes from within. Reliable companies refrain from cheating their contract partners, even if they expect this to be financially advantageous.

Frank (2004) gives several examples of how the virtue of trust is decisive for an efficient operation of markets in the face of market imperfections. In current economic theory, social norms that sustain implicit contracts are labelled social capital, because they are of crucial importance for economic growth. Empirical studies by Knack and Keefer (1997) and Beugelsdijk et al. (2004) confirm this. They find a substantial and robust causal influence of trust on economic growth.

Finally, note that Adam Smith also acknowledged the importance of non-prudent moral sentiments, because in his view few people possess the virtue of prudence. Neither can the rationality of man secure the harmony of society (Berns and van Stratum 1986). According to Smith, God or the 'Author of Nature' therefore has not entrusted human reason to ensure that human beings realize happiness, but instead endowed humans with more immediate instincts to foster such happiness.

Conclusion

Recent experimental research casts doubt on the assumption of self-interested behaviour. Men and women are not cold calculators, each maximizing his or her own well-being. They are also normative-affective beings, whose deliberations and decisions are deeply affected by values (Etzioni 1988). From a moral point of view, the harmlessness of self-interested behaviour can be doubted. In many ethical approaches, such as Kantian ethics and virtue ethics, behaviour that is (solely) motivated by self-interest has insufficient or no moral value. Even in an economic morality that takes social efficiency as the sole standard of evaluating market behaviour, self-interested behaviour is insufficient if the market is subject to market imperfections, such as imperfect information or externalities.

Note

1. Self-interest is sometimes defined as rationality. However, this relationship is not unequivocal. Rationality requires that preferences are complete, transitive and continuous and that choices are determined by preferences. But rationality places no constraints on what a rational individual may prefer (Hausman and McPherson 1996). Therefore, it permits moral preferences and moral choices. Indeed, trying to do one's best to promote non-self-interested goals can be a part of rationality (Sen 1977).

References

Berns, E.E. and R. van Stratum (1986), 'De plaats van de economie in Adam Smith's "*Moral Philosophy*"', in G. Berns (ed.) *Adam Smith: Ethiek, Politiek en Economie*, Tilburg: Tilburg University Press, pp. 176–203.
Beugelsdijk, Sjoerd, Henri L.F. de Groot and Anton B.T.M. van Schaik (2004), 'Trust and economic growth: a robustness analysis', *Oxford Economic Papers*, **56**, 118–34.
Bovenberg, A.L. (Lans) (2002), 'Norms, values and technological change', *De Economist*, **150**, 521–53.
Collard, David (1978), *Altruism & Economy: A Study in Non-Selfish Economics*, Oxford: Martin Robertson.
Etzioni, Amitai (1988), *The Moral Dimension: Towards a New Economics*, New York: The Free Press.
Fehr, Ernst and Simon Gächter (1999), 'Reciprocity and economics: implications of reciprocal behavior for labor markets', paper presented at the Annual Conference EALE, 23–26 September, Regensburg, Germany
Frank, Robert H. (2004), *What Price the Moral High Ground*, Princeton, NJ: Princeton University Press.
Gächter, Simon and Ernst Fehr (1999), 'Collective action as a social exchange', *Journal of Economic Behavior & Organization*, **39**, 341–69.
Graafland, Johan J. (2007), *Economics, Ethics and the Market: Introduction and Applications*, London: Routledge.
Hausman, Daniel M. and Michael S. McPherson (1996), *Economic Analysis and Moral Philosophy*, Cambridge: Cambridge University Press.
Knack, Stephen and Philip Keefer (1997), 'Does social capital have an economic payoff? A cross-country investigation', *Quarterly Journal of Economics*, **112**, 1251–88.

Mandeville, Bernard (1714), *The Fable of the Bees: Or, Private Vices, Public Benefits*, ed. Jack Lynch, www. xs4all.nl/~maartens/philosophy/mandeville/fable_of_bees.html, accessed February 2007.

McCloskey, Deirdre N. (2006), *The Bourgeois Virtues: Ethics for an Age of Commerce*, Chicago, IL: University of Chicago Press.

Peil, Jan (1995), *Adam Smith en de Economische Wetenschap: Een Methodologische Herinterpretatie*, Tilburg: Tilburg University Press.

Rabin, Matthew (1998), 'Psychology and economics', *Journal of Economic Literature*, **36**, 11–46.

Rose-Ackerman, Susan (1996), 'Altruism, nonprofits, and economic theory', *Journal of Economic Literature*, **34**, 701–28.

Sen, Amartya (1977), 'Rational fools: a critique on the behavioral foundations of economic theory', *Philosophy and Public Affairs*, **6**, 317–44.

Sen, Amartya (1984), *Resources, Values and Development*, Oxford: Blackwell.

Sen, Amartya (1987), *On Ethics and Economics*, Oxford: Blackwell.

Smith, Adam (1759), *The Theory of Moral Sentiments*, New York: Prometheus Books.

Smith, Adam (1776), *Inquiry into the Nature and Causes of the Wealth of Nations*, New York: Prometheus Books.

Velasquez, Manuel G. (1998), *Business Ethics: Concepts and Cases*, 4th edition, Upper Saddle River, NJ: Prentice Hall.

See also the entries on: Egoism; Homo economicus.

63 Amartya Sen
Sabina Alkire

The writings of Amartya Sen (b. 1933) trace and draw attention to many interconnections between ethics and economics. Indeed, they have done much to reshape this intersection. Sen spent much of his childhood in Santineketan, Bengal. He studied economics first at Presidency College Calcutta and subsequently at Trinity College Cambridge, where he was awarded a Prize Fellowship. He has taught at Jadavpur University Calcutta, the Delhi School of Economics, the London School of Economics, the University of Oxford, where he became the Drummond Professor of Political Economy and Fellow of All Souls College, Trinity College Cambridge, where he served as Master from 1998–2003, and Harvard University, where he is the Lamont University Professor and Professor of Economics and Philosophy. In 1998 Sen was awarded the Alfred Nobel Prize in Economic Sciences for his contributions in three areas of welfare economics: social choice, welfare distributions and poverty. As of September 2008, Sen had published 25 books and over 370 articles.

In the Royer lectures, later published under the title *Ethics and Economics*, Sen observes that modern economics began in part as a branch of ethics, as suggested by Adam Smith's position as professor of moral philosophy at the University of Glasgow. Sen observes two origins of economics: ethics and engineering. Economics' ethical fastenings address motivation (how one should live) and social achievement (the human good). Engineering techniques, which now dominate economics, shed light on the interdependence between important variables. Sen argues that a better balance needs to be struck between these two complementary branches by strengthening the ethical branch of economics, and further, that well-constructed economic analyses could, in turn, better inform moral philosophy.

This chapter explores five conceptual interconnections between ethics and economics which Sen has developed in writings in philosophy and welfare economics. The first section introduces the need to scrutinize the informational basis of moral principles underlying economic analyses, drawing attention to the field's narrow informational framework. The second and third sections focus on information pluralism, first introducing capabilities and opportunity freedoms as the internally plural space that Sen proposes for the evaluation of social or economic arrangements, then describing process freedoms such as agency and democratic practice. The fourth section, on principle pluralism, argues for the introduction of plural principles into economic analyses rather than relying wholly on Pareto optimality. The fifth section presents Sen's arguments that human motivations are complex, and that assumptions of uniform self-interest or of internal consistency of choice are misleading, as is the neglect of our imperfect obligations and responsibility. The concluding section, on justice, advocates an incomplete, maximizing comparative approach which can rank (or judge as unrankable) existing states of affairs and policy options, based on the features introduced above, such as opportunity and process freedoms, plural principles, incomplete assessments and responsibility.

Due to space constraints, this chapter is unable to survey Sen's related writings on gender, hunger, poverty, human rights, India's development, nutrition, population, identity, violence and other topics of moral concern. Likewise, the space available is insufficient to attend to the secondary literatures that build upon Sen's work. Such constraints make this account incomplete, as the omitted works and secondary literature are, in a number of cases, significant.

Information

Welfare economics regularly draws on moral principles, such as Pareto optimality, or Arrow's independence of irrelevant alternatives. By analysing the information that these principles include and exclude, Sen argues, one can draw attention to their insights and oversights. 'Informational analysis can be used to bring out the content, scope, and limitations of different moral principles. Each moral principle needs some types of information for its use and – no less importantly – "rules out" direct use of other types of information' (Sen 1985, p. 69–70; see also Sen 1974, 1979).

Much of Sen's work can be seen as criticizing the unnecessarily narrow informational foundations of welfare economics and outlining methods to enrich the information that guides economic decisions. For example, Arrow's impossibility theorem (1951) raises fundamental questions regarding the rules by which systematic social welfare judgements are made. In *Collective Choice and Social Welfare* (1970a) and subsequently, Sen challenges some of the informational bases of Arrow's theorem, arguing that a social ordering need not be assumed to be transitive, that incompleteness is sometimes sufficient to identify maximal options, that social choice should consider the intensities of individual preferences, and that interpersonal comparisons are not impossible. Overall, he argues, 'the most likely route of escaping the Arrow dilemma in making social welfare judgements lies . . . in the general direction of enriching the informational input into that analysis' (Sen 1996, p. 55), and much of his writing has followed this route.

To take another example, Sen has systematically drawn attention to three fundamental building blocks of welfare economics: welfarism (which sees the goodness of a state of affairs as a function only of individual utilities), sum ranking (an aggregation procedure that loses information regarding the initial distribution) and consequentialism (which judges states of affairs solely by outcomes, disregarding processes). Taken together, these three constitute the framework for welfare economics in which an act is to be pursued if it produces the maximum utility sum. Sen has powerfully observed how conventional uses of each of these three components exclude certain kinds of information that *should* be routinely considered in a normative framework, such as information about people's freedoms, distribution considerations such as the Rawlsian concerns for the least well off, and process considerations such as human rights or democratic practice.

Well-being and opportunity freedom

In the 1985 Dewey lectures and subsequently, Sen has argued for consideration of two additional kinds of information to inform both ethical and economic decision-making. 'One is in terms of plurality of principles (I shall call this *principle pluralism*), and the other in terms of plurality of informational variables (to be called *information pluralism*)' (Sen 1985, p. 176, emphasis in original). This section and the next introduce information pluralism; the following, principle pluralism.

Ethical and economic assessments of well-being tend to draw on utility, opulence or revealed preferences, each of which Sen has criticized for numerous reasons. Utility refers to a psychological state of happiness defined as desire fulfilment or pleasure, yet Sen argues that these measures may be misleading. The chronically deprived often become reconciled with their suffering and appreciative of small mercies, thus a utilitarian reading of their psychological state may be inflated. Further, human rights advances, or expansions in freedom, would be recognized as contributing to well-being only if they impact individual utility. Opulence approaches evaluate well-being on the bases of the resources that a person has, such as income or Rawlsian primary goods. Yet people have widely varying abilities to convert resources into beings and doings that they value. A physically impaired person may require significantly greater resources to achieve mobility; a pregnant woman may require additional food in order to be well nourished. Resource-based measures are blind to these differences. In the revealed preference approach, preference is inferred from an observed choice. While choice behaviour conveys important information, Sen jests that the ascription of 'preference' here is 'an elaborate pun'(Sen 1971) because it reveals nothing about value or reflected preferences. In contrast to inferences drawn from choice behaviour, people do not always choose what furthers their own well-being; they may choose on the basis of commitment, or may be indifferent between options but choose one. Hence, to rely upon choice (revealed 'preference') data alone risks inaccuracy. Information on utility, resources, and choices should continue to inform analyses, but because of these weaknesses should not, Sen argues, form the exclusive informational basis of well-being evaluation.

Sen argues that we should assess well-being in terms of information on *functionings* – what a person manages to achieve – and *capability*, 'the *real opportunity* that we have to accomplish what we value' (Sen 1992, p. 31, emphasis in original). 'The central feature of well-being is the ability to achieve valuable functionings. The need for identification and valuation of the important functionings cannot be avoided by looking at something else, such as happiness, desire fulfillment, opulence, or command over primary goods' (Sen 1985, p. 200).

Functionings are beings and doings that people value and have reason to value. In themselves functionings are information pluralist. They can include quite elementary achievements, such as being well-nourished and literate, or quite complex achievements, such as earning a world-class reputation in ice hockey. Note that by definition functionings are valuable: they reflect the values that people reasonably hold regarding their achievements. This makes at least some functionings incommensurable in the sense that they cannot be reduced to a common denominator, such as happiness, and mechanically summed. Rather, the relative weights of different functionings is itself a further value judgement.

Capability refers to a person's or group's freedom to promote or achieve valuable functionings. 'It represents the various combinations of functionings (beings and doings) that the person can achieve. Capability is, thus, a set of vectors of functionings, reflecting the person's freedom to lead one type of life or another . . . to choose from possible livings' (Sen 1992, p. 40). Capability extends the information pluralism to account for freedoms, 'checking whether one person did have the opportunity of achieving the functioning vector that another actually achieved' (Sen 1985).

As in other areas, Sen's writings on capability have inspired a considerable secondary literature, both constructive and critical, applied and theoretical. Perhaps the most influential of these is by Martha Nussbaum, who argues that Sen should specify a list of capabilities, such as the ten central human capabilities developed in her own work (Nussbaum 1988, 1990, 1995, 2000). The *Human Development Reports* of the United Nations Development Programme have explored some applications of Sen's approach in measurement and development policy. At present hundreds of academic papers draw upon or further develop Sen's work in different contexts, measures, countries and disciplines each year.

Agency and process freedom

Alongside capabilities, which are in a sense 'opportunity freedoms', we may wish to consider *process freedoms* related to what a person is able to do themselves on behalf of the goals that they value and are motivated to advance.[1]

Sen's influential paper 'The impossibility of a Paretian liberal' (1970b) elegantly illustrates the disregard for individual freedom introduced by an exceedingly mild application of the Pareto principle. In this well-known example, two persons 'Prude' and 'Lewd' have different preferences over whether *Lady Chatterley's Lover* is read by Prude (p), Lewd (l) or No one (n). Prude prefers no one to read it, but certainly does not wish Lewd to relish it, hence holds the ranking (n, p, l). Lewd would like to read it, but would be even more delighted to inflict it upon Prude, so holds the ranking (p, l, n). In a liberal society, one might wish not to inflict it upon unwilling Prude, hence would prefer (n) to (p); also, a liberal society would not withhold it from Lewd, hence would prefer (l) to (n) so the social ranking would be (l, n, p), which is, however, Pareto inferior. Sen concludes that 'while the Pareto criterion has been thought to be an expression of individual liberty, it appears that in choices involving more than two alternatives it can have consequences that are, in fact, deeply illiberal' (Sen 1970, p. 157).

A concern for people's freedom to act in and beyond private spaces is more systematically developed in conceptual and development writings. Sen's capability approach views people, including poor people, as active agents. Agency is an assessment of 'what a person can do in line with his or her conception of the good' (Sen 1985, p. 206). People who enjoy high levels of agency are engaged in actions that are congruent with their values. When people are unable to exert agency, they may be alienated from their behaviour, coerced, submissive, desirous to please or simply passive. If development and poverty reduction activities are to avoid such situations, then 'the people have to be seen . . . as being actively involved – given the opportunity – in shaping their own destiny, and not just as passive recipients of the fruits of cunning development programs' (Sen 1999b, p. 53). This requires attention to the processes by which outcomes are attained, in particular, the extent to which people are able to engage actively and freely as agents.

Sen's account of agency has distinct and plural features: agency is exercised with respect to multiple goals; agency includes effective power as well as direct control; agency may advance well-being or may address other-regarding goals; recognizing agency entails an assessment of the value of the agency goals; and agency introduces the need to incorporate the agents' own responsibility for a state of affairs into their evaluation of it (Alkire 2008).

First, agency is internally plural in that it may be exercised with respect to, and defined in relation to, multiple goals. Second, agency may include effective power and control. Effective power is the person's or group's 'power to achieve chosen results'. In situations of effective power, no matter how choices are actually made and executed, power is 'exercised in line with what we would have chosen and because of it' (Sen 1985, p. 211). Effective power may pertain to individuals, but in some cases it pertains only to groups: 'Given the interdependences of social living, many liberties are not separately exercisable, and effective power may have to be seen in terms of what all, or nearly all, members of the group would have chosen' (ibid., p. 211). Control refers to a person's ability to make choices and to control procedures directly (whether or not they are successful in achieving the desired goal) (ibid., p. 208–9). Third, agency and well-being perspectives are interrelated but remain importantly distinct. In particular, agency does not have to advance well-being at all; it may be other-regarding. Thus, agency has *open conditionality* in the sense that it is 'not tied to any one type of aim' but advances any goals the person thinks important, whether for themselves, their community, the poor or some other entity altogether, such as preserving China's terracotta soldiers. Fourth, agency is, by definition, related to goals that the person values. 'The need for careful *assessment of aims*, allegiances, objectives, etc., and of the conception of the good, may be important and exacting' (ibid., p. 204 italics added). This requirement, in essence, imposes upon agency conditions similar to those for capability, namely that agency pertains to the advance of objectives that 'people value *and have reason to value*'. Fifth, an agent's assessment of a situation or state of affairs, and their subsequent response to it, will include, when relevant, an assessment of their own responsibility in bringing about that situation (Sen 1983, 1985). That is, in Bernard Williams's famed case, Jim is faced with a choice of watching as a bandit kills twenty people, or killing one of them himself and saving the others. Of this situation Sen writes, 'Whereas others have a straightforward reason to rejoice if Jim goes ahead, Jim has no option but to take serious note of his own responsibility in that state and his agency in killing someone himself.'

Agency can be exercised individually or collectively and the collective possibility is worth highlighting. The capability approach reintroduces a number of value judgements into economics that had been expunged by Lionel Robbins, Paul Samuelson and others. For example, the choice of relevant capabilities to pursue is a value judgement, as is the choice of the relative importance and urgency to assign distinct capabilities and different groups within a population. Such value judgements and mobilization are often to be made, or at least informed by and held accountable to, some form of collective agency, such as participation, public debate and deliberation, democratic practices and social movements.

Sen provides three reasons for expanding process freedoms. First, 'Participation . . . has intrinsic value for the quality of life. Indeed being able to do something not only for oneself but also for other members of the society is one of the elementary freedoms which people have reason to value (Drèze and Sen 2002, p. 9). Second, public action can play a vital *instrumental* role in people's claims to political attention. 'In a democracy, people tend to get what they demand, and more crucially, do not typically get what they do not demand' (Sen 1999b, p. 156). Finally, Sen argues that, 'the practice of democracy gives citizens an opportunity to learn from one another, and helps society to form its values and priorities . . . In this sense, democracy has *constructive* importance' (Sen 1999a, p. 10, emphasis in original). The prominent role given to democratic processes to make value judgements shifts the boundary between economics and politics. As in other areas, significant literatures on empowerment, participatory methods, deliberative democracy, political freedoms and other process freedoms interact with and expand upon Sen's writings.

Principle pluralism

In principle pluralism, a welfare objective – whether that of Pareto optimality, or of social welfare maximization, or of expanding capabilities – can be coherently situated within a wider system of thought (indeed an ethical rationality) that evaluates the same state of affairs by additional principles such as efficiency, equity, sustainability, liberty, respect for human rights and situated responsibility (Sen 2000a). In *Inequality Reexamined* Sen writes, 'The real question is not about the kind of equality to ask for *if* that were the *only* principle to be used, but [how] in a mixed framework in which aggregative considerations as well as equality are taken into account, the demands of equality as such are best represented' (Sen 1992, p. 92, emphasis in original). For example Sen's early writings on poverty measurement drew attention to the depth of poverty and inequality among the poor (Sen 1976, 1997). The principle of respect for human rights – a classic deontological considera-tion – could be, Sen showed, included in consequential analysis as 'goal rights' (Sen 1982b, 2004). Similarly, other concerns – for equity, sustainability, responsibility and respect for process freedom – need to and can be incorporated into a consequential analysis.

Sen argues for the development of a form of consequential evaluation, which he describes as 'the discipline of responsible choice based on the chooser's evaluation of states of affairs, including consideration of all the relevant consequences viewed in light of the exact circumstances of that choice' (Sen 2000a, p. 477). Such a structure can, he argues, 'systematically combine very diverse concerns, including taking responsibility for the nature of one's actions (and related considerations that have figured prominently in the deontological literature) without neglecting other types of consequences (on which some of the narrower versions of consequential reasoning – such as utilitarianism – have tended to concentrate)' (Sen 2000a, p. 477). For example, cost-benefit analysis, which tra-ditionally has employed quite a narrow set of principles, could be coherently broadened by such analysis if relevant consequences are understood to include 'not only such things as happiness or the fulfillment of desire . . . but also whether certain actions have been performed or particular rights have been violated' (Sen 2000b, p. 936).

Rationality and motivation

Sen's writings on rationality pierce two persistent assumptions regarding economic behaviour: that of exclusively self-interested motivation and that of internal consist-ency of choice. In the seminal paper 'Rational fools' (1977), Sen inquires how modern economic theory would fare if people were not concerned uniquely with their own self-interest narrowly defined. He defines two possibilities in which a consideration for others' welfare might enter: sympathy and commitment.

In sympathy, concern for others directly affects one's own welfare: if another person's discomfort is reduced (for example, the agent's child's distress), the agent's own welfare is improved. Whereas in earlier forms of revealed preference, sympathy-based behaviour was considered an externality, Sen showed that it could be incorporated without much difficulty.

A commitment is not motivated by one's own-welfare considerations at all, but does affect one's subsequent action. It may reflect various motives, such as altruism or conviction (justice, honesty, care for other species) or an urge to punish. Commitment is a counter-preferential choice, 'destroying the crucial assumption that a chosen alternative must be better than (or at least as good as) the others for the person choosing it' (Sen 1982a, p. 92). Because it 'drives a wedge between personal choice and personal welfare, and much of traditional economic theory relies on the identity of the two' (Sen 1982a, p. 94), commitment-based behaviour requires a reformulation of economic models.

In 'Rational fools' and subsequently, Sen argues that commitment, or intrinsically motivated behaviour, is significant enough to reformulate economic assumptions for several reasons. First, while it may be exhibited only rarely in Smithian exchange, commitment may be of considerable importance in achieving public goods (hospitals, street lights, nature reserves). Clearly some forms of commitment have direct social benefits – for example, as experienced by activists and others who pursue justice and others' well-being regardless of the cost to themselves. Certain commitments to behavioural or moral codes (trustworthiness) are instrumentally valued, as they reduce monitoring and enforcement costs and increase outputs. Behavioural economics and economic psychology have now extensively probed and developed these and related issues. Also, people who are aware of their effective freedom to help the less well off may not only wish to do what they can to help, but may also be under some kind of 'imperfect obligation' to do so. Imperfect obligations are not legally formulated, but rather commend action despite being 'inexactly specified (telling us neither who must particularly take the initiative, nor how far he should go in doing this general duty)' (Sen 2000a, p. 495).

Another pivotal assumption in social choice theory, demand theory, game theory, decision theory and behavioural economics is that choices are internally consistent. Internal consistency of choice is an assumption of revealed preference and many common axioms. In his presidential address to the Econometric Society, Sen raised a series of arguments as to why choices cannot be judged as consistent or inconsistent purely on internal grounds (Sen 1993). Inconsistencies of choice may be reasonable and rational in a number of different situations, he argues. Thus, an evaluation requires information external to the choice, such as the actor's objectives, or the values pursued by the choice. As the (misunderstanding) of people's choices threads through many aspects of economics, Sen traces how a more accurate appreciation of people's behaviour that draws on such external correspondences could be used in different fields.

Justice

No discussion of Sen's work would be complete without acknowledging the tremendous influence of John Rawls (Rawls 1971, 1993; Rawls and Kelly 2001), as well as the fundamental challenge that Sen's emerging theory of justice poses to Rawlsian and similar 'transcendental' theories of justice.

In developing his account, Rawls took as his focal question, 'What is a just society?' This is also the focal question of 'most theories of justice in contemporary political philosophy' (Sen 2006, p. 216). Sen calls this a 'transcendental approach to justice', focusing, as it does, on identifying perfectly just societal arrangements.

Yet real questions of injustice occur in this quite imperfect and messy world. The transcendental approach, which seeks instead to describe a perfectly just society far removed from our own, is not well suited to address these. Sen argues that this is a key weakness because the answers that a transcendental approach to justice gives – or can give – are quite distinct and distant from the type of concerns that engage people in discussions on justice and injustice in the world, for example, iniquities of hunger, illiteracy, torture, arbitrary incarceration, or medical exclusion as particular social features that need remedying. (Sen 2006, p. 218)

This would not be too problematic if we were able to measure the shortfall of each of two alternatives from a perfectly just situation and compare them indirectly in this way. But justice comparisons involve comparisons of capabilities and of other spaces such as procedural equity, and infractions are of different kinds and depths of seriousness, so, Sen argues, transcendental clarity does not yield comparative rankings. The establishment of a transcendental theory of justice thus is insufficient for the kinds of justice assessments we require. As Sen puts it, 'The fact that a person regards the Mona Lisa as the best picture in the world, does not reveal how she would rank a Gauguin against a Van Gogh' (Sen 2006, p. 221).

Sen further argues that a transcendental account of a perfectly just society is not actually necessary to making comparative justice assessments. 'In arguing for a Picasso over a Dali we do not need to get steamed up about identifying the perfect picture in the world which would beat the Picassos and the Dalis and all other paintings in the world' (Sen 2006, p. 222). The case for pursuing transcendental theories is also weakened by the 'extremely demanding institutional requirements of accomplishing pristine justice', which disable realistic assessments of global justice (Sen 2006, p. 226).

In contrast, Sen advocates a 'comparative' approach to justice. This would concentrate on a pairwise comparison and ranking of alternative societal arrangements in terms of justice (whether some arrangement is 'less just' or 'more just' than another). Such a ranking would make 'systematic room for incompleteness' (Sen 2006, p. 223). Incompleteness that derives in part from missing information, in part from the use of plural principles without an 'umpire', and in part from the fact that people will differ in their assessment of the appropriate principles to prioritize. Utilitarians, egalitarians and libertarians, for example, prioritize different principles, and although they should be encouraged to consider non-local views and self-critically explore their own views, in some cases all will agree on the same maximand for quite different reasons. So a maximizing yet incomplete comparative approach could still do considerable work in identifying and rejecting options that are clearly inferior to others according to multiple principles or considerations.

The structure of pairwise assessments of states of affairs that would constitute a framework for comparative justice is not unlike the consequential analysis and extended cost-benefit analysis that Sen advocates for assessments of social welfare.

Note

1. A full discussion of process and opportunity freedoms is found in Sen (2002, Chs 19–21).

References

Alkire, Sabina (2008), 'Concepts and measures of agency, OPH Working Paper No. 9, Oxford: Oxford Poverty and Human Development Initiative.
Arrow, Kenneth (1951), *Social Choice and Individual Values*, New York: John Wiley and Sons.
Drèze, Jean and Amartya Sen (2002), *India, Development and Participation*, New Delhi and New York: Oxford University Press.

Nussbaum, Martha (1988), 'Nature, functioning and capability: Aristotle on political distribution', *Oxford Studies in Ancient Philosophy, Supplementary Volume*, 145–84.

Nussbaum, M. (1990), 'Aristotelian social democracy', in R.B. Douglass, G.M. Mara and H.S. Richardson (eds), *Liberalism and the Good*, New York: Routledge, pp. 203–52.

Nussbaum, Martha (1995), 'Human capabilities, female human being', in M.C. Nussbaum and J. Glover (eds), *Women, Culture, and Development: A Study of Human Capabilities*, Oxford and New York: Clarendon Press/ Oxford University Press, pp. 61–104.

Nussbaum, Martha (2000), *Women and Human Development: The Capabilities Approach*, Cambridge: Cambridge University Press.

Rawls, John (1971), *A Theory of Justice*, Cambridge, MA: Belknap Press of Harvard University Press.

Rawls, John (1993), *Political Liberalism*, New York: Columbia University Press.

Rawls, John and Erin Kelly (2001), *Justice as Fairness: A Restatement*, Cambridge, MA: Harvard University Press.

Sen, Amartya (1970a), *Collective Choice and Social Welfare*, Amsterdam: North-Holland.

Sen, Amartya (1970b), 'The Impossibility of a Paretian liberal', *Journal of Political Economy*, **78** (1), 152–7.

Sen, Amartya (1971), *Behaviour and the Concept of Preference*, London: London School of Economics and Political Science.

Sen, Amartya (1974), 'Informational bases of alternative welfare approaches: aggregation and income distribution', *Journal of Public Economics*, **3** (4), 387–403.

Sen, Amartya (1976), 'Poverty: an ordinal approach to measurement', *Econometrica*, **44** (2), 219–31.

Sen, Amartya (1977), 'Rational fools: a critique of the behavioral foundations of economic theory', *Philosophy and Public Affairs*, **6** (4), 317–44.

Sen, Amartya (1979), 'Informational analysis of moral principles', in R. Harrison (ed.), *Rational Action*, Cambridge: Cambridge University Press, pp. 115–32.

Sen, Amartya (1982a), *Choice, Welfare, and Measurement*, Cambridge, MA: MIT Press.

Sen, Amartya (1982b), 'Rights and agency', *Philosophy and Public Affairs*, **11** (1), 3–39.

Sen, Amartya (1983), 'Evaluator relativity and consequential evaluation', *Philosophy and Public Affairs*, **12** (2), 113–32.

Sen, Amartya (1985), 'Well-being, agency and freedom: the Dewey Lectures 1984', *Journal of Philosophy*, **82** (4), 169–221.

Sen Amartya (1987), *On Ethics and Economics*, Oxford: Basil Blackwell.

Sen, Amartya (1992), *Inequality Reexamined*, New York and Cambridge, MA: Russell Sage Foundation, Harvard University Press.

Sen, Amartya (1993), 'Internal consistency of choice', *Econometrica*, **61** (3), 495–521.

Sen, Amartya (1996), 'On the foundations of welfare economics: utility, capability and practical reason', in Francesco Farina, Frank Hahn and Stephano Vannucci (eds) *Ethics, Rationality and Economic Behaviour*, Oxford: Clarendon Press, pp. 50–65.

Sen, Amartya (1997), *On Economic Inequality, with a Substantial Annexe, with James Foster 'after a Quarter Century'*, Oxford: Clarendon Press.

Sen, Amartya (1999a), 'Democracy as a universal value', *Journal of Democracy*, **10** (3), 3–17.

Sen, Amartya (1999b), *Development as Freedom*, New York: Knopf Press.

Sen, Amartya (2000a), 'Consequential evaluation and practical reason', *Journal of Philosophy*, **97** (9), 477–502.

Sen, Amartya (2000b), 'The discipline of cost-benefit analysis', *Journal of Legal Studies*, **29**, 931–53.

Sen, Amartya (2002), *Rationality and Freedom*, Cambridge, MA: Belknap Press.

Sen, Amartya (2004), 'Elements of a theory of human rights', *Philosophy and Public Affairs*, **234**, 315–56.

Sen, Amartya (2006), 'What do we want from a theory of justice?' *Journal of Philosophy*, **103** (55), 215–38.

See also the entries on: Capability approach; Human development; Justice; Needs and agency; Needs and well-being.

64 Sin
Samuel Cameron

Introduction
Sin is not at the forefront of work by economists. Recent applied work by mainstream economists has, however, mentioned gluttony and sloth. There is also a tendency for academic economics writings on addiction and subjects of a sexual nature to stray into implicitly treating these activities as sins. Yet sin, in general, is not a regular topic in applied economics, though theoretical discussion has shown some emphasis on the converse, those being acts of virtue, particularly altruism. A full treatment of sin within the field of economics requires a debate on the extent to which indulging in sin can be treated as rational choice behaviour. This debate is the subject of the current chapter, which looks at the concept of sin in the context of both the standard rational choice model and the expanded version represented in multiple utility models. It also discusses the function of religions as suppliers of moral standards about what is considered to be a sin.

Archetypal categories of sin
Sins appear to fall into three categories:

- actions
- attitudes (or states of mind or emotions)
- inaction

The obvious examples of actions are purchases, such as buying huge amounts of forbidden goods or actions involving deceit, such as adultery or deceiving subscribers to a pension fund to rob them of their savings.

Envy is a clear example of an attitude. Envy may or may not translate into action. If television advertising creates envy of other people's car ownership, then it may translate into action, with the envious individuals exceeding their prior equilibrium level of car expenditure. However, one can be envious purely in the manner of wishful thinking or indulge in *schadenfreude* when the objects of one's envy lose their value or otherwise fall from grace. Or, as Elster (1982) pointed out, following Aesop's fable *The Fox and the Grapes*, jealousy may manifest in the form of claiming not to want what someone else has because they have it instead of you.

Inaction is represented in the case of sloth, which may manifest as negligence – such as the failure to service a public transport item (thus leading to undesirable actions) or neglect of oneself as in the failure to adequately provide for one's self in terms of savings or insurance or health maintenance. Traditional welfare economics would tend to take the consequentialist line and hence would disregard pure *schadenfreude* and non-actioned feelings of envy. However, the concept of externalities can lead to trouble here, since there is the perennial conundrum as to why we might take account of, say, noise pollution as a negative externality, but not envy.

Economic concepts of sin

The idea and practice of sin seems to lie at the heart of the intersection between economics and ethics. Considered without reference to economics, sin appears to be an inherently ethical subject, although there are many discussions of ethics which make no reference to sin. In fact, economics proceeds, for a very large portion of the time, without referring to sin, although one might argue that sin is implicit in some of the discussions in which negative externalities are invoked.

Economists have been willing to use the term 'sin' in the context of indulgent consumption and taxation and policies to curb it. The direct sumptuary tax argument is clearly stated in the 1892 textbook by Irish public finance economist C.F. Bastable:

> The last important influence that affects the selection of the objects of indirect taxation is the desire to discourage certain forms of outlay that are regarded as pernicious, or to take the mildest view, not promotive of economic or other virtues. This idea which lies at the root of all sumptuary taxes, is represented in modern Finance by the treatment of intoxicating drinks and tobacco. (Bastable 1892, p. 455)

Discussions of sin outside of this field have been rare, until recently, with the exception of Kenneth Boulding (1962), who provides some analysis of the interaction between a saint and a devil. However, he makes no attempt to define the concept of sin from an economic perspective. An exception to the omission of sin in titles of works by economists, albeit quite an old one, is a short paper by Rendig Fels (1971) entitled *The Price of Sin*, which turns out to be an account of how the US military became involved in the supply of prostitutes to soldiers due to the need to maintain efficiency in soldiering. Notably, Fels moved away from the ethical tones used by Bastable and sumptuary tax writers, in that he considered only the effects of prostitution on the productivity of soldiers without worrying about their moral situation.

Papers have appeared, mainly in the addiction field (see Miahon and Miahon 2005) which bring the word 'sin' into economic discourse; and some general theoretical papers have appeared that refer to specific sins in their titles (for example, Bednarek et al. 2006). That said, and notwithstanding these papers' use of the terms 'sinful', 'sloth' and 'gluttony', they are not really about sin at all as it is normally understood. The text of these papers barely mentions sin, despite its presence in the title. They are papers about health-harming behaviour in the context of rational choice models. The introduction of the actual word 'sin', and its components, just confuses the issue, which is really just one of attempting to explain apparently irrational behaviour.

This is not to say that sin per se might not involve irrational behaviour. To fully explore the nature of sin requires reference to shared social values, because the notion of sin involves a judgement of some type about the desirability of an action beyond its effects on the material well-being of the actor. It carries with it the associated phenomenon of guilt, which is a source of disutility. Shared social judgements about sin have historically been in the control of religious oligopolists. The idea of sin is such that one might think it would go away in a secular society, particularly if rising levels of wealth make individuals more materialistic.

Despite this, popular media continually make linguistic references to sinful behaviour. Obvious examples are the British television drama series on the seven deadly sins; a theme which features even more globally in the Hollywood movie *Seven*. In music, there is the

Pet Shop Boys' song *It's a Sin*, inspired by continually being told as an adolescent not to do certain things which are 'wrong'. This is a song by an older generation. Even so, pornography and quasi-pornography is still promoted today by the idea of being dirty or naughty, and hence the notion of pleasure in indulgence in sin is part of the marketing. One might argue that in these cases it is guilt that is being used as a selling strategy without it blossoming into sin as such. In a video of a song aimed squarely at young people, Christina Aguilera expounds her sex-seeking philosophy as indicative of her being 'dirty' and 'naughty': 'its fun and I like it so what's wrong with that'. In case we missed the point, the song video features copious amounts of mud to symbolize the dirt motif. There is also a longer tradition in more 'highbrow' art and culture of individuals, who experience profound guilt feelings about their sinfulness, describing themselves as dirty.

Mention the word 'sin' to most people brought up in the culture of Western religions, and the first thought likely to enter their minds is of the seven deadly sins or the Ten Commandments in the Bible which issue instructions about what one should and should not do. The seven deadly sins and the Ten Commandments are clear ethical guides providing perspectives on how we should lead our lives, particularly in order to be a 'good' person. In economics terms, then, they might form standards or codes if sufficient people obey them. A person who falls short of these prescriptions for good behaviour has committed a sin, and one who persistently falls short without attempting redemption is a sinner. The ultimate payoff for the sinner is being sent to hell or its equivalent depending on the religion in question. There is also the possibility of being held in limbo after death before entrance to hell. Within any religion at any point in time, such a list can function as a price system to be administered by agents of the religion, such as priests or scholars of religious doctrine. It is they who decide on the different relative prices of the various sins. For example, they might decide that adultery is not as serious as murder. They might also decide on the form and value of payments by which to remove a sin from a person. This has taken various forms, from performance of acts (penance), to more or less outright monetary payment, to attempts to pass sin on to others ('sin eaters') at the point of death.

So, let us turn to the issue of fitting sin into rational choice models. Taking a standard neoclassical rational choice model of the consumer, a sin must be something that is either a source of utility (hence a good) or disutility (hence a bad) or a constraint on the attainment of goods and the avoidance of bads. The Aguilera example perhaps illustrates that people may derive positive utility from feelings of indulgence in sin; that is, the fact that an activity was once heavily proscribed makes it more enjoyable than it would otherwise be. This concept of indulgence and heightened pleasure is also apparent in advertising for luxury consumer products, such as chocolate and ice cream.

Sin can thus be viewed as embodied in consumer goods, which brings positive utility from direct effects and negative utility from indirect effects such as social criticism. For example, people brought up to believe an action is wrong will experience the psychic cost of pain when they indulge in that action. In this situation, the bad is a joint product with the good. Of course, the good and bad are not necessarily in fixed proportions at different levels of consumption. Many technical possibilities exist, such as diminishing returns for the good and increasing returns for the bad (guilt, feelings of sin). Or, there may be threshold or tipping effects, such as individuals who sin so much that they become inured to it and therefore no longer experience bad elements in their consumption of the erstwhile sinful good.

Sin may also be represented as a general type of taste capital which can be positive or negative. A person who has been indoctrinated by a strict religion may develop a neurosis which predisposes them to feel continually sinful because they think they are a bad person with no chance of redemption, even in the face of a choice situation which has no sin potential. This is what James ([1902] 1977) referred to as 'sick religiosity'. It also constitutes negative personal capital, as it reduces a person's capacity for satisfaction. Positive personal capital from religiosity may increase one's capacity for satisfaction as the individual will get greater utility from non-sinful (virtuous) choices. This may even involve an all-round gain in utility, simply from believing in the goodness or virtue (absence from sin) of one's choices.

We might then take the economic definition of a sin good as the case in which the negative utility of sinning outweighs the gain implicit in the attractiveness of the sin good. Further, let us assume that individual perception of sin is not a function of being caught – that is, there is negative utility from the act regardless of who knows about it. Otherwise we are not really talking about sin but just code observance of any sort. One must bear in mind that sociological treatments of code observance would incorporate the internalization or learning of costs of feeling guilty. Being caught introduces an independent factor of costs, if a punishment is imposed on the individual due to the decisions of other people in the group. This definition leads us straight into a cul-de-sac, as no one would ever sin except by mistake or miscalculation.

If we rule out the mistake argument, then we are left with the observation that some individuals will find themselves engaging in an act, omission or state of mind to which their reference group attaches the sin label. This has to mean that they personally do not experience the negative utility in sufficient volume to be deterred. The only thing that can put them off is public or explicit punishments which are merely price signals and not full-blown feelings of sin. One type of mistake which could lead to sin is distorted ex ante perceptions of the preferences that will be felt ex post of a decision. For example, a religiously inhibited individual might imagine that they are going to greatly enjoy delving into pornography or prostitution for the first time, but then find it to be a source of negative utility due to their underestimating the depth of their acquired sin capital stock.

Such an individual may perceive that, in the long run, they could engineer a change in their preferences. This is a fundamental issue which mainstream economics has always sidestepped; to wit, if preferences determine utility why should individuals not engage in large-scale attempts to change their own preferences? This takes us to the area of multiple utility models of sin.

Multiple utility models of sin

A literature derived from philosophy has, for some time, suggested more complex (non-monistic) utility functions. This has generated excitement among heterodox economists seeking to undermine the hegemony of the neoclassical paradigm (see White 2006 for a recent example; see Sen 1977 and Schelling 1984 for perhaps the beginning of this vogue). The argument, in the simplest case, is that people have two utility functions. One is a reflection of their immediate preference set. The other is their meta-preference function, which contains their 'preferences about preferences'. For there to be any kind of conflict between these two choice sets there has to be a problem of willpower or self-control.

This model can be relevant for individuals for whom sin is of no relevance whatsoever, as they may have intentions they cannot keep perhaps for pragmatic reasons (such as health) or because they have a personal morality of some sort to pursue. We would not call obeying purely personal morality avoiding sin, as the essence of sin is to involve social judgements of some kind. For completely consistent and devout religious persons, the meta-preference set is the doctrines of their religion. The lower preference set involves sinning, as they are doing things (or not doing things or thinking things) they wish they could avoid.

This approach does not immediately take us to any obvious policy conclusions without invoking some kind of imperative of the religious preference set. Nevertheless, there are people willing to come to such conclusions. Heterodox economist David George (2001, pp. 122–4) briefly discusses pornography as an instance of what he calls 'preference pollution'. In this scenario, free markets impose weakness of will upon us leading to the wrong choice of consumption basket. We end up at a lower level of utility than we might otherwise have obtained, in his view, because we are weak and fall prey to market pressures to consume pornography. Thus, government can make pornography lovers better off by constraining their consumption. This could be in the form of the sumptuary taxes discussed above with reference to the quote from Bastable. The difference here is that rational sinners might be expected, under certain circumstances, to vote for a politician who wants to curb their actions. This is to say, smokers might vote for higher taxes on smoking and pornography consumers for similar measures.

Regulation of sin

In an economic framework individuals may make rational choices in a world where they believe in sin. We can characterize this in different ways which may be more or less useful according to the situation. We now come to the economics and ethics of the role of sin regulatory institutions.

When an individual tries to make choices in which concepts of sin inform their thinking, they are essentially trying to comply with a standard of some sort. That standard might be deemed to be a system of ethics. The choice then can become a two-stage process. In the first stage a system of ethics is chosen and this then becomes a constraint on the second-stage choice process. If one takes the decidedly 'non-economic' view that a person has no choice over the system of ethics chosen, as it is indoctrinated into them at an early age, then the first stage vanishes, and if we wish to keep the analysis within the province of economics we can go back to regarding the unwanted ethics as negative sin capital, as in the discussion above.

On the supply side, we expect there to be competition in the supply of sets of ethical standards. As mentioned, this has historically been the role of religions. Religions have essentially monopolized the concept of sin, in some cases for monetary purposes (see, for example, Schmidtchen and Mayer 1997; Davidson and Ekelund 1997). Religions have ultimately sold their systems of ethics on the basis of a net expected payoff at some future time, which may be in the afterlife. This underlying concept can be found across very different religions (Kuran 1995, 1997; Smith 1999). Strict religions may decree that entrance to heaven (or its analogous concept) is a scarce commodity to be rationed by competition over purity of conduct and belief, so only the truly sin-free can enter it. The logical extreme of this kind of competition is to designate selected individuals as saints for their virtue, which by implication would confer freedom from sin (or in a less strict religion, a suitable redemption from a past life of sin).

Loss of support may dictate changes in the price of sin within religions, as they may be forced into an adapt-or-die situation. Across the spectrum, there must be alternatives to the stereotypical punitive religions which use sin as a control device. Yet even in these religions, which offer uplift as their main output rather than the prospect of salvation from failure, there is still a necessity to deal with sin. Given that the club good of an individual's religion can never have universal membership, the sin of outsiders is a considerable threat to the viability of this kind of religion. Uplift is difficult to sustain in, say, a situation where the club has two members and the rest of the world is drowning in an orgy of evil and dangerous behaviour. At present, the developed economies seem to be going through a period of attraction to such faiths particularly among younger people.

As expounded in Cameron (2005), the doctrines that may be loosely banded under the label of 'Wicca' seek to deal with the sin problem in a way that is common throughout history and across many cultures. The positive nature of these religions comes from the idea that practitioners can acquire power to effect changes in the world that may be broadly termed as magic. Once a person obtains transformative powers they could become psychic or charismatic healers, in line with Wiccan doctrines. But, they could also become potent sinners, using their powers to inflict harm on others for their own ends or as agents of someone who hires them. The universal control mechanism is the claim of a rebound effect of any attempts to do harm to other people through the practice of magic. The rebound effect (that any magically willed, morally wrong act is reciprocated by greater suffering to the perpetrator) serves the role of absolving Wicca (and similar religions) from accusations that it promotes a world of conflict by teaching people techniques to interfere in the lives of others. Some basic microeconomic concepts, explained in detail in Cameron (2005), suggest that the moral force of this rebound law is difficult to sustain except under very unreasonable assumptions.

Conclusion

This chapter has reviewed the position of sin at the intersection between ethics and economics. Sin clearly still plays a part in economic life and the thinking of economists. However, attempts to analyse sin within the confines of the rational choice model have seldom really been about sin as we appear to know it. This is not surprising, as mainstream economics eschews ethical foundations. A much clearer notion of sin is present in models of multiple utility, as some writers in this vein explicitly or implicitly presume that individuals have higher and lower functions where the terms 'high' and 'low' have normative connotations. However, the decision as to which is higher and which is lower obviously requires a proper treatment of ethics. Otherwise, the model of sinning is again just a model of whether one obeys a convention imposed by a reference group.

References

Bastable, Charles F. (1892), *Public Finance*, London and New York: Macmillan.
Bednarek, Heather, Thomas D. Jeitschko and Rowena A. Pecchenino (2006), 'Gluttony and sloth: symptoms of trouble or signs of bliss? A theory of choice in the presence of behavioral adjustment costs', *Contributions to Economic Analysis & Policy*, **5** (1) 6, www.bepress.com/bejeap/contributions/vol5/iss1/art6.
Boulding, Kenneth E. (1962), *Conflict and Defense: A General Theory*, New York and London: Harper Torchbooks.

Cameron, Sam (2005), 'Wiccanomics', *Review of Social Economy*, **63** (1), 87–100.

Davidson, Audrey B. and Robert B. Ekelund (1997), 'The medieval church and rents from marriage market regulations', *Journal of Economic Behavior and Organization*, **32** (2), 215–46.

Elster, Jon (1982), 'Sour grapes-utilitarianism and the genesis of wants', in Amartya Sen and Bernard Williams (eds), *Utilitarianism and Beyond*, Cambridge: Cambridge University Press, Ch.11.

Fels, Rendigs (1971) 'The price of sin', in Harry Townsend (ed.), *Price Theory: Selected Readings*, Harmondsworth: Penguin.

George, David (2001), *Preference Pollution: How Markets Create the Desires we Dislike*, Ann Arbor, MI: University of Michigan Press.

James, William ([1902] 1997), 'The varieties of religious experience: a study in human nature', in R. Coles (ed.), *Selected Writings: William James*, New York: Book of the Month Club.

Kuran, Timur (1995), 'Islamic economics and the Islamic subeconomy', *Journal of Economic Perspectives*, **9** (4), 155–73.

Kuran, Timur (1997), 'Islam and underdevelopment: an old puzzle revisited', *Journal of Institutional and Theoretical Economics*, **153** (1), 41–71.

Miahon, Hugo M. and Sue H. Miahon (2005), 'Sinful indulgences, soft substitutes and self control', *Applied Economics Letters*, **12** (2), 719–22.

Schmidtchen, Dieter and Achim Mayer (1997), 'Established clergy, friars and the pope: some institutional economics of the medieval church', *Journal of Institutional and Theoretical Economics*, **153** (1), 129–49.

Schelling, Thomas C. (1984), 'Self command in practice, in policy, and in a theory of rational choice', *American Economic Review*, **74** (2), 1–11.

Sen, Amartya (1977), 'Rational fools: a critique of the behavioural foundations of economic theory', *Philosophy and Public Affairs*, **6**, 317–44.

Smith, Ian (1999), 'The economics of the Apocalypse: modelling the biblical Book of Revelation', *Journal of Institutional and Theoretical Economics*, **155** (3), 443–57.

White, Mark D. (2006), 'Multiple utilities and weakness of will: a Kantian perspective', *Review of Social Economy*, **64** (1), 1–20.

See also the entries on: Religion; Utilitarianism.

65 Adam Smith
Jan Peil

Typing 'Adam Smith' into a search engine for scientific publications on economics retrieves an extensive literature about the principles of economics dated since the 1970s, when discussions on these principles were revived (compare Peil 1999; Tribe 1999; Wight 2002). Until then the works of Smith (1723–90) were of interest to only a small group of scholars on the history of economic thought. Outside this small circle of experts, Smith's economic analysis and theories were considered outdated. His ideas however – such as those related to human nature and the market mechanism – were often quoted in support of the mainstream approach of (neo)classical economics or to invoke an opponent against whom it was easy to present alternative views on the economics subject matter and methods at hand.

Adam Smith epitomized the trend in economics to conceive of an economy as a self-regulating mechanism: if individuals are free to act in accordance with their (human) nature – that is, in accordance with self-interest – the market mechanism will ensure a stable and optimal equilibrium. Various quotes are frequently used to confirm this interpretation of Smith:

> It is not from the benevolence of the butcher, the brewer, or the baker, that we expect our dinner, but from their regard to their own interest. We address ourselves, not to their humanity but to their self-love, and never talk to them of our own necessities but of their advantages. (*The Wealth of Nations* (*WN*) I.ii.2)

> He, generally . . . neither intends to promote the publick interest, nor knows how much he is promoting it . . . [H]e intends only his own gain, and he is in this, as in many other cases led by an invisible hand to promote an end which was no part of his intention. Nor is it always the worse for the society that it was no part of it. By pursuing his own interest he frequently promotes that of the society more effectually than when he really intends to promote it. (*WN* IV.ii.9; compare *WN* IV.ii.4)

> The natural price is . . . as it were, the central price, to which the prices of all commodities are continually gravitating. Different accidents may sometimes keep them suspended a good deal above it, and sometimes force them down even somewhat below it. But whatever may be the obstacles which hinder them from settling in this centre of repose and continuance, they are constantly tending towards it. (*WN* I.vii.15)

An Adam Smith renaissance

Commemorating the publication of *The Wealth of Nations* in 1776, Horst Claus Recktenwald (1978) noted a revival of the studies of Adam Smith.[1] Referring to the 'bicentenary output', he used the expression 'an Adam Smith renaissance' to indicate that the bicentenary itself could not fully explain the substantial growth of publications about Smith (ibid.). Economists, political scientists, lawyers, philosophers and historians started to (re-)read Smith in relation to topical subjects in fields such as economics and political science. These new readings gave rise to an avalanche of publications dealing with a variety of subjects in which Recktenwald observed four trends: (i) comprehensive re-readings of Smith's works as a coherent whole, (ii) reappraisals of Smith's economic analysis, (iii) reconstructions of the social philosophy behind Smith's economic theory and (iv) rethinkings of Smith's discussions of the role of the state and other socio-political institutions in a market economy.

The renewed interest in Adam Smith's works reflected a revival of disputes about the principles of (economic) science. In economics, the community of scientists was once again disintegrating into rival schools of thought. Though this rivalry has largely given way to disputes inspired by methodologies of pluralism, discussions about the principles of economics are as topical as before. The same is true of economists' interest in Adam Smith. Discussions of his works are related to disputes about, for instance, distinctions between positive and normative economics; between economics, (other) social sciences and ethics; and about core concepts such as rationality, sentiments, institutions and market economy.

It is impossible to deal with all of these in this chapter. The focus will therefore be on two trends in the new Adam Smith readings which are relevant to hermeneutics-based reorientations in economic methodology and to the new rule-based approaches to economic behaviour.[2] The first is a trend towards an integral reading of Smith's works, including the use of a new hermeneutic model of interpretation. In the perspective of this new understanding of interpreting texts, Smith is transformed from a supplier of useful citations into a contributor to today's discussions of principles of economics. The second trend is that of reinterpretation of Smith's works. The first trend is discussed below. The next section then deals with the second trend, in particular the reinterpretation of Smith's conception of the market economy.

From a selective to an integrated reading of Smith's works
In the mid-twentieth century, the common view held that Smith's works consisted of two parts. The first part – *The Theory of Moral Sentiments* (*TMS*), of which the first edition was published in 1759 – was classified as ethics; it was supposedly based on an altruistic view of man.[3] The second part – *The Wealth of Nations* (*WN*), of which the first edition was published in 1776 – was considered a contribution to economic thought. *WN* conceived human behaviour as motivated by self-interest. The first two books of *WN* are said to be Smith's contribution to economic analysis, with economics conceived of as a science distinct from (other) social sciences, ethics and other discourses of economic thought – for example, ethico-political.[4]

According to Schumpeter ([1954] 1972), at that time an authority on the history of economics, Smith's ideas were hardly new. Smith's merit was above all that he accomplished the tremendous job of collecting existing fragments of ideas and presenting these as a coherent whole.[5] Interpreting his economic analysis as a general equilibrium analysis in nucleo, Smith was understood to be a forerunner of Leon Walras (compare Schumpeter [1954] 1972, p. 189). Schumpeter viewed *WN* as '(perhaps) the peak success of the first classical situation', that is, the first of three periods in the history of economics, which was conceived as a development in which general equilibrium analysis took shape.[6]

In line with new trends in economic analysis and new directions in philosophy and economic methodology, interpretations and appraisals of Smith's works have thoroughly changed. In the 1970s, philosophy and methodology became hotspots in economic discourse. Concepts like 'paradigm', 'scientific revolution', 'research programme', 'hard core' and 'rhetoric' fuelled critiques of positivistic understandings of economics. A new rivalry of approaches emerged after a period in which the (neoclassical) synthesis of Keynesian and 'classical' economics, initiated by economists like Paul Samuelson and John Hicks, was conceived as the threshold towards maturity: no more contending doctrines, but science based on sound methods, as in physics. This new rivalry of approaches revived old debates about principles and concepts such as positive economics, *homo economicus* and the market mechanism. However, unlike the old debates, the rivalry departed from the framework of dichotomy: market versus government, positive versus normative, universal laws versus history, egoism versus altruism. A search for new approaches took off in which opposition was substituted for relation. It was in this context of turmoil and reorientation that today's Adam Smith renaissance emerged.

In this renaissance, authors set about re-examining incoherencies and inconsistencies in Adam Smith's economic thought as revealed by former interpretations of his works. Examples are the so-called 'Adam Smith problem', understood as the inconsistency between the altruistic understanding of human nature in *TMS* and the self-interest model of *WN*, and the contradictory methodologies in *WN*, which in Books I and II (on economic science) sets forth the abstract, general equilibrium approach and in Books III, IV and V (on historiography and political economy) offers a contextual, historic-institutional approach. Many of these interpretations have since been deconstructed as misinterpretations caused by anachronistic reading. Today it is common sense to read Adam Smith as an eighteenth-century Scottish moral philosopher who dealt with economics as part of a moral philosophical discourse about the evolving commercial societies.

This change from selective to integrated, contextual readings was supported by the publication of a new edition of Smith's works and correspondence – the so-called 'Glasgow edition' in the 1970s and 1980s. This Oxford University Press edition made Smith's complete works, including both previously published and as yet unpublished works, lecture notes and correspondence, available for the first time.[7]

A new model of interpretation

To avoid misunderstandings about the meaning of 'misinterpretation(s)' of Smith's works it is important to note that with the Adam Smith renaissance a new model of interpretation was introduced. Until that time the common view of Smith was based on the idea that a text has an objective, invariant meaning which corresponds to the intention of the author. An interpretation was thus understood as reproducing the meaning immanent to the text. From this perspective it is hard to explain the Adam Smith revival, in which new interpretations of his works inspired new views in economics. With this conventional approach, any new interpretation was viewed as questioning the old interpretation, leading to the question of which interpretation, the old one or the new one, best reproduced the original content. A plurality of interpretations would indicate that the interpreters had been untrue to the text and its intrinsic meaning, which could be discovered by using appropriate methods. Or it might mean that something was 'wrong' with the text – that is, the text was not unequivocal. For that matter, passages can be found in Smith's work to support many given viewpoints (Viner 1927).

The new model of interpretation is called 'hermeneutical' to distinguish it from other contextual approaches based on the old, positivistic model. In this regard, new readings of Smith's works acknowledge the relevance of the historical context of the texts and the contemporaneous horizon of the reader in interpreting them. However, particularly in the new readings of the early years of the Adam Smith renaissance, it was erroneously assumed that the double hermeneutics of the contemporary and the historical horizon could be separated into two distinct hermeneutics. Recktenwald (1978), West (1978) and Winch (1978), for example, conceive interpretations as perceptions of the self-same immanent content. Besides these interpretations, still based on the old, positivistic model, new readings were presented in which interpretation was understood as a dialogue between reader and author. With these, the double hermeneutics operative in reading a text allowed distinction but not separation.

Present-day economic Smith research is organized as an economic discourse with Smith's views being considered as contributions to an ongoing discussion about the principles of economics. Economists attempt to comment on and interpret, for their own times, the vision of the free market which Smith's manuscripts describe with reference to the historical circumstances of his day. The focus of this research lies on the ways in which Smith's texts illuminate the virtual pattern of the free market in our own era (Peil 1999, pp. 10–23).

Reinterpreting Smith's conception of a market economy

After *WN* had induced the breakthrough of the idea of the competitive market economy, in the first half of the nineteenth century Ricardian economics provided a law-based interpretation aimed at explaining long-term economic performance. By the latter nineteenth century, law-based and rule-based hybrids had replaced the Ricardian interpretation of the market economy. Most prominent on the threshold of the rivalries in the second half of the twentieth century was the auctioneer model of Walras intended to explain situations of general equilibrium produced by the market mechanism through interrelated markets. Since the 1970s, this interpretation of the competitive market economy has been challenged by rule-based interpretations presented by a variety of institutional approaches.

Here we reconsider Smith's contribution to the discussion of the idea of the market economy by re-examining his understanding of three concepts: self-interest, commerce and the invisible hand.

Self-interest
TMS opens with the following passage:

> How selfish so ever man may be supposed, there are evidently some principles in his nature, which interest him in the fortune of others, and render their happiness necessary to him, though he derives nothing from it except the pleasure of seeing it. (*TMS* I.i.1.1)

An interpretation of this first line that corresponds to the 'Adam Smith problem' is that humankind is not purely egoistic in nature but also has altruistic features.

Understanding 'sympathy' – the core concept of *TMS* – as 'compassion', *TMS* appears to oppose *WN*, which – in the old interpretation – supposedly explains economic behaviour from the perspective of egoism or self-interest. Reinterpreting altruism in a framework in which the *homo economicus* is understood as an agent who maximizes a constrained utility function containing preferences of both an altruistic and selfish nature, is no option in solving the problem. Regardless of whether self-interest is conceived in the conventional confined sense or the new enlightened way, Adam Smith disapproves of a rationalistic approach (*TMS* II.ii.3.5, VII.iii.1.4).

Another approach which does not end in the 'Adam Smith problem' and which takes note of Smith's own warnings not to misunderstand his (re)interpretation of the notion of 'sympathy' as compassion, is that the first line of *TMS* does not refer to a framework in which explaining behaviour is conceived as deducing it to given selfish or altruistic propensities.[8] Before the Adam Smith renaissance, scholars like Glenn Morrow (1923, [1923] 1973) and Alec Macfie (1959, 1961, 1967) had already indicated that with his (re) interpretation of 'sympathy' Smith refers to an understanding of humanity which differs profoundly from the atomistic approach that fits the dualism of individualism versus collectivism which emerged in the nineteenth century.

In using 'sympathy' 'to denote our fellow-feeling with any passion whatever', Smith introduced a social understanding of man, which resembles recent findings of neurological research of so-called 'mirror neurons' (compare Rustichini 2005). By discussing an almost never-ending sequence of examples, Smith tried to communicate the idea that in order to understand and explain human behaviour, character and even (self) consciousness we must look at our involvement in everlasting processes of mutual sympathy exchanges. By reading Smith's examples, we are supposed to observe (i) that we constantly experience feelings of approval or disapproval of other people's behaviour, (ii) that these feelings arise from imagining how we would behave and feel if we project ourselves in the position of these people, (iii) that we are conscious of the reciprocity of these processes, (iv) that because of this we long to concur in our behaviour and thinking with what we imagine other people's appraisal will be and (v) that we feel confident with the appraisal – that is, 'the praiseworthiness' – of an imagined impartial spectator when the actual appraisal of people in real life – that is, 'their praise' – differs.

From this psychology-based understanding of the social nature of man it is clear why Smith praises Francis Hutcheson for his insight that behaviour is not the effect of reason but of feelings. The sympathy approach also explains why Smith rejects his teacher's version of a theory of moral sentiments. Smith disagrees with Hutcheson that humanity has a moral sense in addition to the external senses like seeing and hearing (*TMS* VII. iii.2.7–9). According to Smith, there is no evidence for such a sense; moreover, his idea of mutual sympathy exchanges does not need it. The exchanges constantly (re)produce a shared frame of reference for appraisal and – because of this – shared norms for behaviour.[9]

With an eye on this (mutual) sympathy approach of human nature it is apparent that Smith's understanding of human nature goes beyond the debate on whether behaviour is driven by egoism or by altruism. While that debate refers to an atomistic conceived individual with a predetermined frame of behaviour, Smith's sympathy perspective presents a social individual, whose behaviour mirrors the individual's involvement in the (mutual) sympathy exchange processes (*TMS* VII.iii.1.4). In the first approach 'egoism' and 'altruism' express a property of the human frame of behaviour conceived of as given. In the last approach behaviour is driven by a craving for the acclaim of others in the context of a continuous exchange of sympathetic feelings; it is the intersubjectively framed set of values and rules that informs people whether self-interest is afforded or benevolence.

Commerce

Smith uses 'commerce' as a model to convey that a society organized by processes of (mutual) sympathy exchanges is self-regulating and vice versa. Striving for wealth and riches in competition with other people is conceived as an expression of the communication and concurrence immanent in exchanges of (mutual) sympathy. Wealth and riches are perceived as important in light of the expectation that the observation of wealth and riches by others delivers praise. The toil and trouble of labour is made worthwhile by imagining the feelings of sympathy people will express as they observe the results (*TMS* I.iii.2.1, VI.i.3). People of rank and distinction are more easily appreciated, and because of this, rank and distinction take a central role in the quest for praiseworthiness.

In Smith's view, the expected utility of goods is relevant in explaining behaviour, but not in a utilitarian way. Smith claims the discovery of a different approach in his criticism of David Hume's utilitarian view on economic policy (*TMS* IV.1.1–3). The (expected) utility and moreover its role in motivating people's behaviour comes with a background of longing for praise(worthiness) (*TMS* IV.1.1 and 2).[10]

The concept of a commercial society, understood in the perspective of Smith's sympathy-based theory of moral sentiments, differs from the frequently criticized caricature: a world populated by atomistic individuals whose behaviour is determined by the calculus of optimizing their own – that is, solipsistically perceived – utility. Smith's four stages theory of history places the commercial society as the final stage of human history after the age of hunters, the age of shepherds and the age of agriculture (*Lectures on Jurisprudence* (*LJ*), p. 30; *LJ*(A) i.27–35; *WN* III). Society is organized according to the principle of commerce: free exchange between people is ruled by shared beliefs, values and norms (re)produced through the processes of (mutual) sympathy immanent in that very same exchange.[11] This approach of man and society concurs with recent developments in institutional and experimental economics (compare North 1990, 1994; Gintis et al. 2005). It conceives behaviour as rule-governed in contrast to the law-governed approaches of (neo)classical economics, that is, to approaches said to be inspired by Smith.[12]

The invisible hand

Confronted with the concurrence between the self-interested behaviour of actors in a market economy, the observer may – as Smith did – use the metaphor 'the invisible hand' to communicate the observed coordination. Economists interpreted Smith's metaphor as a suggestion for conceiving coordination in the context of markets as a mechanism, or they substituted another metaphor for the invisible hand, as Walras did with his story of the auctioneer. For today's discussion of how to understand the coordination effect of exchanges in a market economy it is important to note that modern economics was shaped by a different understanding of humanity than that proposed by Smith in his moral philosophy of the commercial society. Smith's philosophy was modern in the sense that he believed in the autonomy of man, but his relational understanding expressed in his (mutual) sympathy view differed from the atomistic and functionalistic interpretation mirrored in the *homo economicus* concept.

Economists in search of new approaches to go beyond old dichotomies, such as the individual versus society or market versus government, may find suggestions in Smith's theory of (mutual) sympathy. Unlike, for example, Walras's use of the 'auctioneer', Smith did not need a *deus ex machina* to conceive a market economy as a self-regulating system in which self-interest and general interest are related. From the (mutual) sympathy perspective the difference between 'market price' and 'natural price' is not the difference between short term and long term, as Schumpeter ([1954] 1972, pp. 308–9) indicated. 'Natural price' is of a different order to the 'market price'. Natural price is part of society's prevailing value patterns, which orient people's behaviours and actions, while the market price – irrespective of whether its level differs from or corresponds with the level of the natural price – reflects the actual social values, produced in the actual exchange of the personal interpretations which actors have given to the value patterns in their local situation (Peil 1999, p. 142).[13]

This brief discussion of Smith's conception of a market economy serves as an example of how a re-reading of Smith's works could contribute to today's rethinking of economic behaviour beyond conventional dichotomies.

Notes

1. The full title is *An Inquiry into the Nature and Causes of the Wealth of Nations.* In this chapter *WN* will be used henceforth.
2. For an overview of the discussions since the 1970s revival of Adam Smith studies see for example Brown (1997), Tribe (1999) and Wight (2002). For an impression of the latest developments in Smith readings see the *Adam Smith Review* (2004, 2006 and 2007), Evensky (2005a and 2005b), Haakonssen (2006), Montes and Schliesser (2006) and Raphael (2007).
3. Smith published an expanded and revised edition – the sixth – shortly before his death on 17 July 1790 (compare Raphael and Macfie ([1976] 1991, pp. 15–20).
4. The contents of *The Wealth of Nations* (Smith [1976] 1979) lists five books, in addition to the 'Introduction and Plan of the Work': Book I 'Of the Causes of Improvement in the Productive Powers of Labour, and of the Order According to which its Produce is Naturally Distributed among the Different Ranks of the People; Book II 'Of the Nature, Accumulation, and Employment of Stock; Book III: 'Of the Different Progress of Opulence in Different Nations'; Book IV 'Of Systems of Political Oeconomy; Book V: 'Of the Revenue of the Sovereign or the Commonwealth'.
5. Letwin (1963) criticized this interpretation of Smith's contribution to economics, because it denies the creativity involved in restyling existing theories into a new comprehensive approach: economic behaviour from an encompassing system perspective.
6. Schumpeter ([1954] 1972, pp. 51–2, 143, 380, 753–4, 953).
7. For an overview see references and further reading, below.
8. 'Pity and compassion are words appropriated to signify our fellow-feeling with the sorrow of others. Sympathy, though its meaning was, perhaps originally the same, may now, however, without much impropriety, be made use of to denote our fellow-feeling with any passion whatever' (*TMS* I.i.1.5; see also *TMS* I.iii.1.1 and VII.i.4).
9. For example,

   'Were it possible that a human creature could grow up to manhood in some solitary place, without any communication with his own species, he could no more think of his own character, of the propriety or demerit of his own sentiments and conduct, of the beauty or deformity of his own mind, than of the beauty or deformity of his own face. All these are objects which he cannot easily see, which naturally he does not look at, and with regard to which he is provided with no mirror which can present them to his view. Bring him into society, and he is immediately provided with the mirror which he wanted before. It is placed in the countenance and behavior of those he lives with, which always mark when they enter into, and when they disapprove of his sentiments; and it is here that he first views the property and impropriety of his own passions, the beauty and deformity of his own mind. To a man who from his birth was a stranger to society, the objects of his passions, the external bodies which either pleased or hurt him, would occupy his whole attention. The passions themselves, the desires or aversions, the joys or sorrows, which those objects excited, though of all things the most immediately present to him, could scarce ever be the objects of his thoughts. The idea of them could never interest him so much as to call upon his attentive consideration. The consideration of his joy in him excite no new joy, nor that of his sorrow any new sorrow, though the consideration of the causes of those passions might often excite both. Bring him into society, and all his own passions will immediately become the causes of new passions. He will observe that mankind approve of some of them, and are disgusted by others. He will be elevated in the one case, and cast down in the other; his desires and aversions, his joys and sorrows, will now often become the causes of new desires and new aversions, new joys and new sorrows; they will now, therefore, interest him deeply, and often call upon his most attentive consideration.' (*TMS* III.1.3)

10. Thorstein Veblen pointed out this aspect of consumption years later in observing the behaviour of the rich. Discussing their behaviour in as far as it was focused on demonstrating their riches he named it 'conspicuous consumption'.
11. In *WN* (I.ii.1–2), Smith refers to this understanding of exchange when he discusses humanity's propensity to truck, barter and exchange as the origin of the division of labour. In the *Lectures of Jurisprudence* (for example, *LJ*(A) vi.56) he relates this propensity to humans' natural inclination to persuade:

'If we should enquire into the principle in the human mind on which this disposition of trucking is founded, it is clearly the natural inclination every one has to persuade. The offering of a shilling, which to us appears to have so plain and simple a meaning, is in reality offering an argument to persuade one to do so and so as it is for his interest. Men always endeavour to persuade others to be of their opinion even when the matter is of no consequence to them. If one advances any thing concerning China or the *more distant moon* which contradicts what you imagine to be true, you immediately try to persuade him to alter his opinion. And in this manner every one is practicing oratory on others thro the whole of his life. – You are uneasy whenever one differs from you, and you endeavour to persuade him to be of your mind; or if you do not it is a certain degree of self command, and to this every one is breeding thro their lives.'

12. 'It was Smith who taught Bastiat to speak of the "social mechanism", Cairnes to analyse Ricardo's work as an exercise in mechanistic explanation, and Jevons to describe the science of economics as the "mechanics of self-interest"' (Letwin 1963, p. 225).
13. For a more extended discussion, see Peil (1999, pp. 137–47).

References and further reading

Brown, Vivienne (1994), *Adam Smith's Discourse: Canonicity, Commerce and Conscience*, London: Routledge.
Brown, Vivienne (1997), 'Mere inventions of the imagination: a survey of recent literature of Adam Smith', *Economics and Philosophy*, **13**, 281–312.
Clark, Charles M.A. (1992), *Economic Theory and Natural Philosophy: The Search for the Natural Laws of the Economy*, Aldershot, UK and Brookfield, USA: Edward Elgar.
Cockfield, Geoff, Ann Firth and John Laurent (2007), *New Perspectives on Adam Smith's* The Theory of Moral Sentiments, Cheltenham, UK and Northampton, MA, USA: Edward Elgar.
Evensky, Jerry (2005a), 'Adam Smith's Theory of Moral Sentiments: On Morals and Why They Matter to a Liberal Society of Free People and Free Markets', *Journal of Economic Perspectives*, **19** (3), 109–30.
Evensky, Jerry (2005b), *Adam Smith's Moral Philosophy: A Historical and Contemporary Perspective on Markets, Law, Ethics and Culture*, Cambridge: Cambridge University Press.
Gintis, Herbert, Samuel Bowles, Robert Boyd and Ernst Fehr (eds) (2005), *Moral Sentiments and Material Interests: The Foundations of Cooperation in Economic Life*, Economic Learning and Social Evolution Series, No. 6, Cambridge, MA: MIT Press.
Haakonssen, Knud (2006), *The Cambridge Companion to Adam Smith*, Cambridge: Cambridge University Press.
Letwin, William (1963), *The Origins of Scientific Economics*, London: Routledge.
Macfie, A.L. (1959), 'Adam Smith's moral sentiments as foundations for his wealth of nations', *Oxford Economic Papers*, **11** (3), 209–28.
Macfie, A.L. (1961), 'Adam Smith's theory of moral sentiments', *Scottish Journal of Political Economy*, **8**, 12–27.
Macfie, A.L. (1967), *The Individual in Society: Papers on Adam Smith*, London: Allen and Unwin.
McCloskey, Deirdre (2008), 'Adam Smith, the last of former virtue ethicists', *History of Political Economy*, **40** (1), 43–71.
Montes, Leonidas and Eric Schliesser (eds) (2006), *New Voices on Adam Smith*, London and New York: Routledge.

Morrow, Glenn R. (1923), 'The significance of the doctrine of sympathy in Hume and Adam Smith', *The Philosophical Review*, **32** (1), 60–78.

Morrow, Glenn R. ([1923] 1973), *The Ethical and Economic Theories of Adam Smith: A Study in the Social Philosophy of the 18th Century*, New York: Augustus M. Kelley.

Muller, Jerry Z. (1993), *Adam Smith in His Time and Ours: Designing the Decent Society*, New York: Free Press.

North, Douglass C. (1990), *Institutions, Institutional Change and Economic Performance*, Cambridge: Cambridge University Press.

North, Douglass C. (1994), 'Shared mental models: ideologies and institutions', *Kyklos*, **47**, 3–31.

Oncken, August (1897), 'The consistency of Adam Smith', *Economic Journal*, **7** (27), 443–50.

Peil, Jan (1999), *Adam Smith and Economic Science: A Methodological Reinterpretation*, Cheltenham, UK and Northampton, MA, USA: Edward Elgar.

Peil, Jan (2000), 'Deconstructing the canonical view on Adam Smith: a new look at the principles of economics', in M. Psalidopoulos (ed.), *The Canon in the History of Economics: Critical Essays*, Studies in the History of Economics, Vol. 28, London: Routledge, pp. 68–91.

Raphael, D.D. (2007), *The Impartial Spectator: Adam Smith's Moral Philosophy*, Oxford: Clarendon. Press.

Raphael, D.D. and A.L. Macfie ([1976] 1991), 'Introduction', in D.D. Raphael and A.L. Macfie (eds), *Adam Smith. The Theory of Moral Sentiments*, Oxford: Clarendon Press, pp. 1–52.

Recktenwald, Horst C. (1978), 'An Adam Smith renaissance *anno* 1976? The bicentenary output: a reappraisal of his scholarship', *Journal of Economic Literature*, **16** (1), 56–83.

Rustichini, Aldo (2005), 'Neuroeconomics: present and future', *Games and Economic Behavior*, **52**, 201–12.

Samuels, Warren J. and Steven G. Medema (2005), 'Freeing Smith from the "free market": on the misperception of Adam Smith on the economic role of government', *History of Political Economy*, **37** (2), 219–26.

Schumpeter, Joseph A. ([1954] 1972), *History of Economic Analysis*, London: George Allen & Unwin Ltd

Smith, Adam ([1976] 1991), *The Theory of Moral Sentiments*, ed. D.D. Raphael and A.L. Macfie, *The Glasgow Edition of the Works and Correspondence of Adam Smith*, Vol. 1, Oxford: Clarendon Press.

Smith, Adam ([1976] 1979), *An Enquiry into the Nature and Causes of the Wealth of Nations*, ed. R.H. Campbell, A.S. Skinner and W.B. Todd, *The Glasgow Edition of the Works and Correspondence of Adam Smith*, Vol. 2, Oxford: Clarendon Press.

Smith, Adam (1980), *Essays on Philosophical Subjects*, ed. W.P.D. Wightman and J.C. Bryce; with Dugald Stewart's account of Adam Smith, ed. I.S. Ross, *The Glasgow Edition of the Works and Correspondence of Adam Smith*, Vol. 3, Oxford and New York: Clarendon Press/Oxford University Press.

Smith, Adam (1983), *Lectures on Rhetoric and Belles Lettres*, ed. J.C. Bryce; general editor, A.S. Skinner, *The Glasgow Edition of the Works and Correspondence of Adam Smith*, Vol. 4, Oxford and New York: Clarendon Press/Oxford University Press.

Smith, Adam ([1977] 1987), *Correspondence of Adam Smith*, ed. Ernst C. Mossner and Ian S. Ross, *The Glasgow Edition of the Works and Correspondence of Adam Smith*, Vol. 6, Oxford and New York: Clarendon Press/Oxford University Press.

Smith, Adam ([1978] 1987), *Lectures on Jurisprudence*, ed. Ronald L. Meek, David D. Raphael and Peter G. Stein, *The Glasgow Edition of the Works and Correspondence of Adam Smith*, Vol. 5, Oxford and New York: Clarendon Press/Oxford University Press.

Tribe, Keith (1999), 'Adam Smith: critical theorist?', *Journal of Economic Literature*, **27** (2), 609–32.

Viner, Jacob (1927), 'Adam Smith and laissez-faire', *Journal of Political Economy*, **35**, 198–232.

Werhane, Patricia H. (1991), *Adam Smith and His Legacy for Modern Capitalism*, New York: Oxford University Press.

West, Edwin G. (1978), 'Scotland's resurgent economist: a survey of the new literature on Adam Smith', *Southern Economic Journal*, **45**, 343–69.

Wight, Jonathan B. (2002), 'The rise of Adam Smith: articles and citations, 1970–1997', *History of Political Economy*, **34** (1), 55–82.

Wight Jonathan B. (2004), 'Adam Smith's ethics and the "noble arts"', *Review of Social Economy*, **LXIV** (2), 155–80.

Winch, Donald (1978), *Adam Smith's Politics: An Essay in Historiographic Revision*, Cambridge: Cambridge University Press.

See also the entries on: Self-interest; Utilitarianism; Virtue ethics.

66 Social capital
John Field

The debate over social capital is rich with ethical dimensions. Although precise definitions vary considerably, the concept of social capital draws attention to both the ways in which social norms and values can reinforce people's network assets and the ways in which obligation and trust underpin reciprocity. Empirically, social capital can be shown to have a demonstrable influence on people's health, education, employment, security from crime and the life chances of their children. Moreover, unlike many concepts in the social sciences, the notion of social capital lends itself to practical application. The social capital debate is unusual in that it engages academics in discussions with policymakers, professionals and organizational leaders.

Ethical issues appear to be at the centre of contemporary interest in social capital. Yet at the same time, the ethical dimensions of this interest are often deeply buried. Of course, this is true for many concepts in the social sciences; indeed, it could be argued that the social capital concept is attractive to some because it carries none of the heavy sentimental baggage of older and more conventional terms, such as 'community'. For others, the concept's appeal lies in the way it allows for community and relationships to re-enter economic debates. By placing a value on people's network assets, the concept provides a new language for debating the collective. These ethical dimensions surface occasionally in current debate, but in a somewhat marginal manner which possibly reflects the wider neglect of values and ethics in the dominant forms of contemporary social science.

Rapid evolution
The social capital concept has evolved with remarkable speed. Barely known in the 1980s, by 2000 it was one of the most widely cited terms in the social sciences. Theoretically eclectic, the concept draws on several distinctive traditions, including both neo-Marxism and rational choice theory. To complicate matters further, it has proven extremely controversial, dividing the ranks of social scientists and provoking as much scepticism as enthusiasm from policymakers and professionals.

Although the concept has an earlier history, most contemporary approaches derive from the work of Pierre Bourdieu, James Coleman and Robert Putnam. Bourdieu, influenced by neo-Marxist thinking, developed the concept as part of a wider analysis of how social order is maintained despite highly visible inequalities and injustices. He wrote about the creation by professionals and the service middle class of a 'capital of social relationships' in order to attract clients and advance their careers (Bourdieu 1977, p. 503). He later published a more elaborate theoretical sketch (Bourdieu 1980, 1986) setting out a framework in which people deploy their social capital in tandem with other symbolic assets, such as cultural capital (an appreciation of cultural heritage) or educational capital. All, he believed, rested ultimately on the possession of economic capital.

Coleman sought to create a comprehensive and interdisciplinary theory of social behaviour drawing equally on economics and sociology (Coleman 1994). His work was rooted in rational choice theories of behaviour, which share with classical economics a belief that people's actions are based on the pursuit of their own interests. This rational action theory, however, has often been criticized by sociologists for methodological individualism. The theory assumes that since individual actors automatically do what best serves themselves, social interaction can be reduced to a form of exchange; presenting the obvious questions of why individuals should ever cooperate with one another and why they behave in ways which appear altruistic even in the long term (Misztal 2000). For Coleman, the theory of social capital offered an answer to these problems: cooperation was explained as a form of learned behaviour which appears altruistic, but which represents in fact a capacity for pursuing long-term interests through a series of reciprocal exchanges based on learned trust; it was strongest when underpinned by 'primordial' ties, such as those of kinship.

While Bourdieu and Coleman have certainly shaped scholarly discussion over social capital, Robert Putnam's work on the topic has had a far wider appeal. Putnam, a political scientist who initially explored the concept in the course of a study of government in Italy, made a remarkable public and political impact when he turned his attention to his native United States (Putnam 2000). That impact derived from his diagnosis of the 'collapse of community' in contemporary America, as well as the systematic way in which he gathered evidence to support this thesis. It reflects wider concerns for the future of civic engagement and social cohesion in the United States. Those concerns have reverberated throughout public life since the early nineteenth century, when the French author Alexis de Tocqueville identified civic association as the basis of social solidarity in what was then the world's most democratic and unregulated nation (Field 2003, p. 30).

Putnam's theory of social capital is situated firmly within this intellectual and political context. For him, 'the core idea of social capital theory is that social networks have value . . . social contacts affect the productivity of individuals and groups', as a direct result of the resources created by the existence of 'social networks and the norms of reciprocity and trust that arise from them' (Putnam 2000, pp. 18–19). Whereas Coleman emphasizes the importance of primordial ties, Putnam is much more concerned with the range and diversity of people's networks, arguing that shared membership of secondary associations gives people access to groups and individuals who bring new ideas and new resources that might be unavailable within a relatively bounded group such as a kinship circle. As Barbara Misztal said, while this places Putnam in the tradition of Durkheimian notions of social solidarity arising from the complexities of social ties, he also tends to adopt a view of actors' rationality that draws on rational choice theory (Misztal 2000, p. 119). In addition, he espouses a Tocquevillian enthusiasm for volunteering and sociability as counterweights to a strong state and corporate power, identifying apathy as the enemy of democracy.

The debate has advanced rapidly, addressing not only the topics that interested these early writers, but increasingly encompassing a wide range of academic preoccupations and policy concerns. The role of two international governmental bodies in promoting the concept is worth noting here. Part of the World Bank has taken it up as a factor to be taken into account in anti-poverty strategies (World Bank 2001), and some of the bank's staff have been associated with scholarly writing on social capital and economic development (Dasgupta and Serageldin 2000; Woolcock 1998). Influential publications have also emerged from the Organization for Economic Co-operation and Development (OECD), notably its 2001 report *The Well-Being of Nations* (OECD 2001).

There has also been considerable development in the academic discussion of social capital. As argued some years ago, it is unhelpful to lump different types of social networks and norms together without further differentiation (Schuller et al. 2000; Woolcock 1998). Woolcock (1998) and Putnam (2000) distinguished three types of network tie: bonding ties, which are made up of links between like-minded people with similar backgrounds; bridging ties, which link people from heterogeneous groups; and linking ties, which bring together people of quite different status positions and with command over resources that are not controlled by people within either one's immediate or more proximate circles. More recently, a number of researchers have emphasized the importance of informal social ties, as well as the more formal types of association recorded in the evidence on which Putnam and other scholars have tended to draw (Li et al. 2003).

Though the concept of social capital has, then, developed rapidly in recent years, its status remains ambiguous, as Schuller (2007) notes, for a number of reasons. As well as significant difficulties in reaching an agreed definition, the concept has proven controversial, particularly for neo-Marxists, who believe that it represents economists' efforts to colonize the social sciences (Fine 2000), and for some conventional economists who believe it to be a fuzzy metaphor legitimating sociological intervention in economics proper (Arrow 2000). It has also attracted criticism from some in the social sciences, such as the feminist Maxine Molyneux, who believes that the language of social capital lends itself to a neglect of issues of power and authority (Molyneux 2002).

Certainly it is possible to criticize the concept, or more properly, the ways in which some have used it. Yet it has clearly met a need in the social sciences for terminology which allows for transdisciplinary discussions of people's social relationships and which draws attention to the different consequences of different social arrangements. In particular, by accentuating the importance of norms and values, of reciprocity and trust, it emphasizes issues that conventional economists in particular have preferred to ignore.

Why social capital matters to economists

Much of the literature is concerned with both the generation of social capital and the impact of social capital on individuals, institutions and wider society. Essentially, as we saw above, the basic insight associated with the concept is that capacities for mutual cooperation and reciprocity are learned, and underpinned, through participation in social networks, which then leads people to develop broader identities and reciprocity, which benefits not only themselves but can spill over into wider consequences for institutions and society more generally. Empirical researchers have recently adopted a more differentiated approach to social capital analyses, leading to the insight that different types of relationships appear to have different consequences (Li et al. 2003).

One example, from a plethora of empirical literature, illustrates these rather general remarks. In a quantitative study of longitudinal panel data on black and ethnic minority groups in Britain, Yaojun Li showed that different types of social capital are distributed unevenly between the different sub-groups (the remainder of this paragraph and the next draws on Li 2005). Distinguishing between three types or dimensions of social capital, Li found that black people in Britain show relatively low levels of attachment to their immediate neighbourhood, are active in civic associations at a similar level to Britons as a whole and have stronger than average informal networks. Conversely, Indian, Pakistani/

Bangladeshi and Chinese people in Britain have relatively weak links on all three dimensions of social capital.

Interestingly, Li found that social networks played an even more important role for people from socially disadvantaged black and ethnic minority groups, particularly black and Pakistani/Bangladeshi people, even when other factors were allowed for. Li concluded that while close neighbourhood ties might limit job opportunities, by contrast 'a wide range of social ties unrestricted to neighbours/acquaintances in the immediate neighbourhood is of considerable importance for gathering information or for seeking references. People with strong social networks are also likely to have better social skills' (Li 2005, pp. 17–18).

Li's findings are broadly consistent with other studies which have shown that wide, heterogeneous networks serve as a powerful information resource, which in turn enables people to advance their interests (Field 2005). It also confirms that labour markets are by no means perfect markets, but rather are asymmetrical and shaped by social and cultural factors which cannot really be written off as mere 'externalities', since they appear to be intrinsic to the functioning of the labour market. In this respect Li's work fits neatly into well-established theories of the labour market as a socially embedded set of practices, and is broadly consistent with theories of 'the strength of weak ties' in facilitating the transmission of hot information across different social circles (for example, Granovetter 1973).

However, as far as economics is concerned, the main focus of recent research on social capital has been its role in economic growth, competitiveness and development. As noted elsewhere, this work shows at least some parallels with so-called 'new growth theory', in which endogenous factors such as human capital are viewed as crucial to processes of innovation and growth (van Staveren 2002). While human capital is clearly recognized as playing a central role in innovation, however, this is possible only because of social and cultural processes which facilitate – or block – processes of learning and knowledge creation and exchange (Kim and Nelson 2000). Further, competence and knowledge are themselves frequently embedded in social practices and institutions, such as workplaces and families. This is particularly true for what is often called 'tacit knowledge', which cannot be readily codified and transmitted through formal means, but conversely is very effectively transmitted through informal everyday connections (Maskell 2000; Field 2005). Innovation and knowledge transfer are not simple and unilinear processes, but are rather complex and multifaceted, depending on interaction between a range of individuals and institutions, as well as on mutual understanding of what information is being exchanged, how it can be applied and what is expected in return.

For conventional economists, the diffusion of knowledge can represent a problem. While it is relatively easy to transfer standardized and codified knowledge from one setting to another, this form of knowledge is easily protected in legislation. All potential users compete on equal terms: provided they are willing to pay the owner of the intellectual property, or take the risk of legal action, they can adopt the same methods and innovate in the same ways. While this can lead to productivity gains, it does little to secure sustainable advantage, so the short-term advantage goes to those whose costs are lowest. But much knowledge – as well as the competences and skills required to apply it – does not lend itself to codification, usually because it is embedded in the routines and habits of particular institutions and social networks. It is, in short, dependent on what we might describe as 'tacit human capital' (Vuorensyrjä 2001), which in turn appears to be most productive in certain social settings.

At the very least, social networks reinforced by shared values have a positive effect in reducing the transaction costs of exchanges. Stated simply, shared norms of reciprocity and relationships of trust are considerably cheaper and less stressful than the services of corporate lawyers. But social capital also appears to promote the exchange of innovation and new knowledge, particularly tacit knowledge that lends itself to context-specific forms of application. It also appears to further the exchange of hot information, such as news about a job vacancy (as well as inside information on which job applicant is reliable and honest) or a business process.

Social capital, then, is of considerable potential interest to economists, offering new insights into how actual markets (as opposed to 'the market') operate as socially structured practices involving social actors. Less clear is whether economists can treat social capital as simply another form of capital, along with finance and physical assets such as plants and machinery. Arrow, among others, suggests that the metaphor of capital has probably been stretched too far, since it is hard to measure investment or returns on social capital (Arrow 2000). But other researchers, including Nan Lin, claim that social capital can be defined as 'investment in social relations with expected returns in the marketplace' (Lin 2001). This idea has received some empirical support. For example, a study of longitudinal survey data on educational continuation identified a number of ways in which people use money to invest in social capital (for example, by purchasing residential stability), just as money can be used to invest in human capital (Sandefur et al. 1999). So the debate on social capital's status as a form of economic capital has yet to conclude. However, the main importance of the concept for economists appears to lie in its explanatory and heuristic power: it allows us to ask important questions about people's economic behaviour, which can be understood not as a set of isolated self-interested choices, but as a set of social practices, in which values and relationships play a vital part.

Values and social networks
Social capital appears, on balance, to be a clear 'public good'. It can also be an important positional good for individuals. Yet access to social capital is not equitably distributed across the entire population, and neither does it create equal benefits. In some cases people use their social capital in ways that create negative consequences. The public good argument is therefore somewhat ambiguous, and the policy implications are by no means clear-cut.

A number of studies have shown the distribution of social capital to be highly skewed by social class (Heinze and Strünck 2000; Field 2003). Civic activism is known to be a largely middle-class phenomenon, and as trade unions and workers' clubs continue to decline this appears to be increasingly the case. But it is not simply a matter of unequal distribution of the overall volume of social capital; there are also skewed patterns in the distribution of particular *types* of social capital. In a detailed multidimensional analysis of social capital based on the British Household Panel Survey, one team of British researchers found patterns of stratification in the types of social capital that people possess. In particular:

> The greatest class differences are shown between the service and the working classes, with the
> service class's main channel of social capital generation being through civic engagement and

social networking, and the working class's social capital drawing mainly on neighbourhood networks . . . [T]he working class may be deprived of formal access to social capital but they may on the other hand have a relatively high degree of social capital in informal social capital, in their neighbourhood attachment. (Li et al. 2003, p. 11)

This is consistent with other evidence of systematic differences in the composition of people's network assets, which have been shown to vary significantly by socio-economic status (for example, Glaeser et al. 2000). We might add that there is a marked gender effect, with women appearing to possess stronger stocks of social capital than men with respect to informal, family and neighbourhood ties (Li et al. 2003).

In short, working-class people – and members of minority ethnic groups – generally appear to possess those forms of social capital that are least effective in accessing resources that are unavailable in the immediate vicinity. Disadvantaged groups in contemporary societies tend, as Putnam puts it (2000), to develop forms of social capital that are good for purposes of coping and dealing with immediate pressures; they are not so useful for changing things or benefiting from externally-led transformations. It is not entirely clear why middle-class people and the highly educated are more likely to engage in civic participation, though it is clear that they possess social competences that enable them to create and manage voluntary organizations effectively. If Bourdieu is correct, the middle class also uses civic associations to find new clients, close off similar opportunities to others and protect their place in the social hierarchy. Middle-class civic activism also provides a way to pursue one's interests through lobbying, campaigning and information exchange. People's connections may well constitute a resource, then, but this resource is unequally distributed and can be used to secure positional advantage over others.

This alone justifies questioning the assumption that social capital is a simple public good. However, social capital also possesses what Putnam refers to as a 'dark side' (Putnam 2000). People may use their social connections in some circumstances to promote forms of cooperation that damage the wider public interest. The most obvious examples are organized crime and many forms of terrorism. Feminists might add that patriarchal structures often also depend on highly gendered 'old-boys networks' of various kinds. Indeed, power and inequality can be seen as inherent features of all network structures.

Is it possible to develop strategies for social justice that attend to the power of networks? This question should be turned upside-down, so as to ask what happens if we do not take network assets into account. Rosenfeld, for example, argues that rather than lamenting the equity risks associated with economic development strategies based on clusters and partnerships, it is possible to engage disadvantaged groups and communities in cluster-based strategies for regeneration and innovation (Rosenfeld 2002). It is certainly the case that social capital generation, and particularly access to heterogeneous informal networks, can play an important role in helping the most disadvantaged ethnic and social groups climb out of exclusion. It is equally certain that policies and actions that neglect network assets will do little if anything to promote equity and social justice. In either case, though, equity and power must be taken into account.

References

Arrow, Kenneth (2000), 'Observations on social capital', in Partha Dasgupta and Ismael Serageldin (eds), *Social Capital: A Multi-faceted Perspective*, Washington DC: World Bank, pp. 3–6.

Bourdieu, Pierre (1977), 'Cultural reproduction and social reproduction', in Jerome Karabel and A.H. Halsey (eds), *Power and Ideology in Education*, New York: Oxford University Press, pp. 487–511.

Bourdieu, Pierre (1980), 'Le capital sociale: notes provisoires', *Actes de la recherché en sciences sociales*, **31** (January), 2–3.

Bourdieu, Pierre (1986), 'The forms of capital', in John G. Richardson (ed.), *Handbook of Theory and Research for the Sociology of Education*, Westport, CT: Greenwood Press, pp. 241–58.

Coleman, James S. (1994), *Foundations of Social Theory*, Cambridge, MA: Belknap.

Dasgupta, Partha and Ismael Serageldin (eds) (2000), *Social Capital: A Multi-faceted Perspective*, Washington DC: World Bank.

Field, John (2003), *Social Capital*, London: Routledge.

Field, John (2005), *Social Capital and Lifelong Learning*, Bristol: Policy Press.

Fine, Ben (2000), *Social Capital versus Social Theory*, London: Routledge.

Glaeser, Edward L., David I. Laibson, Jose Scheinkman and Christine L. Soutter (2000), 'Measuring trust', *Quarterly Journal of Economics*, **115**, 811–46.

Granovetter, Mark (1973), 'The strength of weak ties', *American Journal of Sociology*, **78** (4), 1350–80.

Heinze, Rolf G. and Christoph Strünck (2000), 'Die Verzinsung des sozialen Kapitals. Freiwilliges Engagement im Strukturwandel', in Ulrich Beck (ed.), *Die Zukunft von Arbeit und Demotratie*, Frankfurt-am-Main: Suhrkamp Verlag, pp. 171–216 .

Kim, Linsu and Richard R. Nelson (eds) (2000), *Technology, Learning and Innovation: Experiences of Newly Industrializing Economies*, Cambridge: Cambridge University Press.

Li, Yaojun (2005), 'Social capital and labour market attainment of black and minority ethnic groups in Britain', *Proceedings of International Conference on Engaging Community*, http://engagingcommunities2005.org/abstracts/Li-Yaojun-final.pdf, accessed 20 October, 2008.

Li, Yaojun, Andrew Pickles and Mike Savage (2003), 'Conceptualising and Measuring Social Capital: A New Approach', Manchester: Centre for Census and Survey Research, Manchester University, www.iser.essex.ac.uk/bhps/2003/docs/pdf/papers/li.pdf, accessed 20 October, 2008.

Lin, Nan (2001), *Social Capital*, Cambridge: Cambridge University Press.

Maskell, Peter (2000), 'Social capital, innovation and competitiveness', in Stephen Baron, John Field and Tom Schuller (eds), *Social Capital: Critical Perspectives*, Oxford: Oxford University Press, pp. 111–23.

Misztal, Barbara A. (2000), *Informality: Social Theory and Contemporary Practice*, London: Routledge.

Molyneux, Maxine (2002), 'Gender and the silences of social capital: lessons from Latin America', *Development and Change*, **33** (2), 167–88.

OECD (2001), *The Well-being of Nations: The Role of Human and Social Capital*, Paris: Organization for Economic Co-operation and Development.

Putnam, Robert D. (2000), *Bowling Alone: The Collapse and Revival of American Community*, New York: Simon and Schuster.

Rosenfeld, Stuart A. (2002), *Just Clusters: Economic Development Strategies that Reach More People and Places*, Carrboro, NC: Regional Technologies Strategies.

Sandefur, Gary, Ann Meier and Pedro Hernandez (1999), 'Families, social capital and educational continuation', Centre for Demography and Ecology Working Paper 99–19, University of Wisconsin at Madison, Madison, WI.

Schuller, Tom (2007), 'Reflections on the use of social capital', *Review of Social Economy*, **65** (1), 11–28.

Schuller, Tom, Stephen Baron and John Field (2000), 'Social capital: a review and critique', in: Stephen Baron, John Field and Tom Schuller (eds), *Social Capital: Critical Perspectives*, Oxford: Oxford University Press, pp. 1–38.

Staveren, Irene van (2002), 'Social capital: what is in it for feminist economics?' ISS Working Paper No. 368, Institute of Social Studies, The Hague.

Vuorensyrjä, Matti (2001), 'Tacit human capital', in Eero Pantzar, Reijo Savolainen and Paivi Tynjälä (eds), *In Search for a Human-Centred Information Society*, Tampere: Tampere University Press, pp. 57–79.

Woolcock, Michael (1998), 'Social capital and economic development: towards a theoretical synthesis and policy framework', *Theory and Society*, **27** (2), 151–208.

World Bank (2001), *World Development Report 2000/2001 – Attacking Poverty*, Washington DC and New York: World Bank/Oxford University Press.

See also the entries on: Equity; Social economics.

67 Social economics
Mark A. Lutz

Introduction

'Social economics', more than any other concept in the history of economics, has been subject to various meanings and interpretations for decades, even centuries. In addition, the North American meaning has tended to differ somewhat from the European 'sozialoekonomie' or 'economie sociale'. Given the contemporary focus on the North American notion of the term – as articulated in and promoted by the Association of Social Economics and its principal journal, the *Review of Social Economy* – it is perhaps useful to briefly describe it as 'a discipline studying the reciprocal relationship between economic science on the one hand and social philosophy, ethics and human dignity on the other'. Social economics sees itself as value-directed and social justice-driven, ameliorative, reconstructive, holistic and pluralistic.

Before proceeding to review its history, it is appropriate to mention several alternative and often conflicting meanings of 'social economics'. They were proposed by well-known mainstream economists who recognized social economics as a special field of inquiry. Among them, some understood the field as an essentially normative branch of economics, while others saw it in terms of positivism, as a richer description of how the economy works.

Among the former is Leon Walras, whose celebrated *Elements d'Economie Politiques Pure* (1874) distinguished 'pure' and 'applied' economics from 'social' economics where the latter as '*science morale*' deals in the name of social justice with the distribution of wealth, property and taxation. In that category, among other themes, we also find Walras's famous proposal for the nationalization of all land. Frank Fetter (1915), too, saw a distinction between a profit-oriented 'business economy' and a more normative and general welfare-oriented 'social economy'. In the same vein, for Knut Wicksell (1934), the subject of social economics, unlike practical and theoretical economics, was to ascertain which changes in the economic and legal structure of society were necessary to obtain maximum social gain. Similarly, the French economic historian Charles Gide and Charles Rist (1948) singled out social economics as investigating that 'which should be' and 'what needs to be done' to achieve it.

Set against such *normative* perceptions of the discipline, there is also a *positive* view containing several illustrious names. Among them is Austrian economist Friedrich Wieser, whose German text *Theorie der Gesellschaftlichen Wirtschaft* (1914) was translated into English and given the title *Social Economics*. Wieser's social economy was meant in contrast to 'simple economy' because it added to utility and law the further social force of (government) power as the organizing principle of a real-world economy. Similarly, the Swede Gustav Cassel's *Theory of Social Economy* ([1918] 1932) was meant to be of purely positive character to serve as the basis for normative assessments and economic policy.

More recently, the *New Palgrave Dictionary* published among its many volumes one entitled *Social Economics* (Eatwell et al. 1989). After a regretful admission that the designation 'social economics' is neither much in use these days nor does it carry a commonly agreed meaning, the editors decided that the label 'seems appropriate as a title for a collection of articles pertaining to the use of economics in the study of society' (pp. xi–xii). In other words, it treats the discipline, in Gary Becker-type fashion, as nothing more than an application of the tools of rational choice to the non-market domain of social life. A few years later, the *MIT Dictionary of Modern Economics* (Pearce 1992) told us that the concept stands for 'the application of neoclassical theory to social policy' – particularly health, education, crime, housing and welfare services (p. 398). Finally, in contemporary Continental Europe, the translation of the English 'social economy' generally stands as a label for the non-profit sector: cooperatives, credit unions and mutual societies.

The North American social economics movement
In North America, since World War II, the 'social economics' concept has gained a more fixed and distinct (albeit broad) meaning, thanks to the organization in December 1941 of a separate economic association, the Catholic Economic Association, which in the late 1960s was renamed the Association of Social Economics.

Historical context
The real boost to the idea of an independent and academically respectable social economics undoubtedly came with John Maurice Clark's celebrated *Preface to Social Economics* (1936). In it, he claimed that the goal of a meaningful economics is human fulfilment, or 'the well-rounded development and use of human faculties' ([1936] 1967, p. 25). The fact that the book was published on the heels of Clark's presidency of the American Economic Association may have further enhanced the prestige of this new field. Realistically, the impact of Clark's book must also be seen in the context of events taking place at that time. For one, the prolonged worldwide depression must have undermined much of the confidence with which economists followed the road of orthodox theory, thereby clearing the way for a more open-minded assessment of all kinds of alternative approaches.

Then another event took place in the 1930s: Pope Pius XI proclaimed his social encyclical *Quadragesimo Anno* (1931) in which, among other issues, he decried the negative effect of both a purely market-dominated society and a state-directed economy on the quality of life. Both systems create de-personalizing tendencies that produce social alienation and feelings of 'hopelessness'. In that context, the principles of 'solidarism' and 'subsidarity' were first officially offered as a structural remedy for the problem. It appears that the papal encyclical may have nudged a fair number of Catholic social scientists and economists to explore how their own work related to the official social doctrine of the Church. Significantly, *Quadragesimo Anno* triggered a statement by the American bishops, *Church and the Social Order* (1940), and initial discussions of a Catholic Economic Association.

The Association of Social Economics
From the start the new Catholic Economic Association produced its own journal, *Review of Social Economy*, which began by publishing papers presented at their annual proceedings within the overarching framework of the American Economic Association. The Catholic Economic Association's first two decades were characterized by a general stance

that accepted conventional economics with an added emphasis on policy based on a Judeo-Christian ethical foundation. But eventually, most members came to embrace a more distinct view: social economics was to be 'primarily concerned with the rehabilitation of social institutions to improve human efficiency and social order . . . [They saw the pursuit of social justice as an] obligation to reconstruct economic institutions so that they will reflect human dignity and produce effectively for the common good' (Waters 1990, p. 95). Both liberalism and communism, together with the economics they spawned, were rejected in favour of a humanistic and egalitarian capitalism. Mainstream economics, rather than simply being accepted as valid, was subjected to critical analysis of its underlying philosophical, epistemological and methodological premises. These developments were significantly encouraged by the new editor of the *Review*, who pushed for two approaches: a socio-philosophical inquiry into the basic principles of the orthodox economics paradigm, and a social architecture aiming to construct a more just economic system.

In 1970, the Association for Social Economics (ASE) elected to go beyond its identification with Catholic social thought and reach out to interested economists with quite different intellectual backgrounds. Membership grew rapidly, first with an influx of institutionalist economists, then with some neo-Marxists and, a few years later, with humanistic and ecologically-oriented economists. This new pluralism was an extraordinary hallmark of the reformed association, distinguishing it from any other professional economic organization.

By the end of the 1980s, five distinct social economic strands, each with its own history, constituted the basic fabric of the group. The first, and most important among them, was the (Catholic) solidarist branch with roots in nineteenth-century France. It consisted of the work of economists such as Villeneuve-Bargemont (1784–1850) and LePlay (1806–82). Also worth mentioning is the Italian Toniolo (1845–1918), who wrote the two-volume *Treatise on Social Economics* (1907/9) and is said to have been a likely contributor to Pope Leo XIII's encyclical *Rerum Novarum* (1891). Finally, there was the true father figure of modern solidarist social economics, the German Pesch (1854–1926), who published the five-volume *Lehrbuch der Nationaloekonomie* (1905–26). Pesch is said to be the 'first economist to construct an economic theory on the foundation of Aristotelian-Thomist philosophy'. He also seems to have had an important role in the crafting of *Quadragesimo Anno* (Mulcahy 1952).

The second strand was made up of those of the American institutionalist school, who were also the first non-Catholic economists to join the ASE. These were followers of Commons and the German-educated Patten and Ely. Not surprisingly so, since this school shares with Pesch's solidarism some common roots in nineteenth-century German historicism. In addition, Clark's influence was strongly felt and represented early on. Beside this sizeable group of 'classic' institutionalists, there was also a growing influx of the 'Texas School' of institutionalists. Tracing themselves back to Veblen, and more recently to Ayres, their brand of evolutionary economics leaned heavily on an ethics propagated by pragmatist US philosopher Dewey, of instrumental value theory. Over time, it was this group rather than the earlier 'classics' who became the flag-bearers of the institutionalist strand.

Economists more at home with a Marxist-socialist view of social economy became the third strand of the reformed organization. Their Marxism was, however, of a 'softer' kind, more philosophical and normative than deterministic and class-warfare oriented.

In the late 1970s, the ASE welcomed a fourth strand, loosely woven by economists with humanistic bearings. Their roots were said to reach down to the first few decades of the nineteenth century, anchored in the 'new' political economy of Sismondi. Other major standard-bearers were Hobson, Tawney and Schumacher. It should be added that the 'humanism' underlying their normative economics was, generally speaking, not of the secular kind, but more like Mauritain's integral humanism, stressing a transcendental personhood as the source of human dignity.

Last, but not least, a few outstanding scholars interested in the relationship between economics and ecology made strong contributions to the development of modern social economics. One of the earliest voices in this novel area is said to have been Nobel prize-winning chemist turned economist Soddy, who in 1926 pleaded for an 'economics founded upon life' (Daly 1996). But the towering figures were the Romanian mathematician turned American economist Georgescu-Roegen with his 'bioeconomics', and subsequently, his student Daly. The kind of ecological concern expressed by all three is inspired by considerations of human welfare (future generations) rather than a preoccupation with deep ecology. In that sense, their work carries much of the humanistic flavour intrinsic to the other four strands.

In conclusion, we may follow one social economist who some thirty years ago summarized the essence of all social economics orientations succinctly: it recognizes innate traits of human nature that include universal needs and a degree of malleability to attain them; it is normative in that it can judge a comparative superiority of one society over another in achieving universal need satisfaction; and it is critical in addressing society's historical genesis, relative adequacy, probable course of future development and possibilities for change (Hunt 1978).

This is where matters stood until the 1990s. As such, the ASE was relatively immune to postmodern pressures questioning the idea of a human essence or nature and, with it, a normative superstructure with universal reach. To the extent that feminism was represented, it was of the liberal kind. In other words, there was a certain unity in diversity, a moderate pluralism being epistemological and methodological, rather than ontological.

Besides the *Review of Social Economy,* the ASE has published since 1970 a second journal with similar content, *The Forum for Social Economics.* Over the years it has been upgraded to become a refereed journal recognized by the *Journal of Economic Literature.*

Contemporary developments
During the past decade, with nominalism, subjectivism and postmodern philosophy making inroads in the social sciences in general, and in alternative economic thought in particular, a trend is discernible towards a stronger version of pluralism. Diversity in social theory has been increasingly seen as reflecting an intrinsically diverse social reality 'out there'. Many in the ASE, therefore, would now prefer an approach proposed decades ago: social economics as an 'open-ended matrix' approach to the study of schools and strands, implying that there simply are no 'true' and 'best' principles of a social economics – instead there may be a multitude (Samuels 1977, p. 287).

To the extent that such a stronger pluralism takes hold, it would in all likelihood affect the traditional type cohesion and identity of the field. Given this development, a broader description of social economics – as concerned with the role and nature of social values in economic theory and economic life – might be more appealing to many. Whatever that may be, the ASE has definitely succeeded in reaching out to a significantly enhanced constituency. For one, it has strongly reached out to economists overseas, particularly in Europe. In 2005, editorship of the *Review* passed from John B. Davis, who stepped down after almost twenty years of fine leadership, to a group of two Europeans and two Americans. Internationalization has also swept the *Forum of Social Economics*, at which the majority of its ten associate editors are now from abroad.

The organization has been making efforts to increase membership of women as well. Its first woman president took the helm in 1997, and since that time there have been two more. At the *Review*, two of the four editors are women, and on its board, the number of women economists has increased from two to seven since 1995. As a result of this fruitful feminization and internationalization, the *Review*'s base for manuscript submissions has been significantly broadened. Furthermore, there has also been closer collaboration with similar groups in Europe, especially the International Centre for Social Economics, which focuses primarily on income and wealth distribution issues, theoretically, empirically and ethically. The results of some of this research are published in the associated *Journal of Income Distribution*.

Traditional themes and topics of research

The ASE was formed for the purpose of studying the relationship of philosophy, ethics and human dignity to economic thought. According to the ASE website, 'its members seek to explore the ethical foundations and implications of economic analysis, along with the individual and social dimensions of economic problems, and to help shape economic policy that is consistent with the integral values of the person and a humane economy'. A review of some of the primary research topics that have preoccupied the ASE membership, particularly since the late 1960s, provides a better idea about the group's orientation.

Much space in the *Review* and *Forum* has been devoted to a critical discussion of conventional economics. Some of the primary targets have been of a methodological nature, centring on the fact-value distinction and economics' pretension to being value-free. There has also been some questioning of methodological individualism. Similarly, we observe much critical ink chastising atomistic, self-centred and maximizing economic man, an individual cut off from society and culture. In this respect, there has been ongoing concern with the conventional over-reliance on self-interest and the almost exclusive emphasis on competition as a coordinating mechanism. What orthodox economics has overlooked (or certainly neglected) is the social and moral context of the person embedded in society, and with it, the possibilities of cooperation and collaboration. Finally, all schools and strands have been discontented with the state of conventional welfare economics and its preoccupation with allocative efficiency. In fact, one could describe much of social economics simply as an attempt to create an alternative: a *human* welfare-centred economics based on (objective) needs and the necessity of interpersonal comparisons of well-being. It should be noted that all of this fault-finding with mainstream economics is not just negative, but is intended as constructive criticism.

On the constructive side, economics is understood in the sense of provisioning, particularly as a tool for providing vital assistance to the poor and disenfranchised. Historically, there has been much emphasis on alleviating poverty, unemployment and inequality, as well as on eliminating discrimination of all kinds. More recently this has included concerns about gendered household relations and, more generally, the feminization of poverty.

One pivotal value has been the norm of human dignity, even though the strands are not in agreement as to what confers this dignity: society or the transcendental nature of humanity. It has been applied primarily to the workplace and industrial relations. Some have argued that an economic system respecting dignity must do away with the employment contract and operate with industrial cooperatives where workers are their own bosses. The extremely large and highly successful Spanish firm, Mondragon Cooperative Corporation, is often cited as an example of a cooperative enterprise that seems to have overcome the well-known problems that have plagued many worker cooperatives from the beginning.

Corporate globalization and trade are two other much-discussed topics. There has been scepticism about the advantages of a laissez-faire type free trade regime, although members are far from reaching consensus on these issues, especially on the question of how trade and trade policy affects the standard of living of the masses in low-income countries.

Finally, there are the issues of sustainability of economic growth and prospects for future generations in a world of climate change, exhaustion of energy and forest resources, overfishing, scarcity of fresh water, pollution of land, toxification of the sea and population growth.

Internal issues and tensions
As with any professional organization, so also in the ASE, not all members are always on the same page. Some of the underlying tensions have not enjoyed much attention, and certainly have not found resolution. There are obviously many, but here is a selection of three.

The first issue is whether social economics should reckon with only material needs, or also take into account the social and, possibly, even the person's 'higher' needs? In one case, the goal is material welfare for all. In the other, the goal is equal opportunity for a quality life and general human flourishing.

The second issue is the lingering question of how to integrate, or at least accommodate, scholarship of a postmodern kind. In other words, how to fit a view that tends to be anti-humanism, anti-philosophy, as well as anti-universalist ethics into a professional community whose very identity and unity has largely been derived from embracing those tenets.

The third is the need for some clarification of the relationship and potential boundaries with other alternative economic associations. Of particular importance here is the ASE's relative affinity with Socio-Economics, a group founded in the early 1990s by Etzioni and led by prominent social scientists and business economists. Their research is published in the *Journal of Socio-Economics*. In stressing the social, perhaps the main difference between the two organizations boils down to the one being more transdisciplinary and the other more interdisciplinary, leaning heavily on empirical sociology, psychology and ethical decision-making in business.

Conclusion
The dynamic character of social economics cannot be denied. As the economy constantly changes, economic theory will evolve and new social values will continue to emerge, as

will relationships between them. Therefore, it is difficult to offer an intelligent opinion as to where the discipline is heading, except, perhaps, one core aspect: its pluralistic nature. Its strength has been and will continue to be its open nature, providing a ready stage for intellectual dialogue, exchange of ideas and proposals that aim at a more meaningful economics and a more just economy.

References and further reading

ASE, www.socialeconomics.org, accessed 20 October, 2008.
Cassel, Gustav ([1918] 1932), *Theory of Social Economy* (translated by S.L. Barron), New York, NY: Harcourt, Brace and Co.
Clark, John M. ([1936] 1967), *Preface to Social Economics*, New York: Augustus M. Kelley.
Culbertson, John (1984), *International Trade and the Future of the West*, Madison, WI: 21st Century Press.
Daly, Herman (1996), *Beyond Growth*, Boston, MA: Beacon Press.
Davis, John B. and Edward J. O'Boyle (eds) (1994), *The Social Economics of Human Material Need*, Carbondale, IL: Southern Illinois University Press.
Eatwell, John, Murray Milgate and Peter Newman (eds) (1989), *The New Palgrave: Social Economics*, New York: Norton.
Ellerman, David (1990), 'The corporation as a democratic social institution', in Mark Lutz (ed.), *Social Economics: Retrospect and Prospect*, Boston, MA: Kluwer, Ch. 11.
Ellerman, David (1992), *Property and Contract*, London: Blackwell.
Fetter, Frank (1915), *Economic Principles*, New York, NY: The Century Co.
Gide, Charles and Charles Rist (1948), *A History of Economic Doctrine* (2nd English edition, translated by R. Richards and E.F. Row), Boston, MA: D.C. Heath.
Henderson, James P. and John B. Davis (1993), 'The challenges facing social economics in the twenty-first century', *Review of Social Economy*, special issue, **51** (4), 412–15.
Hill, Lewis E. (1990), 'The institutionalist approach to social economics', in Mark Lutz (ed.), *Social Economics: Retrospect and Prospect*, Boston, MA: Kluwer, Ch. 4.
Hunt, E. (1978), 'The normative foundations of social theory', *Review of Social Economy*, **36** (3), 285–309.
Hunt, E. (1990), 'Social economics: a socialist perspective', in Mark Lutz (ed.), *Social Economics: Retrospect and Prospect*, Boston, MA: Kluwer, Ch. 5.
Leo XIII (1891), *Rerum Novarum*.
Lutz, Mark (ed.) (1990a), *Social Economics: Retrospect and Prospect*, Boston, MA: Kluwer.
Lutz, Mark (1990b), 'Social economics in the humanistic tradition', in Mark Lutz (ed.), *Social Economics: Retrospect and Prospect*, Boston, MA: Kluwer, Ch. 7.
Lutz, Mark (1999), *Economics for the Common Good (Two Centuries of Social Economic Thought in the Humanistic Tradition)*, London: Routledge.
Mulcahy, Richard E., S.J. (1952), *The Economics of Heinrich Pesch*, New York: Henry Holt & Co.
O'Boyle, Edward J. (1990), 'Catholic social economics: a response to certain problems, errors and abuses of the modern age', in Mark Lutz (ed.), *Social Economics: Retrospect and Prospect*, Boston, MA: Kluwer, Ch. 3.
O'Boyle, Edward J. (ed.) (1996), *Social Economics: Premises, Findings and Policies*, London: Routledge.
Pearce, David W. (1992), *MIT Dictionary of Modern Economics* (4th edition), Cambridge, MA: Massachusetts Institute of Technology Press.
Samuels, Warren J. (1977), 'Reflections on social economics in a diverse and open economics', *Review of Social Economy*, **35** (3), 283–91.
Soddy, Frederick (1926), *Wealth, Virtual Wealth and Debt*, London: George Allen & Unwin.
Walras, Leon (1874), *Éléments d'Économie Politiques Pure*, Paris: Guillaumin et cie.
Waters, William R. (1990), 'Evolution of social economics in America', in Mark Lutz (ed.), *Social Economics: Retrospect and Prospect*, Boston, MA: Kluwer, Ch. 2.
Wicksell, Knut (1934), Lectures on Political Economy (translated by E. Classen, ed. Lionel Robbins), New York, NY: Macmillan.
Weiser, Friedrich von (1914), *Theorie der Gesellschaftlichen Wirtschaft*, (1st edition), Tübingen: J.C.B. Mohr.

See also the entry on: Catholic social thought.

68   Solidarity

Patrick J. Welch and Stuart D. Yoak

With the expanding global marketplace dramatically changing business relationships it is reasonable to question whether the traditional neoclassical economic model based on self-interest, which was largely adequate for explaining and justifying outcomes of business relationships in more homogeneous geopolitical and cultural settings, is losing its viability in this broader and more complex setting. Alongside concern about the viability of the traditional model, we might also ask whether there is an alternative to which we can turn. The answer is yes.

In addition to the traditional model there is an emerging solidarity-based model for evaluating business behaviours that build on respect for others. Solidarity has been characterized as the 'third principle' between classic economic liberalism and communitarianism. According to Cima and Schubeck, '[solidarity] tries to balance the first two by affirming how individuals, groups, and government ought to see themselves in relationship to each other . . . [It is] based on knowledge, trust, and friendship that moves the parties to do business together' (2001, p. 226).

Globalization and its implications for business relationships

One of the strongest forces stimulating change in business relationships in recent years has been the rapid globalization of economic activity. The magnitude of globalization's expansion can be understood by comparing the growth of countries' exports and imports with the growth of their gross domestic product (GDP). For example, in the United States in 2005, real (inflation adjusted) GDP was slightly more than 50 per cent greater than in 1990, while real exports and imports, respectively, more than doubled and tripled over that same period (Council of Economic Advisors 2006, pp. 282, 311). In China, nominal GDP grew by approximately 36 per cent from 2003 through 2005, while exports and imports grew by approximately 74 and 60 per cent, respectively, according to the Federation of International Trade Associations. Why this great rise in globalization? While a long list of reasons can be offered, the most significant appear to be sellers' quests for larger markets, cheaper materials and lower-cost labour and their improved ability to access and transport materials to and from buyers and suppliers.

Perhaps a more important question is what are the likely consequences of this expanding marketplace. Certainly, one is that businesses now operate in an environment that is more culturally diverse and complex in terms of acceptable practices and standards. Such an environment is less responsive to traditional and more localized remedies to problems and strategies for attaining objectives. In short, what may have worked at home cannot be expected to apply across the world. The complex diversity accompanying globalization has several dimensions that merit attention. One is different standards of income. While in 2002 a worker in the United States might have complained about earning a minimum wage of only $5.15 per hour for working an eight-hour day, workers in Bangladesh were reportedly earning about 14 cents an hour and working ten-hour days (Herubin 2002,

p. 2). A second dimension is different concepts of workers' entitlement to safe working conditions. Stories from Haiti, Thailand, Bangladesh and elsewhere recount employees working nonstop in locations lacking basic toilet and washing facilities, ventilation and safe drinking water (Herubin 2002, p. 2; Arthur 2001, p. 2; Janchitfah 2004, p. 3).[1] A third dimension is different standards for protecting the environment. Examples are preventing the depletion or misuse of environmental resources, which impacts global warming; controlling the extent and growth of dead zones in water because of toxic sewage, which has a direct impact on the potability of groundwater; and monitoring air quality to control particulate and nonparticulate emissions from manufacturing activities. A fourth dimension, which connects to the first three, is diversity in levels and styles of government intervention in business activities. The variety of legislative and regulatory oversight is illustrated by, for example, differences in antitrust enforcement between the United States and the European Union.

This (incomplete) list of the dimensions of diversity resulting from increased globalization of economic activity gives rise to a seminal question: how effective can we expect individual nation-states, international governing treaties, nongovernmental organizations, and other currently existing entities to be in dealing with the increasingly complex problems and opportunities that await us as a result of this changing global environment? While a large percentage of world trade continues to be controlled by the European Union and the United States, and while there are examples of NGOs successfully dealing with international problems,[2] the fact remains that each entity reflects and supports the shared values of a specific group, making it more effective in more homogeneous settings.[3] Consequently, dependence on these groups and the traditional economic theory considered to be the foundation of their success in a homogeneous setting may result in an unstable and fragile context for business transactions in increasingly heterogeneous settings. This instability and fragility stems from the fact that traditional theory that has worked in the past fails to acknowledge different political structures and economic, religious and cultural values. The result, clearly demonstrated by the crisis-ridden transition of the former Soviet Union to a more market-based economic society, is that what works in one milieu might not work in another.

George Soros has written that 'the market has escaped regulators' (quoted in Garten 2001, pp. 225–6). This is especially true in the global economy where the market now extends beyond the jurisdictions of regulators in individual sovereign states. This being the case, both success in, and successful evaluation of, the global marketplace demands a model for business relations that incorporates effective transactions and working relationships with diverse peoples – which might not be a strength of the traditional, more homogeneous model.

The traditional model for business relationships
The traditional model that dominates analysis of business relationships in the global economy is the capitalist model based on privately-owned companies seeking to maximize profit. This model has guided Western economic thinking since the late eighteenth century. Its justification rests on two key elements: first, free markets that are sufficiently competitive remove the need for detailed government oversight and, second, a moral model arguing for an expectation of appropriate behaviour by business people based on Adam Smith's notion of 'sympathy' as set out in his 'The theory of moral sentiments'.

Smith's notion of sympathy and its role in the traditional model can be described as my ability to put myself in your place and to appreciate your feelings when, for example, I overcharge you for a product, or fail to meet my commitment to you in some other way. Understanding and appreciating how you would feel, I will give you what you expect. As a result of this sympathy, I am guided 'as if by an invisible hand', to advance your interests, and in so doing, the interest of all society.

It can certainly be argued that sympathy is a force informing business relationships in today's economy. Today's CEOs and managers can well be expected to empathize with the dismay of stockholders, suppliers, distributors and final buyers when practices not in their best interest are exposed by regulators or the media. But questions can nonetheless be asked about the effectiveness of sympathy and the invisible hand in leading to desirable outcomes in an increasingly global economy.

For one, to what extent does sympathy depend on the homogeneity of the business environment? Put differently, how easy is it to sympathize with someone else when economic relationships are increasingly moving across cultures and the previously largely homogeneous values among participants in transactions become more heterogeneous? Certainly there are values that span cultures, such as sustaining one's well-being and the pursuit of happiness. But there are also values, such as gender equality and opposition to human trafficking, that vary across cultures and can affect one's ability to sympathize with another.

Another question regarding Smith's concept of sympathy in guiding business practices – be they national or international – arises from a short statement in 'The theory of moral sentiments' that has been largely overlooked in the traditional economic presentation of the invisible hand doctrine. Smith writes the following:

> Sympathy . . . cannot, in any sense, be regarded as a selfish principle. When I sympathize with your sorrow . . . it may be pretended, indeed, that my emotion is founded in self-love, because it arises from . . . putting myself in your situation, and thence conceiving what I should feel in the like circumstance . . . My grief is entirely upon your account, and not in the least upon my own. It is not, therefore, in the least selfish. (Smith [1790] 1964, p. 323)

But to what extent do adherents of the traditional model interpret my empathy for the feelings of a person with whom I am dealing in a business-related matter as driven not by genuine sympathy but by my own self-interest? We can add one last question, also tied to Smith, about the traditional model's ensuring that economic agendas lead to desirable outcomes in the new global economy. Despite his position on the invisible hand moving the economy in the right direction, Smith did see a role for government as a judicial administrator and provider of security and public goods. The question to be posed is that while the traditional model flourishes in the stable environment of the nation-state can nationalism meet the needs of an international economy? If not, does it create obstacles to growth in internationalism as countries, in the interest of their businesses or geopolitical agendas, impose tariffs, quotas and embargos? For example, what would be the effect on the global economy and workers in developing countries if the United States, which has a current-account trade deficit approximately eight times larger than the nation with the second largest current-account deficit (*The Economist* 2007, p. 110), committed itself to a policy of significantly shrinking its imports?

What is needed to improve business relationships in the global marketplace?

Several steps are needed if we are to increase stability for business transactions and improve business relationships in the global economy. First we need universal norms and models that span national boundaries and on which business relationships can be built. Second, a dynamic diversity is needed to maximize business success. Neither of these steps can be left to individual nation-states to accomplish because none have a mandate to enforce norms (such as on employing children) in other countries, nor can they ensure respect for a dynamic diversity in other nations and cultures. Third, to preserve the common good, moral leadership in business is needed to replace morally disputable leadership and ineffective government regulatory oversight. Put differently, business leaders can and do make choices about how to treat stakeholders, and there should be prescriptive guidelines on how these choices are made.

These steps call for an evolution away from the traditional model based on individual self-interest toward a solidarity model that incorporates a larger social identity. Analysis of business relationships has demonstrated a transition from a 'shareholder model' which focuses on maximizing the interests in a single relationship between management and investors, to a 'stakeholder model' where multiple parties such as investors, employees and consumers compete with one another for a dominant position to pursue their own interests, and finally to a 'solidarity model' where the interests of all parties are brought together for the common good of the whole.

Solidarity as a new model for business relationships

The solidarity-based model for business relationships, as an alternative to the traditional model, is grounded on an eagerness to conduct business in a worldwide marketplace in which all do not have shared cultural, political and other backgrounds. It is not about trying to make people the same, but rather, recognizing that people and cultures will continue to be different. It is about moving beyond our differences to a new appreciation of the dynamic relationships between stakeholders in business transactions and providing a model that encourages people to work together. Thus, solidarity offers an expanded model of community relations that includes all people in the global marketplace and seeks a social partnership between all stakeholders – be they shareholders, management, labour, customers or nation-states – for mutual benefit.

In a recent review of the principle of solidarity as described by Fr. Henry Pesch, Franz Mueller argues the following:

> [S]olidarity denotes [a] community of interests and responsibilities. It signifies the fact that as the welfare of individual persons and smaller groups depends to a great extent on the welfare of the larger social whole, so the welfare of the whole depends on that of its parts. Instead of being mutually exclusive, the individual and the common good are really correlative. (Mueller 2005, p. 349, emphasis in the original)

The solidarity model presents both a new structure for understanding business relationships and a call for those in business to become leaders of a civic identity that incorporates the global marketplace in which we live and work. As a business model it is functionally based on partnership relations between all stakeholders. Labour, management, investors, customers and the communities in which their transactions take place must, as partners, reach common understandings that encourage and support stable business relations.

David Hollenbach (1999, p. 9) describes solidarity as 'mutual engagement' and a willingness to take others seriously. Solidarity partnerships demand reciprocity and a tolerance of others. In return, these dynamic relationships create new business opportunities and a stable environment for transactions across cultures.

Seen in this light, the solidarity-based model can be a powerful tool for understanding and ordering relationships in the global economy because it enables us to better structure business transactions between diverse stakeholders. The model illustrates the possibility of building a framework for trust and promise-keeping among all parties by fostering mutual respect and reciprocity in human relationships.[4]

What makes the solidarity model a potentially more reasonable vehicle than the traditional model for building and judging economic transactions in the world marketplace is its recognition that without mutual respect trust is far more difficult to establish between diverse stakeholders, and that operating in an environment of mutual respect and trust can be in everyone's best interest. This is increasingly important in today's world economy, because, as a result of its complexity and diversity, the disrespect that undermines trust can take many forms and come from many directions.

Solidarity encourages business transactions that foster a sense of community between all stakeholders. This, in turn, promotes fair competition, acceptable working conditions and high product quality. Alternatively, transactions are discouraged where they restrict or exclude an expanding community, for example, when sellers in less-than-competitive markets take (or take more) consumer surplus from buyers. Thus, solidarity allows the setting of both objectives and limits on business behaviour. In other words, solidarity calls for three types of civic business obligations: negative duties (do no harm); positive duties (expand opportunities for all marketplace participants); and social duties (increase the common good and tolerance).

As the new millennium broke so too did a flood of stories revealing corporate fraud, theft and corruption. Beginning with Enron, Tyco and WorldCom in the United States and followed closely by Vivendi in France and Royal Ahold in the Netherlands, the revelation of widespread corporate mismanagement brought governmental sanctions and calls for a change in business practices.[5] The solidarity model is one example of how business leaders are being called upon to fundamentally change the moral structure of marketplace transactions. Corporate leaders with the vision to embrace a new way of doing business are necessary to get beyond the narrow framework of self-interest found in the traditional model and to realize the potential of marketplace transactions grounded in an intrinsic respect for all stakeholders.

Advancing from self-interest to solidarity might be described as moving from seeing the individual as separate from the community towards seeing the individual as a product of their community. It is a move from egoism towards mutual appreciation and respect. While the traditional economic model interprets self-interest by focusing on how individuals maximize their well-being, solidarity focuses on individuals as part of their community, which allows the 'self' to be seen in a larger sense that incorporates people's intrinsic value. The solidarity model does not ignore self-interest, but rather redefines it; placing self-interest where it rightly belongs, in the larger community. Solidarity makes respect for others a foundation for action in a diverse world, where individuals can more fully realize their own potential by being part of a larger community. Business transactions restructured to improve not only individual well-being, but also the well-being of all – even those one may never meet – ultimately bring greater benefit to the individual and to the community as a whole.

The extreme alternative to this is the isolated cynicism seen in the stakeholder model, where a person does something that helps another only because it is in their own self-interest. While we might sympathize with others because we know how we ourselves would feel in their situation, the fact remains that the intrinsic value of the other person is rendered meaningless. It is their instrumental value in achieving our objectives that matters.

Seen in this way, the solidarity model can be viewed as a step forward from the traditional model. At a time when the global economy is creating significant and ongoing changes in the marketplace and diversity in business is more the rule than the exception, development of a model that moves beyond the concept of self-interest toward a concept of shared respect for all humanity could increase trust and strengthen economic ties in ways that benefit all.

Questions about the solidarity model

There are challenges in transitioning to this new solidarity model which rests on arguments about business leaders' core values, their willingness and ability to implement those values in a global economy, and the benefits of implementing those values. While an introduction to the solidarity model might lead one to concur with its position and support its implementation, the introduction might also prompt questions, several of which are addressed here.

First, what constitutes moral action in business? Morality often reflects individual and cultural norms that are not shared by all people. Thus, the solidarity model must focus on value-based decisions that respect the interests of all parties in the marketplace. Business leaders using the solidarity model may be called upon to demonstrate moral courage to pursue difficult agendas and to take into consideration values of others that they might not initially share in their conception of the greater good for all.

Second, is it naive to expect an across-the-board shift in business leadership towards respectful, solidary behaviour? The answer is no, because this model addresses the same interests of businesses identified by the traditional model. More mutual respect in the global economy leads to less need for oversight of foreign partners in business transactions, which is both costly and time-consuming

Third, is solidarity achievable? Given that the needs of all partners cannot be fully satisfied due to resource scarcity, is it possible to act morally and not harm someone else? That is, if solidarity is not fully achievable, is the vision more idealistic than realistic? There certainly are obstacles to fully achieving solidarity and, yes, solidarity sets high standards for business relationships. But to use this as an argument to dismiss the solidarity model triggers a comparable question about the traditional model. Given less than the perfectly competitive markets essential to Smith's invisible hand doctrine, is it reasonable to expect self-interest to be a reliable regulator of economic activity? In other words, Smith's ideal upon which the traditional capitalistic model is built may be no more achievable than the ideals upon which the solidarity model is built. To use the argument of achievability as a basis for dismissing the solidarity model might well strengthen the argument for dismissing the traditional model as well.

In summary, we can argue that solidarity is something that might be expected in an ideal world, but the real world is not and never will be ideal. This is a fault in the real world of business. But a shared oneness is there too, because without it we would not be able to recognize or rank the extent of the fault. Thus, when speaking of solidarity we are trying to articulate something that, in fact, exists. Knowing this, focusing on solidarity is a step forward towards conceiving a broadly beneficial alternative to what the traditional model offers.

Notes

1. For example, several US producers agreed to monitor an overseas contractor to prevent its abuse of workers and to comply with US labour laws and international human rights standards (Meadows 1999, p. 1, page number from electronic database).
2. This is not to suggest that the cultural settings within, say, the European Union and the United States are strictly homogeneous. Within any culture there will always be conflicting views on specific issues.
3. Companies frequently cited for moving away from the single focused shareholder model for business relationships to a stakeholder model include Ben & Jerry's, Body Shop International and Tom's of Maine.
4. The moral underpinning of the solidarity model draws largely upon two traditions: (i) the ethical writings of Immanuel Kant ([1785] 1969, [1788] 1956) and (ii) the Catholic social tradition. See as examples Kennedy (2002) and Mele (2002).
5. Such as, in the United States, the Sarbanes-Oxley Act of 2002, also known as the Public Company Accounting Reform and Investor Protection Act of 2002.

References

Arthur, Charles (2001), 'Haiti's thirst for justice', *Multinational Monitor*, **22** (1/2), 25–7.

Cima, Lawrence R. and Thomas L. Schubeck (2001), 'Self-interest, love, and economic justice: a dialogue between classic economic liberalism and Catholic social teaching', *Journal of Business Ethics*, **30**, 213–31.

Council of Economic Advisors (2006), *Economic Report of the President*, Washington DC: US Government Printing Office.

The Economist (2007), 'Economic and financial indicators', 21 April, 110.

Federation of International Trade Associations (n.d.), Economic Indicators, http://fita.org/countries/economie_11.html, 1 July 2007.

Garten, Jeffrey E. (2001), *The Mind of the CEO*, New York, NY: Basic Books.

Grow, Brian, Steve Hamm and Louise Lee (2005), 'The debate over doing good', *Business Week*, 3947 (August), 76–8.

Herubin, D. (2002), 'Bangladesh workers protest conditions, pay for making Disney T-shirts', *Knight Ridder Tribune Business News*, (9 October).

Hollenbach, David' S.J. (1999), 'The common good in a divided society', Lecture, Santa Clara University, Ignation Center, Bannan Institute, Santa Clara, CA.

Janchitfah, Supara (2004), 'Opinion: human trafficking puts thousands of girls, women at risk every day', *Knight Ridder Tribune Business News*, 7 March.

Kant, Immanuel ([1785] 1969), *Foundations of the Metaphysics of Morals*, trans. Lewis W. Beck with critical essays ed. R.P. Wolff, Indianapolis, IN: Bobbs-Merrill.

Kant, Immanuel ([1788] 1956), *Critique of Practical Reason,* trans. Lewis W. Beck, New York, NY: Liberal Arts Press.

Kennedy, Robert G. (2002), 'The virtue of solidarity and the purpose of the firm', in S.A. Corthrighth and Michael J. Naughton (eds), *Rethinking the Purpose of Business: Interdisciplinary Essays from the Catholic Social Tradition,* Notre Dame, IN: University of Notre Dame Press, pp. 48–64.

Meadows, Shawn (1999), 'Four firms settle in Saipan's "Sweatshop" case', *Bobbin*, **41** (2), 8–10.

Mele, Domenec (2002), 'Not only stakeholder interests: the firm oriented toward the common good', in S.A. Corthrighth and Michael J. Naughton (eds), *Rethinking the Purpose of Business: Interdisciplinary Essays from the Catholic Social Tradition,* Notre Dame, IN: University of Notre Dame Press, pp. 190–214.

Mueller, Franz H. (2005), 'The principle of solidarity in the teachings of Father Henry Pesch, S.J.', *Review of Social Economy*, **63** (3), 347–55.

Nocera, Joe (2006), 'The paradoxes of businesses as do-gooders', *New York Times*, 11 November, C1.

Sarbanes-Oxley Act (2002), Public Law No. 107-204, 116 Stat. 745, Washington DC: US Government.

Smith, Adam ([1790] 1964), 'The theory of moral sentiments', in Lewis A. Selby-Bigge (ed.), *British Moralists*, Indianapolis, IN: Bobbs-Merrill, pp. 257–336.
Zadek, Simon (2004), 'The path to corporate responsibility', *Harvard Business Review*, (December), 125–231.

See also the entries on: Corporate social responsibility; Self-interest; Adam Smith.

69 Sustainability
J.B. (Hans) Opschoor

Orientation

'Sustainability' is a quality or characteristic of a process, condition or structure (an 'object' hereafter), namely that it can be sustained (that is, maintained, supported, provided for) for an extended period of time, without net loss of valued qualities inside or outside of the system in which the object functions (compare Holdren et al. 1995).

This definition is rather formal and empty. To become meaningful the objects of sustainability must be specified. Originally the notion of sustainability related to natural resources. The range of objects has since grown to include activities such as agriculture and mobility, development, cities, livelihoods, societies as a whole and even world orders. These objects rest on or are produced or reproduced by underlying processes and systems. This renders the question of an object's sustainability a complex one, as in reality it depends on the continued ('sustained') functioning of these systems and processes. To make this complexity manageable it has been suggested that the concept be distinguished according to three main aspects: economic, social and ecological or environmental (for example, Lele 1991). In this contribution, we pay special attention to the environmental aspects and to the sustainability of development – both viewed through economists' lenses.

Sustainability is not only a many-faceted characteristic of objects, it is also approached from a variety of viewpoints including different disciplinary and paradigmatic (if not ideological) points of departure. This has triggered various discourses on sustainability.

Related to sustainability as an objective, interest has shifted to processes of transition *towards* sustainability, with more gradualist processes realizing increasingly less unsustainable states of the objects studied. This is because institutional and cultural change may be necessary for an object to become sustainable. On the institutional side, *un*sustainability has its roots in the economic system. Moreover, (un)sustainability is an issue in the discourse about globalization, especially in its neoliberal forms.

Sustainability can be a characteristic of an object, but it has evolved into much more: a criterion and even a societal objective. Definitions of sustainability contain references to human interests and values. There are also other ethical considerations: human interests and values do not necessarily incorporate the interests of all possible categories of stakeholders (that is, those of non-human species).

Environmental/ecological sustainability

In the eighteenth century sustainability referred to practices in forestry: ways of harvesting trees that left the forests intact. The World Conservation Strategy (IUCN, UNEP and WWF 1980) broadened this to the *sustainable use* of natural resources as a pattern of use that can continue forever. The World Commission on Environment and Development (WCED) generalized the concept of sustainability to relate to development in general (WCED 1987).

The most important innovation in the notion of sustainability is that it looks at inter-temporal and even intergenerational aspects. Costanza and Patten (1995, p. 195) hold that the objects, or states, of which the sustainability is examined have their own intrinsic or 'natural' time scales; '[a] sustainable system . . . [is] one that attains its full expected life span within the nested hierarchy of systems within which it is embedded'. From this perspective an ecologically sustainable economy is one that maintains its essential eco-logical processes and life support systems (IUCN, UNEP and WWF 1980). Daly (1996) elaborated this intertemporal concern in three requirements: (i) to keep rates of renewable resource use below their regeneration rates; (ii) for non-renewables, to keep use patterns within time spans needed to develop renewable alternatives; and (iii) to keep pollution within acceptable levels of damage.

Economic welfare depends on the deployment of a variety of resources: human capital (labour and skills), physical (or 'produced') capital and natural capital. In generating eco-nomic welfare, these types of capital may be substituted for one another at least to some degree. Thus, it is conceivable for welfare levels to remain constant (or rise) in the future, while natural stocks *decline* – as long as this deterioration of natural capital is compen-sated by increases in human or physical capital so that total capital remains constant or increases. The degree to which any deterioration of natural capital would be compatible with sustainable welfare depends on the degree of actual substitutability and technologi-cal innovation. Expectations on these vary tremendously, which has prompted a range of perspectives on sustainability with diverging implications for environmental quality and natural resources. In the 'strong sustainability' perspective, *natural* capital is to be kept constant over time; in the 'weak sustainability' perspective, the *overall or aggregate* level of stocks is to be preserved. In-between positions may call for preservation (at least) of, for example, 'essential' natural resources.

Resource use is embedded in societal-biospheric systems of which often little is known in terms of their dynamics. These dynamics may induce inherent uncertainties, and give rise to more vulnerable, less secure or even insecure livelihoods (for example, through famines, droughts, financial crises). Sustainability requires a flexible attitude of going 'with' complexity in the natural environment, rather than attempting to control it as in the blunt, mechanistic practices of most post-1945 recipes for society-environment interactions. It also requires principles for dealing with uncertainty, which have been translated into notions such as the 'precautionary approach'.

Alternative discourses on sustainability
There are disciplinary biases in what is considered important in relation to sustainabil-ity: the sustainability of human activities depends inter alia on technological, economic, political and cultural forces and ecological ones. All of these dimensions have their own disciplines, and within these disciplines, perspectives or approaches (may) differ. Sustainability as a concept particularly poses problems for many in the social sciences. Dangers and pitfalls identified include the application of natural science metaphors to social realities and ecological reductionism (Becker and Jahn 1999). Moreover, as needs change over time and vary across cultures, the objects of sustainability vary as well (Redclift and Woodgate 1997).

Furthermore, environmental sustainability is a criterion or objective in addition to others, notably social justice (Dobson 1999). Because the environment has elements that are scarce, distributional issues may arise (including associated questions related to power asymmetries). There is also the issue of justice to the environment. In short, there may be clashes between the interests of the poor now and of future generations, and between both and the rest of nature. Ideological stances will thus influence positions taken with respect to the meaning and scope of sustainability. In this context, Jacobs (1999, p. 137) has identified a set of 'fault lines' or tensions that have triggered different discourses on sustainability: (i) a protectionist versus a development focus; (ii) equity first or sustainability first; (iii) sustainability as an environmental concern versus sustainability as a social concern, including the protection of communities and cultures.

Fundamental critiques of the concept of sustainability are found in political economy and political ecology, and 'green economics' has recently rearticulated these. Lunn (2006) observes that sustainability has been interpreted in too narrow a way as tied to economic growth or, at best, to environmental conditions in a 'prevalent consumptive model' dominated by economistic views in the 'global capitalistic society'. She pleas for developing broader social and cultural aspects in contributions to 'achieving sustainability'. Similarly, Springett (2006) sees sustainability as having largely been incorporated in the rhetoric of 'eco-modernism and green business' in a paradigm of growth-oriented economic policy which actually induces *un*sustainability. She argues in favour of a more critical ('a more dialectical', 'counter-hegemonic') discourse on sustainability.

These are powerful articulations of what others might describe as a 'hijacking' by mainstream economists or economic interests of the notion of sustainability by essentially reducing it to some economic aspects and by applying it only within the context of economic activities as we know them and within the prevailing economic order.

Sustainable development

The WCED has defined sustainable development popularly as development that meets the needs of the present generation while not jeopardizing the possibilities for future generations to meet their needs. More precisely, 'sustainable development is a process of change in which the exploitation of resources, the direction of investments, the orientation of technological development, and institutional change are in harmony and enhance both current and future potential to meet human needs and aspirations' (WCED 1987, p. 46). WCED also mentions conservation based on moral obligations to other living beings and future generations (for example, ibid., p. 57), yet the emphasis is on resources for development (for example, ibid., p. 155). Strictly speaking, the WCED definition only calls for concern for sustainability in its weak form.

Economics-oriented definitions have described sustainable development as development without growth in throughput beyond the environmental carrying capacity; or as a state of non-decreasing per capita welfare across generations; or the amount of consumption that can be continued indefinitely without degrading capital stocks. From a North-South perspective, Pronk and Haq (1992) defined it as economic growth that provides fairness and opportunity for all the world's people without further destroying the world's finite natural resources and carrying capacity.

In a way, 'sustainable development' is a political and global response to the problems raised by the Club of Rome around 1970, on the (physical) limits to (economic and population) growth. The growth-versus-environment debate took a remarkable turn just before the UN Conference on Environment and Development (1992) with the presentation of the so-called 'Environmental Kuznets Curve' which pictured an inverted U pattern in which growth in income per capita would initially yield rising environmental pressure that would level off as incomes grew further, to, beyond some threshold, even decline. Pursuing economic growth would thus (it was suggested) eventually improve environmental conditions: sustainability would be an inherent product of growth. Meanwhile, the generality of this has been challenged (Arrow et al. 1995; Opschoor 1995). Environmental sustainability remains a profound developmental concern.

In line with the broad WCED definition of sustainable development as 'a process of change', sustainability now is increasingly regarded as a goal to be pursued in a process of development – perhaps even a more fundamental societal 'transition' towards sustainability. Sustainable development then becomes 'development *towards* sustainability' (for example, Lunn 2006; Springett 2006; compare the notion coming from the global South of 'making development more sustainable', Munasinghe 2000).

The fuzziness implicit in the various definitions of sustainable development has to some extent been clarified in the 'principles' of sustainable development of the 1992 Rio Declaration. These link environmental concerns with the right to development, and establish a human right to 'a healthy and productive life in harmony with nature', explicitly extended to future generations. They also establish that states have the right to exploit their own natural resources without causing damage to the environment of other states. Poverty eradication is an essential precondition for sustainable development. The special needs of developing countries and the different shares in causing environmental degradation of developing and developed nations make for 'common but differentiated' responsibilities for each of these categories of states. Furthermore, a 'precautionary approach' is called for, whereby cost-effective interventions to reduce or prevent serious or irreversible damage to the environment will not be blocked by a lack of full scientific certainty on their need or effectiveness. These 'Rio principles on sustainable development' are now finding their way into international legislation and agreements (Schrijver and Weiss 2004).

Globalization and (environmental) sustainability

Even though most countries are committed to sustainable development there is insufficient progress to reverse the loss of the world's natural resources (UN 2005). Land is becoming degraded at an alarming rate; and plant and animal species and habitats are being lost in record numbers. Fisheries and other marine resources are over-exploited. Forests are disappearing.

The question then arises of what the prospects are for halting and reversing these trends. Driving forces such as economic growth and the level and orientation of consumption are profoundly related to features of the – market-based – economic system (see, for example, Opschoor 1994). Sustained (ongoing) economic growth is not necessarily sustainable. One needs to put actual patterns of development in the context of globalization as it is now developing, that is, in a neoliberally institutionalized form.

Globalization in its neoliberal manifestations tends to maximize rather than optimize economic growth. In the absence of adequate and enforceable standards and regulations ensuring the delivery of environmental goods and services, economic growth ignores ecological constraints and renders the overall economy-environment system prone to unsustainability. Firms operating in increasingly competitive markets can survive and develop only by processes of cost-shifting (and cost-avoiding), thereby passing on the social costs of environmental degradation in the form of externalities to others. These others include other generations and other species. Similarly, globalization tends to increase inequalities, to crowd out care and to erode social cohesion. Without deep-reaching additional environmental policies and institutions to address and curb inherent market failures, these links between economic growth and environmental pressure would push the world economic process further on an unsustainable track (Reed 2002; Rees 2006).

Supporters of the economic mainstream (for example, as assembled in the World Economic Forum, including financial and economic institutions, such as the International Monetary Fund, the World Trade Organization and the World Bank) believe that providing more scope for economic forces and market mechanisms will eventually increase welfare and ultimately reduce inequality and unsustainability. This reductionist, economistic understanding of 'development' is currently being broadened by taking into account institutional features necessary to make a market economy operate in a socially and ecologically more responsible way (for example, World Bank 2001).

In response to this type of globalization civil society worldwide has become active in fields such as human rights and ecological issues. To challenge the World Economic Forum, the World Social Forum was established, bringing together organized civil society to confront, often radically, neoliberal development strategies with their consequences in terms of inequality and unsustainability (for example, WCC 2005).

Less radical proposals for alternative, more sustainable development include *managed globalization* and *partnerships for the global public good.* Behind these is the idea that if equity and sustainability are relevant societal aspirations then there is a need for governments capable of imposing 'managed' forms of globalization driven by political and societal concerns and not only by efficiency-oriented considerations. Countervailing power needs to be brought in from the political domain. New alliances ('global partnerships') are proposed between civil society organizations, the corporate sector, and governmental and intergovernmental agencies of various kinds and at various levels (for example, Kaul et al. 2003).

Ethics and sustainability
Sustainability has become a value-laden concept. Obviously, sustainability is not necessarily a required property of each and every object. Views on this vary across time and place, and 'contextual' ecological as well as cultural variation give rise to different choices. Moreover, sustainability is a consideration relevant in evaluation and decision-making, alongside others, such as equity and human welfare.

The WCED definition of sustainable development recognizes two broad perspectives on equity:

- intra*generational equity to which poverty or inequality, as well as the issue of environmental externalities, is related;
- inter*generational (or intertemporal) equity which includes issues related to opportunities for economic welfare across generations.

Beyond these is a third ethical dimension:

- fairness or responsibility in relation to *non-human* species and other forms of biodiversity.

The ethical content of sustainable development as promulgated internationally has been analysed by distinguishing an 'ethics of outcomes' (in terms of distributions of goods and services) and an 'ethics of responsibilities' (involving the duty to avoid causing harm). In terms of intragenerational equity the two may differ sharply in their implications, but this is less so in an intergenerational setting (compare Hurka 1996). The WCED definition of sustainable development appears to reflect both positions, which leads to ambiguity. In the intergenerational setting, Hurka distinguishes (i) utilitarianism (giving equal weight to equal gains to individuals wherever and whenever they live), (ii) egalitarianism (constraining inequalities in distribution or in access to resources) and (iii) a 'satisficing' approach (implying duties to ensure to others reasonably good conditions). Utilitarianism comes into the WCED focus on relationships with non-human species and ecosystems, but on the whole the WCED seems to adopt egalitarianism, which is a potentially powerful stance on intergenerational equity, very much in line with an intertemporal extension of Rawlsian views on justice. Hurka argues, instead, for a satisficing interpretation (elements of which he also recognizes in the WCED report) based on limits (reflecting safety or precaution in ecological terms and fairness in ethical terms). Hurka rejects strict utilitarianism because of its excessively demanding nature and acceptance of an uneven distribution of outcomes.

When it comes to non-human elements in nature and societal/human relationships with these, a fundamental distinction is that between ethical positions accepting the 'intrinsic values' of (elements of) nature and those regarding the latter as having only 'instrumental value' vis-à-vis humans and society. This second position exists in the (conflicting) forms of exploitative, romantic or (intergenerationally) responsible attitudes towards nature; the first is found reflected in, for example, stewardship or 'partnership' ethics and 'deep ecology' ethics (for details see UNT 2002). From a largely instrumental perspective, WCED discusses species and ecosystems as 'resources for development', and their conservation as 'crucial for development' (WCED 1987, p. 147). Species and ecosystems should, they say, be safeguarded 'to the extent that this is technically, economically and politically feasible' (ibid., p. 148). The UN Millennium Declaration (UN 2000) took this further and identified a set of 'fundamental' values including 'respect for nature'. Surprisingly, the declaration also advanced 'a new ethic of conservation and stewardship'.

Several attempts have been made to elaborate normative stances towards nature. Two of these are presented here: the 'Declaration towards a Global Ethic' and the 'Earth Charter'.

The Declaration towards a Global Ethic, endorsed by the Parliament of the World's Religions in 1993, is a result of the Global Ethic Project (Küng 1993). Among its assertions are the following:

- respect for the community of living beings and for the planet and its preservation;
- generosity, based on the notion of 'the human family', equal partnership between men and women, and absence of domination or abuse;
- a 'culture of non-violence, respect, justice and peace';
- the striving for a social and economic order in which all have an equal chance to reach their full potential as human beings.

The starting point is the intrinsic dignity of the human person, the inalienable freedom and equality of all and the necessary solidarity and interdependence amongst all people.

The declaration proposes a sense of responsibility and duty, explicitly including respect for non-human life forms. Duties towards future generation are also included, though less explicitly.

The Earth Charter (2000) is the result of a worldwide secular process that emerged in response to the WCED (1987). In essence, its aim is a just, sustainable, participatory and peaceful global society. The charter's key commitments include the following:

- respect for earth and life in all its diversity and care for the community of life;
- building democratic societies that are just, participatory, sustainable and peaceful;
- securing the earth's bounties and beauty for present and future generations.

The charter comes closer than the WCED to a strong sustainability perspective and to acknowledging the relevance of intrinsic values in non-human life forms and other categories of biodiversity. Together with the WCED and the 'Declaration towards a Global Ethic', the charter underlines the importance of intragenerational equity. It also aims to tie in with official initiatives in the development domain (Witoelar 2005).

Sustainability: some comments in conclusion

Sustainability is a catch-all concept referring to characteristics of complex real-world entities. The sustainability of an object has also become a normative concept: a criterion for assessment or an objective to be attained. The sustainability concept has the merit of drawing attention to the intertemporal and intergenerational aspects of goals that society finds worth pursuing.

'Sustainable development' is a synthesis of concerns about ecological sustainability and other needs and aspirations of societies – especially the poor – now and in future. At the operational level some convergence has been reached in the focus on a few of sustainability's key aspects, particularly ecological, social and economic ones.

There now appears to be a global understanding that there can be no ongoing concern about environmental sustainability without an effective commitment to addressing issues of poverty and inequity, and vice versa (Sachs et al. 2002).

From a political economy perspective there are profound reasons to be concerned about the prospects of sustainability as well as equity of development, in an economic context dominated by neoliberalist ideologies and global market forces.

References

Arrow, Kenneth, Bert Bolin, Robert Costanza, Partha Dasgupta, Carl Folke, Crawford S. Holling, Bengt-Owe Jansson, Simon Levin, Karl-Goran Maler, Charles Perrings and David Pimentel (1995), 'Economic growth, carrying capacity and the environment', *Science*, **268** (195), 520–1.

Becker, Egon and Thomas Jahn (eds) (1999), *Sustainability and the Social Sciences: A Cross-Disciplinary Approach to Integrating Environmental Considerations into Theoretical Reorientation*, London and New York: Zed Books.

Costanza, Robert and Bernard C. Patten (1995), 'Defining and predicting sustainability', *Ecological Economics*, **15**, 193–6.

Daly, Herman E. (1996), *Beyond Growth: The Economics of Sustainable Develoment*, Boston: Beacon Press.

Dobson, Andrew (ed.) (1999), *Fairness and Futurity: Essays on Environmental Sustainability and Social Justice*, London: Oxford University Press.

Earth Charter Initiative (2000), *The Earth Charter*, www.earthcharter.org, 4 June 2007.

Holdren John P., Gretchen C. Daily and Paul E. Ehrlich (1995), 'The meaning of sustainability: biogeophysical aspects', The World Bank for the United Nations University, Washington DC, http://dieoff.org/page113. htm, 1 September 2007.

Hurka, Thomas M. (1996), 'Sustainable development: what do we owe to future generations?' *Unasylva*, **47**, 38–43.

IUCN, UNEP and WWF (1980), *World Conservation Strategy: Living Resource Conservation for Sustainable Development*, Gland, Switzerland: The World Conservation Union.

Jacobs, Michael (1999), 'Sustainable development as a contested concept', in Andrew Dobson (ed.), *Fairness and Futurity: Essays on Environmental Sustainability and Social Justice*, London: Oxford University Press, pp. 21–45.

Kaul, Inge, Pedro Conceição, Katell le Goulven and Ronald U. Mendoza (eds) (2003), *Providing Global Public Goods: Managing Globalization*, New York: Oxford University Press.

Küng, Hans (1993), 'Declaration towards a Global Ethic', endorsed by the Parliament of the World's Religions, http://astro.temple.edu/~dialogue/Center/mission.htm, 1 September 2007.

Lele, Sharachchandra M. (1991), 'Sustainable development: a critical review', *World Development*, **19** (6), 607–21.

Lunn, Clare E. (2006), 'The role of green economics in achieving realistic policies and programmes for sustainability', *International Journal of Green Economics*, **1** (1/2), 37–49.

Munasinghe, Mohan (2000), 'Development, equity and sustainability in the context of climate change', in Mohan Munasinghe and Rob Swart (eds), *Climate Change and its Linkages with Development, Equity, and Sustainability*, Paris: Intergovernmental Panel on Climate Change/World Meteorological Organization.

Opschoor, J.B. (1994), 'Market forces and environmental degradation', in W. Zweers and J.J. Boersema, *Ecology, Technology and Culture,* Cambridge: White Horse Press.

Opschoor, J.B. (1995), 'Ecospace and the fall and rise of throughput intensity', *Ecological Economics*, **15**, 137–40.

Pronk, Jan and Mahbubul Haq (1992), *Sustainable Development: From Concept to Action. The Hague Report*, New York: United Nations Development Programme.

Redclift, Michael and Graham Woodgate (eds) (1997), *The International Handbook of Environmental Sociology,* Cheltenham, UK and Northampton, MA, USA: Edward Elgar, pp. 55–71.

Reed, David (2002), 'Poverty and the environment: can sustainable development survive globalization?' *Natural Resources Forum*, **26**, 176–84.

Rees William E. (2006), 'Globalization, trade and migration: undermining sustainability', *Ecological Economics*, **59**, 220–25.

Sachs, W. and H. Agrawal (eds) (2002), *Fairness in a Fragile World: Memorandum for the World Summit on Sustainable Development*, Berlin: Heinrich Böll Foundation.

Schrijver, Nico and Friedl Weiss (ed.) (2004), *International Law and Sustainable Development: Principles and Practice*, Leiden and Boston, MA: Martinus Nijhoff.

Springett, Delyse (2006), 'Managing the narrative of sustainable development: "discipline" of an "inefficient" concept', *International Journal of Green Economics*, **1** (1/2), 50–65.

UN (2000), *UN Millennium Declaration*, resolution adopted by the General Assembly, A/55/L.2, 8 September.

UN (2005), *The Millennium Development Goals Report*, New York: United Nations.

UNT (2002), 'A very brief history of the origins of environmental ethics', University of North Texas, www.cep. unt.edu/novice.html, 3 August 2006.

WCC (2005), 'Alternative globalization addressing peoples and Earth (AGAPE): a background document', Justice Peace and Creation Team, World Council of Churches, Geneva.

WCED (1987), *Our Common Future*, New York: Oxford University Press.

Witoelar, Erna (2005), 'The Earth Charter and the United Nations Millennium Development Goals', in *Earth Charter, Towards a Sustainable World: The Earth Charter in Action*, Amsterdam: KIT (Royal Institute of the Tropics), pp 86–8.

World Bank (2001), *World Development Report 2000/2001: Attacking Poverty*, New York and Oxford: Oxford University Press.

See also the entries on: Global financial markets; Justice; Inequality.

70 Teaching economics
Jonathan B. Wight

Introduction

Ethical considerations intersect with economics education on a number of planes. Nonetheless, in terms of curricula, only a handful of economics departments offer courses specifically focused on ethics.[1] This chapter addresses the ways in which instructors can incorporate ethical components into teaching principles and field courses in order to broaden economic understanding and to enhance critical thinking. It examines three pedagogical issues: the artificial dichotomy between positive and normative analysis; the limiting scope of efficiency in outcomes analyses; and the incorporation of alternative ethical frameworks into public policy debates.

Charles Dickens began his satirical novel *Hard Times* (1854) with the exhortation of a successful businessman to a schoolmaster: 'Now what I want is, Facts. Teach these boys and girls nothing but Facts.' The speaker, Thomas Gradgrind, was 'A man of realities. A man of facts and calculations.' Such is the caricature of an economic technocrat who can explain the price of labour and predict its future movements using purely objective means – eschewing any reliance on moral analysis or judgement. By the mid-twentieth century, neoclassical economists also had an allegedly 'scientific' way of evaluating government policies, by measuring welfare gains and losses using cost-benefit analyses.

Unfortunately, these achievements rely upon a model of individual choice that severely restricts the scope of human identity, social relations in society and the ethical dimensions that inform them. As taught by Adam Smith and others, however, economics is inextricably a part of moral philosophy because humans are not aloof islands of exchange (as depicted in textbooks): rather, they live, work and thrive in social settings. Humans have innate instincts for self, for others and against others that serve useful functions, yet whose claims must be internally adjudicated by a moral agent. Smith, in rejecting a narrow focus on selfish individualism and hyper-rationality, noted that humans are endowed with social sentiments that aid survival and procreation. He observes, 'It is thus that man, who can subsist only in society, was fitted by nature to that situation for which he was made' ([1759] 1982, p. 85). For a classroom supplement that develops these ideas for students, see the academic novel by Jonathan B. Wight (2002).

Understanding individual and social conceptions of 'right' and 'wrong' is essential for the analysis of choice. Re-introducing ethical considerations to the classroom might better prepare students for the study of how economic agents actually behave, demonstrate how public policy analysis can be enriched by alternative welfare and ethical formulations and provide critical thinking exercises desirable for liberal arts and business educations. We begin by arguing that science itself relies upon such ethical components.

Normative and positive analyses

Economics teachers generally start by distinguishing between the goals of analysing the world as it currently exists or has existed (positive economics) and of analysing the world as it might exist under different policies (normative economics). This dichotomy is a prominent feature of modern economics and is a useful starting point. But students who are taught that it is possible to model economic behaviour without introducing a number of important ethical judgements will be dangerously misled. Ethics – the study of right and wrong, or good and bad – is infused into the ways that science operates and progresses. Attempting to delineate a value-free science would likely be destructive of it. Students should recognize that while science cannot eliminate ethical judgements, it also suffers when moral considerations dominate the search for truth (as during the Middle Ages).

The role of ethics in positive economics can be briefly described, beginning with how scientists come to conceptualize the world to be studied. In ancient times peoples observed the irregular events of nature and assumed that omnipotent beings (gods) were responsible for producing them. Adam Smith noted that 'thunder and lightening' were ascribed to 'the invisible hand of Jupiter' (Smith [1795] 1982, p. 49). Somewhat similarly, scientific researchers have an incomplete understanding and approach their investigations with imperfect preconceptions. What researchers currently believe (either consciously or unconsciously) affects what they can 'see' and what subjects they believed to be important for investigation (Brugger and Brugger 1993, cited in Weisstein n.d.).

Scientists thus approach their tasks not as empty vessels but as jumbles of sometimes conflicting worldviews. Preconceptions are intricately tied to moral values and philosophies. For example, classical economists held the view that markets – including labour markets – always cleared at an equilibrium price. This belief was central to the contemporaneous moral judgement about the virtue of hard work and the vice of relying on charity. Yet, these are not 'facts' about the world so much as limiting pre-scientific worldviews. John Maynard Keynes, in introducing *The General Theory of Employment, Interest, and Money*, wrote:

> The composition of this book has been for the author a long struggle of escape . . . from habitual modes of thought and expression . . . The difficulty lies, not in the new ideas, but in escaping from the old ones. ([1936] 1964, p. viii)

Bringing presuppositions to light is an important part of helping students to learn how to think critically. Worldviews play an important role in the initial formulation of models, and are central to the allocation of resources. Science could not proceed without individual and social judgements about the relative importance of different research programmes and competing theories for testing.

Once a researcher has developed a hypothesis and received funding to gather data, there are a number of additional steps requiring ethical judgements. 'Facts' do not fall from the trees into the laps of researchers. Economic facts must be defined, which entails a normative consideration of the goals of the research. For instance, if the subject of inquiry is the labour market, one would need to define 'unemployment'. If the definition is set too stringently, those in need of assistance will be undercounted; if it is set too leniently, there will be an overcount. Pure science cannot provide the definition of unemployment, since it is a moral (or political) judgement as to what type of definitional errors one should be willing to accept.

Facts then must be collected and analysed. Since resources for doing so have opportunity costs, a judgement must be made as to which subset of facts to collect and what degree of accuracy to accept. Observing the data often alters the data (known in physics as Heisenberg's uncertainty principle), hence methods of data gathering are subject to ethical norms and constraints. The choice of acceptable statistical errors in data analysis is a step often overlooked by researchers (who simply rely upon industry norms). However, the industry norm for acceptable Type I and Type II errors is not determined by scientific means, but is a collective normative judgement.

Conclusions about the findings must then be publicly debated through a peer review process. This entails a commitment to honesty and to rhetorical elements that are often unconsciously normative (McCloskey 1998). Science itself cannot provide a sufficient reason why investigators should tell the truth. One can argue – and students should consider – whether science progresses more efficiently when researchers ascribe to honest conduct because of duty or identity considerations (as discussed below) or due to simple calculations of self-interest. In mentoring young people, teachers are role models in the socialization of future scholars – which to Adam Smith meant inculcating students with examples of virtuous conduct that become internalized over time.

Finally, factual conclusions about the world often give rise to public policies that change the world, so that discovery and change are linked. In short, it is difficult to conceive of a positive economic researcher being isolated from important ethical concepts and principles.

Welfare analysis

Economists would also like to say something useful about how to make the world a better place. But this normative analysis is often approached from a single ethical framework – consequentialism – and from one narrow aspect of consequentialism, that relating to consumer and producer welfare. Modern textbooks, and probably most teachers, pay little attention to the underlying ethical framework that is implicit in neoclassical welfare theory.

Economists have an overriding but largely unconscious bias toward efficiency as a moral value (Hausman and McPherson 1993, p. 675). Teachers often address the term as if it were a scientific concept rather than a normative one. This is a serious mistreatment, reflecting perhaps the blinkers of worldview. 'Efficiency' is the implied superiority of one situation to alternative states of affairs; to analyse efficiency, the term must first be defined in relation to a goal. Choosing a goal is completely normative. Utilitarians such as Jeremy Bentham focused on the goal of net utility (measured by pleasure and pain). Neoclassical economists focus on maximizing the potential satisfaction of consumer and producer preferences. The modern formulation has several notable advantages, mainly that it can be quantified using market (and hedonic) price information. Yet it also has disadvantages.

Teachers of economics should advise students that efficiency and the related concepts of consumer and producer surpluses, and deadweight losses, are constructed using important ethical judgements that are open to debate. The difference between 'efficiency' as defined by economists and 'efficiency' as defined by wider moral norms provides an interesting contrast for discussion. One classroom technique for demonstrating this is to have students participate in a mock medical triage.

Tell the students they will play the role of a doctor at a remote hospital. The hospital has in stock only ten doses of a life-saving serum; it is impossible to get more in the short run. Two busloads of patients now arrive simultaneously. Bus A holds ten passengers who each need a life-saving serum, and who if administered the serum, will each certainly survive. Without the serum each will definitely die. Bus B holds ten passengers who also need the serum to survive. But due to their worsened conditions, their survival rate will be only 50 percent even if they receive the serum. I ask students, 'If you were the doctor, what should your goal be? Based on that goal, and given the resource constraints, how would you allocate the serum?'

Virtually all students adopt a Hippocratic ethical perspective. They answer that the goal should be to save as many lives as possible. Given this goal, they would perform a triage and allocate the scarce serum to patients on Bus A and thereby save 10 lives. By contrast, if they gave the serum to Bus B passengers, half would die and that would mean only 5 lives saved. I follow this up by then providing additional information: the passengers on Bus A are from a nursing home with an average age of 85 years; the passengers on Bus B are from an orphanage with an average age of 5 years. The new information leads many students to re-evaluate the goal. A new goal is not to save 'lives' but 'life years extended'. In saving a child they would extend life by perhaps 80 years; in saving an elderly person, they would extend life by perhaps only 5 years. Allocating the serum to children would save 400 life years, even though half of the children are not expected to live (compared to 50 life years if the serum goes to the elderly). Almost all students now switch their allocation of serum to Bus B patients.

This discussion helps students realize that being 'efficient' as a doctor is not simply a scientific determination; it is an ethical one. It requires choosing a goal that is most morally defensible. The analysis becomes more complex when I then announce that the life-saving serum is actually not under the control of the doctor. Rather, it is owned by a for-profit pharmacy that will sell it to the highest bidders. The passengers on Bus A are elderly and well-off financially. I ask students how they think the market would allocate the serum. Based on a market-efficient solution, and assuming selfish individualism, the serum would be sold to Bus A passengers and all of the children would die.

Students are surprised and upset to discover that the 'efficient' solution from the economic perspective (maximizing economic welfare) is not 'efficient' from the social perspective (maximizing life years extended), at least in the short run. Suddenly, the interpretation of consumer and producer surpluses takes on new importance. Students now see that economists and others in society often have competing notions of 'efficiency'. Defining and debating the desired goal is a critical step, yet it is one that many teachers simply bypass in assuming economic efficiency to be the most important goal. Many teachers would no doubt justify this approach by arguing that economists have a comparative advantage in assessing economic efficiency, and that teachers from other departments can best address alternative public policy goals. Such reductionism likely hurts the critical thinking process and ill prepares students for leadership positions.

A concluding segment of this exercise requires extending the timeframe of analysis. Students now examine potential outcomes 10 years in the future, comparing the market price system (allocation to highest bidder) with a command and control system (allocation by medical triage). Students come to appreciate the paradox that while markets might not extend the most life years in the short run, they have the potential to do so in the long run through profit incentives for production and product innovations (assuming competitive conditions). By contrast, the command and control mechanism could theoretically save more lives in the present, yet produce shortages and fail to create incentives for long-run production, research and development. It could also lead to corruption and black-market activity. Hence, the ethical analysis of market outcomes is far more interesting and complex than a short-run period would indicate.

In summary, teachers who focus on efficiency and neglect other outcomes (life years extended, equity, freedom and other values) may inadvertently bias student perceptions about the acceptable or desirable goals in society (Frank 1996; Frank et al. 1993). Economic efficiency is an indispensable concept for students to master, yet it does not have an elevated place above other possible goals when analysing public policies. It is ultimately a normative concept, not a scientific one.

Non-consequentialist perspectives

The preceding section highlighted the role of ethical judgement in the selection and definition of consequentialist goals, such as efficiency. But the analysis of public policy goes deeper than simply choosing goals. Alternative ethical frameworks add depth to the analysis, and students often utilize these unconsciously. Teachers might briefly describe these in class. The major non-consequentialist ethical frameworks are illustrated in the schema below, based on Solomon (1998, p. 121):

(1) Economic Agent → (2) Action → (3) Outcomes

The (1) economic agent takes (2) an action that produces (3) certain outcomes. The neoclassical welfare model utilizes an outcomes-based ethical framework, which asserts that economic systems and policies should be evaluated on the basis of consequences alone. More specifically, efficiency is judged by the degree to which consumer and producer welfare is potentially maximized. One criticism, noted previously, is that alternative outcomes should be considered when assessing economic policies.

More subtle but important criticisms of the neoclassical approach come into view when students consider the antecedent steps. Processes (1) and (2) bring to light issues of duty and character that provide alternative frameworks for ethical analysis. These can be briefly described. Immanuel Kant's categorical imperative defines one's duty as the obligation to carry out actions that one's reason determines to be moral. The consequences of acts are irrelevant to the determination of moral value. Kant's approach leads to the conclusion, for example, that it is immoral to treat another person as a means to an end, regardless of how desirable the end might be. This ethical framework permeates modern philosophy and is reflected in both law and tradition.

Proponents of natural law and rights-based theories rely on a similar construct. The United Nations' Universal Declaration of Human Rights (1948), for example, establishes 'the inherent dignity' and 'equal and inalienable rights of all members of the human family'. According to this view, policies that infringe basic rights cannot be justified by appeals to beneficial economic outcomes. This is relevant for many public policy debates. For example, students often instinctively support the Living Wage Movement, and oppose sweatshop labour, because of adherence to rights-based considerations. That is, if all persons are created equal, there is thought to be some minimum level of compensation and standard of working conditions that is compatible with dignity. Economists can demonstrate that unemployment may rise if wages are set higher than equilibrium, but to students concerned with human rights, the efficiency argument is a non sequitur. Rather than ignore the issue – thereby implying that only consequentialist ethics matters – teachers can use the issue as an opportunity to briefly outline the differing ethical frameworks, and thereby place neoclassical welfare analysis within its proper context.

Other duty-based ethical systems rely not on rationality or rights, but on adherence to divine law. The pope opposes stem cell research, for instance, because he considers it a violation of God's commandments. While medical advances may occur, these desirable outcomes have no bearing on the moral question of protecting those who are vulnerable. Like Kantians, the pope would argue that it is morally wrong to use others as a means to our ends, regardless of how beneficial those ends might be. Cost-benefit calculations are rejected as a flawed method of moral analysis.

Lastly, the Aristotelian character-based or virtue-based framework addresses important aspects of meaning and identity that shape human behaviour. This approach focuses on (1), the economic agent, and on the motivations that guide behaviour. According to this view, the right action is one that upholds the ideal human person. Adam Smith, who was clearly a consequentialist in his analysis of public policies, also promoted virtue ethics when writing about individual choice. Smith believed that a good society required not only good institutions and policies, but also the cultivation of virtuous character and moral imagination ([1759] 1982). To some degree, the outcome-based and virtue-based ethical systems operate side-by-side. That is, if people are virtuous, this will often produce positive outcomes for society. But people do not have to be virtuous to produce good outcomes. A shopkeeper who is inherently dishonest might discover that acquiring a reputation for honesty generates more business and larger profits in the long run. Hence, from a superficial perspective, it may appear that it doesn't matter why the shopkeeper is honest, either through calculation or character, since the ultimate result is the same.

But Smith argued that the two approaches are starkly different in terms of motivations and ultimate effects. A calculating person will always wonder whether it makes sense to steal, producing conduct of a 'much inferior order' ([1759] 1982, p. 263). By contrast, a person of character is honest for the love of virtue. Virtue includes an appropriate regard for one's own interests. However, one's interests are circumscribed by moral norms and conscience. Smith had no illusions that business people were virtuously motivated, which is why he strongly emphasized the importance of checks and balances using competitive markets. Still, virtue plays a role in the invisible hand by lowering transaction costs and enhancing wealth.

Conclusion: reconciling ethical views
One complaint that teachers may raise against discussing ethics in economics is that it lies outside the boundary of their specialization. A second is that economic theory provides definitive guidance to policymakers regarding what is efficient. Expanding the discussion to alternative ethical frameworks, as suggested here, might open a Pandora's box, because in a relative sense no ethical approach can be found superior to any other.

These are troubling concerns, but the alternative – to ignore ethics – seems even more problematical. Indeed, the American Economic Association warned against producing graduates who were '*idiot savants*, skilled in technique but innocent of real economic issues' (Barber 1997, p. 98). Public policy debates occur within a multidimensional ethical framework. Economists play an important role in assessing efficiency, but it abrogates pedagogical duty to argue that this limited approach is sufficient for helping students reach conclusions about complex public policy issues.

Yet how can students reconcile conflicting ethical views? Students may ask, for example, how a president could endorse the use of torture in interrogating prisoners (justified by a predominant concern for outcomes) and at the same time oppose stem cell research (based on a predominant duty to uphold human rights). These are incongruous ethical stances. Such incongruity is common, however, and to force students into positions of internal consistency would likely offer a false model. Kenneth Boulding (1969) disclosed how conflicted he was in the autumn of 1968 when, as President of the American Economic Association, he had to decide whether to keep the ASSA convention in Chicago, where police abuses of human rights had been alleged at the Democratic Convention held there that summer. Many exerted pressure to boycott the city in protest. Boulding concluded that as an individual his duty would be to stay away from Chicago; however, he came to see that leaders have a different obligation, namely to consider the outcomes for all members. He thus decided to hold the meetings as scheduled. Through a critical thinking process, students too can come to recognize when it is appropriate to rely on one, versus another, ethical approach. A rational consistency can be foolish (to borrow from Sen 1977).

If the goal is to develop critical thinking skills, students should be aware of the ethical dimensions of positive economics; they should be able to place the study of economic efficiency within the context of wider normative goals; and – whether or not they are experts – they should understand the duty-based and virtue-based modes of thinking that inform many worldviews, and learn how to debate public policy issues using them. Teachers interested in introducing some of these ideas into the classroom have available in Wight and Morton (2007) a mix of ten lessons that contain step-by-step instructions.

Note

1. For example, Princeton, Notre Dame, Richmond, California-Riverside Erasmus, Nijmegen, Gothenburg, Lahore and others. Some philosophy departments also offer courses on economics and ethics (for example, the University of Wisconsin-Madison and City University of New York).

References

Barber, William J. (1997), 'Reconfigurations in American academic economics: a general practitioner's perspective', *Daedelus* (Winter), 87–104.
Boulding, Kenneth E. (1969), 'Economics as a moral science', *American Economic Review*, **59** (1), 1–12.
Dickens, Charles (1854), *Hard Times,* The Literature Network, www.online-literature.com/dickens/hard-times/2/, 18 July 2007.
Frank, Robert H. (1996), 'Do economists make bad citizens?' *Journal of Economic Perspectives*, **10** (Winter), 187–92.
Frank, Robert H., Thomas D. Gilovich and Dennis T. Regan (1993), 'Does studying economics inhibit cooperation?' *Journal of Economic Perspectives*, **7** (Spring), 159–71.
Hausman, Daniel M. and Michael S. McPherson (1993), 'Taking ethics seriously: economics and contemporary moral philosophy', *Journal of Economic Literature*, **31**(June), 671–731.
Keynes, John Maynard ([1936] 1964), *A General Theory of Employment, Interest, and Money*, New York: Harcourt, Brace & World.
McCloskey, Deirdre (1998), *The Rhetoric of Economics*, 2nd edition, Madison, WI: University of Wisconsin Press.
Sen, Amartya (1977), 'Rational fools: a critique of the behavioral foundations of economic theory', *Philosophy and Public Affairs*, **6** (Summer), 317–44.

Smith, Adam ([1759] 1982), *The Theory of Moral Sentiments*, reprinted in D.D. Raphael and A.L. Macfie (eds), Indianapolis, IN: Liberty Fund.

Smith, Adam ([1795] 1982), 'The history of astronomy', in William P.D. Wightman and J.C. Bryce (eds), *Essays on Philosophical Subjects,* Indianapolis, IN: Liberty Fund, pp. 33–105.

Solomon, W. David (1998), 'Normative ethical theories', in Charles K. Wilber (ed.), *Economics, Ethics, and Public Policy*, Lanham, MD: Rowman & Littlefield, pp. 119–38.

United Nations (1948), *Universal Declaration of Human Rights*, www.un.org/Overview/rights.html, 12 July 2007.

Weisstein, Eric W. (n.d.), 'Rabbit-duck illusion', MathWorld: A Wolfram web resource. http://mathworld.wolfram.com/Rabbit-DuckIllusion.html, July 2007.

Wight, Jonathan B. (2002), *Saving Adam Smith: A Tale of Wealth, Transformation, and Virtue*, Upper Saddle River, NJ: Prentice Hall.

Wight, Jonathan B. and John S. Morton (2007), *Teaching the Ethical Foundations of Economics*, New York: The National Council on Economic Education.

See also the entries on: Code of ethics for economists; Efficiency; Epistemology; Positive versus normative economics; Rhetoric.

71 Trust
Bart Nooteboom

What is trust?

We need trust when we are vulnerable to the behaviour of others (Deutsch 1962). Trust enables us to believe that despite such vulnerability 'things will go well'. But we are vulnerable to many things, in many ways; and trust may emerge for different reasons.

First there is the question of whom we can trust. We can trust people, but also organizations and institutions (such as the legal-judicial system, in 'system trust') (Luhmann 1979). For collaboration between firms, we must be able to trust the people we are dealing with, as well as the corresponding organization. If we trust people but they are not backed by their superiors and co-workers, our trust becomes less meaningful. Conversely, we may trust an organization, for example, on the basis of its reputation. But if its policy is not reliably implemented by its people, that trust too has little meaning. In small owner-managed firms, personal and organizational trust come together in one. In larger companies, we must be able to trust the people, the organization and between them the connections which arise in the positions and roles of people, organizational procedures and organizational culture (Ring and van de Ven 1994).

Second is the question of what in people or organizations we can trust. We can trust competence, that is, the ability to act according to agreements and expectations. We can also trust intentions, meaning the will to act 'properly', with attention and commitment and 'benevolence' (lack of opportunism, absence of cheating). This distinction goes back to Parsons (Lane 2000). The difference between trust in competence and trust in intentions is important. If something goes wrong due to a lack of competence, we react differently to when something goes wrong due to cheating. In the first case we may invest in better competence, for example, with training or advice. In the latter case we might set up a tighter contract. We might trust in others' competence but not in their intentions, or vice versa. Concerning partners, we need to trust both their competence and their intentions. Concerning rivals, if we do not trust their intentions, we may hope they are *not* very competent. If we trust the integrity of the police, we would like to also trust their competence. If we think the police are corrupt, we may hope they are *not* competent. We want competent partners and incompetent rivals.

Trust suffers from 'causal ambiguity'; that is, when something goes wrong, we often do not know what went awry and why. It may have been due to a mishap, an accident, a lack of competence, a lack of attention or opportunism. This has important implications, as we will see.

Is there a difference between trust and control? (In this regard see Das and Teng 1998, 2001; Bachmann 2000; Maguire et al. 2001; Reed 2001; Klein Woolthuis et al. 2005.) Can we speak of trust when 'proper' behaviour is enforced by contract or by hierarchy? What about when trust is based on control by material incentives, such as profit? If we define trust widely as the expectation that despite risk in relations 'things will go well', for whatever reason, this would include control. Control causes people to behave well because they are forced to do so by, for example, contract or the governing hierarchy, or because it is profitable for them to do so. Is that trust? Or should we speak of trust only if expectations of 'proper behaviour' go beyond control, to the confidence that people will act in a reliable fashion not because they must, but because they want to, based on intrinsic motives of ethical conduct or solidarity? Then trust is defined as the expectation that things 'will go well' even if the partner has both the opportunity and the incentive to cheat or to be sloppy (compare Bradach and Eccles 1984; Chiles and McMackin 1996). Here, trust means, for example, that we would not expect partners to walk out ('exit') the moment a more profitable opportunity arises elsewhere. We expect them to first warn us, and give us an opportunity ('voice') to jointly improve the relationship (Hirschman 1970; Helper 1990).

These intricacies cause great confusion about trust. When X is said to be trustworthy, the intended meaning might be that X is competent. Yet another person might take this to mean that X will not cheat. If the speaker means intentions rather than competence, the meaning might actually be that X is bound by a contract, or that it is in X's own interest to act properly, or that X will be loyal even if both the opportunity and the incentive arise to cheat. What one means by a statement of trust, therefore, depends on culture and circumstances. This ambiguity has caused many tragic and costly misunderstandings. A simple question as to what extent people are trustworthy, without clarification of exactly what is meant, will inevitably lead to different interpretations for different people, depending on the context. In surveys, answers to questions of trust are highly dependent on how the question is formulated, framed and positioned with respect to other questions.

To avoid this confusion, I propose use of the words 'trust' and 'trustworthiness' only to refer to dependability beyond the power of control, and use of the terms 'reliance' and 'reliability' when the meaning includes control (Nooteboom 2003). In other words, reliance is based on control or on trust, or on both.

Problems of collaboration

Successful collaboration has many benefits and is indispensable especially for innovation, hence the present trend of 'open innovation'. Clearly, however, collaboration also has its problems.

One problem is a potential lack of mutual understanding or 'absorptive capacity'. This is especially the case in processes of innovation, when knowledge and competencies are under development. Things are new and unfamiliar, and a common language must still be derived. On the one hand we need partners with different knowledge, at some 'cognitive distance', in order to learn from them and produce novelty together. But we also need to understand them to be able to collaborate, so the cognitive distance must not be too large. This leads to the idea of an 'optimal cognitive distance', which should be large enough to yield novelty, but not so large as to block mutual understanding and ability to collaborate (Nooteboom 1999).

The ability to understand and collaborate with others is not fixed, but increases with experience in collaboration with people who think differently. Such experience enables us to deal with larger cognitive distance, and it increases our innovative performance. People who are open and tolerant and have built up experience in using diversity creatively therefore have what could be termed an innovation bonus. In sum, there is economic benefit in an ethic and capability of openness and of understanding people who think differently. Cognitive distance can then be transformed from a problem into a competitive advantage.

A second problem in collaboration for innovation is risk of 'spillover', that is, competitive advantage from commercially valuable new knowledge or competence may 'leak' to competitors. Partners may thus become competitors. One partner may also be linked with one or more competitors, providing routes for sensitive knowledge to escape to them. Such spillover risk may or may not be present. Often the risk is overestimated. The risk is small if competitors cannot absorb any information they might receive, or if by the time they would be able to make use of the knowledge, new insights have made the knowledge obsolete. As such, a rapid speed of change can enhance openness.

A third risk arises from dependence on a partner, whereby loss occurs when the relationship breaks. In other words, costs are involved when switching to a different partner. Investments that are useful only in a specific relationship have to be made anew for a new partner. These so-called 'specific investments' can be in facilities, installations, instruments and training (Williamson 1975), but also in mutual understanding and the building of trust (Nooteboom 2003). Often, understanding and trust are built up in a specific relationship and apply only then and there. People are generally willing to make specific investments only when they expect that the relationship will last sufficiently long, and will be sufficiently fruitful, to make the investment worthwhile.

The implication is that people should not go for maximum flexibility, but rather, for optimal flexibility of relationships. Maximum flexibility yields superficial associations. Yet economic and strategic policy is increasingly based on a rhetoric of flexibility. The implicit claim hereby is that greater flexibility is associated with more innovation, as it enables 'novel combinations'. But we make specific investments in a relationship only when we are confident that the partnership will last long enough to recoup the investment. So the value of flexibility must be seen as being limited. Too high flexibility discourages the specific investments needed for collaboration, especially for innovation.

Limits of trust

To deal with relational risks we can try to impose control, but control is never perfect, especially in innovation. Innovation implies too great uncertainty to manage all risks by contract, monitoring and control. Innovation requires creativity, which necessitates freedom of action. Thus, where control ends trust needs to begin. But trust cannot be unconditional, because trustworthiness has limits. People may not be trustworthy, by inclination, by experience or because of the conditions they must cope with.

Trustworthiness also requires reciprocity, give-and-take. That might necessitate the surrender of some opportunities for profit, for the sake of the partner or the relationship. It is unrealistic to expect sacrifices if they entail disaster for a partner, in the form of loss of a job (for personal trust) or bankruptcy of the firm (for trust in a firm). Can we expect even our best friends to sacrifice themselves for our sake? Is that an ethical expectation? Aristotelian ethics requires tolerance of the 'fragility of goodness' (Nussbaum 2000). The implication is that generally people are less trustworthy when their existence or job 'is on the line', and firms are less trustworthy when subject to intense pressures of price competition. The more intense the competition, therefore, the less trustworthy firms will be (Pettit 1995). As a result, we may trust someone under certain conditions but not in

Table 71.1   Sources of reliability

	Micro (Relational)	Macro (Institutional)
Control		
Opportunity control	Hierarchy, managerial 'fiat'	Contracts, legal enforcement
Incentive control	Dependence, hostages, bonus schemes	Reputation
Trust	Empathy, identification, routinization, friendship	Values, social norms of proper conduct, moral obligation, sense of duty, bonds of kinship

Source: Adapted from Nooteboom (2003).

another situation. We must be aware of the survival pressures on partners and of their ability to withstand such pressure.

In a trusting relationship, partners discuss problems openly ('voice') (Hirschman 1970; Zand 1972; Helper 1990). When that does not work and the relationship cannot be repaired, one withdraws from the relationship ('exit'). Trust is not equivalent to just 'being nice' to each other. In fact, partners can express intense differences of opinion precisely because they trust each other. And trust deepens when conflict is resolved using 'voice' (Six 2005). In other words, trust needs to be active. It requires effort, attention and commitment to build and maintain.

A second limit to trust, of a very different sort, is that it may go too far. Partners may take a relationship and its continuation for granted, so that they become blind to more innovative or profitable alternatives. In other words, too much trust and loyalty can generate rigidity and lack of innovation. This is sometimes seen in family businesses. Family relations can also be a source of strong tension and conflict when intertwined in business, because exit from the relationship is not an option, and criticism is often hidden to protect sensibilities.

If a long-term relationship is exclusive, cognitive distance declines over time, and partners no longer have anything new to tell each other. The relationship then runs out of innovative steam (Wuyts et al. 2005). However, if the relationship is nonexclusive and partners tap into other, non-overlapping sources of variety, the relationship is continually fed with new impulses and insights and can remain innovative over a longer time.

Foundations of reliability

How can we solve problems of collaboration? What instruments are there to manage or 'govern' relational risks? On what basis can we rely on partners: based on control or trust or both? There are underlying psychological mechanisms that *cause* people to trust, or not. Even though trust is often based on information, there is no certainty about behaviour. One has to surrender to uncertainty with a 'leap of faith' or by accepting the 'suspension' of doubt. This idea goes back to Simmel (Lane 2000; Möllering 2006).

The focus chosen here, however, is on rational *reasons* for people or business partners to be reliable. Table 71.1 provides an overview. In the two columns, the table distinguishes reasons for reliability on two levels: within a relationship (micro) and within its institutional environment (macro). The rows in the table distinguish between control and trust.

One type of control is *opportunity control*. Here the action space is limited, either by contracts invoking the law (outside of a relationship) or by hierarchy (power within a relationship). A second type of control is *incentive control*, in which actions are shaped by rewards. Within a relationship this may be a result of dependence, for example, a partner who is dependent is more inclined to take the interests of the other into account. Dependence may be due to the unique value the partner offers or to specific investments that have been made in the relationship. A partner may also be dependent on another because the one has control over something that is of value to the other, but not to themselves. The partner in control of this 'hostage' would not hesitate to destroy it if the other partner behaves badly. Such 'hostages' may take the form of a minority shareholding that could be sold to someone wanting to use it for a hostile takeover of the partner. More often, the hostage has the form of commercially sensitive information that could be leaked to a competitor of the partner. Another form of incentive control is reputation, which is a matter of self-interest: the partner behaves well because bad behaviour would destroy the prospect of an ongoing relationship as well as possibly fruitful relations with others.

Ethics, empathy and routinization

Beyond control, the lower part of the table presents some bases for trustworthiness. Trust and trustworthiness begin where control ends, and may help to reduce the need for control. Trustworthiness may be the result of shared social *norms and values*. This is where ethics comes in. One reason why ethics is important in economics is that it forms part of the basis of trust. Values and norms may be based on an ethic that is shared prior to the relationship, but they may also develop as the relationship progresses.

Another ethical principle associated with trust is that trust works as a default: trustworthiness is taken for granted until violated. Distrust keeps one from engaging in relationships that may prove distrust wrong, showing that in fact people are trustworthy to a greater or lesser extent. Trust, on the other hand, is subject to correction: when in fact people turn out to be less trustworthy than assumed, one can revise one's expectations.

A further ethical principle associated with trust concerns the importance of openness (Zand 1972) and of granting the benefit of the doubt, in view of the 'causal ambiguity' of trust. When something goes wrong, the cause is not immediately apparent: a mishap or accident, a shortfall of competence, lack of attention or outright opportunism. Rather than immediately assuming the worst, trust obliges one to extend the benefit of doubt and allow partners to explain. Conversely, when a mishap or shortfall of competence occurs, partners must immediately be informed, with the offer to jointly prevent or redress damage. Openness and allowance, even encouragement, of partners to voice intentions and concerns, and willingness to accept partners' influence form key preconditions for trust (Zand 1972).

Another principle with ethical implications is *empathy*, defined as the ability to place oneself in the shoes of another, to understand their needs, weaknesses and strengths, to understand what 'makes the partner tick'. Empathy enhances trust, providing insight on why things might go wrong and what motives or pressures might cause a partner to fall short or to succumb to pressures of circumstance. Empathy can yield forgiveness. It may also lead to *identification*, which is the sense of a shared destiny and an incorporation of partners' needs or goals into one's own (McAllister 1995; Lewicki and Bunker 1996) and 'ticking in the same way'.

Trust and trustworthiness may also arise from sheer *routinization*, where things are taken for granted since nothing has gone wrong before. In this case, we might lose awareness of the possibility of failure (Gulati 1995; Nooteboom et al. 1997). Where identification and routinization are ingrained, trust can be taken too far. Relationships then are taken for granted and fail to be subjected to critical scrutiny, which may yield a lack of flexibility and closure to novel opportunities.

Third parties, or go-betweens, can play a valuable role in managing collaboration (Nooteboom 2003). For the control of conflict there is the possibility of arbitration or intermediation. But the roles of go-betweens extend beyond that. Where there is causal ambiguity, a go-between may help to clarify a situation. Furthermore, regular review of a partnership by a go-between can prevent misunderstandings from triggering vicious cycles of mistrust that escalate beyond repair. Another role for a go-between is to support a reliable reputation mechanism: to verify accusations of opportunism or incompetence and broadcast them to all relevant parties. However, go-betweens may themselves be unreliable, leading the issue of reliability to reappear on a different level (Shapiro 1987).

In sum, there are many ways to manage relational risk. There is no single best way. Solutions need to be tailored to conditions. Table 71.1 offers a toolbox from which to configure instruments suited to specific situations, taking due care that instruments reinforce rather than contradict one another. Where there is a lack of adequate outside institutions (legal system, reputation mechanisms, shared behavioural norms and values) the foundations of reliability must be built into specific relationships. If sources of trustworthiness are absent one must be able to fall back on control. Contracts make no sense without an appropriate legal and judiciary basis, and they are of limited value where there is insufficient information and knowledge on contract design or compliance monitoring. Due to the volatility of technology and markets this is particularly the case in partnerships for innovation. Reputation mechanisms can be valuable, but they cannot be taken for granted. As indicated earlier, one may need intermediaries to make partnerships work. Such intermediaries might already be in place, in the form of professional or trade associations. If not, they have to be arranged as part of the relationship.

Trust and control can both replace and support one another. More trust allows for less control. But since trust and control are both limited, one needs to start where the other ends. Contracts should not go so far as to break down the basis of trust. Trust may precede as well as follow contracts (Klein Woolthuis et al. 2005).

It is important to achieve some balance of dependence and power among partners. Unbalanced relationships are difficult to sustain. Balance is not needed for each instrument separately, but it should be achieved in the mix. If one partner is more dependent because specific investments in the relationship lie mostly on their side, balance may be achieved by sharing the ownership of those assets, or by compensation with another instrument, for example, by holding a 'hostage' from the other party. Unbalanced relationships are especially problematic when the most dependent party lacks self-confidence or suffers from the 'Calimero syndrome' of feeling small and vulnerable. This often jeopardizes relationships between small and large firms.

Conclusions

Uncertainty is too great to manage risk by contractual control only. Trust is therefore needed. But trust cannot be unconditional. Survival pressures limit the trustworthiness of partners. Therefore, some balance is needed between trust and control in managing relationships. Too much trust, for instance, in routinized relationships, can lead to rigidity and smother innovation.

For control, we might choose a contract or hierarchy based on (majority) ownership, reputation, a balance of mutual dependence or hostages. Trust may be based on a shared ethic, with common norms and values of conduct, on routinization, or on personalized relations of empathy or identification. Trust may be supported by go-betweens, to solve conflicts, but also to prevent their occurrence by helping to reduce the causal ambiguity inherent in trust and to eliminate mistaken suspicions of opportunism arising from mere mishaps. Also in view of causal ambiguity, it is important for partners to exercise 'voice', to signal problems and suspicions, giving associates opportunities to redress them. Partners need the ability to imagine themselves in the shoes of, for example, customers, and to look at themselves from the perspective of others.

The chosen instruments of trust and control must be well mixed. Heavy emphasis on contracts for the sake of control can destroy the basis of trust. An attractive instrument of control is a balance of dependence. People hereby invest in competence to make themselves of unique, indispensable value to their partner, who responds in the same fashion, yielding an association of unique value. The problem is that such associations are vulnerable to unforeseen shifts, such as changes in technology and markets. Therefore, any balance of dependence must be complemented by a reputation mechanism or trust.

Trust and ethics are connected in many ways. Trust often requires shared norms and values. In view of causal ambiguity, trust requires openness, ability to extend the benefit of doubt and empathy.

References

Bachmann, Reinhard (2000), 'Conclusion: trust – conceptual aspects of a complex phenomenon', in Christel Lane and Reinhard Bachmann, *Trust within and between Organizations*, Oxford: Oxford University Press, pp. 298–322.

Bradach, Jeffrey L. and Robert G. Eccles (1984), 'Markets versus hierarchies: from ideal types to plural forms', *Annual Review of Sociology*, **15**, 97–118.

Chiles, Todd H. and John F. McMackin (1996), 'Integrating variable risk preferences, trust and transaction cost economics', *Academy of Management Review*, **21** (7), 73–99.

Das, T.K. and B.S. Teng (1998), 'Between trust and control: developing confidence in partner cooperation in alliances', *Academy of Management Review*, **23** (3), 491–512.

Das, T.K. and B.S. Teng (2001), 'Trust, control and risk in strategic alliances: an integrated framework', *Organization Studies*, **22** (2), 251–84.

Deutsch, Morton (1962), 'Cooperation and trust: some theoretical notes', in Marshall R. Jones (ed.), *Nebraska Symposium on Motivation*, Lincoln, NE: University of Nebraska Press, pp. 275–319.

Deutsch, Morton (1973), *The Resolution of Conflict: Constructive and Destructive Processes*, New Haven, CT: Yale University Press.

Gulati, Ranjay (1995), 'Does familiarity breed trust? The implications of repeated ties for contractual choice in alliances', *Academy of Management Journal*, **30** (1), 85–112.

Helper, Susan (1990), 'Comparative supplier relations in the US and Japanese auto industries: an exit/voice approach', *Business and Economic History*, **19**, 1–10.

Hirschman, Albert O. (1970), *Exit, Voice and Loyalty: Responses to Decline in Firms, Organisations and States*, Cambridge, MA: Harvard University Press

Klein Woolthuis, Rosalinde, Bas Hillebrand and Bart Nooteboom (2005), 'Trust, contract and relationship development', *Organization Studies*, **26** (6), 813–40.

Lane, Christel (2000). *Trust within and between Organizations*, paperback edition, Oxford: Oxford University Press.

Lewicki, Roy J. and Barbara B. Bunker (1996), 'Developing and maintaining trust in work relationships', in Roderick M. Kramer and Tom R. Tyler (eds), *Trust in Organizations: Frontiers of Theory and Research*, Thousand Oaks, CA: Sage Publications, pp. 114–39.

Luhmann, Niklas (1979), *Trust and Power*, Chichester: Wiley.

Maguire, Steve, Nelson Philips and Cynthia Hardy (2001), 'When "silence = death", keep talking: trust, control and the discursive construction of identity in the Canadian HIV/AIDS treatment domain', *Organization Studies*, **22** (2), 285–310.

McAllister, Daniel J. (1995), 'Affect- and cognition-based trust as foundations for interpersonal cooperation in organizations', *Academy of Management Journal*, **38** (1), 24–59.

Möllering. Guido (2006), *Trust: Reason, Routine, Reflexivity*, Amsterdam: Elsevier.

Nooteboom, Bart (1999), *Inter-Firm Alliances: Analysis and Design*, London: Routledge.

Nooteboom, Bart (2000), 'Institutions and forms of co-ordination in innovation systems', *Organization Studies*, **21** (5), 915–39.

Nooteboom, Bart (2003), *Trust: Forms, Foundations, Functions, Failures and Figures*, paperback edition, Cheltenham, UK and Northampton, MA, USA: Edward Elgar.

Nooteboom, Bart, J. Berger and N.G. Noorderhaven (1997), 'Effects of trust and governance on relational risk', *Academy of Management Journal*, **40** (2), 308–38.

Nussbaum, Martha (2000), *The Fragility of Goodness*, 2nd edition, Cambridge: Cambridge University Press.

Pettit, Philip (1995), 'The virtual reality of *homo economicus*', *The Monist*, **78** (3), 308–29.

Reed, Michael I. (2001), 'Organization, trust and control: a realist analysis', *Organization Studies*, **22** (2), 201–28.

Ring, Peter S. and Andrew H. van de Ven (1994), 'Developmental processes of cooperative interorganizational relationships', *Academy of Management Review*, **19** (1), 90–118.

Shapiro, Susan P. (1987), 'The social control of impersonal trust', *American Journal of Sociology*, **93**, 623–58.

Six, Frederique E. (2005), *The Trouble about Trust: The Dynamics of Interpersonal Trust Building*, Cheltenham, UK and Northampton, MA, USA: Edward Elgar.

Williamson, Oliver E. (1975), *Markets and Hierarchies*, New York: Free Press.

Wuyts, Stefan, Massimo Colombo, Shantanu Dutta and Bart Nooteboom (2005), 'Empirical tests of optimal cognitive distance', *Journal of Economic Behaviour and Organization*, **58** (2), 277–302.

Zand, Dale E. (1972), 'Trust and managerial problem solving', *Administrative Science Quarterly*, **17** (2), 229–39.

See also the entries on: Institutions; Social capital.

72 Utilitarianism
Johan J. Graafland

Introduction

The basic principle of utilitarianism is 'the greatest happiness for the greatest number'. Or, more formally, an act is right if and only if the sum total of utilities produced by that act is greater than the sum total of utilities produced by any other act the agent could have performed in its place (Velasquez 1998, p. 73). Recent improvements in measuring happiness have increased the popularity of utilitarianism among economists. According to Layard (2003, p. 50), utilitarianism is the only ethical standard that provides an overarching principle by which to solve conflicts between principles.

A practical method of applying utilitarianism is by cost-benefit analysis. The basic procedure of cost-benefit analysis is as follows. If we must decide whether to perform action A, the rule is perform A if the benefits for present and future populations exceed those of the next best alternative course of action; if this is not the case, do not perform A. For this purpose, numerical values are assigned to costs and benefits of performing an action. After adding these, one should accept the project with the greatest net benefits.

Utilitarianism has great practical value. It is consistent with the value of efficiency and in harmony with the way policymakers often make up their minds by looking at the beneficial and harmful consequences of a particular act. It also stimulates decision-makers to conduct a systematic overview of the benefits and costs of an act. Economic policy bureaus increasingly use cost-benefit analysis to evaluate policy options. Still, the method is subject to serious moral criticism. In particular, utilitarianism on occasion seems to disregard the human rights of individuals, to neglect distributive justice and to legitimize immoral preferences. This reduces its applicability and legitimacy as a moral standard.

This chapter examines utilitarianism in relation to ethics and economics. First, it describes three characteristics of utilitarianism: consequentialism, welfarism and sum ranking. It then recounts several criticisms of utilitarianism as an ethical theory. The conclusion places utilitarianism in a hierarchy of values.

Characteristics of utilitarianism

Utilitarianism essentially combines three elementary requirements: consequentialism, welfarism and sum ranking (Sen 1987, p. 39).

Consequentialism

Consequentialism asserts that actions, choices or policies must be morally judged exclusively in terms of the resulting, or consequent, effects, rather than by any intrinsic features they may have. Outcome matters – not process, intention or motivation. Since the consequences of an action are almost always uncertain, most utilitarians speak of the expected outcomes of actions. The expected outcome of an action is calculated by multiplying the value of the outcome by the probability of its occurring. In a consequentialist argument, the entire focus is therefore on future consequences of choices, actions or policies.

Utilitarianism does not look back to the past, as deontological theories might, to judge whether a certain policy can be justified.

Welfarism
Utilitarianism's second characteristic is welfarism. Welfarism is the answer to the question, 'What are good consequences?' What is the value of an outcome? Welfarism requires that the goodness of a state of affairs be a function only of the utility or welfare obtained by individuals in that state. But what is welfare? In this respect, there are different varieties of utilitarianism (Beauchamp 1982, pp. 138 ff.) Some take welfare to be a mental state, like happiness or pleasure. This is expressed by Jeremy Bentham, who claimed that pleasure is a kind of sensation. Since all pleasures and all pains are structurally similar sensations, it should be possible to calculate a net total sum of utility.[1] Thus, Bentham applies a monistic concept of utility by assuming that all values can be measured on the same scale of pleasure (and pain). The other major exponent of utilitarianism, John Stuart Mill (1871), also believed pleasure and prevention of pain to be the only desirable ends, but he distinguished higher and lower pleasures and argued that higher pleasures are qualitatively different from lower pleasures. Pluralist utilitarian philosophers such as G.E. Moore go one step further and argue that there is no single goal and that many other values besides happiness possess intrinsic worth, such as friendship, knowledge, love, courage, health, beauty and moral qualities such as fairness (Beauchamp 1982, p. 141).

Economists try to avoid taking a position in this philosophical debate by arguing that any assessment of individual welfare should be based on a person's own judgement, because it is difficult and perhaps impossible to determine objectively the value of an outcome. Utility should instead be equated to the satisfaction of individuals' actual preferences. Thus, economists prefer a formal theory of well-being instead of a substantive theory. Formal theories find out which things are intrinsically good for people by deriving their preferences from their behaviour (Hausman and McPherson 1996, p. 72). Utility is understood as a formal attribute, a common denominator, according to which all specific quests for satisfaction can be ranked. This approach, then, avoids the discussion between hedonistic and pluralistic views of intrinsic value. What is intrinsically valuable for an individual is that which each individual actually prefers to obtain.

In order to measure individual preferences, cost-benefit analysis uses individuals' willingness to pay as a monetary metric for utility. The willingness to pay for a certain policy is usually derived from studies of market transactions in which individuals voluntarily trade commodified versions of goods against money. Apart from the fact that it is costly to ask people how much they would pay or how much compensation they would require, economists consider market information reliably to reflect authentic individual preferences. Valuations expressed in questionnaires or public debate may, after all, be biased by strategic considerations. In accordance with the theory of revealed preference, economists attempt to define preferences in terms of real choices. Choosing x when one might have had y at a lower cost reveals a preference for x over y.

Sum ranking
The third and most decisive characteristic of utilitarianism is sum ranking. Sum ranking means that the effects of an action on the utilities of all who are affected by it must be aggregated and numerically ranked. This allows identification of the choice, action or policy that maximizes

the total sum of utilities. Even though individualistic experiences or valuations form the sole basis for evaluating an action or policy, utilitarianism is not an egoistic ethical theory. The fundamental thesis of utilitarianism is that one should do whatever maximizes the total sum of utilities. Actions and policies are evaluated on the basis of the benefits and the costs they will impose on all who are affected. So, utilitarianism requires decision-makers to be strictly impartial, disinterested and perfectly sympathetic spectators who identify with and experience the desires of all others as if those desires were their own (Rawls 1999, p. 24).

Sum ranking may have drastic consequences. An example is development aid. Maximizing total welfare means that the marginal utility of different persons should be equalized. Assuming declining marginal utility from income, substantive variants of utilitarianism hold that income should be redistributed until the marginal utility from additional income is equal for all persons. If we can agree that suffering and death from lack of food, shelter and medical care are bad, utilitarianism then implies that development aid should be substantially raised if it succeeds in preventing this suffering without sacrificing anything of comparable moral importance. As Singer (1972, p. 30) states, one ought to give to the poor up to the point at which by giving more one would begin to cause more suffering for oneself than one would prevent for the receiver of the gift. Aiding the poor is in this strict utilitarian reasoning not a supererogatory act, but a moral duty: we ought to give money to lift the poor from their need, and it is wrong not to do so.

Criticisms of utilitarianism
Utilitarianism and cost-benefit analysis are subject to several serious criticisms. These criticisms can be categorized according to the three characteristics of utilitarianism mentioned above. Table 72.1 presents an overview.

Problems of consequentialism
A first fundamental criticism of consequentialism is that it fails to consider the intentions of the person performing the act, only the consequences of the act. Immanuel Kant stated

Table 72.1   Problems of utilitarianism

Consequentialism	Welfarism		Sum Ranking
	(All variants)	(Formal variant)	
No consideration of intentions	Well-being is not the only valuable thing, agency is disregarded	Immoral preferences Non-rational preferences No community valuation	No distributive justice How to discount the utility of future generations or non-human beings?
Disregards retributive justice	Utility does not adequately represent well-being		Is over-demanding
Consequences are difficult to predict	Problem of incommensurability No intrinsic value of rights		

Source: Adapted from Table 7.1 in Graafland (2007).

the importance of intentions for a moral evaluation of actions, as did other philosophers such as David Hume and Adam Smith. In Kant's view, the intention of an action is morally good only if the person's intention is to uphold moral law (Henson 1979, p. 40). In contrast to Kant, Hume argues that a good intention means that a person likes to do the right actions voluntarily; acting well merely because obligation requires it is not sufficient. Being moved by natural sympathy rather than obligation is clearly virtuous. Yet, natural sympathy has no clear moral place in Kant's philosophy.

A second problem is that consequentialism abstracts from considerations of retributive justice. Retributive justice refers to the just imposition of punishments upon those who do wrong. Take, for example, the fining policy of antitrust regulatory bodies. In a utilitarian framework, the entire focus is on the consequences of such a policy in the future. Will the fines deter companies from illegal anti-competitive practices? What if companies are unable to pay the fines and go bankrupt? To what extent will that make the victims happier? But the question of whether the companies deserve to pay compensation for the harm done to others is not taken into account. Thus, utilitarianism disregards the idea that justice should be done by punishing criminals for their harmful behaviour towards victims in the past.

A final problem is that consequences of an action, and hence the costs and benefits it generates, are difficult to predict and subject to different degrees of uncertainty. In contrast to the first two criticisms, this third criticism is not a fundamental problem that invalidates the logic of utilitarianism. Still, the uncertainty involved in predicting the possible consequences of a policy strongly diminishes the value of utilitarianism as an ethical standard compared to other, more deontological ethical standards.

Problems of welfarism
Utilitarianism can also be criticized because of problems resulting from considering welfare as the sole type of good consequences. Let us first discuss the problems that hold for all forms of utilitarianism. Next we describe problems that hold more specifically for the formal variant.

First, welfare, or happiness, as the effect or result of an action or policy is not the only relevant argument in an evaluation of that action or policy. Utility is, at best, a reflection of a person's well-being, that is, feelings about the consequences. But a person's success cannot be judged exclusively in terms of this well-being (Sen 1987, p. 40). Sen distinguishes between well-being and agency. If we view people in terms of agency, the focus is on their ability to form goals and commitments and on the way they perform. Although well-being and agency are related, they are also distinct. Sen gives the example of a commitment to fight for the independence of one's country. When that goal is realized, one also feels happier, but this achievement does not consist only of that happiness. MacLean (1994, p. 172) provides another example, that of rescue missions undertaken on the battlefield to retrieve the corpses of slain soldiers. Great risks are sometimes taken in such missions. It strains credibility to say that the benefit of retrieving corpses outweighs the cost to the soldiers who die in the effort. It is rather a matter of devotion and the sentiment of belonging to each other that require certain attitudes and actions. A commitment to one's family or one's friends can sometimes be a burden and exact a heavy personal toll. Sen (1987, p. 44) therefore concludes that a welfarist calculus which concentrates only on the well-being of the person, ignoring the agency aspect, loses something of real importance.

Second, utility may not adequately represent well-being, because what people perceive as pleasure or pain depends on their circumstances. Judging well-being by the mental metric of utility can become biased if the mental reactions reflect defeatist compromises with harsh reality (Sen 1984, p. 309). A homeless beggar may learn to manage to suppress intense suffering, but that does not imply that a correspondingly small value should be attached to the beggar's loss of their home. Valuation of well-being, thus, sometimes requires a more direct method of assessing the value of the consequences than the utility effects.

A third fundamental criticism is that welfarism assumes that different values are reducible to one basic value, namely utility. Values are, however, often incommensurable and pluralistic in nature, relating to several generic goods rather than only to a single one (Anderson 1993, p. 1).[2] Anderson offers two underlying reasons for incommensurability: (i) diversity in modes of valuation, meaning that people care about things in different ways, such as loving, respecting, using, tolerating and honouring; and (ii) diversity in social roles, meaning that a valuation depends on the social context. Diversity in modes of valuation is also apparent in cases of hierarchical incommensurability, where some values are seen as incomparably higher than others. Kant famously proclaimed that rational human beings have dignity and whatever has dignity is 'above all price, and therefore admits of no equivalent' (Kant 1997, p. 435). This implies that the safety of human lives cannot be traded against money. Cost-benefit analysis is unable to deal with these different types of valuation. The distinction between higher and lower goods may support norms that prohibit certain trade-offs between them.

A fourth criticism is that the utilitarian approach views rights merely as instrumental to achieving utilities. No intrinsic importance is attached to the fulfilment of rights. Utilitarianism might therefore imply that certain actions are morally right when in fact they violate people's rights. To illustrate, the utilitarian accepts torture if the torturer gains more than the tortured loses (Sen 1984, p. 194). In contrast, rights ethics would argue that the right to personal liberty of the tortured may not be violated. Furthermore, any pleasure derived from a violation of the rights of others is illegitimate and should not count in the total sum of utilities. Rights set absolute constraints on what types of measures are morally acceptable (Nozick 1974, p. 29).

Besides these fundamental criticisms of utilitarianism in general, additional criticisms apply especially to the formal variant of welfarism, which equates welfare with the satisfaction of the actual preferences of individuals.

First, individuals may have morally unacceptable preferences according to, say, standard group norms (Beauchamp 1982, p. 142). Utilitarianism based purely on subjective preferences is satisfactory, then, only if a range of acceptable values can be formulated, where acceptability is agent-neutral and thus not a matter of preferences. This is inconsistent with a pure preference approach, because this approach logically ties human values to preferences, which are by their nature not agent-neutral.

Second, relying on actual preferences or 'willingness to pay' scales assumes that individuals are rational in the sense that satisfaction of their preferences maximizes their well-being. Rationality is a rather strong assumption (Etzioni 1988, p. 114; Conlisk 1996, pp. 670 ff.; Rabin 1998, p. 24). People may prefer something that is bad for them because of ignorance or false beliefs (Hausman and McPherson 1996, p. 76). Conflicts between first-order preferences and meta-preferences may give rise to inconsistent behaviour, making it impossible to identify an agent's actual preferences. Some people want things precisely because they cannot have them (Schwarz 2004). Moreover, some parties are adept at manipulating people's preferences (for example, by advertisements) (Hausman 1992, p. 21). In order to value preferences for a certain state, any decision based on utilitarianism should therefore also be informed by the reasons behind the individual preferences. Cost-benefit analysis is only responsive to given wants, without evaluating the reasons people have for wanting the goods in question.

Third, one could doubt whether individual preference satisfaction should be the sole basis for evaluating social welfare. In communitarian ethics, individual preferences are not grounds for evaluation. What one ought to do is determined by the community. Whether moral rules serve the community well or ill is the critical factor in their acceptability. Only if communal relationships are good can individuals within the community develop their capacities. Communitarians, therefore, argue that individuals should develop a community ethos, based on the acknowledgment of a common fate and history and a patriotic identification with fellow citizens. Then they will be prepared to comply with the elementary civil duties that support the community (Vandevelde 2001, p. 20). These duties may go against individual preferences. Therefore, one could not take individuals' utility functions as the basis of evaluation.

Problems of sum ranking

A first criticism of sum ranking is that it may result in injustice and overrun the rights of minorities. In utilitarianism, principles of justice are dependent upon utility: a distribution of individual rights are only just if they maximize total utility. For instance, if a slave society produces the greatest happiness for the greatest number, the practice of slavery is just and morally obligatory (Beauchamp 1982, p. 159). This illustrates, once again, that utilitarianism disregards the intrinsic value of rights and the distinctness of individuals.

That applying utilitarianism may result in an unjust social distribution can be illustrated for cost-benefit analysis. If income or wealth is unequally distributed, the preferences of those with greater incomes will carry more weight than the preferences of those with lesser incomes, because the rich people would be more prepared to pay a high price for improving their utility than poor people. Thus, cost-benefit analysis reproduces the inequality of the status quo in its results. As such, the method can legitimate a policy that offends our intuition of distributive justice. Cost-benefit analysis sometimes counters this problem by using equivalence scales that correct for differences in the value of one unit of money for different groups of people. For example, the poor person's price may need to be valued more highly than the rich person's price by multiplying the first by a factor $s>1$. But how large should this factor be? The choice is arbitrary. Utilitarianism does not give a definitive solution to the problem of how to weigh the utilities of different income groups. Hence, cost-benefit analysis is not neutral on distributive questions.

Problems with distribution also arise if the utility of future generations or non-human beings is affected. Utilitarians often give less weight to the interests of future generations by applying a discount factor, but provide no grounds for determining the value of this factor. Also the interests of non-human beings might be given a lower weight than the interests of human beings; but again utilitarianism cannot provide a satisfactory answer to the question of how high this weight should be. These issues of fairness cannot be justified in utilitarian terms (Hausman and McPherson 1996, p. 103).

A third problem of sum ranking is that it is over-demanding. Utilitarianism requires that, other things being equal, I should value a certain utility equally, whether it is to be experienced by me, or by my friend, my relative or a complete stranger. Because of its impartiality, utilitarianism may become very demanding, especially in the non-ideal case when most people fail to live up to the moral duties it implies (Crisp 1998, p. 17). An example is that of famine relief, when only a few persons are actually contributing. If just a few people contribute, those who do contribute have to contribute much more to fight the famine. Even if a rich person has already donated half their income to the relief effort, their loss of utility from giving an additional amount is still less than the rise in utility of those who could survive thanks to the support. Utilitarianism holds that this support is obligatory, since it maximizes total utility. According to Williams (1973, p. 116), this might endanger the personal integrity of the donator. He believes that people have certain 'ground projects' that are so central and important to their lives that they should not be required to give them up just because the utilitarian calculation happens to come out that way. Compelling a person to give up ground projects robs them of their personal integrity. This has become known as 'the integrity objection' (Crisp 1998, p. 28). In order to diminish the problem of utilitarianism being over-demanding, Scheffler (1994, p. 20), for example, proposed that each agent be allowed to give a higher weight to their own interests than to the interests of other people. However, again utilitarianism provides no procedure for determining the exact amount of this weight.

Conclusion

As the moral objections show, utilitarianism fails to give a fully satisfactory theoretical account of our moral intuitions. Still, as long as we remain aware of the criticisms, the application of utilitarianism to economic policies by means of cost-benefit analysis does have profound advantages and is of great practical use. The method is consistent with the way many people make decisions, namely, by looking at the beneficial and harmful consequences of a particular action. Furthermore, it takes economics one step further towards normative economics. In economic welfare theory, sum ranking is not allowed. Hence, only policies that make one or more people better off without making anyone worse off are allowed (Pareto improvement). True Pareto improvements are, of course, very rare, because often there is no such thing as a free lunch. The Pareto principle is therefore strongly biased to the status quo. Unlike purely Paretian welfare economics, utilitarianism allows comparisons of policy alternatives that are not Pareto superior to each other (Hausman and McPherson 1996, p. 114). Also, in evaluating economic policies, some of the problems of utilitarianism, such as incommensurability, may be less pressing than in personal decisions (Leist 1994, p. 184). With respect to the problem of measurement, the strong assumptions of utilitarianism may be relaxed in cases where measurements prove impossible and where a systematic qualitative overview of the benefits and costs suffices to identify the policy producing the greatest net benefits.

In cases where cost-benefit analysis leads to controversial results, one could replace utilitarianism by extra welfarist approaches that broaden the concept of well-being, but remain consequential in nature. Extra welfarist approaches can avoid the problem of immoral or irrational preferences, they are less vulnerable to the criticisms of sum ranking, and they can be combined with communitarian valuations and a decision-maker approach (Hurley 2000, p. 64). Another option is rule utilitarianism, which applies utilitarianism only to rules instead of actions. The utilitarian standard is then reformulated as: a rule is right if and only if the sum total of utilities produced by that rule is greater than the sum total of utilities produced by any other rule the agent could apply in its place. Restricting utilitarianism to rules ensures that the protection of rights and justice is taken into consideration. Only in cases of conflict between different rules would one resort to act utilitarianism to decide what to do (Beauchamp 1982, p. 154). A final possibility is to place utilitarianism in a hierarchy of ethical standards, in which other ethical standards are used as absolute side constraints before applying utilitarianism. An example of such a lexicographic weighting procedure is the well-known rule of thumb that perfect duties and the correlated rights have greater weight than justice and that justice has greater weight than maximizing total utility (Velasquez 1998, p. 128; Graafland 2007, p. 267).

Notes

The author thanks Mandy Bosma and Bert van de Ven for their comments on an earlier version of this article.

1. Research shows that the happiness that people report closely corresponds to activity in the brain. According to Layard (2003), this means that happiness corresponds to an objective reality and is not a vague concept.
2. The pluralist variant of utilitarianism acknowledges that goods such as knowledge, love and beauty have intrinsic value independent of the pleasure they produce. Still, the pluralist variant must assume commensurability between these plural goods in order to assess an action's rightness in terms of the greatest aggregate good.

References

Anderson, Elizabeth (1993), *Value in Ethics and Economics*, Cambridge, MA and London: Harvard University Press.
Beauchamp, Tom L. (1982), *Philosophical Ethics: An Introduction to Moral Philosophy*, New York: McGraw-Hill.
Conlisk, John (1996), 'Why bounded rationality?', *Journal of Economic Literature*, **34**, 669–700.
Crisp, Roger (ed.) (1998), *J.S. Mill: Utilitarianism*, Oxford: Oxford University Press.
Etzioni, Amitai (1988), *The Moral Dimension: Towards a New Economics*, New York: The Free Press.
Graafland, Johan J. (2007), *Economics, Ethics and the Market: Introduction and Applications*, London: Routledge.
Hausman, Daniel M. (1992), *The Inexact and Separate Science of Economics*, Cambridge: Cambridge University Press.
Hausman, Daniel M. and Michael S. McPherson (1996), *Economic Analysis and Moral Philosophy*, Cambridge: Cambridge University Press.
Henson, Richard G. (1979), 'What Kant might have said: moral worth and the overdetermination of dutiful action', *Philosophical Review*, **88** (1), 39–54.
Hurley, Jeremiah (2000), 'An overview of the normative economics of the health sector', in Anthony J. Culyer and Joseph P. Newhouse (eds), *Handbook of Health Economics*, 1, Amsterdam: Elsevier pp. 56–118.
Kant, Immanuel (1997), *Grundlegung zur Metaphysik der Sitten*, trans. Thomas Mertens, Amsterdam: Boom.
Layard, Richard (2003), 'Happiness – has social science a clue?', Lionel Robbins Memorial Lectures 2002/3, Centre for Economic Performance, London School of Economics and Political Science, London.
Leist, Anton (1994), 'Comment on Douglas MacLean', *Analyze & Kritik*, **16** (2), 181–5.
MacLean, Douglas (1994), 'Cost-benefit analysis and procedural values', *Analyze & Kritik*, **16** (2), 166–80.
Mill, John S. (1871), *Utilitarianism*, Oxford: Oxford University Press.
Nozick, Robert (1974), *Anarchy, State and Utopia*, New York: Basic Books.
Rabin, Matthew (1998), 'Psychology and economics', *Journal of Economic Literature*, **36**, 11–46.
Rawls, John (1999), *A Theory of Justice*, revised edition, Boston, MA: Harvard University Press.
Scheffler, Samuel (1994), *The Rejection of Consequentialism*, revised edition, Oxford: Clarendon Press.
Schwartz, Barry (2004), *The Paradox of Choice*, New York: HarperCollins.
Sen, Amartya (1984), *Resources, Values and Development*, Oxford: Blackwell.
Sen, Amartya (1987), *On Ethics and Economics*, Oxford: Blackwell.

Singer, Peter (1972), 'Famine, affluence and morality', *Philosophy and Public Affairs*, **3**, 229–43.

Vandevelde, Antoon (2001), 'Charles Taylor en de discussie tussen liberalen en communautaristen', *Wijsgerig Perspectief*, **41** (3), 15–28.

Velasquez, Manuel G. (1998), *Business Ethics: Concepts and Cases*, fourth edition, Upper Saddle River, NJ: Prentice Hall.

Williams, Bernard (1973), 'A critique of utilitarianism', in J.J.C. Smart and Bernard Williams (eds), *Utilitarianism: For and Against*, Cambridge: Cambridge University Press, pp. 77–150.

See also the entries on: Jeremy Bentham; Efficiency; Justice.

Introduction

Thorstein Veblen (1857–1929) is the most original economic thinker that the United States has produced. He co-founded the original institutional economics with John Rogers Commons. His work was intended as a complete reconstruction of economic theory along evolutionary and cultural lines. In the 1890s Veblen published a series of articles criticizing neoclassical economics. His criticisms focused on two main areas of disagreement with the mainstream. The first was that the economists of his day had not followed the lead of Darwin and others and transformed their discipline into an evolutionary science. Second, he criticized neoclassical economics' outdated preconceptions, which he claimed were based on natural law and animistic modes of thought. These essays were republished as a collection entitled *The Place of Science in Modern Civilization* in 1919.

However Veblen is best known for his classic work on consumption theory, set out in *The Theory of the Leisure Class* (1899). In this book Veblen introduced his theory of economic evolution based on the transformation of institutions. He also developed a cultural theory of consumption based on pecuniary emulation and conspicuous leisure and consumption. Veblen then turned his attention to the conduct of business in the United States economy. Employing data from the reports of the Industrial Commission (1898–1902), Veblen wrote a comprehensive study of the conduct of business enterprise and its methods of finance in his book *The Theory of Business Enterprise* ([1904] 1978). In this work Veblen introduced his distinction between the business activities of firms aimed at making profits and the industrial activities of firms aimed at making serviceable output. In other words, Veblen developed a theory of human behaviour in which biological instincts provide the motivating force of behaviour and culture, in turn structuring the institutions that shape the actual behaviour of individuals. Veblen ([1914] 1964) explored the instinct of workmanship, the parental bent and idle curiosity most intently, but also discussed predatory instincts and emulatory instincts.

As an undergraduate at Carleton College, Veblen studied economics with the noted marginalist John Bates Clark. Veblen's later educational experiences focused his economic thought on evolutionary and cultural analyses and similarly affected his ethics. In particular the influence of Charles Pierce at The Johns Hopkins University, where he began his graduate studies, drew him to pragmatism. His work with William Graham Sumner at Yale University, where Veblen completed his doctoral degree, was central to his interest in cultural analysis. Pragmatic philosophy and cultural analysis combined with his evolutionary perspective made up the main components of Veblen's alternative to neoclassical economics.

Pierce's influence on Veblen's ethical thought is evident in his first published article, 'Kant's Critique of Judgment' (Veblen 1884). Here Veblen argues that in Kant's system of thought moral reasoning and moral action are a fiction unless people are able to act efficaciously in the world (ibid., p. 176). Therefore, attempting to extend Kant's analysis Veblen argues, 'Judgment must come in, if experience is to be of any use, and morality anything more than a dream' (ibid.) Judgement is the reasoning that must mediate between knowledge and moral action, according to Veblen. The kind of judgement necessary for this task is inductive reasoning, by which thinkers place particular things under universal laws. However, Veblen goes beyond this, seeing moral decisions as made up of known particulars but absent of knowledge of the universal law that covers the particulars. He calls this 'reflective judgement' because it goes further than the known and seeks a universal not known from experience.

Reflective judgement attempts to systematize particulars as if they were governed by a system of law or intelligent cause. This is similar to Charles Pierce's explication of abductive reasoning. Pierce used the notion of abduction to describe processes of reasoning for creating new laws or rules to explain particulars. Pierce argued that humans have an innate ability to draw these kinds of inferences as a result of evolutionary processes, but Veblen is silent on the source of the ability to draw inferences. However, the process of judgement that results, according to Veblen, is adaptive reflective reasoning.

This works in the following way. People take particulars and infer from them what universal laws would constitute sufficient cause for these particulars. These judgements are collected and adapted to other inferences to create new concepts. These new concepts must be logically connected to other concepts in our system of understanding; this is the process of adaptive judgement. Eventually as our confidence in the logical connection of these inferred constructs grows we start to treat these concepts as part of the system of principles, as actual knowledge of the way the world works. Unlike Pierce, Veblen does not argue that this is the creation of new knowledge. He notes that for Kant:

> [T]he principle of adaptation cannot give us any new data, nor can it tell us anything new about the data we have. All it can do is guide us in guessing about the given data, and leave it to experience to credit or discredit our guesses. That is, it is a regulative, not a constitutive principle of knowledge according to Kant. (Veblen 1884, p. 190)

Thus, our confidence must be tempered by the knowledge that such laws are only probabilistic and cannot be known with certainty.

The consequence of this for ethical reasoning is that at best, people can infer concepts and incorporate them into their understanding of the natural laws of action and then base their actions and decisions about ethical and moral issues upon them with a reasonable degree of efficaciousness to those actions. Or at the very least, moral and ethical judgements are not completely illusory.

Christian ethics

Veblen's most explicit discussion of ethics is in his article 'Christian Morals and the Competitive System' (1910). Here he compares the moral principles underlying generic Christianity with the moral principles underlying the competitive market system.

Veblen observes that the competitive system is based on eighteenth-century natural law and natural rights philosophy. The ethics and morality on which the system is founded developed along with the handicraft industry that gave rise to the competitive system. These were absent in the medieval society that preceded it. Ethics are, after all, the character of the cultural constructs, institutions or habits of thought that support the underlying material conditions of the society in which they emerge. As such, they are transitory in character.

The specific morals of the competitive system identified by Veblen are 'the egoistic principles of natural rights and natural liberty. These rights and this liberty are egoistic rights and liberty of the individual. They are to be summed up as freedom and security of person and of pecuniary transaction' (Veblen [1910] 1964, p. 213). These morals make sense in the context of the handicraft industry and petty trade between individuals on equal footing.

Veblen notes that the growth of industrial machine-based industry and modern industrial financial practices have rendered much of this moral system inconsistent with material practices. As a result he anticipates, but does not speculate on, the direction in which these morals might evolve or change.

The other source of ethics emerges in Veblen's discussion of Christian morality. Veblen argues that the central and elemental features common to all the variants of Christianity are non-resistance (humility) and brotherly love (Veblen [1910] 1964, p. 203). Veblen sets aside all divine or supernatural origins or warrants for these ethics and assesses them for their functionality in the society in which Christianity emerged. He sees the emergence of Christianity under the crushing weight of Roman authority and the powerlessness of the subject population as essential to the survival of Christians. He also sees brotherly love or mutual succour as an ethic likely to emerge in a subject population at a low level of material existence. The continuation of these ethics during the medieval period is supported by the continued low material level of existence of the underlying population, slightly altered by the fact that the now-Christian rulers of the period adopted a morality of 'coercive control and kindly tutelage', which was not, however, uniquely characteristic of Christianity. Veblen thus explains Christian morality as a culturally constructed institution adapted to the particular material circumstance of medieval European culture. This is the same explanation for the origin of ethics as for the competitive system. In this regard, Veblen's explanatory framework for ethics is certainly consistent with Sumner's cultural explanation of folkways (Sumner [1906] 1940, pp. 17–27, 37–43, 46–50, 61–3, 66–75).

However, Veblen opens another possibility for the origin of ethics in his discussion of brotherly love or 'the impulse to mutual service'. Veblen notes that this impulse is not unique to Christians. In fact, he observes that it was common among the more peaceable societies of savages (as opposed to later barbarian stages of culture). Because of the ubiquity of this ethic in peaceable savage societies, Veblen suggests that it might be part of human nature. He describes such traits as 'congenital and hereditary traits of the species which assert themselves instinctively, impulsively, by force of the mere absence of repression' (Veblen [1910] 1964, p. 204). Veblen speculates that this impulse is 'something of a kind [that] appears to prevail by mere force of hereditary propensity' (ibid., p. 205) He adds, 'it recurs throughout the life of human society with such an air of ubiquity as would argue that it is an elemental trait of the species rather than a product of Christendom' (ibid.) He continues by arguing that the presence of brotherly love in Christian morality is a cultural reversion to an atavistic trait of human nature.

Two sources of ethics
Thus in Veblen's view ethics derives from two sources. One is the material circumstances of life. This reflects Veblen's predisposition toward cultural analysis. But alongside that

is Veblen's argument that some ethics are biologically derived, evolutionarily structured instincts motivating human behaviour. When not repressed, such instinctual proclivities emerge as drivers of actions, expressing themselves as guides to ethical behaviour. This second source incorporates Veblen's evolutionary proclivities and his use of instinct psychology.

Veblen's theory of instincts was central to his economic theorizing. Among the instincts Veblen discussed are idle curiosity, the parental bent, workmanship, and predatory and emulative drives. Veblen argued that these evolved to motivate behaviour. Behaviour so motivated is then, in some sense, natural. But since instincts are merely motivations that manifest in culturally formed behaviour, they have no special warrant as ethical as a result of being biologically motivated. For example, the parental bent is an instinctual motivation to care for children. But the actual child-rearing behaviour will be a result of each particular culture's standards for proper childcare. In fact, the immense diversity in child-rearing practices demonstrates there is no natural standard for good child-rearing practices as opposed to poor child-rearing practices. Similarly, the drive for emulation assists in education and acculturation, but as Veblen demonstrated it can also just as easily lead to status emulation. The predatory instinct can assist in provisioning or manifest as the use of force and fraud upon other people to their detriment. Similar observations could be made about the impact of idle curiosity and the instinct of workmanship on human behaviour.

This does not mean Veblen's economic analysis of human behaviour was ethically neutral. In *The Theory of the Leisure Class* Veblen explored consumption behaviour. He observed that consumption behaviour in the United States was motivated by pecuniary emulation. Basically people consume based on standards of appropriate consumption determined by their income level. The leisure class sets the standards at the top of the social hierarchy. They engage in conspicuous consumption and conspicuous leisure, which demonstrates their ability to spend money in ostentatious ways without the need for productive work. Because of the technological advances of modern industrial culture the items that lend themselves to conspicuous display become less expensive and less rare as a result of mass production. Thus, in a fairly short time those with lesser income can acquire these items, causing the items to lose their ability to serve as signifiers of high status. Frequent changes in fashion with regard to such status goods leads to a constant need to consume to ever-greater levels in order to sustain the system.

It is impossible to read *The Theory of the Leisure Class* without noting the sarcastic tone with which Veblen describes the excesses of the leisure class in terms of consumption and leisure activities. Clearly he sees all of this activity as conspicuous waste. Neither is the term 'waste' ethically neutral for Veblen. Rick Tilman described Veblen's ethics in terms of evaluating whether a person, thing or behaviour contributes to 'the generic ends of life, impersonally considered' (Tilman 2004, pp. 7, 258). Veblen himself, in his popular writings, suggested that 'live and let live' was an appropriate ethic for people and particularly for the actions of nations.

Yet the generic ends of life broadly considered as an ethic seems amorphous and overly vague. By exploring Veblen's explicit writing on Christian ethics and his economic writings, more specific ethical positions can be discerned. In his description of the underlying ethics of Christianity, Veblen argues that brotherly love, or as he also describes it, the impulse to mutual service, is shared by people in both the peaceable savage state and all the various Christian communities. This implies that individuals working together for mutual support is both a recurring moral motif and a recurring behaviour under a variety of social orders. Consequently it is safe to conclude that Veblen considers ethics as addressing community life rather than individual action. In particular, people working together to provide for their survival and sustenance – what we might describe as social provisioning behaviour – is desirable.

The opposite is also amply demonstrated in his writings. In *The Theory of the Leisure Class* consumption for the purpose of differentiating one self from others by employing status comparisons based on abstaining from contributing any productive effort to community provisioning is ridiculed and described as waste. In *The Theory of Business Enterprise* Veblen describes how the machine process in modern industry leads to increased output of the means of life. But he also notes that production for profit leads to business behaviour directed at earning the highest possible rate of return by any means, regardless of its impact on society's ability to adequately provision itself. Similarly these same business principles applied in the context of higher education frustrate the instinct of idle curiosity and the pursuit of disinterested scholarship. Imperial politics and the belligerence to which it leads (described in Veblen's *Imperial Germany and the Industrial Revolution* as well as his popular writings) is definitely considered to be damaging to the well-being of the common folk.

For Veblen, behaviour directed at enhancing the survival and provisioning of the community, improving the lot of the common folk, is good. Bad behaviour is that which leads to waste, invidious distinctions, benefits for the few at the expense of many, or systematic efforts to frustrate human potential.

Liberal ethics

Veblen discusses 'live and let live' in his post-World War I essays, especially those collected in *The Vested Interest and the Common Man*. In these writings he notes, 'peace means the same thing as Live and Let Live' (Veblen [1919] 1964, p. 139). Clearly peace is good according to Veblen. Yet these essays describe how continuation of peace is made unlikely by the statesman's return to business as usual with regard to dynastic politics derived from the notion of the divine right of kings. He compares the motivation of statesmen to vested interests in the ownership of property and control of business. These vested interests all derive free income from their inalienable right to exploit their property. The exercise of these rights is enhanced by dynastic politics in that the expansion of the state and its range of control of resources is for the benefit of vested interests but not necessarily the common folk, who are put at risk to acquire them.

Veblen expresses the possibility of the machine process that dominates industrial economies undermining belief in the animistic habits of thought supporting the goals of the vested interest. This is by virtue of its creating a necessity among workers to understand cause-and-effect reasoning in their daily lives. Such optimistic moments in Veblen's writing occur at the end of *The Theory of Business Enterprise*, in the last chapter, in which he discusses the natural decay of business enterprise by the discipline of the machine process (Veblen [1904] 1978, pp. 374–82). Veblen engages in Utopian ruminations of this type in his popular essays collected in *The Engineers and the Price System* (1921). But his optimism is always tempered (Veblen [1904] 1978, p. 400) as he writes in *The Instinct of Workmanship*, 'history records more frequent and more spectacular instances of the triumph of imbecile institutions over life and culture than of peoples who have by force of instinctive insight saved themselves alive out of a desperately precarious institutional situation' (Veblen [1914] 1964, p. 25).

While Veblen articulates his moral position in his discussion of how modern industrial economies operate, he writes approvingly of activities that promote provisioning and of a policy of live and let live regarding one's neighbours applied individually and to nations. He clearly disapproves of activities that are wasteful, exploitative of others or involve invidious distinction, predation, force and fraud.

References

Sumner, William Graham ([1906] 1940), *Folkways*, New York: New American Library.

Tilman, Rick (2004), *Thorstein Veblen, John Dewey, C. Wright Mills and the Generic Ends of Life*, New York: Rowman & Littlefield.

Veblen, Thorstein ([1884] 1964), 'Kant's critique of judgment', *The Journal of Speculative Philosophy*, 18 (July); reprinted in Leon Ardzrooni (ed.), *Essays in Our Changing Order*, New York: Augustus M. Kelley, pp. 175–93.

Veblen, Thorstein ([1899] 1931), *The Theory of the Leisure Class*, New York: Modern Library.

Veblen, Thorstein ([1904] 1978), *The Theory of Business Enterprise*, New Brunswick, NJ: Transactions Press.

Veblen, Thorstein ([1910] 1964), 'Christian morals and the competitive system', *The International Journal of Ethics*, 20 (January); reprinted in Leon Ardzrooni (ed.), *Essays in Our Changing Order*, New York: Augustus M. Kelley, pp. 200–218.

Veblen, Thorstein ([1914] 1964), *The Instinct of Workmanship*, New York: Augustus M. Kelley.

Veblen, Thorstein ([1915] 1964), *Imperial Germany and the Industrial Revolution*, New York: Augustus M. Kelley.

Veblen, Thorstein ([1919] 1964), *The Vested Interest and the Common Man*, New York: Augustus M. Kelley.

Veblen, Thorstein ([1919] 1990), *The Place of Science in Modern Civilization*, New Brunswick, NJ: Transactions Press.

Veblen, Thorstein ([1921] 1933), *The Engineers and the Price System*, New York: Viking.

See also the entries on: Consumerism; Institutions; Immanuel Kant; Religion; Max Weber and the Protestant work ethic.

74 Virtue ethics
Irene van Staveren

Aristotle's virtue ethics

Virtue ethics has its roots in Aristotle's *Nichomachean Ethics*. Here, Aristotle offers a contextual and personhood-based ethics which he developed in response to the more universalist and abstract ethics of his master, Plato. Virtue ethics is not so much concerned with the question of what is the right thing to do, but rather the question what is the good life – human flourishing, or *eudamonia*. The good life is a pluralist type of good and not reducible to a single dimension, such as pleasure (utility) or right (a set of rules). The key to *eudamonia* is, as Aristotle argued, the self-sufficiency of the virtues. Humans seek to follow the good for itself, they have a plurality of commitments that are incommensurable and not instrumental for any other goal, as Aristotle explained more than 2000 years ago:

> If, then, there is some end of the things we do, which we desire for its own sake (everything else being desired for the sake of this), and if we do not choose everything for the sake of something else (for at that rate the process would go on to infinity, so that our desire would be empty and vain), clearly this must be the good and the chief good. (Aristotle 1980, pp. 1–2)

Examples of virtues are benevolence, civility, courage, fairness, generosity, honesty, justice, patience, prudence, self-discipline and tactfulness. Each virtue represents a mean between two extremes. For example, courage is the mean between cowardice and rashness. Hence, the virtuous mean is not a fixed norm and has no universal standard but is contextual. It cannot be found by following a moral rule or doing one's duty or obeying a law, explains Aristotle (1980, p. 12): 'The good, therefore, is not something common answering to one Idea.' Instead, Aristotle recognized human life as full of contingencies, and hence the mean can be found only through trial and error in relationships with others, in an ever-changing social environment.

> First, then, let us consider this, that it is the nature of such things to be destroyed by defect and excess, as we see in the case of strength and of health . . . exercise either excessive or defective destroys the strength, and similarly drink or food which is above or below a certain amount destroys the health, while that which is proportionate both produces and increases and preserves it. (Aristotle 1980, p. 30)

Virtue, according to this passage, like health, is a mean between two extremes. The main characteristics of virtue ethics, hence, are that the good is understood as having no universal standard, that the good cannot be found through individual reasoning only, and that moral behaviour is imperfect and continuously adapting to changing social circumstances, developing through habituation. This implies that it is not easy to hit the mean, hence, to be virtuous. Indeed, Aristotle acknowledges that people often fail to find a balance between excess and deficiency due to 'weakness of the will, indecisiveness, guilt, shame, self-deception, rationalisation, and annoyance with oneself' as formulated by Michael Stocker (1997, p. 66).

Modern virtue ethics

Since the Middle Ages ethics has been dominated by theories emphasizing rightness, actions and obligation. This is very much so for the two main ethical theories next to virtue ethics. One is utilitarianism, in which the good is perceived in acts that generate the greatest happiness for the greatest number – a consequentialist ethics. The other competing ethical theory is deontology, which finds the good in duties and obligations – a principled ethics. Virtue ethics received renewed interest in the second half of the twentieth century, in particular with a groundbreaking article by Elizabeth Anscombe, first published in 1958, entitled 'Modern moral philosophy'. In this pamphlet she points out a basic inconsistency of the dominant moral philosophy, namely, its concern with moral laws without a lawgiver and the strong moral judgements that are based on this, in terms of 'ought', duty and obligations. She says, instead,

> [I]t would be a great improvement if, instead of 'morally wrong', one always named a genus such as 'untruthful', 'unchaste', 'unjust'. We should no longer ask whether doing something was 'wrong', passing directly from some description of an action to this notion; we should ask whether, e.g., it was unjust; and the answer would sometimes be clear at once. (Anscombe [1958] 1997, p. 34)

Today, we find virtue ethics forming the basis of various contextual ethical approaches, in particular communitarianism and the ethics of care. Communitarians understand the development of moral values as occurring in human interaction within communities, that is, in day-to-day practices, rather than as stemming from a set of given moral norms that should constrain human behaviour. A key notion of communitarianism, developed by Alasdair MacIntyre, is that of a moral practice. He defines moral practice as follows:

> [Moral practice is] cooperative human activity through which goods internal to that form of activity are realized in the course of trying to achieve those standards of excellence which are appropriate to, and partially definitive of, that form of activity, with the result that human powers to achieve excellence, and human conceptions of the ends and goods involved, are systematically extended. (MacIntyre 1987, p. 187)

A quite different branch of virtue ethics is found in the ethics of care, which has strong feminist roots and therefore tends to be critical of the support for patriarchal traditionalism found in the work of some communitarians. In the ethics of care, not communities but relationships between persons are central. The ethics of care expresses contextual values developing between persons on the basis of contingent needs arising from human vulnerability. One of its main proponents, Joan Tronto, explains that care is a response to people's needs in such a way that it furthers the network of relationships around the person in need of care. Care may be given to closely related people, such as one's own children or friends, but also to strangers, as in helping an elderly person to cross the street or in voluntary work for the homeless. As in communitarianism, care also refers to practices, which, according to Tronto (1993, pp. 127–37), consist of four stages: attentiveness to needs (caring about), taking responsibility (taking care of), showing competence (care giving) and responsiveness (care receiving). Both ethics of care and communitarianism emphasize the personal level, character traits and social context in practices, characterizing the two approaches as belonging to the tradition of virtue ethics.

Virtue ethics also has shortcomings compared to the two other main ethical theories of utilitarianism and deontology. Its concern with the good person makes it difficult to evaluate situations, structures and institutions. Virtue ethics was developed for individuals, not for organizations or society. But it is a misinterpretation to assume that virtue theory is only about good intentions: it is the combination of moral motivation by the intrinsic goodness of virtues themselves *and* reason about the good means that need to be employed in the process to achieve virtue. Aristotle developed his theory for a small-scale community, the *polis*, largely ignoring social inequalities between people. He aimed his theory at 'the good man' in the *polis*, excluding the non-citizens of Athens, such as foreigners, slaves and women – a very particularistic position which has rightly been criticized (see, for example, Freeland 1998). Current developments in virtue ethics try to go beyond these limitations and explore relationships with the other ethical traditions. It shares with utilitarianism a concern with good ends, while having its concern with human dignity and practical reason in common with deontology.

Virtue ethics in economic thought

Adam Smith recognized the importance of virtuous character traits for the functioning of markets in his *Theory of Moral Sentiments*. The key concept of this theory is 'sympathy', which he remarked is not motivated by self-interest: 'Sympathy, however, cannot, in any sense, be regarded as a selfish principle' (Smith [1759] 1984, Part VII. III, p. 317). Sympathy is expressed in close human interaction and involves emotions, Smith explains. He was very much aware of the contextuality of virtues. For benevolence, he gave the example of how much to care for someone – what would be too little and what too much? He was very much aware that rules of justice are not sufficient for guiding moral behaviour in our society, but that a flourishing society needs more: 'Mere justice is, upon most occasions, but a negative virtue, and only hinders us from hurting our neighbour . . . Where the necessary assistance is reciprocally afforded from love, from gratitude, from friendship, and esteem, the society flourishes and is happy' (idem. Part II. II.ii, p. 85). Moreover, Smith has argued that the economy rests on a careful balance between three virtues: prudence, justice (or propriety) and benevolence.

> Concern for our happiness recommends to us the virtue of prudence; concern for that of other people, the virtues of justice and beneficence; of which, the one retains us from hurting, the other prompts us to promote that happiness . . . If virtue, therefore, does not consist in propriety, it must consist in either prudence or benevolence. Besides these three it is scarce possible to imagine that any other account can be given of the nature of virtue. (Smith [1759] 1984, pp. 262, 267)

Others have shared Smith's insight on the supportive role of virtues in the economy and linked each virtue to a particular economic domain: liberty to the market with exchange relationships, justice to the state with redistribution, and benevolence to the unpaid or care economy, with gift relationships, or reciprocity (see van Staveren 2001). Hirschman's (1970) distinction between exit, voice and loyalty is a good example of a similar combination of virtues and the economic domain.

Deirdre McCloskey contributed to a revival of attention to virtues in economics in various publications, for example, an article called 'Bourgeois virtue' (1994) and her book *The Bourgeois Virtues: Ethics for an Age of Commerce* (2006). In the book, she returns to the classical seven virtues of love, faith, hope, courage, temperance, prudence and justice. Whereas neoclassical economics narrows all virtues to one, prudence, McCloskey argues that the whole set of seven needs to be cherished if markets are to function well. The neoclassical assumption that rational agents strive to maximize their utility reduces love and other virtues to a preference that satisfies one's own utility through someone else, which she aptly labels 'altruistic hedonism' (2006, p. 115). She admits that she was, once, a believer in neoclassical economic theory's key concept of utility maximization and used it widely in her work in economic history. But she now recognizes the concept as being too narrow and reducing economic agents to selfish utility maximizers, ignoring virtue and vice, and thereby even ignoring the wise insights of the founding father of economics on the interconnectedness of economic behaviour and virtues. McCloskey characterizes both utilitarianism and deontology as ethical monism, and instead favours virtue ethics as a wider ethical perspective as more adequately describing the ethics underlying human behaviour, including economic behaviour.

Taking the virtue ethical perspective on economics, McCloskey portrays the virtue of hope as the virtue of the forward-looking entrepreneur making investments (a typical Keynesian view, although McCloskey does not refer to Keynes), while courage is pictured as the virtue of the Schumpeterian dynamic economy in which entrepreneurs take delight in ventures and the exercise of their ingenuity, rather than just striving for endless accumulation. McCloskey interprets prudence, following Aristotle, as the virtue of practical knowledge of means, as good reasoning. Indeed, prudence seems quite helpful for flourishing in economic life, making the right production decisions, finding and keeping buyers for one's products and making sufficient revenues to feed and clothe one self and loved ones, without ignoring saving for bad times and investing for the replacement and technological improvement of one's stock of capital. Prudence, hence, is a virtue of competence, McCloskey claims, and should not be reduced to self-interest as is the case in modern economics.

Returning to Smith's three basic virtues and accompanying forms of economic interaction, I have suggested in my work on virtues and economics that we may understand the economy as a careful balance between the three economic value domains of freedom/market, justice/state and the caring/care economy (van Staveren 2001). In each domain, economic agents further the domain's values and can do so only by exhibiting domain-specific virtues. In the domain of freedom, free exchange requires but also enhances agents' independence, self-esteem and self-fulfilment, whereas in the domain of justice, distributive rules protect rights and express a particular conception of fairness. In the domain of caring, gifts of labour time and other resources serve to support generous relationships, requiring and furthering trust and sympathy. Arthur Miller's famous play *Death of a Salesman* beautifully illustrates the failure of economic behaviour in markets when lying, cheating and rudeness take the place of honesty, faithfulness and friendship. The tragedy of the salesman is not that he becomes successful through ruthlessness but that he is unable to make profits, become competitive and innovative, precisely because of his entirely instrumental behaviour (van Staveren 2007). In other words, the neoclassical definition of rationality, based on self-interest and individual utility maximization, lacks a concept of virtue without which economic behaviour cannot result in successful exchange. It is virtue that makes rationality meaningful, by providing to it the perspective of human flourishing in an uncertain and continuously changing social environment where humans acknowledge that they depend on one another. But virtue is a mean, as Aristotle said. Hence, too much or too little does not contribute to flourishing. Therefore, a balanced economy, one that contributes to the flourishing of its members, should strike a mean between the three virtues in economic life, implying an organic whole of the market, state and care economy.

These general views on virtue ethics and economics bring us to more specific questions of how virtues relate to markets. Recent economic literature, in the mainstream as well as in heterodox economics, shows an interesting picture emerging, building further on Adam Smith's position that markets need the virtues in order to function well. Virtue ethics is receiving more attention in economics now that the neoclassical paradigm, based on its assumptions of perfect information and self-interested utility maximization, has been broadened by developments such as behavioural economics, game theory, institutional economics and feminist economics.

Virtues and the market
Recent literature shows the emergence of two positions on the relationship between virtues and the market. The first position is the one from communitarianism, posing virtues and the market as opposites. The second is a set of pragmatic positions emerging from social capital research, the feminist economics of care and experimental economics, in which virtues and the market are regarded as interrelated and sometimes even mutually supportive.

Communitarianism: opposition
As we saw above, communitarian philosophers view morality as developing in the moral practices of communities. The economy, however, is not regarded as a moral practice by communitarians – to the contrary, as MacIntyre explains. He and other communitarian writers tend to perceive the economy, in particular the market, as non-moral or even as going against shared values and undermining virtue. MacIntyre admits that the household economies of the past may have been moral practices, with small-scale economic activity integrated into family life and small communities. But today's market economy has become a domain of instrumental behaviour, he claims. The modern economy with its stock markets, far-advanced division of labour and widespread international trade is no longer a moral practice, he finds, while its agents pursuing self-interest and efficiency are no longer moral agents (MacIntyre 1987).

Elizabeth Anderson's critique of markets focuses on market boundaries, the dividing line between (non-moral) markets and (moral) non-markets. Markets, she agrees with MacIntyre, tend to reduce value to prices and provide strong incentives through competition for instrumental behaviour. From this perspective, Anderson (1993) criticizes markets for marriage, sex, children and pregnancy. Anderson distinguishes between economic goods and moral goods. Economic goods are characterized by five criteria, all of which reflect use-value: impersonal relations, freedom to pursue personal advantage, exclusivity and rivalry in consumption, purely want-regarding, and dissatisfaction expressed through 'exit' (Anderson 1990, p. 225). In contrast, she recognizes moral goods as diverse, reflecting a variety of moral motives and characterized by shared values.

Amitai Etzioni is a third communitarian thinker about markets and virtue. He proposes a duality between virtues and the market similar to Anderson's. He claims that humans act from two motives, 'moral principles' and 'pleasure'. These he conceptualizes as the 'We' paradigm and the 'I' paradigm (Etzioni 1988). The two reflect a divided self, Etzioni explains in recent work, which leads agents to 'inconsistencies and tendencies to zig-zag as resulting from their being subject to these two competing super-utilities' (Etzioni 2003, p. 113).

It is clear in the communitarian positions on virtues and markets that they are opposites, and markets are perceived not just as morally neutral but as potentially negatively affecting morality by undermining virtue.

Pragmatic approaches

Recent literature on social capital reveals the importance of various virtues, particularly the virtues of trust (to trust others rather than to distrust them, though not to naively believe anything people say) and trustworthiness (being worthy of other people's trust, hence, not cheating but also not making promises one cannot keep). The virtue of trust has been widely recognized as supportive of markets (Nooteboom 2002). Trust replaces the need for contracting and monitoring and fills the gap of imperfect information about what may happen in the future. It also tends to reduce transaction costs under conditions of uncertainty, while enabling collective action as well as positive externalities between workers in organizations and labour markets more generally, and between entrepreneurs in clusters and networks of innovation. High-trust societies therefore tend to do better economically than low-trust societies. But economic performance also depends on the kind of trust. Social capital research generally distinguishes two types of trust. The first is the bonding ties of communities expressing strong trust within groups but distrust between groups; the second is bridging ties across individuals and groups expressing generalized trust in others, including strangers. It is in particular the second type of trust, generalized trust, which seems to support markets by enhancing trade and innovation (van Staveren and Knorringa 2007).

In feminist economics, the virtue of caring, and the related virtue of responsibility, has been recognized as a key component in explaining labour market behaviour. First, when uncritically taken as a preference, caring has been used to explain the gender division of labour in households. In neoclassical household economics, women's higher unpaid workload is attributed to their presumably stronger preference or natural comparative advantage for caring work compared to men (Becker 1991). Feminist economists, however, criticize this biological explanation of the gender division of labour. This has led to a second way in which caring has been conceptualized, namely as an unequal social norm, ascribing virtues of care and delegating caring work to women and not to men (Folbre 1994). Recent feminist economic work on caring emphasizes a third, more nuanced, conceptualization of caring. This is the view that caring is a human motivation, present in men and women, and expressed through work attitudes and effort, consumption and savings and risk strategies in investment and production, with macroeconomic impacts (Himmelweit 1999; van Staveren 2005). This third strand of work on caring suggests that caring has a positive impact on labour productivity through intrinsic motivation. Care has a negative impact on female labour supply, because of the time constraint that unpaid work imposes on women's decision to engage in paid work. At the same time, through risk diversification and the substitution of paid employment in times of economic crises, caring tends to function as a buffer against market volatility and helps households to sustain minimum levels of livelihood.

In a book on the state of the art in experimental game theory, focusing on ethics, Gintis et al. (2005) redefine rationality in an Aristotelian way. Based on numerous results from experiments with well-known games in economics, such as the public goods game, the ultimatum game and the dictator game, they develop a notion of rationality that lies between the two extremes of self-interest and altruism. They call this virtuous mean 'strong reciprocity', defined as 'a predisposition to cooperate with others, and to punish (at personal cost, if necessary) those who violate the norms of cooperation, even when it is implausible to expect that these costs will be recovered at a later date' (Gintis et al. 2005, p. 8). Evidence from experiments supports the position that most people are strong reciprocators, and only a minority of people show either self-interested or altruistic behaviour. Interestingly, the authors not only found this meta-virtuous behaviour in repeated games, relying on the mechanism of reputation, but they also established it in non-repeated and anonymous settings.

A rethinking of economic motivation makes particular sense when we also reject the neoclassical economic assumptions of perfect information (or probabilistic knowledge) and independent agency. Acknowledging fundamental uncertainty, vulnerability, human fallibility and human interdependence, it becomes clear that self-interest does not necessarily provide the best guide for behaviour. We simply do not know what actions will maximize our interests, and often we do not even know what our interests really are in a changing and uncertain environment. In other words, in a more realistic view of economics, rationality must be understood as strong reciprocity, implying a concern with human flourishing through cooperation in fallible human practices.

Conclusion

The influence of virtue ethics on economics is traced particularly to Aristotle and Adam Smith. Nonetheless, during much of the past century the dominance of the neoclassical paradigm has driven this influence to the margins of the discipline. Recent developments in mainstream and heterodox economics, have shed renewed light on virtue ethics in economics, with impacts on core concepts such as work and rationality.

References

Anderson, Elizabeth (1990), 'The ethical limitations of the market', *Economics and Philosophy*, **6**, 179–205.
Anderson, Elizabeth (1993), *Value in Ethics and Economics*, Cambridge, MA: Harvard University Press.
Anscombe, Elizabeth ([1958] 1997), 'Modern moral philosophy', in Roger Crisp and Michael Slote (eds), *Virtue Ethics*, Oxford: Oxford University Press, pp. 26–44.
Aristotle (1980), *Nichomachean Ethics*, Oxford: Oxford University Press.
Becker, Gary (1991), *A Treatise on the Family*, enlarged edition, Cambridge, MA: Harvard University Press.
Etzioni, Amitai (1988), *The Moral Dimension: Toward a New Economics*, New York: Free Press.
Etzioni, Amitai (2003), 'Toward a new socio-economic paradigm', *Socio-Economic Review*, **1** (1), 105–18.
Folbre, Nancy (1994), *Who Pays for the Kids? Gender and Structures of Constraint*, London: Routedge.
Freeland, Cynthia (1998), *Feminist Interpretations of Aristotle*, University Park, PA: Pennsylvania State University Press.
Gintis, Herbert, Samuel Bowles, Robert Boyd and Ernst Fehr (2005), *Moral Sentiments and Material Interests: The Foundations of Cooperation in Economic Life*, Cambridge, MA: MIT Press.
Himmelweit, Susan (1999), 'Caring labour', *Annals of the American Academy of Political and Social Science*, **561** (0), 27–38.

Hirschman, Albert (1970), *Exit, Voice and Loyalty: Responses to Decline in Firms, Organizations, and States*, Cambridge, MA: Harvard University Press.

MacIntyre, Alisdair (1987), *After Virtue: A Study in Moral Theory*, 2nd edition, London: Duckworth.

McCloskey, Deirdre (1994), 'Bourgeois virtue', *American Scholar*, **63** (2), 177–91.

McCloskey, Deirdre (2006), *The Bourgeois Virtues: Ethics for an Age of Commerce*, Chicago, IL: University of Chicago Press.

Nooteboom, Bart (2002), *Trust: Forms, Foundations, Functions, Failures and Figures*, Cheltenham, UK, and Northampton, MA, USA: Edward Elgar.

Smith, Adam ([1759] 1984), *The Theory of Moral Sentiments*, Indianapolis, IN: Liberty Fund.

Staveren, Irene van (2001), *The Values of Economics: An Aristotelian Perspective*, London: Routledge.

Staveren, Irene van (2005), 'Modelling Care', *Review of Social Economy*, **63** (4), 567–86.

Staveren, Irene van (2007), 'The irrationality of utility maximization or the death of a salesman', in Stavros Ioannides and Klaus Nielsen (eds), *Economics and the Social Sciences: Boundaries, Interaction and Integration*, Cheltenham, UK, and Northampton, MA, USA: Edward Elgar, pp. 141–62.

Staveren, Irene van and Peter Knorringa (2007), 'Unpacking social capital in economic development: how social relations matter', *Review of Social Economy*, **65** (1), 107–35.

Stocker, Michael (1997), 'The schizophrenia of modern ethical theories', in Roger Crisp and Michael Slote (eds), *Virtue Ethics*, Oxford: Oxford University Press, pp. 66–78.

Tronto, Joan (1993), *Moral Boundaries: A Political Argument for an Ethics of Care*, London: Routledge.

See also the entries on: Aristotle; Ethics of care; Feminism; Adam Smith.

75 Max Weber and the Protestant work ethic
Pippa Norris and Ronald Inglehart

Studies in recent years have revived interest in the impact of values. In particular, comparative work has utilized the newly available range of cross-national survey datasets. Yet the theoretical antecedents of this work are rooted more deeply in political sociology, notably in the controversial claims Max Weber made more than a century ago about the role of religious values in the birth and growth of modern industrial free-market economies.

Weber's argument about the origin of modern capitalism is among the most influential in the history of the social sciences, attracting confirmation and refutation by sociologists, historians, psychologists, economists and anthropologists throughout the twentieth century (Lehman and Roth 1993; Lessnoff 1994; Chalcraft and Harrington 2001; Jones 1997; Swedberg 1998). The central puzzle addressed by Weber concerns why the Industrial Revolution, economic modernization and bourgeois capitalism arose first in the West, and specifically in Protestant and not Catholic Western societies, rather than elsewhere. Weber argued that legal and commercial changes, institutional developments and technological innovations in Europe were insufficient by themselves in providing an adequate explanation. After all, other societies developed banking, credit institutions and legal systems, as well as the foundations of science, mathematics and technology. He noted that the material conditions for capitalism existed in many earlier civilizations, and a merchant class engaged in trade and commerce arose in China, Egypt, India and the classical world well before the Protestant Reformation (Weber [1904] 1992, p. 19). What they lacked, however, Weber believed, was a particular and distinctive cultural ethos.

For Weber, it was the values associated with the Protestant Reformation and Calvinist doctrine that gave birth to the spirit of Western capitalism. Ascetic Protestantism preached people's duty to work diligently, to pursue financial rewards and to invest prudently. The aim of working and accumulating resources was not just to meet minimal material needs – and still less to display profits in the form of material gains and enjoy hedonistic and worldly pleasures. Rather, work was regarded as a moral duty pursued for its own sake: 'Labour must, on the contrary, be performed as if it were an absolute end in itself, a calling' (ibid., p. 62). The Protestant ethic interpreted ethical activities, not as monastic asceticism renouncing this life, but rather as fulfilment of worldly obligations. In turn, the virtues of hard work, enterprise and diligence, Weber argued, provide the underlying cultural foundation for capitalist markets and investment. 'Honesty is useful, because it assures credit; so are punctuality, industry, frugality, and that is the reason they are virtues' (ibid., p. 52).

Weber thus understood the Protestant ethic to be a unique set of moral beliefs about the virtues of hard work and economic acquisition, the need for individual entrepreneurial initiative and the rewards of a just God. Its specific values emphasized self-discipline, hard work, prudent reinvestment of savings, personal honesty, individualism and independence, all of which were thought to generate the cultural conditions most conducive to market economies, private enterprise and the bourgeois capitalism of the West.

It should be stressed that Weber did not claim that the restless go-getting entrepreneurial class of merchants and bankers, shopkeepers and industrial barons were also the most devout ascetic Protestants. On the contrary, he argued, 'those most filled with the spirit of capitalism tend to be indifferent, if not hostile, to the Church' (Iannaccone 1998). He therefore did not expect an individual-level relationship to exist between personal piety, church-going habits and adherence to the Protestant work ethic. Instead, this cultural ethos was thought to be pervasive, influencing the devout and atheist alike, within Protestant societies. Any attempt to analyse Weberian theory should therefore be tested at the macro level, and not the individual level.

The Weberian thesis, like any classic in the literature, attracted widespread debate and criticism during the last century.[1] Much of that work focused on understanding the historical relationship between Protestantism and the subsequent rise of capitalism. For example, Tawney and later Samuelson questioned the direction of causality in this relationship, arguing that the early growth of capitalism in late-Medieval Europe preceded and encouraged subsequent cultural shifts, such as greater individualism and the more acquisitive attitudes that were conducive to the adoption and spread of Protestantism (Tawney 1926; Samuelson 1993; Blum and Dudley 2001). Historians have disputed whether economic activities actually flourished most, as Weber claimed, where Calvinism was predominant in the seventeenth century Dutch Republic (Ter Voert 1997).

Economists have since examined whether contemporary religion generates cultural attitudes conducive to economic development and growth. For example, Guiso et al. (2003) provide limited evidence in support of this argument, finding that religiosity is linked to attitudes such as social trust, which is conducive to the working of free markets and institutions. But when comparing specific economic attitudes within Christian denominations, in both Protestant and Catholic cultures, their results were mixed (see also Greenfield 2001; Furnham et al. 1993; Barro and McCleary 2003).

Political sociology has studied these issues as well. Inglehart showed a strong linkage between macroeconomic growth rates and some of the core values of the Weberian Protestant ethic (which are not unique to Protestant societies today) – including the emphasis on values of individual autonomy and economic achievement (Inglehart 1997, Ch. 7).

We lack the historical evidence with which to examine cultural conditions at the time when capitalism was burgeoning in the West. But if Weber's thesis is correct, we might expect the culture of Protestantism to have left an enduring legacy in values that still remains visible today. To develop these arguments further, we focus here on the core Weberian hypothesis, namely that, compared with those living in all other religious cultures (especially Catholic societies), Protestant societies display the strongest work ethic, conducive to modern capitalism, as exemplified by their valuing the virtue of work as a duty, as well as favouring markets over the state. Moreover, Weber stresses that an important aspect of Protestantism concerns the teaching of broader ethical standards, including honesty, willingness to obey the law and trustworthiness, which serve as the foundation of business confidence, good faith dealings and voluntary contract compliance.

Since Weber's claim concerns societal-level cultural effects, we focus on analysing macro-level values when classifying societies by their predominant religious culture. We describe the mean distribution of attitudes by religious culture, then use multivariate models to control for factors already demonstrated to be closely related to the strength of religious values and practices. This includes the level of human development. We suspect that societies sharing a common Protestant heritage still display an affinity in basic values, but that the forces of development have subsequently transformed the cultural legacy of religious traditions. As Inglehart argued,

> In Western history, the rise of the Protestant Ethic – a materialistic value system that not only tolerated economic accumulation but encouraged it as something laudable and heroic – was a key cultural change that opened the way for capitalism and industrialization. But precisely because they attained high levels of economic security, the Western societies that were the first to industrialize, have gradually come to emphasize Postmaterialist values, giving higher priority to the quality of life than to economic growth. In this respect, the rise of Postmaterialist values reverses the rise of the Protestant Ethic. Today, the functional equivalent of the Protestant Ethic is most vigorous in East Asia and is fading away in Protestant Europe, as technological development and cultural change become global. (Inglehart 1997, Ch. 7)

If this is true, we would interpret the Protestant ethic as a set of values that are most common in societies of scarcity. They may be conducive to an emphasis on economic growth, but as they reflect an environment of scarcity, they would tend to fade under conditions of affluence.

Evidence of the Protestant ethic

Work ethic
What values are intrinsic to capitalism, and how can the Protestant work ethos best be measured? Social psychological studies have used detailed multi-item scales to gauge orientations towards work, although a systematic meta-review of the literature found that generally small groups have been tested, rather than nationally representative random samples of the population (Jones 1997). These studies suggest that scales measuring attitudes towards work need to be multidimensional, since the Weberian thesis predicts that the Protestant ethic involves a range of personal values conducive to early capitalism (Miller et al. 2002).

Table 75.1 examines whether Protestant societies differ from other religious cultures in the priority given to the intrinsic and material rewards of work, as well as attitudes towards work as a duty. The results are striking and consistent across all three measures. Contrary to the Weberian thesis, compared with all other religious cultures, *those living in Protestant societies today display the weakest work ethic*. The contrasts between Protestant and the other religious cultures are consistent across scales, though they are usually modest in size, with the important exception being the difference with Muslim cultures, which display by far the strongest work ethic. An important reason for this pattern emerges from the comparison of the same scales by type of society: post-industrial economies today have the weakest work ethic because rich nations place the greatest importance on the values of leisure, relaxation and self-fulfilment outside of employment. Industrial societies place moderate value on the rewards of employment. But in the poorer developing nations, where work is essential for life, often with long hours and minimal leisure time and an inadequate welfare safety net, people place by far the highest emphasis on the value of work. The contrasts between rich and poor societies in attitudes towards work as a duty are greater than those generated by religious culture.

Table 75.1   Mean scores on the work ethic scales

	Intrinsic rewards	Material rewards	Work as a duty
All	54	55	72
Type of religious culture			
Protestant	50	49	68
Catholic	52	52	72
Orthodox	51	55	73
Muslim	70	70	90
Eastern	53	52	75
Type of society			
Post-industrial	50	46	65
Industrial	53	55	74
Agrarian	61	63	81
Difference by religious culture	0.537***	0.542***	0.628***
Difference by type of society	0.330**	0.496***	0.794***
Number of societies	73	73	46

Notes:
All scales have been standardized to 100 points. The significance of the difference between group means is measured by ANOVA (Eta) without any controls. *** Sig. 0.001.
Intrinsic rewards: 'An opportunity to use initiative; A job in which you feel you can achieve something; A responsible job; A job meeting one's abilities; A job respected by people in general; A job that is interesting.'
Material rewards: 'Good hours; Generous holidays; Good pay; Not too much pressure; Good job security.'
Work as a duty: Agrees or agrees strongly: 'People who don't work turn lazy; Work is a duty to society; It is humiliating to receive money without work; Work should always comes first.'

Source: The World Values Survey/European Values Survey, Waves III and IV (1995–2001).

If we limit the comparison to Catholic and Protestant societies – which is the main focus in Weber's work – some modest differences do emerge on individual items within the composite scales. Catholic societies, for example, place slightly greater weight on the value of pay and holidays. Protestant cultures give greater priority to jobs requiring initiative, as well as those generating interest and a sense of achievement. But overall Protestant societies score slightly *lower* on the summary work scales than Catholic cultures, not higher as the original Weberian thesis predicts.

Yet these results could prove spurious if there is some other characteristic of Protestant societies that could influence these patterns, such as greater levels of higher education or an older age profile of the populations in these nations. To test for this, we used regression analysis at the individual level, coding the predominant religious culture in each society as a dummy variable. The Protestant culture is the reference category. The results confirm the significance of the observed cultural patterns, even after controlling for levels of human and political development and the social background of respondents. Growing affluence and the development of the welfare state in richer countries mean that work is no longer such a necessity of life, and people turn increasingly towards other opportunities for individual self-fulfilment. Yet even after accounting for these various factors, all other religious cultures prove significantly more work-oriented than Protestant societies, with the strongest coefficients being in Muslim nations.

Of course these results have limitations. Contemporary survey data cannot tell us how cultural attitudes have changed since previous centuries, and we lack historical evidence from the time of the Reformation. It is entirely possible that a strong orientation towards work as a duty characterized the Protestant societies of northern Europe during the rise of bourgeois capitalism – and that this ethos gradually dissipated precisely because these societies were the first to become rich – shifting towards an emphasis on more leisured lifestyles in subsequent centuries. Though some historians doubt the thesis, Weber's analysis could be correct for the historical era in which he claimed that the Protestant ethos fuelled the capitalist spirit (Samuelson 1993). But it seems clear that *today*, contemporary Protestant societies place relatively little value on the virtues of labour, both in terms of material and intrinsic rewards, especially compared with contemporary Muslim societies. Systematic survey evidence from a broad range of societies indicates that by the late twentieth century the work ethic was no longer a distinctive aspect of Protestant societies. Quite the contrary, they are the societies that emphasize these characteristics least of any cultural region in the world. Any historical legacy, if it did exist in earlier eras, appears to have been dissipated by processes of development.

Attitudes towards capitalism
What about broader attitudes towards some of the key principles of capitalism, such as attitudes towards the role of the market versus the state? We have already noted that Guiso et al. (2003), who drew on the first three waves of the World Values Survey, concluded that religiosity was associated with personal trust, which social capital theory claims to be broadly conducive to effective free markets and better governed institutions (Putnam 1995). This logic suggests that a cultural trait affects certain values or beliefs, and those beliefs in turn influence economic decision-making and thus economic outcomes. Yet the linkages in this chain of reasoning between social trust and economic growth remain controversial (Keely 2003). Guiso et al.'s more direct comparison of economic attitudes among Christian denominations, however, found mixed results: 'Protestants are more trusting and favor incentives more, Catholics are more thrifty and favor private property and competition more' (Guiso et al. 2003, p. 228).

To test these ideas, we compare economic values related to support for capitalism by focusing on four 10-point scale items: (i) the priority people give to maintaining individual economic incentives compared to achieving greater income equality; (ii) whether people should take responsibility for themselves rather than the government providing for everyone; (iii) whether competition is regarded as good or harmful; and (iv) preferences for the role of the state or the private market in ownership of business and industry. Table 75.2 summarizes the mean distribution of responses by type of religious culture and type of society.

Comparing only Protestant and Catholic societies, Protestants are slightly more pro-capitalist in orientation on three of the four indicators. This provides some limited support for the Weberian thesis. Yet comparisons across all religious cultures show a more mixed pattern, according to the particular dimension under comparison. Overall, compared with all religious cultures, those living in Protestant societies gave the least support to the position that individuals should be responsible for providing for themselves, rather than the

Table 75.2   Economic attitudes by religious culture and society

	Favour economic incentives over economic equality	Favour individual responsibility over state responsibility	Favour competition	Favour private ownership
All	5.9	5.6	7.5	6.1
Type of religious culture				
Protestant	5.8	5.1	7.6	6.8
Roman Catholic	5.6	5.6	7.2	6.2
Orthodox	6.4	6.4	7.5	5.4
Muslim	6.4	5.4	8.0	5.6
Eastern	5.7	5.9	7.6	5.6
Type of society				
Post-industrial	5.7	5.3	7.2	6.8
Industrial	5.8	5.8	7.4	5.8
Agrarian	6.4	5.4	8.0	5.6
Difference by religious cultures	0.120***	0.131***	0.097***	0.182***
Difference by type of society	0.088****	0.080***	0.110***	0.177***
Number of respondents	188,401	204,949	187,400	172,549

Notes:
The mean scores on the following 10-point scales were recoded so that low = left side, high = right side of the questionnaire cards:

Q141-4: *'Now I'd like you to tell me your views on various issues. How would you place your views on this scale? 1 means you agree completely with the statement on the left; 10 means you agree completely with the statement on the right; and if your views fall somewhere in-between, choose any number in-between.'*

Q141: (1) 'We need larger income differences as incentives for individual effort.' Or (10) 'Incomes should be made more equal.'

Q143: (1) 'The government should take more responsibility to ensure that everyone is provided for.' Or (10) 'People should take more responsibility to provide for themselves.'

Q142R: (1) 'Private ownership of business and industry should be increased.' Or (10) 'Government ownership of business and industry should be increased.'

Q144R: (1) 'Competition is harmful. It brings out the worst in people.' Or (10) 'Competition is good. It stimulates people to work hard and develop new ideas.'

The significance of the difference between group means is measured by ANOVA (Eta).
*** Sig. 0.001

Source: The World Values Survey/European Values Survey, Waves II to IV (1990–2001).

government being responsible for ensuring that everyone is provided for. This response is consistent with the extensive welfare states and cradle-to-grave protection that exist in Protestant Scandinavia and northern Europe, along with the relatively high level of trust in government commonly found in the Nordic nations (Norris 1999).

Compared with all other cultures, Protestant societies rank towards the middle on attitudes towards favouring economic incentives over economic equality. They were more positive than average towards the value of competition, and they were highest of all cultures on support for private ownership of business and industry, rather than state ownership. While this last finding could be interpreted as approval of a key dimension of capitalist economies and private property, the overall pattern remains mixed. The evidence thus does not provide consistent support for the thesis that those living in Protestant societies today are more strongly committed to free-market economic values and a minimal role for the state. Many factors may influence capitalist attitudes in any given society, such as the public's experiences with government services, benefits offered by the welfare state and the performance of public-sector industries.

Ethical standards

Yet the Weberian thesis might still apply to contemporary Protestant societies if we found that certain ethical standards, which grease the wheels of capitalism, were more pronounced in them. Willingness to obey the law, voluntary compliance with the payment of taxes, honesty in public transactions and lack of corruption are all standards of public life that are widely believed to play an important role in the economy. Indeed, during the last decade the issue of corruption has witnessed a marked revival of interest among many international developmental agencies, including the World Bank and Transparency International. Widespread bribery and corruption in the public sector are now commonly regarded as key problems in economic development, since they funnel the benefits of international aid to governing elites.

Is it true that religious cultures play a critical role in setting certain ethical standards that encourage business confidence, investment and contract compliance? The World Values Survey contains four 10-point scale items that are designed to test the public's ethical attitudes, including the degree to which people believe that certain actions are either always justified, never justified or somewhere in between. For the comparison, we take the strictest standard, which is regarding certain actions as never justified. The items we compared included claiming government benefits to which one is not entitled, avoiding paying one's fare on public transport, cheating on taxes and accepting a bribe during the course of one's duties.

There was broad consensus about these ethical standards. Table 75.3 shows that overall almost two-thirds of the public thought that claiming false benefits, avoiding fares and cheating on taxes were never justified, with this proportion rising to three-quarters concerning bribery. Comparison across religious cultures shows Protestant societies as only moderately ethical on all four scales; usually slightly more ethical than the Catholic societies but not displaying the highest ethical standards across all groups. Indeed, by contrast, the Eastern religious cultures showed the highest disapproval of moral infringements. Thus, any argument that today Protestant societies display higher ethical standards that may be conducive to business confidence and good governance is not supported by this analysis.

Conclusions

There are many reasons why we might expect the moral and ethical values taught by the world's major faiths to exert an enduring impact on the publics living in these societies. Those who are brought up as active adherents to these religions will be most exposed to the teachings of religious leaders and interpretations of moral standards in holy texts. But through a broad process of diffusion everyone in these societies might be affected by these cultural values. The claims of Weberian theory suggest that the church's values

Table 75.3   Ethical scales by religion (% 'never justified')

Type of religious culture	Claiming government benefits to which one is not entitled	Avoiding paying a fare on public transport	Cheating on taxes if one has the chance	Accepting a bribe in the course of one's duties
All	61	59	60	74
Religious culture				
Protestant	67	61	56	76
Catholic	57	54	57	71
Orthodox	54	47	50	72
Muslim	66	71	75	81
Eastern	68	75	79	80
Type of society				
Post-industrial	66	63	56	75
Industrial	55	50	57	71
Agrarian	65	69	71	79
Difference by religious culture	0.114***	0.171***	0.176***	0.081***
Difference by type of society	0.108***	0.155***	0.120***	0.065***
Number of societies	75	75	75	75

Notes:
Q: *'Please tell me for each of the following statements whether you think it can always be justified (10), can never be justified (1), or something in-between.'*
Figures presented are for percentage *'Can never be justified'*.
The significance of the differences between groups without any controls is measured by ANOVA (Eta).
*** Significant at the 0.001 level.

Source: The World Values Survey/European Values Survey, Waves III and IV (1995–2001).

are important, not just in themselves, but also because cultural factors may have a decisive impact on patterns of economic growth and development. In particular, Weber argued, after the Reformation the ethos of Protestantism in Europe fuelled the spirit of capitalism.

But do denominational cultures continue to exert a decisive influence on economic attitudes and moral standards today? If secularization has weakened the strength and vitality of religion in affluent nations, then instead of the church imposing clear and distinct ethical standards and rules for society, we might expect contemporary modern societies to display a 'bricolage' or a patchwork of diverse moral values, beliefs and practices derived from many sources (Dobbelaere 1999; Voye 1999).

We have no historical evidence that would unravel the relationship discussed by Weber between Calvinistic values found in Western Europe at the time of the Reformation and the subsequent rise of the merchant class of bourgeois shopkeepers, industrialists and business entrepreneurs during early capitalism. We can, however, examine whether any legacy from Protestantism continued to stamp an enduring cultural imprint on economic attitudes in Protestant societies in the late twentieth century that distinguished these cultural societies from those of other world religions. Our comparison reveals that those living in contemporary Protestant societies display the weakest work ethic today, not the strongest, of all the major religious cultures. Those living in Protestant nations give roughly equal weight to the importance of work and leisure. Regarding attitudes towards broader economic issues, the differences are modest. Compared to Catholic cultures, Protestant societies are slightly more pro-free market on most questions. Nevertheless, Protestant societies are not *the* most pro-market across all religions.

Any analysis of the relationship between economic development and ethical values needs to address the classical issues raised by Max Weber a century ago. New tools are now available for empirical analysis using cross-national survey datasets. The findings reported here cannot be regarded as definitive, since that would require historical evidence which is simply unavailable, but contemporary patterns nonetheless throw new light on this classic debate. The results provide little support for the core claims made by Max Weber, but this does not mean that a Protestant culture has no significant impact on ethical values. Although there is considerable evidence that religiosity has eroded in many affluent nations, religious cultures nevertheless continue to display the imprint of their distinct moral value tradition.

Note

1   For a summary of the many critiques made over the years see Giddens (1992)

References

Barro, Robert J. and Rachel M. McCleary (2003), 'Religion and economic growth', National Bureau of Economic Research (NBER) Working Paper No. 9682, issued May 2003, www.nber.org/papers/w9682.
Blum, Ulrich and Leonard Dudley (2001), 'Religion and economic growth: was Weber right?' *Journal of Evolutionary Economics*, **11** (2), 207–30.
Chalcraft, David and Austin Harrington (2001), *The Protestant Ethic Debate: Max Weber Replies to His Critics, 1907–1910,* Liverpool: Liverpool University Press.
Dobbelaere, Karel (1999), 'Towards an integrated perspective of the processes related to the descriptive concept of secularization', *Sociology of Religion*, **60** (3), 229–47.
Furnham, Adrian, Michael H. Bond, Patrick Heaven, Denis Hilton, Thalma Lobel, John Masters, Monica Payne, R. Rajamanikam, Barry Stacey and H. Vandaalen (1993), 'A comparison of Protestant work-ethic beliefs in 13 nations', *Journal of Social Psychology*, **133** (2), 185–97.
Giddens, Anthony (1992), 'Introduction', in *Max Weber: The Protestant Ethic and the Spirit of Capitalism*, New York: Routledge.
Greenfield, Liah (2001), *The Spirit of Capitalism: Nationalism and Economic Growth*, Cambridge, MA: Harvard University Press.
Guiso, Luigi, Paola Sapienza and Luigi Zingales (2003), 'People's opium? Religion and economic attitudes', *Journal of Monetary Economics*, **50**, 225–82.
Iannaccone, Laurence R. (1998), 'Introduction to the economics of religion', *Journal of Economic Literature*, **36** (3), 1465–96.
Inglehart, Ronald (1997), *Modernization and Postmodernization*, Princeton, NJ: Princeton University Press.
Jones Jr, Harold (1997), 'The Protestant ethic: Weber's model and the empirical literature', *Human Relations*, **50** (7), 757–78.
Keely, Louise (2003), 'Comment on: "People's opium? Religion and economic attitudes"', *Journal of Monetary Economics*, **50** (1), 283–7.
Lehman, Hartmut and Guenther Roth (eds) (1993), *Weber's Protestant Ethic: Origins, Evidence, Contexts*, New York: Cambridge University Press.
Lessnoff, Michael (1994), *The Spirit of Capitalism and the Protestant Ethic: An Enquiry into the Weber Thesis*, Aldershot, UK and Brookfield, USA: Edward Elgar.
Miller, Michael J., David J. Woehr and Natasha Hudspeth (2002), 'The meaning and measurement of work ethic: construction and initial validation of a multidimensional inventory', *Journal of Vocational Behavior*, **60** (3), 451–89.

Norris, Pippa (ed.) (1999), *Critical Citizens: Global Support for Democratic Governance*, Oxford: Oxford University Press.

Putnam, Robert D. (1995), *Making Democracy Work*, Princeton, NJ: Princeton University Press.

Samuelson, Kurt (1993), *Religion and Economic Action: The Protestant Ethic, the Rise of Capitalism and the Abuses of Scholarship*, Toronto: University of Toronto Press.

Swedberg, Richard (1998), *Max Weber and the Idea of Economic Sociology*, Princeton, NJ: Princeton University Press.

Tawney, Richard H. (1926), *Religion and the Rise of Capitalism*, New York: Harper & Row.

Ter Voert, M. (1997), 'The Protestant ethic in the Republic of the Seven United Netherlands: fiction or fact?' *Netherlands Journal of Social Sciences*, **33** (1), 1–10.

Voye, Liliane (1999), 'Secularization in a context of advanced modernity', *Sociology of Religion*, **603**, 275–88.

Weber, Max. ([1904] 1992), *The Protestant Ethic and the Spirit of Capitalism*, New York: Routledge.

See also the entries on: Market; Protestant ethics; Religion

Index